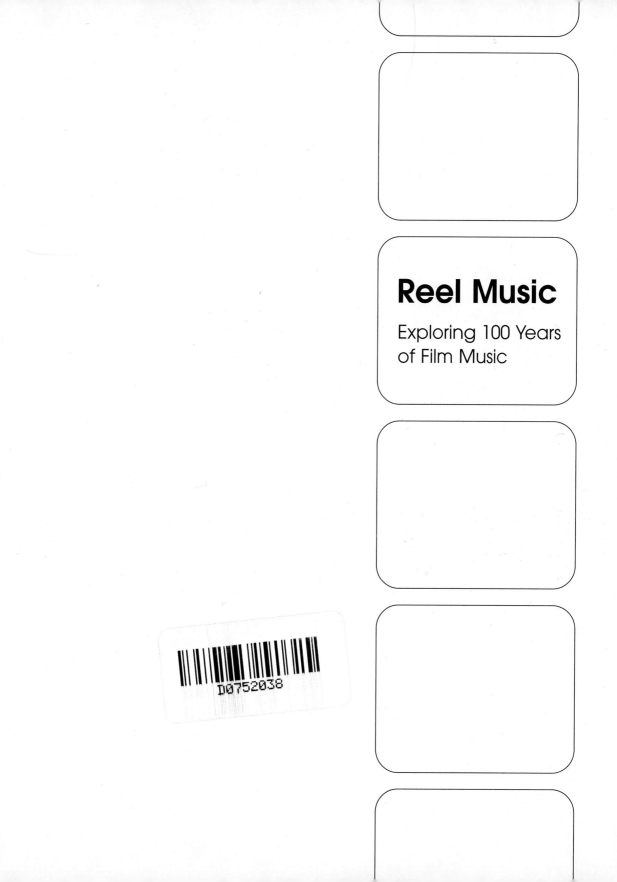

Reel Music

Exploring 100 Years
of Film Music

W. W. Norton & Company
New York · London

Reel Music

Exploring 100 Years
of Film Music

Roger Hickman
California State University
Long Beach

W. W. Norton & Company has been independent since its founding in 1923, when William Warder Norton and Mary D. Herter Norton first published lectures delivered at the People's Institute, the adult education division of New York City's Cooper Union. The Nortons soon expanded their program beyond the Institute, publishing books by celebrated academics from America and abroad. By mid-century, the two major pillars of Norton's publishing program—trade books and college texts—were firmly established. In the 1950s, the Norton family transferred control of the company to its employees, and today—with a staff of four hundred and a comparable number of trade, college, and professional titles published each year—W. W. Norton & Company stands as the largest and oldest publishing house owned wholly by its employees.

Editor: Maribeth Anderson Payne
Assistant Editor: Allison Courtney Fitch
Project Editor: Thomas Foley
Copy Editor: Richard Wingell
Managing Editor, College: Marian Johnson
Production Manager: Benjamin Reynolds
Book Designer: Rubina Yeh
Photo Researcher: Neil Ryder Hoos

Composition by TSI Graphics, Inc.
Manufactured by the Courier Companies—Westford Division

Cover illustration: Phil Banko/Corbis

Library of Congress Cataloging-in Publication Data

Hickman, Roger.
   Reel music: exploring 100 years of film music/by Roger Hickman.
      p. cm.
   Includes bibliographical references and index.
   ISBN 0-393-92574-9
   1. Motion picture music—History and criticism. I. Title: Exploring 100 years of film music.
II. Title: Exploring one hundred years of film music. III. Title.

ML2075.H5 2005
781.5´42´09—dc22

                                                      2004059539

W.W. Norton & Company, Inc., 500 Fifth Avenue, New York, N.Y. 10110
www.wwnorton.com
W.W. Norton & Company Ltd., Castle House, 75/76 Wells Street, London W1T 3QT

7 8 9 0

To my parents, Ralph and Edith,

Thank you for making me turn off the television and go outside.

Thank you for making me practice the violin.

Thank you for dropping me off at the movies every Saturday morning.

Thank you for the worldly wisdom to understand why you dropped me off at the movies every Saturday morning.

Thanks for all your patience and support.

All my love.

Contents

Part 5   A New American Cinema, 1960–1976

Part 6   The Classic Revival, 1977–1988

Part 7   Fin de Siècle and the New Millennium, 1989–2004

Preface

The study of film music has made rapid strides since Luke Skywalker's fanfare first resounded in movie theaters across the United States in the summer of 1977. Writing one year earlier, composer Peter Odegard, my mentor, criticized two major histories of twentieth-century music for their superficial treatment of film music. One of a handful of voices attempting to bring greater recognition to film composers active in Hollywood and around the world, Odegard argued: "It is in fact the most widely dispersed repertoire being performed today, and hence, in its peculiar way, the most influential."[*]

In 1977, the stunning success of the soundtracks for *Star Wars* and *Saturday Night Fever* expanded film music's level of dispersion and sphere of influence even further. Consequently, today's audience members, eagerly purchasing CD soundtracks even before a film has been released, are much more aware of music in film. The traditional description of film music as being "unheard" is no longer appropriate, as film music has engendered a large listening audience independent from the films.

Today, many historians recognize the impact that film has had on the music of the twentieth and twenty-first centuries. In addition to its role in shaping popular music, film has produced a repertoire that, for a large percentage of Americans, is the classic orchestral music of our time. Performances of film music excerpts have moved from the realm of pops orchestras to that of major symphonies, where the compositions of John Williams and Miklós Rózsa are now presented alongside those of Beethoven, Brahms, and Stravinsky. Indeed, films have often played a significant role in introducing the sounds of modern concert music to general audiences, as noted by Odegard: "Musical effects that would shock the public in the concert hall will be accepted in a film situation without question."[†]

From its inception, film has had a significant impact on music. What has changed in the last thirty years is the recognition of this relationship by music historians, who now regularly write articles and books, as well as teach classes about film music. There are numerous reasons for this change. On the most practical level, the study

---

[*] Peter Odegard, Review of *Dictionary of Contemporary Music* by John Vinton (1974) and *The New Oxford History of Music,* vol. 10: *The Modern Age 1890–1960* (1960), in *Journal of American Musicological Society*, 19 (1976), 155.

[†] *ibid.*

of film music has been facilitated in recent years by numerous technological advancements. Since 1977, the VCR, video rentals, cable movie channels, DVDs, and the proliferation of soundtrack recordings have become important tools of the film music scholar. Today, the study of film music is more acceptable in part because it can be studied more thoroughly.

The current interest in film music can also be attributed to the attitudes of postmodern critics, who no longer distrust any art form that has popular appeal. But above all, we need to acknowledge the work of a small number of pioneers who wrote about film music and laid the foundation for the field. Books by respected authors such as Kurt London and Roy Prendergast explored the world of film music, expanded our understanding of the field, and inspired further studies.

For the Student

A course on film music will increase your understanding and enjoyment of both music and film. Like any book designed for a music appreciation class, this text will introduce a number of musical concepts that can be applied to a wide variety of music. Indeed, topics such as themes, thematic transformation, dissonance, timbre, style, and emotions, which are part of many musical experiences, may be more readily grasped in the context of a film than with abstract music. Throughout your studies of film music, you should constantly ask yourself why the director and composer made certain choices, whether they were successful in achieving their goals, and what alternatives they might have chosen. In this way you will expand your critical thinking capabilities and accumulate tools that you can apply when listening to music of all types.

Since most of the material in this text is organized in a chronological fashion, you will also learn a good deal about film history, including general information on trends and specific information about a large number of representative films. In selecting the films for this study, I have avoided defining the qualities of a great film score *a priori* and then limiting our scope to films that reflect my judgment. It would be easy for a music historian to focus only on those films that have a musical approach similar to the conception of theatrical music by Richard Wagner. Rather, I have sought out the most highly regarded films from any given period and examined how they use music. Hence, our coverage includes movies with non-traditional and non-symphonic music.

The foremost goal of this text is to study how music functions in a given film, regardless of its musical style. In the process, you will discover that music establishes psychological moods, guides our emotions, and reveals aspects of an unfolding narrative. By the end of this study, you will have gained a greater understanding of both music and film; it is likely that you will never watch or listen to another movie in quite the same way again.

For the Instructor

This textbook is designed for non-music and non-film majors at the university level. Majors in music and film can also benefit from instruction based on this text, but a strong background in either of the two disciplines is not required. The material of the first four chapters (Part 1) introduces basic concepts and terminology for drama, film, music, and film music. In addition, the Glossary provides explanations for many of the technical terms used in this text.

The coverage of the historical chapters (Parts 2–7) extends from the early experiments of Thomas Edison up to the present time. Underlying this overview is the premise that film is an art form, a modern counterpart to Richard Wagner's conception of the total artwork. Viewing film as an art, we see that its history follows many of the natural cycles found in all art forms, including a classic age, a period of innovation, the emergence of a classical canon of works, and a neoclassic revival. In addition, film is subject to the same trends as other contemporary art disciplines, all of which have been shaped in part by the historical events of the twentieth and early twenty-first centuries.

The text is admittedly slanted toward Hollywood. Students are familiar with American films, and Hollywood films have created an enormous variety of musical treatments. But discussions of international films are also included in order to acknowledge some outstanding accomplishments in film music outside of Hollywood and to remind our students that there is a vast and wonderful repertory of films produced throughout the world.

Text Overview

Entitled "Exploring Film and Music," the first part can be discussed in class or assigned as homework. It is suggested that some class time be spent assisting non-music majors with the concepts of music and how music is used in films. The four introductory chapters of Part 1 treat the following topics:

Chapter 1 ("Wagner's Prelude") discusses the innovations of Wagner in the areas of theater and theater music and links these innovations to film.

Chapter 2 ("Drama and Film") presents basic concepts and terminology of drama and film.

Chapter 3 ("Elements of Music") focuses on musical terminology for non-music majors and includes a section on reading music notation.

Chapter 4 ("Listening to Film Music") examines how music functions in a film, concluding with an analysis of a specific scene.

Throughout the textbook, incipits of important music themes are included for reference. Non-majors are encouraged to follow the notation so that they can use this tool in their studies. Chapter 3 begins with a simple discussion of music notation and how it works. For ease of following while listening, I have simplified some of the musical themes in the text. The principal theme for *E.T. the Extra-Terrestrial*, for example, is shown with eighth notes rather than the more visually complicated (and accurate) sixteenth notes.

In each of the historical units, the discussion centers on the general context of film music, major film composers, and significant works. Numerous Composer Profiles provide basic lists of films, and Close-Ups discuss nonmusical issues that may be of interest to burgeoning film connoisseurs.

Discussions of individual films are treated in three different ways.

- Featured Films: Each historical unit contains one chapter devoted to a single film. The six films were chosen based on their quality, their representation of an era, and their variety of music treatments.
- Viewer Guides: Most chapters contain a Viewer Guide, which describes in detail how music functions in an individual scene. These scenes are selected with an eye to highlighting major composers, films, and approaches to film composition. In all, there are twenty-four Viewer Guides.
- Numerous other major films are mentioned in the text, but an effort has been made not to overwhelm students with too many names. Discussions are deliberately limited, and, at the end of each chapter, a Suggested Viewing section contains the names of additional films recommended for study. Not all of the suggested films have extended musical scores, but they are among the best films produced at any given time period and represent significant historical trends.

Course Overview

Film is a temporal art and, as such, occupies time during a lecture. Just as it is difficult to imagine a poetry class in which no poems are read or a music class in which no music is heard, so too is it difficult to imagine this class with no time given over to viewing part of a film. How much time to devote to watching films is a decision for each instructor. The Featured Films and the Viewer Guides contain timings for both VHS tapes and DVDs that will aid the instructor in class or the student at home. Since VHS players and cassettes have minor discrepancies, allow for some variation from the timings given in the text.

This text was created for a semester-long course comprising forty-five hours of lecture time. One could devote a single hour lecture to each chapter except the Feature Film chapters, which could be presented in two lectures. The text would thus be covered in forty-two hour-long classes, leaving three classes for exams and holidays.

Modifications of this formula are necessary for those teaching classes longer than an hour; like many instructors, I teach both ninety-minute and three-hour classes. More significant variations can be made to devote time to an instructor's area of interest. Since Part 1 is written as a reference tool for students, it may not require as much lecture time. Similarly, the silent era (Part 2) has fewer films with original music and could be taught in less than six hours. The instructor may choose to apply these additional lecture hours to later units, where examples are more abundant. In addition, some instructors may want to assign the Featured Films as homework and devote lecture time to discussions of other films.

Exams

The essential material of the text is contained in Parts 2–7. As noted earlier, Part 2 has only two Viewer Guides. By contrast, Part 3, which covers the Golden Age of film scoring, contains six Viewer Guides. Each of the remaining Parts contains four Viewer Guides. As a result, it is possible to divide the course content into thirds (Parts 2–3, 4–5, 6–7) or halves (Parts 2–4, 5–7). If you choose to have two midterms, there would be eight Viewer Guides and two Feature Films for each exam. If you choose to have just one midterm, there will be twelve Viewer Guides and three Featured Films for each.

Listening

It is often a good practice to have students listen to film music before watching the film. In this manner they can focus on the musical qualities and have a sense of familiarity when the film is shown. If you are considering requiring the purchase of CDs, I strongly recommend one of the following collections, all of which would coordinate well with this text:

- *Cinema Century* (4 CDs) produced by Silva Treasury ($30)
- *Cinema Century 2000* (4 CDs) produced by Silva Treasury ($30)
- *Music in Film: National Public Radio Milestones of the Millennium* (1 CD) produced by Sony ($12)

Critical Thinking

Film music can provide numerous opportunities for evaluating students' critical thinking, in both class discussions and written papers. Class discussions can be lively—almost everyone has opinions about film. Have your students discuss the mood that is created by the music and how that mood is achieved. Encourage students to use precise terminology in defending their views. Have them think of other moods that might have been used in a film.

You can challenge students' listening and critical thinking skills by asking specific questions: Why does the film *Rebel Without a Cause* use dissonant sounds? What difference is created when the *Star Wars* theme is played by French horns instead of trumpets? Why did John Williams choose to feature a solo violin in *Schindler's List*? I have enjoyed many classroom debates over the issue of music in *2001: A Space Odyssey*. Show the opening ("The Dawn of Man") as is, without music, and then repeat the scene along with a recording of Alex North's original music. Have them discuss how the music changes the impact and argue about which approach is more successful.

Each instructor will have his or her own ideas about written projects. Try to avoid having the students write biographies or plot descriptions. The Viewer Guides in this text are not meant to be models for student papers. Encourage them to design papers that have a thesis that they can support in a formal writing style.

Historical Apologies

As a music historian, I have had to make some accommodations to conventions in film history and criticism. Conforming to standard practice, I have chosen the year that a film is first publicly shown as the official date for a film. I have also avoided the word "decade" in my terminology. Normally, one writes of a decade as extending from a year ending in 1 to a year ending in 0, such as 1931–1940. Film historians and critics tend to speak of films as coming from the 1930s, meaning 1930–1939, a designation that I adopt in the text. Historians will be glad to know that for me the twenty-first century began in 2001, just as the title of Kubrick's film implies.

Acknowledgments

For a first-time author, the journey from conception to publication is similar to watching a *Lord of the Rings* movie: the experience is long, unexpected turns and detours invigorate the process, and one is never sure when it will end or even if it has ended. The five-year adventure leading to the appearance of *Reel Music: Exploring 100 Years of Film Music* could not have succeeded without the support of a strong fellowship whose number certainly exceeds nine.

Foremost I would like to thank the excellent staff at W. W. Norton & Company. Music Editor Maribeth Payne has skillfully guided and encouraged me through the entire process, and Assistant Editor Courtney Fitch, my constant e-mail companion, has answered all questions large and small with patience and good humor. My sincere appreciation is also extended to Thomas Foley (Project Editor), Neil Hoos (Photo

Permissions Manager), Benjamin Reynolds (Production Manager and Proofreader), Rubina Yeh (Art Director), and Marian Johnson (Managing Editor, College).

The final form of *Reel Music* is largely indebted to the guidance of a number of distinguished writers and scholars. I have benefited greatly from the wisdom and advice of a select group of reviewers: Rick Altman, Professor of Cinema and Comparative Literature at the University of Iowa; Stephen Douglas, Burton Heritage Chair and Professor of Music and Film Faculty at George Mason University; Julie Hubbert, University of South Carolina; David E. James, UCLA School of Cinema-Television; Professor Jerome S. Kleinsasser; Michael V. Pisani of Vassar College; and David Sterritt, Ph.D., of Columbia University. In particular, I wish to express my deep gratitude for the thorough and painstaking work of copyeditor Richard Wingell, who had to deal with an array of grammatical, organizational, and typographical challenges.

I am also grateful for the support provided by C. S. U. Long Beach and for encouragement from Don Para, Dean of Fine Arts, and John Carnahan, Chairman of the Music Department. I also benefited from the encouragement of colleague Kristine Forney, who played an important role in facilitating this publication. I also owe a special thanks to Maureen, who has encouraged, proofread, and advised throughout this long journey. Her keen judgment and sense of humor are reflected everywhere, beginning with the title page.

Part 1

Exploring Film and Music

Wagner's Prelude

Max Steiner is generally considered the father of American film music. He composed the first extended score in the sound era for *King Kong*, and his prolific output includes some of the most beloved American films, including *Gone With the Wind* and *Casablanca*. Yet when he was told that he had invented movie music, Steiner responded:

> Nonsense. The idea originated with Richard Wagner. Listen to the incidental scoring behind the recitatives in his operas. If Wagner had lived in this century, he would have been the number one film composer.

Steiner's reply is both surprising and revealing. At first glance, Richard Wagner seems far removed from film composition. Wagner was a nineteenth–century German opera composer who died in 1883, a dozen years before the official birth of cinema. He is revered as one of the giants of Western classical music. By contrast, film music is only recently considered a subject worthy of serious study. The connection between the two seems tenuous. But Steiner's remarks are typical of the attitude of film composers in general. From the earliest scores for silent films, through the classic works of Erich Korngold, to *Star Wars* and beyond, Wagner has been a source of inspiration for many of film's finest composers.

Figure 1.1 Richard Wagner

Wagner's *Gesamtkunstwerk*

Wagner's influence on film is not limited to music; a number of his theatrical innovations have had an impact as well. One of his greatest achievements is the revolutionary concept of the total artwork, which he termed the *Gesamtkunstwerk*. Wagner argued that the individual arts could not achieve their highest level of perfection by themselves and suggested that drama was the greatest unifying artform: "The highest conjoint work of art is the Drama: it can only be at hand in all its possible fullness, when in it each separate branch of art is at hand in its own utmost fullness."*

In his music dramas, Wagner sought to bring together the finest elements of all the arts—brilliant philosophy and literature in the libretto; stunning visual elements in the scenery, costumes, and lighting; and the best of performing arts in the acting and music. To this end, Wagner created some of the most celebrated works in the history of Western arts, including the masterpieces *Tristan und Isolde* and the cycle of four operas *Der Ring des Nibelungen*.

One of the challenges facing Wagner in creating a total artwork was that the arts do not naturally mix. In general, the arts can be divided into two basic types, visual and temporal. The visual arts, sometimes referred to as the spatial arts, occupy space and can theoretically be seen in their entirety in a given moment. The principal types of visual art are painting, photography, sculpture, and architecture. The temporal arts occupy time and can be perceived only as they unfold in time. The principal types of temporal art are literature, music, and dance.

Throughout western civilization, attempts have been made to combine divergent types of art. The most successful efforts have been within the temporal arts. The union of music and poetry creates song; the combination of music and drama creates operas and musicals; and the mixture of drama, music, and dance produces ballet.

It is more problematic to combine the temporal arts with the visual arts, since they occupy different dimensions. Before the late nineteenth century, the principal efforts to combine the visual and temporal arts took place in the theater, where the visual elements of a drama could be linked with the unfolding of the temporal arts. Descriptions of such productions extend back to antiquity. In his *Poetics*, Aristotle includes both spectacle (visual) and song (music) as two of the six basic elements of tragedy.

Theatrical dance, with its emphasis on the visual art of dancing combined with music and drama, can also be seen as a type of total artwork. The Ballet Russes in the early twentieth century united the talents of a variety of artists, including the dancer Nijinsky, the composer Stravinsky, and the artists Chagall and Picasso. The production of *The Rite of Spring* can truly be considered a total artwork. Similarly, the American masterpiece *Appalachian Spring* by Aaron Copland, Isamu Noguchi, and

---

* *Richard Wagner's Prose Works*, trans. William Ashton Ellis. New York: Broude Brothers, 1892, I/184.

Martha Graham and the more recent productions by John Cage, Robert Rauschenberg, and Merce Cunningham combine the efforts of numerous outstanding artists.

Wagner as Auteur

Yet these works are different from Wagner's conception. Dance productions are largely collaborations among several artists, whereas Wagner created a single vision for all of the arts by maintaining strict control over each of them; he wrote his own librettos that expressed his philosophies, he meticulously directed the staging and acting, he dictated the visual elements of scenery, costumes, and lighting, and he composed the music.

Figure 1.2 *Appalachian Spring* with music by Aaron Copland, set design by Isamu Noguchi, and choreography by Martha Graham

In order to implement his ideals fully, Wagner even built his own theater, the Festival Theater at Bayreuth, where he exerted total control over his productions. Among his theatrical innovations are the following, many of which we take for granted today:

- The auditorium was darkened during the performance.
- He widened the distance between the audience and the stage with a double proscenium.
- He created an orchestra pit that extended beneath the stage, so that the audience would not see the musicians.
- Members of the orchestra were not allowed to tune their instruments in the pit.
- The audience was asked not to applaud during the performance.
- He insisted upon acting rehearsals before singing rehearsals began.
- Unique and detailed scenery and visual effects were created for each scene in a production.
- He eliminated box seats and created a classless theater, in which every seat had equally good sight and sound. The fanlike arrangement is now known as "continental" seating.

A number of these innovations were aimed at creating the illusion that the audience was not sitting in a theater. Darkening the hall, removing the musicians from sight, and not letting the drama be interrupted by applause helped the audience lose its sense of attending a theatrical event. These developments were at the forefront of a general theatrical revolution in which drama was enhanced by greater sensory appeal, action became more important than words, and the director became the central figure, replacing the writer.

The foundations of modern theater were established just prior to the emergence of film, and a number of the innovations observed in Wagner's productions were also assimilated into the art of film. Perhaps the most important of these is his role as the dominant director. In film, the term *auteur* is used to describe the central role of the director, the creative force that forges all the artistic elements into one principal goal. Theater historians Oscar Brockett and Robert Findlay summarize Wagner's position: "It is primarily from this demand for artistic unity and its corollary—the all-powerful director or *regisseur* [auteur]—that Wagner's enormous influence on the modern theater stems." [†]

Figure 1.3 Siegfried Wagner, son of the composer, conducts in the sunken pit at the Festival Theater at Bayreuth

Wagner and the Music Drama

Theodor Adorno, one of Germany's foremost philosophers and critics after World War II, described Wagner's music dramas as "Das Kino der Zukunft" ("cinema of the future"). In a history of film, Wagner is one of a number of worthy subjects to consider; in a history of film music, Wagner plays a fundamental role. His music dramas provided practical and artistic solutions for film composers, including issues involving musical style, dramatic support, and unity. Detailed explanations of these subjects will appear in later chapters, but you can get a sense of Wagner's dramatic music by listening to the overture to *The Flying Dutchman*. As you listen, imagine that you are listening to film music, not to an opera overture. In particular, listen for the colorful use of instruments, the emotional moods created by the music, and the recurring melodies. What images does the music suggest?

In the legend of *The Flying Dutchman*, a ship is doomed to sail in a storm for eternity. The only hope for salvation occurs one day every seven years, when the ship is visible to mortals. If the captain can find true love on that day, the curse will be broken. In the overture, the dark mood of the story is supported by the prominent use of low brass instruments and the sound of stormy waves created by strings and woodwinds. Most important is the contrast of mood between the stormy opening Dutchman theme and the subsequent Redemption theme. Ultimately,

Figure 1.4 The crew of the Black Pearl are destined to meet the Flying Dutchman in *Pirates of the Caribbean: Dead Man's Chest* (2006)

[†] Oscar G. Brockett and Robert Findlay, *Century of Innovation: A History of European and American Theatre and Drama Since the Late Nineteenth Century*, 2nd ed. Boston: Allyn & Bacon, 1990, 29.

the Redemption theme will be heard in a triumphant setting, foretelling the conclusion of the opera.

Wagner's influence on film music is enormous. He established many of the distinctive characteristics of postromantic music, including colorful orchestration, strong emotional qualities, a rich harmonic vocabulary, and a texture dominated by melody. With these elements, Wagner was able to support his dramas by underscoring the emotional qualities, establishing moods, and creating specific visual images. His most

Composer Profile

Richard Wagner (1813–1883)

Wagner is one of the most influential Western composers. His innovations and influence extended well beyond opera, and he is viewed as a critical figure in ushering in the era of modern music. In addition to his influence on film music in general, his music has appeared in numerous movies. The first film with synchronized sound, *Don Juan* (1926), was preceded by a recorded performance of Wagner's *Tannhäuser* Overture by the New York Philharmonic. The *Ride of the Valkyrie* has appeared in over thirty films, the *Liebestod* from *Tristan und Isolde* in over twenty, and the Bridal Chorus from *Lohengrin* has appeared in too many to enumerate. For many moviegoers, the music of Wagner is best known from the Bugs Bunny animated short "What's Opera, Doc?" (1957).

Selected Films with Music by Wagner

The Birth of a Nation 1915: *The Ride of the Valkyrie*
The Gold Rush 1925: *Tannhäuser*
L'Âge d'or 1930: *Tristan und Isolde*
Dracula 1931: *Der Meistersinger*
Mad Love 1935: *Siegfried*
The Lady Eve 1941: *Der Meistersinger*
Humoresque 1946: *Tristan und Isolde*
Brute Force 1947: *Lohengrin*
Unfaithfully Yours 1948: *Tannhäuser*
The Blue Gardenia 1953: *Tristan und Isolde*
Nosferatu 1979: *Das Rheingold*
Apocalypse Now 1979: *The Ride of the Valkyrie*
Excalibur 1981: *Parsifal, Tristan und Isolde*, and *Siegfried*
Romeo and Juliet 1996: *Tristan und Isolde*

significant contribution, however, was his ability to achieve musical unity without sacrificing the dramatic flow of the story.

Although both drama and music occupy time, each has its own structure; drama builds upon its plot, and music is shaped through repetition and contrast. When music is completely subordinate to dramatic form, it tends to be dull and insipid, and when music dominates, drama often moves in a ponderous, interrupted manner. Traditionally the solution to this problem was to create periodic breaks in the plot in order to allow for musical reflection, which can then take on recognized musical forms. Such compromises can be seen in the chorus in Greek plays, the solo aria in opera, the song in musicals, and the pas-de-deux in ballet. These musical reflections are equivalent to the soliloquies in Shakespearean tragedies, which are also set in formal structures.

Wagner's innovation was the creation of a continuous musical flow. By avoiding closed musical structures, Wagner allowed the drama to move in a natural manner, without interruptions for reflection. In his dramas, he created musical themes that represent various characters and aspects of the story. Called leitmotifs, these themes appeared for the most part in the orchestra and hence could propel the drama forward without stopping the action and at the same time create a sense of musical unity. In the overture to *The Flying Dutchman*, two principal themes, or leitmotifs, can be identified—the Dutchman and Redemption themes. During the opera, these melodies represent the essential conflict of the story, as Wagner is able to reflect both the details and the overall theme of the drama with music.

Film composers were quick to apply these techniques to the new art form. To be sure, not all films use leitmotifs or even a postromantic musical style. In a great many films, these would be inappropriate. But Wagner's influence on what will be termed the "classical" film score is substantial. Every facet of the classical score—the use of a symphony orchestra, the prevalent postromantic musical style, the musical support of the drama, and the sense of unity through leitmotifs and thematic transformation—has precedents in the music dramas of Richard Wagner.

Trailer

Max Steiner, quoted at the beginning of this chapter, suggested that if Wagner had lived in the twentieth century, he would have been a film composer. While several other twentieth-century observers have echoed this opinion, the idea remains mere fanciful speculation. But in keeping with this spirit, we might add that if Wagner had been a film composer, he would probably have wanted to be the director, cinematographer, writer, and possibly actor as well. What is important in Steiner's reflection is his reverence for Wagner. Like many of the major composers in the history of film music, Steiner was well grounded in Wagner's ideas and style and believed that he was applying the master's techniques to the new medium of film. Although Wagner's name will appear only sporadically in the following pages, he remains one of the most influential figures in the history of film music.

Important Names and Terms

Richard Wagner
auteur
Gesamtkunstwerk
leitmotif

Suggested Listening

The Flying Dutchman (*Die fliegende Holländer*): The story of this opera by Wagner is
described earlier in this chapter. Listen for the way the principal melodies
guide you through the drama.

Der Ring des Nibelungen: Known as the Ring Cycle, this is a set of four music
dramas. Wagner wrote the libretto and composed the music. Although lengthy
(over sixteen hours), it is fascinating storytelling and clearly influenced both
the *Star Wars* and the *Lord of the Rings* trilogies.

2

Drama and Film

In the late nineteenth century, technology paved the way for a new type of total art-work—moving pictures. Once pictures moved, they occupied time; once they occupied time, the visual arts crossed into the realm of the temporal arts, thereby combining visual images with both drama and music. For evidence of the diverse artistry involved in the creation of film, one need only observe the Academy Awards, where Oscars are given to an array of artists, including writers, actors, cinematographers, directors, set designers, costume designers, makeup artists, and musicians. Film has become the modern world's counterpart to Wagner's *Gesamtkunstwerk*.

The complex interconnection of the diverse arts found in film is a topic that is too broad for this text. Yet the study of film music necessitates an understanding of how music functions within a dramatic framework. Since the scope of this book is limited to narrative films, we will consider some of the basic elements of drama and film before proceeding to those of music.

Elements of Drama

Western drama can be described in terms of its basic elements. Since the time of Aristotle's *Poetics* (c. 350 BCE), numerous and varied interpretations of those elements have appeared. For our limited purposes, we will discuss five elements that are frequently associated with drama: plot, character, setting, theme, and mood.

Plot

Any narrative—novel, play, poem, or film—presents a story. Many of these stories are original, stemming from the imagination of a creative writer. But quite frequently, legends, history, or current events serve as inspiration for the storyteller. A substantial number of narrative films are adaptations of existing stories, including novels (*Gone With the Wind*, 1939), short stories (*2001: A Space Odyssey*, 1968), plays (*A Streetcar Named Desire*, 1951), poems (*The Charge of the Light Brigade*, 1936), legends (*The Adventures of Robin Hood*, 1938), and earlier films (*The Ten Commandments*, 1956).

Stories can be told in a variety of ways. Some simply start at the beginning and continue until the story is over. Others may incorporate jumps in time or location that reveal important information about the story. The structure of a story is called the **plot**. The plot provides the basic framework for the drama and for the temporal unfolding of the artwork.

Two basic plot structures are commonly encountered in Western fiction—causal and episodic. The **causal plot** contains the following four principal sections:

- **Exposition**: the necessary background information for the story to unfold
- **Complications**: a series of events stemming from a conflict; each complication leads to the next, generally building in intensity
- **Climax**: the moment of greatest tension, when the complications come to a head
- **Resolution** (or **denouement**): the end of the story, in which the complications are resolved, and the loose ends are tied together

One of western civilization's earliest stories, Homer's *Iliad*, provides an excellent example of this structure. Set during the Trojan War, the exposition describes a quarrel between the leader of the Greeks, King Agamemnon, and his greatest warrior, Achilles. By refusing to fight, Achilles sets in motion a series of complications that leads to the slaying of his best friend, Patroclus, at the hands of Hector, Troy's greatest hero. In the dramatic climax, Achilles fights and kills Hector. The resolution section provides the most powerful and moving portion of this tragedy, as Hector's father, King Priam, comes to Achilles to plead for his son's body, and the two powerful men weep at the senselessness of war.

Although the **episodic plot** is similar in a number of respects to the causal, the difference between the two approaches is significant. Rather than moving through a series of complications, an episodic plot presents a succession of events that do not build directly from one to the next. These episodes often function as brief subplots,

Table 2.1

Traditional plot structures

CAUSAL PLOT	EPISODIC PLOT
exposition	exposition
complications	episodes
climax	climax
resolution	resolution

and their ordering is seemingly random. An example of an episodic plot is Homer's *Odyssey*, in which Odysseus has a number of adventures during his long journey home. Stories involving travel—*Don Quixote, Gulliver's Travels, Huckleberry Finn*—frequently have an episodic structure.

Both these basic formulas are subject to numerous variations and nuances. Some stories have multiple plots, each with its own structure. **Flashbacks** can interrupt the chronological flow of the story, bringing new insights to the current situation. A story that maintains a strict chronological timeline is called **linear**, while a plot that incorporates either logical or illogical jumps of time is called **nonlinear**. **Epic** stories tend to have a long string of complications that lead to a number of climaxes, while conveying a larger story of a person's life or a major event. Another common variation of the standard structure is the omission of the resolution. A chilling effect can be created by abruptly ending at the climactic moment, leaving the audience in shocked disbelief, such as the final moments of *Bonnie and Clyde* (1967).

Character

The term **character** is applied in a number of ways in drama. In its most general use, a character is simply someone in a story. The principal character is called the **protagonist**, and it is primarily through his or her eyes and experiences that we follow a story. Many plots involve a principal adversary, called the **antagonist**, who generates a conflict that sets a series of complications in motion. The interplay between these two key figures often creates the basic tension of a story.

Figure 2.1 Indiana Jones, an idealized hero

For a drama to maintain interest, the characters in a story need to appeal to an audience through their psychological makeup, the conflicts that they endure, and the changes that they undergo. We admire some characters for being ideal heroes like Indiana Jones, but we are also attracted to other characters that are more like ourselves or people we know. Among the techniques that contribute to characterization in film are the character's actions, physical appearance, and language, the camera technique, and, of course, the music.

Setting

The term **setting**, which refers to both the location and the time frame in which a story takes place, can have an important influence on a narrative. The contemporary suburban setting in films such as *American Beauty* (1999), *Edward Scissorhands* (1990), and *Halloween* (1978) contributes to the mood and impact of these diverse stories. In movies such as *Midnight Cowboy* (1969), *Mean Streets* (1973) and *Lost in Translation* (2003), the sights and sounds of city life are essential to the unfolding dramas. By way of contrast, the scenic background for John Ford's westerns shot in Monument Valley, such as *The Searchers* (1956), makes a quiet yet indelible impression on the viewer.

Figure 2.2 Woody Allen often plays characters with many human frailties

Settings can have a strong psychological effect. The contrast between Superman's bright Metropolis and Batman's dark Gotham City contributes greatly to the divergent moods of these movies. Some stories unfold in restrictive settings that create a sense of being trapped. The survivors in *Lifeboat* (1944), the refugees in *Casablanca* (1942), and Joe Gillis (unable to leave a Gothic Hollywood mansion) in *Sunset Blvd.* (1950) are confined by their environments, and the audience shares their sense of hopelessness. The terror in *Jurassic Park* (1993) is similarly intensified by the setting on an isolated island with nowhere to run or hide.

In some instances, the setting can run counter to the mood or action of a story. War movies, such as *Platoon* (1986), often give fleeting glimpses of the beauty of nature. Similarly, *The Mission* (1986), *The Last of the Mohicans* (1992), and *Braveheart* (1995) juxtapose stunning landscape panoramas with scenes of horrific violence. In these films, this contrast serves as a reminder about the beauty of the natural world, which stands in direct opposition to the cruelty of man.

The time period for a particular story can also be significant. A movie set in a defined historical era is often referred to as a **period film**, a term that suggests attention to details of costumes, scenery, and manners. Films such as *Amadeus* (1984), *The Age of Innocence* (1993), and *Shakespeare in Love* (1998) provide us with fascinating glimpses of the past. Plots are sometimes set in historical eras that underwent rapid change, thereby creating a sense of uncertainty and even chaos. Ingmar Bergman's *The Seventh Seal* (1957) is set during the years of disillusionment following the Crusades, and Akira Kurosawa's *Seven Samurai* (1954) takes place during the decline of Japan's feudal system. Similarly, Kirk Douglas portrays one of the West's last cowboys struggling to adjust to modern America in *Lonely Are the Brave* (1962). In all of these stories, the vision of changing traditions has a clear parallel to contemporary American life.

Fantasy films enjoy a wide variety of time settings. Science fiction movies, such as *2001: A Space Odyssey* (1968), are filled with visions of the future. By contrast, two of Hollywood's most popular film trilogies are set in the mysterious past. *The Lord of the Rings* takes us to the mythical world of Middle-earth, at a time before the histories of man were recorded. Similarly, *Star Wars*, despite its futuristic images, is set "a long time ago." This simple statement fires the imagination and encourages us to speculate about how these stories connect to our own history.

Theme

A **theme** is the central idea underlying a given story. A plot gives us the basic actions of a story, and the theme provides us with its intellectual meaning. In *Citizen Kane*, for example, the essential facts of the story are presented in the opening newsreel. But it is the fascinating retelling of the story from five different perspectives that adds details and slowly reveals the principal theme, a theme that is tied to the word "Rosebud."

In this strict literary use of the term, not all films have themes. Some, such as slapstick comedies or light musicals, simply provide entertainment. By contrast, other films may have themes that are too obvious and heavy, and these are often dismissed as propaganda. The racist theme found in *The Birth of a Nation* (1915), for example, mars this otherwise brilliant work of art.

The most highly regarded films tend to deal with serious issues, such as religion, patriotism, and morality. Underneath the hilarious physical comedy of *City Lights* (1931) are the poignant themes of selflessness and the beauty of love. *To Kill a Mockingbird* (1962) teaches us about prejudice with a dual story of racism and fear of someone who is different. The numerous episodes of *Apocalypse Now* (1979) do not directly affect the overall plot, but each contributes to one of the underlying themes of the movie, a vision of how the United States lost the Vietnam War. Films such as these impart meaningful messages that can have a profound impact on an audience.

Mood

A movie may be funny, sad, whimsical, profound, optimistic, dark, or any of countless other emotions and combinations of emotions. This quality of a film is called **mood** or **tone**. The mood of the film does not necessarily have to match the mood of the story and theme. For example, *M*A*S*H* (1970) is a powerful pacifist film about the Korean War created at a time when the United States was divided about the Vietnam conflict. But the biting criticism of the war is presented within a prevailing comic mood, as is suggested by its theme song, "Suicide Is Painless."

During the course of a film, the director has a number of tools that he can employ in order to create specific moods. Among the most powerful are the visual elements and music. The overall mood is often suggested at the onset. When a film begins with a title and credits, music and visual elements can adumbrate the general tone for the ensuing narrative. The music accompanying the opening credits of *Gone With the Wind* (1939), *Psycho* (1960), and *The Graduate* (1967) establishes appropriate moods for those films. In *Catch-22* (1970), the absence of music during the opening credits helps to create a sense of seriousness, which will underlie the entire black-humor drama.

In some films, the director will omit the title and credits or add them unobtrusively after the story has begun. In these instances, source music or underscoring (see Chapter 4) might still be used to establish a central mood. A comparison of the two versions for *Touch of Evil* (1958), for example, illustrates the importance of the opening moments of a film. In the studio release, the titles are presented along with Henry Mancini's blaring big band tune. In Welles's original conception, now available on DVD, the credits are omitted, and the music projects an entirely different mood while establishing a stronger sense of realism (see Chapter 18).

Elements of Film

Film can be divided into two broad categories, nonfiction and narrative. **Nonfiction** films, encompassing the documentary, propaganda, factual, and instructional sub-categories, are beyond the scope of our text. This limitation, however, does not imply that there is less art in the creation of these films. Indeed, some of the most critically acclaimed films are nonfiction, and many incorporate strong musical scores. Narrative films, the principal product of the modern movie industry, present stories. Even though the plot of a narrative film may use real characters and actual events, the content is selected and manipulated by the writer and director, and the film is therefore considered fiction.

Film Genres

Narrative films can be organized into **genres**—categories based on similar stories and other conventions. Definitions of genres and sub-genres vary from writer to writer. A significant number of films avoid generic conventions altogether, and many others reflect characteristics of two or more genres. Despite these difficulties, recognition of genres is essential to the study of film and film music. Generic conventions often play a prominent role in musical choices, including how much music and what style of music will be used. The following are the most common genres and sub-genres of narrative films:

> action/adventure: crime, disaster, martial arts, swashbuckler, war
> animation
> comedy: dark, romantic, screwball, sentimental, slapstick
> drama: biopic (biography), historical (often epic), melodrama
> horror: monster, psychological thriller
> musical
> mystery: courtroom, detective, film noir
> romance
> science fiction
> western

Cinematography

The creation of a film occurs in three stages—preproduction, production, and post-production. The preproduction phase, largely controlled by the producer, involves the planning and preparation of the film, and may take several years. Once production begins, the film is in the hands of the director, who oversees the activities of the production crew, actors, and cinematographer. Of the many varied artistic elements of this phase, let us consider some aspects of cinematography.

A photographer takes still pictures, and his art is called photography. The cinematographer takes moving pictures, and his art is called **cinematography**. Film shares a number of characteristics with both photography and painting. All three present a framed image. In film, the visual element is called the *mise-en-scène*, a term that is borrowed from theater. This term encompasses aspects such as lighting, costumes, and décor, the relationship of these elements to each other, and how they are photographed. For the casual moviegoer, visual elements may be secondary to the story, and indeed, they are often intended to be unobtrusive. But visual elements have an enormous psychological impact on the viewer and can play a critical role in the presentation of the plot, the development of the characters, and the perception of the theme.

Figure 2.3 The *mise-en-scène* in *Laura*

Like the photographer, the cinematographer needs to consider the shot's composition, the camera's proximity to the subject, and the camera angle, lighting, and lenses. Unlike his counterpart, the cinematographer also needs to deal with movement, both of the subject and of the camera. There are numerous technical terms covering these aspects, which will be introduced as needed in the text. But one important element of cinematography needs some elaboration—point of view.

Point of View

The term "point of view" can be used in multiple ways. In drama, the unfolding of a plot is often seen through the perspective of a particular character. In *Gone With the Wind*, the Civil War and Reconstruction are seen through the point of view of the female protagonist, Scarlett O'Hara. The film opens and closes with her, and her transformation and her love for the land are the central issues of the film.

In cinematography, **point of view** (abbreviated as POV) refers to the perspective of the camera eye. Usually, a narrative film is shot through what is termed the **omniscient POV**. Often set at a distance from the action, the camera moves at the will of the director. Through this relatively objective point of view, we are allowed to see the action as an observer, and hence often know more about a situation—the identity of the antagonist, what is around the corner—than do the principal characters.

At times, the cinematographer may let us see through the eyes of one of the characters—this is called a **subjective POV**. In *Jaws* (1975), we see dangling legs from the underwater perspective of the shark. In *Lady in the Lake* (1947), the audience sees predominantly through the eyes of the protagonist, whose face appears on the screen when he looks into a mirror. In most instances, subjective POV is used briefly, allowing the audience to know what a character observes, such as a written note or a critical detail.

Film Editing

During **postproduction**, the film is given its final shape through the editing process and the addition of sound effects and music. In **editing**, the shots created during production are joined together. A **shot** is an uninterrupted length of film, and the precise moment when one shot ends and another begins is called a **cut**. Editing decisions, such as which shots to use, the length of shots, and the ordering of the shots, contribute greatly to the impact of the film.

Figure 2.4 The protagonist's image appears in a mirror in *Lady in the Lake*

From the viewer's perspective, many of the cuts will be accepted as natural, allowing us to see a continuous scene from a variety of perspectives. In showing a conversation, for example, a director can cut deftly between the people who are talking, the reactions of the listeners, what one of the characters might be looking at, something that is unknown to the people talking, such as impending danger, or a general view of the setting of the conversation. In fact a continuous shot without cuts might strike an audience as monotonous. To experience a film with a minimum of cuts, watch Alfred Hitchcock's *Rope* (1948), in which Hitchcock creates the sense that the entire movie was shot in one long, uninterrupted take.

Cuts also separate changes of scene that lead the viewer to other locations and times. In *The Birth of a Nation* (1915), D. W. Griffith presents a powerful Civil War scene in which two best friends, one from the South and one from the North, die in each other's arms. Griffith brilliantly cuts across both time and location to show the two families hearing the news of the deaths. In an instant, Griffith has given us a powerful lesson about the personal costs of war.

With the aid of cutting, a film can show several events occurring simultaneously. The alternation of shots from two or more sequences is called **crosscutting**. One of film's classic clichés is the tension-building crosscutting between someone in danger and someone racing to the rescue. Crosscutting can also allow for the development of multiple plot strands. Much of the plot of *The Empire Strikes Back* (1980) involves crosscutting between scenes of Luke Skywalker training with Yoda, Han Solo and Princess Leia avoiding the Imperial forces, and Darth Vader plotting against the heroes. All three strands eventually come together in an extended climax.

Because of the flexibility cutting provides, film can incorporate flashbacks and embrace nonlinear plots much more readily than theatrical drama can. Mike Nichols effectively uses a jumble of stream-of-consciousness flashbacks in the film *Catch-22* (1970) to show the irrationality of war. Recent filmmakers have excelled in a variety of unusual storytelling techniques. One of the most fascinating is used in Christopher Nolan's *Memento* (2000), a story that is essentially told backward.

Another editing technique is called **montage**. The exact definition of this term varies, but for our purposes montage refers to a section of film comprising a number of brief shots edited together in order to show a condensed series of events. The juxtaposition of these multiple images emphasizes their relationship, both similarities and differences. Montage is an effective device for showing travel, the passing of time, and the frenetic chaos of battle.

Trailer

The effect of a montage and of cuts in general can be greatly enhanced by the use of music. Although some composers begin work on musical ideas while a film is still in production, the bulk of the scoring must wait until after the final editing is completed, when time is usually limited. The craft of film composing is demanding, and the output of some film composers working under pressure is genuinely remarkable. A detailed examination of how music functions within a film follows in Chapter 4, but first we must explore a few musical concepts that will aid you throughout the remainder of the text.

Important Terms

causal plot	setting	subjective point of view
episodic plot	period film	postproduction
flashback	genre	editing
linear	cinematography	shot
nonlinear	*mise-en-scène*	cut
epic story	point of view (POV)	crosscut
protagonist	omniscient point of view	montage
antagonist		

3

Elements of Music

One does not need to know how to read music, play a musical instrument, or analyze a musical score in order to listen to and talk about film music. But since this book contains examples of musical notation and discussions of music that use technical terms, an introduction to music notation and explanations of some important musical concepts and terms are in order.

The expression "to read music" has two principal meanings: the knowledge of the note names and rhythmic values, and the ability to play notes on a musical instrument while looking at such notation. The difference between the two definitions is similar to the distinction between reading words on a page and typing. There are people who know how to read without knowing how to type, and it is possible to type without knowing how to read—for example, when we need to type a foreign word or phrase. The same is true with musicians. There are people who can read note names and rhythms but cannot play them on a musical instrument, and there are those who can play an instrument but cannot play from written notation. With the aid of computers and Midi keyboards, there are growing numbers of musicians who cannot read music but are still successful as performers and composers.

Music Notation

For the purposes of this text, you will not be required to read music by either of the above definitions. But being able to follow a brief musical line is helpful as you listen and is much simpler than it might seem at first. In general, musical sound has three properties: pitch, duration, and color. The traditional music notation developed in Western civilization denotes the first two of these properties. Think of music notation as a graph; pitch is indicated on the vertical axis and duration on the horizontal.

Pitch is the term for how high or low a musical note is. The musical **staff** has five horizontal lines. The higher a note appears on the staff, the higher the pitch. In Example 3.1, you see that the melodic line at first goes lower and then turns upward. In listening to this melody, you should be able to hear the same descent and ascent in the musical line. Also important to pitch is the first symbol on the staff—the **clef sign**. This symbol designates pitches on the staff and tells us whether the basic range is high or low; Example 3.1 contains a treble clef, which suggests a high range, and Example 3.2 is set with a bass clef, which indicates a lower range.

In addition to seeing the general direction of a melody, you can also tell if two adjacent notes are the same pitch (Example 3.2, notes 1 and 2), close together (most of Example 3.2), or have a wide interval between them (most of Example 3.1). These two melodies are American patriotic tunes. One is "The Star-Spangled Banner," and the other is "America the Beautiful." Can you tell which is which just by looking at the notation?

When following musical notation, you do not have to know the exact duration of individual notes. There are two ways of tracking the music on a staff while listening. The first is simply to follow note by note. For every note that you hear, there is one note indicated on the staff. Be sure to skip the symbols for rests and be aware that the curved line connecting identical pitches, such as the last two notes of Example 3.2, is called a **tie** and indicates that these two pitches will be heard as one note.

The other helpful technique for following written notation is to count beats. A single vertical line appears at regular intervals on the musical staff; it defines a basic temporal unit called a **measure** (or bar). The second symbol shown on the

Example 3.1

Example 3.2

music staves in Examples 3.1 and 3.2 is a **time signature**, which tell us how many beats there are in a measure (the top number) and what type of note receives a beat (the bottom number). In Example 3.1, the time signature tells us that there are three beats in a measure and that a quarter note is equal to one beat. The symbol for Example 3.2 represents "common time," which has four beats in a measure and a quarter note for a beat. Knowing how many beats there are in a measure and counting along with the music are useful tools in keeping your place, especially when the music is moving quickly.

Elements of Pitch and Duration

Music is commonly described as having five basic elements. Three of these elements deal with the organization of pitch—melody, texture, and harmony. The remaining two elements, rhythm and timbre, deal with the properties of duration and color. It is not the intention in this section to introduce all of the concepts of listening to music in general. Rather, the focus here will be on those aspects that will be most beneficial for listening to film music.

Melody

A **melody** is a succession of pitches that is heard as a unit. The term sometimes suggests that the unit is easily recognized and somewhat memorable, in which case one can also use the word **tune** or describe a melody as being **tuneful**. The shape or contour of a melody contributes greatly to its nature and impact on the listener. In the melodies shown in Examples 3.1 ("The Star-Spangled Banner") and 3.2 ("America the Beautiful"), the divergent directions of the melodic contour are easily seen. The first also has a wider **range** (the distance between the highest and lowest note of a melody), and it moves by wider **intervals** (the distance between one pitch and the next) than does the second melody. When a melody contains a significant number of large intervals, as in Example 3.1, it is called **disjunct**, while a melody that moves primarily in small intervals, as in Example 3.2, is called **conjunct**.

Because of the limits of the human voice, vocal melodies tend to be limited in range and are frequently conjunct. By necessity, a vocal melody also comes to periodic momentary rests that allow the singer to breathe. These rests define melodic units called **phrases**; the ends of phrases are called **cadences**. In a number of respects, musical phrases are similar to phrases and clauses in writing. Some are independent, some are incomplete, and some are questioning. Musical cadences are the equivalent of punctuation marks. The endings that seem to be incomplete, similar to commas or question marks, are called **open cadences**. Those that are clear and complete, like periods and exclamation points, are considered to be **closed cadences**.

Melodies composed for instruments can have a greater range and variety of contour. Instruments are capable of large ranges and wide leaps and can hence create a disjointed melody. Some instruments are also capable of playing an endless string of notes without breathing, creating melodies that lack clear phrase structures. Instruments can also play melodies in vocal style, with limited ranges, conjunct motion, and regularly recurring phrases; such melodies are often described as **lyrical**.

The theme from *Gone With the Wind* (1939) shown in Example 3.3 is an instrumental melody that can be divided into two eight-measure phrases; the first ends with an **open cadence**, and the second comes to a **closed cadence**.

Two other terms are frequently encountered in discussions of melody—motive and theme. A **motive** is a small melodic idea that can serve as part of a larger melody or stand on its own. Both of the two larger, eight-measure phrases in Example 3.3 contain four two-measure motives. The motives have a similar shape; each begins with a wide leap upwards (disjunct motion) followed by a descent. The use of motives has two purposes. First, it helps make the tune more memorable, and second, the motive can be isolated and developed on its own. After the initial statement of the melody in Example 3.3, there is a contrasting section. Listen carefully and you will hear that the motive continues to play a prominent role in this section, building tension as we wait for the expected return of the main theme.

Motives can also function as independent melodic ideas. John Williams needs only two low notes to create a memorable and frightening motive in *Jaws* (1975). Similarly, we will hear how Bernard Herrmann constructs a powerful musical score in *Citizen Kane* (1941) based largely on two five-note motives representing power and youthful innocence. While motives may lack the broad appeal of full-length melodies, they are useful building tools.

Example 3.3 Tara's Theme from *Gone With the Wind*

A musical **theme** is a melody that recurs within a given work, usually with special significance to the drama. Some themes have no specific meaning and represent the general spirit of a movie, such as the popular songs that introduce many films. Other themes are more specific and refer to various aspects of a story. The theme from Example 3.3 represents Tara, the plantation that belongs to Scarlett O'Hara. John Williams's motive from *Jaws* is associated with the shark. These themes are considered to be **leitmotifs**, a concept that will be explored more fully in the next chapter.

Texture

When we listen to melodies in film music, we usually hear a musical accompaniment in the background, subordinate to the principal tune. But there are also moments when we can hear a melody without any other musical sounds, and passages in which two or more equal melodies are played. The relationship of a melodic line to other musical material in a given passage is called **texture**. Film music usually presents a single dominant melody with accompaniment or music that seemingly has no dominant tune. In either case, this texture is considered to be **homophonic**. Examples of such a texture include the music for the opening credits of *Gone With the Wind*, *Star Wars*, and *Psycho*.

The presentation of a single melodic line without any other musical material is called **monophonic**. This texture is not common in film music. It is heard mostly as a brief contrast, often used for dramatic effect. A single woodwind instrument slowly playing the principal theme from *E.T. the Extra-Terrestrial* (1982) suggests childlike simplicity. In *The Empire Strikes Back* (1980), a sense of fear and power is created when the Darth Vader theme is suddenly intoned in unison by the full symphony orchestra. A monophonic texture can also be used to suggest the distant past—for example, singing Gregorian chant to suggest the Middle Ages—or distant lands, where monophonic textures are more common.

The presence of two or more equal melodies is called a **contrapuntal** texture or simply **counterpoint**. In such passages, the melodies are usually similar to each other, as is the case in a round such as "Frère Jacques." This texture is called imitative counterpoint, often abbreviated to **imitation**. Most often imitative counterpoint is encountered when a brief musical motive is played alternately by two or more musical instruments. Contrapuntal settings of longer themes are unusual in film music, but can be effective, such as in a climactic scene of *A Place in the Sun* (1951). Here the imitative counterpoint suggests a chase. Such passages recall the structure of a musical form called a **fugue**, which is characterized by extensive imitative counterpoint.

Harmony

Harmony is the element of music that is created when two or more pitches are produced at the same time. Harmony is an essential aspect of Western music after 1400, but it is unusual in music from non-Western cultures, which is based on monophonic textures. An important harmonic term is **chord**, which denotes the sound of three or more pitches at any given moment in a musical work. Some chords sound beautiful and restful to the ear, while others are harsh and disturbing. The latter sound, called **dissonance**, is created when the pitches of a chord clash with each other. The resultant sound is especially effective for dramatic moments.

Example 3.4 presents the opening chords of Bernard Herrmann's score to *Psycho* (1960). The bottom three notes of the chords, taken by themselves, create a traditional harmony. But the top note clashes with the bottom one, and the resultant dissonance establishes the dark mood of the story of a disturbed psychological state.

Traditional Western harmony depends on dissonances and their resolution. The movement from dissonance to consonance suggests conflict and resolution. But there are a number of films that employ continuous dissonance without resolution. The resultant sound conveys a disturbing mood, suggesting that something is wrong, such as the irrational psychological states in *Spellbound* (1945) and *Psycho*, the pains of being a teenager in *East of Eden* (1955), the upside-down world of *Planet of the Apes* (1968), and the terror of *Alien* (1979).

Hearing dissonance and resolution is an important step in listening to harmony. More advanced listening skills need to be based on some knowledge of Western music theory. The following discussion gives some background for further listening, but like so many listening skills, you cannot learn to hear harmony by reading a book. Listening skills can be developed only by practice.

In discussions of harmony and melody, the word **interval** appears frequently. This term refers to the distance between two pitches, whether they are played simultaneously or in succession. In traditional Western harmony, the intervals of thirds and sixths are generally considered to be stable, while intervals of seconds and sevenths are unstable and create dissonances. In a melody, intervals of fourths and fifths are considered to be strong. The opening theme from *Star Wars*, for example, contains a number of fourths and fifths that contribute to the heroic quality of that theme.

Terms designating intervals also contain modifying words, such as major, minor, or perfect. Hence you may read about a major third or a minor second. For our purposes it is not necessary to know the meanings of these modifying terms, so this topic will not be addressed. But there is one special interval that deserves some attention. Known as a diminished fifth, augmented fourth, or **tritone**, this interval creates great tension both melodically and harmonically in traditional Western

Example 3.4 *Psycho* opening chords

music. The harshness of the Rowing theme from *Ben-Hur* (1959) can be attributed in part to the melodic outline of two tritones.

Fundamental to all music systems is the interval of an **octave**, the distance between a pitch and its repetition in a higher or lower range. In Western music, the octave is divided into twelve equal intervals called **half steps**. From these twelve pitches, two seven-note scales have been created, using a combination of whole and half steps. These scales are commonly referred to as **major** and **minor**.

It is not necessary to learn scale patterns in order to listen to film music, but you should be aware that the difference between major and minor harmonies is significant. The majority of music that you will hear is set in major keys. Minor keys often provide a darker, more menacing sound. Luke Skywalker's theme, heard at the beginning of *Star Wars*, is in a major key. By contrast, the dark qualities of Darth Vader's theme are partially due to its minor scale. The minor key can also be used to underscore the transformation of a character. When Luke Skywalker is sad or in trouble, John Williams transforms Luke's theme by playing it slower and placing it in a minor key, suggesting troubled thoughts or danger.

In modern art music, it is not uncommon to abandon these two seven-note scales and employ melodies and harmonies using all twelve pitches found in the octave. Such harmonic treatment is called **chromatic**. Other cultures have subdivided the octave into a variety of different patterns, some with more than twelve pitches and some with less. These systems may sound odd and exotic to the ear. The **microtones** (units smaller than a half step) heard in a gamelan band from Indonesia can sound both disturbing and fascinating to the Western ear. Such sounds are particularly effective in suggesting an exotic location or a non-Western philosophy.

Rhythm

Rhythm is the element of music dealing with time. Musical time may have a floating, unmeasured character, or it may be structured on a series of recurring pulses called **beats**. Floating, unstructured rhythm is more common in non-Western musical cultures, and can be found occasionally in Western music. The playing and sustaining of a single low pitch when a character enters a room is a cliché suggesting danger. In quite a different circumstance, the seemingly timeless sound of Ligeti's *Lux aeterna* is a perfect match for the mysterious monolith in *2001: A Space Odyssey* (1968).

For the most part, music in the Western tradition is organized around recurring beats. The speed at which pulses are heard is called **tempo**. A fast tempo generates excitement and suggests conflict, while a slow tempo indicates calm and might accompany a love scene. In film music, we often encounter tempos in which the beat is exactly equivalent to one second. This tempo is common because it makes it easy to calculate how much music is needed to match the length of a specific scene.

Beats often occur in regular patterns of strong and weak pulses. Such patterns are called **meter**. In films, most music features meters with two or four pulses. The strongest beat is always the first of the group. For the most part, melodic material supports the established meter. But it can also contradict the given pulse by creating accents on weak beats or between beats. This rhythmic effect is called **syncopation**. In twentieth-century American popular music, the placement of notes just before or after a pulse creates a rhythmic conflict that generates a fresh, energetic character.

Timbre

Timbre is the technical term for the color or tone quality produced by voices, instruments, and various combinations of the two. This element often plays a critical role in the overall impact of a film score. Many composers initially write their music at the piano and then assign the various musical ideas to voices and instruments, a task that is called **orchestration**. Someone who specializes in this last activity, an **orchestrator,** can provide valuable assistance to a composer by suggesting possible instrumental combinations for a given passage and by completing the time-consuming job of writing out individual orchestral parts according to the direction of the composer.

Voices

A wide variety of colors can be achieved with human voices. Among the factors contributing to vocal color are voice types (male or female, tenor or bass), how many singers are heard (a soloist or a chorus), what text is being sung, and what performance style is used. In considering performance style, think of the vast difference in vocal color between a performer of Italian opera and a performer of Beijing opera, or the difference between the sound of Barbara Streisand and the voice of Bob Dylan. There are many memorable uses of voices in film music, including the strong male chorus in Sergei Prokofiev's *Alexander Nevsky* (1938), the demonic full choir in John Williams's *The Phantom Menace* (1999), and the haunting solo soprano in Ennio Morricone's *Once Upon a Time in the West* (1968).

Symphonic Instruments

The instruments of the symphony can be divided into four groups: strings, brass, woodwinds, and percussion. The principal string instruments are usually played with a bow, which gives the sound a great deal of flexibility. Strings can play lyrical love themes or agitated combat music. Their versatility can be heard in *Psycho* and *The Red Violin* (1999). Both films employ an orchestra consisting only of strings, but the color effects are dramatically different. String instruments can also be plucked by the finger, a technique called **pizzicato.** This plucking sound is also heard with the

Table 3.1

Instruments of the orchestra

STRINGS	BRASS	WOODWINDS	PERCUSSION
violin	trumpet	flute/piccolo	timpani
viola	French horn	oboe	snare drums
cello	trombone	clarinet	cymbals
string bass	tuba	bassoon	xylophone
harp			piano

harp, a string instrument often used to suggest elegance. Because of its association with heaven, the harp is sometimes heard when someone is dying—for example, Darth Vader in *Return of the Jedi* (1983).

Brass instruments can generate great power and force. They are often heard in marches and fanfares. Movies about ancient Rome usually feature elaborate brass fanfares. At the outset of *Star Wars*, the trumpets play Luke Skywalker's theme, creating the effect of an opening fanfare. The return of this theme after the brief string interlude, however, is given to the French horns, creating a deeper, nobler, and more heroic feeling.

While the strings and brass are often heard as unified families of instruments, the woodwinds are generally heard either with the entire orchestra or isolated as soloists. The colors of this family of instruments are more varied than those of the strings and brass, and composers use solo woodwind colors for effective contrast. In particular, the oboe and clarinet are quite expressive and are used to create a sense of poignancy in film music.

Percussion instruments are often added to generate excitement or add a touch of color to the orchestral sound. In *Seven Days in May* (1964), Jerry Goldsmith creates a terse musical score by limiting the underscoring to percussion instruments, suggesting the military setting of the story. Also considered a percussion instrument is the piano, whose presence in the traditional symphony orchestra is unusual. The piano is capable of producing many colors, as can be heard in jazz numbers (the closing credits to *Big*, 1988), works in concerto style (*Exodus*, 1960), and modern musical sounds (*Wait Until Dark*, 1967).

Symphonic instruments have a standard musical color that is produced through the normal process of playing. But there are also a number of special sounds that can be created with unusual performance techniques. Table 3.2 can help you with the terminology for these special sounds.

Table 3.2

Special color effects

EFFECT	INSTRUMENT	HOW CREATED	RESULTING SOUND
mute	brass, strings	an object (mute) is placed at the end of the brass instrument or on the bridge of the string instrument	muffled, restrained
trill	piano, winds, strings	the quick alternation of two adjacent pitches	fast oscillating sound
pizzicato	strings	pitches are plucked by fingers	guitar-like
harmonic	strings	lightly touching a pitch with a finger	high, soft, ringing
tremolo	strings	bow is moved back and forth quickly	intense
glissando	strings, harp, piano	series of successive pitches, played quickly	swooping
flutter-tongue	winds	fluttering the tongue while blowing into an instrument	jarring, oscillating sound
prepared piano	piano	small objects are placed into the strings of a piano	percussive sounds, some with no pitch

Instruments of Popular Music

Popular music often features the same instruments that can be heard in the symphony orchestra. The violin can be featured as a country fiddle, the pizzicato string bass is a common jazz sound, and the clarinet, trumpet, and trombone are frequently heard in jazz ensembles. When these instruments are heard in popular settings, their color is often altered, sometimes with a more cutting edge, such as the beautiful trumpet theme heard at the beginning of *Chinatown* (1974).

The saxophone is a versatile instrument that can be heard in both jazz and rock ensembles. Leonard Bernstein employs a saxophone at the beginning of *On the Waterfront* (1954) to link the dissonant, harsh opening music to the popular style of jazz. Bernard Herrmann adds to the unsettling mood of *Taxi Driver* (1976) with an extended saxophone solo.

The instruments of a rock ensemble can be used for a variety of effects, creating a hip, slick sound or an intense, loud sound to accompany violence. As with jazz, rock music can be combined with other musical sounds. In *Dirty Harry* (1971), Lalo Schifrin combines the dissonance associated with modern concert music with an underlying rock beat. The sound of a drum set generally indicates a musical link to popular music.

Electronic Instruments

A number of musical instruments generate sound through electronics. The earliest electronic instruments heard in film music are the theremin and ondes martenot (see Figures 3.1 and 3.2). Similar in sound, these instruments produce oscillating pitches that create an eerie, unreal sound. Miklós Rózsa employs a theremin in *The Lost Weekend* and *Spellbound*, both from 1945, to portray psychological problems. The keyboard of the ondes martenot makes it a more practical instrument, and its sounds can be heard in numerous film scores, including Maurice Jarre's *Lawrence of Arabia* (1961).

Elaborate electronic music labs established in the 1950s were capable of generating a seemingly endless variety of new sounds. Film music ventured into these new sounds cautiously, but the landmark film *Forbidden Planet* (1956) used a completely electronic score created in a studio by Bebe Barron.

Another early pioneer in electronic sounds was Walter/Wendy Carlos, who abandoned the electronic studio in favor of the Moog synthesizer. After establishing the popular appeal of the synthesizer with the album *Switched-On Bach*, Carlos used the synthesizer in the score to Kubrick's *A Clockwork Orange* (1971). Since that time, the synthesizer has greatly transformed the sound of film scores. Vangelis won an Oscar for his synthesized score to *Chariots of Fire* (1981), in which he used the synthesizer to reproduce the sounds of traditional instruments. But the synthesizer can also create new sounds such as those heard in Vangelis's *Blade Runner* (1982). In combination with computers, the synthesizer remains a valuable tool for its ability not only to replace acoustic instruments, but also to create new musical sounds (see Close-Up on page 359).

Figure 3.1 Leon Theremin with his electronic theremin

Figure 3.2 Maurice Martenot with an ondes martenot

Historical Instruments

Western civilization created a number of musical instruments, now obsolete, that are effective in suggesting an earlier time period. A story set in the sixteenth or seventeenth century may feature the sounds of recorders (wind instruments similar in sound to flutes), viols (bowed string instruments), or lutes, and mandolins (plucked string instruments, similar to the guitar). But the most distinctive antique-sounding instrument is the harpsichord, a keyboard instrument that looks like a small piano. The sound of the plucked strings of the harpsichord immediately suggests an earlier time. The instrument is also used in *Who's Afraid of Virginia Woolf* (1966), where it suggests the intellectual façade of a dysfunctional university couple.

Folk and Ethnic Instruments

Musical instruments from other cultures often play a role in establishing the location of a story. Ethnic instruments, such as those shown in Table 3.3, can perform in a style indigenous to their region, but they may also be combined with Western

Figure 3.3 A harpsichord

instruments. In this way a film composer can suggest another culture while maintaining a musical style that is familiar to Western audiences. The combinations of a symphony orchestra with an Indian sitar in *Gandhi* (1982) and a cello with a Chinese erhu in *Crouching Tiger, Hidden Dragon* (2000) provide fresh musical solutions to the depiction of non-Western music in a Western art medium.

In creating an ethnic ambience, musical authenticity is not necessary. John Debney, in his score to *The Passion of the Christ* (2004), employs a wide variety of instruments, including the plucked oud from the Middle East, the duduk, an Armenian flute, and the Chinese erhu. The combination of these instruments has no basis in historical fact, but their unique timbres create a sound that effectively suggests the time and region for the story.

Table 3.3

World instruments

INSTRUMENT	REGION	CHARACTER	MOVIE FEATURING INSTRUMENT
African drums	Africa	Variety of drums, primarily played by hand	*The Naked Prey* (1966)
Andean flute	South America	Similar to pan flute; can have a percussive sound	*The Mission* (1986)
bagpipes	Scotland, Ireland	Nasal wind instrument with bag for air supply	*Braveheart* (1995)
banjo	United States	Plucked string instrument with bright tone	*Bonnie and Clyde* (1967) *Deliverance* (1971)
erhu	China	String instrument with nasal vocal quality	*Crouching Tiger, Hidden Dragon* (2000)
gamelan	Indonesia	Percussion ensemble with hypnotic, repetitive character	*The Year of Living Dangerously* (1982)
koto	Japan	Plucked string instrument	*Tora! Tora! Tora!* (1970)
oud	Middle East	Plucked string instrument	*The Passion of the Christ* (2004)
shakuhachi	Japan	Wind instrument similar to recorder	*Legends of the Fall* (1984)
sitar	India	Plucked string instrument	*Gandhi* (1982)
taiko drums	Japan	Drums beaten with sticks	*Pearl Harbor* (2001)
zither	Europe	String instrument, strummed and hammered	*The Third Man* (1949)

Trailer

The musical terminology presented in this chapter may seem daunting at first. Since music is perceived aurally, it is often difficult to understand these concepts by simply reading. But the ideas put forth in this chapter are not as complex as they might appear, and, with the aid of your instructor, you should find yourself more comfortable with discussions of music in a relatively short time. As you read through the remaining chapters, you may want to review this chapter periodically and refer to the glossary for definitions of musical terms. For now, we will turn our attention to how music functions in a narrative film.

Important Terms

melody	monophonic	rhythm
conjunct	contrapuntal	tempo
disjunct	imitation	meter
cadence	fugue	syncopation
phrase	harmony	timbre
lyrical	chord	orchestration
motive	dissonance	orchestrator
theme	interval	electronic instruments
texture	tritone	historical instruments
homophonic	major and minor	ethnic instruments

Suggested Listening

Peter and the Wolf by Sergei Prokofiev. In this children's classic, you can hear individual instruments and follow the story through Prokofiev's use of leitmotifs.

Young Person's Guide to the Orchestra by Benjamin Britten.

Listening to Film Music

Music is one part of the total sound fabric that can be heard in film. In the simplest terms, film sound can be divided into three categories: dialogue, sound effects, and music. Dialogue tends to be the principal focus of our conscious listening, while the other two elements generally invade our senses through our peripheral hearing. In many films, music and sound effects, both of which are added during postproduction, work together to create a sound ambiance for the unfolding of a drama.

Yet music is also a unique sound in film. Both dialogue and sound effects are essential to the realism of a film narrative. Music, however, is often introduced as an outside element, a sound that is not part of the story itself. Such music is sometimes referred to as "background" music, but this designation does not do justice to the powerful and often critical role that music plays in film.

Because the presence of music is often secondary to dialogue and sound effects, it may be difficult at first to listen to film music. With practice and some understanding of the roles of film music, peripheral hearing can be sharpened, adding to the pleasures of watching films. To this end, we will consider five basic topics concerning film music: placement, borrowings, styles, function, and unity.

Placement

One of the subtle arts of filmmaking is the placement of music. The appearance or disappearance of music at a precise moment can make an audience laugh, cry, gasp, or feel tension. In order to support and not distract from the dramatic intention of the director, a film composer must have a keen sense of drama and frequently a good sense of humor.

Music as the Opening and Closing Frames

In many films, music is heard during the opening and closing credits, thereby providing a musical frame for the film as a whole. In accompanying the main title and the opening credits, music can fill a variety of functions:

- Alerting the audience, often with brass fanfares, to the beginning of the film
- Introducing the dominant musical theme of the film as a whole
- Presenting several musical themes that will be heard in the film; when the music contains a series of tunes from the film, as is common in musicals, it is called a **medley**.
- Establishing the mood of the film as a whole or of the opening scene
- Foreshadowing significant aspects of the story

Music for the closing credits may similarly reflect the mood at the end of a film or simply create a cheerful ambiance for the exiting audience. Frequently, the closing credits reprise a number of important musical ideas from the film, but it is also common in recent filmmaking for the closing credits to include a new song, which could lead to a possible Oscar nomination for Best Song and boost potential sales of a soundtrack recording.

One of the traditions of the epic genre is the inclusion of additional music designated as overture, intermission, and entr'acte. An **overture** is meant to precede the beginning of the film, the intermission separates the two parts of the film so the audience can take a brief break, and the **entr'acte** immediately precedes the resumption of the film, functioning like an overture to the second part. In these extended formats, the film often takes on the following structure:

overture
main title and opening credits
first part of the film
intermission (with or without music)
entr'acte
second part of the film
closing credits

In a sense, these epic films contain a double overture—the overture proper and the music for the main title and opening credits. Of the two, the music during the opening credits is usually more significant for the film as a whole, but the overture can still help establish a mood and acquaint the audience with themes from the film. Similarly, the music for the entr'acte generally has greater musical weight than that for the intermission.

Music within the Narrative

Music appearing during the narrative portion of the film is considered to be either source music or underscoring. **Source music**, or **diegetic music**, is heard as part of the drama itself—for example, when musicians are performing at a party or concert, or when a radio or phonograph is playing in the film. In a way, source music could also be considered a kind of sound effect. As with sound effects, the audience does not have to see the actual source of the sound. Just as the sounds of cars on a distant street can be understood as real, so too the sound of an unseen dance band or jukebox is considered to be diegetic. While the use of source music might seem to be the simplest music in film, it can be subtle and quite sophisticated. In Hitchcock's *Rear Window* (1954), there is no underscoring. All the music comes from radios and musical instruments in the neighborhood apartments, and the impact is just as strong, if not stronger, than what would have been produced by traditional underscoring.

Much of the music that you hear in films is called **underscoring** or **non-diegetic** music. Underscoring has no logical source in the drama itself. Performed by an unseen orchestra, jazz band, rock group, or singers, underscoring creates a general mood and guides us emotionally and psychologically through the course of a film. The following is a good rule for distinguishing between these two basic types of film music. If there is a reasonable expectation that a character in the film can hear the music, then it is source music. If only the audience can hear the music, then it is underscoring. Hence, if you are watching a film about survivors in a lifeboat in the middle of an ocean and you hear a full symphony orchestra, you are listening to underscoring.

A passage of underscoring from its entrance to its end is called a **cue**. The number and length of cues in a given film vary greatly. In some films there is no underscoring at all. In other films, music plays almost continuously, a technique that is referred to as **wall-to-wall** music. The beginning of a cue may coincide with other sound effects so that the viewer may be unaware that music has been added, and cues often fade quietly without notice. But in some instances, the dramatic entrance or the abrupt stopping of music can have a strong emotional impact on the audience. In horror films such as *Halloween* (1978), tensions can be raised both when music starts and when it disappears. Whether obtrusive or subtle, the placement of musical cues is a delicate craft that contributes greatly to the effectiveness of the film score.

Borrowings

Film music is either original or borrowed. Original music, as the name implies, is newly created for a specific film, while borrowed music is based on music that was previously composed. Despite the terminology, there can be a great deal of originality in the art of borrowing music. Two terms are commonly used when discussing borrowed music: arrangement and adaptation. An **arrangement** borrows a melody from another source, and the film composer provides it with an original setting suited to the film. After "As Time Goes By" is introduced as source music in *Casablanca* (1943), Max Steiner subjects the tune to a variety of arrangements in the underscoring, as it becomes the principal love theme for the film. Other melodies frequently heard in movies include the American traditional song "Red River Valley," the melancholy "Auld Lang Syne," and regional songs such as "Dixie" and the "Marseillaise."

An **adaptation** borrows a complete passage from another source, including both melody and accompaniment. Alterations in the orchestration (Scott Joplin's rags in *The Sting*, 1973) or length (Richard Strauss's *Also Sprach Zarathustra* in *2001: A Space Odyssey*, 1968) are typical adaptations of a musical composition to fit the needs of the film. There are two terms that are used to describe film scores that depend largely on adaptation. In the silent film era, scores that are a pastiche of borrowed music were referred to as **compilation scores**. In the sound era, the term **adapted score** refers to film music that is substantially borrowed, such as the music for *The Sting* and *2001: A Space Odyssey*. The principal differences between the two terms are the eras from which they originate and the amount of music in the film score. The compilation score from the silent era suggests non-stop, wall-to-wall music, while the adapted score from the sound era uses music more sparingly.

Musical Style

Anyone who has shopped for CDs is aware that music can be divided into a myriad of styles. All of these styles are defined by distinct characteristics created by the musical elements discussed in Chapter 3: melody, harmony, texture, rhythm, and timbre. Whether listening to Baroque, punk rock, or Japanese music, you will hear musical qualities that are shared by other music in that style. Knowledge of the basic characteristics of musical styles can be a great aid in listening to film music. To begin with, we will divide film music into five basic musical styles, which can be seen in Table 4.1. Of these, the first three—postromantic, modern, and popular—are the most common.

Table 4.1

Basic musical styles in film

ELEMENTS	POSTROMANTIC	MODERN	POPULAR	HISTORICAL	ETHNIC
melody	great variety of melodies	avoids tunes; often disjunct	central role for tunes	appropriate to era	appropriate to region
texture	melody-dominated	variety of textures	melody-dominated	appropriate to era	monophonic
harmony	traditional	dissonant	traditional	appropriate to era	no harmony
rhythm	strong pulse; regular meter	irregular pulses and meter	strong beat; syncopation	appropriate to era	often complicated
timbre	full orchestra common	often small, colorful ensembles	popular music ensembles	historical instruments	indigenous instruments

The generalizations in the table are by necessity very broad. Most students will be able to describe and recognize a great variety of subtypes of popular music, whether in jazz (New Orleans, big band, bop) or rock (Motown, disco, rap). Each of these subtypes has its own distinct characteristics, but in general popular music tends to be melody-oriented, have a strong beat, and incorporate syncopated rhythms.

The term "modern" is problematic. In this case, it is not meant to be synonymous with "recent." Although it may seem strange to refer to something from 1913 as "modern," the term is a common way to refer to music predominantly by concert composers (composers writing for performances in opera and concert halls) that is consciously written in a new experimental style, as opposed to postromantic or popular styles. As with popular music, there are many subtypes of modern music, ranging from the accessible American nationalism of Aaron Copland to the intense expressionism of Arnold Schoenberg. The avant-garde movement of the 1950s, which emphasized radical and experimental sounds, also exerted a strong influence on film scores. In general, modern musical styles sound disoriented, distorted, and disjointed. An element critical to the modern sound is harmonic dissonance created by a clash of pitches. Such sounds can be found in both traditional film scores and popular music, but these dissonances usually resolve. In a modern score, the dissonances can seem unrelenting, and the resultant musical tension is continuous. Also characteristic of modern scores is the frequent use of a small, colorful group of instruments.

Perhaps the easiest way to identify the postromantic style is by eliminating the other two possibilities. If the music is not popular and does not sound modern, then it is likely postromantic style. In this context, the term refers to the prevalent musical style created by Wagner. The style encompasses the basic elements of Romanticism, such as the emphasis on melody and a wide range of emotions. It also allows for the incorporation of colorful orchestrations and strong dissonances. Such qualities are ideally suited for the needs of film; the style is flexible, powerful, and unobtrusive. The generation of composers after Wagner exerted a great influence on film composers. Among the most prominent of these figures are Richard Strauss, Gustav Mahler, and Sergei Rachmaninov.

The remaining two styles of film music—historical styles and ethnic styles—are used more sparingly. These styles can help set the time and place of a film. Historical styles are frequently heard as source music. A story set in the Middle Ages, such as *The Name of the Rose* (1986), might incorporate Gregorian Chant, while Renaissance music rings through a film such as *Shakespeare in Love* (1998). Historical styles can also create a special ambiance that matches a particular story. The film score for *The Four Seasons* (1981), which takes its title from a Baroque composition by Vivaldi, abounds in works by this Venetian composer. Similarly, the score for *A Little Romance* (1979), in which the goal of the journey is to kiss under a bridge over a Venetian canal, includes numerous Vivaldi quotations.

Ethnic music—music from a non-Western culture—can likewise be heard as source music or incorporated into the underscoring in order to suggest a location in a distant country or the presence of someone from another culture. In some instances, an ethnic style may emerge at the slightest suggestion in the film. For example, characteristics of Asian music are heard during Neo's training in martial arts in *The Matrix* (1999) after he realizes that he knows kung fu. In *Pay It Forward* (2000), a gamelan band accompanies Trevor's plan, because at some point it is described as "Tibetan."

Films can feature more than one musical style. Many contain both postromantic underscoring and popular source music or music in a wide variety of musical styles. In Lalo Schifrin's score to *Enter the Dragon* (1973), for example, we can hear elements of postromanticism, modern, popular, and ethnic styles. In this text, a score that is characterized by the juxtaposition or combination of widely divergent musical styles will be described as an **eclectic** score.

Function of Film Music

One way to study the role of music in film is to begin with an analysis of the drama in terms of its basic elements as described in Chapter 2. The next step is to consider whether and how music contributes to these areas. In our brief overview, we will begin with a discussion of mood, as establishing mood is perhaps music's quintessential role in film.

Establishing a Mood

Since music appeals directly to the emotions, all music projects some kind of mood. Even deliberately unemotional music still suggests a mechanical, uncaring world, and the absence of music creates a stark, realistic atmosphere. In some movies, the musical mood remains consistent throughout a film, no matter what is occurring in the story. In these instances, the music creates an overall ambiance that serves as a detached backdrop to the unfolding drama. The relentless somber mood of John Williams's music for *Schindler's List* (1993), for example, reminds us of the reality of the Holocaust. A similar effect can be heard in films that rely on popular music, such as *The Graduate* (1967) and *8½* (1963); in the first, the music creates a consistent mood of youthful uncertainty and in the second, of a superficial lifestyle.

In the typical Hollywood film, the musical mood changes with the developments of the story. Still, there is often an overriding mood, usually suggested in the music for the opening credits. The music for the beginning of such diverse films as *Gone With the Wind, Citizen Kane, The Magnificent Seven, Breakfast at Tiffany's, Psycho, The Graduate, Star Wars,* and *Forrest Gump* establishes the essential mood of the film as a whole.

There are also times when the music depicts a mood that deliberately does not match what is happening on the screen. This is called **running counter to the action**. In the final scene of *Glory* (1989), the triumphant sound of the music conflicts with the slaughter seen by the audience. And in one of the most unforgettable scenes in all of film, the climax of *The Godfather* (1972), we hear sacred organ music while we observe the systematic slaying of Michael's foes.

Supporting the Plot

In addition to creating an overall mood, music can also support a plot by reinforcing its emotional content. In many Hollywood films, music reflects the emotions of a given scene or moment. When a character becomes angry, we hear the music rise in intensity; when someone is sad, we hear a plaintive, longing melody; and when victory is at hand, we are swept away by triumphant music. These emotions are often projected without the actor saying a word; the plot is moved forward by the music.

Because of the abrupt nature of film editing, music can play a critical role by showing the relationship between two or more shots. Leading up to the climactic showdown in *High Noon* (1952), director Fred Zinnemann crosscuts between the protagonist, Will Kane, and the approaching antagonists. By having the music play continuously over the cuts, Zinnemann creates a single mood that connects the contrasting movements. A director may also choose to change the music with the cuts to reinforce the differences between the shots.

The rapid number of cuts in montage often necessitates the use of music to create a sense of unity. Usually a single musical mood is projected, such as the passing of summer to "The Sounds of Silence" in *The Graduate*, the ticking of a clock near the climax of *High Noon*, and the playful bicycle scene in *Butch Cassidy and the Sundance Kid* (1969). Some exceptions to this norm are the breakfast montage from *Citizen Kane* (1941), in which each change of shot is accompanied by a musical change, and the first battle sequence in *Braveheart* (1995), where the rhythmic sound effects from the battle replace musical sounds.

In addition to suggesting the emotional qualities of a given story, music can also reflect physical movement and recreate natural sounds. A sudden impact, such as a slap in the face or an object hitting the ground, can be accompanied by an accent in the orchestra, often referred to as a **stinger**. Sometimes when we see a person or object rise, the music ascends, and when the person or thing goes down, the music descends. Music can also suggest natural sounds, such as splashing water, thunder, the ticking of a clock, gunfire, or a speeding train. Such mimicking of movement and sound is quite common in cartoons. Since films are supposed to be more realistic, composers tend to be careful not to match the music too closely to the action. When the music is too obvious—for example, accenting every step of someone walking—it is appropriately termed **Mickey Mousing**.

Figure 4.1 The mirroring of physical movement in film music is called "Mickey Mousing"

Establishing Character, Setting, Point of View, and Theme

In addition to setting moods and creating emotions, music can reinforce the characterization and setting of a given story. The appearance of a dashing romantic character can be accompanied by a passionate melody, a soldier can be supported by a strong march, and a worldly woman might appear accompanied by a raspy saxophone playing in the background. In a similar fashion, the time and place of a story can be supported by music, as described in the discussion of musical styles. In *Around the World in 80 Days* (1956), the audience can close its eyes and still know the locale of each episode, based on the idiomatic sounds of the musical score.

Since various characters may have conflicting emotions in any given scene, the musical mood can suggest a point of view. While the camera may present an omniscient POV, the music can direct us to feel the emotions of a single character. In *The Mission* (1986), for example, the slave trader Mendoza is seen with a village celebration in the background. While the villagers are dancing joyfully, the music reflects the darkness of Mendoza's mood after he discovers that his brother is sleeping with his mistress.

The underlying theme of a film can also be aided by music. Music can show a change of character, reflect a prevailing mood, and underscore the essential message of the film. In *Citizen Kane*, the music projects the contrasting emotions of the youthful and older Kane, creates a prevailing mood of darkness, and through leitmotifs constantly reminds us of the essential conflict between innocence and power that underlies the story.

Musical Unity

Film scores can be unified by a consistent mood, timbre, and style. The string timbre of *Psycho* (1960), the voices of Simon and Garfunkel in *The Graduate* (1967), and the surf-oriented rock music of *Pulp Fiction* (1994) create a unified sound for their respective films. In other movies, such as *Wuthering Heights* (1939), *Laura* (1944), *Breakfast at Tiffany's* (1961), *Doctor Zhivago* (1965), and *E.T. the Extra-Terrestrial* (1982), a single memorable theme dominates the score, creating a different kind of unity.

Leitmotif

Musical themes can represent the overall mood or underlying idea of a film, without any specific connection to the drama. But some themes, called leitmotifs, can be identified with a person, object, or idea in a story. Since not all musical themes are leitmotifs, caution should be taken in applying the term. One must observe a clear and consistent relationship between a musical idea and its onscreen counterpart in order for a musical theme to be considered a leitmotif.

One of the best-known leitmotifs in film is the two-note oscillating motive that accompanies *Jaws* (1975). Throughout the film, the audience is alerted to the shark's presence by these two notes. Also memorable are the numerous leitmotifs in the original *Star Wars* trilogy, including the opening fanfare that represents Luke Skywalker, the strong theme of Obi-Wan Kenobi and the Force, and the dark theme of Darth Vader. Through a leitmotif, the audience can be told what a character is thinking. In *Gone With the Wind* (1939), for example, we see a silent Scarlett O'Hara and hear the Tara theme. Without a word, we know that she is thinking of her plantation.

Thematic Transformation

Thematic transformation helps to create variety and gives support to dramatic situations. In the simplest terms, a leitmotif can be altered when it recurs during a film. The alteration can be a change of instrumentation, tempo, or harmony. Through these transformations, the changing mood or state of a character can be depicted. In *Return of the Jedi* (1983), the death of Darth Vader is accompanied by his theme. Vader's leitmotif, generally heard in the low brass with a terrifying edge, is now played gently, suggesting the transformation of his character just before his death. The melody can be heard in woodwinds, string harmonics, and the harp. The high register of the instruments and the timbre of the harp (the instrument of angels) are musical clichés for death.

Gone With the Wind

With this general overview of the many roles of film music in mind, let us consider a specific scene. *Gone With the Wind* (1939) is generally considered to be one of Hollywood's greatest films, and Max Steiner's music is a paradigm of the classical Hollywood score. Steiner writes for a full symphony orchestra, employs a post-romantic style, supports the nuances of the drama with music, and unifies the score with leitmotifs. The scene described in the Viewer Guide can be divided into three parts.

In the first, Scarlett pulls Ashley into a room and confesses her love to him. He rejects her, saying that he is marrying Melanie. Throughout the scene, the music follows Scarlett's changing moods, as within a matter of minutes she shifts from playful to tentative to passionate, and finally to anger. While she expresses her love for Ashley, we hear a theme that functions as a leitmotif for their relationship played lyrically by the strings (see Example 4.1). When Ashley does not respond as Scarlett had expected, this theme becomes distorted, revealing Scarlett's changing emotional state. After Ashley leaves, Scarlett hurls a vase across the room. In the music, we can hear the flight of the vase and its impact. The abrupt silence reinforces our surprise when we see that Rhett Butler has been present throughout.

In the second and third parts, the music often reflects the emotions of people other than Scarlett, hence the musical mood runs counter to what Scarlett is feeling. After Scarlett leaves the room in tears, the news is announced that war has been declared. The orchestra plays "Dixie," a Southern patriotic tune. The music matches the jubilant mood of the house, but it is in stark contrast to the tearful Scarlett that we see on the screen. Later, as Charles proposes to Scarlett, the music returns to Scarlett's point of view. Rather than supporting Charles's love and joy or the general jubilation of the household, the music reveals Scarlett's detached emotional state. As she watches Ashley and Melanie kiss, we hear her love theme and a high-register violin note that suggests Scarlett's isolation.

The second part closes when Ashley goes off to join the army, accompanied by a faint trumpet fanfare. For the final portion of this scene, we see Scarlett at her wedding ceremony. The diegetic music from the church organ reflects a solemn mood that once again runs counter to Scarlett's comically tragic demeanor. This mock seriousness continues, as we hear a trumpet play "Taps" (borrowed music) and read that Charles died in a non-heroic manner.

In all these emotional contradictions and in Scarlett's quickly changing emotions, Steiner has given us an important aspect of the story that contributes to the overall theme. At this time, Scarlett is young, impetuous, and self-centered, as summed up in her classic response when told that war has been declared: "Don't you men ever think about anything important?" Scarlett will change greatly during the course of this film. She will become independent and strong-willed, a transformation that will be reflected in Max Steiner's music.

Viewer Guide

Gone With the Wind: Scarlett Declares Her Love

Timing

28:30–35:50 (0:00 at Overture); DVD Chapters 11–12

Key Points

- Scoring for full symphony orchestra
- Music reflects a variety of emotional states
- Use of leitmotifs and thematic transformation
- Arrangements of well-known tunes: "Dixie" and "Taps"

Setting

Scarlett (Vivien Leigh), having heard rumors that Ashley (Leslie Howard) will marry Melanie (Olivia de Havilland), comes to a party at Live Oaks to win him over. Just after the men have had a heated debate about war with the North, she pulls Ashley into a room to confess her love. During this excerpt we also encounter Rhett (Clark Gable) and Charles (Rand Brooks).

Leitmotif

Example 4.1 Ashley and Scarlett's Love theme

PLOT	MUSIC
Scarlett runs downstairs and invites Ashley into a room.	The descending music mirrors her downward motion. The music becomes more lyrical as they enter the room, suggesting tenderness.
Ashley asks what she wants, and Scarlett declares her love for him.	At first, the music is hesitant; the Love theme begins as she talks.
Ashley asks her to forget him and confesses his love for Melanie.	The Love theme becomes distorted and grows more passionate. With Ashley's sentiments, the mood softens a bit.
Scarlett accuses Ashley of being false and slaps him.	The music grows in intensity; a single chord is sustained after the slap.
After he leaves, she throws a vase.	Her building anger is reflected in the music. The music follows the flight of the vase.
"Has the war started?"	No music for the dialogue with Rhett
Scarlett leaves the room and hears Melanie defend her.	No music
People cheer; war has been declared.	"Dixie"
Charles talks to Scarlett and declares his love for her.	"Dixie" continues. As Charles speaks, the music becomes tender.
Scarlett agrees to marriage and watches Ashley kiss Melanie outside.	The music is emotionally reserved during the proposal. The Love theme for Ashley and Scarlett accompanies the kiss. A trumpet appears at the end as Ashley goes off to join the army.
At the ceremony, Scarlett cries.	Source music: church organ
We read that Scarlett is a widow.	A trumpet plays "Taps."

Trailer

The preceding scene from *Gone With the Wind* should be watched several times. With each viewing, you should be able to hear more details about the music. As you become more aware of these details and of the general concepts in this chapter, you will develop listening skills that will aid you in watching other films. The material of this chapter forms a critical foundation for the study of film music and should be reviewed periodically. Once you have grasped these fundamentals, you will be ready to explore over one hundred years of film music.

Important Terms

medley

overture

entr'acte

source music (diegetic music)

underscoring (non-diegetic music)

cue

wall-to-wall music

arrangement

leitmotif

thematic transformation

adaptation

compilation score

adapted score

eclectic score

running counter to the action

Mickey Mousing

Part 2

The Silent Film Era, 1895–1928

5

Birth of an Art Form, 1895–1907

The history of film music begins with the first coordination of music and moving pictures. The initial practical efforts in this endeavor were undertaken by Thomas Edison, the great American inventor. Edison's goal was not to create a new art form, but rather to capitalize on the commercial potential of combining the phonograph with moving pictures. His vision became reality in 1895, when he created the Kinetophone. But this moment in film history is overshadowed by two separate public showings of films in the same year, both of which included live musical performances. Within a dozen years of these three separate events, moving pictures began to illustrate narratives, movie theaters called nickelodeons proliferated throughout the United States, and music established a clear association with the new art and entertainment medium.

SIGNIFICANT EVENTS

1879	Muybridge exhibits the Zoopraxiscope in Stanford's home
1888	Edison produces a commercially viable phonograph
	Edison meets with Muybridge
1891	Edison introduces the Kinetoscope
1894	Edison opens the first Kinetoscope parlor
1895	Edison unveils the Kinetophone
	Max Skladanowsky presents his films to an audience in Berlin
	The Lumière brothers present their films to an audience in Paris
1896	Edison premiers the Vitascope
1902	*A Trip to the Moon*
1903	*The Great Train Robbery*
1905	The first nickelodeon opens in Pittsburgh

Early Developments

Edison, who invented the phonograph in 1876, unveiled a commercially viable version of the invention in 1888. Immediately Edison vowed to work on moving pictures: "I wanted to do for the eye what the phonograph does for the ear." To this end, Edison met with Eadweard Muybridge in that year and proposed a cooperative venture that would lead to the coordination of moving pictures and recorded sound.

Eadweard Muybridge

A leading photographer of the American West, Muybridge had over fifteen years of experience working with moving images. Initially he had been hired by Leland Stanford, the former governor of California, to settle a bet. Racing enthusiasts had long debated whether or not a horse lifted all four legs off the ground while running, and Stanford decided to settle the issue with the aid of photography. Muybridge

Close-Up: Controversial Early Figures

Murder and Monopoly

The two leading names in the early history of American film are tinged with controversy. Eadweard Muybridge (1830–1904) was an eccentric artist. He was born in England with the name Edward James Muggeridge; the peculiar spelling of his name evolved over the years. He spent much of his life in the United States and is recognized as one of the great photographers of the old West. Especially well known are his images of Yosemite (1868 and 1872) and his monumental panorama of San Francisco (1878).

Muybridge was also one of the first photographers to develop a shutter for the camera, a critical step in capturing motion. His collaboration with Leland Stanford, the former governor of California, led to several technical improvements, and soon his camera was able to capture what the human eye could not see. Published in important science journals, Muybridge's images generated a great deal of excitement.

But his work was put on hold when he was tried for murder. Muybridge had married a twenty-one year-old photo retoucher named Flora Stone. She had divorced her husband in order to marry Eadweard, but soon became involved with another man, Harry Larkyns. Outraged, Muybridge shot and killed her lover at close range. During the trial his lawyer argued that an accident on a stagecoach had left him mentally unbalanced, and Muybridge was acquitted.

He went back to work with Stanford, but after some disputes, Stanford withdrew his support. The photographer took a position at the University of Pennsylvania, where he used fellow teachers, models, and other artists as subjects for his studies of motion. Although some of the views, such as a nude woman throwing a baseball, seem silly and bordering on pornography, the intent was serious, as evidenced by the lined backdrop used for measuring movement (see Figure 5.1). Muybridge created over one hundred thousand images, many of which were issued in two publications, *Animals in Motion* and *The Human Figure in Motion*.

Albert Einstein called Thomas Edison (1847–1931) "the greatest inventor of all time." At the age of twenty-one, Edison received his first patent for the stock ticker.

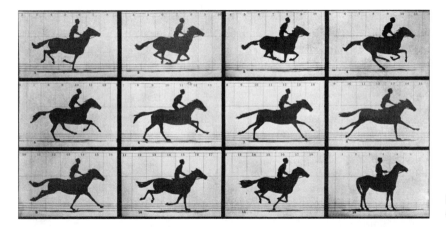

Figure 5.1 Muybridge's photos of a horse in motion

placed twelve cameras at specified intervals next to a racetrack. When a running horse broke the trip wires, twelve successive photos were taken. Through this process it was eventually shown with certainty that a horse does leave the ground while

After perfecting numerous devices for the operation of the telegraph, he founded a research laboratory in New Jersey. Here, the "Wizard of Menlo Park" developed the the phonograph, the incandescent lamp, and the carbon microphone used in the telephone.

Yet Edison has a dubious role in film history. The principal moving force behind the development of moving pictures at the Edison lab was not Edison, but an English amateur photographer, W. K. L. Dickson (1860–1935). His first crude camera was used to photograph fellow worker Fred Ott in a comical sneeze. Seeing the result of this work, Edison decided to focus on the Kinetoscope. He chose to develop a device for an individual viewer rather than projections that could be shown to an audience. This approach allowed for a simpler coordination of film and phonograph, and Edison believed that it was a better financial investment. Dickson created the first studio, a small building called the Black Maria, directed the early films, and even appeared as an actor in several of them.

Unhappy that new faces were entering the motion picture arena, Edison attempted to block others from working in the field. In 1902, a Supreme Court decision concluded that since Edison did not invent motion pictures, he could not own a patent on the process. Angered by the decision, Edison turned his attention to controlling the marketplace. In 1909 he consolidated Vitagraph, Biograph, Pathé, Méliès, and other companies into the Motion Picture Patents Company. The key to this trust was George Eastman, who was bullied into a restrictive contract that prevented him from selling his film to anyone who did not cooperate with Edison's company. The Eastman Company would survive and thrive in future years, but George committed suicide in 1932 following a lengthy illness.

Edison assumed dictatorial powers in the field. He limited films to no more than two reels, and he would not allow actors' names to appear in the credits, in order to keep them from demanding more money. Some filmmakers were forced to sign contracts to work for Edison. Others, who were reportedly threatened with bodily harm, fled west, eventually making a new home in Hollywood in order to avoid Edison's gangsters. Finally William Fox decided to fight Edison, and in 1917 an antitrust action dissolved Edison's company. Edison quit the business in order to pursue other ventures.

running. Stanford won his $25,000 bet at a cost of at least $40,000.

The issue soon extended beyond idle curiosity; animal and human motion had become an important subject in both France and the United States. Muybridge continued to improve his shutter-release mechanism, increased the number of cameras used for a scene, and explored new subjects, including the movement of unclothed men and women. Having established his technique for capturing motion and freezing it on film, he then took the critical next step of reconstructing the appearance of motion by showing the images in rapid succession. Using a projection device that he called a Zoopraxiscope, Muybridge toured the United States and England, showing moving images to distinguished audiences of artists, dignitaries, and intellectuals.

Figure 5.2 A Kinetoscope parlor in San Francisco in 1895

The Kinetoscope

Edison wanted to capitalize on Muybridge's expertise and reputation in the field of motion pictures and suggested a cooperative venture. The photographer declined Edison's offer, believing that the coordination of pictures and sound was impractical. The Wizard of Menlo Park was left to work on the project on his own. Indeed the combination proved to be difficult. After three years of laboratory work, Edison unveiled the Kinetoscope, a peephole viewer for a single person to observe moving pictures without sound. In 1894, the first Kinetoscope parlor was established in New York, at a site that is now occupied by Macy's, and soon similar establishments appeared throughout the United States. In a photo of a San Francisco Kinetoscope parlor from 1895 (Figure 5.2), Kinetoscopes for viewing are on the right, and phonographs for listening, with earphones and handkerchiefs dangling in front, are on the left.

Once a public forum for viewing had been established, it became necessary to create a steady stream of new films. W. K. L. Dickson, the Edison lab assistant who had played a critical role in the creation of the Kinetoscope, built the first movie studio and began shooting the first significant repertory of silent moving pictures. The subjects of these films tended to be sensational and somewhat earthy. *The Kiss* (1896), perhaps the most famous of the early works, is a recreation of the climactic scene of a Broadway show, using the actual cast members. By modern standards the scene is somewhat comical, but it created a minor moral furor at the time. Other Dickson films include Sandow, the father of modern body building,

Figure 5.3 *The Kiss*

flexing his muscles, an unsavory cockfight, and a tantalizing view of young women (and their ankles!) engaged in a pillow fight.

The Kinetophone

During this time, Edison continued to work on his original goal of creating visual images that would accompany recorded sound from a phonograph. On May 23, 1891, the year in which the Kinetoscope was publicly unveiled, a writer for the *Orange Chronicle* reported:

Figure 5.4 A Kinetophone with a viewer and earphones

> A large number of the ladies were, by special invitation, driven down to the laboratory, where Mr. Edison himself was present and exhibited to them the Kinetoscope, the new invention that he is about perfecting, by which the gestures of a speaker are accurately reproduced, while the spoken or sung words are reproduced by the phonograph.

Strictly speaking, if the invention observed by the ladies coordinated film with sound, then it was probably a Kinetophone, which is simply a Kinetoscope with a phonograph placed in its cabinet. The Kinetophone finally debuted in 1895 and, as seen in the center of Figure 5.2 and in Figure 5.4, came equipped with both a viewer and earphones. Dixon shot the first known films with sound in 1894 or 1895. In one experimental film, several frames of which are shown in Figure 5.5, Dixon plays a tune from the opera *The Chimes at Normandy* on the violin into a recording horn, while two men dance in the foreground. Recordings for the Kinetophone—our first examples of film music—tend to be of popular dance tunes, such as the "Pomona Waltz," "Continental March," and "Irish Reel." These tunes primarily accompanied images of dancers.

Figure 5.5 Dixon's experimental sound film

Projectors and Public Viewing

Edison's vision of film was limited by his original goal of combining moving pictures with music played on his phonograph. The individual peephole approach of the Kinetoscope and Kinetophone was the most practical means to these ends. But Edison soon discovered that others had created a great sensation by projecting films to an audience. Not concerned with using recorded music, these innovators employed live musicians to accompany their public showings. Quick to recognize the financial advantages of this alternate approach, Edison soon turned his energies towards projection as well.

The Lumières and Max Skladanowsky

Europeans were the first to explore the projection of films to a paying audience. In 1894, Louis and Auguste Lumière created the Cinématographe, a device that was capable of taking moving pictures, printing film, and projecting images onto a screen. Because the camera weighed only twelve pounds, it could be taken outdoors, and it shot the first moving images outside a studio. On December 28, 1895, the Lumière brothers showed a series of films to an audience consisting primarily of photographers and inventors. Included in the show were *Departure from the Lumière Factory*, their first motion picture from 1894, *The Arrival of a Train at La Ciotat Station*, which created an enormous sensation as the train seemed to roar toward the audience, and *The Sprinkler Sprinkled*, a brief comedy sketch.

Figure 5.6 *Departure from the Lumière Factory*

In later years, the Lumière cameras were turned on historical events, such as the coronation of Czar Nikolai II in Moscow and the inauguration of President McKinley. They also filmed reenactments of historical events, including *The Life and Passion of Jesus Christ*. Hundreds saw Lumière films at the Paris Exposition of 1900, but the brothers abandoned film production in that year in order to work on other ventures. Louis is reported to have said: "The cinema is an invention without a future."

The often-overlooked works of Max Skladanowsky paralleled and actually preceded those of the Lumière brothers. On November 1, 1895, Skladanowsky projected films before a paying public, nearly two months before the Lumière debut. His fifteen-minute show included acts from a local circus and city scenes from Berlin. Dismissing these films as primitive, film historians have bypassed this event and named December 28, 1895, the date of the Lumière showing, the "birth of cinema."

Figure 5.7 A poster advertising Edison's Vitascope c. 1896 shows a pit orchestra in front of the screen

Significantly, live music played a role in both presentations. For the Lumière debut, a pianist played what has been described as improvisations on popular melodies. In subsequent presentations of these films in London, musical performances by a harmonium (a reed organ) and an orchestra have been documented. For the Skladanowsky show, an orchestra played a variety of popular and light classical works, including polkas, marches, and waltzes.

Thomas Edison and the Vitascope

Because of the popularity of public viewings in a theater setting, Edison abandoned the individual peephole approach of the Kinetoscope. In 1896 he unveiled his pro-

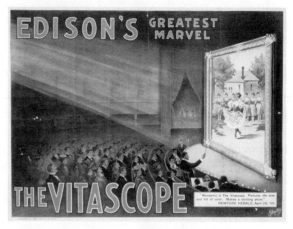

jector, the Vitascope, and, as depicted in a poster from that year, the event was accompanied by an orchestra. Edison proceeded to sell his Vitascope to vaudeville theaters, which began showing films as part of their shows, a practice that increased substantially after a strike of vaudeville performers in 1900. In these venues, the vaudeville orchestras often accompanied the film presentations as they would any other act.

Narrative Film

The first moving pictures did not tell stories. The art form was originally conceived as an extension of photography. Both film and photography focused on similar subjects—people, city life, important events—and both created a heightened sense of reality. The principal difference between the two was simply that the subjects in films moved. It is not surprising that the early history of film is dominated by figures from France and England, the main centers for photography in the nineteenth century, and that many of the important pioneers in filmmaking are also significant in the history of photography. But films soon began to present recreations of historical events and brief comic skits, tentative steps towards the telling of stories. The two figures most closely associated with the beginnings of narrative films are Georges Méliès and Edwin Porter.

Georges Méliès

One of the observers at the first Lumière showing was a young magician, Georges Méliès. Inspired by Houdini, Méliès owned the Théâtre Robert-Houdin, where he performed magic shows. Méliès obtained his own camera-projector and began showing Edison films during his show. Not content with these brief diversions, he built a studio and began making his own motion pictures. Characterized by elaborate sets and costumes, fantastic stories, and bevies of beautiful girls, these extended visions were well suited to a magic show. During these showings, the theater orchestra provided musical accompaniment. Several films even contained dance and musical sequences. For at least one film, *Kingdom of the Fairies* (1903) a newly composed score was created. In all, Méliès made over five hundred films, in which he explored camera techniques such as slow motion, dissolves, fade-outs, and superimpositions.

Figure 5.8 A fanfare before launching in *A Trip to the Moon*

His most famous work is *A Trip to the Moon* (1902). While this is not the first film narrative, its substantial length (over ten minutes), elaborate sets and costumes, and fantastic story make this a landmark work in the presentation of a story. In each of its fifteen scenes, the camera is stationary, while the actors (Méliès appears as the principal astronomer) and scenery move in front of it. The character of a theatrical magic show is evident. Particularly notable is the seventh scene, in which moving sets, a fire, and a superimposed celestial view create a magical lunar vision. The film was originally shown with both narration and musical accompaniment.

Edwin Porter

Edwin Porter's *The Great Train Robbery*, considered to be the first major American narrative film, appeared in the following year (1903). Porter had worked as a projectionist and began directing films for the Edison studio at the turn of the century. Earlier that year, he created an extraordinary work in *The Life of an American Fireman*, which mixes actual footage of fire with acted scenes. But it was *The Great Train Robbery* that captured the public's attention. In a way, this film falls within the tradition of recreating historical events. Although partially based on a stage play by Scott Marble from 1893, it was also inspired by an actual theft. On August 19, 1900, Butch Cassidy and his gang stopped a train in Wyoming, uncoupled several cars, robbed the passengers, and made off with five thousand dollars. This film is a retelling of that event. While westerns for modern audiences are fantasies set in the past, this plot was current news and audiences went wild, especially when one of the bandit's pointed his gun at the camera and shot straight at the audience.

The greatest dramatic achievement in this work is the telling of the story with discontinuous action. By moving from the escaping bandits to the discovery of the crime and then to a dance hall, we get a sense of simultaneous events. Noteworthy is the length of the dance-hall sequence. The scene is unnecessary for the drama and can be considered an early example of the insertion of a dance or musical diversion into a melodramatic tale. One bit of unintended humor in the film is the appearance of a cowboy, a bandit wearing a white hat, who stumbles and obviously does not know how to mount a horse. Ironically, this actor, who doubles as the passenger who gets shot, would later become one of the first famous western stars—Bronco Billy.

Georges Méliès and Edwin Porter were the early creative forces behind film narratives. Both continued to work through the first decade of the twentieth century, but

Figure 5.9 Dancers and musicians (back right) in *The Great Train Robbery*

neither was able to sustain the energy or excitement of their early landmark works. Méliès produced a significant number of films, but the public seemed to tire of his magical special effects. He made his last film in 1914, declared bankruptcy in 1923, and died in a sanitarium in 1938.

Edwin Porter made films for Edison until 1909. His films became more sophisticated in their storytelling, and he increasingly used larger casts and more elaborate scenery. But Porter grew weary of the hectic pace of filmmaking and eventually quit the business, leaving the future of American filmmaking to be shaped by the hand of one of his actors, D. W. Griffith.

Music

As we saw in the first public showings by the Lumière brothers and Skladanowsky, music attended the birth of film. Over the next dozen years, the complex relationships of the variety of film types, venues for film presentations, and roles of music did not engender a uniform musical practice. In looking at the diverse music from this fascinating era, we need to consider three separate issues: who (or what) made the music, when was the music used, and what type of music was played.

Musical Accompaniment

The size of the venue for film presentations was a significant factor in determining the size of the accompanying musical ensemble. Many of the earliest films were presented as part of a theatrical entertainment, such as a magic show or a vaudeville performance. In these situations, it was natural for the theater orchestra to introduce or accompany the film as an extension of their normal duties. In the first decade of the twentieth century, however, the principal venue for film presentations shifted from theaters to nickelodeons, small shops that showed films exclusively, usually for the admission price of a nickel. The first nickelodeon was established in 1905 in Pittsburgh, and by 1907, nearly three thousand had been created in the United States. Within three years, that number had increased to over ten thousand.

In the confines of the nickelodeon, an orchestra or even a small ensemble of musicians was often impractical. The variety of sounds that could be heard in early movie theaters included the following possibilities:

- Films were shown in silence.
- Films could be shown without music, but with added sound effects, narration, or a lecture by a "professor," a practice that thankfully did not endure.
- Music might be played continuously in the background, often by a mechanical device such as a phonograph or player piano. In some instances, the music was not played in the theater, but rather in front of the shop, where the volume would be boosted in order to attract attention. Music played this way was known as "ballyhoo music."
- A single pianist filled a variety of musical needs for a film presentation.
- A small number of musicians could perform with the pianist. Most important were a drummer, who also provided a variety of sound effects, and a singer, who entertained between films.

Figure 5.10 The interior of the first nickelodeon in Pittsburgh

Placement of Music

Many theaters provided musical entertainments before and after a film and perhaps during reel changes as well. In some theaters, this was the only function of music, and the musicians rested during the film. For these musical interludes, a pianist might perform a light diversion, a local music store might send a singer to present some of the latest tunes, or the audience might enjoy a sing-along.

With the growing concern for sound effects in the early nickelodeon years, music was sometimes added during a film when musical sound was indicated, even if the film was otherwise shown without music. Early examples of this source music might include the sound of a piano when a piano was played or touched in a film, the playing of dance music when the film presented dancers, or the sound of a trumpet when a battle was depicted. The dance sequence in *The Great Train Robbery*, for example, could have been enhanced by live musicians playing dance music for this extended scene (Figure 5.9).

In some theaters, music was performed continuously during a film. The exact role of continuous music naturally varied. Besides creating an overall mood for the film entertainments, the music might reflect the mood of an individual film or a particular scene. A chase might have fast music, a battle could be supported with loud music, and lovers might be accompanied by a lyrical melody. There is also evidence that some musicians enhanced the films by reflecting aspects of character, setting, and physical movement in their musical choices.

Clearly, the quality of such musical performances was uneven. The following review from the September 4, 1909 issue of *Moving Picture World* describes the music enthusiastically:

> Never at a moving picture theater have I heard or seen a girl enter so completely into the spirit of the pictures shown. She absolutely adapts her music to them. Every emotion, every sentiment, every movement, every mood illustrated on the screen is duplicated by the tones of the piano. It is a perfect concordance of sound, movement, and thought . . . so with the drummer. He is absolutely master of the necessary effects. No animal is shown which does not find his peculiarities of articulation illustrated by some one of the drummer's battery of weird and startling instruments. He almost makes men and women talk, almost; they groan, they laugh, kiss, whisper, under his magic touch.

In another review (*Moving Picture World,* July 3, 1909), a grimmer picture is painted.

> The piano and some sound effects are usually considered sufficient: and oh, and oh, the piano and the players we sometimes hear and sometimes see! The former is more often than not out of tune, and the latter, though he can strike the keys with something like accuracy and precision, if not violence, cannot play music, or if he can, he does not. In other words, speaking generally, the musical end of the moving picture house programme is, as a rule, so unsatisfactory that we think it our duty specially in this article to call attention to it.

Types of Music

A variety of music would have been heard in the early years of film, ranging from well-known classics and popular melodies to improvisations in traditional or popular style. Popular music seems to have been preferred. Edison chose popular dance melodies for the Kinetophone, and the earliest public showings of films featured popular music, which provided an energetic, cheerful, and decidedly modern ambiance. Likewise, vaudeville theaters and nickelodeons tended toward popular musical styles.

Indeed, the early years of film in America coincide with the explosion of the publication of popular songs coming primarily from a cluster of music publishers in New York known as Tin Pan Alley. The combination of popular songs and films was natural. At a time when radio was in its infancy and household phonographs were rare, nickelodeons became a valuable tool in the spread of new songs. There is even a significant repertoire of song films—films that were created to illustrate a popular song that would be played or sung with the film or slide show. It was common for song films to alternate with narrative films in a nickelodeon.

Popular music was also employed to accompany narrative films. Well-known popular melodies were chosen, not necessarily for the mood that they projected, but sometimes because their titles reflected an aspect of the story. For example, a scene showing the effects of too much alcohol might be accompanied by "How Dry I Am," or, in the case of a seaman, "What Shall We Do with a Drunken Sailor?" This tradition continued into the sound era. In *The Wizard of Oz* (1939), for example, Schumann's "Happy Farmer" introduces life on the Kansas farm, and Dorothy's longing to return to Kansas is accompanied by the song "There's No Place Like Home."

Despite the wide variety of musical practices and frequent abuses in these early years, the combination of live music and film created a special effect. Narrative film depends upon the illusion of reality—making the audience forget that it is in a theater observing a two-dimensional screen—and live music greatly adds to this illusion. Music would have distracted from the noise of the projector, which otherwise would be a constant reminder that the images are emanating from a machine. More important, the energy of live musicians would have helped compensate for the lack of live actors. When film first appeared, the ghostly appearance of actors on a screen could have been a mere intellectual curiosity, but the energy and emotion of musicians helped drama bridge the gap from live theater to canned film.

Trailer

With the advent of sound films, the vibrant quality of live music was abandoned. Today, there is a growing appreciation for silent films performed with live musicians, and, upon occasion, even sound films have been performed with a live ensemble. In 2002, the revised *E.T. the Extra-Terrestrial* premiered with an orchestra conducted by John Williams and received an overwhelming response. Such is the power of live music and film, a quality that was lost when music too was canned in the late 1920s.

Important Names and Terms

Thomas Edison

Eadweard Muybridge

Zoopraxiscope

W. K. L. Dickson

Black Maria

Kinetoscope

Kinetophone

Louis and Auguste Lumière

Cinématographe

Max Skladanowsky

Vitascope

Georges Méliès

Edwin Porter

nickelodeon

ballyhoo music

song films

Suggested Viewing

Landmarks of Early Film, distributed by Image Entertainment. The first volume of this set contains an excellent sampling of early films, including works by Muybridge, Edison, the Lumière brothers, and the films *A Trip to the Moon* and *The Great Train Robbery.*

A video of "Dixon Experimental Film," discussed on page 55 can be found in the DVD collection, *More Treasures From American Film Archives, 1894–1931,* produced by the National Film Preservation Foundation, 2004.

6

The Foundations of Modern Film, 1908–1919

In the dozen years following the first public viewings of films in 1895, the commercial viability of the new art form was established. During the next dozen years, the fledgling industry would undergo rapid change. Inventors would create the necessary technological advances, entrepreneurs would capitalize on the financial rewards, and artists would express themselves in a new discipline that combined elements of the visual arts, dramatic arts, and musical arts.

The physiognomy of modern filmmaking took shape in the 1910s. During this time, the length of films expanded from one-reel shorts (a reel usually runs twelve to fifteen minutes) to feature films with multiple reels. The size of movie theaters also grew; the first large movie palace was built in 1912. Emerging from anonymity, a number of actors became stars. Names such as Mary Pickford, Douglas Fairbanks, and Charlie Chaplin drew audiences to the new theaters, and movie magazines and gossip columns focused on the lives of the leading men and women. As the financial potential grew, so did the studio system. After breaking

SIGNIFICANT FILMS

1908	*L'Assassinat du Duc de Guise*
1912	*Queen Elizabeth*
1915	*The Birth of a Nation*
1916	*Intolerance*
	The Fall of a Nation
1919	*Broken Blossoms*

Edison's grip on filmmaking, studios built their own empires. Much of the building was in the west, most notably in Hollywood, where there was an abundance of cheap land and plenty of sunshine for filming.

Perhaps the most significant development during these years was the emergence of the United States as the dominant center of filmmaking. In the early years of the twentieth century, the history of European and American film is intertwined, and Europe arguably produced the finest works. The ascent of American films is largely a consequence of World War I, which halted film production in Europe. European films never regained equal footing with their American counterparts in the commercial aspects of the industry. Quick to fill the European void were a number of creative Americans, including the first major American director, D. W. Griffith.

D. W. Griffith

Appearing on the scene when the industry was still in its infancy, D. W. Griffith elevated the medium from a short diversion to a sophisticated art form. Generally regarded as the single most important figure in American film, he stands as the first great artist in the field.

His rise to this position was remarkably quick. In an eight-year time span he rose from novice to master. Entering the industry as a hopeful young writer, he soon found himself acting for both Edison and Biograph. In 1908 he directed his first film for Biograph, and before the year was out he was directing all the films for this company. By the time he began work on *The Birth of a Nation* in 1915, he had made approximately 450 films. Most of these were one-reel works, but he also created a number of two-reel and four-reel films. This output is prodigious by any standard, and the sheer number of productions allowed him to develop his craft.

In these early works, Griffith fine-tuned his skills at using the visual, dramatic, and musical arts. Griffith became the first true auteur of film, controlling all aspects of filmmaking. In the area of visual arts, Griffith, with the assistance of cameraman Billy Bitzer, explored a wide range of effects, including close-ups, panoramas, and the moving camera. Griffith also exploited the unique abilities of film to enhance storytelling. By mastering the technique of crosscutting, he was able to build tension and to show simultaneous action in a way that is not possible on the stage. He also worked with a permanent ensemble of actors. During his unprecedented rehearsals prior to filming, he abandoned the theatrical gestures used in live theater and created a new style of acting suited to film. Having a strong background in music, Griffith also worked closely on the composition of original scores for his films.

All of these elements came to fruition with *The Birth of a Nation*, film's first masterwork, which is discussed in detail in Chapter 7. Before the end of the decade, Griffith created two other masterpieces. In 1916 he produced *Intolerance*, which would prove

Figure 6.1 D. W. Griffith

to be a major turning point in his career. Trying to recapture the success of the large battle scenes in *The Birth of a Nation*, Griffith transformed a simple melodramatic story of a mother who must fight to keep her child and save her husband from execution into a spectacular film combining four distinct stories. In addition to the contemporary story, Griffith added monumental scenes from the siege of Babylon, the tragic tale of the Huguenots, and brief reenactments of scenes from the life of Christ. The crosscutting between these four powerful stories is brilliant, but it left audiences bewildered. The film was a financial disaster, and Griffith lost all of the money he had earned with *The Birth of a Nation*. Still, the film stands as a virtuoso display of Griffith's talents, and because of the extent of its impact on other filmmakers, it has been called the most influential film of the silent era.

The following years were difficult for Griffith. A variety of partnerships and legal relationships failed to create a secure environment for his work. In 1919 he joined Douglas Fairbanks, Mary Pickford, and Charlie Chaplin in forming the United Artists Corporation. The first film under this umbrella was one of his finest, *Broken Blossoms* (1919). The poignant tale of interracial love and its brutal destruction achieved a high degree of popularity, and Griffith had another moneymaking film. But such works were rare, and the great master entered the 1920s on the decline, as he continued to lose money. His last film, *The Struggle*, one of his few sound films, was shot in 1931. In 1948, at the age of seventy-three, a bitter Griffith died quietly in a Hollywood hotel.

Developments in Film Music

The diversity of music created for films during this time makes generalization difficult. By 1920, a significant number of theaters still provided no music at all, while others featured full symphony orchestras. Still, several trends can be observed:

- The organ became the most common movie theater instrument.
- The size of musical ensembles in movie theaters tended to expand.
- Compilation scores incorporating excerpts from nineteenth-century classics became common.
- Cue sheets and music anthologies provided help for theater musicians.
- Original scores were created for specific films.

Musical Accompaniment

During these formative years, music performed by a single pianist gave way to a greater variety of accompaniments. Responding to the growing needs of theaters and musicians, Wurlitzer, America's largest organ maker, began producing special instruments designed for movie theaters. In addition to the greater volume

Close-Up: Founding Fathers of American Film

Shaping American Film

In addition to D. W. Griffith, a number of other prominent figures helped shape the landscape of American film during the 1910s. In the early years of the decade, films were often one-man productions, with a single individual dealing with all financial and artistic matters. Soon, these duties were divided between a producer who handled financial matters and a director responsible for the artistic side. Other roles were more clearly defined when studios were established (see Close-Up on page 122), where specialized production teams worked on individual aspects of the film. Wielding supreme power over this kingdom was the studio head. Producers and directors, like actors, were often attached to one studio, but each could also work independently. Two other roles can be seen in the commercial production of film: the distributor who controls the leasing of a film to theaters, and the theater owner who provides the direct link to the public.

William Fox (1879–1952) entered the business with a chain of theaters. He achieved a hero's status with his successful efforts to break Edison's control of the business. Soon he created his own monopoly—the Twentieth Century Fox studio. Eventually his monopoly was broken, and, after some jail time, he retired from the business.

Adolph Zukor (1873–1976) also began with a chain of theaters but soon turned to distribution and brought some of Europe's finest films, including *Queen Elizabeth* (1912), to the United States. He was one of the founders of Paramount and led the studio to its initial height. After a major financial setback, he turned over the controls but continued to work there until he was one hundred years old. He died at the age of 103.

Jesse Lasky (1880–1958) produced the first film on the West coast (*Squaw Man*, 1914) and is credited as the founder of Hollywood. He joined Zukor in creating the Paramount studio, but unlike Zukor he was let go by the company after financial woes hit the studio, and he worked independently thereafter.

Thomas Ince (1882–1924) acted in some of Griffith's earliest films and soon began directing his own works. Fleeing Edison control, he went to Cuba, Texas, and finally California. He established Hollywood's first great studio, Triangle Pictures, which would become MGM. Here, Ince created the factory system with distinct production units and defined the role of producer. In one of Hollywood's darker moments, he was killed on board the yacht of William Randolph Hearst. It was suggested that Hearst shot him, thinking that he was Charlie Chaplin, the suspected lover of Hearst's mistress, Marion Davies.

Mack Sennett (1880–1960) began his career with D. W. Griffith, and soon his talents led him into directing comedies. Founding the Keystone Company, he produced a film a day, many featuring the famous Keystone Kops. He also discovered Charlie Chaplin and played an important role in the careers of other comic actors, including Harold Lloyd and W. C. Fields.

Charlie Chaplin (1889–1977), born in London, became the greatest comedy star of the American silent screen. He had a phenomenal impact on the industry, and his immense popularity made him the first actor to earn a million-dollar contract. His mustache, cane, and tramp character are still among film's best-known trademarks. Eventually, he became his own director and producer. He continued making silent films (with synchronized music and sound effects) well into the age of talkies. His greatest work perhaps is *City Lights* (1931), for which he was producer, director, star, and composer.

Winsor McCay (1867–1934), a talented artist and newspaper cartoonist, spent much of his career working under William Randolph Hearst. He drew political cartoons and several popular comic strips, including "Little Nemo in Slumberland," which was made into a Broadway musical. More significantly, McCay experimented with animated pictures and is a critical pioneer in the field. *Gertie the Dinosaur* (1914) featured the first animated cartoon personality and enjoyed wide popular success.

and enormous variety of colors an organ can produce, additional mechanical devices were created for the instrument so that musicians could produce nonmusical sound effects, such as the sound of a rooster, car horn, telephone, or gunshot. Soon other companies joined in, producing instruments with fanciful titles such as "One-Man Motion Picture Orchestra" and "Pipe-Organ Orchestra." The Fotoplayer Style 50, made by the American Photo Player Company, was twenty-one feet long and capable of a wide variety of effects, including the lowing of cattle, street traffic noises, crackling flames, and the sound of machine guns and cannons.

Figure 6.2 Roxy Rothapfel and a theater organ with five keyboards, a pedal keyboard, and an array of stops

Throughout the 1910s, new theaters were larger and more ornate. Musical ensembles often increased in size as well. A group of five to ten musicians, including a pianist, could achieve an effective accompaniment, similar in sound to what one hears on recordings of old radio shows. The process of creating the music for such an ensemble is more complicated than it is for a single keyboard player, as individual parts have to be copied for each performer. But these difficulties are compensated by the richer and more varied tone colors and by the sheer power of a larger ensemble. By the end of the decade, a number of theaters featured symphony orchestras of over fifty musicians. While most theaters still relied upon pianos and organs, the association of symphony orchestras with quality productions was clearly established by 1920.

Compilation Scores

Music for silent films can be divided into three types: adaptations of works from the classical repertoire; arrangements of well-known patriotic, religious, or popular tunes; and newly composed material. All three types can be found in many film scores, since original music provided important transitions between passages of adapted or arranged material. Musical scores based largely on borrowed material are considered to be compilation scores.

Because of the increasing number and size of films and the growing need to write wall-to-wall music, musicians frequently adapted classical works. The benefits of this approach include the availability of parts already in print; the freedom from having to compose new music for each film; the saving of rehearsal time, since many of the orchestra performers would already know the classical excerpts; the audience's potential familiarity with the music; and the lack of copyright protection for these older works. Many theaters developed extended libraries of musical works, often organized by emotional content. Max Winkler, a pioneer in compiling music for films, describes the process:

In desperation, we turned to crime. We began to dismember the great masters. We began to murder the works of Beethoven, Mozart, Grieg, J. S. Bach, Verdi, Bizet, Tchaikovsky, and Wagner—everything that wasn't protected by copyright from outright pilfering. The immortal chorales of J. S. Bach became an 'Adagio Lamentoso' for sad scenes. Extracts from great symphonies were hacked down to emerge again as 'Sinister Misterioso' by Beethoven, or 'Weird Moderato' by Tchaikovsky. Wagner's and Mendelssohn's wedding marches were used for marriages, fights between husbands and wives, and divorce scenes; we just had them played out of tune, a treatment known in the profession as 'souring up the aisle.' If they were to be used for happy endings, we jazzed them up mercilessly.*

These borrowings were drawn predominantly from the works of nineteenth-century composers. The resultant Romantic style of film music corresponds roughly to the tastes of concertgoers in early twentieth-century America. Although there would be exceptions to the dominance of Romanticism, such as ensembles that improvised in a popular style and the rare film that required modern music, the fundamental reliance of American film music on the musical idiom of the late nineteenth century would continue for at least two more decades.

Cue Sheets and Anthologies

Filmmakers, theater owners, and musicians became increasingly concerned about the relationship of music to the drama. The emotions of a given scene needed to be supported by corresponding music. Moreover, the ability of music to build a sense of character, to mirror physical gestures on the screen, and to create a sense of time or place—especially useful for exotic settings—was beginning to be recognized.

Efforts to facilitate this coordination followed two directions: the creation of guides to help theater music directors select appropriate music, and the composition of new scores for individual films. Two types of guides appeared: cue sheets created to accompany a specific film and anthologies of musical excerpts. The first cue sheets appeared in 1909, and leading the way was the Edison Film Company.

Wanting to maintain more control over the music played for his films, Edison published specific suggestions for individual scenes. Describing each scene of the film, the cue sheet would indicate what type of music would be appropriate to the various moods. These suggestions were especially valuable if they arrived prior to the film, so that the musicians could prepare music ahead of time. That was not always the case, and many musicians had to guess the mood of a scene as they watched the film for the first time in performance.

Also in 1909 the first significant anthology was published with the fanciful title *Motion Picture Piano Music: Descriptive Music to Fit the Action, Character, or Scene of*

---

* Max Winkler, "The Origins of Film Music," *Films in Review*, 2/10, December, 1951, 40.

Moving Pictures. Unrelated to any specific film, the anthology contains excerpts of music that match general moods, settings, or characters. Rather than picking random works from the classical repertoire, a theater pianist could select passages from the anthology based on the needs of a film. Over the next fifteen years, numerous anthologies were created, including the following popular examples:

- *Sam Fox Moving Picture Music,* 1913–14. This three-volume anthology contains seventy simple musical excerpts for piano, composed and compiled by J. S. Zamecnik. A Czech immigrant, Zamecnik was the music director for the Hippodrome Theater in Cleveland and would continue to be an active film composer into the 1930s.
- *Kinobibliothek* (generally referred to as *Kinothek*), 1919. Compiled by Giuseppe Becce, *Kinothek* was published in Berlin and eventually became the most widely used anthology in America. It contains numerous musical excerpts, many newly composed by Becce, organized into groups delineated by moods (solemn, mysterious, passion) and action (flight, battle, storm). The Italian-born Becce spent most of his career in Germany and scored a number of films during the next two decades, including two of Germany's greatest silent films, *The Cabinet of Dr. Caligari* (1920) and *The Last Laugh* (1924).
- *Motion Picture Moods for Pianists and Organists,* 1924. This anthology by the conductor and composer Erno Rapée correlates 370 musical excerpts keyed to a variety of moods found in films. In Figure 6.3, we see "Agitato No. 3," with a note that the music would be "suitable for gruesome or infernal scenes, witches, etc." The excerpt borrows heavily from a well-known song by Schubert, *Der Erlkönig*. On the left, an index appears as a quick guide for finding other types of music that would establish a mood—"funeral" and "happiness," accompany action—"battle" and "fire-fighting," mimic sounds—"birds" and "chimes," and provide source music, as suggested by the various dances.

Figure 6.3 A page from Rapée's *Motion Picture Moods for Pianists and Organists*

Original Musical Scores

The second development in improving film music was the creation of specific musical scores for individual films. Between 1910 and 1914, over 100 scores, mostly written for piano accompaniment, can be documented. The Kalem Company, a production company known for the high quality of its films, was a leading force in the creation of scores in the early 1910s, many of them composed by Walter Cleveland Simon. By mid-decade, the number of original scores began to decline due to complications from the length of feature films and from the growth of orchestras with varying instrumentations.

Camille Saint-Saëns

One of the first completely original film scores for orchestra was created for the Film d'Art in Paris. Dedicated to producing films of high artistic quality, this company engaged the leading stage actors in France to perform quality dramas based on history or mythology. For their first production, *L'Assassinat du Duc de Guise* (1908), the company turned to one of France's most prestigious composers—Camille Saint-Saëns. Best known for his symphonies, concertos, operas (*Samson and Delilah*), and numerous popular works, such as *The Carnival of Animals* and *Danse Macabre*, Saint-Saëns also composed incidental music for stage plays. He had composed music for three plays in 1902, including Racine's *Andromaque*, which he dedicated to the leading actress Sarah Bernhardt.

Figure 6.4 Camille Saint-Saëns

Saint-Saëns published the music for *L'Assassinat du Duc de Guise* separately as Opus 128. In the published version, the theatrical titles are retained for each of the five movements. Rather than using the traditional tempo designations, Saint-Saëns labeled the movements introduction, scene 1, scene 2, scene 3, scene 4, and scene 5.

The concert version of *L'Assassinat du Duc de Guise* reveals four important aspects about the first film score. First, the published version is written for twelve instruments: flute, oboe, clarinet, bassoon, French horn, a string quintet, piano, and harmonium. This combination of instruments is unusual for concert music, but is typical of good theater orchestras. Second, as one might expect from a great master of Romanticism, the musical style is based on nineteenth-century traits, including an emphasis on melody and a strong emotional content. Third, the frequent mood changes within each movement mirror the dramatic action. The film recounts the murder of the French duke by King Henry III in 1588, and the music aptly supports this tragic tale. Most convincing are the fourth and fifth scenes depicting the brutal attack and the horrified reaction of the Duke's lover. Fourth, recurring themes among the five movements suggest that Saint-Saëns employed a simple system of leitmotifs—that is, themes associated with characters in the film. In other words, the basic elements of the classical film score are already present in Saint-Saëns's initial conception.

Figure 6.5 *L'Assassinat du Duc de Guise*

Joseph Carl Breil

The use of original orchestral film scores by the Film d'Art inspired similar productions in the United States. In 1912, Adolph Zukor brought the Film d'Art's *Queen Elizabeth* to America. The arrival of this four-reel film created a great sensation, as it proved that feature-length films could hold the attention of American audiences. Starring the legendary Sarah Bernhardt, this film had been shown in France with an original score. Zukor, who modeled his Famous Plays Company on the Film d'Art, commissioned Joseph Carl Breil to create music for the American showings. Breil responded with a finely crafted and well-received orchestral score. Writing in the *San Francisco Chronicle* on July 12, 1914, a critic describes Breil's music for *Queen Elizabeth* with enthusiasm:

Figure 6.6 *Sarah Bernhardt in Queen Elizabeth*

> Briel [*sic*] was the first composer of quality to be attracted to the motion picture as an inspiration to composition. For Frohman's "Famous Players," he wrote the synchronizing score to *Queen Elizabeth*, which attracted the attention of musicians generally by the modern spirit in which it was penned. Each of the principals in the cast was given a "motive," such as Wagner identified his mythological characters with, and these themes, characteristic of the personages in the drama of the Stuart Queen, the Duke of Essex, the Duchess of Nottingham, Earl of Nottingham, and the rest of the persons [in] the play, including the masculine Queen herself, were woven ingeniously in the texture of Breil's orchestral score.

For this film, Breil first composed a piano score and later rewrote the music for an ensemble numbering up to fifteen, making this one of the earliest film scores for an orchestral ensemble in the United States.

Breil continued to compose film scores, completing scores for two more American releases of French films in 1912, and creating music for *The Prisoner of Zenda* (1913) and for an Italian import, *Cabiria* (1914), featuring the future dictator Benito Mussolini

Composer Profile

Joseph Carl Breil (1870–1926)

America's first significant film composer, Breil began his career as a singer and opera composer. He had completed a short opera and several light operas when he was asked to compose music for *Queen Elizabeth* in 1912. In later years, he would be most closely associated with the works of D. W. Griffith.

Important Film Scores

Queen Elizabeth 1912	*Tess of the Storm Country* 1922
The Birth of a Nation 1915	*The Phantom of the Opera* 1925
Intolerance 1916	

in a small role. In 1915 he scored eight films, including *The Birth of a Nation,* and in the following year he created the music for *Intolerance.* Like the score for *Birth of a Nation*, the music for *Intolerance* contains extensive borrowings from classical sources, including a chorus from Verdi's *Aida*, a quartet singing an arrangement of "My Wild Irish Rose," and music from the ballets of Delibes.

Victor Herbert

Film composition attracted one prominent figure in American music in the early twentieth century, the Irish-American cellist, conductor, and composer, Victor Herbert. Best known for his popular operettas, such as *Babes in Toyland* and *Naughty Marietta*, Herbert composed a symphonic score for *The Fall of a Nation* (1916), produced by the author of the novel *The Birth of a Nation*, Thomas Dixon. Herbert's score, which avoids borrowed material, has been cited as the first fully original American film score. Descriptions of Herbert's score praise his use of recurring themes associated with individuals in the film. Unfortunately, Herbert, voicing his frustrations over the continued revisions required by altered instrumentation, local censorship, and the varying speeds of projectors, abandoned the medium and wrote no other film scores.

Trailer

The difficulties faced by Herbert and Breil were substantial, but their efforts helped to establish the viability of original orchestral film scores in U. S. filmmaking. Within a decade, most major silent films in this country appeared with newly composed orchestral scores. The film that sparked this trend was D. W. Griffith's *The Birth of a Nation*.

Important Names and Terms

D. W. Griffith
United Artists
Wurlitzer organ
compilation score
Max Winkler
cue sheets
music anthologies
Motion Picture Piano Music
J. S. Zamecnik
Sam Fox Moving Picture Music
Giuseppe Becce

Kinobibliothek
Erno Rapée
Motion Picture Moods for Pianists and Organists
Film d'Art
Camille Saint-Saëns
Kalem Company
Walter Cleveland Simon
Joseph Carl Breil
Victor Herbert

Suggested Listening

Saint-Saëns, *L'Assassinat du duc de Guise*, Opus 128. Harmonia mundi, HMA 1951472.

Suggested Viewing

Treasures of the American Film Archives and *More Treasures From American Film Archives, 1844–1931*. These CD sets contain a rich collection of early silent films, as well as interesting films from other genres. Informative notes accompany the set.

Cabiria (1914): This is the oldest feature-length film to be reunited with its original music, which is performed on a piano in the DVD produced by Kino Video.

7

The Birth of a Nation

The Birth of a Nation presents a perplexing dichotomy. On the one hand, it is film's first great masterpiece, elevating the technique of filmmaking to an art form. On the other hand, it presents a repugnant defense of Southern segregation, glorifying the formation of a terrorist organization—the Ku Klux Klan. The disparity between these two aspects compels us to consider what makes art great. Can we separate the technique from the content of an artwork? Is this film, as the American Film Institute suggests, the greatest American silent film? Give some thought to these issues after viewing this historic and controversial film.

The Narrative

Appearing fifty years after the close of the Civil War, *The Birth of a Nation* is a twelve-reel epic film. The plot extends from the idyllic days before the Civil War, through the war, to the time of Reconstruction. The film is divided into two parts. The first half is a powerful story of the Civil War and its tragic impact on two families. Griffith took great pains to recreate several events of the war, most strikingly the assassination of Abraham Lincoln (Kino 1:18:35), which is remarkable for its historical accuracy. In addition, Griffith studied contemporary photos of the war in order to add a high sense of realism. The most spectacular and successful moments of the film are the panoramic battle scenes. For the climactic scene of the Civil War, Griffith chose to recreate the battle of Petersburg (Kino 46:15), the one battle that most closely resembled the modern trench warfare of World War I. The relationship between what was on the screen and current events in Europe would not have been lost on an audience in 1915.

Figure 7.1 The assassination of President Lincoln

These historic recreations create the backdrop against which numerous melodramatic scenes are played, revealing Griffith's masterful crosscutting techniques. Many of these scenes would have been the subjects of separate films in earlier years, but they are held together by a coherent storyline and by a brilliant buildup of tension, which can be observed in three rescue scenes. In the first, black Union soldiers attack the town of Piedmont (Kino 34:00). Visions of the destruction and ruthlessness of the attack are crosscut with scenes of the approaching rescue by Confederate soldiers. Once the rescue is successful, the audience is confident that such scenes will end happily.

In the second rescue scene, Flora, the younger daughter of the Cameron family, runs from the lascivious advances of the black renegade Gus (Kino 2:12:15). Crosscutting reveals that her brother Phil is coming to her rescue, and the audience expects another happy ending. This expectation heightens the shock when Flora jumps to her death, and Phil arrives in time only to cradle the dying child. This failed rescue takes the audience out of its comfort zone and increases the anxiety for the final climactic scene, which depicts two simultaneous crises. Both of these rescues are successful, but not before brilliant crosscutting builds enormous tension.

The second half of the film is based on *The Clansman*, a 1905 novel by the white supremacist Reverend Thomas Dixon. In this portion of the film, Griffith slips into historical inaccuracies. Although he suggests that he has recreated a historic vision of the State House of Representatives of South Carolina, his images are actually based on political cartoons of the time, not photos (Kino 1:54:05). In addition, historical events are distorted and manipulated to conform with Griffith's southern point of view. In both halves of the film, racism is rampant. The negative caricatures of blacks, the intense evil of Silas Lynch and the rapist Gus, the stupidity of the radical liberal whites (Senator Stoneman, with his wig and clubfoot, is clearly a parody of Thaddeus Stevens), and Griffith's apparent refusal to use black actors cannot be dismissed. If it is any consolation, the racist content was recognized in 1915, and the film faced opposition in newspapers, in court, and in the streets.

The Music

The dramatic and visual achievements of *The Birth of a Nation* are sufficient justification for this film's artistic reputation. Less known, but also significant, is its land-mark use of music. Griffith worked closely with Joseph Carl Breil in the creation of a compelling, three-hour musical score in which all three types of music used for silent film can be heard—adaptations of classical works, arrangements of well-known melodies, and original music. Each type fills a specific function in the film.

Figure 7.2 Breil underscores the ride of the KKK with Wagner's *Ride of the Valkyrie*

Adaptations

The extended quotations of classical music usually accompany large action scenes. The principal exceptions are a stately passage from a Mass attributed to Mozart that is used for the overture and denouement, and an ominous section from Bellini's overture to *Norma* played during Lincoln's assassination. Otherwise, Breil chose excerpts from the most agitated sections of the works he selected and placed them during extended scenes of action and violence. Among the most prominent adaptations are passages from Weber's *Der Freischütz*, Suppé's *Light Calvary* Overture, Beethoven's Symphony No. 6 (the storm), and Wagner's *Ride of the Valkyrie*. The last of these serves as a spir-ited leitmotif for the ride of the KKK. In certain versions of the music, three notes of Wagner's tune played by a bugle serve as their rallying call.

Arrangements

The arrangements of well-known melodies are used primarily to arouse emotions and set moods. Southern tunes, such as "Dixie," "Maryland, My Maryland" (the same melody as "O Christmas Tree"), and "Old Folks at Home" express stirring patriot-ism for the South while reminding the viewer of the story's setting. Other patriotic melodies include "The Star-Spangled Banner" (which was not the national anthem of the United States until 1931), "America the Beautiful," and "The Battle Hymn of the Republic." Popular tunes, such as "The Girl I Left Behind Me," are also effective in creating lighter moments for the story.

Some of the borrowed tunes underline the story. When the Southerner Cameron seeks refuge in a cabin with former Union soldiers, their acceptance of each other is suggested by the playing of "Auld Lang Syne," a song associated with reconciliation after the Civil War (Kino 2:39:40). Earlier, Breil quotes a popular tune, "Where Did You Get That Hat?", when Ted pokes fun at Duke's hat (Kino 9:25). This tune poignantly recurs when the two boys die in each other's arms on the battlefield (Kino 39:45). Unfortunately,

Breil also uses tunes to support the film's racist theme. Slaves are shown happily dancing (Kino 14:00) to "Turkey in the Straw" (also known as "Zip Coon"), and later scenes of African-Americans in power are mockingly accompanied by minstrel tunes, melodies associated with blackface entertainers of the nineteenth century (Kino 1:45:05).

Original Music

The greatest strength of Breil's score lies in the original music. Breil creates numerous leitmotifs, several of which are shown in the Featured Film Guide. These themes reinforce Griffith's characterizations. The two principal Stoneman themes reflect divergent personalities. The music for Senator Austin Stoneman, set in a minor key, is stern and formal, suggesting his questionable role in the drama. His daughter Elsie, by contrast, has a playful tune that suggests her innocence. The mulatto Silas Lynch, the principal antagonist, is given a dark theme dubbed "The Motif of Barbarism." The young Flora Cameron has several childlike themes, and the Cameron family has a radiant, lyric theme suggestive of the old South. The two budding romances— between Margaret Cameron and Phil Stoneman and between Elsie Stoneman and Ben Cameron—are also accompanied by tender melodies. The latter melody was the best-known original music from the film. Taking on an independent life, it was published as "The Perfect Song," becoming the first hit theme from a movie. Ironically, it would later be used as a theme song for a radio show featuring two white comedians playing African-Americans —"Amos 'n' Andy."

In spite of the monumental achievement of Breil's score, it was subject to the same type of treatment as all silent film scores. A seven-piece orchestra accompanied the first showing of the film in Riverside, California, on January 1 and 2, 1915. We do not know what music was played. For the official premiere of the film in Los Angeles at the Cluny Theater, Breil's score was replaced by music created by the theater's musical staff, headed by Carli Elinor. Reportedly played by an orchestra of fifty members and several vocal soloists, the supporting music consisted primarily of excerpts from the classics. Breil's score was first heard in its intended form at the New York debut. But in the years that followed, the original music was performed only at select theaters around the United States, and, because of Griffith's periodic reediting of the film, Breil made continual alterations to his work.

The existence of multiple versions of both the film and the score has made the coordination of the original music with the film on a video a difficult process. A 1933 reissue, in which Griffith cut over an hour of the film, provides valuable information about the original music. For this version, Griffith added a recorded musical score and sound effects. Since Breil had passed away in 1926,

Figure 7.3 Sheet music for "The Perfect Song" from *The Birth of a Nation*

Figure 7.4 Best friends die as the music plays a tune associated with their friendship

Griffith enlisted the aid of another of his favorite music collaborators, Louis F. Gottschalk. The two essentially retained and reworked the score that had been created by Griffith and Breil. Especially noteworthy are the insights into Breil's orchestration, which includes a vocal rendition of "Dixie."

There are a number of different video copies of *The Birth of a Nation* available today, some with the music by Breil and some with newly created music (see Table 7.1). It is strongly recommended that you view a video with music based on the Breil score. As indicated, a reconstructed score by Eric Beheim can be heard on a number of DVD and VHS versions of the film. Our Featured Film Guide (beginning on the following page) is based on the Kino DVD.

Table 7.1

Videos of *The Birth of a Nation*

MUSIC BASED ON BREIL'S SCORE

Kino International (DVD and VHS): arranged by Eric Beheim

Image Entertainment (DVD): arranged by Eric Beheim

Thames (VHS): arranged by John Lanchbery

Triton (DVD): synthesized arrangement by R. J. Miller

Delta Entertainment (DVD) and KVC Home Video (VHS): synchronized score of Breil adapted by Gottschalk and D. W. Griffith in 1933

NEWLY CREATED SCORES

Blackhawk Films (VHS): newly composed orchestral score by Fraser MacDonald

Republic Entertainment (VHS): newly composed orchestral score by Fraser MacDonald

Madacy Entertainment (VHS, DVD): an assortment of classical works

Vci Home Video (VHS): newly composed orchestral score

Video Entertainment Corp (VHS): organ accompaniment

NO SOUND

United American Video Corp.

The Birth of a Nation (1915)

Directed by D. W. Griffith
Music by Joseph Carl Breil

Principal Characters

Austin Stoneman, leader of the House of Representatives
  (Ralph Lewis)
Elsie Stoneman, daughter of Austin (Lillian Gish)
Ben Cameron, oldest son of the Cameron family (Henry
  Walthall)
Flora Cameron, little sister of Ben (Mae Marsh)
Silas Lynch, mulatto who oversees Reconstruction (George Siegmann)

Principal Leitmotifs

Example 7.1 Barbarian/Lynch

Example 7.2 Stoneman

Example 7.3 Elsie

Example 7.4 Cameron family

Example 7.5 Love of Phil and Margaret

Example 7.6 Love of Ben and Elsie

Exposition

0:00–14:50/Chapters 1–3

SCENE DESCRIPTION	MUSIC
Title, opening credits and disclaimers	Mozart Gloria from Mass in G, K. 232
Africans are brought to America.	Barbarian theme
An abolitionist meeting	Hymn-like music
Senator Austin Stoneman is shown with his daughter Elsie.	The Stoneman theme is followed by Elsie's theme.
The two Stoneman brothers (Phil and Tod) compose a letter for their Southern friend Ben Cameron.	Elsie's theme alternates with contrasting material.
We meet the Cameron family from Piedmont, South Carolina, including daughters Margaret and Flora and sons Ben, Duke, and Wade.	"Old Folks at Home," by Stephen Foster, alternates with the Cameron theme.
The Stoneman sons visit the Cameron family; friendships renew and love begins.	Elsie's theme, contrasting material, and a touch of the Cameron theme
Tod and Duke horse around.	"Where Did You Get that Hat?" followed by playful music
Phil and Margaret walk through the cotton fields.	Idyllic music and their Love theme
Ben, grabbing a photo of Elsie, falls in love with the image.	Lyric music and the Love theme for Ben and Elsie
A brief visit to the slave quarters	"Turkey in the Straw"

Complications: Gathering Storm

14:50–32:25/Chapters 4 and 5

SCENE DESCRIPTION	MUSIC
The families read the newspaper account.	Weber's *Der Freischütz*
Stoneman and Charles Sumner talk; soon we see Lydia Brown begin to seduce Stoneman.	Several melodic ideas associated with ambition and lust
Phil and Tod leave Piedmont.	Love theme of Phil and Margaret
Lincoln signs proclamation asking for volunteers; Phil and Tod enlist.	"We Are Coming, Father Abraham"; playful music follows.
Confederate ball celebration, with scenes of the Cameron sons preparing to go to war; the flag from Bull Run is brought in.	Dance music with "Comin' thro' the Rye" followed by "The Bonnie Blue Flag"
The Confederate soldiers are called, and the Cameron sons say goodbye and leave with the troops.	Military and Southern patriotic tunes include the *Light Cavalry Overture* by Suppé, "Maryland, My Maryland," and "Dixie."
Elsie rejoins her father.	Mostly Elsie's theme

Complications: War

32:25–58:30/Chapters 6–8

SCENE DESCRIPTION	MUSIC
Ben reads a letter from Flora, who is in Piedmont. Suddenly, Union guerrillas attack Piedmont, but the town is rescued. The Cameron family gathers in their home.	Sad music and Flora's playful theme give way to the Barbarian theme and Weber's *Der Freischütz*; "Maryland, My Maryland" at end.
Ben looks at a portrait of Elsie.	Ben and Elsie's Love theme
On the battlefield, Tod and Duke die together. The families receive news of the deaths. The Cameron women donate clothes for the war. Elsie becomes a nurse.	Ominous music and a reprise of "Where Did You Get That Hat?"; mournful music with scenes of families
Sherman marches through Georgia, destroying Atlanta. Wade Cameron is killed.	"Marching through Georgia," action music, and Grieg's *In the Hall of the Mountain King*

Confederate food train is behind Union line. General Lee orders rescue.	*Light Cavalry* Overture and "Reveille"
The Battle of Petersburg commences, and Ben is captured. Several views of the dead are shown.	Battle music with fragments of patriotic tunes, including "Dixie" and "The Bonnie Blue Flag"; "Taps" accompanies scenes of the dead.

Complications: Peace

58:30–1:26:30/Chapters 9–11

SCENE DESCRIPTION	MUSIC
The North is victorious. The Cameron family learns of Wade's death.	Sad music
Ben, in a Union hospital, meets Elsie, and they fall in love. Mrs. Cameron appeals to Lincoln for Ben's life and secures a pardon. She visits Ben before returning home.	"Kingdom Coming," Elsie's theme, Ben and Elsie's Love theme, and the Cameron theme
Lee surrenders to Grant.	"America the Beautiful"
Ben leaves Elsie for home. Flora prepares to meet her brother, and the two reunite.	"Kingdom Coming"; Flora's music, "Comin' thro' the Rye," "Home, Sweet Home," and "My Old Kentucky Home"
Stoneman and Lincoln argue about the treatment of the South.	Stoneman theme and phrases of "America"
The South begins to rebuild.	"The Girl I Left Behind Me"
President Lincoln is assassinated	Bellini's overture "Norma"

Complications: Reconstruction

1:26:30–1:57:00/Chapters 12–15

SCENE DESCRIPTION	MUSIC
Historical notes and more disclaimers by Griffith.	Solemn music
Stoneman is now the "uncrowned king" in Washington. He appoints Silas Lynch, a mulatto, to oversee Reconstruction. Sumner argues in vain for a more moderate approach. Lynch eyes Elsie.	Stoneman's theme, the Barbarian theme (now given to Lynch), and the Lust theme are prominent throughout.

Lynch moves to Piedmont and begins to assist former slaves. Lynch and Ben meet.	Various minstrel tunes; Lynch theme
The Stonemans move to Piedmont.	Elsie theme
The Stonemans arrive. Several comic scenes between the servants. Elsie and Flora meet.	Predominantly playful music with Elsie's theme
Lynch appears, and Ben refuses to shake hands. Lynch and Stoneman attend a rally of the Southern Union League. Lynch recruits the former slaves to vote.	The Lynch theme dominates; the Stoneman theme is also heard. More minstrel tunes are heard at the rally.
Lynch observes Ben giving a dove to Elsie. Meanwhile Margaret rejects Phil, and Elsie attempts to reject Ben, but later relents.	Ben and Elsie's Love theme dominates; Phil and Margaret's Love theme is also prominent.
Election Day and Lynch becomes the Lieutenant Governor.	Minstrel tune, the Lynch theme, and celebration music
Ben narrates a series of outrages.	Agitated music
A scene from the House of Representatives	Minstrel songs

Complications: Death of Flora

1:57:00–2:20:30/Chapters 16–18

SCENE DESCRIPTION	MUSIC
The renegade Gus observes Flora. Ben and Lynch meet again. Ben threatens Lynch.	Flora's playful themes followed by agitation featuring the Lynch theme
Ben observes children playing with sheets and is inspired. The Klan is created and springs into action.	Tunes associated with the Klan
Lynch is told of this event and ambushes a group from the Klan.	Lynch theme
Stoneman is furious about the Klan. Elsie breaks off her engagement with Ben and Flora consoles her brother.	Stoneman theme dominates at first, then Ben and Elsie's Love theme. Flora's theme also appears.

Gus observes Flora in the woods. He attempts to rape her, and she runs to the edge of a cliff and leaps. She dies in the arms of her brother, who has arrived too late. Ben laments.	Flora's theme and the Lust theme; the music turns toward resignation with a slower version of Flora's theme.
Phil argues with his father.	Stoneman theme mixed with lament

Complications: Tensions Rise

2:20:30–2:40:40/Chapters 19–20

SCENE DESCRIPTION	MUSIC
Gus hides in Joe's gin mill and kills someone looking for him. Gus is then captured and executed by the Klan.	Beethoven's Symphony No. 6; a lament returns.
Lynch is furious and calls on the Union soldiers. Stoneman leaves town quietly.	Continued agitated music with Lynch and Stoneman themes
The Klan prepares for action while Ben honors Flora.	Klan music begins to incorporate Wagner's *Ride of the Valkyrie*.
Lynch becomes drunk with power.	Beethoven's Symphony No. 6
Elsie laments. Dr. Cameron is arrested, and Margaret appeals to Elsie for help. The servants help, and Phil Stoneman shoots a black soldier. They all escape.	Sorrow music followed by action music
Elsie waits for her father, and soldiers give chase to Dr. Cameron. Lynch celebrates, and the Cameron group takes refuge in a cabin. Their hideaway is observed.	Continued agitated and action music. "Auld Lang Syne" is used for the cabin scene.

Climax

2:40:40–3:03:30/Chapters 21–23

SCENE DESCRIPTION	MUSIC
Elsie turns to Lynch for help, but he tells her that he wants to marry her and locks her in the room. Crosscutting reveals the gathering Klan.	Lynch theme mixed with agitated music, Elsie's theme, and Tchaikovsky's *1812 Overture*

Stoneman returns, and Lynch tells him of his plan to marry Elsie. Stoneman is furious. Crosscuts show the Klan riding.	Lynch theme and Herold's *Zappa* Overture
With crosscuts, we see Elsie appealing for help and the Klan coming to the rescue. Meanwhile, the Cameron group is under siege. Clansmen see the cabin situation and go for help.	Weber's *Der Freischütz*, Wagner's *Rienzi* Overture, and the *Ride of the Valkyrie*.
Ben rescues Elsie. The soldiers are closing in on the cabin, but the Klan rides to another rescue.	*Ride of the Valkyrie* and the *Rienzi* Overture

Resolution

3:03:30–3:06:45/Chapter 24

SCENE DESCRIPTION	MUSIC
The blacks are disarmed and disenfranchised.	"Dixie"
The two pairs of lovers contemplate a better life.	Both Love themes and Mozart, Gloria from Mass in G, K. 232
Closing statement.	"The Star-Spangled Banner"

Trailer

Breil's score for *The Birth of a Nation* was a remarkable achievement, both for its size and quality. His use of borrowed material reflected some of the trends in silent film music of that time, but the extensive amount of new material with unifying leitmotifs set a model for the future. In the following years, other composers would build upon and refine the techniques explored by Breil in this controversial masterpiece.

Important Names and Terms

Thomas Dixon

The Clansman

"The Perfect Song"

Carli Elinor

Louis F. Gottschalk

8

The Golden Age of Silent Film, 1920–1928

Building upon the foundations of the 1910s, film entered its first golden age in the early 1920s. By the middle years of the decade, an impressive number of masterworks had been produced both in America and in Europe. Indeed, the production of outstanding films from 1925 through 1928 rivals that of any other similar period in film history. Without a doubt, these silents are golden.

Musical Accompaniment in the 1920s

Prior to the advent of sound, the movie theater was the largest employer of musicians in the world. Most of the musicians played keyboard instruments—organ or piano. According to a 1922 survey of theaters featuring music, an organ was the primary accompaniment instrument in over 45 percent of the houses, a piano in about 25 percent, and an orchestra in nearly 30 percent. The survey's definition of an orchestra is somewhat loose and includes

SIGNIFICANT FILMS

1920	*The Cabinet of Dr. Caligari*
1925	*Battleship Potemkin*
1927	*Napoléon*
1929	*The New Babylon*

Table 8.1

Classic silent films, 1920–1928

1920:	*The Cabinet of Dr. Caligari*	1926:	*Faust*
	The Mark of Zorro		*What Price Glory*
1921:	*The Four Horsemen of the Apocalypse*		*Don Juan*
	The Sheik	1927:	*The General*
1922:	*Nosferatu*		*Sunrise*
	Foolish Wives		*Napoléon*
1923:	*The Ten Commandments*		*Metropolis*
	The Hunchback of Notre Dame		*Wings*
1924:	*Greed*		*Seventh Heaven*
	The Thief of Bagdad		*The Jazz Singer*
1925:	*Battleship Potemkin*	1928:	*The Passion of Joan of Arc*
	The Big Parade		*The Crowd*
	The Phantom of the Opera		*The Wind*
	Ben-Hur		*The Wedding March*
	The Gold Rush		

what should be termed chamber groups. Among the ensembles playing in the theater, a small group of two to five performers was the most common size (about 65 percent), moderate sizes of five to ten were frequent (just over 28 percent), and large sizes were rare (just over 1 percent had twenty-five to fifty performers).

Musical activities were quite elaborate in the big theaters known as "movie palaces." Palaces such as Sid Grauman's Chinese Theatre in Los Angeles were built in every region of the country. The greatest movie palaces were in New York. Here Samuel "Roxy" Rothapfel bought or built a number of grand theaters, including the Rialto, Rivoli, Capitol, Roxy, and Radio City Music Hall. The Roxy Theatre, built in 1927 with a seating capacity of 6,214 (see Figure 8.1), has been described as the largest theater since the fall of the Roman Empire. Each seat was electronically wired to a panel of lights so that ushers could identify empty seats. Outside the auditorium, there was a luxurious waiting room with a capacity for two thousand, a kitchen, fully staffed nursery and hospital, radio broadcast booth, and private apartments.

Patrons attending performances at such lavish venues could expect to be entertained by a full symphony orchestra performing overtures and entr'acte music. The music library was said to hold over fifty thousand scores. In addition, singers and dancers were often part of an extravagant revue before the featured film. The legendary Rockettes from the Radio City Music Hall are the last legacy of the Rothapfel era. Unfortunately, the Roxy was built just at the end of the era. The conversion to

Figure 8.1 The interior of the Roxy Theatre in New York

films with synchronized music in the late 1920s brought about an abrupt end to these theatrical entertainments, and theater orchestras were quickly disbanded.

Film Composers in America

Following the enormous success of Joseph Carl Breil's score for *The Birth of a Nation*, original orchestral film scores became more common. During the 1920s, a new musical score accompanied almost every major film. The three leading film composers in America were conductors and composers for New York movie palaces—William Axt, Erno Rapée, and Hugo Riesenfeld.

Figure 8.2 Dancers at the Capitol Theatre in New York

William Axt

William Axt, the music director for the Capitol Theatre, frequently collaborated with another composer, David Mendoza. Mendoza describes their process of creating a compilation score:

> Our first step is to preview the picture, thus getting an accurate idea of the mood, atmosphere, and general type of music required for the film. . . . Directly after the preview of the picture we plot out a cue sheet . . . The musical library is next visited. The filing cabinets here classify practically all existing music—sacred, profane, old-fashioned, and jazz. One classification tabulates all music according to composers: Bach, Beethoven, Irving Berlin, and so on. Another lists everything according to mood: joy, anger, sorrow, and the like. Another gives the style of the music . . . There are still other files, including one arranging all music nationally. In each listing one can find the score both for orchestra and for piano. Some orchestrations are made up largely of original music or original "blendings" composed by Mr. Axt or myself. Other scores consist almost entirely of carefully interwoven excerpts from various existing music.*

Once films were created with synchronized music, Hollywood sent most of their films to New York to be scored. In particular, the Capitol Theatre and William Axt maintained a close relationship with Hollywood's MGM studio, which eventually absorbed the entire Capitol music library of over thirty thousand scores. In this relationship William Axt worked on many of MGM's greatest silent films. All of the films listed in his Composer Profile were produced at MGM with the notable exception of

---

* David Mendoza, "The Theme Song," *American Hebrew,* March 15, 1929, 124.

William Axt (1888–1959)

Born in New York, William Axt was the assistant conductor at the Manhattan Opera House under the music direction of Oscar Hammerstein. In 1919, he was appointed music director of the Capitol Theatre. Known as "Dr. Billy," he received a doctorate in music from the American University in Chicago and Los Angeles. He later worked for MGM and was the central musical figure in their transition from silent film to sound.

Important Film Scores

Greed 1924	*Faust* 1926
The Big Parade 1925	*The Wind* 1928
Ben-Hur 1925	*Dinner at Eight* 1933
Don Juan 1926	*The Thin Man* 1934

Don Juan. In the late 1920s, Axt began working directly for MGM. According to *Film Composers in America*, "William Axt ushered [MGM] into the sound era almost single-handedly, scoring more films through 1934 than all their other composers together."

Erno Rapée

The Hungarian-born Erno Rapée (1891–1945) conducted orchestras at the Roxy, Rivoli, and the Capitol; he also served as the music director at Radio City Music Hall. These orchestras were large—the Capitol Theatre orchestra numbered seventy-one performers, including forty-seven string players—and their quality was excellent. In addition to accompanying films, theater orchestras played major symphonic works, including tone poems by Richard Strauss. As a conductor, Rapée was heard by millions on the radio in performances on the "Roxy Hour." Well-known for his anthology of music for film, *Motion Picture Moods for Pianists and Organists*, Rapée also composed a number of important scores for films such as *Sunrise, What Price Glory,* and *Seventh Heaven.* In addition, Rapée was a gifted songwriter; his "Charmaine" from *What Price Glory* enjoyed enormous popularity and sparked the trend of using original popular tunes in movies. He continued to compose film scores into the 1930s, primarily for the Warner Bros. Studio.

Hugo Riesenfeld

Hugo Riesenfeld (1879–1939) was also prominent as a conductor, directing orchestras at the Rialto, Rivoli, and Criterion. He felt that his orchestras were equal in quality to the New York Philharmonic, and considering how well the movie theater musicians were paid and the number of repeated performances, he may well have been correct. In addition to conducting, Riesenfeld created musical scores for such classics as *Dr. Jekyll and Mr. Hyde* (1920), *The Hunchback of Notre Dame* (1923), *Les Misérables* (1925), and the synchronized version of *Sunrise* (1927), which will be discussed in Chapter 9. He later became the music director at United Artists and served as an important musical figure in the early sound era.

Among the other prominent composers for silent films in America are the following:

- Louis F. Gottschalk (1869–1934), the nephew of the prominent American composer Louis Moreau Gottschalk, composed scores for a trio of early films based on the *Wizard of Oz* story (1914) and for several of D. W. Griffith's works, including *Broken Blossoms* (scored for violin and harp, 1919) and *Orphans of the Storm* (1921). He also composed music for Rex Ingram's *The Four Horsemen of the Apocalypse* (1921).
- Louis Silvers (1889–1954) composed music for D. W. Griffith's *Way Down East* (1920) and for the sensational *The Jazz Singer* (1927). Later, he would serve as music director for Twentieth Century Fox and would be awarded the first music Oscar for his contributions to *One Night of Love* (1934).
- J. S. Zamecnik (1872–1953) was music director for a movie palace in Cleveland. He created a pioneer anthology of film music and distinguished himself with scores for several well-known films, including *The Wedding March* (1928), and two films that won Oscars for Best Picture—*Wings* (1927) and *Cavalcade* (1933).

European Films

Returning from its hiatus during World War I, Europe saw a flurry of creative activity during the 1920s. Strong centers of filmmaking appeared in many countries, including Germany, the Soviet Union, and France. While no one European country matched the production of the United States, especially in the commercial aspects, a significant number of the films produced in these international centers are from the artistic point of view among the finest of the era.

Germany

Germany began a creative period of filmmaking in 1920 that extended until Hitler took control of the industry in 1933. German films tend to have a strong visual component, which can be seen in such masterworks as Fritz Lang's *Metropolis* (1926) and F. W. Murnau's *Nosferatu* (1922). The first important work of the German school is *The Cabinet of Dr. Caligari* (1920), directed by Robert Wiene. A product of the expressionist movement, *The Cabinet of Dr. Caligari* stands as a true total artwork with clear

Close-Up: Great Producers and Directors

The Golden Age of Silent Film

During the 1920s, a number of outstanding producers and directors contributed to the growing American industry. Particularly strong is the impact of German directors, several of whom emigrated to Hollywood during the Nazi regime. The following are among the most prominent names of the era.

Irving Thalberg (1899–1936) became the model for the powerful studio producer, controlling all aspects of production and reigning supreme, even over directors. Known as the "Boy Wonder," he was a major figure at Universal Studios before the age of twenty-one. Moving to the newly formed MGM, he became the dominant figure in production in that studio. He had a number of well-publicized clashes, most notably with director Erich von Stroheim and studio head Louis Mayer. A heart attack in 1932 slowed his activities, and his sudden death from pneumonia at the age of thirty-seven shocked Hollywood. In 1937, the Academy of Motion Pictures Arts and Sciences created the Irving G. Thalberg Award for high-quality achievements in production, the only award that is not given as an Oscar but rather in the image of Thalberg himself.

Cecil B. DeMille (1881–1959) began directing films in 1913 with partners Jesse Lasky and Sam Goldwyn. His prolific output culminated in the 1920s with two of Hollywood's most lavish films—*The Ten Commandments* (1923) and *The King of Kings* (1927). After a downturn in his activities during the 1940s, he concluded his career with three outstanding films: the religious epic *Samson and Delilah* (1950); *The Greatest Show on Earth* (1952), which won an Oscar for Best Picture; and *The Ten Commandments* (1956), a remake that became the biggest box-office success of the decade.

King Vidor (1894–1982) rose quickly in the Hollywood directorial ranks. His first feature film appeared in 1919, and within five years he was working for MGM, making such acclaimed films as *The Big Parade* (1925)

and *The Crowd* (1928). His successes continued into the sound era, when he directed *Hallelujah* (1929) and *The Champ* (1931). He was also one of the uncredited directors of *The Wizard of Oz* (1939). Among his later films are *Northwest Passage* (1940) and *War and Peace* (1956).

Fritz Lang (1890–1976) is principally remembered for directing dark and twisted stories. He helped create the script for Wiene's *The Cabinet of Dr. Caligari* (1920), for which he is credited with formulating the brilliant framed plot. In 1927, Lang filmed the science fiction masterpiece *Metropolis,* and he entered the sound era with the sensational *M* (1931), an extraordinarily dark film about a child murderer, which made Peter Lorre an international star. In Hollywood, he made a number of serious westerns, but is best remembered for his contributions to the film noir movement.

Eric von Stroheim (1885–1957) is one of the most enigmatic and brilliant directors to work in Hollywood. He began working with D. W. Griffith and has a small role in *The Birth of a Nation*. He soon created a sensation by making silent films with great sexual tension, such as *Foolish Wives* (1922). In 1924, he completed one of the most monumental films in Hollywood history, the forty-two-reel film *Greed,* which lasts for over ten hours. MGM cut this film down to ten reels, destroying the other thirty-two reels. The lost material is still the subject of much debate and speculation. Thereafter, Stroheim worked primarily as an actor. In this capacity he can be seen in Jean Renoir's *Grand Illusion* (1937) and Billy Wilder's *Sunset Blvd.* (1950).

Friedrich Wilhelm Murnau (1888–1931) is one of the most influential directors coming from the silent film era. While in Germany, he created a horror masterpiece, *Nosferatu* (1922). He immediately followed with several more masterpieces, including *The Last Laugh* (1924) and *Faust* (1926). *Sunrise* (1927), Murnau's first film in Hollywood, is considered by many to be the greatest of all silent films.

ties to drama, visual arts, and music. Expressionism is a predominantly German movement that delves into the darker regions of the subconscious mind. Expressionistic dramas explore topics such as perversion, nightmares, and insanity. Expressionistic paintings use distorted images and heavy black lines to give the impression of a disturbed world. Expressionistic music, most closely associated with the works of Arnold Schoenberg, avoids rational tonal centers and creates a nightmare-like sound with its totally dissonant treatment.

All three aspects of the expressionist movement converge in *The Cabinet of Dr. Caligari*. What appears to be a horror film is really a vision of insanity. The opening frame sets up the deception. The audience is led to believe that the young hero Francis is telling a daring tale of murder and detective work. It is only in the final frame that we understand that Francis is insane, not Dr. Caligari. The entire film has been a fantasy seen through the eyes of a patient at an insane asylum. His distorted view of life is reinforced by the expressionistic stage sets, make-up, and costumes. Only in the framing scenes, when we are not seeing through the eyes of Francis, are the expressionistic visual elements minimized.

Figure 8.3 *The Scream* by Edvard Munch is a forerunner of expressionism

The original music, which unfortunately is lost, was composed by Giuseppe Becce. The music has been described as expressionistic in style, but only a handful of examples survive as themes in Becce's musical anthology. When *The Cabinet of Dr. Caligari* was brought to America, it premiered at Rothapfel's Capitol Cinema in New York. Rothapfel, working with Erno Rapée, decided to complement the dramatic and visual style with modern music, using excerpts from works by Schoenberg, Stravinsky, Debussy, Prokofiev, and Richard Strauss. From this repertoire, several leitmotifs were crafted: A theme from Richard Strauss's *Till Eulenspiegel* accompanied Dr. Caligari, and Debussy's *Prelude to the Afternoon of a Faun* underscored Cesare. Bernard Rogers, writing for *Musical America*, April, 1921, praised the daring use of modern music:

Figure 8.4 *The Cabinet of Dr. Caligari* helped open the door for modern music in film

Properly, the American premiere of *Caligari* employed music calculated to heighten its exotic character, to underline its fantastic aspects . . . As briefly back as five years Stravinsky or Schoenberg in the movie-house belonged to the inconceivable. Today it calmly happens, and the audience calmly swallows the pill. It would have been far simpler in preparing accompaniment for this film, to dish up the old safe and sickening potpourri. The more admirable, then, is the departure made by Messrs Rothapfel and Rapée. The thing took more than courage; it meant double labor and it meant considerable expense. Four rehearsals were called. But the tune was worth the toll. The acrid air of Stravinsky has been borne into the film theater. It may clear the sweet murk before the last reel is run.

Rothapfel's choice of music was deservedly applauded, but the total effect of the film was diluted by the appearance of a narrator both before and after the show, mirroring the frame within the film itself. Compounding this intrusion was the added happy ending; the narrator assured the audience that Francis was now cured, happily married, and working as a jeweler in Hostenwall.

The Soviet Union

Soviet filmmaking began in earnest in 1919, after the revolution. D. W. Griffith's *Intolerance* greatly impressed Nikolai Lenin, who felt that film could be the most influential of all the arts. He had copies of *Intolerance* sent to Soviet filmmakers for study. Sergei Eisenstein, the leading Soviet director, built upon many of Griffith's techniques. Most impressive are his ability to use close-ups of individuals to give a sense of the larger mass and his terse cutting technique, called montage. The montage depicting the massacre on the steps of Odessa in *Battleship Potemkin* (1925) remains one of the great scenes in film history (49:00).

Edmund Meisel's score for *Battleship Potemkin* is in its own right as powerful as the film itself. Indeed, when the film was imported to Germany, the movie was found acceptable, but the music was banned because it might incite powerful rebellious emotions. Using dissonant harmonies, a pounding percussion section, and nearly intolerable dynamics, the score stands as one of the great symphonic works for silent films. Herman G. Weinberg, writing in the *New York Herald Tribune* on April 29, 1928, describes a performance of *Battleship Potemkin* in the United States:

> For the New York presentation of *Potemkin* at the Biltmore the original accompanying score by Dr. Edmund Meisel, of Berlin, was used. Of the film itself, one need say little here. It has made cinema history already. The music was almost passed over entirely by the critics of the metropolitan press, which was a mistake, for the score is as powerful, as vital, as galvanic and electrifying as the film. It is written in the extreme modern vein, cacophonies run riot, harmonies grate, crackle, jar; there are abrupt changes and shifts in the rhythm; tremendous chords crashing down, dizzy flights of runs, snatches of half-forgotten melodies, fragments, a short interpolation of jazz on a piano and a melody in the central portion of the film when the people of Odessa stand on the steps waving to the sailors on the cruiser Potemkin and others go out on fishing boats with provisions for them—that is one of the loveliest that I have ever heard. It sings! It soars and endears itself to the heart. It is full of gratitude and the love of man for man. It is one of the warmest, tenderest passages that has found its way into the cinema-music repertoire.

The last year of the decade produced the first film score by the Soviet Union's leading composer, Dmitri Shostakovich. Best known for his fifteen symphonies, chamber music, and operas, this former movie theater pianist created a score for the silent film *The New Babylon* in 1929. Typical of many of his symphonic works, the music of *The New Babylon* is filled with musical quotations. Since the film is set in Paris, French waltzes, cancans, and patriotic tunes are mixed with Shostakovich's dissonant, satirical sound. The result is a powerful score that can easily stand at the side of his other creations. Shostakovich would continue composing for sound films, scoring thirty-four more films in later years.

Figure 8.5 An image from the Odessa steps montage in *Battleship Potemkin* that was accompanied by Meisel's powerful score

France

French cinema was perhaps the most artistically minded school in the 1920s. In the hands of directors like René Clair and Jean Renoir (the son of the impressionistic painter Auguste Renoir), French films tended to be innovative, experimental, and energetic. Following the lead of Saint-Saëns, a number of prominent French composers created film scores. The grand old man of modern French music, Erik Satie, composed a musical score for René Clair's *Entr'acte* (1924); the American composer Virgil Thomson described the film as the "best union of movies and music that has ever been made." A highly repetitive score that remains detached from the images accompanies *Entr'acte*, so named because it was shown between the acts of a dadaist ballet by Picabia.

Among the other prominent French composers who wrote for films are Jacques Ibert, Darius Milhaud, and Arthur Honegger. Milhaud, a leading figure of a group of composers known as *Les Six*, composed music for Marcel L'Herbier's experimental film *L'Inhumaine* (1924), with a scene depicting a riot at a concert similar to the one at the premiere of Stravinsky's *Rite of Spring*. Milhaud, the most prolific composer of art music in the twentieth century, wrote music for films into the 1960s. Arthur Honegger, another member of *Les Six*, composed numerous film scores, including the music for Abel Gance's two greatest works, *La Roue* (1923) and *Napoléon* (1927).

The latter epic was the first and only completed film of a projected series of six works showing the life of this national hero. *Napoléon* explores many remarkable film techniques, the most spectacular of which is the three-screen Polyvision system that foreshadows wide-screen effects that appeared in American films in the 1950s. Honegger's score features both lyrical romantic sections and

Figure 8.6 The three-screen climax of *Napoléon* was accompanied by stirring patriotic music by Honegger

modern dissonant passages. The emotional highlight is the music that accompanies *Les Mendiants de la Gloire,* which contains a stirring setting of the *Marseillaise.* Within any particular section, there is little contrast, since Honegger's music sets overall moods rather than mirroring dramatic action. This general detachment from the drama will characterize the approach of many European filmmakers well into the 1970s.

Trailer

By the middle of the 1920s, the art of making silent films had been perfected, both in America and in Europe. With grand movie palaces, finely crafted films, and lush musical scores, the industry appeared ready for a lengthy period of excellence. But the future of the silent film world was soon threatened by the success of a new technological advancement, synchronized recorded sound.

Important Names and Terms

movie palace

Roxy Rothapfel

William Axt

David Mendoza

Hugo Riesenfeld

Louis Silvers

expressionism

Sergei Eisenstein

montage

Edmund Meisel

Dmitri Shostakovich

Erik Satie

Jaques Ibert

Darius Milhaud

Arthur Honegger

Abel Gance

Suggested Viewing

Drama: *Orphans of the Storm* (1921), *The Big Parade* (1925), *Greed* (1924), and *The Crowd* (1928)

Horror and Science Fiction: *Nosferatu* (1922) and *Metropolis* (1927)

Comedy: *The Gold Rush* (1925) and *The General* (1927)

American Classics: *The Ten Commandments* (1923), *The Hunchback of Notre Dame* (1923), *Ben-Hur* (1925), and *King of Kings* (1927)

European Classics: *The Passion of Joan of Arc* (1928)

9

The Transition to Sound, 1926–1928

Beginning in 1926, a number of films were issued with recorded music and sound effects. Although they had sound, these films are still considered to be part of the silent era, since they contain no spoken dialogue. At this time, recorded sound was seen merely as an enhancement of silent films, and a number of films created before 1926 were reissued with synchronized sound well into the early 1930s. But the technological achievement of sound signaled the imminent demise of the silent era. Pandora's box was opened in 1927, when Al Jolson ad-libbed a few spoken lines in *The Jazz Singer*. In the next year, Warner Bros. produced ten all-talking pictures, and within two years, the silent film era had come to an end.

Silent films with synchronized music and sound effects represent a brief phase in the history of filmmaking, but the surviving works give us a tantalizing glimpse of how music must have sounded in the great movie palaces of the silent era. In this chapter, we will examine four films with synchronized sound: *Don Juan*, the first feature film to break the so-called sound barrier; *The Jazz Singer*, the first narrative with spoken dialogue; *Sunrise*, one of the first films created using the sound on film technique; and *City Lights*, one of the last great silent films.

SIGNIFICANT FILMS

1926	*Don Juan*
1927	*The Jazz Singer*
	Sunrise
1931	*City Lights*

The Vitaphone

Attempts to synchronize recorded sounds with moving pictures can be traced back to the early years of film, but it was not until 1926 that the two prerequisites of dependable equipment and proper marketing made the concept a practical reality. The first workable system was the Vitaphone, a product of the perseverance of Sam Warner and the ingenuity of Western Electric.

The essence of the Vitaphone system was the coordination of visual images shown by a projector with recorded music and sound effects played on a phonograph. The length of a reel of film was timed to match that of one side of a record. This type of coordination worked best with non-specific sounds, such as background music and general sound effects. The quality of sound did not equal that of a live orchestra, but audiences in the largest theaters quickly adapted to the technological novelty, and for those who attended the 98 percent of theaters in America that did not employ an orchestra, the recorded sound of a group like the New York Philharmonic was an exciting advancement.

Figure 9.1 The Vitaphone coordinated the length of a reel of film with that of a side of a record

Don Juan

The premiere of the Vitaphone system in New York on August 6, 1926, opened with a number of short films, or "shorts," filmed with live-recorded sound. The first featured a spoken introduction by Will Hays praising this historical moment. In this brief segment, we can see that the Vitaphone was capable of recording a speaking voice, but we can also see the constraints placed upon the speaker by having to stand near the microphone. This constraint is acceptable for a speech, but is too restrictive for acting.

The other shorts are musical numbers presented in the style of a revue. The New York Philharmonic opens the set with the overture to Wagner's *Tannhäuser*. Concert violinists, opera singers, and a vaudeville performer (Roy Smeck playing steel guitar, ukulele, and banjo) are featured in these precursors of MTV. The most successful of the musical shorts was Giovanni Martinelli's emotional performance of "Vesti la giubba" from *Pagliacci,* which helped secure a permanent place for recorded music in film.

Following the shorts was the feature film *Don Juan,* starring John Barrymore. The drama, with its humorous amorous complications, swashbuckling duels, romantic passions, and a record 191 kisses, was a perfect choice for the debut of the system. Supporting the film is a musical score composed primarily by William Axt and recorded by the New York Philharmonic.

Figure 9.2 The Vitaphone and *Don Juan* make headlines

In the riveting opening Prologue (see Viewer Guide below), leitmotifs reflect the nature of several principal characters. Don Juan as a boy has a childlike melody played gently in the clarinets. The theme for Don Jose, Don Juan's father, based on a stately Spanish dance rhythm, is intoned by the French horns. The dwarf servant has an impish melody derived from a clarinet theme in *Till Eulenspiegel* by Richard Strauss. Finally, the Spanish lover has a dashing, passionate theme played primarily in the strings.

Through most of the prologue, the music reflects the point of view of Don Jose. At the beginning, the music supports his passionate embrace and kiss of his wife, although she is clearly uninterested and impatient for him to leave. Once outside, Don Jose's theme is transformed into a march by changing the meter from triple to quadruple. After his return, Don Jose's theme undergoes further transformations suggesting the stages of his emotions—anxiety, anger, rage, and controlled revenge. Donna Isobel's emotions surface in the music only after her lover has been sealed in the wall. We hear the intensity of her lament as we watch Don Jose's laugh, a moment that underscores Don Jose's cruelty. At the end of the scene, Don Jose's theme is heard once again, but with the gentle orchestration of Don Juan's theme. Quietly, William Axt has begun to transfer the father's theme to the son, just as his attitude is about to be assumed by Don Juan—indeed, Barrymore plays both roles.

Viewer Guide

Don Juan: Prologue

Timing

1:30–11:40 (0:00 at studio logo)

Key Points

- Synchronized score for full symphony orchestra
- Leitmotifs representing individual characters
- Music reflects emotions and suggests a point of view
- Source music (trumpets)

Setting

In this Hollywood version of the Don Juan story, we discover that all the legendary lover and seducer of women really needed was to meet the right woman. Preparing us for this turn of events, the opening prologue shows Don Juan as a young boy and why his father (John Barrymore plays both the father and Don Juan as an adult) raised him to mistrust women.

Principal Leitmotifs

Example 9.1 Don Juan as a boy

Example 9.2 Don Jose

Example 9.3 The Dwarf

Example 9.4 The Lover/Infidelity

PLOT	MUSIC
Workers are removing a chest from a vault in the wall.	The music moves from the overture to the prologue themes.
We see Don Juan, his father Don Jose, and his mother Donna Isobel.	Don Juan theme, Don Jose theme, then back to the Don Juan theme
We see the mischievous dwarf servant.	Dwarf theme
Don Jose orders the workers out and embraces his wife, then his son, and then, with passion, his wife again.	Don Jose theme, Don Juan theme, and then the Don Jose theme grows in intensity, matching his passion.
Don Jose prepares to leave the castle. He talks with the dwarf servant and waves farewell to his son, who is standing on the balcony.	Source music: trumpet fanfare; the Don Jose theme transformed into a march, then the Dwarf theme and the Don Juan theme.

The wife's lover appears, ascends a rope, and joins Donna Isobel. The dwarf signals for Don Jose to return.	Lover theme
Don Jose rides back to the castle. He ascends the stairs. The lover is forced to hide in the space in the wall.	The Don Jose theme is transformed, becoming hasty and angry; a fragment of the Lover theme gives way to Don Jose's music.
Don Jose thrusts open the door and looks for the lover.	A sustained note coincides with the opening door; another transformation of Don Jose's theme is heard in the trumpet.
Don Jose sees his wife signaling to her lover. He seethes, and calls for workers to seal up the wall. The workers build the wall back up with the lover still inside.	A loud chord suggests the emotional jolt of Don Jose's realization; another transformation of his theme suggests his anger, and then the music builds tension, primarily with motives of Don Jose and the Lover.
Don Jose stops the workers as they are about to place the last block into the wall, sealing up the lover. He asks his wife if there is anything of value in the wall, and she shakes her head.	The music suggests Don Jose's control over his anger and his revenge. When Donna Isobel disavows her lover, an accent is heard in the orchestra, and the tempo speeds up a bit, suggesting Don Jose's disgust with his wife.
The wall is sealed, to the delight of the dwarf. Donna Isobel breaks down and cries for the life of her lover, but Don Jose merely laughs at her protestations.	A loud chord creates a scream as the lover is entombed; the Dwarf theme appears briefly, and then the Lover theme is heard, reflecting Donna Isobel's emotions.
Don Jose throws his wife out and orders Don Juan to remain with him. Donna Isobel passes the dwarf as she leaves, and Don Jose tells his son that women cannot be trusted.	Don Jose's theme is played strongly. The Dwarf theme appears, and we then return to Don Jose's theme, but played gently, along with the childlike music of Don Juan.

The Jazz Singer

The success of *Don Juan* and the Vitaphone system led to another significant film, *The Jazz Singer* (1927). In this film, Warner Bros. explored a different format. For the premiere of *Don Juan*, the studio had created a number of musical shorts recorded live that were shown prior to the feature film itself. In *The Jazz Singer*, the story centers on a vaudeville performer, allowing several segments of live music to be inserted into the narrative. During two of these segments, Al Jolson improvised dialogue, including the famous first words in a narrative film: "Wait a minute! Wait a minute! You ain't heard nothin' yet."

Live music appears in four segments interpolated into the film:

- Segment 1 (14:30): Jolson sings "Dirty Hands, Dirty Face" by Jimmy Monaco (1923) and "Toot, Toot, Tootsie!" by Ted Fio Rito, Dan Rosso, and Ernie Erman (1921). Between the songs he speaks his first lines (see Viewer Guide on page 103).

- Segment 2 (39:00): Jolson sings two versions of "Blue Skies" by Irving Berlin (1926), a traditional version and a jazzy version. Between the verses, Jack carries on a dialogue with his mother.
- Segment 3 (1:10:40) Jolson sings "Mother of Mine" by Louis Silvers (1927) during a dress rehearsal.
- Segment 4 (1:26:00) Jolson sings his famous "My Mammy" by Walter Donaldson (1918) in a stage performance that serves as the film's finale.

Figure 9.3 Jolson sings "My Mammy" with a visible conductor and a microphone (left front)

The still photo in Figure 9.3 shows Jolson at the end of the film singing "My Mammy." Here we see his signature routine, but with some added details not visible in the film. Especially note the conductor in front, reminding us that the orchestra had to be present during the recording. Also observe the microphone to the left, from which Jolson could not stray.

Most of *The Jazz Singer* is shot as a silent film, with synchronized music and sound effects, as in *Don Juan*. The underscoring, created by Louis Silvers, is a compilation score; almost all the music is borrowed from other sources. Silvers carefully selected musical excerpts to support this sentimental tale about a young man torn between his career and his religion. Scenes in the cantor's house are scored with the solemn sounds of Russian or Jewish melodies, including traditional songs. Even the orchestration, with its frequent separation of a solo instrument (often the cello) from the full orchestra, creates the effect of a cantor and his congregation.

Outside the cantor's world, popular tunes and a general popular style predominate. The opening "East Side, West Side" reflects the location of the scene in New York City. "Give My Regards to Broadway" resounds as Jackie learns that he will be singing on a Broadway revue. Popular tunes also help set the date of the scene. When Jackie is a boy, tunes from the early part of the century are heard, such as "My Gal Sal" (1905) and "Waiting for the Robert E. Lee" (1912). In the later scenes when Jack is an adult, the popular tunes are drawn primarily from the 1920s.

The score contains several leitmotifs, most notably for Jackie's mother and Mary. The application of leitmotifs is for the most part simple and lacks the thematic development heard in *Don Juan*. The biggest weakness of the score is the peculiar use of the love theme from Tchaikovsky's *Romeo and Juliet* to underscore the intense arguments between Jackie and Cantor Rabinowitz, played by the Swedish actor Warner Oland, who would later portray ace Chinese detective Charlie Chan (6:45 and 42:15). Adding to the awkwardness of these moments are obtrusive sound cuts that butcher the natural flow of the original work.

In the story, Jack Robin (Al Jolson) is an entertainer who is given an opportunity to sing in a revue on Broadway. Revues were high-class entertainments with a series of musical acts but no plot. Elaborate dance routines and comic sketches were also commonly included. Similar types of entertainment aimed at lower-class audiences were called vaudeville and burlesque. For a performer burlesque and vaudeville were the minor leagues, a training ground for those hoping to be discovered by a revue. In the final two musical numbers of the film, Al Jolson appears in blackface, a practice that was popular in the nineteenth century but had just about died away by 1927. To our modern sensibilities this practice seems to be overt racism, but many of the white entertainers of the nineteenth century felt that this custom paid homage to the energy and creativity of black performers.

The scene outlined in the Viewer Guide below is set in a café where Jack Robin is about to sing for his supper. At this early stage of his career, Jack is hoping to break into vaudeville. While he sings, he attracts the attention of Mary, who will serve as a love interest and help promote his career. Supporting the café ambiance, Silvers presents a number of popular tunes. The initial view of the café is accompanied by an arrangement of "Hop, Skip," composed by Irving Caesar (1926). At Al Jolson's first appearance, Silvers introduces a fragment from "My Mammy," Jolson's signature song, and then quotes "Dirty Hands, Dirty Face," which Jolson is about to sing live. After Jolson's performance, Silvers quotes two popular tunes, "I'm Lonely Without You" by Harry Warren (1926) and " If a Girl Like You Loved a Boy Like Me" by Gus Edwards (1905), the titles of which suggest the imminent love relationship between Jack and Mary.

Viewer Guide

The Jazz Singer: Jack Robin Sings for His Supper

Timing

13:00–21:30 (0:00 at the studio logo)

Key Points

- The film uses both synchronized music and music recorded live
- The popular songs sung by Jolson are by a variety of composers
- Most of the underscoring music is borrowed from other sources, not original
- Popular music reflects the public world of America, unlike the Jewish melodies quoted in the underscoring heard in the cantor's house

Setting

Jack Robin (Al Jolson) ran away from home when he was young and has grown to be a talented singer. Still looking for a break, he sings for his supper at a club, where he will be seen by Mary (Mary McAvoy).

Leitmotif

Example 9.5 Love—"If a Girl Like You"

PLOT	MUSIC
The scene opens at Coffee Dan's.	Silvers's arrangement of "Hop Skip" by Caesar
We see Jack Robin eating. He is asked to sing.	Silvers quotes "My Mammy," Jolson's signature song; "Dirty Hands, Dirty Face" is played in the underscoring.
Jack sings two songs separated by the first spoken dialogue in a narrative film. Mary enters and is attracted to the voice.	"Dirty Hands, Dirty Face" and "Toot, Toot, Tootsie!" are performed in a live recorded segment.
Jack returns to his table and is asked to join Mary.	The music returns to synchronized sound with an arrangement of the tune "I'm Lonely Without You" by Warren.
Mary and Jack exchange compliments, and Mary suggests that she might help his career.	Silvers quotes "If a Girl Like You" by Edwards, which becomes a leitmotif for their love relationship.

Sound on Film

A competing sound system called Movietone, developed by General Electric for the Fox studios, soon appeared. The significant advantage of this system is that the recorded sound is placed on the film itself, rather than on a phonograph record. Movietone proved to have superior sound quality, and its coordination of visual movement with sound was more consistent, which is critical to spoken dialogue. Fox began with a series of shorts, including the famous Fox Movietone newsreels.

Sunrise

The highly acclaimed *Sunrise*, created by the renowned German director F. W. Murnau, is the first full-length feature film using this system. In 1928, the first Academy Awards gave two Oscars for Best Picture—Best Production (*Wings*) and Best Artistic Quality of Production (*Sunrise*). In 1929, however, the latter award was dropped, and the Best Production award was renamed Best Picture. As a result, most histories of the Oscars list *Wings* as the first Best Picture winner, even though *Sunrise* was considered by most to be on an equal footing or superior to the popular aviation film. *Sunrise* failed to make the AFI Top 100 List, and it has only recently been made available commercially. Still, as late as 1970, one poll listed *Sunrise* as the second greatest film of all time after *Citizen Kane*, a film that is influenced by *Sunrise*, and many critics today consider *Sunrise* to be the greatest of all silent films.

Close-Up: The Academy Awards

And The Winner Is . . .

The Academy Awards was the brainchild of Louis B. Mayer (1885–1957). After beginning his career in the family enterprise—the junk business, Mayer set his sights on the burgeoning film industry and made a small fortune distributing *The Birth of a Nation* to New England theaters. In 1917 he moved to Hollywood and founded the Metro Pictures Corporation. Seven years later, a merger produced Metro-Goldwyn-Mayer (MGM), the largest and most prestigious studio in Hollywood. Here he created the studio of the stars, and by 1938 he was the highest paid officer of any corporation in the United States.

One of Mayer's most enduring accomplishments is the founding of the Academy of Motion Picture Arts and Sciences in 1927. The stated purpose was "to improve the artistic quality of the film medium, provide a common forum for the various branches and crafts of the industry, foster cooperation in technical research and cultural progress, and pursue a variety of other stated objectives." In other words, this non-profit organization was founded on the concept of film as a total artwork, dependent on a large number of individual artists. Originally, five branches were recognized—actors, directors, writers, technicians, and producers. The current number is thirteen—actors, administrators, art directors, cinematographers, directors, executives, film editors, composers, producers, public relations men, short-subject filmmakers, soundmen, and writers.

One of the first accomplishments of the Academy was the creation of the Oscar awards for outstanding achievement in the industry. The first ceremony was held in 1928 and awards were given for the following areas:

Production, two awards—Production and Quality of Production
Acting, two awards—Actor and Actress
Director, two awards—Director and Comedy Direction
Writing, three awards—Adaptation, Original Story, and Title Writing
Cinematography
Interior Decoration
Engineering Effects
Special Awards: *The Jazz Singer* and Charlie Chaplin

Because of the dual awards for production, two films won what we would now call the Best Picture award—*Wings* and *Sunrise*. In 1929, the Academy eliminated one of the production awards; the single winner in that year was *Broadway Melody*. The Academy also eliminated the awards for Comedy Direction, Title Writing, and Engineering Effects, and merged the remaining two writing awards into one.

The Academy is not the only institution that gives awards to films. Today, among the awards of other organizations that are closely watched are the Golden Globe Awards, given by the Hollywood Foreign Press Association, and the Cannes Festival Awards in France.

Like many of the major films from this time period, *Sunrise* has two principal musical scores, one by Erno Rapée for live theatrical performances, and a second by Hugo Riesenfeld for the synchronized version. The Riesenfeld score, now available in the Fox DVD release, is remarkable for its emotional range, rich lyric content, and dark moods. Typical of a compilation score, it includes several passages from nineteenth-century classics. Most notable are Liszt's *Les Préludes*, used for the opening credits; Wagner's *Siegfried Idyll*, a passage associated with marriage, heard when the wife thinks that her husband wants to reconcile with her (23:05); and Gounod's *Funeral March of a Marionette,* best known as the theme song for the television series *Alfred Hitchcock Presents*, played in the humorous scene when the couple thinks that they have broken a Venus de Milo statuette (56:15).

Murnau often referred to *Sunrise* with the subtitle *A Song of Two Humans.* The musical reference echoes Murnau's subtitle to his earlier film *Nosferatu* (1922), *eine Symphonie des Grauens* (a symphony of terror). In keeping with the idea of song, the musical score for *Sunrise* abounds in the song-like texture of melody and accompaniment. The middle portion of the film, in which the Man and the Wife (Janet Gaynor won the first Best Actress Oscar for her portrayal) reconcile in the city, presents a succession of song melodies, culminating with the principal love song (45:10). The love theme then remains the dominant musical idea for the remainder of the film. The only other recurring theme in the film is the seductive waltz theme of the Woman from the City (12:00), which begins with a disturbingly wide leap.

Composer Profile

Hugo Riesenfeld (1879–1939)

Hugo Riesenfeld was born in Vienna and played violin in the Vienna Opera Orchestra. After serving as concertmaster for the Manhattan Opera House, he directed the orchestras at a number of major theaters in New York and created scores for a number of major films. He later became music director at United Artists and continued to score films well into the golden age of sound film. In 1929 he composed music for twenty-nine films, but his numbers declined during the 1930s. His last scores were composed in 1938.

Important Film Scores

Dr. Jekyll and Mr. Hyde 1920	*Old San Francisco* 1927
The Hunchback of Notre Dame 1923	*The King of Kings* 1927
Les Misérables 1925	*Sunrise* 1927
Beau Geste 1926	

The most memorable musical moments in the film are the dark moods that, like the cinematography, adumbrate the film noir movement of the 1940s. When we first see the Man, an ostinato melody, a short melodic idea that is repeated unchanged in the lower register, suggests his obsession for the Woman from the City (6:30). As he goes to a rendezvous in the swamp, the music reverts to two alternating chords played in a low register by bassoons (11:10). The visual and musical combination for this scene creates a stunning effect. The chords return when the Man takes his wife out on the lake with the intent of murdering her (23:50), a mood broken only by the sound of bells. The tolling of bells is heard at several critical moments in the plot, suggesting an underlying religious theme.

Figure 9.4 Folk dance music and the Love theme are played simultaneously in *Sunrise*

Another notable aspect of the score is the layered effect created by two or more distinct musical sources. In the fair scene (59:50), source music emanates from a variety of places, contributing to the cacophonous sound that one might encounter at a fair. Near the climax of the story, the love theme is heard in the lower strings, while source music from a folk dance intrudes (1:13:30). Similarly, the love theme is soon overwhelmed by musical sounds depicting a raging storm (1:14:40). Once the storm abates, another intriguing musical moment occurs, as the sound of a French horn substitutes for the Man calling for his missing wife (1:20:15). The same effect will recur at the climactic moment of the story.

City Lights

While the rest of Hollywood was embracing talkies, Charlie Chaplin decided to keep his Little Tramp character silent for two more films, *City Lights* (1931) and *Modern Times* (1936). These are considered the last great silent films, despite their sophisticated use of a synchronized sound track. For both films, the talented Charles Chaplin produced, directed, acted, and composed the music. Chaplin's music for *City Lights* is light and popular in nature and provides appropriate moods. The energetic music heard in the opening scene recurs several times to underscore other scenes featuring physical comedy, most notably the classic boxing match (1:02:30). Adding to the humor, Chaplin's music occasionally employs tasteful Mickey Mousing and quotes well-known tunes, such as "How Dry I Am." The latter is a double pun, since one of the characters, the millionaire, is drunk and both he and Chaplin's character have fallen into the water.

The heart of the story is the love between the Little Tramp and the Blind Girl, which provides a link for the numerous comedic scenes. Chaplin gives the girl a love theme called "La violetera," or "Who'll Buy My Flowers?", the only major theme in the film that is not original. The recurrence of the theme lends a unity to the score and provides a sentimental balance to the humor. The sincerity of the final revelation is underscored by lush string sounds, bringing the film to a happy, tearful conclusion.

Chaplin also wrote music for the *Gold Rush* (1925; synchronized music was added in 1942), *Modern Times* (1936), *The Great Dictator* (1940), *Monsieur Verdoux* (1947), and others. He had help from professional musicians for these works, including the future film composer David Raksin (*Modern Times*) and Meredith Willson (*The Great Dictator*), who would create the Broadway hit *The Music Man*. Although Chaplin never won an Oscar for acting, he was given an Academy Award for his music to *Limelight*. This film was created in 1952, but it first appeared in the United States twenty years later, and that is when he received the Award. In 1972, Charles Chaplin won, despite competition from John Williams (*The Poseidon Adventure* and *Images*), the award for Best Original Dramatic Score.

Figure 9.5 Sentimental music composed by Chaplin accompanies the final scene in *City Lights*

Trailer

Despite the appearance of Chaplin's masterworks and a few other isolated silent films in the early 1930s, the silent film era had clearly come to an end in 1928. In the years that followed, problems with sound technology would limit the amount of music in film. But within a few years, music began to play an important role. By 1936, the year of Chaplin's *Modern Times*, the Golden Age of sound films had arrived, and music had once again achieved a prominent position in Hollywood filmmaking.

Important Names and Terms

synchronized sound
Vitaphone
revue
vaudeville

Movietone
F. W. Murnau
Charlie Chaplin

Part 3

The Sound Era Begins, 1928–1944

10

The Early Years of Sound, 1928–1933

The depression following the stock market crash of 1929 had a major impact on the entertainment business. Live theater suffered the most; vaudeville, revues, and operetta were all dealt mortal blows. Movie houses were also greatly affected. In order to draw larger audiences, theaters lowered ticket prices, showed double and even triple features, and instituted giveaways. One frequent gimmick was "Dish Night," in which a dish was given to each adult paid admission. After a number of such evenings, it was possible to have acquired a complete set of dishes just by going to the movies. The only entertainment medium to thrive was radio, which posed an additional challenge to the film industry, since people could choose to be entertained at home rather than go out to the movies.

Compounding these problems, the advent of sound created havoc for the movie business. Theaters were not equipped with speakers or sound systems, actors had to take speaking lessons and limit their movement in order to speak into stationary microphones, and cameras became less mobile—they were placed in large glass booths so that their mechanical sound would not be recorded. At first many in the industry disliked sound. But since talking pictures attracted large audiences, studios hastened to resolve the technological problems of sound.

SIGNIFICANT FILMS*

1928	*Lights of New York*
	Steamboat Willie
1929	*In Old Arizona*
	Hallelujah
	Blackmail
	The Broadway Melody ★
	The Hollywood Revue of 1929
1930	*The Blue Angel*
1931	*Cimarron* ★
1933	*King Kong*
	42nd Street

* The Academy Awards did not begin giving Oscars until 1927–28 and did not add the Best Score category until 1934. Throughout this text we will denote Best Picture winners ★, Best Music winners (score or song) ♫, and Best Music nominations (score or song) ✉. For more on the Academy Awards, see the Close-Up on page 105.

111

One of the major problems facing the industry was the inability to mix sounds. The technology that allows various recorded sounds to be combined during postproduction had not yet been created. Hence, all sounds for a film—dialogue, sound effects, and music—had to be recorded at the same time, which was a complicated process. As a result, many of the films from the early sound era employ little music. Even after the technology that allows for sound to be recorded on multiple tracks and mixed together was created, there was not an immediate rush to bring back wall-to-wall music. A gradual increase in the number and length of musical cues can be detected in films from 1932 and 1933, but overall the role of music remains somewhat limited in the early years of sound. The major exception to this trend is Max Steiner's stunning musical score for *King Kong* (1933), which heralds the emergence of the classical film score.

Early Sound Films

Because of the many technical problems facing filmmakers, the quality of films in the early years of sound is relatively weak. While the landmark films made at the end of the silent era—*Don Juan*, *The Jazz Singer*, and *Sunrise*—are for the most part excellent works, the first two historically significant films of the all-talking era, *The Lights of New York* (produced by the Vitaphone system, 1928) and *In Old Arizona* (produced by Movietone, 1928) do not rise beyond their technical liabilities. *The Lights of New York* incorporates both underscoring, which is heard weakly in the background, and source music, including an extended live musical number (22:30). *In Old Arizona* contains much less music, but the Cisco Kid does sing "My Antonia" while out on the prairie. Singing cowboys had recently become a rage on the radio, and this film is the forerunner of what will become a dominant trend in westerns from the 1930s through the 1950s. Unfortunately, the music is unable to counterbalance the poor acting, limited staging, and uninspired dialogue in both of these films.

Figure 10.1 No music accompanies this scene of rape and murder in Hitchcock's *Blackmail*

Blackmail

One landmark film that overcame these early technical limitations is England's first talkie, Alfred Hitchcock's *Blackmail* (1929). Hitchcock, one of English cinema's greatest figures, learned his filmmaking techniques during the silent film years. His ability to tell a story without words remained with him throughout his career. *Blackmail* is fascinating for its glimpses into the young director's creative mind and for its inclusion of both silent and sound scenes. When filming began, *Blackmail* was shot as a silent film, but when sound equipment was acquired in mid-production, the film was converted to sound. As a result, some of the scenes are shot as silent film, while others contain dialogue.

The most noticeable difference between the silent and sound scenes is the use of music. Silent scenes are presented with synchronized music created by Hubert Bath and Harry Stafford. The most extended musical cues accompany movement, including the racing van music in the opening sequence (1:10); the disoriented sounds during Alice's dazed walk after killing the artist, which mixes distorted phrases of the artist's song with fragments of the march of law (37:55); and the return of the opening theme for the final chase scene that leads the actors to the top of the British Museum (1:13:00).

The scenes with dialogue have no music, unless it is performed live, such as the artist's piano playing and singing of Billy Mayer's "Miss Up-to-Date" (1929) just prior to the attempted rape (27:00). Also apparent in the dialogue scenes is the camera's lack of mobility. Although Hitchcock deftly moves from one style to another, the seams between the two styles are still visible. One further complication of the sound film was the leading actress Anny Ondra, a Czech actress. Since the film was originally silent, her heavy accent was not a concern, but with added sound, her voice was not acceptable. Hence, another actress had to read her dialogue into a microphone out of camera range while Ondra lip-synched the words on camera.

Hallelujah and The Blue Angel

In most films of the early sound era, music is limited to incidental roles—accompanying the opening and closing credits, functioning as source music, and underscoring an occasional montage. The absence of music can create a stark sense of realism that is effective for certain genres, such as crime (*The Public Enemy*, 1931), war (*All Quiet on the Western Front*, 1930), and horror (*Dracula*, 1931). Still, a number of dramatic films were able to incorporate music creatively. Most notable are two critically acclaimed movies that feature musical numbers—*Hallelujah* (1929) and *The Blue Angel* (1930).

Figure 10.2 Music was dubbed in postproduction for this outdoor scene in *Hallelujah*

Hallelujah is the first film by a major studio to use an all-black cast. During the silent era, films showing African-Americans, such as those created by Oscar Micheaux, were shown to predominantly black audiences, while the studios essentially ignored this segment of the public. The renowned director King Vidor finally convinced MGM to produce this film by donating his services without pay. The result is a fascinating glimpse at the lives of African-Americans. Most compelling are the scenes showing sung religious revivals, including a baptism (53:40). Since much of the film was shot outdoors, the music and spoken words were recorded in a studio and painstakingly dubbed into the film during postproduction.

The Blue Angel helped launch the brilliant international career of Marlene Dietrich. In this German-made film, she plays a seductive singer in a cabaret called The Blue Angel. Here a strict schoolmaster, Professor Rath, played by Emil Jannings, who had won the first Best Actor Oscar in 1928, succumbs to her charms, leading to his rapid downfall. Frederick Hollander provided the music for the film with the assistance of Franz Waxman. Both would later become significant figures in Hollywood. Dietrich's songs were recorded live, as would be done in a musical. The highlight is the classic "Falling in Love Again," which Dietrich sings wearing a slinky costume and a white top hat (52:00). The basic theme of the story

Figure 10.3 Marlene Dietrich sings in top hat in *Blue Angel*

is foreshadowed in Hollander's music for the opening credits, in which a tune that can be associated with the professor (the words begin "Be ever faithful, ever honest") is overwhelmed by Dietrich's melody. Throughout the film, source music is carefully chosen to reinforce this central theme.

Musicals

Films with musical numbers enjoyed great popularity in the early years of the sound era. For models of musical entertainments, Hollywood looked to Broadway, where there were two basic types of musical shows:

- Productions featuring a series of unrelated performances, such as the revue or vaudeville
- Dramatic works that inserted musical numbers into a dramatic plot, such as operetta and the nascent musical comedy

Figure 10.4 Joan Crawford dances the Charleston in *The Hollywood Revue of 1929*

Revues were popular in the early sound era. Films appeared with names such as *Hollywood Revue, Show of Shows, Paramount on Parade,* and *Gold Diggers. The Hollywood Revue of 1929* is considered the best of these shows, although it is sorely lacking by modern standards. The film was shot at the MGM studios in the middle of the night, after production on all the other films had stopped. Not a lot of attention was given to precision in the dance routines, and many of the jokes fall flat. But there are a number of memorable segments, including Joan Crawford singing and dancing the Charleston (6:45), a comedy routine based on the balcony scene of *Romeo and Juliet* shot in two-part Technicolor (1:23:40), and

the theme song, "Singin' in the Rain," which was popularized in a 1952 musical named after the song (1:29:50).

A number of operettas were brought to the screen, beginning with Sigmund Romberg's *Desert Song* in 1929. But interest in that type of entertainment was waning, and the simplicity of the musical comedy, or "musical" as it became known, appealed to Hollywood filmmakers. Over sixty musicals were created in 1928 alone. Particularly noteworthy is *Broadway Melody*, which won the Academy Award for Best Picture—the only true musical to win the award until 1951. This film, advertised as "all talking, all singing, all dancing," served as a model for future musicals; its plot centers on a backstage romance, and its music features a number of popular tunes with music by Nacio Herb Brown and lyrics by Arthur Freed. The musical highlights include "Broadway Melody," "You Belong to Me," and "The Wedding of the Painted Doll," all of which reappear in *Singin' in the Rain*.

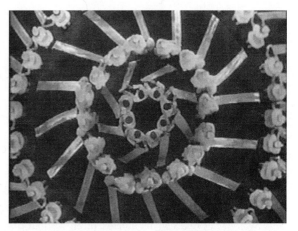

Figure 10.5 A signature Busby Berkeley shot from above the dancers

Hollywood soon produced so many musical films that the public grew weary of them. The more than seventy musical films produced in Hollywood in 1930 saturated the market, and for the next few years such works were box-office poison, but only temporarily. The enormous popularity of *42nd Street* (1933) revived the genre. Featuring a backstage story, effective humor, elaborate dance routines created by Busby Berkeley, innovative visual images such as overhead angles, and entertaining songs by Harry Warren and Al Dubin, the film is a milestone of film musicals.

Early Sound Cartoons

The rich and varied history of cartoon music is certainly worthy of an independent study. Within the limitations of this text, the histories of music for cartoons and narrative films meet only in animated features. Still, a few words about early sound cartoons are appropriate at this point, since cartoons and cartoon composers influenced film music.

The All Singing, All Dancing, All Squeaking Mouse

Walt Disney created a great sensation with *Steamboat Willie* (1928), starring Mickey Mouse. This is not Disney's first Mickey cartoon—it is actually the third—nor is it the first cartoon with sound. But this parody of the Buster Keaton film *Steamboat Bill Jr.* (1928) fully exploited sound technology and had enormous audience appeal. Music and sound effects are at the heart of this short, while dialogue is minimal. The two most prominent melodies in the cartoon are "Steamboat Bill," an Irish folksong appearing at the beginning, and "Turkey in the Straw," featuring a virtuoso performance by Mickey extracting musical sounds from various animals. The coordination of movement and music in this cartoon was painstaking, but the process helped pave the way for advancements in the timing of music and film.

Figure 10.6 Mickey makes music with animals in *Steamboat Willie*

Disney worked on more sophisticated musical settings in a cartoon series entitled *Silly Symphonies*. The first, and one of the most popular, is *The Skeleton Dance*. More a series of sight gags than a story, *The Skeleton Dance* combines elements of the compilation score with music mirroring specific gestures of the skeleton crew. Other *Silly Symphonies* relate short stories, often without dialogue or singing, such as the two versions of *The Ugly Duckling* (1931 and 1939). Singing is featured in several cartoons, including the operatic *The Goddess of Spring* (1934) and the classic *The Three Little Pigs* (1933), with its hit song, "Who's Afraid of the Big Bad Wolf?"

Carl Stalling

When Disney first conceived of adding sound to his animations, he consulted with Carl Stalling. A silent film organist and orchestra director, Stalling (1888–1974) joined the Disney studio and created the music for many of the early cartoons. In making "The Skeleton Dance," Stalling helped develop an early version of the click track, a

Table 10.1

Major cartoon series in the early sound era			
SERIES TITLE	INITIAL DATE	PRINCIPAL CREATIVE FORCE	PRINCIPAL COMPOSERS
Mickey Mouse	1928	Disney	Carl Stalling; Bert Lewis
Silly Symphonies	1929	Disney	Stalling; Lewis
Looney Tunes	1930	Harman-Ising (note pun)	Stalling
Merrie Melodies	1931	Harman-Ising	Stalling
Woody Woodpecker	1940	Walter Lantz	Darrell Calker
Tom and Jerry	1940	Hanna-Barbera	Scott Bradley

system in which holes placed in a film create a clicking sound that can be made audible to the conductor and musicians of a studio orchestra. Because of the success of this system in coordinating music with action, it was adopted by the movie studios and became part of the standard process in postproduction scoring.

Stalling left Disney in 1930 and in 1936 began working for Warner Bros., where he remained for twenty-two years. During this time he composed music for two major cartoon series, *Looney Toons* and *Merrie Melodies*, in which he provided musical support for such popular characters as Bugs Bunny, Porky Pig, Tweety Bird, and the Roadrunner. Behind the visual cartoon antics of these characters are musical scores incorporating children's tunes, popular melodies, jazz, borrowed classics, and modern music. Stalling, like several of the other composers listed in Table 10.1, explored a number of modern compositional techniques ranging from serialism to avant-garde, predating and paving the way for their use in Hollywood feature films. Scott Bradley, the composer for *Tom and Jerry*, once remarked: "I hope Dr. Schoenberg will forgive me for using his system to produce funny music."

King Kong

In 1931, the Oscar for Best Picture went to *Cimarron*, a story about the early years of Oklahoma. As in the other films from the early sound era, music is used sparingly during the film. But in one distinctive scene near the end, an orchestra can be heard playing during a party scene (1:51:00), and this music was viewed as something special. A young composer from Austria, Max Steiner, was responsible for the music. According to Steiner, "The next morning, the papers came out and reported that the picture was excellent. And what about the music—it said that it was the greatest music that ever was written. Their [the producers'] faces dropped, and I got a raise of fifty dollars." Music had begun to return to film, and the distinguished career of Max Steiner was launched.

Shortly thereafter, Steiner was asked to save *King Kong*. The producers were concerned that if the monster did not terrify audiences, the elaborate production would be an expensive disaster. Desperately needing help, producer Merian C. Cooper turned to Max Steiner and paid fifty thousand dollars out of his own pocket for the recording of music. The investment paid off. Steiner created a powerful score, complete with raucous brass and pounding percussion. The amount of music was astonishing for the time; one observer described *King Kong* as "a concert of Steiner music with pictures." The narrative of the film begins without music; Steiner withholds underscoring for over twenty minutes. Music enters quietly only when the ship encounters a mysterious fog (20:35). From that point, the concert begins. Other than the titanic battle between Kong and the tyrannosaurus rex and Kong's final confrontation with airplanes, the music is unrelenting.

Max Steiner successfully captures the varied moods of the story. Using a heavy orchestration dominated by brass and percussion, Steiner adds harsh harmonies, brass flutter-tonguing, and stuttering repeated chords to create a terrifying sound. But the music goes beyond this one-dimensional view of Kong; it also gives him a human personality. By the time the climactic conflict is waged on the Empire State Building, Kong is seen as a tragic figure. Steiner's music projects a tremendous sense of sadness at the death of the magnificent animal.

The extensive musical score is unified by leitmotifs and thematic transformation. The two principal themes represent Beauty and the Beast. Each undergoes a number of transformations. The Beast motive is a three-note chromatic descent (see Viewer Guide). Because of its simplicity, it can easily be combined with other material. When Kong attacks the Third Avenue el train, for example, Steiner creates the sounds of the train in the orchestra, and then adds the Beast motive in counterpoint as the train is demolished (1:31:05).

Composer Profile

Max Steiner (1888–1971)

Steiner was a child prodigy. Born in Vienna, he conducted his first operetta at age twelve, graduated from the Vienna Imperial Academy of Music at thirteen, completing four years of work in one, and composed a successful operetta at sixteen. In that same year, he became a professional conductor, and began working in London. Ziegfeld helped bring Steiner to the United States in 1914, where he conducted and orchestrated Broadway musicals. Steiner was invited to Hollywood in 1929 to work on a film version of the Broadway show *Rio Rita*, and he remained in the service of RKO. In 1933 he worked on thirty-three films, and he would become one of Hollywood's most prolific composers, scoring over three hundred films. Most of these films were for Warner Bros., where he worked from 1937 to 1953. Steiner won three Academy Awards and was nominated for fifteen other Oscars.

Important Film Scores

King Kong 1933	*Casablanca* 1942 ★ ✉
The Informer 1935 ♫	*Since You Went Away* 1944 ♫
The Charge of the Light Brigade 1936	*The Treasure of the Sierra Madre* 1948
Dark Victory 1939 ✉	*The Caine Mutiny* 1954 ✉
Gone With the Wind 1939 ★ ✉	*The Searchers* 1956
Now, Voyager 1942 ♫	*A Summer Place* 1959

★ = Best Picture Oscar   ♫ = Best Music Oscar   ✉ = Music Oscar Nomination

The Beauty theme appears in two main forms. In the scene outlined in the Viewer Guide, it is initially a lovely waltz tune as John declares his love. After Ann is abducted, a terrorized version of her theme appears, in which the tempo is faster and the theme is reduced to four descending notes. Since four descending notes are also embedded in the Native theme, Steiner is able to merge the two themes during the sacrificial dance. In this shared theme, the first two measures are the terrorized version of the Beauty theme, the third measure is both the condensed statement of the Beauty theme and the second measure of the Native theme, and the last measure is from the Native theme.

Typical of Steiner's scores, the music frequently mirrors physical movement. In the Viewer Guide scene, the music parallels Ann and the natives ascending the altar stairs, the natives descending those steps, and later the natives ascending the wall. Similarly, the music mimics each step of King Kong before we see him. Elsewhere in the film, musical chords accompany the steps of the chief when he first observes the intruders (28:05), accents called stingers coincide with physical impacts, and the music rises and falls with ascending and descending images, as heard during the escape from the cliff (1:11:00). Such obvious mimicking of a physical movement (Mickey Mousing) is now considered a weakness in film music.

Viewer Guide

King Kong: Abduction and Sacrifice

Timing

Excerpt: 31:40–43:45 (0:00 at studio logo); DVD Chapters 11–14

Key Points

- Prominent use of brass and percussion
- Music reflects range of emotions from love to terror
- Steiner's use of thematic transformation
- Source music: drums and later full orchestra
- Mickey Mousing effects: music follows the physical movements

Setting

Carl Denham (Robert Armstrong), an adventure photographer, has chartered a boat to locate the legendary Skull Island, home of King Kong. He has also hired a beautiful young woman, Ann Darrow (Fay Wray), to be used as a model in his film. Once they begin to explore the island, the natives are attracted to Ann, believing that she would be a good sacrifice to Kong. Also attracted to Ann is the ship's first mate, John Driscoll (Bruce Cabot).

Principal Leitmotifs

Example 10.1 Beauty (Ann) in love

Example 10.2 Beauty (Ann) terrorized, with Native theme

Example 10.3 Native theme

Example 10.4 Beast/King Kong

Example 10.5 Courage

PLOT	MUSIC
The boat is anchored off Skull Island. John expresses his concern for Ann's safety and then declares his love for her. Interrupting their kiss, the captain calls John to the bridge.	The sound of the timpani, representing drumming from the island, accompanies a mysterious melody that foreshadows the Sacrificial Dance theme. Following a statement of the Courage motive, the Love theme emerges, interrupted by the captain's calls.
While John is gone, natives kidnap Ann and take her back to the island. Discovering what has happened, the sailors prepare to go to the island.	The music builds tension, climaxing with a loud chord as Ann is seized. The Courage motive is heard as she is abducted. The timpani plays during the search, suggesting native drumming on the island.
The natives prepare Ann for the sacrifice.	The Sacrificial Dance theme mixes with Ann's terrorized theme and a bit of King Kong's motive.
The natives open the gate, lead Ann up the altar stairs, tie her to the posts, and close the gate, leaving Ann alone on the altar. The natives ascend the wall, and the chief orders the Kong gong to be sounded.	Dramatic music accompanies the opening of the door. The music ascends as Ann is led up, descends when the natives go, and ascends when the natives climb the wall. Ann's theme and the native theme continue, the latter played slowly with a prominent timpani as the gate is closed. Rapidly repeated chords, associated with terror, are heard as the natives watch Ann. When the chief speaks, the music stops.
King Kong approaches, terrorizing Ann. She pulls herself free, only to fall into King Kong's hand.	Musical chords suggest Kong's approaching footsteps; Kong's theme is intermixed with Ann's theme, along with terror sounds.

Steiner establishes these important moods and thematic relationships during the opening credits. At the outset, the two principal motives are juxtaposed; the Beast motive is intoned by the low brass, supported by a gong, suggesting a jungle setting, and a fragment of the Beauty theme tumbles downwards in sequential motion. Music from the sacrificial dance is then introduced, which includes the variation of Ann's theme and an inverted statement of the Beast motive, ascending instead of descending. Following stuttering repeated chords associated with terror, a transformed version of the Beast motive emerges. The slower tempo and its setting primarily in the strings foreshadows the sadness that underlies the ending of the film. The use of a harp also suggests the telling of a story.

The Major Studios and Their Composers

Hollywood studios can be divided into two groups, the Big Five and the Little Three. Each studio had its own style and its own approach to music.

The Big Five

RKO: This studio played an important early role in the Golden Age. Radio-Keith-Orpheum, or RKO, emerged as a major studio in 1928 and created such masterpieces as *King Kong*, the Astaire-Rogers musicals, and *Citizen Kane*. During its declining years, Howard Hughes bought the studio, and it eventually was sold to Desilu Television in 1955. Max Steiner worked for RKO from 1930 to 1936. Roy Webb became the principal composer after Steiner's departure.

Warner Bros.: Propelled by its early success with talkies, Warner Bros. specialized in gangster films, biographies, and musicals. By 1936, both Korngold and Steiner were on the impressive roster of composers. Hugo Friedhofer worked as the principal orchestrator. *Gone With the Wind* was their greatest achievement.

MGM: Established in the 1920s by a merger of three companies, Metro-Goldwyn-Mayer created the best film factory in Hollywood, with the most sparkling array of stars. Its musicals of the 1940s and 50s were considered the finest in Hollywood. Herbert Stothart was the leading composer in the 1930s, winning an Academy Award for *The Wizard of Oz*.

Twentieth Century Fox: William Fox founded the Fox Company in the nickelodeon days and brought it into prominence with some outstanding productions and early success with the Movietone sound system. In 1935 Fox merged with Twentieth Century to form a new cor-poration. Alfred Newman was the dominant musician in this studio. In the 1950s, the studio began hiring composers for individual film projects, including Herrmann, Waxman, Friedhofer, and Raksin. Lionel Newman, Alfred's brother, became director of music in 1961.

Paramount: Paramount was the first studio to establish nationwide distribution. As a result, it became the dominant force in the early studio years, with the largest array of popular stars, including Mary Pickford. Among its early successes are *The Ten Commandments* (1923) and *Wings* (1927). The studio suffered during the Great Depression and was declared bankrupt in 1933. Reorganized in 1935, it specialized in B films, but continued making quality films as well. Victor Young was the leading composer at the studio.

The Little Three

Universal: Established in 1912, the studio gained prominence in the early 1930s following its production of *All Quiet on the Western Front*. It specialized in horror films, comedies, and musicals. The studio used a corporate approach to music, often involving several composers on the same project. Franz Waxman became the head of music in 1936, and later Charles Previn took charge of the so-called music factory.

Columbia: A small studio, Columbia specialized in B films. It gradually emerged as a power in the 1940s and 50s, primarily due to its early investment in television.

United Artists: UA was not a studio but rather a distributing company for artists who produced their own pictures. The founders were D. W. Griffith, Charlie Chaplin, Mary Pickford, and Douglas Fairbanks. The company has survived competition from the giant studios up to the present day.

Trailer

The musical score for *King Kong* was a remarkable achievement. At a time when film-makers had seemingly accepted a limited role for music, Steiner's score proved that a good film composer could have a profound effect on the success of a film. In saving *King Kong*, Max Steiner also reestablished the basic characteristics of the classical score, which would become one of the key elements of Hollywood's second Golden Age.

Important Names and Terms

sound mixing
singing cowboy
Alfred Hitchcock
Hubert Bath
Harry Stafford
King Vidor
Frederick Hollander

operetta
musical comedy
Walt Disney
Silly Symphonies
Carl Stalling
click track
Max Steiner

Suggested Viewing

Best Picture Winners: *All Quiet on the Western Front* (1930), *Grand Hotel* (1932), and
    Cavalcade (1933)
Crime: *Little Caesar* (1931), *The Public Enemy* (1931), and *Scarface* (1932)
Drama: *Morocco* (1930) and *The Lost Squadron* (1932)
Horror: *Dracula* (1931) and *Frankenstein* (1931)
International: *L'Âge d'or* (1929), *Le Million* (1931), *M* (1931), and *The Private Life of*
    Henry VIII (1933)

11

Entering a New Golden Age, 1934–1938

After the studios began to recover from financial turmoil in the middle 1930s, Hollywood entered a second Golden Age. Although many films, such as Best Picture winners *It Happened One Night* (1934) and *You Can't Take It with You* (1938), continued to limit music to incidental roles, other films increased the amount of underscoring, as music once more became an important part of the director's artistic palette. In particular, music had a significant impact in action/adventure, drama, and horror films. By 1938, an impressive roster of composers worked for Hollywood, including Max Steiner, Erich Korngold, Franz Waxman, Alfred Newman, Herbert Stothart, Dimitri Tiomkin, Victor Young, and Miklós Rózsa. Most of these composers came from Europe, but a number of Americans also played prominent roles in the shaping of Hollywood music.

The Classical Film Score

In the hands of the above composers, the general characteristics of the classical film score were established during the middle to late 1930s. Among the features of the classical score are the following:

- Extensive use of music
- Exploitation of the full range of orchestral colors

SIGNIFICANT FILMS

1935	*Mutiny on the Bounty* ★
	The Informer ♫
	Bride of Frankenstein
1937	*Snow White and the Seven Dwarfs* ✉
1938	*The Adventures of Robin Hood* ♫

- Reliance upon the melody-dominated postromantic style
- Establishment of the principal themes and moods during the opening title and credits
- Musical support for dramatic moods, settings, characters, and action
- Frequent borrowing of familiar melodies
- Unity through leitmotifs and thematic transformation

We will observe these characteristics in three films from 1935 representing different genres: *Mutiny on the Bounty* (historical), *The Informer* (dramatic), and *The Bride of Frankenstein* (horror). All three are based on novels.

Mutiny on the Bounty

Best Picture winner *Mutiny on the Bounty* is an early representative of a wave of nautical adventure films, and it is the first such film to be shot on location rather than in a studio water tank. The story, taken from a 1932 novel by Charles Nordhoff and James Norman Hall, is based on historical events. In 1789, First Mate Fletcher Christian led a mutiny on board the HMS *Bounty* against a vindictive and cruel Captain Bligh. While history supports the accuracy of some of the details of this unfortunate incident, the real motivations and characterizations are open to speculation. Little is known about the mysterious protagonist, Fletcher Christian, and Captain Bligh, the antagonist, was by all historical accounts a brilliant navigator. He later went on to serve with distinction with Admiral Nelson, retired as a rear admiral in the British Navy, and served as a governor in Australia.

Regardless of historical accuracy, the story is engaging and entertaining. The plot unfolds in three locations, each of which features distinct source music. In England, a solo violin is heard at the local tavern (02:15); on board the ship, sailors frequently break into song; and in Tahiti, native drumming, dancing, and singing add an exotic character (1:08:00). England and Tahiti are treated as distinct poles; England, and by extension Bligh's ship, is stern and dutiful, whereas Tahiti evokes love and warmth.

Herbert Stothart, one of the most prolific film composers of the 1930s and 40s, provided an effective musical score that contributes to the film's popular and artistic success. The music reflects the two opposing moods of the plot, both of which are juxtaposed during the music for the opening credits. In setting the English portions of the film, Stothart includes marches and navy tunes, including "Anchors Aweigh," "Rule Britannia," and (at appropriate moments) "What Shall We Do with the Drunken Sailor?" By contrast, the Tahiti

Figure 11.1 A mustacheless Clark Gable and Charles Laughton square off in *Mutiny on the Bounty*

scenes are accompanied by lush string sounds, fitting music for scenes of Tahitian maidens swarming the ship, eagerly seeking English sailors. The combination of beautiful natural scenery and a sumptuous musical score became a standard feature of the exotic adventure story.

The Informer

The Informer, originally a 1925 novel by Liam O'Flaherty, is set in Dublin during the Irish Troubles of the 1920s. The drama centers on Gypo, a simple-minded Irishman who was rejected for service by the Irish Republican Army. In a weak moment, Gypo informs on a friend and collects a reward from the British. Once the friend is killed, remorse sets in, and Gypo turns to drink, squandering all his ill-gotten money. Eventually, the IRA executes Gypo, but he is redeemed at the last moment by the forgiveness of his friend's mother.

Figure 11.2 A Catholic motet sounds as Gypo is forgiven in *The Informer*

Max Steiner, who composed numerous scores in the middle years of the decade, won his first Oscar for *The Informer*. The score has less musical underscoring than *King Kong*, but the music is more thoroughly integrated into the drama. Each character has a distinctive theme so that, as Steiner described it, a blind man could tell who was on the screen. The dominant theme that accompanies Gypo has a march-like character that suggests the inevitable fate awaiting him.

Like Stothart in *Mutiny on the Bounty*, Steiner uses source music to set the location of this film. Most notable is the extended Irish tenor solo that continues uninterrupted even while the British soldiers are searching the singer (2:50). Another striking use of voices, suggesting an unseen choir, is the final motet, reinforcing Gypo's religious redemption through a mother's forgiveness (1:30:20).

As he did in *King Kong*, Steiner uses music to mirror physical action. In the opening scene, for example, Steiner's tempo for Gypo's theme coincides with his steps. Later, when Gypo is waiting for his execution, the dripping of water is accompanied by the plucking of a harp (1:17:00), and this sound continues through the final scene. The tension created by the relentless reiteration also suggests the inevitable conclusion of events, linking the sound and mood to Gypo's initial leitmotif.

The Bride of Frankenstein

The Bride of Frankenstein is a sequel to *Frankenstein*, the classic 1931 horror film. Both films were adapted from Mary Wollstonecraft Shelley's 1818 novel *Frankenstein; or, the Modern Prometheus*. The literary connection is reinforced in the opening scene, where Mary Wollstonecraft Shelley is shown discussing her book with her husband Percy Bysshe Shelley and their friend Lord Byron, while a storm rages outside, paralleling the storm at the end of the film during the creation scene. The story then unfolds, beginning with the revelation that the monster did not really die as we had presumed, a cliché resurrected in the 1980s with such horror-film characters as Michael Myers and Jason Voorhees. Subsequently, Dr. Frankenstein, who disavowed his earlier creation, is forced to bring to life a female partner for the monster by the demented Dr. Septimus Pretorius.

One of the greatest of all horror films, *The Bride of Frankenstein* is noted for its stylized expressionistic images, exuberant self-parody, and the brilliant musical score by Franz Waxman. Waxman matches the hyperbole of the film with an energetic score that also contains a strong sense of parody.

The two principal leitmotifs represent exaggerated versions of their characters (see Viewer Guide on page 130). The Monster's motive, consisting of only five notes, includes a harsh harmonic clash on the fourth note. The dissonance, which could be termed a "wrong-note" harmony, a term suggesting the accidental playing of two

Composer Profile

Franz Waxman (1906–1967)

Born in Germany, Waxman began working in the German film industry and contributed arrangements for *The Blue Angel* (1930). After being beaten by Nazi hooligans, Waxman emigrated to the United States and was soon working in Hollywood. One of film's finest and ablest craftsmen, he scored films from the 1930s into the 1960s, adapting to many of the changes in musical taste. He won two Oscars for Best Musical Score and was nominated an additional nine times, with at least one nomination in every decade of his career.

Important Film Scores

The Bride of Frankenstein 1935
Captains Courageous 1937
Rebecca 1940 ★ ✉
Humoresque 1946 ✉
Sunset Blvd. 1950 ♫
A Place in the Sun 1951 ♫
The Spirit of St. Louis 1957
Taras Bulba 1962 ✉

★ = Best Picture Oscar   ♫ = Best Music Oscar   ✉ = Music Oscar Nomination

adjacent pitches, is purposefully jarring. The loud dynamics, the sustaining of the dissonant sound, and the use of flutter-tonguing techniques in the brass add to the overly horrific effect. By contrast, the theme for the bride is a lush, lyric melody that is far more beautiful than she is, perhaps depicting how she is seen through the eyes of Frankenstein's Monster. Indeed the first three notes of her theme are identical to the initial phrase of the popular melody "Bali Ha'i" from *South Pacific* (1949) by Richard Rodgers, where it is used to suggest the beauty of a Pacific island.

In keeping with the spirit of parody, Waxman underscores several scenes with dance music. The opening scene with the three literary figures is accompanied by an aristocratic minuet (1:35). The sweet sounds of the minuet belie both the storm outside and the dark nature of the story within Mary Shelley's imagination. The melody is heard delicately played by the strings followed by a statement with the bell-like sounds of the celesta, giving the theme an angelic, music-box quality just after Mary is referred to as an angel. During the initial flashback, a stormy passage develops the minuet theme, but the minuet returns politely at the end, as if the intrusion had been merely an extended middle section. Among the other dance sections are a funeral procession (10:00), a pastoral scene (25:35), and a vigorous march (27:50).

Perhaps the most endearing moments of the film are the episodes containing the miniature people held in bottles and the Monster's encounter and eventual friendship with a blind hermit. Waxman engages in a good deal of humor in the bottle sequence (22:00), including saintly organ music for the archbishop and Mendelssohn's "Spring Song" for the ballerina. During the encounter with the hermit, the monster first hears him playing Schubert's "Ave Maria" on the violin (34:48), one of several religious references in the film. The gentle melody is later picked up in the underscoring, including an extended statement by an organ, which underscores their tearfully warm relationship. The maudlin mood is broken by the arrival of hunters. Later, as the Monster takes refuge in the graveyard (44:40), we hear for the only time a version of the Monster's theme without its characteristic dissonance, which coincides with the vision of the crucified Christ. The subsequent macabre waltz (48:30) in the crypt, another dance used for parody, contains a mixture of the Pretorius and Bride motives.

The most celebrated music of the film occurs during the climactic creation scene (see Viewer Guide on page 130). Throughout the early portions of the scene, the timpani provides a steady rhythmic pulse. The drumbeat, which does not coincide with the tempo of the other music, can be heard as the bride's heart, struggling for life. Later, the music mimics the sounds of both wind and electricity. All three of the film's principal leitmotifs can be heard in an aura of magical sounds created by an array of instruments, including the organ, celesta, harp, vibraphone, and bells. The music climaxes when lightning strikes the kite. Immediately the timpani beat quickens, providing an aural clue that the bride is alive before we have a visual confirmation and hear the exuberant cry of the excitable Dr. Frankenstein.

The Bride of Frankenstein: The Creation

Timing

Excerpt: 1:03:15–1:14:00 (0:00 at studio logo); DVD
Chapters 15–17

Key Points

- Colorful orchestration
- Dissonant leitmotif for Frankenstein
- Beautiful leitmotif for the bride of Frankenstein
- Music mimics a heartbeat, wind, and electricity

Setting

The demented Dr. Pretorius (Ernst Thesiger) forces Dr. Henry Frankenstein (Colin
Clive), the creator of the Monster (Boris Karloff), to assist in the creation of a woman
mate for the Monster (Elsa Lanchester). The two doctors make the final preparations as the Monster waits impatiently.

Principal Leitmotifs

Example 11.1 The Monster

Example 11.2 Bride of Frankenstein

Example 11.3 Pretorius

PLOT	MUSIC
Karl informs Pretorius and Henry that the storm is rising. They unravel some of the bandages from the bride's face and order the kites to be flown.	The scene is initially lightly underscored. The Bride motive accompanies her close-up and returns during the preparations. The Pretorius theme is also gently played. A timpani pulse is heard throughout.
The roof opens up, and an electrical machine descends to just above the bride's body. The kites begin to fly.	Descending music is heard leading to another statement of the Bride theme. Imitations of wind and electricity sounds can be heard in the orchestra along with the Bride motive.
A brief montage shows the principal characters running the machines.	The music combines with electrical sound effects.
The bride's body rises to the roof.	The Bride theme is heard three times; each statement successively higher, and the last is accompanied by a colorful halo of sound.
The Monster appears on the roof, fights with Karl, and kills him.	The Monster motive and action music
Lightning strikes the kite, and the bride's body is lowered.	Music presents the climactic statement of the Bride theme (the culminating statement of the previous phrases), and the timpani pulse suddenly quickens, suggesting life.
The scientists are quick to unwrap the body. At first a finger moves, and then the eyes are seen. Henry excitedly pronounces: "She is alive! Alive!"	Fragments of the motive are heard, but all becomes silent, including the timpani, when she moves her hand. A jolting chord accompanies the unveiling of the eyes.
They lift the bride, but her head falls to the side. She abruptly appears dressed, and Pretorius introduces "The Bride of Frankenstein."	The Bride motive is heard, and the music falls with her head. The Bride theme, accompanied triumphantly and religiously by bells, accompanies Pretorius's proclamation.
The Monster enters and sees his bride. He cautiously asks, "Friend?" The bride screams and is moved away from the Monster. The Monster makes a second attempt and holds her hand, but he is again rejected.	The Monster and Bride motives alternate. The music supports the Monster's tentativeness and the delicate situation as observed by Henry and Pretorius. The Bride melody accompanies the handholding.
Elizabeth approaches. The Monster moves to the lever that will destroy the building. Elizabeth calls for Henry, and the Monster allows him to leave with her.	The tension is subtly underscored in the music, and the exit of Henry and Elizabeth is accompanied by scurrying sounds.

The Monster pulls the lever, and explosions demolish the tower. Henry and Elizabeth look on from a safe distance.

Following the Monster motives, the music suggests the collapsing building with descending motion and cymbal crashes. Both Monster and Bride motives can be heard. At the end, we are left with the Bride melody as it was heard when she first came to life.

The Adventures of Robin Hood

In 1935, Warner Bros. needed someone to adapt music by Felix Mendelssohn for a production of Shakespeare's *A Midsummer Night's Dream*. In a coup, the studio brought to Hollywood Erich Korngold, one of Europe's brightest young composers. He soon began to divide his attention between Vienna and Hollywood, and in a trilogy of action films—*Captain Blood* (1935), *Anthony Adverse* (1936), and *The Adventures of Robin Hood* (1938)—Korngold established a model for underscoring action films.

The Adventures of Robin Hood is an episodic story based on the lives of two medieval figures—Richard the Lion-Hearted and Robin Hood. The framework for the story, King Richard's absence from England to lead a crusade and his ultimate return, is based on historic events. Prince John, who would eventually become king, was indeed an abusive figure, and he was later forced by English barons to sign the Magna Carta.

As for Robin Hood, historical research suggests that there may have been such an outlaw, but he likely did not give money to the poor, and his adventures took place over a century after the death of King Richard. The mixture of these stories, largely based on legends, creates an exciting romantic swashbuckler. The lavish nature of this costume drama is enhanced by the brilliant colors produced by three- -strip Technicolor (see Close-Up on page 226), the first film by Warner Bros. to use this process.

Korngold's score to *The Adventures of Robin Hood* is remarkable for its length (he underscored nearly three-quarters of the film), colorful orchestration, dramatic support, and thematic transformation. A number of critics have hailed the work as the first masterpiece of film music. Essential to its conception are the swashbuckling fight scenes, for which Korngold employed a style incorporating the following characteristics:

- A full symphonic orchestration, emphasizing brass and percussion
- Loud dynamics
- Passages of quick notes
- Irregular and hard accents
- Occasional motivic references

These elements combine to create a hectic character, suggesting the chaos of battle. With the addition of sound effects, this simple formula became a cliché for future action films, including *Star Wars*.

Erich Korngold (1897–1957)

Erich Korngold, like Max Steiner, was a child prodigy. His father, Julius Korngold, was the leading music critic in Vienna, and Erich had the opportunity to meet some of the greatest musical figures of the time. Gustav Mahler pronounced Erich a genius when he was only ten. Richard Strauss described Korngold's music with "awe and fear." The great Italian opera composer Puccini noted, "The boy has so much talent he could easily give us some and still have enough left for himself." Among his other notable admirers was the founder of musical expressionism and serialism, Arnold Schoenberg. In 1928, one European newspaper conducted a poll and named Schoenberg and Korngold the two greatest living composers. Korngold's operatic masterpiece is *Die Tote Stadt* from 1920.

When the Nazis confiscated Korngold's home in Austria, he used the money he had earned in films to move his family to safety, and he soon became known primarily as a film composer. Unlike Steiner, Korngold was selective about his film assignments and worked on one or two films a year from 1935 to 1947. Once he was labeled a film composer, his reputation declined and interest in his concert works waned. One of his most popular works today is the beautiful Violin Concerto from 1945, which derives its principal themes from melodies originally written for films.

Important Film Scores

Captain Blood 1935	*The Sea Hawk* 1940 ✉
Anthony Adverse 1936 ♪	*The Sea Wolf* 1941
The Adventures of Robin Hood 1938 ♪	*Kings Row* 1942

★ = Best Picture Oscar   ♪ = Best Music Oscar   ✉ = Music Oscar Nomination

---

Outside of the fighting sequences, the score contains an abundance of tuneful melodic ideas. Korngold was well versed in the principles of Wagner. His father, Vienna's leading music critic, was a strong advocate for the German opera composer. The use of leitmotifs in *The Adventures of Robin Hood* is more complicated than what we observed in *Don Juan* and *The Informer*. The association of themes with individuals is looser, and motivic relationships between themes often suggest underlying connections between characters.

Much of the melodic material in the score is derived from the Robin Hood theme (see Viewer Guide on page 135), initially heard in a quick trumpet fanfare when Robin is seen for the first time (3:15). The first few notes of his theme form an independent motive that is frequently heard in fighting sequences and can be found imbedded within other themes, such as the opening notes of the jovial Little John melody (20:10).

Similarly, the love theme of Robin and Marian bears a strong resemblance to the Robin Hood theme. The love theme also shares a similar contour with the first four notes of the King Richard theme, which allows Korngold to suggest a close association between the two. Indeed, during the primary romantic scene (1:10:10), the love theme actually becomes subordinate to Richard's theme, just as Marian decides to stay and help Richard rather than leave with Robin.

The film opens with a rousing march associated with Robin and his Merry Men. Korngold adds a number of unusual melodic twists to the theme, suggesting the arrogant nature of our hero (and of the actor Errol Flynn) and projecting the spirit of fun that underlies much of the film. The theme reappears in several prominent moments. In the attack on the caravan (33:20), the theme is heard in its entirety, including a contrasting lyric section that coincides with the serene overconfidence of Sir Guy.

Once Robin's men drop into action from the trees, swooping sounds from the woodwinds and harp punctuate motives of the theme. At the end, Robin swings in with a fragment of his fanfare. The music for this scene is effortless; it is musically satisfying and supportive of the action at the same time. Shortly thereafter, the march theme is again altered, this time into a boisterous waltz (39:40), transforming Sherwood Forest into the Vienna Woods.

A master of orchestration, Korngold makes full use of all of the instrumental families; his score sparkles with a variety of colors matching the bright Technicolor film. Especially noteworthy is the ever-changing instrumentation heard in the lyric section preceding the attack on the caravan. Two other scenes illustrate Korngold's remarkable sense of orchestral color. When Robin is led to the gallows (1:04:35), harp glissandos combine with delicate sounds in the woodwinds, strings, and brass to create a dark, ominous mood. In the climactic final scene (see Viewer Guide on page 135), the Merry Men March is distorted, matching their disguises, and combined with source music—church bells and brilliant trumpet fanfares. The latter are played in a different key than the underscoring, creating a layered effect in the music.

Musicals

Following the success of *42nd Street* (1933), the three types of musical films observed in the late 1920s—revues, operettas, and musical comedies—reemerged in the 1930s. But revues went out of fashion, and the elaborate nature of operettas—for example, a series of delightful works featuring the engaging team of Jeanette MacDonald and Nelson Eddy—limited the number of possible productions. So filmmakers embraced the simplicity of musicals, producing both newly created works and adaptations of existing Broadway shows.

The extravagant qualities of the revue were assimilated by many of the new musicals. The leading figure in such spectacles was the choreographer and director who had

The Adventures of Robin Hood: Climax and Resolution

Timing

Excerpt: 1:29:45–1:41:15 (0:00 at studio logo);
DVD Chapters 25–28

Key Points

- Colorful orchestration
- Use of leitmotifs
- Simultaneous source music and underscoring
- Use of action music to accompany fighting

Setting

In the absence of King Richard (Ian Hunter), Prince John (Claude Rains), with the help of Sir Guy of Gisbourne (Basil Rathbone), has taxed the poor unmercifully. Robin of Locksley, known as Robin Hood (Errol Flynn), organizes a band of outlaws to fight the forces of Prince John. Just prior to the climax, King Richard returns to England and escapes an assassination attempt. He makes plans with Robin to sneak into Nottingham castle in order to prevent the unlawful coronation of Prince John and to save Lady Marian (Olivia de Havilland) from execution.

Principal Leitmotifs

Example 11.4 March of the Merry Men

Example 11.5 Robin Hood

Example 11.6 Love

Example 11.7 Richard the Lion-Hearted

Example 11.8 Little John

PLOT	MUSIC
Disguised as priests, Robin, Richard, and their men proceed toward the castle. Humorous dialogue is exchanged on the way.	The March of the Merry Men is played quietly, suggesting that they are in disguise and sneaking into the castle. The sound of bells serves both as source music and as a reminder that the men are dressed as clergy. Prominent bassoons enhance the humor of the dialogue.
Prince John is preparing for the coronation. Sir Guy suggests that Richard must be dead, and they hear the approaching priests. Marian is seen captive in the dungeon.	A contrasting portion of the march is heard. The bell sound is now clearly diegetic. Processional chords continue in the harp.
The priests enter the hall, and the men file into strategic positions. Prince John makes his entrance.	The march theme is combined with source music— bells and trumpet fanfares. More fanfares accompany Prince John.
The Bishop challenges John's authority; Richard reveals his identity.	The March theme is developed until Richard appears, when we hear the first four notes of his theme.

Robin calls his men into action and general fighting ensues. Robin goes to look for Marian.	Energetic fighting music is punctuated by motives from Robin Hood's theme.
Sir Guy and Robin engage in a lengthy duel. At the climax, Robin kills the Sir Guy.	Fighting music combined with Robin's theme continues. The music subtly follows physical movement during the duel. A woodwind trill precedes the climactic moment.
Robin rescues Marian.	The Love theme is played.
Richard bans Prince John.	Richard's theme follows the Love theme. The music stops briefly for John's sentence.
Robin promises loyalty and requests pardons for his men. Richard then gives permission for the union of Robin and Marian.	Robin Hood's theme projects a climactic, triumphant mood.

created the sensational dance sequences in *42nd Street*, Busby Berkeley. He continued to push the musical to its limits, with huge production numbers featuring bevies of beautiful women, fantastic stage sets and costumes, and creative camera angles.

Hollywood also produced less spectacular, more intimate musicals. These were often vehicles for star performers such as Shirley Temple and Gene Autry, "the Yodeling Cowboy." Among the most popular musicals of the decade are those featuring the dancing duo of Fred Astaire and Ginger Rogers, including *The Gay Divorcee* (1934), *Top Hat* (1935), and *Shall We Dance* (1937). Essential to the success of these films is the music, which featured songs by three of the greatest popular composers of the time: Cole Porter, Irving Berlin, and George Gershwin. Fred Astaire was an adequate singer and had a warm, engaging personality, but it was his dancing, with its elegant mixture of ballet and popular styles, that packed the theaters. He is considered one of the greatest dancers of the century, even by the standards of classical ballet, and he is the prototype of the song-and-dance man who remained a staple of musicals into the 1950s.

Animated Features

Walt Disney created an enormous sensation with his first full-length animated feature, *Snow White and the Seven Dwarfs* (1937). Dazzling audiences with its realistic animation, stunning colors, and delightful music, this work became the top moneymaking film in the history of the industry to that point. During that decade, only *Gone With the Wind* (1939) would be more financially successful. In the tradition of earlier Disney cartoons, music plays continuously through the film and includes a number of delightful

The Animated Feature

Although Walt Disney (1901–1966) is viewed as the foremost figure in animation and children's entertainment, some of his early efforts fell short. In the years before Mickey Mouse, Disney was unsuccessful with three separate series of cartoons—*Laugh-O-Grams*, *Alice in Cartoonland*, and *Oswald the Rabbit*. Mickey Mouse was created in 1928, and a large part of his success was due to Disney's foresight into the potential of technology. He quickly adapted sound in his third Mickey Mouse cartoon, *Steamboat Willie* (1928). The sound of Mickey whistling, clanking, and speaking (the high-pitched voice was Disney himself) brought the house down.

In 1931 Disney took another important technological step. He signed an exclusive seven-year contract with Natalie Kalmus to use Technicolor, and produced a sensational cartoon series called *Silly Symphonies*. In 1937 Disney rushed to complete his first feature-length animation before his contract was to expire, allowing other cartoonists access to Technicolor. The result, *Snow White and the Seven Dwarfs,* was an immense success, the most successful musical of the decade at that time, bringing in record-setting box-office receipts. Within five years,

Disney created four additional masterworks: *Pinocchio* (1940), *Fantasia* (1940), *Dumbo* (1941), and *Bambi* (1942).

Fantasia stands out as Disney's only non-narrative feature film, and initially it was a box-office failure. In the Academy Award ceremony of 1941, David Selznick presented Disney with the Thalberg Award and praised his work on *Fantasia*. Walt began weeping and replied to the audience, "Maybe I should have a medal for bravery. We all make mistakes. *Fantasia* was one, but it was an honest one. I shall now rededicate myself to my old ideals." Little did Disney know that *Fantasia* would become one of his all-time biggest moneymakers through subsequent releases. A remake, *Fantasia 2000*, was released in an IMAX version on January 1, 2000.

During World War II Disney quit making feature films in order to make cartoons supporting the war effort. The studio survived on government contracts, which commissioned the work. Donald Duck became his new star. A second flurry of Disney feature animations occurred in the 1950s (*Cinderella, Alice in Wonderland, Peter Pan, Lady and the Tramp,* and *Sleeping Beauty*), and a third creative spurt began in 1989, beginning with *The Little Mermaid*. In all of these works, music plays an integral role.

---

songs. A clear distinction is made between the developed songs sung by the humans, such as "I'm Wishing" and "Someday My Prince Will Come," and the simple tunes for the dwarfs. The title of "Heigh-Ho, Heigh-Ho, It's Off to Work We Go" contains all the words used in the song. The use of brief, simple tunes was established in earlier cartoons, such as "Who's Afraid of the Big Bad Wolf?"

Between 1940 and 1942, the Disney studios produced four more full-length animated films (see Table 11.1). Except for *Fantasia*, these films were box-office sensations, as *Pinocchio, Dumbo,* and *Bambi* became the top three moneymaking movies of the 1940s. All three films included outstanding music and received Academy recognition.

Figure 11.3 The Seven Dwarfs "Heigh-Ho" homewards

Table 11.1

Disney's first animated features

YEAR	ANIMATED FEATURE	COMPOSERS	SCORE	SONG
1937	*Snow White and the Seven Dwarfs*	Churchill, Harline, and Smith	✉	
1940	*Pinocchio*	Harline and Smith	♫	♫
1940	*Fantasia*			
1941	*Dumbo*	Churchill and Wallace	♫	✉
1942	*Bambi*	Churchill and Plumb	✉	✉

Trailer

By 1938, Hollywood was enjoying some of its finest moments. During the early years of the Golden Age, music established a prominent position in numerous film genres, including dramas, horror films, adventure and action films, romances, and animations. These accomplishments would be on full display during Hollywood's greatest year, 1939.

Important Names and Terms

Herbert Stothart
Franz Waxman
Erich Korngold
Technicolor
Busby Berkeley
song-and-dance man

Suggested Viewing

Comedy: *It Happened One Night* (1934) ★, *A Night at the Opera* (1935), *Modern Times* (1936), *You Can't Take It with You* (1938) ★, and *Bringing Up Baby* (1938)
Action/Adventure: *The Lost Patrol* (1934) ✉, *Captain Blood* (1935), *Anthony Adverse* (1936) ♫, and *The Charge of the Light Brigade* (1936) ✉
Biopic: *The Great Ziegfeld* (1936) ★ and *The Life of Emile Zola* (1937) ★
Drama: *Manhattan Melodrama* (1934), *A Tale of Two Cities* (1935), *Dodsworth* (1936), *Camille* (1936), *Stella Dallas* (1937), *A Star Is Born* (1937), *Captains Courageous* (1937), *The Good Earth* (1937), *Lost Horizon* (1937) ✉, and *Jezebel* (1938) ✉
Musical: *Top Hat* (1935), *Show Boat* (1936), and *Shall We Dance* (1937)

12

Hollywood's Greatest Year, 1939

The heart of the Golden Age was 1939, during which a remarkable number of out-standing films were produced in Hollywood. The American Film Institute (AFI) includes five films from 1939 in its list of America's one hundred greatest films: *Mr. Smith Goes to Washington*, *Stagecoach*, *Wuthering Heights*, *The Wizard of Oz*, and *Gone With the Wind*. This is the largest number of films from any single year on the AFI list, only one less than the entire decade of the 1980s.

The classical film score, as defined by Steiner, Korngold, and Waxman, is a key element in many of the films from this year. Because of this association, the classical score has become synonymous with the phrase "The Hollywood Sound." But Hollywood does not speak with just one voice; a variety of musical approaches can be heard in Hollywood films, even in 1939. In view of the preeminence of these five films and the fact that all five scores were nominated for Oscars, we will look at the music for each. In some we find typical classic film scores, while in others we hear a different Hollywood sound.

Adapted Scores

The borrowing of existing music for film scores is part of a tradition that began in the silent era. Recognizing

SIGNIFICANT FILMS

Mr. Smith Goes to Washington ✉
Stagecoach ♫
Wuthering Heights ✉
The Wizard of Oz ♫ ♫
Gone With the Wind ★ ✉

the different techniques involved in adapting previously composed music and composing original scores, the Academy began in 1938 to award two Oscars for musical scores—Best Score, implying that a large portion is adapted, and Best Original Score, for newly composed music. In 1939, both *Mr. Smith Goes to Washington* and *Stagecoach* were nominated in the first of these categories.

Mr. Smith Goes to Washington

In the context of the abundant music in films such as *Gone With the Wind*, the musical score for *Mr. Smith Goes to Washington* by Dimitri Tiomkin seems meager. In his numerous films with director Frank Capra, including classics such as *It Happened One Night* (1934), *You Can't Take It with You* (1938), *Meet John Doe* (1941), and *It's a Wonderful Life* (1946), Tiomkin added little underscoring. The major exception in their collaborative efforts is the richly scored exotic epic *Lost Horizon* (1937).

Several important genre conventions contribute to the limited role of music in these films, as we see in *Mr. Smith Goes to Washington*. This film is marginally related to the screwball comedy. Comedies in general tend to minimize underscoring. Screwball comedies—films having lunatic characters who create chaos and mayhem in sane society—usually employ music only for the credits, source music, montages, and perhaps an occasional musical joke. More significantly, *Mr. Smith Goes to Washington* is a populist film. The heroes of populist films are ordinary people pitted against the rich, politicians, or both. In keeping with the simple nature of these protagonists, music in populist films is traditionally minimized. In addition, there is another Hollywood cliché that limits music. It is generally felt to be inappropriate to underscore scenes set in formal government buildings, such as courtrooms or, in the case of this film, the U.S. Senate.

In conformance with these traditions, underscoring is heard only once in scenes in the Senate, near the end of Mr. Smith's filibuster. Much of the other music in the film stems from source music, such as the bands at the boys' camp and at political rallies. In keeping with the populist tradition, Tiomkin's underscoring contains little original music and is primarily based on well-known patriotic or American folk melodies. American tunes abound during the montage of Mr. Smith's AWOL bus tour of Washington, D.C. (20:50), culminating in one of Hollywood's most patriotic moments at the Lincoln Memorial. Melodies representing the little man of America include "My Darling Clementine," "I Dream of Jeannie with the Light Brown Hair," and "The Red River Valley." The last tune is set

Figure 12.1 A patriotic moment in *Mr. Smith Goes to Washington*

effectively with sounds of nature in the accompaniment, when Mr. Smith and Saunders write a bill for a boys' camp near controversial Willet Creek (51:20).

Stagecoach

The music for *Stagecoach*, the first great western, bested that of *Mr. Smith Goes to Washington*, winning the Oscar for Best Score in 1939. Richard Hageman is the principal creator of the *Stagecoach* score; he provided an energetic sound based primarily on American folk and cowboy tunes. Most prominent is his setting of "Rio Grande," inevitably heard during travel montages. In these sections we hear several devices that became traditions in later films. His setting of the tune incorporates a fast-paced accompaniment, while the tune itself is presented in a broad, lyric manner, a sound that will become a cliché in later western musical scores. The combination of music and beautiful landscapes will also become an essential part of the western.

Figure 12.2 The distant stagecoach rides under the watchful eyes of Indians

Other prominent music includes "I Dream of Jeannie with the Light Brown Hair," which becomes a leitmotif for Lucy; "Shall We Gather at the River?", which underscores the vision of the ladies of the Law and Order League; and a traditional Indian war theme, complete with beating drums. The Indian theme, particularly the drums, is as much a part of the Native American stereotype as feathers and war paint.

In one of the most effective moments (1:09:20), we see the stagecoach in the distance accompanied by its principal theme. As the camera pans to the left, we discover that the stagecoach is being watched by an Indian war party. The shock of this revelation is reinforced by the music, which intrudes with loud drumming and the Indian theme. When the camera pans back to the stagecoach, the innocent stagecoach theme returns, indicating that the passengers are unaware of the impending danger.

Original Scores

The competition for the Best Original Score in 1939 was fierce. Vying for the award were twelve films with music by a number of Hollywood's finest composers and one of America's foremost concert composers, Aaron Copland (see Chapter 13). Among the favorites for the award were Alfred Newman's lush score for the passionate romance *Wuthering Heights*, Herbert Stothart's beloved score for *The Wizard of Oz*, and Max Steiner's monumental score for *Gone With the Wind*.

Wuthering Heights

Alfred Newman, one of the most important figures in film music history, worked on twelve films in 1939, for which he received a record four Oscar nominations. Foremost among these films is one of Hollywood's greatest love stories, *Wuthering Heights*, based on the mid-nineteenth-century novel by Emily Brontë. The title is derived from the name of the manor house located high on the English moors. According to Brontë's novel, "wuthering" is the local word for the fierce winds that blow during storms in this region. The setting is ideal for a tempestuous love story.

While the storyline and the weather continually focus on the stormy aspect of the relationship between Heathcliff and Cathy, the music, predominantly set for strings, serves as a constant reminder of the warmth and endurance of their love. The principal leitmotif, known as Cathy's theme, is one of the most beautiful melodies written for the screen. It dominates the film just as their love dominates the story. At one point the theme is even heard as a waltz tune played by a dance orchestra (1:14:45). In Cathy's death scene (1:32:00), Newman's music does not reflect the emotions of the dialogue or the changes in mood. Even Cathy's death is barely noted in the music. The love theme overwhelms all other emotions, and suggests, as does the *Liebestod* from Wagner's *Tristan und Isolde*, that there is joy in death, which will lead to the ultimate consummation of their love.

Composer Profile

Alfred Newman (1901–1970)

Newman began working in vaudeville at the age of thirteen. By the time he was seventeen he was conducting Broadway shows. In 1930 he came to Hollywood at the request of Irving Berlin in order to conduct Berlin's music for a film. In the following year he conducted Chaplin's music for *City Lights* and composed the notable music for *Street Scene* (1931). Newman soon developed a reputation as Hollywood's finest conductor and became general music director at Twentieth Century Fox. He scored around 225 films, received forty-five Academy nominations, and earned nine Oscars, more than any other composer. A number of his family members have also been active in Hollywood, including brothers Lionel and Emil, sons David and Thomas, and nephew Randy.

Important Film Scores

The Prisoner of Zenda 1937 ✉
Gunga Din 1939
Wuthering Heights 1939 ✉
The Grapes of Wrath 1940
How Green Was My Valley 1941 ★ ✉
The Song of Bernadette 1943 ♫

Gentleman's Agreement 1947 ★
All About Eve 1950 ✉
Call Me Madam 1953 ♫
Love Is a Many-Splendored Thing 1955 ♫
How the West Was Won 1963 ✉
Airport 1970 ✉

★ = Best Picture Oscar   ♫ = Best Music Oscar   ✉ = Music Oscar Nomination

In the opening of the story (see Viewer Guide), the filmmakers add a storm that is not in the novel as background to the unexpected visit to Wuthering Heights by a traveler. The storm not only gives us a visual image of why the manor was named "wuthering," but also reflects the mood of the inhabitants within. Newman balances the intensity of the storm depicted by the brass with a sense of the supernatural in the tremolo strings. The latter dominates as the traveler enters the house, where we hear the Wuthering Heights theme ominously intoned. This theme bears a strong resemblance to a famous melody from Tchaikovsky's ballet *Swan Lake*, another supernatural tale in which lovers consummate their relationship in death. Later in the prologue, when the traveler first hears Cathy's voice, the leitmotif is sung by celestial voices, further suggesting that Cathy is not of this world.

Viewer Guide

Wuthering Heights: Prologue

Timing

Excerpt: 00:55–10:10 (0:00 at title); DVD Chapter 1

Key Points

- Prominence of strings
- Ominous, dark underscoring
- Lyric character of the Cathy theme
- Use of voices to suggest ghostly apparition

Setting

A traveler (Miles Mander) is lost in a storm and seeks refuge at Wuthering Heights. Here he will meet Heathcliff (Laurence Olivier) and will hear the story of Heathcliff's love for Cathy (Merle Oberon).

Principal Leitmotifs

Example 12.1 Cathy

Example 12.2 Wuthering Heights

PLOT	MUSIC
In a fierce winter storm, a traveler struggles through a gate and into an isolated house seeking refuge.	The dark and eerie music, with biting dissonances, suggests both the stormy weather and the mood inside the house.
The traveler comes into the house and is attacked by a dog. He enters a room with a fire, and four people stare at him.	Strings play ominous tremolos (quick notes played as fast as possible). The Wuthering Heights theme is presented quietly.
The traveler asks for help, but the hospitality is cold. Heathcliff finally offers him a room for the night.	The music fades, and the ensuing dialogue has no underscoring.
The traveler enters his room as the sounds of the wind continue. He settles into the dusty bed.	The music (primarily in the strings) returns quietly and somewhat tentatively. Fragments of Cathy's theme are heard.
The window shutter is banging. As the traveler attempts to close the shutter, he hears a female voice outside. He calls Heathcliff into the room.	Cathy's theme is played in the strings and sung by a wordless choir. The music is more forceful when he calls out, centering on the opening leap from the Cathy theme.
Heathcliff rushes in and orders the traveler out of the room. He runs to the window and pleads with Cathy to come to him. He then dashes out the door into the storm.	The music is loud as Heathcliff yells at the traveler. Cathy's theme returns in the strings. The music quickens as Heathcliff runs out of the house.
The traveler speaks with the old servant of the house. She begins to tell the story of Heathcliff and Cathy.	Cathy's theme is heard in the clarinet against a pulse like a heartbeat. After a brief pause, the Wuthering Heights theme returns.

The Wizard of Oz

The greatest film musical of the 1930s, and many would argue of all time, is *The Wizard of Oz*. There are two creative forces behind the music: Harold Arlen wrote the original songs, and Herbert Stothart adapted the songs and composed the underscoring. Both won Academy Awards, Arlen for "Over the Rainbow" and Stothart for Best Original Score.

The songs of Arlen, a replacement for the ailing Jerome Kern, are at the heart of the musical. The musical highlight is Dorothy's rendition of "Over the Rainbow," sung early in the film (5:50). The producers almost cut the song because it slowed down the pace of the opening scene. As a compromise, the song was shortened by omitting the opening verse. The chorus is in a simple A–B–A form with a closing tag. Despite the deletion of the verse, "Over the Rainbow" remains the most fully developed song in the film.

Most of the other songs are brief tunes within larger musical scenes. The operatic Munchkin Land scene features "Ding, Dong, the Witch Is Dead," "Follow the Yellow Brick Road," and "We're Off to See the Wizard." The trip to Emerald City alternates verses of "If I Only Had a Brain" and "We're Off to See the Wizard." While the tunes may not be developed fully, they are catchy enough to be enjoyed by children and adults alike. Indeed, these songs are closer in style to the simple tunes heard in cartoons and in the animated feature *Snow White and the Seven Dwarfs* than they are to the songs in standard film musicals. It is not coincidental that the one fully developed song takes place in the adult world of Kansas, while the abbreviated songs occur in the colorful, cartoon-like world of Oz.

Figure 12.3 Dorothy sings "Over the Rainbow" as Toto listens attentively

Composer Profile

Herbert Stothart (1885–1949)

Stothart began composing as a student at the University of Wisconsin. He wrote for Broadway in the 1920s, working with Oscar Hammerstein, and came to Hollywood in 1929. The leading musical figure at the MGM studio for twenty years, he composed music for many highly acclaimed films. He received a total of twelve Academy nominations and one Oscar.

Important Film Scores

Viva Villa! 1934
Mutiny on the Bounty 1935 ★ ✉
A Tale of Two Cities 1935
A Night at the Opera 1935
The Good Earth 1937

The Wizard of Oz 1939 ♫
Northwest Passage 1940
Mrs. Miniver 1942 ★
National Velvet 1944

★ = Best Picture Oscar   ♫ = Best Music Oscar   ✉ = Music Oscar Nomination

Stothart makes good use of a number of Arlen's tunes in the underscoring. The melody of "Over the Rainbow" reflects Dorothy's fundamental change during the story. Initially, the song represents Oz. It is first heard in the underscoring just after she arrives in Oz, identifying this new land as the place "over the rainbow." Later, however, the tune represents her home in Kansas. The critical turning point occurs when Dorothy, trapped by the witch, has only a few minutes to live (1:18:00). As she thinks of Auntie Em, "Over the Rainbow" is heard in the underscoring, suggesting that Dorothy has learned that her home is the true land over the rainbow. Originally this point was made clearer, as Dorothy sang a moving, tearful reprise of her song. Unfortunately, this poignant moment was cut from the film, but it can still be heard on the Deluxe Edition soundtrack CD from Rhino Records (B0000033JH).

The music to *The Wizard of Oz* shares elements with *Mr. Smith Goes to Washington* and *Stagecoach*. In all three films, the music relies heavily on borrowed material. In addition to employing Arlen's songs in the underscoring, Stothart quotes well-known music, including "There's No Place like Home," Brahms's *Lullaby*, Schumann's "Happy Farmer," and Mussorgsky's *Night on Bald Mountain*. Unlike the music for the other films, however, the score for *The Wizard of Oz* is more extensive and contains a good deal of original music. The underscoring for the tornado scene combines borrowed and new material, as the music portrays both the terror and the humor of the situation (17:10). In this scene, we also hear the only originally composed leitmotif in the film. Formerly associated with Miss Gulch, this snippy little melody turns nasty as it is given over to the Wicked Witch of the West when her image on a broomstick replaces that of Miss Gulch on a bicycle.

Example 12.3 Miss Gulch/Wicked Witch of the West

Gone With the Wind

Upstaging all the other 1939 films is the epic *Gone With the Wind*, based on Margaret Mitchell's popular novel. Shot in lavish three-part Technicolor, this film brought together the finest visual, dramatic, and musical art of the time. Hollywood rewarded the work with nine Academy Awards, a record that has been surpassed by the eleven Oscars for *Ben-Hur* (1959), *Titanic* (1997), and *The Lord of the Rings: The Return of the King* (2003). Considering the strength of the opposition, the number of awards for *Gone With the Wind* is remarkable. Moreover, one could argue that the Selznik epic actually deserved at least one more Oscar. The masterful music by Max Steiner was overlooked by the Academy in favor of *The Wizard of Oz*. Although Stothart's score is effective, Steiner's achievement is considerably more substantial.

The Hays Code

In the 1920s, movies were still a relatively new phenomenon. The impact on audiences of scenes of violence, evil deeds, and immoral romances was unknown. In a way, the situation was similar to today's concerns with the Internet. During the 1920s, a number of highly publicized scandals involving silent film stars fueled the moral debates. Fearing government censorship, in 1922 Hollywood created the Motion Picture Producers and Distributors of America, Inc., for the purpose of improving its moral image. Will Hays was asked to head this organization.

Will Hays (1879–1954) was a lawyer who had served as Chairman of the Republican National Committee and as Postmaster General in Harding's administration. During the 1920s, he helped the organization create a list of "Don'ts" and "Be carefuls." In 1930 the Hays Code was published, based on the following general principles:

1. No picture shall be produced which will lower the moral standards of those who see it. The sympathy of the audience shall never be thrown to the side of crime, wrongdoing, evil, or sin.
2. Correct standards of life, subject only to the requirements of drama and entertainment, shall be presented.
3. Law, natural or human, shall not be ridiculed, nor shall sympathy be created for its violation.

A long list of practical rules followed. The code sought to eliminate profanity, the gratuitous use of liquor, sex outside of proper family relations, and nudity. By 1934, the Catholic Church had begun to exert great influence on the Hays Office, and the Hays Code became a powerful force in the industry. The best-known debate concerned Rhett's final line in *Gone With the Wind*: "Frankly, my dear, I don't give a damn." After trying a variety of alternate phrases such as "I don't give a hoot" and "my indifference is boundless," Selznik opted to pay a $5,000 fine and retained the classic line. The Hays Office closed in 1945, but the Code remained in effect until 1966. In 1968, a rating system took its place.

Gone With the Wind, one of twelve films that Steiner scored in 1939, contains one of the most extensive musical scores ever created in Hollywood. Steiner composed the monumental three-hour and forty-five-minute score in four weeks. During that period, he also worked on another score and supervised the recordings of both films. In order to hold this intense schedule, the studio had a doctor at Steiner's side for twenty hours a day.

As observed in the other films in this chapter, source music and quotations of familiar melodies are common in *Gone With the Wind*. Source music can be heard in several extended passages, such as the dance orchestras at 12 Oaks (17:50) and Atlanta (38:00), the organ music at religious services (34:50), the tearful rendition of "Dixie" by a confederate band (49:40), and the solemn voices of the African-American chorus (1:05:20). Borrowings or quotations of well-known tunes are also plentiful. Particularly effective are the distorted versions of Southern tunes such as "Dixie" when the South begins to suffer defeat. In one powerful scene in Atlanta, the camera rises slowly, revealing a thousand confederate bodies and eventually a tattered confederate flag (1:15:05). The scene is supported by an intense musical score, featuring a somber

"Dixie," distorted versions of other Southern patriotic tunes, and strong dissonances that build to a stirring climactic statement of "Taps."

The original music for *Gone With the Wind* also tends to be tuneful. Avoiding short motivic themes, as heard in his scores to *King Kong* and *The Informer*, Steiner creates a number of full-length melodies to represent individuals and relationships. The most important of these is the Tara theme (Example 12.4). This beautiful melody is associated not with romantic love or patriotism, but with Scarlett's love for her plantation. *Gone With the Wind* begins and ends with Scarlett, and all of the events are seen through her eyes. The character of Scarlett is a strong contrast to that of Melanie. Melanie, with her unchanging goodness, is an idealized vision of how people should be; Scarlett, with her anger, jealousy, and deceit, is a realistic person who resembles how we really are.

Figure 12.4 "Taps" and distorted Southern melodies combine with the scene of the field of dead and wounded in *Gone With the Wind*

Scarlett undergoes continual disappointment. The one constant through all these events is her love for Tara, her source of strength. As she rebounds from every setback, thoughts of Tara, accompanied by the theme, give her renewed energy. At the end of the film, despite all her growth, all her triumphs, and her realization that she loves Rhett, she endures yet one more devastating blow. She deals with Rhett's rejection by feeling the weight of the loss, setting her feelings aside with a reference to her adolescent days—"tomorrow is another day," and turning her thoughts to the source of her strength, Tara. The return of the theme at the end rounds off the film and reassures us that Scarlett's indomitable spirit will triumph.

Examples 12.4–12.9 Leitmotifs from *Gone With the Wind*

Example 12.4 Tara

Example 12.5 Gerald O'Hara

Example 12.6 Mammy

Example 12.7 Melanie

Example 12.8 Rhett

Example 12.9 Rhett and Scarlett

Some of the other major leitmotifs reflect the nature of the characters that they represent. Two of the themes suggest an ethnic background: a jig underscores Gerald O'Hara's Irish heritage, and a syncopated theme, the distinctive rhythmic sound of African-American music, accompanies the lively character of Mammy. Character traits are suggested by the serene melody for Melanie and the confident theme of Rhett Butler. The lyric nature of the other themes reflects the romantic quality of the love relationships. As with the Tara theme, all of the melodies are used with restraint. Perhaps the most beautiful theme of the score, the love theme of Rhett and Scarlett, is not heard for nearly half of the film. It slowly emerges to dominance in the second half, and at the end, it retains a fresh, vibrant quality.

Trailer

Gone With the Wind, with its epic story, colorful cinematography, and lush musical score, will always be seen as the pinnacle of the opulent Hollywood style of filmmaking from the late 1930's. But as we have already observed, filmmaking is a rapidly changing industry. The sounds of modern music would soon be challenging the traditions of the classic Hollywood film score.

Important Names and Terms

Frank Capra   Richard Hageman
Dimitri Tiomkin   Alfred Newman
populist films   Harold Arlen

Suggested Viewing

(All films are from 1939.)

Action/Adventure: *Gunga Din* and *Beau Geste*
Biopic: *Young Mr. Lincoln*
Drama: *Goodbye Mr. Chips, The Women,* and *Dark Victory*
Romance: *Intermezzo*
Comedy: *Ninotchka*
Western: *Destry Rides Again*
Horror: *Son of Frankenstein*

13

Modern Voices, 1936-1944

Hollywood's Golden Age, which extended well into the 1940s, produced an array of outstanding films, as is evident by the list of movies in the Suggested Viewing section at the end of this chapter. The paradigm of the Hollywood style created in the late 1930s, which includes a lengthy score set in the postromantic style, continued to exert a strong influence on American filmmaking even through the end of the 1950s. Yet, as is typical of all artistic cycles, change was inevitable. Although the major challenges to the film industry would take place after World War II, adumbrations of the demise of the classic age can be seen in a number of films from 1940 and 1941.

For film music, the manifestation of this imminent transformation was the emergence of a new musical sound that was influenced by the modern styles of contemporary concert composers. The term "concert composer" refers to composers who write primarily symphonies, chamber music, and operas for performances in concert halls.

In America, concert composers did not usually write for films. The assembly-line production of Hollywood studios required specialists who devoted themselves to film music almost exclusively. These composers wrote quickly and effectively but had little time for concert music. Composers of concert music did not fit well into the Hollywood system, and when they tried, they tended

SIGNIFICANT FILMS

1936	*Things to Come*
1938	*Alexander Nevsky*
1939	*Of Mice and Men* ✉
	La Noche de los mayas
1940	*Our Town* ✉
1941	*The Devil and Daniel Webster* ♫
	Citizen Kane ✉
1943	*Hangmen Also Die* ✉

to resent their lack of artistic control over the final product. Still, the modern styles and techniques of concert music gradually slipped into the palette of Hollywood composers, partially because of a number of concert composers who were enticed to Hollywood and partially because of the creative efforts of several studio composers.

International Films

In Europe a significant number of leading concert composers also wrote film music. As a result, modern styles and compositional techniques can first be detected in scores from traditional film centers, such as France, England, and the Soviet Union. In addition, there would be some notable contributions from emerging national film schools from around the world.

France

In France, the transition into the sound era was made smoothly, without sacrificing visual imagery. Although French sound technology lagged behind American standards, music became an effective tool for the French auteur. As in Hollywood, the amount of music in French films varied, as can be seen in scores by Joseph Kosma for two critically acclaimed films directed by Jean Renoir. *La Règle du jeu* (*Rules of the Game*, 1939) is devoid of music other than occasional examples of source music and brief excerpts from music by two composers of the Classic era, Mozart and Monsigny. By way of contrast, *La Grande illusion* (1937) masterfully blends striking visual images with colorful, mood-evoking music. In general, a number of musical traits can be detected in French works that will characterize European film music well into the 1970s:

- Music is used sparingly
- Source music plays a prominent role
- Music tends to sustain a single mood
- Leitmotifs are used less frequently than in American films

England

The English film industry retained its close ties to America during the 1930s. The films of England's Alfred Hitchcock began to create a sensation in the United States in 1935 with *The Man Who Knew Too Much* and *The 39 Steps*. In 1939 Hitchcock moved effortlessly from his British studio to Hollywood. Perhaps the finest English score of the 1930s is *Things to Come* (1936) by Sir Arthur Bliss. This fascinating futuristic vision—the plot extends from 1940 to 2036—is supported by a number of excellent marches. Particularly noteworthy is the music for the opening montage, which juxtaposes the joys of Christmas with the coming of war. Another prominent English composer, Richard Addinsell, wrote several successful scores, and his piano music to *Suicide Squadron* (1941), popularly known as the *Warsaw Concerto*, received widespread attention in the United States.

The Soviet Union

In the totalitarian governments of Europe, films were seen as propaganda tools. Germany's industry declined as it fell under the control of Hitler in 1933, and the documentary films of Leni Riefenstahl proved to be the only enduring products of the Nazi period. Italian films likewise subordinated artistic value to pro-Mussolini political views. Only the Soviet Union created narrative films that served propaganda purposes effectively and still maintained a high level of artistic quality. Two outstanding concert composers wrote music for films in the Soviet Union. Dmitry Shostakovich (1906–1975), who scored his first movie in 1929, wrote music for fifteen additional films during the 1930s, including *The Great Citizen* (1938), which was largely created by Stalin himself.

The other great Soviet composer is Sergei Prokofiev (1891–1953). Prokofiev left the Soviet Union after the Revolution, and he returned in 1936 after establishing himself as a major international musical figure. During his transition back to the Soviet Union, Prokofiev composed music for the 1934 satirical film *Lieutenant Kije*. While the film was never completed, the music has become one of the standards of twentieth-century concert music. Prokofiev continued to write for films in the 1930s and 1940s. He collaborated with Sergei Eisenstein on two landmark Soviet films *Alexander Nevsky* (1938) and *Ivan the Terrible* (Part I, 1945 and Part II, 1946).

Alexander Nevsky

Alexander Nevsky is a powerful historical drama about the legendary thirteenth-century Russian leader who defeated both the invading Swedish and German armies through brilliant tactical maneuvers. The film focuses on the German conflict. The invaders are portrayed as brutal beasts, cruelly throwing Russian babies into fires (29:00). The prominent Christian symbols on their uniforms and the evil character of the German religious leader serve as strong reminders of the Soviet distrust of Christianity. The film climaxes with the famous battle on the frozen Lake Chudskoye, where the outflanked Germans drown when the ice breaks under the weight of their heavy armor. This inspiring story served as a warning for the twentieth-century Soviet audience, which was preparing for yet another German invasion.

For the most part, Prokofiev uses music to set general moods. In the Battle of Lake Chudskoye, for example, joyful music is heard when Alexander joins the battle (1:04:50), even though the outcome is still in doubt, and the mood does not mirror any of the visual action. Elsewhere, Prokofiev's music has some stunning moments, such as the intense accompaniment to the German crusaders' slaughter of Russians in Pskov (22:10) and the solo soprano voice soaring over the field of dead after the battle (1:25:10). The greatest strength of the score lies in the stirring choruses, representing the voices of the people.

Developing National Industries

While filmmaking was dominated by America and the leading powers of Europe, a number of national schools began to emerge during the 1930s in eastern Europe (Poland, Hungary, and Czechoslovakia), Asia (India, China, and Japan), Australia, and Latin America (Brazil and Mexico). In the shadow of Hollywood, Mexican film-makers struggled for independence, eventually creating a distinctive original style in the 1940s. In the mid-1930s, Silvestre Revueltas (1899–1940), one of Mexico's major composers, began to score films. He completed seven film scores before his untimely death in 1940. The music for *La Noche de los mayas* (1939) has become one of the composer's most enduring works. An energetic composition requiring at least eleven percussionists, the colorful score abounds in folk melodies, dance rhythms, and modern dissonances; it clearly establishes him as one of the principal nationalist composers of the mid-twentieth century.

Figure 13.1 A lament is heard while the women look for the dead in *Alexander Nevsky*

Modern Music in Hollywood

In the United States, two styles of concert music exerted an influence on Hollywood—expressionism and American nationalism. In addition, a new musical style emerged in the scores of films dealing with darker subjects, which will be denoted in this text as the film noir style. All three styles began to appear in American films during the early 1940s.

Expressionism

In the 1930s and 40s, Hollywood invited a number of prestigious composers to write for films. MGM contacted both Igor Stravinsky (1882–1971) and Arnold Schoenberg (1874–1951), considered by many to be the two leading composers of the century. Both eventually lived in Hollywood, but neither actually completed a studio score. Stravinsky worked on several aborted film projects. Some of his musical drafts were later reused in published compositions, including *Four Norwegian Dances* and *Symphony in Three*

Movements. In a frequently told Hollywood anecdote, Schoenberg is said to have requested $100,000 for a score, a year to compose it, and a voice in the how the film was created. Needless to say, the studios did not meet those demands.

Despite never writing a film score, Schoenberg exerted a strong influence on Hollywood both as a teacher and as a model for composing expressionistic music. Characterized by continuous dissonant harmony and disjunct melodies, expressionism was one of the most radical sounding musical styles in the first half of the twentieth century. Schoenberg, who is the principal figure associated with this style, developed in the 1920s a technique known as serialism that systematically maintains the style and sound of expressionism. There is a significant compositional difference between expressionism and serialism, but most listeners cannot distinguish them by ear. In this text, the two terms will be linked together.

Hanns Eisler (1898–1962), a German student of Schoenberg, was the first to bring expressionism into Hollywood film studios, and he is credited for writing the first film score using serialism. In the sparsely scored *Hangmen Also Die* (1943), the dark, dissonant sound created by serial techniques represents the German repression of Czechoslovakia. A socialist, Eisler was among the first Hollywood figures called before the House Un-American Activities Committee under suspicion of promoting Communism. With his name tarnished and commissions at a standstill, Eisler voluntarily deported to East Germany.

American Nationalism

Another distinctive style of concert music was brought to Hollywood through the works of Aaron Copland (1900–1990). America's leading nationalist composer, Copland is best known for his ballets *Appalachian Spring, Rodeo*, and *Billy the Kid*, as well as for the *Fanfare for the Common Man* and a number of symphonies and concertos. In these works, Copland established a distinctive American style. Essential to this sound are broad melodies featuring strong intervals, syncopated rhythms, colorful orchestration, and a modern but relatively conservative harmonic system. His music influenced a number of film composers, including Hugo Friedhofer, Leonard Bernstein, and John Williams; he also created four outstanding scores for narrative films.

All four of Copland's film scores are connected with American stories, two of which will be discussed in Chapter 15. In 1939, he wrote music for a film adaptation of John Steinbeck's 1937 novella *Of Mice and Men*. Much of the film is presented without underscoring, but the score for the final dramatic section builds in a symphonic manner (beginning at 1:38:05), culminating in a powerful musical climax for the tragic ending. The steady, inexorable movement in the orchestra reflects the inevitable conclusion. This outstanding film received Oscar nominations for both Best Picture and Best Original Score in Hollywood's greatest year.

Copland also received an Oscar nomination in 1940 for his contribution to the film adaptation of Thornton Wilder's 1938 Pulitzer Prize-winning play, *Our Town*. In this film, the static quality of Copland's music is particularly effective, as the slow but firm pace of the music bathes the drama in American sounds, matching the lyrical portrayal of a New Hampshire town and the stories of its inhabitants. The final twenty minutes of the film has nearly continuous music, beginning at 1:07:35. During this span, Copland deftly underscores the moods of eternal triumph, the pain of life and death, and the joy of life renewed in the unfortunate Hollywood happy ending added to this classic American drama.

Forerunners of Film Noir

Beginning in the early 1940s, a darker mood can be detected in Hollywood films, as the foundations of film noir are established in lighting, images, stories, and music. Film noir will be addressed more fully in Chapter 15, but in essence the music for this emerging style mixes the postromantic style with elements of expressionism, such as angular melodies, dark instrumental colors, and dissonance. A prototype for the genre of film noir can be seen in *The Maltese Falcon* (1941), for which Adolph Deutsch provided a sparse but moody score. Even more indicative of future musical directions is Roy Webb's dissonant score for *The Stranger on the Third Floor* (1940). But the figure

Composer Profile

Bernard Herrmann (1911-1975)

Born in New York, Bernard Herrmann was trained at the Juilliard School of Music. By the age of twenty, he had founded and was conducting a chamber orchestra. He went on to guest conduct for the New York Philharmonic and a number of other prestigious orchestras. Beginning in 1934, he worked as an arranger and conductor for CBS Radio, and it was there that he met Orson Welles. Herrmann provided musical numbers for Welles's infamous *War of the Worlds* broadcast in 1938, and when Welles decided to make *Citizen Kane*, Herrmann was invited to compose the musical score. In later years, Herrmann would collaborate with other great directors, including Alfred Hitchcock and Martin Scorsese.

Important Film Scores

Citizen Kane 1941 ✉	*The Man Who Knew Too Much* 1956
The Devil and Daniel Webster 1941 ♫	*Vertigo* 1958
The Magnificent Ambersons 1942	*North by Northwest* 1959
The Ghost and Mrs. Muir 1947	*Psycho* 1960
The Day the Earth Stood Still 1951	*Taxi Driver* 1976 ✉

★ = Best Picture Oscar   ♫ = Best Music Oscar   ✉ = Music Oscar Nomination

that played the largest role in the creation of a film noir musical style is Bernard Herrmann.

Herrmann is the first major Hollywood film composer to incorporate the modern sounds of contemporary concert music in consistent fashion. Coming from radio, he made a remarkable film debut in 1941 with two scores, both of which earned Oscar nominations. Characteristic of both are frequent dissonances, small musical ensembles, and new and colorful musical sonorities. Among the innovative new sounds in his score for *The Devil and Daniel Webster* are the recorded sounds of telegraph wires that help to create an eerie effect associated with the devil (15:25). Other musical highlights include a macabre waltz (1:17:15) and the layered violin tracks for a series of variations on "Pop Goes the Weasel" (50:30). Herrmann won the Academy Award for this creative score, but he will always be best remembered for his other 1941 film, *Citizen Kane*.

Citizen Kane

Citizen Kane is universally acknowledged as America's greatest film and can be seen as the high point of the Golden Age. Yet many of the qualities that define its greatness run counter to the general trends of the time. The plot is a unique conception, as a single story—the rise and fall of Charles Foster Kane—is told from six perspectives:

- Newsreel: the public view
- Thatcher: the guardian
- Bernstein: the business partner
- Leland: the best friend
- Susan: the second wife
- Raymond: the butler

After the initial public view of Kane, each of the retellings focuses on more intimate details of the various stages of his life: Thatcher knew him as a boy, Bernstein began business with him, Leland was his best friend until the marriage scandal, Susan lived with him through his declining years, and Raymond witnessed his last days. An anonymous reporter named Thompson, whose face is never shown fully, links these stories together as he searches for the meaning of "Rosebud," Kane's last word before dying. Although his efforts are eventually futile, the audience is given the last puzzle piece in the final moment, completing our understanding of Charles Kane.

Also breaking with contemporary practices are the cinematographic effects. Most striking is the stark contrast between bright light and darkness. This effect is used primarily in scenes with the reporter Thompson, such as the discussion after the newsreel and his visit to the Thatcher Library (Figure 13.2). The camera angles also create many unique shots throughout the film. The low perspective of the camera during Leland's flashback suggests Kane's rise to power and his greatness. The scene with

Kane and Leland after the election loss was shot from beneath the floor. These effects, combined with the use of deep focus, which enables images in the foreground and background to stay in focus, reflected images, and montage, help make this film one of the most creative and influential works in film history.

The Music

Orson Welles starred in *Citizen Kane*, produced it, and helped write the script. He did allow Bernard Herrmann to compose the music. Like the classic film scores of the Golden Age, the music for *Citizen Kane* supports the drama, captures the moods, and contributes a sense of unity to the film. But Herrmann

Figure 13.2 The use of strong light and dark shadows in the Thatcher Memorial Library

Close-Up: Welles vs. Hearst

The Fact and Fiction of *Citizen Kane*

The story of *Citizen Kane* is based on the life of the newspaper mogul William Randolph Hearst. Many of the events depicted in the film mirror incidents in Hearst's career, including the following:

- Hearst was kicked out of Harvard.
- Taking over the *San Francisco Examiner*, Hearst mixed hard-hitting investigative reporting with yellow journalism, a term that designates a sensational and irresponsible approach to newspaper reporting.
- Hearst began expanding his newspaper empire by moving into New York and stealing the top writers from a rival newspaper, Joseph Pulitzer's *New York World*.
- Articles in Hearst's papers helped lead the country into the Spanish-American War.
- Hearst had an affair with an entertainer, the actress Marion Davies, and he promoted her career as he became a force in the film industry.
- Hearst was active in politics and had failed political aspirations.

- In 1937, Hearst had lost almost all of his fortune and temporarily relinquished control of his empire.
- A lavish spender, Hearst built a $30 million mansion on a 240,000-acre lot in San Simeon, California, and filled it, along with several warehouses, with antiques and artworks.

Given these parallels and the use of some sayings that were actually spoken by Hearst, the connection between the two is undeniable. Hearst certainly understood that the film was a parody of his life and tried to suppress the film and destroy the career of Orson Welles. His principal objection to the film was not his unflattering image, but the distasteful depiction of Marion Davies in the character of Susan. Davies was not without talent as an actress, and she appeared in a number of first-rate films. Contrary to the film, Hearst and Davies never married, and she remained a close and faithful friend to him. Moreover, the film dwells on Susan's drinking—Davies did have a drinking problem—which gives her characterization a mean-spirited edge, for which Welles later expressed regret.

also introduces a number of disturbing elements in his choice of orchestration, harmony, and melody.

For the opening montage, Herrmann avoided the typical full symphonic orchestration, and wrote for a small ensemble featuring flutes, bassoons, muted brass, and vibraphone. Tone clusters (highly dissonant chords created by playing a group of adjacent pitches, as if created by banging a fist on the piano keyboard), other dissonances, and the use of the lower ranges of the instruments create a dark and somber mood that matches Welles's foreboding images and parallels the starkness of the story and of the black-and-white photography.

In general, Herrmann's melodic material lacks warmth. The tenderest melody of the film, the waltz tune associated with Kane's first wife, is short-lived. In the breakfast montage (51:50), we hear the waltz melody dismantled through a set of variations, just as we watch their marriage disintegrate. Each of the six breakfast scenes is accompanied by a variation of the waltz. The opening contains the original version, and its romantic quality reflects their feelings just after the wedding. In the succeeding scenes, the music turns humorous, agitated, dark, and ominous. For the final segment, the musical motion is suspended, just as the emotions of their marriage have dissipated. A number of reports have suggested that Welles cut this scene to fit the musical needs of a theme and variations structure. While he may have accommodated some of Herrmann's needs, the music too has obviously been altered to fit the timing of the montage.

Two five-note themes (see Viewer Guide) underlie much of the drama. Both of these motives are prominent in the breakfast montage. The Waltz theme is a four-note variation of the Rosebud theme. During the course of the variations, the Power motive begins to appear more prominently, reflecting the growing success of Charles Kane. In addition to providing unity to the musical score, these motives reveal the film's underlying theme. *Citizen Kane* is the story of a man who rises to a position of great wealth and power. The Power motive appears when we see him on the rise, view his vast possessions, or observe his ruthless treatment of those he loves—for example, such as when he fires his best friend and when he dominates Susan.

But the focus of the film is on something that Kane lost—"Rosebud." Rosebud is the name of Kane's childhood sled. Herrmann reveals this secret early in the film. The Rosebud motive is heard at the opening when Kane says his last word, when he drops the glass ball with the winter scene, and when we first see Charles as a young boy playing with his sled (see Viewer Guide).

Figure 13.3 Deep focus allows both the foreground and background to be clear

Figure 13.4 Low registers and dissonances set the opening tone for *Citizen Kane*

Rosebud stands for much more than a child's possession; it represents the innocence and happiness that Kane lost during his rise to power. Kane's relationship with Susan, whom he symbolically meets (55:10) while on the way to look at items from his youth, including his sled, represents an effort to reach out and recapture what he has lost. Herrmann reinforces this association by initially associating Susan with the Rosebud theme. But the Power motive eventually dominates, as the sweet innocence of Susan is crushed by Kane's power.

Figure 13.5 Charles holds Rosebud between himself and Mr. Thatcher

Thatcher Memoirs

Like each of the five personal stories of Kane's life, the Thatcher portion of the film is set in a frame (see Viewer Guide). Since Thatcher is dead, his view of Kane is related through the memoirs maintained in a locked vault with a guard and a no-nonsense librarian. Flashbacks show three visions of Kane's life: as a boy who has just come into a fortune, as an idealistic young man running a newspaper, and as an older man who has lost much of his fortune. Throughout the excerpt, music is used sparingly; there are a number of extended dialogue scenes without underscoring. Also noteworthy are the various color combinations produced by small ensembles.

The music centers on the two principal motives. The Power motive is heard frequently. At times the motive remains in the background as a subtle reminder of the critical role of wealth in the story. At other times, it is quite pronounced, such as during the mocking statements following Charles's final verbal jabs at Thatcher in his newspaper office, immediately followed by a sad statement as we jump to the year 1929. The Rosebud theme appears in its most joyous form when we first see young Charles playing in the snow. Later it is heard quietly as we see the boy's sled abandoned in the snow. At this point, an alert listener would know the secret of Rosebud.

Other music in this scene is used for humorous effect. When the exasperated Thatcher reads Kane's opinion that it would be fun to run a newspaper, a nineteenth-century can-can dance accompanies a montage showing Kane's newspaper attacking Thatcher. Careful listening can detect that the can-can theme is related to the Power motive. Also humorous is Herrmann's quotation of the Gregorian chant *Dies irae* for the framing scenes, a theme that is similar in shape to the Power motive. The *Dies irae* is a sacred melody sung in the Catholic Church for funeral services. At the beginning, the low brass solemnly intone the tune presenting it as Berlioz does in his *Symphonie fantastique*, but the muted instruments immediately mock the pretentiousness of the memorial library.

Citizen Kane: **The Thatcher Memoirs**

Timing

Excerpt: 17:15–30:15 (0:00 at logo); DVD Chapters 5–8

Key Points

- Role of leitmotifs
- Orchestration for small ensembles
- Nineteenth-century dance music for montage
- Extended dialogue without underscoring

Setting

A newspaper reporter named Thompson (William Alland)
is trying to solve the Rosebud mystery. He goes to the memorial library dedicated to
Walter Parks Thatcher (George Coulouris) and reads notes about the life of Charles
Foster Kane (Orson Welles). In the course of the episode, we will encounter, among
others, Jedediah Leland (Joseph Cotton), Mr. Bernstein (Everett Sloane), and Kane's
Mother (Agnes Moorehead).

Principal Leitmotifs

Example 13.1 Power

Example 13.2 Rosebud

PLOT	MUSIC
We see a sculpture of Thatcher. A librarian recites rules to Thompson.	Muted brass intone the *Dies irae* in mock seriousness. Chords continue through the dialogue.
Thompson and the librarian enter the vault, where the librarian recites rules to Thompson. The librarian shuts the door on Thompson.	The Power motive plays as they enter. A loud chord coincides with the closing of the vault door.
Thompson begins to read, and a flashback takes us to 1871, where young Charles is playing in the snow. He throws a snowball at the house.	The Power motive is heard slowly; the tempo then accelerates into a lush string setting of the Rosebud theme. The music stops after the stinger with the snowball impact.
We learn how Charles came into his fortune, as Mrs. Kane assigns guardianship of the boy to Thatcher, over the objections of Mr. Kane.	No music
Thatcher asks to meet the boy, and they go outside to talk to Charles.	The Power motive is followed by other background music, which quietly disappears.
Trying to understand what he is being told, Charles finally attacks Thatcher with his sled. The scene closes with a view of the sled.	No music until after the attack, when we hear the Rosebud theme. With the vision of the abandoned sled in the snow, woodwinds quietly play the Rosebud theme.
A young Charles is given a new sled, and, years later, his fortune. Charles expresses little interest in his inheritance, except for owning a newspaper.	No music
A montage shows the fun of running a newspaper at Thatcher's expense.	The orchestra plays a nineteenth-century can-can dance.
Thatcher confronts Charles. We learn of Charles's unscrupulous methods and hear him defend the little people.	No music until the Power motive mocks Thatcher at the end.
We jump to 1929 and see an elderly Charles relinquishing a large portion of his fortune to Thatcher. Along with Bernstein, they reminisce and philosophize about the past.	The scene opens with a statement of the Power motive played slowly and sadly in the muted brass. Music disappears until the end, when the Power motive is played one more time in the muted brass.

Trailer

The darker tones of *Citizen Kane*, *The Maltese Falcon*, and *The Stranger on the Third Floor* appear as ominous shadows in the Golden Age. Although at its productive peak, Hollywood was facing a number of emerging problems. In the same year as *Citizen Kane*, the sociologist Leo Rosten painted a grim picture of Hollywood's future:

Other businesses have experienced onslaughts against their profits and hegemony; but the drive against Hollywood is just beginning. No moving picture leader can be sanguine before the steady challenge of unionism, collective bargaining, the consent decree (which brought the Justice Department suit to a temporary armistice), the revolt of the independent theater owners, the trend towards increased taxation, the strangulation of the foreign market, and a score of frontal attacks on the citadels of the screen.*

The pending problems were serious, but World War II delayed the consequences. Hollywood suddenly had a more important challenge, and like the country itself, the American film industry enjoyed one of its finest moments.

Important Names and Terms

concert composer
Joseph Kosma
Sir Arthur Bliss
Richard Addinsell
Sergei Prokofiev
Silvestre Revueltas
Igor Stravinsky
Arnold Schoenberg

serialism
Hanns Eisler
American nationalism
Aaron Copland
film noir style
Bernard Herrmann
Orson Welles
William Randolph Hearst

Suggested Viewing

Social Drama: *The Grapes of Wrath* (1940), *How Green Was My Valley* ★ ✉ (1941), *Meet John Doe* (1941), and *Kings Row* (1942)

Drama: *Mrs. Miniver* (1942) ★, *Now, Voyager* (1942) ♫, *The Magnificent Ambersons* (1942), *For Whom the Bell Tolls* (1943) ✉, *The Song of Bernadette* (1943) ♫, *Going My Way* (1944) ★ ♫, and *Since You Went Away* (1944) ♫

Romance: *Pride and Prejudice* (1940)

Biopic: *The Pride of the Yankees* (1942) ✉

Mystery: *The Stranger on the Third Floor* (1940), *Rebecca* (1940) ★ ✉, *Suspicion* (1941) ✉, and *The Maltese Falcon* (1941)

Adventure: *The Thief of Bagdad* (1940) ✉, *The Mark of Zorro* (1940) ✉, *The Sea Hawk* (1940) ✉, and *The Sea Wolf* (1941)

Western: *The Ox-Bow Incident* (1943)

Comedy: *The Philadelphia Story* (1940) and *The Lady Eve* (1941)

Musical: *Yankee Doodle Dandy* (1942) and *Meet Me in St. Louis* (1944) ✉ ✉

* Leo Rosten, *Hollywood: The Movie Colony.* New York: Harcourt, Brace, 1941, p. 78.

14

Casablanca

The bombing of Pearl Harbor on December 7, 1941, is the defining moment in twentieth-century American history. By the end of World War II (1945), the United States had become a superpower, and every aspect of American life was transformed. During the war, European film production was either curtailed or converted to serve the wartime needs of those countries. In the United States, President Franklin Roosevelt decided to let the film industry remain independent, and Hollywood responded splendidly. Patriotic films were produced to help boost morale, documentaries kept the public informed, and training films helped build stronger armed forces. Moreover, theaters sold war bonds and stars entertained the troops, supported charity and relief efforts, and even enlisted. Hollywood had its finest moment as a social institution; it also made record profits.

War movies filled the screen with images of courageous American soldiers pitted against villainous Germans and "Japs." Other major film genres of the 1930s were retooled to incorporate war themes. Backstage musicals, instead of featuring Broadway hopefuls, now dealt with USO entertainers. Detectives began to pursue spies and become agents of espionage. Horror films showed zombies created by evil Axis scientists. Even comedies and cartoons lampooned the enemy and, at the very least, provided needed diversion from the strains of the war.

Typical of the conversion process was a drama entitled *Everybody Comes to Rick's*. The original script told of Rick, an owner of a café in French Morocco that was a hangout for European refugees. His life there would be totally disrupted by the arrival of Lois Meredith, a seductress who had ruined both his marriage and his law practice in prewar Paris. An official report on the possibilities of this story was filed at Warner Bros. on December 8, 1941, the day after the Pearl Harbor bombing. The studio saw great potential for a film version, but changed the story to incorporate themes of separation and sacrifice. The woman, now named Ilsa, was seen as an innocent victim of events in the war, and Rick was recast as a former freedom fighter, who is inspired to support a new cause. The drama was also given a new name—*Casablanca*.

The Narrative

The story of *Casablanca* takes place within a forty-eight-hour period in December 1941. American audiences would have known the significance of the date and understood that these events occurred during the first week of December—that is, prior to December 7, since the United States is not yet involved in the war. When Rick describes America as sleeping, we know that the country, just like Rick, is about to be awakened into action.

On July 10, 1940, France surrendered and signed a peace treaty with Germany. In the terms of the accord, Germany was to occupy the northern regions of France, including Paris, while the French, from their new capital in Vichy, would govern the southern regions and the French territories in North Africa. Although ostensibly independent, the Vichy government acted as an extension of Nazi Germany and was at odds with the forces of Free France led by General Charles de Gaulle. Casablanca, located in Morocco, North Africa, was under the control of the Vichy government at the time of this story.

In 1942, as the film was being shot, the allied forces under General Eisenhower took control of Casablanca. Film production rushed to capitalize on the free publicity, and released the movie on Thanksgiving Day. Attention on Casablanca was further boosted by a conference in January 1943, during which Roosevelt finally broke off relations with the Vichy government. The timing could not have been better for the film.

Many of the films that were hastily revised seem dated by their wartime settings. But the changes in *Casablanca* elevate this melodrama to a timeless tale of love and sacrifice. At the beginning of the film, Rick is seen as a self-centered, detached man. He has no friends, either male or female, and he does not believe in any cause other than himself. Everything changes with the entrance of his former lover Ilsa and her husband Laszlo. Ilsa rekindles his emotions, and he moves through the cycle from bitterness and anger to love and passion. But at the end, Laszlo's influence is just as strong; Rick sacrifices the joys of being reunited with Ilsa for the greater needs of the world around him. This transformation from selfish to selfless was an important war message in the early 1940s, but it also transcends time and retains its appeal to modern audiences. The American Film Institute rates *Casablanca* as America's second greatest film, after *Citizen Kane*.

The Music

Max Steiner's music plays a critical role in the film as a whole and in the development of Rick's character in particular. In portions of the film, Steiner provides an emotionally charged underscoring with frequent quotes of national melodies, particularly the French "Marseillaise" and the German "Deutschland über Alles" and "Die Wacht am Rhein." But source music, predominantly American popular music, also plays a critical role in the film. A list of the borrowed popular music heard in *Casablanca* appears in the Feature Film Guide. All the popular tunes are borrowed except for "Knock on Wood," which was created for this film.

The principal popular tune in the film is "As Time Goes By," one of the most memorable tunes in all of film history. Although Steiner made this tune famous, he did not compose it. "As Time Goes By" was written by Herman Hupfeld for a 1931 revue. At the time, Steiner did not like the song and asked to write an original tune instead. An attempt was made to accommodate his wishes, but Ilsa had spoken the title of the tune, and the scene could not be re-shot because Ingrid Bergman had changed her hair for her role in *For Whom the Bell Tolls*. So Steiner worked with the theme as given to him, and he later admitted that the tune grew on him.

Exposition

The opening credits are presented against a map showing the location of Casablanca in relationship to Africa and Arabia. Steiner's music also helps establish the locale. Following a typical Steiner fanfare, the melody, with a percussive accompaniment and crashing gongs, suggests an Arabic setting. The tune is not original, as Steiner had composed it for an earlier film *The Lost Patrol* (1934), which is set in a Mesopotamian desert. After two phrases of the Arabian melody, the French "Marseillaise" is fervently intoned, reminding us of the French control of Morocco and fueling patriotic emotions. On the last chord, Steiner strikes a sour note, as the movie segues into a narrator's description of these dark days for Europe.

Figure 14.1 The sound of American popular music distinguishes Rick's Café Americain

For the opening of the story, Steiner's music masterfully sets the mood, reinforces the locale, underscores the action, and establishes the principal struggle between France and Germany. At first, a tortuous melody is heard, accompanied by heavy repeated chords, often creating harsh dissonances. The music suggests the weariness of the travelers described by the narrator. The sound of an oboe (the snake-charmer's instrument) playing an Arabian tune accompanies our initial vision of Casablanca, but the mood is abruptly interrupted by a German announcement, punctuated by the opening notes of "Deutschland über Alles." Dramatic action music underscores a brief montage showing a roundup of the usual suspects.

At the conclusion of the montage, a man is shot and killed beneath a poster of Marshal Philippe Petain, the prime minister of the Vichy government, with the printed words: "Je Tiens Mes Promesses Meme Celles Des Autres" ("I Keep My Promises, Just as I Keep the Promises of Others"). While the camera focuses on the three words of the French Revolution—"liberté, egalité, fraternité" (freedom, equality, brotherhood), the "Marseillaise" is played in a minor mode, reflecting the sad state of Free France. Many moviegoers would have known that the Vichy government replaced this well-known three-word patriotic French Revolution saying with a new slogan— "travail, famille, patrie" (labor, family, country).

Rick and Ugarte

The events surrounding Rick and Ugarte are set in Rick's Café Americain. All of the music for this nearly thirty-minute segment is diegetic, stemming from the pianist Sam and members of the band. There is no non-diegetic music, not even during the action of Ugarte's arrest.

The reliance on popular music for this portion of the story serves several purposes. Tunes such as "Knock on Wood" are catchy and enjoyable, and the film brilliantly interweaves these entertaining songs into the drama without interrupting the dramatic flow. In addition, popular tunes help date the story, and they distinguish Rick's Café from the rest of Casablanca. More importantly, source music creates an atmosphere of superficiality that shrouds Rick's Café. In this time of trouble, visitors come to Rick's to make deals, gamble, drink, find romance, and be entertained. Rick barricades himself in this superficial world, and the absence of underscoring reflects his lack of emotions.

Figure 14.2 Sam and the band perform "Knock on Wood"

Rick and Ilsa

Ilsa and Laszlo enter and shatter Rick's artificial world. When Ilsa asks Sam to play "As Time Goes By," the film's most famous melody makes its initial appearance. At the moment that Rick sees Ilsa, underscoring returns (33:30) for the first time since the exposition. An orchestral stinger suggests that Rick is stunned by Ilsa's appearance. The oboe then picks up the tune, now transformed into their Love theme, and from this point forward, "As Time Goes By" dominates the score. During the subsequent awkward conversation that refers to the Paris days, mention is made of the Germans, and the music turns dark with a quotation of "Deutschland über Alles," against which a phrase of the Love theme can be heard in counterpoint. This is our first musical depiction of the events in Paris, where the German invasion disrupted their relationship.

After the guests leave, Rick has an alcohol-induced flashback to Paris (38:55). As he slips into his memories, the orchestra picks up the Love theme that Sam is playing on the piano. Following the "Marseillaise," Steiner provides a lush fantasy based on individual phrases of "As Time Goes By." Two moments of source music intrude into the montage—a tango at a dance club and Sam's singing of a portion of the song. Other music heard in the section includes the two German melodies in dark, sinister settings and a somber "Marseillaise" at the train station. The variations on "As Time Goes By" during the montage and the emotional climaxes that accompany the kiss and the reading of the rain-drenched letter are among Steiner's finest moments.

After the flashback (41:50), Sam's piano playing reemerges, helping us understand that the flashback was in Rick's mind. Ilsa abruptly enters, accompanied by the same stunned chord heard when Rick first saw her. In the troubled conversation that follows, "As Time Goes By" dominates, and a brief entrance of Laszlo's theme (49:45) foreshadows his role in the later stages of the story.

Figure 14.3 Rick drinks just before the Paris montage

Rick and Laszlo

A good portion of this segment takes place in a rival café, The Blue Parrot. Within these confines, we hear Arabian popular music in striking contrast to the sounds of Rick's Café Americain. One of the most compelling musical moments of the film takes place when Laszlo asks Rick for help (1:12:00). Downstairs, the German soldiers begin singing "Die Wacht am Rhein," and Laszlo responds by leading a rousing rendition of "Marseillaise." The two melodies are heard in counterpoint until the French tune overwhelms the German. At its conclusion, Major Strasser of the German Gestapo is convinced that Laszlo must die, a moment that is underscored by "Deutschland über Alles." From this point, Laszlo begins to take a more prominent role in the story. Similarly, his theme, heard at the end of this segment, becomes more pronounced as the plot moves to its climax.

Figure 14.4 Laszlo leads a stirring rendition of the "Marseillaise"

Climax and Resolution

"As Time Goes By" remains the dominant musical theme until the end of the film. When Laszlo and Ilsa talk about Paris, Ilsa suggests that she was lonely, and a single cello plays the Love theme. In Rick's apartment, Ilsa confronts Rick and the theme appears in the style and orchestration heard in the Paris montage, underlining the rekindling of their love. Subsequently, the Love theme appears at every new step in the plot—Laszlo's first arrest, when Rick is waiting for Captain Renault, at the arrival of Laszlo and Ilsa, and as Rick pulls a gun on Renault. Love is guiding every step of this climax. In the final farewell, Steiner gives yet another potent setting to "As Time Goes By," as the lovers make a sacrifice for the greater cause (1:36:10).

Although the love theme dominates the closing musical material, the patriotic melodies—Laszlo's theme and the "Marseillaise"—are given prominence. At the end, we are left with only the latter, as Rick and Renault go off to fight for Free France. The music here parallels the statement of the tune in the opening credits, but it is now given a firm and confident cadence.

Featured Film

Casablanca (1942)

Directed by Michael Curtiz
Music by Max Steiner

Principal Characters

Rick Blaine, disillusioned café owner (Humphrey Bogart)
Ilsa Laszlo, former lover of Rick (Ingrid Bergman)
Victor Laszlo, a leader of the underground fight against
    Germans (Paul Henreid)
Ugarte, a petty crook who has stolen two letters of
    transit (Peter Lorre)
Captain Renault, police captain in Casablanca (Claude Rains)
Major Strasser, head of Germans seeking Victor Laszlo (Conrad Veidt)

Principal Themes

Example 14.1 "As Time Goes By"/Love Theme

Example 14.2 Laszlo

Example 14.3 "Marseillaise"

Example 14.4 "Deutschland über Alles"

Other Popular Music Appearing in *Casablanca*

"It Had To Be You," Isham Jones and Gus Kahn (1924)

"Shine," Ford Dabney (1924)

"Knock on Wood," M. K. Jerome (1942—composed for the film)

"The Very Thought of You," Ray Noble (1934)

"Baby Face," Benny Davis and Harry Akst (1926)

"Love for Sale," Cole Porter (1930)

"Tango delle Rose," F. Schreirer, A. Bottero (1928)

"Avalon," Al Jolson, Vincent Rose, B. G. DeSylva (1920)

"Can't Help Loving That Man," Jerome Kern (1927)

"Perfidia," Alberto Dominguez (1922)

"You Must Have Been a Beautiful Baby," Harry Warren (1938)

Exposition

0:00–6:30; DVD Chapters 1–2 (chapter numbers are derived from Warner Home
    Video release of 2003)
[timings begin at the studio logo]

SCENE DESCRIPTION	MUSIC
Opening credits appear against a map of Africa and Arabia.	Following the logo fanfare, an Arabian theme reinforces the locale. A stirring statement of the "Marseillaise," coinciding with Steiner's name, ends on a sour chord, coinciding with Curtiz's name.
A narrator describes the fate of the refugees fleeing from France. We enter Casablanca.	Repeated dissonant chords suggest the weariness of travel. In Casablanca, a snake charmer's oboe is heard.

Following an announcement that two German couriers have been murdered, a montage shows a roundup of the usual suspects.	A phrase of "Deutschland über Alles" punctuates the announcement. Action music supports the roundup.
A man is detained and then shot as he tries to escape. He is holding a Free France flyer, and we see the French slogan over the Ministry of Justice.	The music sustains low pitches during the questioning and then springs into action as he runs. The "Marseillaise" is played sadly in minor as we see the symbols of Free France.
A pickpocket provides some humor.	A trombone slide reinforces the humor of the moment.
Refugees watch an incoming plane.	The refugee theme returns.
Major Heinrich Strasser meets Captain Louis Renault and is told that there will be an arrest tonight.	No music

Complications: Rick and Ugarte

6:30–25:20; DVD Chapters 3–9

SCENE DESCRIPTION	MUSIC
We enter Rick's café and see desperate people trying to get out of Casablanca. In the gambling room, we see some of the wealthy customers.	Sam sings "It Had To Be You," and the band continues to play the tune until we are taken into the gambling room.
Rick is working at a table. He refuses entrance to a German banker.	Music returns when the café door opens with the tune "Shine."
Ugarte talks to Rick and suggests that he has killed the German couriers. He gives Rick two valuable letters of transport for temporary safekeeping.	Music fades out when Ugarte begins to talk.
Rick hides the letters in Sam's stack of music. Ferrari, a rival club owner, enters.	Music returns as Sam and the band perform "Knock on Wood."
Ferrari tries to buy the café and Sam. Rick dismisses a former girlfriend and talks with Renault.	The piano continues with "The Very Thought of You," and the orchestra joins in to extend the tune.
Renault tells of the imminent arrest and of the arrival of a prominent freedom fighter, Victor Laszlo. Rick is warned not to interfere.	Sam plays "Baby Face." The music stops when they shut the door.

Strasser enters the café, Ugarte is arrested, and Strasser questions Rick.	The music stops when Ugarte begins shooting. Music returns for the interview, but fades when Rick advises the Germans not to invade New York.

Complications: Rick and Ilsa

25:20–51:00; DVD Chapters 10–17

SCENE DESCRIPTION	MUSIC
Victor Laszlo enters the café with his wife Ilsa. Sam is startled by her appearance. Laszlo speaks with both Renault and Strasser.	Sam plays "Love for Sale." The music stops when Strasser appears.
A freedom fighter informs Laszlo that his contact, Ugarte, has been arrested.	A singer with guitar performs "Tango delle Rose."
Ilsa asks Sam to come to her table, and then requests songs from the old days.	Sam plays "Avalon" initially, but finally sings "As Time Goes By."
Rick sees Ilsa. He joins Laszlo, Ilsa, and Renault for a drink. References are made to the Paris relationship. Laszlo and Ilsa leave.	After a stinger, "As Time Goes By" is played in the orchestra, dominating the remainder of this scene. At the mention of Germans, "Deutschland über Alles" is quoted.
After closing the café, Rick begins to drink heavily. He asks Sam to play "As Time Goes By."	At first Sam plays "Can't Help Loving That Man," but finally plays the love song.
In a flashback montage, we see the earlier relationship between Rick and Ilsa in Paris.	As Rick sinks into his memories, "As Time Goes By" is played in the orchestra. The "Marseillaise" announces our shift to Paris. A free fantasy based on the Love theme suggests the joy of their love. At a dance club, we hear "Perfidia."
The Germans are approaching Paris; the three friends drink champagne. The Germans are about to arrive, and Rick and Ilsa make plans to meet. They kiss as if it were the last time.	"Die Wacht am Rhein" is played with a dark and heavy character. Sam sings the Love theme at Le Belle Aurore, and the melody is picked up in the underscoring. "Deutschland über Alles" intrudes with the Germans.
Rick waits in the rain at the train station. Sam brings a note from Ilsa saying that she will not join him. He leaves without her.	The "Marseillaise" plays sadly as Parisian citizens gather to flee. "As Time Goes By" passionately underscores the reading of the note.

At the conclusion of the flashback, Ilsa enters Rick's place. She tries to explain what happened, but Rick insults her and she leaves.	Her entrance again brings an orchestral stinger. "As Time Goes By" dominates the underscoring. The Laszlo motive is heard when Ilsa refers to him.

Complications: Rick and Laszlo

51:00–1:15:30; DVD Chapters 18–24

SCENE DESCRIPTION	MUSIC
Laszlo and Ilsa meet with Renault and Strasser. Laszlo is threatened, and they learn that Ugarte is dead.	The "Marseillaise" announces our shift to the office of the Prefect of Police. No music is heard thereafter.
Rick is at the Blue Parrot. Outside, he sees Ilsa and apologizes. Ilsa joins Laszlo inside the Blue Parrot, as they seek a way out of Casablanca. Ferrari suggests that Rick might have the two letters of transit.	Exotic Arabian source music is heard in the Blue Parrot, a striking contrast to the popular American sounds in Rick's. Outside of the café, there is no music.
At Rick's, a brief scuffle breaks out with a German soldier. Rick talks to a young, recently married Bulgarian woman who is willing to sleep with Renault in order to get exit visas.	Sam, joined by band members, plays "You Must Have Been a Beautiful Baby." Music stops with the fight.
Laszlo and Ilsa enter, and Rick helps the Bulgarian couple win at the roulette wheel so that they can purchase the visas.	Music resumes as Sam plays "It Had To Be You" and then "As Time Goes By." No music is heard in the gambling room.
Renault is disappointed at the loss of a sexual encounter. Laszlo asks Rick for the letters of transit, but he refuses, saying only "Ask your wife."	Back in the bar, Sam plays "The Very Thought of You." No music is heard in Rick's room.
The Germans begin singing, but are drowned out when Laszlo leads a rousing "Marseillaise." Renault closes the café, and Strasser threatens Ilsa.	Steiner combines "Die Wacht am Rhein" with the "Marseillaise." "Deutschland über Alles" underscores Strasser's anger. At the end, we hear the Laszlo theme.

Climax and Resolution

1:15:30–1:42:30; DVD Chapters 25–32

SCENE DESCRIPTION	MUSIC
Laszlo and Ilsa talk about her relationship with Rick.	Laszlo's theme and "As Time Goes By" are used in the underscoring.
After Laszlo leaves, Ilsa confronts Rick and asks for the letters of transit. She pulls a gun, and they ultimately embrace.	The orchestral stinger returns when Rick sees Ilsa. "As Time Goes By" dominates the emotional underscoring, with a brief reference to Laszlo's theme.
Ilsa explains what happened in Paris and expresses a desire to stay with Rick. Laszlo enters the café and asks Rick to take his wife away from Casablanca. The police enter and arrest Laszlo.	No music is heard initially. "As Time Goes By" returns in the underscoring. The mood is broken as Laszlo enters, with his theme. The Love theme is played as Ilsa leaves, and the music fades. Dramatic music accompanies the entrance of the police, and the Love theme closes the scene.
Rick tells Renault that he is taking Ilsa out of Casablanca and has a plan to rid everyone of Laszlo. He sells his café to Ferrari.	Again, there is no music in Renault's office, and Arabian source music is heard at the Blue Parrot.
That night, set against the fog, Renault enters the café. Soon, Laszlo and Ilsa arrive.	The Love theme opens the scene, but fades with Renault's entrance. Both the Laszlo and Love themes are heard when the couple arrives.
Renault arrests Laszlo, but Rick pulls a gun on Renault. Renault calls Strasser.	The silence of the arrest is dramatically broken when Rick pulls the gun, accompanied by the Love theme. Fragments of "Deutschland über Alles" are heard with Strasser.
The three arrive at the airport, where Rick announces that Laszlo and Ilsa will leave together. Rick says goodbye to Ilsa.	No music is used as they arrive, but the Love theme passionately plays under the farewell scene. Laszlo's theme can also be heard.
After a crosscut to Strasser, Rick offers an explanation for Laszlo. The two leave for the plane.	A dramatic chord is heard with the crosscut, and then Laszlo's theme is played. The Love theme and Laszlo's theme continue.

| Strasser arrives and Rick shoots him. Renault tells the other police to round up the usual suspects in the murder of Strasser. | Dramatic chords are heard as Strasser uses the phone. When he is shot, a dissonant chord (with brass flutter-tonguing) signifies his death. "Deutschland über Alles" and "As Time Goes By" are combined again in counterpoint. |
| Renault and Rick watch the plane leave and then go off. | The "Marseillaise" triumphantly closes the film. |

Trailer

Casablanca is considered to be the finest product of the war years. Building on trends established in the 1930s, this film assimilated many of the qualities of Hollywood's Golden Age, including an outstanding musical score. In particular, Steiner's music is impressive for its ability to interweave popular music into a basic postromantic musical style. Although Steiner and other studio composers would continue to create film scores in the classic tradition for another decade, most of our attention in the next unit will be on the challenges to the traditional Hollywood sound, which became more pronounced after the close of World War II.

Important Names and Terms

Everybody Comes to Rick's
Vichy government
"Marseillaise"
"Deutschland über Alles"
Herman Hupfeld
"As Time Goes By"

Part 4

The Decline of the Hollywood Studio System, 1944–1959

15

Postwar Trends, 1944–1949

The years following World War II brought significant changes in filmmaking. The initial euphoria of victory and the return home of the American armed forces led to Hollywood's single most profitable year in 1946. But the troublesome prewar issues in the film industry did not vanish, and a dark cloud soon settled over Hollywood. A double blow was struck in 1948. Paramount lost an antitrust case and had to divest itself of its lucrative theater chain. In that same year, television established itself as a serious competing force with successful showings of the political conventions and the Rose Bowl football game.

Cynicism and pessimism became prominent themes in films, and the critically acclaimed films from the postwar years tended to deal with serious social issues. The themes of the Best Picture winners from 1945 to 1950 mark a strong departure from the sunny optimism of 1944's winner, *Going My Way* with Bing Crosby:

The Lost Weekend (1945): alcoholism

The Best Years of Our Lives (1946): difficulties of veterans

Gentleman's Agreement (1947): anti-Semitism

Hamlet (1948): Shakespeare's classic drama of indecision and murder

SIGNIFICANT FILMS

1944	*Laura* ★
	Double Indemnity ✉
1945	*The Lost Weekend* ★ ✉
	Spellbound ♫
1946	*The Best Years of Our Lives* ★ ♫
1947	*A Double Life* ♫
1948	*Hamlet* ★ ✉
	The Red Shoes ♫
1949	*The Heiress* ♫

All the King's Men (1949): the corruption and power of Huey Long
All About Eve (1950): intrigues on Broadway

Supporting these prevailing themes of anxiety and social problems was a correspondingly serious musical tone. Scores for films dealing with social issues created before the war often resorted to simple adaptations of American folk tunes like "Red River Valley" in Alfred Newman's score for *The Grapes of Wrath* (1940). In the postwar years, scores for films about social issues like *The Lost Weekend* and *The Best Years of Our Lives,* create a much more disturbing mood through increased dissonance, smaller instrumentation, and the avoidance of lyrical melodic material. In this chapter, we will focus on three important developments from the late 1940s: music composed for film noir, the appearance of several outstanding scores reflecting the American nationalist musical style, and the resurgence of European centers, which produced a number of significant films and scores.

Film Noir

Film noir is a significant movement in American filmmaking. The term, first employed by French film critics in 1946, designates both a style of filmmaking and a film genre. Viewed as a style, film noir is dark and pessimistic. The images are black and white with strong contrasts of light and dark, creating deep shadows. Clearly indebted to *Citizen Kane,* the style can be found in a variety of films, including the melodramatic *Mildred Pierce,* the psychological thriller *Spellbound,* and the study of alcoholism, *The Lost Weekend,* all from 1945.

The term can also be applied to a sub-category of the detective or crime genre. The typical film noir plot is modeled after detective stories from the 1930s by American novelists such as Dashiell Hammett and Raymond Chandler. These authors created an American detective who was distinct from his refined, cerebral English counterpart. The American detective was tough, pragmatic, not necessarily above flouting the law, and smart enough to resolve complicated cases with dogged determination and a strong jaw. Scenes often take place at night, frequently in a city with rain-slicked streets, and the stories contain multiple twists. Most of these films feature voice-over narration by one of the main characters. Women in film noir tend to be alluring, sexually active, and dangerous. Typically, the detective falls in love with the "dame," but he remains strong enough to kiss and tell, if she is guilty. The prototype of the genre is *The Maltese Falcon* (1941), but the movement clearly burst on the scene in 1944 with three classics: *Double Indemnity, Murder, My Sweet,* and *Laura.*

Arriving at the peak of Hollywood's Golden Age, film noir introduced disruptive elements that ran counter to the prevailing trends of Hollywood. New visual techniques challenged classical traditions, happy endings, in which the boy gets the girl and good triumphs over bad, were replaced with tragic and ambiguous conclusions, and disturbing musical sounds, previously reserved for horror films, underscored starkly realistic portrayals of life.

Music for film noir has a number of distinctive characteristics. The following are typical elements of a film noir score:

- one prevailing mood, generally dark and pessimistic
- minimal musical cues
- orchestration for small ensembles
- prominent low-pitched instruments, such as the bass clarinet
- emphasis on the lower registers of the strings
- use of a non-traditional orchestral sound, often a wavering pitch
- angular, disjunct melodies
- harsh dissonant harmonies
- the use of jazz, the musical sound of cities at night, as source music and sometimes underscoring

Just as the visual groundwork for the movement can be seen in films such as *Stranger on the Third Floor* (1940), *The Maltese Falcon* (1941), and *Citizen Kane* (1941), so too are the musical characteristics evident in the scores of these works and others by Roy Webb, Adolph Deutsch, Bernard Herrmann, Franz Waxman, and Hanns Eisler.

Laura

One of the most significant musical scores created for film noir is David Raksin's *Laura* (1944). The plot of this film has many of the traditional features of the genre, but the principal woman, Laura, is treated in a unique manner. Instead of portraying her sexual activity within a negative social stereotype, she is given the character of a modern, sophisticated woman. Essential to building her positive image is the music, which relies heavily on the idiom of popular music.

Director Otto Preminger originally wanted to use Duke Ellington's "Sophisticated Lady" as the principal theme song for *Laura*, but Raksin objected. Given the weekend to create a substitute, Raksin responded by composing the hauntingly beautiful Laura theme, one of the most popular melodies of the decade. The melody is stated in its most complete form during the opening credits, and the material is rich enough to provide virtually all of the musical material for the entire film. Like the music in many film noir stories, contrasts of mood are held to a minimum. But rather than creating an overriding mood of pessimism, the score projects an elegant, sophisticated music style appropriate for a modern woman.

Prior to this time, popular music had been relegated to musicals and comedies, or as source music in dramas. For the most part, popular music was associated with the sophisticated rich and the younger generation. These traditional roles can be observed in an early scene of *Laura*, in which Waldo narrates Laura's rise to prominence at a restaurant (15:15). In the moments where we see Waldo talking to Mark in the restaurant, Laura's theme is heard as source music played by a trio of musicians. But during the flashback montages, the underscoring picks up the tune and projects the image of a young woman rising through high society. The overall flow of the music as the story weaves in and out of the present is brilliantly seamless.

Figure 15.1 Mark's infatuation with the image of Laura is suggested by the music

In *Laura*, popular music extends beyond its typical functions and underscores dramatic moments as well, thereby opening the door for an expanded role for popular music in future films. Most striking is the scene in which Mark returns to Laura's apartment on a rainy night and becomes obsessed by the sense of her presence (41:20). Heard extensively in the underscoring, Laura's theme helps us understand that Mark has fallen in love with a dead woman. Raksin enhances the impression of Mark's irrational drunken state by manipulating the recording in order to introduce a wavering quality, a frequent film noir sound. This technique is particularly disturbing when a warbling piano plays Laura's theme (44:05). The music subsequently suggests Mark falling asleep and the passing of time; it will quietly disappear when Laura enters the apartment, very much alive—or is the rest of the film a dream?

Film Noir Scores by Miklós Rózsa

A leading figure in the creation of a film noir musical style is Miklós Rózsa. The Hungarian-born musician emerged in the 1940s as one of Hollywood's finest composers, earning much of his reputation for film noir scores, including *Double Indemnity* (1944) and *The Killers* (1946). The music for the earlier film can be heard as a model for the genre. It is dominated by a single dark theme, often heard in string tremolos or in the low woodwinds. Although Rózsa also includes a love theme, it is overwhelmed by darker tones. In one intriguing scene, Rózsa links the sound of film noir to Schubert's *Unfinished Symphony*, performed as source music by the Hollywood Bowl orchestra (1:26:45). Indeed, the symphony, an early Romantic masterpiece, shares a number of characteristics with film noir music, including the exploitation of the low register, a volatile emotional character, and harsh dissonances.

Rózsa also incorporated a film noir style into three major films dealing with psychological problems: *The Lost Weekend* (1945), *Spellbound* (1945), and *A Double Life* (1947). The first of these, starring Ray Milland, received an Oscar for Best Picture for its brutally realistic look at alcoholism. Hollywood, at that time, tended to glamorize drinking, but *The Lost Weekend* focused on the destructive consequences of alcohol addiction. In underscoring the irrational cravings of an alcoholic, Rózsa added an electronic instrument called the theremin to the orchestra. Its eerie wailings, in combi-

Miklós Rózsa (1907–1967)

Rózsa was born in Hungary and studied film composition in Germany. He came to Hollywood with Alexander Korda, the great Hungarian producer and director who was a major force in English films of the 1930s. One of Rózsa's earliest scores, *The Thief of Bagdad* (1940), created a great sensation, and his music for *The Jungle Book* (1942) became the first film score recorded and sold as a record album by RCA Victor. His use of modern musical sounds in film noir films of the 1940s helped usher in a new musical style. During the next decade, Rózsa would create his best-known works in a series of historical and religious films, headed by *Ben-Hur* (1959). In all, Rózsa received twelve Academy nominations and won three Oscars.

Important Film Scores

The Thief of Bagdad 1940 ✉
The Jungle Book 1940 ✉
Double Indemnity 1944 ✉
The Lost Weekend 1945 ★ ✉
Spellbound 1945 ♫
The Killers 1946 ✉

A Double Life 1947 ♫
Asphalt Jungle 1950
Quo Vadis 1951 ✉
Julius Caesar 1953
Ben-Hur 1959 ★ ♫
El Cid 1961 ✉ ✉

★ = Best Picture Oscar   ♫ = Best Music Oscar   ✉ = Music Oscar Nomination

nation with dissonances, are critical to the impact of the film, including the film's two most powerful moments. In one of these, Don Birnam, a writer, is trying to pawn his typewriter to get money for a drink, but finds that all the pawnshops are closed for Yom Kippur (1:03:50). In the other, Birnam has a delusion in which a mouse, eating through the wall, is devoured by a bat, causing the wall to ooze blood (1:24:30). Rózsa's creative effort earned an Oscar nomination, but the award went to his other outstanding score from 1945, *Spellbound.*

Like the score for *Double Indemnity*, the score for *Spellbound* features both a romantic love theme and a darker, more disturbing theme. But unlike the earlier film, love eventually triumphs in *Spellbound*, and the lush Love theme is omnipresent, perhaps to a fault. In one extended scene, we observe Constance (Ingrid Bergman) getting up in the night to look for a book (19:25). The Love theme is

Figure 15.2 Birnam's cravings for alcohol are suggested by the theremin

heard first in a solo cello, and it is repeated, building in intensity, for almost six minutes, until we finally see her in John's arms and erotic images of doors opening wide.

The mood of this scene is broken by one of John's psychotic spells, accompanied by the Dementia theme. Capturing the nightmare-like character of these spells, Rózsa includes the theremin in the orchestration. His eerie swoops and warbles effectively create a sense of the irrational state of John's mind. The theremin is heard when John sees lines (the tablecloth, the robe, the train tracks) and white (shaving cream, milk, snow). Most striking is the dream analysis scene, which combines Rózsa's disjointed music with a set design by the celebrated surrealistic artist Salvador Dalí (1:22:30).

Figure 15.3 A set designed by Salvador Dalí and music by Miklós Rózsa create a fitting mood for the nightmare dream sequence in *Spellbound*

Rózsa received his second Oscar for the score to *A Double Life* (1947). The movie can be seen as the combination of two popular trends of the late 1940s, Shakespeare films (*Hamlet* won the Best Picture Oscar in 1948) and film noir. Many of Shakespeare's plays are well suited for film noir effects, and *Othello* serves as the appropriate play within a play for this film. Instead of the theremin, Rózsa incorporates the instruments and styles of Renaissance music, often including a harpsichord. Renaissance music serves a dual purpose; the style suggests the time period of Shakespeare, and distorted versions of it underscore the actor's demented state. At one point, he is at a party observing a pianist, but we hear disturbing Renaissance music (44:30). Clearly, his stage life is impinging on his real life. Another effective element of the score is the adaptation of music by Gabrieli, a Venetian contemporary of Shakespeare, as source music for *Othello*, a play that opens in Venice. Rózsa's mixture of Renaissance and modern musical sounds matches the double life of the protagonist.

American Nationalism

A number of excellent film scores appeared in the late 1940s that reflect the musical style of American nationalism. Aaron Copland composed his last two film scores in 1949, and Hugo Friedhofer created a memorable score to one of the most highly acclaimed films in the postwar years, *The Best Years of Our Lives*.

The Best Years of Our Lives

The Best Years of Our Lives (1946) was the biggest box-office hit since *Gone With the Wind* and the winner of seven Oscars, including Best Picture and Best Scoring of a Dramatic Picture. Inspired by an article in *Time* magazine, *The Best Years of Our Lives* interweaves the stories of three veterans arriving home after the war. MacKinley Kantor, a future Pulitzer Prize winner, created a blank verse novel entitled *Glory for Me*, based on the articles, and screenwriter Robert E. Sherwood fashioned the story into a script for director William Wyler.

Figure 15.4 Homer uses his hand hooks to play "Chopsticks" with Hoagy Carmichael

While sharing the bond of a common war experience, the three veterans in the story come from different branches of the armed forces, are in different stages of relationships with women, and have different financial backgrounds. In addition, the youngest has had both hands amputated and replaced by mechanical hooks. Harold Russell, a real-life paratrooper who lost both hands in a grenade explosion, played the role of Homer Parrish. His ability to manipulate his hooks in such ordinary tasks as lighting a match and playing a "Chopsticks" duet with songwriter Hoagy Carmichael (2:09:50) is part of the film's fascination. For this role, Russell won two Oscars—Best Supporting Actor and a special award for bringing hope and courage to veterans. He is the only actor ever to win two Oscars for one role.

The music for *The Best Years of Our Lives* is by one of the quiet masters of film music—Hugo Friedhofer. His gift for orchestration is readily apparent in many passages, such as the music accompanying Fred's nightmare (50:40). The strength of his score, however, is in the overall mood, which is indebted to the style of Aaron Copland. Friedhofer assimilated many of the features of Copland's American nationalist style—melodies built on disjunct intervals, non-traditional harmonies, syncopated rhythms, and warm orchestrations—and applied them to a story about a troubled America. Rather than conjuring up nostalgia for an unspecified past, the music is applied to contemporary issues of veterans' adjustments, urban life, and changing values. Friedhofer's choice of style contributes a positive tone to the serious plot, which ultimately shows that all three men can overcome their difficulties through honest American values and, of course, the steadfast love of three women.

Each of the three principal characters has a theme associated with his individual story. Al Stephenson, an older army sergeant, returns home to his wife, two grown children, and a job at the bank. He has a serious drinking problem, but he is able to bring to his work a strong supportive voice on behalf of veterans. His primary theme, first heard on a solo cello as he approaches his front door (19:20), is "Among My Souvenirs," which we later hear as source music played by Hoagy Carmichael. In one humorous scene, the tune is heard in a variety of settings, including a military march, as a hungover Al wakes up in his house for the first time (1:01:30).

Fred Derry, a younger Air Force bombardier, returns to his bride, only to find her less than devoted. Friedhofer employs a Gershwinesque theme for Fred (55:00), which also suggests his wife's loose lifestyle. Ultimately she leaves him when he cannot find a decent job.

Hugo Friedhofer (1902–1981)

California-born Hugo Friedhofer, a former cellist in a silent film orchestra, worked in the 1930s as an orchestrator for other film composers, including Max Steiner (for whom he orchestrated over fifty scores), Erich Korngold, and Alfred Newman. In 1944 he began composing scores for Twentieth Century Fox, and he would eventually receive nine Oscar nominations, winning the award for *The Best Years of Our Lives*.

Important Film Scores

The Best Years of Our Lives 1946 ★ ♫   *Boy on a Dolphin* 1957 ✉

The Bishop's Wife 1947 ✉   *An Affair to Remember* 1957 ✉

Joan of Arc 1948 ✉   *The Young Lions* 1958 ✉

★ = Best Picture Oscar   ♫ = Best Music Oscar   ✉ = Music Oscar Nomination

---

Homer, the sailor who has lost his hands, has difficulty accepting the unconditional love of his girlfriend Wilma. While Homer does not have his own theme, Wilma has a sprightly tune first heard in the scene outlined in the Viewer Guide. Homer's little sister also has a brief theme, built on a children's tune similar to "It's raining, it's pouring."

While these three themes distinguish the three stories, a number of other themes link them together. The title theme is a strong melody presented initially with French horns, suggesting their common heroic background as veterans. This theme returns with each character at various times, including renditions played by English horn just before several major events.

The title theme spawns a number of related motives that are developed throughout the film, including the two identified in the Viewer Guide as Love and Memories. The Love motive, with its ascending octave, suggests both the warmth and strength of love. This theme is particularly prominent in scenes with Fred, a married man who falls in love with Al's daughter Peggy. The memory theme, generally heard over a descending accompaniment, resembles the opening of "Taps" and usually accompanies Homer's thoughts of the war.

Many of the above musical ideas are present in the scene in the Viewer Guide. In addition, two other prominent shared themes appear in that segment. The first half of the scene features a Boone City theme, which cackles with excitement as the veterans return to their home town of Boone City. The same motive is reused in other contexts latter in the film. The second melody, the Home theme, is initially heard as the cab approaches Homer's home. There it warmly mixes with Wilma's theme, but ends quietly as Homer waves goodbye to his friends.

The Best Years of Our Lives: Coming Home

Timing

Excerpt: 11:10–15:10 (0:00 at logo); DVD Chapters 3–5

Key Points

- American nationalist musical style
- Use of leitmotifs

Setting

Three veterans—Al Stephenson (Fredric March), Fred Derry (Dana Andrews), and Homer Parrish (Harold Russell)—return home from the war. Although they have just met on the bomber that is taking them to their hometown of Boone City, a close bond develops between them.

Principal Leitmotifs

Example 15.1 Title Theme: Best Years

Example 15.2 Boone City

Example 15.3 Love

Example 15.4 Memories

Example 15.5 Home

Example 15.6 Wilma

PLOT	MUSIC
Homer wakes up and sees the sunrise. He thinks about his past and future.	We hear in succession: the Love motive in imitation, the cadence of the Best Years theme, the Memories motive, and the Home theme.
All three veterans look through the bombardier's window at their hometown.	A trumpet plays the Boone City theme; quick, stuttering motion depicts their excitement about returning home.
Homer sees the high school football stadium.	The strings play the Boone City motive in legato style.
They fly over the airport and observe many now-obsolete Air Force planes.	Friedhofer mixes motives from the Boone City, Best Years, and Memory motives.
In a taxi, the three veterans see some familiar sights and the new world of postwar America.	The Boone City theme alternates between legato statements and fast, energetic passages.
The taxi arrives at Homer's street. Homer suggests that they all go out for a drink, but Al and Fred decline.	The strings gently play a variation of the Home theme. As Homer exits the taxi, the Home theme is played in its full form.
Homer's little sister sees him first and yells excitedly to her parents. She runs next door to tell Wilma.	Excited quick motives lead to a lyric statement of the Best Years theme as Homer embraces his sister.

Wilma runs to greet Homer, but as she joyfully hugs him, he does not put his arms around her.	Wilma's theme appears first in a solo violin and then is picked up by strings. The mood darkens a bit with Homer's stiffness.
Homer waves goodbye to Al and Fred, and the family becomes aware of his hook. The mother tries to hide her crying; Homer enters his house.	The Memory motive returns and mixes with the Home theme.

Aaron Copland

The figure most closely associated with American nationalism, Aaron Copland, composed his last two scores for films appearing in 1949—*The Red Pony* and *The Heiress*. Like his earlier films, both are based on well-known American literary works. John Steinbeck's *The Red Pony* contains four related stories about a boy coming of age on a California ranch. Originally written in 1937, the collection was expanded in 1945. The film is largely based on the story entitled "The Gift." For this film, Copland composed his most extensive film score and some of his most beloved music, frequently heard in a concert suite.

The Heiress contains considerably less music than *The Red Pony*. Still, the sparse but effective scoring for this compelling drama earned the composer his only Oscar. Based on the Henry James novel *Washington Square* (1881), *The Heiress* tells of a fortune seeker wooing a wealthy but unattractive spinster. Proving that his "western" sound is equally suitable for portraying life on the East Coast, Copland provides us with numerous cues that compliment the nostalgic vision of life in nineteenth-century New York.

For much of the film, the music remains somewhat detached emotionally, reflecting the moods of the father and of the mature Catherine. The romantic scenes in the first half of the film contain the only lyrical melodic material. Morris earnestly sings a nineteenth-century song "Plaisir d'amour" (26:00), and Copland uses the tune as a leitmotif for their early relationship. There is no original love theme. When we see them together, we either hear disjunct and largely unemotional music or a setting of the song, which carries a superficial connotation.

At the end of the film (1:41:35), Morris's declarations of love are appropriately devoid of musical support, signifying Catherine's cold and calculated response. After the door is bolted on Morris (1:52:50), the music builds to an intense climax. This musical ending is critical to the film's theme. Copland could have provided triumphant music, heralding Catherine's newfound assertiveness. There could also be a suggestion of humor or irony in this scene that parallels Catherine's disappointment at the door earlier in the film. Instead, the angular melodic line, the intense dissonances, and the slow pace create a cold, dispassionate conclusion. In the end, Catherine has achieved her father's goals of confidence and sound judgment, but she has also inherited his sense of cruelty. The final tragic mood belongs to both her and Morris.

Copland makes effective use of "Plaisir d'amour" (you may recognize it through a version of this song by Elvis Presley), but the film presented the tune one more time than he had intended. At the last moment, the producers replaced Copland's music for the opening credits with a rather insipid arrangement of the tune. Infuriated, Copland asked to have his name removed from the credits—the request was not honored—and he refused to accept his Oscar. This would be his last film score.

Close-Up: Producers and Directors

Great Names of the 1940s

Audiences are generally attracted to a film because of the featured stars. We see movies because of the presence of Denzel Washington, Tom Cruise, or Nicole Kidman. But sometimes, the producer and director can also attract an audience. Names such as George Lucas and Steven Spielberg have great appeal, and we approach their films with definite expectations as to content and quality. The same is true of the films from the 1940s. Indeed, some of the producers and directors achieved such prominence that they could work independently, without a contract with any single studio. The following list includes two independent producers and five major directors whose style and quality were well known to audiences.

David Selznick (1902–1965) began work at MGM as a script reader and rapidly rose through the ranks. Opinionated, he was fired even though he had married the daughter of Louis Mayer. He later worked for Paramount and RKO before returning to MGM as a producer to replace the ailing Thalberg. Later Selznick founded his own independent company and produced some of the great films of the era. Best known for *Gone With the Wind* (1939), which used three directors and fifteen screenwriters, he was also responsible for bringing Alfred Hitchcock to Hollywood, and they collaborated

on *Rebecca* (1940). Both of the above films won Academy Awards for Best Picture, the only time a producer has won that award in two consecutive years.

Samuel Goldwyn (1882–1974) married the sister of producer Jesse Lasky and together in 1913 they formed the Jesse L. Lasky Feature Play Company, which became Paramount Pictures. Later he founded his own company, but when the company merged with Metro Pictures, creating Metro-Goldwyn-Mayer (MGM), Goldwyn was shut out of the studio. He then became an independent producer, and films beginning with the words "Samuel Goldwyn Presents" soon earned a reputation for high quality. Among the major works produced by his company are *Wuthering Heights* (1939), *The Pride of the Yankees* (1942), *The Best Years of Our Lives* (1946), and *Guys and Dolls* (1955).

John Ford (1895–1973), the son of Irish immigrants, was born in Maine. He began working in Hollywood as a stunt double, and is said to be one of the Ku Klux Klan members on horseback in D. W. Griffith's *The Birth of a Nation*. Ford began directing films in 1917 and specialized in westerns. His later films are noted for their complex characters and populist subjects. His four Oscars, the most for any director, are for *The Informer* (1935), *The Grapes of Wrath* (1940), *How Green Was My Valley* (1941),

International Films

In Europe, the traditional film centers quickly began to rebuild their industries, and soon important films were produced in France, Italy, and England. French auteurs created a number of outstanding works in the postwar years. Particularly noteworthy is the collaboration of director Jean Cocteau with the composer Georges Auric, a member of the prestigious group of composers known as *Les Six*. Auric created evocative settings for two of Cocteau's masterpieces, the fairy story *Beauty and the Beast* (1946) and the updated Greek myth *Orphée* (1949).

and *The Quiet Man* (1952). He also remained a leading director of westerns, including such classics as *Stagecoach* (1939), *The Searchers* (1956), and *The Man Who Shot Liberty Valance* (1962).

William Wyler (1902–1981), a Swiss immigrant, began his film career as a publicity writer during the silent film era and worked his way up to directing for Universal Studios and later for Sam Goldwyn. Known for his fine craftsmanship and perfectionism, he received more Oscar nominations (twelve) than any other director and won Academy Awards for Best Director and Best Picture for *Mrs. Miniver* (1942), *The Best Years of Our Lives* (1946), and *Ben-Hur* (1959). He was trained as a violinist at the Paris Conservatory, and music often played a significant role in his films. During World War II, he enlisted in the Air Force and endeared himself to the American public for his filming of bombing raids.

Frank Capra (1897–1991) was born in Sicily and moved to California at the age of six. He received a degree in chemical engineering from the California Institute of Technology in 1918, and he tried several careers before he settled into filmmaking. He began making films for Columbia Pictures, and there he achieved his greatest successes that helped establish this studio. His best-known films were comedies in which an idealistic individual wins out against huge odds. He won Academy Awards for *It Happened One Night* (1934), *Mr. Deeds Goes to Town* (1936), and *You Can't Take It with You* (1938). Also much beloved are *Mr. Smith Goes to Washington* (1939), *Meet John Doe* (1941), and *It's a Wonderful Life* (1946).

Alfred Hitchcock (1899–1980) established himself as the foremost British director in the silent film era. Retaining the visual sense he developed in silent films, he gained a reputation in the United States with *The Man Who Knew Too Much* (1934) and *The 39 Steps* (1935). Hitchcock began directing films in America collaborating with Selznick on *Rebecca* (1940), for which he received his only Academy Award for Best Picture. He continued to produce popular thrillers, climaxing with *Rear Window* (1954), *Vertigo* (1958), *North by Northwest* (1959), *Psycho* (1960), and *The Birds* (1963). He became a household figure by producing a weekly television mystery series from 1955 to 1965.

Italy

Italian film began to reemerge in the late 1940s. Essentially dormant since 1913, Italy boldly asserted itself immediately following the end of the Nazi occupation. Roberto Rossellini's *Open City* (1945) lacks the finesse of Hollywood films, particularly in the use of music, but its gritty, realistic portrayal of Italian freedom fighters more than compensates. Rossellini daringly began shooting this film even as the Nazis were leaving Rome. Rejecting the happy endings of Hollywood plots, Italian filmmakers created a new style termed neorealism, characterized by visions of people, society, and situations as they really are, not as we would like them to be, often filmed outdoors. The most recognized film of this movement is Vittorio DeSica's *The Bicycle Thief* (1948). Focusing on ordinary people and using amateur actors, this simple story unfolds against the backdrop of postwar social problems. Alessandro Cicognini's music utilizes an operatic theme whose unchanging nature suggests the inability of Antonio to shape his own destiny.

England

By the end of the 1940s, a number of English-made films began to receive Hollywood recognition. *Henry V* (1946), *Great Expectations* (1947), *Hamlet* (1948), and *The Red Shoes* (1948) were all nominated for Best Picture Awards. Laurence Olivier adapted *Henry V* and *Hamlet* for film. *Hamlet*, for example, was reduced from a four-hour Shakespeare drama to a two-and-a-half-hour, black-and-white film. The action was filmed in a studio, not on a stage, and interior monologue sometimes replaced spoken soliloquies. *Hamlet* won the Oscar for Best Picture, becoming the first foreign film to win that coveted award. Hollywood was stunned, and the major studios threatened to pull out their support of the award ceremonies in the future. No British film was nominated for Best Picture in 1949, despite the appearance of *The Third Man*, considered by some to be England's greatest film. The haunting music in this film, played on the zither by Anton Karas, adds greatly to the film noir vision of decadent postwar Vienna.

British composers also began to receive American recognition in the 1940s. The scores to *Henry V* and *Hamlet* were created by William Walton, one of England's most renowned composers, and both received Academy nominations. In each, the music extends far beyond the supportive role of the source music found in stage productions. Walton assigns musical motives to characters and judiciously underscores some of the dialogue and soliloquies with appropriate music, including Hamlet's famous "To be or not to be" (1:02:40). One of the most fascinating scenes is the "play within the play." Walton scores the accompaniment to sound like Renaissance dance music, but effortlessly moves into orchestral underscoring when the King reacts to the stage depiction of his murderous deed (1:16:15).

Walton's brooding score did not win the award in 1948; it went instead to an energetic score for the ballet tale *The Red Shoes* by Walton's compatriot Brian Easdale (1909–1995). A composer of music for film, stage dramas, and opera, Easdale employed a contemporary musical idiom not unlike that of his countryman Benjamin Britten. Much of *The Red Shoes* is source music, as the story tells the tragic tale of two young rising stars, a composer and a ballerina. The film features dance scenes with excerpts from several traditional ballets and an extended performance of a new ballet entitled "The Red Shoes." Easdale's music for the new ballet successfully captures the idealistic, bold compositional style of a young composer and intensifies the strong emotions of the principal characters. Ballet stories, which were popular at this time in England, also influenced American films. In the 1950s, films such as *An American in Paris*, *Singin' in the Rain*, *Carousel*, and *Oklahoma* contained substantial ballet scenes.

Figure 15.5 The *Red Shoes* ballet

Trailer

By the end of the 1940s, the United States had turned from the certainty of moral victory at the end of World War II to the uncertainty of a rapidly changing world. Hollywood, with its production ranging from optimisic films created within the traditions of the Golden Age to dark films showing disturbing realistic subjects accompanied by new musical sounds, reflected the country's insecurities. The American film industry, like its European counterpart, would never be the same again, as both entered the turbulent and creative period of the 1950s.

Important Names and Terms

film noir	surrealism	Anton Karas
David Raksin	Hugo Friedhofer	William Walton
Miklós Rózsa	Georges Auric	Brian Easdale
theremin	neorealism	

Suggested Viewing

Film Noir: *Murder, My Sweet* (1944), *The Killers* (1946) ✉, *The Big Sleep* (1946), *Out of the Past* (1947), *The Lady from Shanghai* (1947), *Force of Evil* (1948), and *Champion* (1949).

Thriller/Adventure: *Notorious* (1946), *The Treasure of the Sierra Madre* (1948), and *Key Largo* (1948)

Drama: *Mildred Pierce* (1945), *It's a Wonderful Life* (1946), *Humoresque* (1946) ✉, and *Johnny Belinda* (1948) ✉

Romance: *The Ghost and Mrs. Muir* (1947) and *The Bishop's Wife* (1947) ✉

Western: *Red River* (1948) and *She Wore a Yellow Ribbon* (1949)

Musical: *Easter Parade* (1948)

16

Country, Rock, and All That Jazz, 1950–1956

For Hollywood, it was the worst of times. For film history, it may have been the best of times. In the 1950s, the American film industry, dealt major legal blows and facing fierce competition from television (see Close-Up on page 198), suffered from decreasing revenues and increasing costs. The grand old man of the studios, Louis B. Mayer, resigned from MGM in 1951; several studios began to sell their lots or convert to television production; and movie stars broke away from studio contracts. Like any other business, movie studios responded to these money woes by cutting expenses. By 1959, the average number of movies produced in Hollywood was around 250 a year, about one-half the level at the end of the 1940s. Production staffs were cut drastically. Adding to the Hollywood hysteria was the witch hunt of the House Un-American Activities Committee (HUAC—see Close-Up on page 212), which helped bring the industry to its lowest point.

American filmmakers faced these challenges and responded with a remarkable array of excellent films. The AFI includes twenty films from the 1950s on its list of America's Greatest One Hundred Movies, the most from any decade. And if one considers the tremendous production of classic films in international centers, headed by legendary directors such as Fellini (Italy), Bergman (Sweden), and Kurosawa (Japan), then the decade may indeed be seen as one of the finest in the history of filmmaking.

SIGNIFICANT FILMS

1951	*An American in Paris* ★ ♫
	A Streetcar Named Desire ✉
1952	*High Noon* ♫♫
	Singin' in the Rain ✉
1955	*The Man with the Golden Arm* ✉
	Blackboard Jungle

Close-Up: Television

"People will soon get tired of staring at a plywood box every night" —*Daryl Zanuck, 1946.*

Zanuck's prediction is fascinating for its classic miscalculation, shared by many in the film industry, and for its date (television had already been available publicly for almost ten years). The history of television can be traced back to the nineteenth-century, prior to the first public showing of films. Practical developments took longer than those in the film industry, but in 1927, the same year as *The Jazz Singer*, television images were sent from Washington DC to New York City, and Philo T. Farnsworth of the United States applied for a patent on his invention. By the next year, the first American home had a television set with a one-inch-square screen, and regular broadcasts had begun in the US. Experiments in broadcasting took place in both England and the US during the late 1920s and early 1930s. RCA set up 150 receivers in New York homes in 1936, and the first broadcast entertainment was the cartoon *Felix the Cat*.

Film's greatest year, 1939, was also a significant year for television: NBC began regular broadcasts for the East Coast; the first musical was shown—Gilbert and Sullivan's *The Pirates of Penzance*; and the first professional baseball game and the first college football games were televised. The war interrupted television's progress, but after the war, it moved at an accelerated pace. In 1948, the presidential conventions were shown, the Rose Bowl game was broadcast, and "Uncle Miltie"—Milton Berle—appeared for the first time. Television sets were set up in homes all over America. There were fewer than ten thousand television sets in 1945; by 1950 there were six million, and by 1960, sixty million. In 1951, broadcasts were finally shown coast-to-coast, and Lucille Ball began her astonishing reign as the queen of comedy. Within five years of Zanuck's reassuring prediction, the popularity of television was threatening to destroy the movie industry.

Figures 16.1–16.3 Television sets from different eras: (1) 1928, (2) 1939, and (3) 1950

The most significant development in film music during the 1950s is the expanding role of popular music. Hollywood quickly learned that popular music was less expensive than symphonic scores, attracted young audiences, and created additional revenue through sales of records. During the late 1940s and early 1950s, the number and variety of popular music styles began to increase rapidly. Newer forms of jazz, such as bebop, created a more agitated and disturbing mood than earlier jazz styles. Characterized by hard accents, rapid notes, and increased volume and intensity, these newer styles of jazz became associated with young hoodlums and the seedier aspects of life. Other important trends in popular music of the 1950s include country and western, ideal for westerns, and rock and roll, a natural for movies aimed at teenagers.

Changing Sounds of Jazz

Popular music has been part of the movie-going experience since the beginning of the silent film era. Jazz played a central role in the first talkie, *The Jazz Singer*, and the sounds of American and Latin American popular music can be heard in films throughout the 1930s and 1940s. For most of these films, popular music was restricted to incidental roles, such as the source music in *Casablanca*. But the role of popular music, and especially jazz, was expanded in a number of films inspired by film noir, such as *Laura* (1944) and *Champion* (1949). In the 1950s, several film composers continued to exploit the sounds of jazz, using the newer jazz styles to portray moods of sexual intensity and violence. The impact was often disturbing.

A Streetcar Named Desire

In using popular music of any type, whether waltzes, jazz, or rock, one has to deal with an inherent lack of contrast in mood. Hence, popular music as underscoring is most commonly heard in scenes without dialogue, such as montages. When popular music underscores dialogue and action, it often sustains a single mood that does not necessarily reflect the emotions of the characters.

Alex North uses these effects well in *A Streetcar Named Desire (1951)*, director Elia Kazan's adaptation of the classic Tennessee Williams play. The setting of New Orleans, the birthplace of jazz, allows North ample opportunity to include jazz as source music. Jazz naturally emanates from barrooms, restaurants, and the radio, providing a fitting atmosphere for this tale of lust, instability, and passion. The music often remains in the background, not directly connected to the intense dialogue or physical action.

Figure 16.4 Stella descends the stairs in a steamy scene accompanied by a saxophone

Jazz underscoring also suggests the sexually charged atmosphere of Stanley's house. The saxophone, which was rapidly becoming the standard instrument to depict an attractive female, now accompanies Marlon Brando in his many poses with a wet shirt or bare chest. The restrained but sultry music underlying Stanley's famous yelling of Stella's name, her slow descent on the staircase, and their embrace as she is carried off into the house provides a new, earthy dimension to the film love scene (40:15). Into this coarse world comes Blanche, who is often lost in her own world, as suggested by the more elegant and aristocratic popular music that she hears—the waltz. The clash of these two worlds and musical styles is symbolically depicted when Stanley grabs the radio, which had been playing a waltz, and throws it out the window (38:30).

When necessary, North subtly moves away from popular music in order to underscore moments of extreme emotions. The most powerful of these is Stanley's rape of

Composer Profile

Alex North (1910–1991)

American-born Alex North was the son of Russian parents. Trained at the Curtis Institute, Juilliard, and the Moscow Conservatory, he studied with Aaron Copland and began composing for theater and dance, receiving commissions from Martha Graham and Agnes de Mille. After the war, he wrote incidental music for the Broadway production of Arthur Miller's *Death of a Salesman*, which proved to be his gateway to Hollywood. When director Elia Kazan decided to convert *Death of a Salesman* into a movie in 1951, he asked North to provide the score. In that same year, Kazan again teamed with North in a filmed version of Tennessee Williams's *A Streetcar Named Desire*, and it is this score that caught the attention of Hollywood. The low point of his career was the decision by director Stanley Kubrick not to use any of the nearly fifty minutes of music that North had composed for *2001: A Space Odyssey* (1968). North has received fifteen Academy nominations and was awarded an honorary Lifetime Achievement Award in 1986.

Important Film Scores

Death of a Salesman 1951 ✉
A Streetcar Named Desire 1951 ✉
Spartacus 1960 ✉
Cleopatra 1963
Who's Afraid of Virginia Woolf? 1966 ✉
Under the Volcano 1984 ✉
GoodFellas 1990

★ = Best Picture Oscar   ♫ = Best Music Oscar   ✉ = Music Oscar Nomination

his sister-in-law while his wife is having a baby. The music begins innocently, as a quiet blues melody drifts down from the nearby tavern (1:42:00). But as the emotions begin to rise, North deftly changes to non-diegetic music. At the climactic moment (1:50:00), the music erupts, and ripping horn glissandos provide a substitute for the unheard screams of Blanche.

The Man with the Golden Arm

Elmer Bernstein, one of the great names of film music, created a stir with one of his first film scores, *The Man with the Golden Arm*. Recordings of music from the film became bestsellers, further cementing a permanent role for popular music in film. As in *A Streetcar Named Desire*, jazz elements in *The Man with the Golden Arm* stem from logical sources. The principal character, Frankie Machine (Frank Sinatra), has learned to play drums while rehabilitating from drug addiction and is seeking to make a living in the world of jazz. Jazz emanates naturally from numerous sources. Bernstein also employs traditional symphonic scoring, but the intense sounds of jazz, often with a prominent drum part, portray Frankie's cravings for drugs and illustrate the anguish of his final withdrawal (1:42:00). Once again Hollywood provided a happy ending, suggesting that all the protagonist really needed to kick his addiction was to meet the right woman.

High Noon

Dimitri Tiomkin, one of Hollywood's veteran composers, introduced a major innovation to film music when he included a country and western song in his landmark score to *High Noon* (1952). The ballad, released four months before the film, created a great sensation and quickly reached the top of the *Billboard* charts. Not only did record sales provide a new source of income, but every playing of the tune on the radio or phonograph served as free publicity for the movie as well. *High Noon* would become the first film to win Academy Awards for both dramatic scoring and song.

Theme songs quickly became a rage, preferably those whose titles were identical to the film. *Love Is a Many-Splendored Thing* repeated *High Noon*'s double Oscar in 1955, and popular new melodies appeared in numerous dramatic films, such as *The High and the Mighty*, *The Bridge on the River Kwai*, and *Around the World in Eighty Days*. Even Hitchcock's remake of the 1934 film *The Man Who Knew Too Much* (1956) was altered in order to include Doris Day's Oscar-winning hit song "Que Será, Será."

Considered by many to be Hollywood's greatest western, *High Noon* is a classic showdown between good and evil. The film lacks many of the standard features of westerns at this time; there are no Indians, no scenes of the wide-open west, and relatively little violence. The essence of the drama is not the showdown itself, but the tensions leading up to the climax. Will Kane, having just resigned as Marshal (thus becoming Citizen Kane) is leaving town with his Quaker bride. News arrives that

Frank Miller is coming with his gang at noon to take revenge against Will and retake control of the town. Part of the fascination with this film is that it is set in real time.

Will decides to stay and save the town; he expects his friends and the community to help him. But as time ticks towards noon, his wife, his ex-lover, his deputy, his friends, and virtually everyone in the town abandons him. Most compelling is the scene in the church, in which good Christians debate what to do. A number want to help, but they become resigned to inaction because the majority feels that the problem will disappear if nothing is done. The symbolic parallel to the attitudes of appeasement toward Hitler's Germany is clear, but the drama can also be seen as representing the silence of Hollywood during the onslaught of the Congressional hearings on Communism. The sacrificial death of one man was seen as a reasonable price for the security (not freedom) of their society.

Figure 16.5 Will and Amy wed with the ever-present clock in the background

Composer Profile

Dimitri Tiomkin (1894–1979)

Born in Russia, Tiomkin was trained at the St. Petersburg Conservatory of Music and played piano in Russian silent film theaters. He came to the United States in 1925 and performed on the vaudeville circuit. In 1928 he played the European premiere of George Gershwin's Piano Concerto in F, but a broken arm nearly ten years later ended his concert career. He began writing for Hollywood during the 1930s and became a dominant figure in the 1950s. He is one of Hollywood's most honored composers, with four Oscars and numerous nominations to his credit.

Important Film Scores

Lost Horizon 1937 ✉
You Can't Take It with You 1938 ★
Mr. Smith Goes to Washington 1939 ✉
Meet John Doe 1941
It's a Wonderful Life 1946
High Noon 1952 ♫ ♫
The High and the Mighty 1954 ♫ ✉

Dial M for Murder 1954
Giant 1956 ✉
The Old Man and the Sea 1958 ♫
The Alamo 1960 ✉ ✉
The Guns of Navarone 1961 ✉
Town Without Pity 1961 ✉
55 Days at Peking 1963 ✉ ✉

★ = Best Picture Oscar   ♫ = Best Music Oscar   ✉ = Music Oscar Nomination

The Ballad

The score for *High Noon* centers on Tiomkin's ballad "Do Not Forsake Me," sung by the well-known country and western singer Tex Ritter. During the opening credits, instead of the standard orchestral introduction, Tiomkin presents the ballad, which oddly appears to be too short. This is the only time that the tune is heard in its entirety. The apparent simplicity of the ballad is deceptive. Tiomkin offsets the standard quadruple meter of country and western music with a three-four measure during the first phrase and a two-four measure in the second. While the tune still continues to flow smoothly, these metric alterations prevent it from sounding too square or predictable. The tune itself is an A-B-A structure. The distinctive parts are the opening, with the words: "Do not forsake me, oh my darlin'," the middle contrasting phrase, and the closing cadence with the words: "till I shoot Frank Miller dead."

The ballad is not restricted to the opening credits. During the film, Ritter's voice sings parts of the ballad seven times. The sound of the solo voice with its sparse accompaniment serves as a constant reminder of Will Kane's isolation. Each entrance of the voice coincides with a vision of the marshal being abandoned, beginning with his wife's departure. Only in the final moment, after his wife has courageously given up her religious convictions to help save her husband, do we see Will and Amy together during the song. Eschewing the typical Hollywood ending, the quiet fading of the song as the two ride out of town reinforces the seriousness of the drama.

Tiomkin's ballad is well integrated into the orchestral underscoring. There are four principal themes in the film, two of which are derived from the song. Will and Amy's theme is taken from the first phrase. For Frank Miller and his gang, Tiomkin uses the middle portion of the tune, with its repetitive, menacing character. Helen has an independent theme with a strong Spanish flavor. Perhaps the most interesting motive is also the simplest, the ticking motive for the clock. The drama is set against the tension created by the passing of time. Clocks are conspicuous in the background of many of the interior shots, and the frequent close-ups of clocks are accompanied by Tiomkin's pulsating motive.

Final Moments Before Noon

The finest musical moment in the film occurs just before the climax (see Viewer Guide on p. 204). During the last two minutes before noon, Kane writes out his last will and testament. A montage, showing us the variety of characters in the drama, is synchronized with the music; the images change every one or two measures. Thirty measures, occupying 120 seconds, tighten the tension with the incessant ticking pulse and Frank's menacing motive. The mounting intensity peaks as we look at the chair where the convicted Frank Miller vowed to take revenge, and the shrill whistle of the arriving train diverts us from the climax.

The silence that follows is unsettling. Once Will walks into the street, the audience expects to hear Tex Ritter's voice again, but there is no sound. Finally breaking the silence is the noise of the wagon taking Amy and Helen to the train station. Will's isolation is complete. After showing Frank's arrival, the film returns to Will's image in a remarkable shot. Pulling backwards and upwards, the camera reveals Will standing alone in an empty town. Tiomkin underscores the eeriness of the solitary figure with a colorful setting of the Will and Amy motive, complete with string harmonics, piano, and bells.

Tiomkin effectively captures the menacing character of Frank Miller and his gang in a march that precedes the initial confrontation. The pounding piano, low brass, and percussion evoke the sound of Shostakovich, the prominent composer from Tiomkin's native country. Following the shooting of Ben Miller, Tiomkin reprises the Will and Amy motive as Amy leaves the train. By now, the audience associates this theme with the words "Do not forsake me, oh my darlin'," and the motive builds anxiously as Amy runs to rejoin her husband. Mixed into the background is a musical suggestion of the departing train heard in the accelerating snare drum.

Viewer Guide

High Noon: Final Moments Before Noon

Timing

Excerpt: 1:08–1:17:00 (0:00 at logo); DVD Chapters 19–22

Key Points

- Ticking motive creates tension during the montage
- Leitmotifs are drawn from the theme song
- Orchestra underscores tension and action
- Silence suggests Will's isolation
- Colorful orchestrations

Setting

Will Kane (Gary Cooper) has unsuccessfully tried to obtain help from his friends and other townspeople in order to fight Frank Miller and his gang, who will arrive at noon. Even his bride (Grace Kelly) is going to the train station with Helen, Kane's ex-girlfriend, in order to leave town at noon. Realizing that he will likely be killed in the ensuing battle, Kane draws up a last will and testament.

Principal Leitmotifs

Example 16.1 Will and Amy

Example 16.2 Frank Miller

Example 16.3 Helen

PLOT	MUSIC
Will begins writing.	No music; ticking from the clock.
Will looks at the clock at two minutes before noon. A montage shows the clock, the train, the church, the saloon, the empty town, individuals, and finally Frank's chair.	The musical pulse is sustained throughout, synchronized with the clock's pendulum. Frank's motive is heard repeatedly, and the music grows in volume and dissonance until the train whistle is heard.
Will finishes, releases a prisoner, and goes outside. He stands alone and watches Amy and Helen go to the train station on a wagon.	No music.
Frank arrives and meets his gang. He sees Helen leaving. Putting on his gun, he leads his gang towards town.	Music returns with: "Let's get started then." The low brass help establish a menacing mood. Frank's motive appears and mixes briefly with Helen's.
Will stands waiting, and a tracking shot shows his complete isolation.	An eerie setting of Will and Amy's motive, accompanied by the piano and string harmonics, creates a foreboding mood.
The adversaries march toward their inevitable encounter.	A cymbal crash breaks the mood, and a menacing march ensues with a pounding pulse in the piano.
Ben Miller smashes a window, alerting Will to their presence. Will hides until they pass, calls to them, and shoots Ben Miller. The fight has begun.	The music suddenly becomes quieter, suggesting Will's hiding. Just before the fight both of the principal motives are heard.
Amy hears the gun shot and runs from the train. She sees a dead body in the street and is relieved that it is not Will's.	After a brief statement of Frank's motive, Will and Amy's theme is played with great urgency. Tiomkin also mixes in the sound of the departing train in the snare drums. Tension builds with the return of Frank's motive as Amy sees the body, but releases when she sees that it is not her husband.

Rock and Roll

The history of rock and roll begins in 1955 when Bill Haley's "Rock Around the Clock" became the first rock tune to top *Billboard*'s hit chart, a position that it maintained for eight weeks. *Billboard* is a trade magazine founded in 1894, and it began publishing its "Music Popularity Chart" in 1940 with its first number one song, Frank Sinatra's "I'll Never Smile Again." The dominant performers through the next fifteen years included Bing Crosby, Perry Como, Patti Page, and the Andrews Sisters. But after 1955, rock music was king. By the end of the decade, the foundations of classic rock had been laid by a number of legendary performers, including Elvis Presley, Chuck Berry, Jerry Lee Lewis, Roy Orbison, Fats Domino, and Little Richard.

Blackboard Jungle

The rock phenomenon was fueled in part by Hollywood movies. "Rock Around the Clock" was released in 1954 with only moderate success. It was propelled to the top of the charts when it appeared in *The Blackboard Jungle* (1955), a film that deals with juvenile delinquency in a high school. Haley's rendition of the song is heard only during the opening and closing credits, but the melody also appears in the underscoring during a savage attack on two teachers by teenage hoodlums (36:15). For adults, the association of rock music with rebellious youth was clear, but teenagers quickly adopted this exciting new kind of music.

Hollywood saw the financial potential of the new genre, and turned to rock music to lure younger audiences to the movies. Stars of rock and roll, both white and black, soon appeared on the screen. Two films filled with rock came out in 1956. Fats Domino, The Platters, and Little Richard perform in *The Girl Can't Help It*, in which curvaceous Jayne Mansfield squeaks out "Rock Around the Rock Pile." Columbia Pictures' *Rock Around the Clock* features not only Bill Haley and the Comets, but also the Platters and Freddy Bell and His Bellboys. By the end of the 1950s, a rebellious young rock star had also become a movie star. *Love Me Tender* (1956), *Jailhouse Rock* (1957), and too many others brought Hollywood stardom to Elvis Presley.

Musicals

Entering the 1950s, Hollywood, and specifically MGM under the leadership of Arthur Freed, continued to produce a large number of elaborate, high-quality musicals. Although the number would diminish towards the end of the decade, the golden age of Hollywood musicals would extend into the 1960s. Stage adaptations are the most common type of musical in the 1950s, but the three most highly acclaimed musicals of the decade are original productions: *An American in Paris* (1951), *Singin' in the Rain* (1952), and *Gigi* (1958).

An American in Paris contains a dazzling score by George Gershwin that features several previously composed songs by Gershwin and excerpts from his 1928 symphonic poem, *An American in Paris*. The musical highlights of the film include several extended dancing sequences and a performance of the third movement of Gershwin's Piano Concerto in F (1:05:30), with a day-dreaming Oscar Levant humorously playing the piano solo, conducting the orchestra, playing violin and percussion, and also leading the bravos at the end. *An American in Paris* became only the second musical to win an Academy Award for Best Picture; *Broadway Melody* (1929) was the first, and seven years later, *Gigi* would become the third.

Singin' in the Rain

Although receiving relatively little Academy recognition, *Singin' in the Rain* (1952) is the best musical of the decade and one of the all-time great American films. The impetus for the film came from producer Arthur Freed. Having just completed a catalogue of songs in MGM's collection that were composed by Nacio Herb Brown with lyrics by himself, Freed asked writers Adolph Green and Betty Comden to create a movie using these tunes from ten or twenty years ago. The result is a humorous tale of Hollywood during the transition from the silent film era to sound. Not only are the situations based on actual problems faced during this time, such as microphone placement, ridiculous dialogue, and soundproof booths for the camera, but also specific silent film scenes are mimicked, and the characters of Roscoe Dexter and R. F. Simpson are modeled after Busby Berkeley and Arthur Freed.

Musical numbers account for well over half of this 103-minute film. Nacio Herb Brown composed most of the songs during the late 1920s and 30s. Several of them, such as the title song, appeared in multiple films prior to *Singin' in the Rain*. Dancing

Figure 16.6 Gene Kelly sings and dances in *Singin' in the Rain*

sequences extend many of the songs. Donald O'Connor's "Make 'em Laugh" (27:40) and Kelly's "Singin' in the Rain" (1:07:50) are justifiably listed among the greatest dance routines in all of film, and "Good Morning, Good Morning" features an energized romp by the trio of stars (1:01:45). A relatively brief *pas de deux* follows "You Were Meant for Me" (44:15), but the dancing highlight is the thirteen-minute "Gotta Dance" segment (1:15:30). This complete interruption of the story, highlighted by a *grand pas de deux* featuring Gene Kelly and Cyd Charisse, is a remarkable artistic achievement. Unheralded in most discussions of this film is the excellent orchestral score by Lennie Hayton.

The Disney Renaissance

The Disney studios, which had taken a break from animated features during the war, created another remarkable series of great animation films beginning in 1950 with *Cinderella*. In keeping with the Disney tradition, music plays an important part in *Cinderella*, and it

Table 16.1

Major Disney animated features from the 1950s

YEAR	ANIMATED FEATURE	COMPOSER	SCORE	SONG
1950	*Cinderella*	Oliver Wallace and Paul Smith	✉	✉
1951	*Alice in Wonderland*	Wallace	✉	
1953	*Peter Pan*	Wallace		
1955	*Lady and the Tramp*	Wallace		
1959	*Sleeping Beauty*	George Bruns	✉	

received two Academy nominations—for Best Scoring of a Musical Picture and Best Song ("Bibbidi-Bobbidi-Boo"). As shown in Table 16.1, Disney continued to create outstanding animated features throughout the decade. The musical highlights of this series are the song-filled *Alice in Wonderland* and *Sleeping Beauty*, with substantial music adapted from Tchaikovsky's ballet.

Trailer

The early 1950s witnessed a rapid change in the sounds of popular music. At that time, the dominance of jazz styles was challenged by the skyrocketing popularity of rock and roll. Film music benefited greatly from this expanding array of musical styles. Musicals tended to retain the popular styles of earlier decades, but a significant number of other films began to incorporate the new styles of popular music, both as source music and underscoring.

Important Names and Terms

Alex North
Tex Ritter
Elmer Bernstein
rock and roll

Billboard
Arthur Freed
Lennie Hayton

Suggested Viewing

Drama: *Greatest Show on Earth* (1952) ★, *From Here to Eternity* (1953) ★, *Wild One* (1954), *Picnic* (1955) ✉, and *Baby Doll* (1956)
Romance: *Quiet Man* (1952), *Lili* (1953) ♫, *Love Is a Many-Splendored Thing* (1955) ♫ ♫, and *Love in the Afternoon* (1957)
Western: *Rio Grande* (1950) and *Shane* (1953)
Musical: *Gigi* (1958) ★ ♫ ♫

17

Expanding Modern Styles, 1950–1956

The serious tone of American films in the 1940s was often supported by music that incorporated elements of modern musical styles. The disturbing musical qualities heard in films such as *Citizen Kane* continued to support film noir stories through the 1950s, until the musical style, like the genre itself, was eventually assimilated into the new American cinema of the 1960s. The other two major trends in modern scores of the 1940s—American nationalism and expressionism—would continue to exert influence in the 1950s, but expressionism would give way to the new modern voices of avant-garde music.

SIGNIFICANT FILMS

1950	*Sunset Blvd.* ♫
	La Ronde
	Rashômon
1951	*A Place in the Sun* ♫
	The Day the Earth Stood Still
1954	*On the Waterfront* ★ ♫
	Seven Samurai
1955	*East of Eden*
	Rebel Without a Cause
1956	*Forbidden Planet*

Film Noir

Franz Waxman entered the 1950s as one of Hollywood's most respected composers, with over fifteen years of studio experience and six Academy nominations. In the early 1950s, he finally was recognized with back-to-back Oscars for *Sunset Blvd.* (1950) and *A Place in the Sun* (1951). Calling upon his experience with dark stories such as *Rebecca* (1940), Waxman employed an effective film noir style in both these films.

Sunset Blvd.

Like *Spellbound*, *The Lost Weekend*, and *A Double Life*, *Sunset Blvd.* is a story about dementia. In addition to the visual aspects of film noir, it contains several links to the detective genre, including extended night scenes and the use of a narrator—the murder victim, Joe Gillis. A biting satire about Hollywood, the story centers on an aging former silent film star, Norma Desmond, played by real-life silent film star Gloria Swanson. Supported by other Hollywood film figures, such as actor/director Erich von Stroheim, director Cecil B. DeMille, comedian Buster Keaton, and Hollywood reporter Hedda Hopper, *Sunset Blvd.* presents a harsh view of the fleeting, seductive, and all-consuming nature of fame.

Figure 17.1 Music in the style of Richard Strauss accompanies Norma's descent of the staircase in *Sunset Blvd.*

At age fifty, Norma Desmond decides to make a comeback playing Salome. Although some may wish to argue that the age of fifty is hardly over-the-hill, the filmmakers have turned Norma into a rather grotesque caricature. Waxman helps us feel the absurdity of her delusional self-image by frequently assigning her a sultry saxophone solo that contradicts her physical and mental condition. In the original biblical story, Salome is a beautiful young woman, renowned for her alluring Dance of the Seven Veils. For musicians, the most famous retelling of this story is the expressionistic opera by Richard Strauss (1905), which is based on an Oscar Wilde play from 1893. In the opera, Salome's dementia plays a pivotal role. After having John the Baptist beheaded for spurning her advances, she dances with and erotically kisses the Prophet's severed head on a silver platter, before being crushed by soldiers. While not as gruesome as the opera, the plot of *Sunset Blvd.*, in which insanity drives a woman to murder, has some obvious parallels.

In maintaining the aura of Norma's delusion, Waxman does not assign her a rational theme, but instead gives her an exotic Salome theme. When the theme is first heard in the opening credits, it is set against a percussion accompaniment that is reminiscent of Strauss's music for the Dance of the Seven Veils. The Salome theme dominates the film, just as Norma controls everything in her world. It is heard in the low woodwinds when she first appears (13:40), and a saxophone plays the theme when Joe, the reporter, recognizes her (16:30).

Two of the more striking appearances of the Salome theme are related to Desmond's comeback. When she is on the set, a lighting man shines a spotlight on her, and the actors and crew gather around in admiration (1:09:15). This should be a moment to bask in, but her theme remains subdued, accompanied only by an odd vibrating sound. The disquieting music suggests that she is unable to grasp reality, even at a moment of potential triumph. Later, a montage shows her preparing for the comeback with a series of beauty treatments, and a lyric statement of her theme is presented in counterpoint with a frantic, scurrying violin line (1:16:20). At the end of the film, her theme returns in a full orchestration in the style of Strauss, as she makes her final descent down the staircase (1:16:20).

Another significant musical idea borrowed from Richard Strauss is a simple trill, a quick oscillation between two pitches. In the opera, the trill signifies Salome's insanity, a detail that Waxman does not overlook. Linking the trill with the film noir cliché of a wavering pitch, Waxman frequently employs an oscillating sound in the score to signify Norma's insanity. In one scene, the sound is attributed to the wind blowing through the pipes of an organ (18:20). The trill subtly becomes more pronounced in the film leading to the final scene, when Norma hears that the cameras have arrived. In a direct quote from the opera, a trill begins in the woodwinds, signaling Norma's complete descent into her fantasy world (1:45:45).

A Place in the Sun

Sunset Blvd. presents a typical film noir story, in which the two leading figures are trapped: Norma Desmond by her dementia, and Joe Gillis by his dependence on Norma and her mansion. A similar quality characterizes *A Place in the Sun* (1951). George Eastman (Montgomery Clift), a young man eager to find a place in the sun, finally breaks through formidable social barriers when the wealthy socialite Angela (Elizabeth Taylor) falls in love with him. Unfortunately, George is trapped by a previous relationship with Alice Tripp (Shelley Winters), a worker on the factory assembly line, and the consequences are tragic.

In projecting the relationship between George and Angela, Waxman provides a versatile love theme that can be played passionately by the orchestral strings or in a sultry manner by a solo saxophone. The steamy nature of the latter setting, in combination with Liz Taylor's close-ups, creates a mood of passion and desire. Unfortunately, director George Stevens objected to what he considered to be the overuse of jazz and had Victor Young and Daniele Amfitheatrof rewrite a significant portion of Waxman's score.

Figure 17.2 Waxman turns to a film noir style for the scene at the lake in *A Place in the Sun*

The mood of the film alters dramatically when a doctor denies Alice's request for an abortion (44:10). Emphasizing the shamefulness of the situation, the doctor's visit takes place at night, and the figures remain in dark night shadows as George drives her home. Alone in his apartment, George begins to contemplate murdering Alice, prompted by a radio newscast (50:55). In portraying George's dark thoughts, Waxman introduces film noir elements, including strong dissonances and colorful orchestration. Most compelling is a pulsing heartbeat that builds tension as George is lost in his thoughts.

The film noir style reappears when George begins to carry out his sinister plan. Knowing that Alice cannot swim, he takes her out on a rowboat to the middle of a lake. As the lake darkens, the pulse returns (1:09:00). George eventually decides he cannot commit the murder, but as passions rise and the musical pulse quickens, Alice falls and drowns. The scene is similar to one in Murnau's *Sunrise* (1927), an important ancestor of film noir (see Chapter 9). The dark musical style makes a final appearance when George takes flight in order to escape the police, underscored by a fugal passage played in the lower register of the strings (1:33:35).

Close-Up: Blacklisting

Hollywood Under Attack

One of the darkest moments for Hollywood was the investigation by the House Un-American Activities Committee (HUAC) into Communist influence in the American film industry. Following World War II, the United States found itself thrust into the Cold War with the Soviet Union. Having paid the price of Europe's failed appeasement policies with Germany prior to the war, the United States was not about to appease Communism. Communism, which had been a viable political stance in the United States before the war, was now seen as subversive. While the rhetoric of the committee may have sounded patriotic, it allowed the political extreme right to punish and intimidate a Hollywood that, although clearly not Communistic, did have leftist tendencies.

The hearings were held in two phases, beginning in 1947 and 1951. The initial hearings called a number of witnesses. Friendly witnesses, such as Louis B. Mayer, Gary Cooper (*High Noon*), and Ronald Reagan (the head of the Screen Actors Guild), were not under suspicion and were treated with respect. The HUAC also called eleven unfriendly witnesses. One of these was the German playwright Bertolt Brecht, known for his works such as *Threepenny Opera* (1927) and *Mother Courage and Her Children* (1939). Brecht had contributed to the script of *Hangmen Also Die* (1943) and was involved in a number of other productions. He quietly left the country and returned to East Germany.

The remaining unfriendly witnesses, known as the Hollywood Ten, refused to answer questions and pleaded the Fifth Amendment. By today's standards, this position would have been sufficient for their defense, but almost all of the Hollywood Ten spent six to twelve months in prison and were prevented from returning to work.

In 1951, the HUAC continued its investigation, primarily targeting screenwriters. Those who were labeled Communists were denied work or blacklisted in Hollywood. Some worked under pseudonyms, but most had their careers ruined. Among those who were investigated are the following:

John Garfield: Garfield was a major Hollywood star. Having appeared in many films, including *Gentleman's Agreement* (1947) and *Force of Evil* (1949), he was a large public target for the investigation. He refused to cooperate and was blacklisted. He died of a heart attack in 1952; his family blamed his death on the stress caused by the HUAC.

Charlie Chaplin: Chaplin was out of the country during the hearings. He was labeled a Communist and not allowed to reenter the United States until 1972.

American Nationalism

The American nationalist style is most closely associated with the concert music and film scores of Aaron Copland and with Hugo Friedhofer's masterful score to *The Best Years of Our Lives* (1945). Although Copland completed his last narrative film score in 1949, elements of his style continue to appear in the works of other film composers up to the present time. As in the 1940s, American nationalism in the 1950s is primarily associated with American stories, such as those set in small towns or in the old west.

Elia Kazan: Kazan was a director whose films, such as *A Streetcar Named Desire* and *Rebel Without a Cause,* had a great impact on Hollywood. Kazan agreed with the purposes of the HUAC, and in a controversial decision named other Communists in the industry. His film *On the Waterfront* can be viewed as a defense of his testimony. His position in Hollywood history is still debated.

Clifford Odets: Odets is one of America's finest playwrights. Although his plays often contained leftist tendencies, he was eventually cooperative and was not accused of being a Communist. He continued to work in Hollywood throughout the 1950s.

Lionel Stander: Stander was a character actor in Hollywood when he was brought before the committee. He was defiant—when asked if he knew of anyone engaged in un-American activities in Hollywood, he replied "Only the members of the HUAC." He later worked in Europe, appearing in a number of spaghetti westerns. He eventually returned to America, where he endeared himself to America in the role of the chauffeur in the television series *Hart to Hart.*

Sam Jaffe: Jaffe, who had appeared in movies such as *Lost Horizon* (1937) and *Gunga Din* (1939), was nominated for Best Actor in 1950 for his role in *The Asphalt Jungle* (1950). He was blacklisted and spent many years teaching mathematics in high school. Only later did he return to acting in roles such as Dr. Zorba on the *Ben Casey* television series.

Lee Grant: Grant was blacklisted for not testifying against her husband, screenwriter Arnold Manoff. She later returned to acting and received both an Oscar and an Emmy.

Musicians were not an important target for the committee. Yip Harburg, the lyricist for *Wizard of Oz* ("Over the Rainbow") and such popular songs as "Brother, Can You Spare a Dime?", "It's Only a Paper Moon," and "Lydia, the Tattooed Lady," was blacklisted and given only menial work thereafter. Composers Hanns Eisler, Sol Kaplan, and George Bassmann were blacklisted, and their Hollywood careers ended. Jerry Field, also blacklisted, later returned to score *Advise and Consent* (1962), *The Wild Bunch* (1969), and the television series *Barnaby Jones.* Both Elmer Bernstein and Alex North, who had strong leftist connections, were "graylisted," meaning that their careers were slowed but not halted. Two hundred and twelve of the 324 names on the blacklist were still actively working in Hollywood at that time; most of them would soon lose their jobs.

Leonard Bernstein

American nationalism was a strong force in the music of Leonard Bernstein (no relation to Elmer Bernstein). One of the great figures of American music, Leonard Bernstein is better known outside the world of film music. Leonard's immense popularity, flamboyance, and talent allowed him to develop three separate musical careers as a concert pianist, conductor, and composer. As a conductor, he was the much-beloved leader of the New York Philharmonic, and he later conducted the Vienna Philharmonic. His crowning moment may be the monumental performance of Beethoven's Ninth Symphony in Berlin, celebrating the fall of the Berlin Wall. As a composer, he is best remembered for *West Side Story*, which was adapted for film in 1961. He composed his only original film score, for *On the Waterfront* (1954), which has become recognized as one of America's greatest movies.

On the Waterfront

Inspired by a Pulitzer Prize–winning newspaper series entitled "Crime on the Waterfront," Elia Kazan's *On the Waterfront* deals with graft and mob influence on the Longshoremen's Union. Filmed on location in Hoboken, New Jersey, the plot focuses on the heroic efforts of Terry Malloy (Marlon Brando) to confront corruption. Malloy is not a courageous figure like Marshal Kane from *High Noon* (1952). Rather, he is portrayed as a dimwitted ex-boxer, who fulfills a small role in the organization. In the opening scene, he discovers that he has helped set up the murder of his friend Joey. The film deals with his transformation, and his redemption through a woman's love.

Bernstein supports the realism of the film with a stark, disturbing score. He incorporates aspects of Copland's style, including disjunct melodies and an emphasis on small, colorful musical ensembles. Two features, however, distinguish his sound from that of Copland. Bernstein employs more dissonance, and, as he will again do so brilliantly in *West Side Story*, he adds elements of jazz, including syncopated rhythms and the prominent use of drums and saxophone, instruments associated with jazz. Copland describes Bernstein's ability to work in the two styles:

> Bernstein represents a new type of musician—one who is equally at home in the world
> of jazz and in the world of serious music. George Gershwin made something of an
> attempt to fill that role, but Bernstein really fills it—and with ease.[*]

These divergent styles can be observed at the beginning of the film. As is typical with a modern musical style, the music for the opening credits is played by a small number of instruments. A solo French horn, an instrument often associated with heroes, intones the initial statement of the Waterfront theme. A solo flute and trombone repeat the theme canonically, and finally muted trumpets and woodwinds play fragments of the theme's cadential phrase. As the film opens, the music departs dramatically

---

[*] Aaron Copland, *Copland on Music*. New York: W. W. Norton & Co., 1963, 172–3.

from these gentle sounds, as the drums and piano violently pound out syncopated rhythms. A saxophone blares out a theme associated with Joey and violence, and soon the entire orchestra joins the percussive sound. The music comes to an abrupt halt as the last strokes of the timpani suggest the impact of Joey's body hitting the ground.

The score is largely unified by three principal themes (see Viewer Guide). The Waterfront theme is used sparingly. It functions as a musical frame for the film, appearing in its most complete form at the beginning and end. The love theme is first heard in the park when Edie says that she remembers Terry from her youth (29:20). This disjunct melody is often heard gently scored for individual instruments, and it can even be heard as source music when they dance (43:40). It also grows in passionate intensity with full orchestration in several scenes, such as their first encounter on the rooftop (35:20) and when Terry breaks her door down (1:16:15).

The Violence theme is the dominant motive of the film. Because of its presence in the opening scene, it is also associated with Joey. It is heard when we see Joey's pigeon coop on the rooftop, and it also appears as source dance music (45:30). Later, and more subtly, it develops into a melody heard when Charley and Terry talk in the cab (1:13:50). One of the more intriguing sounds in the film occurs when Terry tells Edie about his role in Joey's murder (1:02:10). No dialogue or music is heard, just the pounding of the machines at the dock. Yet the rhythm of these sounds is identical to that of the Violence theme, and when the music finally enters, it is synchronized with the dock sounds.

The musical highpoint of the film occurs at the climax (see Viewer Guide). Terry is beaten badly by Friendly's men, accompanied by an intense version of the Violence theme, combining the dissonances of modern music and the syncopated rhythms of popular music. Later, a plaintive, dissonant version of the Violence theme returns in the woodwinds as we see his bloodied face. When Terry says "Put me on my feet," the Waterfront theme is stated heroically by a solo horn, and then repeated quietly by a harp and vibraphone. The full orchestra begins to accompany his courageous walk and builds to a Coplandesque climax. The American nationalist sound suggests the courage of one American, standing up to the forces of the mob-controlled union. While the wide leaps of the melody and the powerfully moving bass line are sounds clearly indebted to Copland, the intensity of the dissonances is pure Bernstein.

Expressionism

Musical expressionism and serialism are the most radical styles of mainstream concert music prior to World War II. Unlike film noir style, the dissonance is much more unrelenting. The great silent film *The Cabinet of Dr. Caligari* (see Chapter 8) was accompanied by an expressionistic score, but for the most part the style was deemed appropriate only for certain scenes and cues, and not for a complete film. In the 1940s, Hanns Eisler introduced the sound to Hollywood films, and in the 1950s, Leonard Rosenman became the leading film composer to work within this style.

On the Waterfront: Climax

Timing

Excerpt: 1:38:10–1:47:20 (0:00 at logo); DVD Chapters
26–28

Key Points

- Musical style of Copland at climax
- Dissonant harmonies
- Syncopated rhythms
- Use of leitmotifs

Setting

Terry Malloy (Marlon Brando) has testified against the mob before a Senate hearing. He is considered a stool pigeon and has become an outcast. But rather than hiding,
he goes to the docks wearing Joey's jacket and ready for work. The foreman chooses
everyone on the docks to work except for Terry, who remains standing alone.

Principal Leitmotifs

Example 17.1 Waterfront

Example 17.2 Violence/Joey

Example 17.3 Love

PLOT	MUSIC
Terry stares at John Friendly's office.	A solo French horn intones the Waterfront theme, similar to the beginning of the film.
Terry walks to the office and challenges Friendly as workers watch.	No music
Terry and Friendly fight. Losing, Friendly calls for help from his thugs, and Terry is beaten badly.	A version of the Violence theme is played loudly, with dissonances, repeated chords, and syncopated accents.
The workers stare sadly. Father Barry arrives with Edie. They go to Terry. The longshoremen refuse to work unless Terry joins them; Joey's father pushes Friendly into the water.	Silence signals the end of the fight. A soulful variation of the Violence theme follows. Music stops with the arrival of Father Barry.
The workers ask Terry to join them and see his beaten face.	The soulful string sound returns, followed by woodwinds with the Violence theme.
Father Barry and Edie help Terry to stand, and he heroically walks to work.	The Waterfront theme is heard in various instruments building to a grand climax.

In 1955, Rosenman debuted as a film composer with three sensational scores. The score for the least known of the three, *The Cobweb*, contains music created by serial techniques. The other two films, considered to be among the best of the decade, star James Dean—*East of Eden* and *Rebel Without a Cause*. Both deal with the angst of being a teenager.

In the 1950s the teenager was a relatively new phenomenon. The term itself had first appeared in print in 1941, signaling the nation's recognition that it had developed a large distinct population of youths who were between childhood and adulthood. In earlier generations, this gap did not exist; children became adults in their early teens and were expected to work, bear children, and handle responsibilities like all other adults. During the Depression (1930s), there was not enough work for younger adults, so teens began to be herded into another relatively new cultural institution, the high school. With ample free time, fewer responsibilities, active minds, growing bodies, and raging hormones, this segment of the population often resorted to rebellious activities, much to the dismay of older generations.

Leonard Rosenman (1924–2008)

A key figure in expanding the role of modern music in film, Leonard Rosenman studied music with Roger Sessions, Ernst Bloch, and Arnold Schoenberg. Rosenman was an active composer of concert music when he was asked to write the score for *East of Eden* (1955), primarily because his piano student, the future movie star, James Dean, insisted on it. Rosenman has since had a long career scoring for both film and television. His television credits include work on *The Defenders, Marcus Welby,* and *The Twilight Zone,* and he won Emmies for two TV movies, *Sybil* (1976) and *Friendly Persuasion* (1979). For his work in film he was nominated for an Oscar four times and won the award twice.

Important Film Scores

East of Eden 1955
Rebel Without a Cause 1955
The Cobweb 1955
Beneath the Planet of the Apes 1970
Barry Lyndon 1975 ♫
Bound for Glory 1976 ♫
Cross Creek 1983 ✉
Star Trek IV: The Voyage Home 1986 ✉
RoboCop 2 1990

★ = Best Picture Oscar   ♫ = Best Music Oscar   ✉ = Music Oscar Nomination

East of Eden

Concern over this phenomenon led to a series of films dealing with rebellious teenagers, including *The Wild One* (1954), *East of Eden* (1955), *Blackboard Jungle* (1955), *The Delinquent* (1957), and *West Side Story* (1961). In the adaptation of the Steinbeck novel *East of Eden,* Rosenman uses an expressionistic style to suggest the disturbed, angry state of the antihero Cal. Although asked to tone down his use of Modernism by director Elia Kazan, Rosenman still managed to insert extended passages that clearly evoke the style of Schoenberg and Berg. Particularly powerful is the scene in which Cal takes his brother to confront their mother, setting off the dramatic climax of the film (1:35:00). The clash of musical styles when Cal leaves the room and encounters the honky-tonk piano is jolting, reflecting Cal's inner conflict. Providing a counterbalance to the dissonant sounds in the film is one of Rosenman's most beautiful lyrical themes, representing Cal's love interest.

Rebel Without a Cause

Nicholas Ray's *Rebel Without a Cause* is based on a 1944 case study of a teenage delinquent. The film focuses on three dysfunctional families trying to raise troubled youths. In telling this story, Ray attacks the essence of 1950s values—the family unit—by exposing its underlying weaknesses, such as neglect, ineffectual parenting, and sexual repression. The story is cast in the framework of classical tragedy. The events roughly take place within twenty-four hours, corresponding to the Aristotelian unity of time, and the plot divides into five clearly defined acts. Part of the fascination of this film is the real-life tragedies of its three stars. Natalie Wood drowned at age forty-three, Sal Mineo was murdered near his home at age thirty-seven, and James Dean, who exploded on the Hollywood screen in 1955 with three major films, died that same year in a car accident at age twenty-four, just months before *Rebel Without a Cause* opened in the theaters.

It is easy to link *Rebel Without a Cause* with *East of Eden*. Both star James Dean, both deal with teenage problems, and both have dissonant scores by Leonard Rosenman. A significant difference between the two is the love interest. In *East of Eden*, Cal falls in love with Abra, a pure young woman who brings a sense of redemption to Cal. Rosenman's score balances a beautiful love theme reflecting Abra's spirit with the dissonant aura surrounding Cal. In *Rebel Without a Cause*, Jim falls in love with Judy, an adolescent who is struggling with her own sexual energies. Here Rosenman responds by blending expressionistic harmonies with the sounds of jazz.

Two themes dominate the score. Judy's theme is frequently presented in a jazz idiom, and a solo saxophone often represents her. The other principal theme, the Rebel theme, has no clear association. It is generally heard behind scenes featuring Jim and Plato, a lonely youth who has befriended Jim. Both themes are presented during the opening credits. Judy's theme is used as a fanfare, the Rebel theme enters in jazz style, and Judy's theme returns in a lush, romantic setting. The first four notes of the Judy theme are distinctive, and they are often heard in developmental and improvisational passages.

Principal themes

Example 17.4. Judy

Example 17.5. Rebel

Expressionistic sounds reach a peak in three episodes: the vision of the exploding earth at the planetarium (27:00), the knife game (35:15), and most dramatically at the "chickie run" (52:05). In the latter, the music achieves an intense climax after Buzz is killed. Judy stares over the edge of the cliff at the wreckage, possibly considering suicide. At that moment, Jim offers her his hand and the music softens into a romantic setting of Judy's theme, marking a major turning point in their lives.

Figure 17.3 The Love theme emerges during this scene with Judy, Jim, and Plato at the cliff side after the death of Buzz

Avant-garde

The term avant-garde is applied to a variety of art movements in the twentieth century. Consciously trying to create unique new styles, avant-garde artists and composers explored the limits of their disciplines in creative and often colorful manners. The movement was particularly prevalent in the 1950s and 1960s. In listening to avant-garde music, it is difficult to distinguish between the various compositional techniques. Because of this, we will apply the term avant-garde loosely and specify a distinct type of technique only when it is clearly audible.

The Day the Earth Stood Still

One audible type of avant-garde music from the 1950s is electronic music, which found a natural home in science fiction films. Bernard Herrmann, who had experimented with electronic sounds in *The Devil and Daniel Webster* (1941), makes extensive use of the theremin in *The Day the Earth Stood Still* (1951). Moving beyond the typical film noir use of the instrument, Herrmann creates a unique musical style with an unusual orchestra, including thirty brass instruments, four pianos, four harps, electric violin, electric piano, and two theremins. Absent from the score are the standard orchestral strings and woodwinds. With these forces, Herrmann shapes a futuristic musical sound that evokes a consistently ominous, terrifying, and unworldly mood.

Figure 17.4 Electronic music and Robby the Robot are part of the fascination of *Forbidden Planet*

Forbidden Planet

Moving beyond the use of a single electronic instrument, *Forbidden Planet* (1956) is set to an all-electronic musical accompaniment by the wife-husband team of Bebe and Louis Barron. Pioneers in electronic music, they established one of the first electro-acoustic music studios in 1948; the renowned avant-garde composer John Cage

composed his first electronic works there. For *Forbidden Planet*, the Barrons created a score that could function as underscoring, even mimicking the steps of the invisible monster, and as the sound effects of a futuristic world. In addition to setting the mood of twenty third-century technology, the electronic music contributes to the disturbing atmosphere of this fatal planet.

International Films

International filmmaking achieved new heights in quality and influence during the 1950s. France once again took center stage, but a strong school also appeared in Japan, led by the films of director Akira Kurosawa.

France

A limited use of music can be seen in the films of directors Henri-George Clouzot, Robert Bresson, and Jacques Tati. Clouzot, often referred to as the French Hitchcock, proved that no underscoring is necessary to create intense thrillers. The only music in *The Wages of Fear* (1953) and *Diabolique* (1955) is heard during the opening credits or as source music. In each film, the music of the opening credits introduces some aspect of the story, through the Latin American sounds in the former and the boys' choir in the latter. For Bresson and Tati, music creates general moods. Bresson uses brooding music for his intimate *Diary of a Country Priest* (1951), and Jacques Tati provides lively popular sounds for his comic masterpieces *Mr. Hulot's Holiday* (1953) and *My Uncle* (1958).

Music plays a much more prominent role in the films of Max Ophüls. *La Ronde* (1950) is a delightful amorous vision with parallels to the light hearted Rococo painting movement of the eighteenth century. The music by Oscar Straus lends unity to the episodic story. The principal waltz theme, associated with the merry-go-round, becomes a leitmotif for lust and love, and recurs in each episode. The choice of a waltz is perfect, as the dance swirls in circles like the film itself. The tune is subject to numerous transformations; we hear the waltz piped from the merry-go-round, sung by the narrator (3:55), played as an elegant waltz for aristocratic couples (45:40), and even transformed into a march for the young French soldier (10:35). A light, melodic style also plays an important part in Georges Auric's music for another dazzling masterpiece by Ophüls, *Lola Montès* (1955).

Japan

Akira Kurosawa, Japan's foremost director, created two masterful films in the early 1950s—*Rashômon* (1950), which first brought him international acclaim, and *Seven Samurai* (1954), the model for Hollywood's *The Magnificent Seven* (1960). The scores for these two films, by Fumio Hayasaka, present two opposing musical approaches. *Rashômon* is set primarily in a European style, with Western instruments and harmonies, and would have been quite accessible to European audiences. In one extended scene during the woman's story, 38:30, Hayasaka even adapts Ravel's *Bolero* to a Japanese setting. In general, traditional Japanese melodic styles and instruments play a small role in this film.

By way of contrast, the score to *Seven Samurai* features the traditional sounds of Japanese music. Often relying on Japanese instruments and voices, the music centers on folk-like melodies that are presented without contrasts. The dramatic effect of the music comes from the texts, their general moods, and their placement. Still, as with much Asian music of the decade, Western influences are difficult to avoid. Western instruments can be heard playing some of the melodies, and the dominant monophonic Japanese style occasionally gives way to Western harmony—as in the Hollywood ending.

Trailer

Heading into the late 1950s, film scores in the classic traditions of the late 1930s were still part of the Hollywood sound. One of the greatest film scores reflecting these traditions, *Ben-Hur*, appeared in 1959. Yet the two trends noted in Chapters 16 and 17, the expanded use of popular and modern musical styles, would have an enormous impact on the future of film music, as evidenced by a number of films created at the end of the decade.

Important Names and Terms

Leonard Bernstein	Bebe and Louis Barron
Elia Kazan	Oscar Straus
Leonard Rosenman	Akira Kurosawa
avant-garde	Fumio Hayasaka
electronic music	House Un-American Activities Committee (HUAC)

Suggested Viewing

Film noir: *Asphalt Jungle* (1950), *D.O.A.* (1950), and *Kiss Me Deadly* (1955)
Thriller/Mystery: *Strangers on a Train* (1951), *Rear Window* (1954), *Dial M for Murder* (1955), and *Night of the Hunter* (1955)
Horror: *The Thing* (1951) and *Them!* (1954)
Drama: *All About Eve* (1950), *The Bad and the Beautiful* (1952), and *The Caine Mutiny* (1954) ✉

18

The Close of the Decade, 1956–1959

By the mid-1950s, television had become a permanent fixture in the American home. Feeling threatened, Hollywood launched a two-pronged attack. The first was an unsuccessful attempt to undermine the new industry. No movies were to be shown on television, and no movie stars were to appear on a television program—a stigma that still lingers today. Studios soon softened their hard line by lifting the ban on actors in 1956 and selling the rights to pre-1948 movies to television. The other response was to lure people out of their living rooms with innovations. Some of the experiments, such as 3-D films, were short-lived, but other changes were more lasting. The two most visible and enduring technical changes in film during the 1950s are the use of color film (see Close-Up on page 226) and the advent of wide-screen cinematography. In conjunction with stereophonic sound, these visual effects successfully created a theatrical experience that television could not match.

Two competing systems made possible the birth of wide-screen films—Cinerama and CinemaScope. Cinerama is a process requiring three cameras, three projectors, and a large curved screen. It debuted in 1952 with *This is Cinerama*, a travelogue with stimulating visual effects. *How the West Was Won* (1962), with Alfred Newman's rousing score, is the system's greatest creation.

SIGNIFICANT FILMS

1956	*Around the World in 80 Days* ★ ♫
1957	*The Bridge on the River Kwai* ★ ♫
	The Seventh Seal
1958	*Big Country* ✉
	Vertigo
	Touch of Evil
1959	*North by Northwest*
	Anatomy of a Murder
	Some Like It Hot

Despite these spectacular results, Cinerama proved to be too costly and impractical. A second and more successful system, called CinemaScope, requiring only a single camera, was used for the 1953 religious epic *The Robe* (see Chapter 19). This Twentieth Century Fox production is the first major narrative film to employ this simpler system, and soon other studios adopted rival wide-screen formats with names such as VistaVision, Todd-AO, and Panavision.

The Birth of the Blockbuster

The blockbuster film—lavish, lengthy, and spectacular—burst onto the screen in 1956 with three wide-screen epics: *Around the World in 80 Days, War and Peace,* and *The Ten Commandments.* Because of costs, the extravagant epic would enjoy a limited life span. Still, some of these films from the 1950s can be considered to be among Hollywood's greatest productions, containing some of Hollywood's finest music. Religious films (see Chapter 19) are the most sensational epics of the period, but the same traits can be seen in a variety of films, including comedies, musicals, westerns, and war stories. Most notable are *Around the World in 80 Days* and *The Bridge on the River Kwai,* both of which won Academy Awards for Best Picture and Best Scoring of a Dramatic Picture.

Around the World in 80 Days

Around the World in 80 Days (1956), shot in color with Todd-AO and recorded with stereophonic sound, is a travelogue with a narrative. Built on an episodic plot—Phileas Fogg wagers that he can, with the assistance of his servant Passepartout, travel around the world in eighty days—the film takes us on an exuberant tour of some of the world's most scenic spots. Accompanying the beautiful wide-screen effects is a colorful and tuneful score by Victor Young, one of Hollywood's finest composers.

Figure 18.1 The balloon glides over Paris to the melody of "Around the World in 80 Days"

Each area of the world is accompanied by appropriate music, either using ethnic instruments or evoking Western stereotypes of regional styles. Quotations of well-known tunes suggest locations, such as "Rule Britannia" for England, "Auprès de ma blonde" for France, and numerous familiar melodies for the United States. The most memorable music in the score is the waltz tune, "Around the World in 80 Days." Typical of the treatment of popular melodies in film scores, the tune is initially heard in an extended travel montage in which a balloon soars over French locales (30:20). Later, the melody is treated as the love theme between Fogg and a princess from India, played by Shirley MacLaine. Lacking opening credits, the film is one of the earliest to include lengthy closing credits that last for over six minutes, allowing Young the opportunity to reprise numerous musical highlights, including the waltz.

The Bridge on the River Kwai

Although the scoring to *Around the World in 80 Days* is clearly in the tradition of the Golden Age, its inclusion of a dominant popular tune points to the future of epic film scores. *The Bridge on the River Kwai* (1957), one of director David Lean's finest works, also features a single memorable tune known as the "Colonel Bogey March." Ironically, although film composer Malcolm Arnold, an English concert composer, won an Oscar largely on the strength of this tune, he did not compose it. The original melody was composed by Kenneth Alford in 1914. Arnold did provide it with a sensational setting, beginning with whistling and then adding the sounds of a band and a newly composed countermelody (7:30). The effect of adding winds and percussion is not only musically satisfying, but it also suggests the pride of the English, who are imagining a formal British parade while they march in a stark Japanese prison camp.

Composer Profile

Victor Young (1900–1956)

Born in Chicago, Young spent most of his early years in Poland, where he studied at the Warsaw Conservatory. Returning to America, he worked in vaudeville theaters and created music for silent films. In 1936 he began working for Paramount Studios, where he remained until his death. He was nominated for twenty-two Oscars, but won only one award posthumously in 1956 for *Around the World in 80 Days*.

Important Film Scores

Golden Boy 1939 ✉
Northwest Mounted Police 1940 ✉
The Dark Command 1940 ✉
For Whom the Bell Tolls 1943 ✉
Love Letters 1945 ✉ ✉
Samson and Delilah 1950 ✉
The Quiet Man 1952
Shane 1953
Around the World in 80 Days 1956 ★ ♫

★ = Best Picture Oscar   ♫ = Best Music Oscar   ✉ = Music Oscar Nomination

"We're Not in Kansas Anymore"

Dorothy's observation is a delightful understatement, as the audience is taken visually from the drab black-and-white world of Kansas to the stunningly colorful world of Oz. Color in films such as *The Wizard of Oz*, *The Adventures of Robin Hood*, and *Gone With the Wind* may seem quite startling in comparison to earlier films, but two things are important to remember. Color film is not an invention of the late 1930s, and color at this time did not take over completely, as the vast majority of films in the 1940s and early 50s were shot in black and white.

Attempts to bring color to film began in the late nineteenth century. In *The Great Train Robbery* (1903), selected objects, such as the dresses of some of the dancing girls, were handpainted frame by frame. Most striking is the use of color for the explosion and the final gunshot. A different and more typical color effect can be seen in *The Cabinet of Dr. Caligari*, where the night scenes are paler, and the scenes in Mary's bedroom are awash with a blue tint.

The Technicolor Corporation, so called because the inventors had attended the Massachusetts Institute of Technology, was founded in 1917, and held a monopolistic hold on all color equipment in American films. It introduced a two-color process, favoring red and green hues, in the 1920s; this system is found in a number of films from that time, including a striking scene in *The Phantom of the Opera* (1925). By 1933, Technicolor had developed a much superior three-color process, focusing on red, blue, and yellow. Among the early experiments with this process was the first color cartoon, Disney's *Flowers and Trees* (1932).

Unfortunately, the color process was expensive, requiring special film and cameras. The cost, combined with other technical problems and the financial crunch of World War II, prevented the use of color from becoming widespread. Throughout the 1940s, color was reserved for the most lavish spectacles. In the 1950s, the appearance of a cheaper and more efficient color system designed by Eastmancolor and the competition from black-and-white television forced the film industry to convert quickly to color. By 1960, black-and-white films were in the minority, and separate Oscars for non-color films were discontinued in 1967.

Filmed on location in Sri Lanka in CinemaScope, the film would seem to invite extensive underscoring with broad, lyric melodies. But the score seldom settles into a lush style, and the few combinations of beautiful scenery and music are brief, such as Shears, an escaped American prisoner, boating down the river (58:05). The most extended lyric statement occurs when the two adversaries admire the completed bridge at sunset (2:05:30). For the most part, music is used sparingly, and many cues use a modern, dissonant style in keeping with a story about the futility of war.

Popular Music

The box-office appeal of *Around the World in 80 Days* and *The Bridge on the River Kwai* can be attributed in part to their use of popular melodies, a waltz tune and a British march. Three other highly regarded films from the late 1950s, *Some Like It Hot, Anatomy of a Murder*, and *Touch of Evil*, also incorporate popular music, but in distinctly different ways.

Some Like It Hot

Some Like It Hot (1959), rated by the American Film Institute as America's greatest comedy, is a hilarious cross-dressing farce. As in many great comedies, music plays a significant role. Hollywood veteran Adolph Deutsch, who received three Oscars for his adaptations of Broadway musicals, was an excellent choice for this film. In the story, Tony Curtis and Jack Lemmon don women's apparel and join an all-women jazz band in order to escape execution by Spats Columbo. The featured soloist of the band is Hollywood's foremost sex symbol, Marilyn Monroe, and she performs several musical numbers.

The underscoring by Deutsch serves two opposing roles—to make the story seem serious and to underline the humor. In order to make the plot appear plausible, Deutsch calls upon traditional symphonic scoring to support the perceived danger from Spats

Composer Profile

Adolph Deutsch (1897–1980)

London-born Adolph Deutsch began his career as a Broadway conductor in the 1920s. He started scoring films in the early 1930s, and he joined the staff at Warner Bros. in 1938, where he remained until moving to MGM in 1946. Although he worked on a number of memorable films in his early years, his Academy recognition, including three Oscars, was for film adaptations of Broadway musicals.

Important Film Scores

The Smiling Lieutenant 1931
The Maltese Falcon 1941
Little Women 1949
Annie Get Your Gun 1950 ♫
Show Boat 1951 ✉
Seven Brides for Seven Brothers 1954 ♫
Oklahoma! 1955 ♫
Some Like It Hot 1959
The Apartment 1960 ★

★ = Best Picture Oscar   ♫ = Best Music Oscar   ✉ = Music Oscar Nomination

and his gang, just as one would hear in a serious drama. But elsewhere, Deutsch freely incorporates popular music to underscore the fun. Melodies from Marilyn's songs appear both in the underscoring and in the music for the opening credits, much as would be heard in a musical. Other popular music cues include a scurrying saxophone line for Joe and Jerry's narrow escapes, the use of the tango "La Cumparsita" as the love theme for Osgood and Daphne/Jerry, and a muted trumpet that accompanies Marilyn's steamy scenes.

Figure 18.2 Jack Lemmon and Tony Curtis play in an all-girl band in *Some Like It Hot*

Anatomy of a Murder

In 1959, director Otto Preminger wanted to incorporate the sound of jazz in *Anatomy of a Murder*. Turning away from Hollywood composers, he hired the greatest contemporary figure in jazz, Duke Ellington, to compose the entire score for a big band. Typical of courtroom dramas, there is no music during the trial portions of this film. Ellington's music is primarily heard as source music, during transition scenes, and at the end, where it closes the film on an extremely high note. Although used sparingly, music has a strong impact. Justified by the jazz piano playing of lawyer Paul Bielger (James Stewart), the often-intense sound contributes to the overall mood of overt sexuality in the film that introduced frank discussions of rape, semen, and "panties." Subject matter, which in 1959, was still considered too risque by many audience members for a major motion picture.

Figure 18.3 The studio version includes credits during the opening shot of *Touch of Evil*

Touch of Evil

One of the most fascinating films to appear in the late 1950s, described as the last great film noir, is Orson Welles's *Touch of Evil* (1958) with music by Henry Mancini. Controversy surrounds the film. Welles left production at the last moment to work on another project, and the studio editors did not follow his instructions in creating the final cut. Welles later disowned the film and left a lengthy memo detailing how the film should appear. In 1998, *Touch of Evil* was restored following the intent of Welles's memo, so two versions of the film are now available—the original studio release and the Welles version.

No new scenes were added in the revision, and both versions run the same length. The DVD for the latter has a longer running time only because of an opening state-

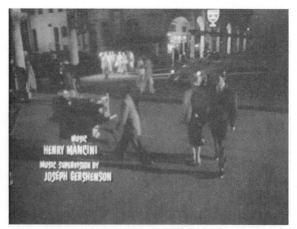

ment about the revision and the addition of closing credits. Within the film, the order of several scenes is altered with crosscutting, but the major difference between the two versions is the lack of credits in the Welles opening scene (compare Figure 18.3 and the image in the Viewer Guide) and the treatment of music at the beginning and end of the film.

The opening scene is a stunning visual accomplishment, as the first four minutes are presented without a cut. Beginning with a close-up of a time bomb, an uninterrupted crane tracking shot takes us backwards to the border between the United States and Mexico. In the studio version, this scene contains credits and a lively big band tune by Henry Mancini. In the Welles version, the credits and most of Mancini's music are eliminated. Replacing the opening number, diegetic music emanates from a number of sources, such as a car radio and barrooms. Musically, the sound is more cacophonous and less satisfying than Mancini's energetic beginning, but for the effect of the film, Welles's opening is more realistic and allows us to focus on the people, the location, and, of course, his extraordinary camera shot.

In both versions, a mixture of Mexican and American popular musical styles can be heard. The studio version begins with the ticking of the bomb followed by bongos and the ticking of drumsticks. The bongos, an instrument associated with Latin American music, are played almost throughout this otherwise American-dominated beginning. Welles reverses the opening sounds so that we first hear bongos and the drummer and then the sound of the ticking bomb. Latin-American music from a club is heard, but a car radio, tuned to American rock, drowns out all other sounds. The remainder of the scene is fascinating for the interplay between musical sounds and cultures, as we move in and out of proximity to the car in this border town. As the car finally leaves our sight, we hear a marimba gently underscoring a brief romantic moment for the newlyweds. Also audible is the bongo sound, suggesting the imminent explosion of the time bomb.

A variety of other popular musical styles are heard throughout the score. Country and western music is heard at the hotel (32:35), rock music is heard as Mexican youths abduct Susan (Janet Leigh) (1:09:40), and intense jazz accompanies the murder of Uncle Joe Grande by Hank Quinlan (Orson Welles) (1:23:20). Another unique musical sound is provided by the player piano, called a pianola. A standard feature of film noir scores is an unusual musical sound, most often a wavering pitch. But it can also be a disturbing musical sound, such as the zither in *The Third Man* (1949). The pianola fills that function in this film. Associated with Quinlan's old relationship to Tana (Marlene Dietrich), the instrument plays the same nostalgic tune whenever Hank visits her. At the end of the film, the music returns in the underscoring as Tana gazes at Hank's body in the river. In this final moment of the film, we hear the other major musical difference between the two versions. In the studio version, Mancini's music is brought back for an obtrusive Hollywood ending. Welles allows the pianola to linger hauntingly, and the film segues quietly into closing credits.

Touch of Evil: Beginning

Timing

Excerpt: 0:00:0–4:10 (0:00 at logo)

Key Points

- Use of popular music styles
- Differences between source music and underscoring

Setting

Mexican-born policeman Ramon Vargas (Charlton Heston), taking a break from fighting the Grande crime family, has just married an American, Susan Vargas (Janet Leigh). He will shortly have more dealings with the Grande family and with a possibly corrupt American police chief, Hank Quinlan (Orson Welles).

PLOT	STUDIO VERSION	WELLES VERSION
Universal International logo	Opening motive is played by a big band.	Opening motive is played by a big band.
A time bomb is planted in the back of Rudi Linnekar's car.	Ticking is heard followed by bongos. The drummer mimics the ticking. The opening motive returns.	Bongos and the drummer start immediately. Latin-American music from a nightclub enters.
Rudi and his mistress get in the car and begin to drive.	The big band continues with a theme based on the opening motive.	American rock music blares from the car radio.
The car drives onto the street and heads for the border.	The opening of the tune continues, still played loudly.	Live music emanating from barrooms obscures the car radio momentarily.
The car pauses, and Mike and Susan cross in front.	The music softens, as saxophones play the descending interval from the opening.	As the couple walks away from the car, a trumpet from a barroom gains prominence.

The car moves and passes the couple, only to be stalled again, allowing Mike and Susan to go by.	The louder music returns as Mike and Susan walk away from the car again.	The car radio is heard as the car passes, and the trumpet solo returns. When Mike and Susan walk away from the car, the music grows fainter.
The border guards talk to Mike and Susan.	Music gets softer for the dialogue, featuring a solo saxophone.	Music comes from the car radio.
Rudi's girl complains of a ticking noise.	The bongos and main theme reenter.	Music from the car radio continues.
Mike and Susan kiss. The car explodes in the background.	The opening motive is heard.	A marimba plays gently, followed by the bongos just before the explosion.

Composer Profile

Henry Mancini (1924–1994)

Henry Mancini is one of Hollywood's most beloved composers. Trained as a piccolo player and pianist, Mancini attended Juilliard and played piano in Glenn Miller's big band. He was asked to make arrangements for the film *The Glenn Miller Story* (1954), for which he received an Oscar nomination. His reputation rests largely on the quality of his theme songs, both for movies and television (*Peter Gunn* and *Mr. Lucky*), but his scoring abilities and versatility are exceptional. He received four music Oscars, two for Best Song and two for Best Score, and fourteen other nominations.

Important Film Scores

The Glenn Miller Story 1954 ✉
Touch of Evil 1958
Breakfast at Tiffany's 1961 ♫ ♫
Days of Wine and Roses 1962 ♫
Charade 1963 ✉ ✉

The Pink Panther 1963 ✉
Wait Until Dark 1967
10 1979 ✉ ✉
Victor/Victoria 1982 ♫

★ = Best Picture Oscar   ♫ = Best Music Oscar   ✉ = Music Oscar Nomination

Modern Styles

A number of films from the late 1950s continue to reflect the variety of modern styles. Three such films will be presented here: the first major western to incorporate elements of the American nationalist style, *Big Country* (1958), and two Hitchcock films with innovative scores by Bernard Herrmann, *Vertigo* (1958) and *North by Northwest* (1959).

Big Country

An influential new western sound can be heard in Jerome Moross's score for *Big Country*. Moross, who is also known for his works for theater and ballet, created the definitive western sound of the next generation for this epic story. With obvious parallels to the American nationalism of Aaron Copland, Moross captures the sense of wide-open spaces and the grandeur of the old west with a style that will be ably assimilated by Elmer Bernstein in the 1960s.

The film begins with an exhilarating rapid string figure that underlies a brass fanfare. This leads to a jaunty theme characterized by syncopated rhythms and a stuttering accompaniment, a key element of this style. Normally syncopation is heard in the melodies of popular music, while the accompaniment maintains a steady rhythmic pulse, as in the drum beat of rock music. By staggering the bass notes of the accompaniment so that they do not always coincide with the pulse, Moross creates a sense of cockiness and an energy that can be linked both to the bigness of the west and to the big men who tamed it. Typically the tune is heard as one or more cowboys are riding against the beautiful backdrop of western scenery. In its most breathtaking moment, the music is played softly in a moderate tempo as the lone figure of the Major knowingly rides into a trap. As he is joined by Leech (Charlton Heston) and then the rest of his loyal ranch hands, the pulse begins to quicken and soon the brass join in with a vigorous statement of the main theme (2:29:30).

Vertigo

Among the most highly regarded films at the end of the decade are two of Alfred Hitchcock's most memorable works: *Vertigo* (1958) and *North by Northwest* (1959). Hermann, who composed for Hitchcock into the 1960s, created the scores for both films. The psychological thriller *Vertigo* unfolds in three parts. The first and shortest shows Scottie's initial bout of vertigo. During the opening credits, Herrmann establishes an ominous mood with a six-note ostinato offset by dark brass chords, wavering sounds, and imitations of the ostinato. Once the action begins, scurrying strings, cacophonous wind chords, and glissandos combine with dizzying visual effects to dramatize Scottie's attack.

The second phase of the movie follows immediately. Surprisingly, over an hour elapses without vertigo returning as a factor. During this time, a fascinating mystery unfolds, and both its resolution and our expectation that vertigo will play a part, as suggested by the title of the movie, build enormous tension. Since many of the scenes contain little dialogue or action, Herrmann's moody musical cues, often repetitious in character, are essential in sustaining suspense. Most striking are the combination of high strings and the bass clarinet at Carlotta's grave (22:50), the disturbed sounds as Madeline leaps into the bay (41:40), and the wavering, distorted sounds heard in the forest (59:45).

Figure 18.4 Dizzying music accompanies the opening bout of vertigo

Once Madeline dies (1:16:30), the third portion of the film commences. Gradually the audience learns that the second portion of the film has been a deception—a carefully calculated misdirection. As the second and real mystery is unraveled, Herrmann continues to employ music primarily for moods. At the end, Scottie conquers his vertigo, but the results are still tragic. Hitchcock abruptly ends the film without resolution, leaving many questions unanswered. The final section of the film contains a number of film noir clichés, including the detective's indignation over the culpability of his lover and the nighttime setting. Herrmann's music also features some of the film noir traditions as well, with its sustained moods, use of low woodwinds, and wavering tones.

North by Northwest

North by Northwest is an action thriller that calls for more traditional scoring. The most famous musical moment in this film is the absence of music. During an attack on the hero by a crop duster, Hitchcock allows the sound of the plane to create realistic tension without musical assistance (1:11:30). Elsewhere, Herrmann supplies two exceptional musical themes. The action theme, established during the opening credits, is a vigorous dance with alternating duple and triple meters. Called a fandango by Herrmann, the music can be linked to a variety of Spanish, Italian, and South American dances. Indeed, Herrmann makes a brief motivic reference in the opening credits to a saltarello, an Italian dance from the finale of Mendelssohn's "Italian" Symphony. Later, the dance music is used to underscore action and chase scenes. The finest orchestration and manipulation of the theme accompanies Thornhill's arrival at the Frank Lloyd Wright house in South Dakota (1:54:45).

Figure 18.5 There is no music during this dramatic moment in *North by Northwest*

The other principal musical idea is the love theme, appearing first in the scene in the train's dining car (46:10). Often heard in the clarinet or oboe, Herrmann's theme captures the warmth and sincerity of their nascent love. In comparing the musical settings for this love scene with that in *A Place in the Sun* (Chapter 17), we can hear that instrumentation makes a significant difference. Both films contain beautiful melodies, but in the earlier film, Franz Waxman employs a saxophone, emphasizing the youthful and hedonistic aspects of the relationship. In Herrmann's setting, the sound of the clarinet and oboe is more mature, more genuine, and just as sexy.

International Films

During the late 1950s, international attention focused on two major new auteurs, Federico Fellini from Italy and Ingmar Bergman from Sweden. Both were to employ music in distinct manners. Also significant at this time was the recognition in the United States of the burgeoning school of filmmaking in India.

Italy

Italian filmmaking joined France at the forefront of world cinema in the 1950s, led by the masterful works of Federico Fellini. Providing music for the Italian auteur was Nino Rota who composed sixteen film scores for Fellini, including the international sensations *La Strada* (1954), *Nights of Cabiria* (1957), *La Dolce vita* (1960), and *8½* (1963).

La Strada appeared in the United States in 1956, when it won the first Oscar in a new category, Best Foreign Language film, an award that would also be bestowed upon both *Nights of Cabiria* and *8½*. The main theme of *La Strada* is haunting, much like the principal character herself. The melody is derived from the Larghetto of Dvořák's Serenade, Opus 22, and became a national sensation in Italy. Much of the other musical material in the film is source music, including some raucous circus marches. In all four of these films, popular music plays a major role, generally creating an ambiance of detachment and decadence. The music rarely interacts with the drama, and the vague delineation between source music and underscoring reinforces the superficiality of the characters' lifestyles.

Sweden

Joining the ranks of great auteurs in the 1950s is Sweden's foremost director, Ingmar Bergman. Bergman was thrust into the international light in 1957 with two brilliant works, *The Seventh Seal* and *Wild Strawberries*. Erik Nordgren supplied the musical scores for both. The sparse score to *Wild Strawberries* is essentially romantic and sentimental in style. In contrast, Nordgren's music for the apocalyptic vision of *The Seventh Seal* is dark and ominous. Although sparse, the music helps to create Bergman's atmosphere through the use of low voices and the low, dark registers of wind instruments and percussion. The dissonant opening choral statement of *Dies irae* ("Day of Wrath") supported by brass instruments sets the mood of the film. The frequent combination of the low register of the clarinet and a bass voice is haunting. For the most part, the instrumental groups are small, and he never calls upon the warm sound of string instruments.

Figure 18.6 A game of chess with Death is accompanied by dark, foreboding music in *The Seventh Seal*

India

India's film industry also achieved international recognition in the 1950s. An already strong school of filmmaking gained new energy after the country became independent in 1947. Satyajit Ray's first film, *The Song of the Road* (*Pather Panchali*, 1955), won the Jury Prize at Cannes in 1956, and Mehboob's *Mother India* (*Bharati Mata*, 1957) received India's first Academy nomination for Best Foreign Language Film. Centered in Bombay, or "Bollywood" as it is generally known, the Indian film industry would become the most prolific in the world by 1971. Indian films are distinctively formulaic, particularly in the incorporation of musical numbers. Indian critics have described the formula as "a star, six songs, and three dances," a loose structure that is applied to even the most serious dramas. The music for these films provides a fascinating mixture of three distinct styles: traditional Indian, European, and popular American. At first, the abrupt insertion of a song-and-dance sequence into a serious dramatic moment may seem odd to Western observers, but the tradition has endured and produced many outstanding and entertaining film.

Trailer

The principal focus of the first four chapters of Part 4 has been on the growth of popular and modern musical styles in film music, both in America and abroad. Both styles were used in a variety of innovative fashions, and both would continue to be a strong force in film music in the decades ahead. We should also recognize, however, that traditional symphonic scores were also composed during the 1950s. Especially noteworthy were those created for Hollywood's religious epics, culminating with *Ben-Hur*.

Important Names and Terms

Cinerama

CinemaScope

blockbuster

David Lean

Malcolm Arnold

Jerome Moross

Adolph Deutsch

Duke Ellington

Henry Mancini

Federico Fellini

Nino Rota

Ingmar Bergman

Erik Nordgren

Bollywood

Suggested Viewing

Epic: *Giant* (1956) ✉

Drama: *The Spirit of St. Louis* (1957) and *The Old Man and the Sea* (1958) ♪

Thriller: *The Man Who Knew Too Much* (1956) ♪

Drama: *Sweet Smell of Success* (1957)

19

Ben-Hur

In the 1950s, with the threat of nuclear holocaust hanging over the world, religious stories proved to be popular subjects for films in this country and abroad. Mindful of the scrutiny of the HUAC, Hollywood produced a series of spectacular epics set in the ancient world or in antiquity that promoted strong religious and democratic values. Although the civilizations of Egypt and ancient Rome were fascinating and admired for their accomplishments, they also represented totalitarian states similar to the Soviet Union. Knowing that the struggle for freedom in each of these regions eventually toppled empires, American audiences found inspiration in the underlying themes. In case the connection was too subtle, Cecil B. DeMille addressed the issue directly in a filmed prologue to *The Ten Commandments*, a movie in which Moses's last speech is directed not at religion, but at liberty.

The Religious Epic

Common to each of the epics listed in table 19.1 is a strong musical score in the tradition of Hollywood's Golden Age, generally by a veteran composer. All of the films received a nomination for Best Scoring of a Dramatic Picture except *The Robe* composed by Alfred Newman—a snub that

SIGNIFICANT FILMS

1951	*Quo Vadis* ✉
1953	*The Robe*
1956	*The Ten Commandments*
1959	*Ben-Hur* ★ ♪

compelled fellow composer Franz Waxman to quit the Motion Picture Academy—and *The Ten Commandments*, composed by newcomer Elmer Bernstein.

Table 19.1

Epic films set in the ancient world or antiquity

YEAR	EPIC	COMPOSER	OSCAR
1949	*Samson and Delilah*	Victor Young	✉
1951	*Quo Vadis*	Miklós Rózsa	✉
1951	*David and Bathsheba*	Alfred Newman	✉
1953	*The Robe*	Alfred Newman	
1953	*Julius Caesar*	Miklós Rózsa	✉
1956	*The Ten Commandments*	Elmer Bernstein	
1959	*Ben-Hur*	Miklós Rózsa	♫

Quo Vadis

The best of the epic scores created in the B.C. (before CinemaScope) era is Rózsa's *Quo Vadis*. A trained musicologist, Rózsa studied the music and instruments of antiquity. While the score is unavoidably compromised with modern practices, he captured the spirit of the Roman era with modal harmonies and parallel chords, which will be discussed more fully in our study of *Ben-Hur*. Some of his melodic material is modeled directly on examples of Gregorian chant, the music of the early Christian Church, and indirectly on the music of ancient Greece. While Rózsa includes traditional love themes for the three separate love relationships and action music, these standard cues are created in such a way that they do not disturb the stylistic integrity of the score as a whole.

One of the difficulties facing Rózsa was the lack of information about Roman music. We know that the two principal solo instruments of the ancient world were the lyre and the aulos, a wind instrument; Rózsa imitates their sounds with the harp and English horn. Rózsa also distinguishes between the Roman and Christian cultures. For the Romans, who were fond of brass instruments, Rózsa uses a brass choir for marches and fanfares. Early Christian music was primarily sung, and in the first Christian service observed by Marcus (1:03:30) we hear a solo voice answered by a chorus. Responsorial singing was common to both Jewish and early Christian services. Most striking is the music for the opening credits, in which these two elements are pitted against each other, as they are in the story. Christian voices sing, while in the background Roman trumpets play fanfares.

The Robe

Because of the grandeur of their stories and their pageantry potential, religious epics were well suited for the new wide-screen systems. The wide-screen era begins with *The Robe* (1953), Hollywood's first CinemaScope feature film. Forgoing the standard opening Twentieth Century Fox fanfare, Newman composed a solemn passage to accompany the unveiling of the new system and to set a serious tone for Rome in the early years after the death of Christ. The music accompanying the opening credits features a wordless chorus that exploits the innovative multi-channel stereophonic system. The chorus returns triumphantly at the end of the film singing the word "Alleluia," as Marcellus (Richard Burton) and Diana (Jean Simmons) willingly give up their lives in the name of the Lord.

Just as many of the scenes take full advantage of the new potential for visual effects, Newman created a number of the musical cues to make maximum effect of the enhanced sounds of stereo. One of his finest cues underscores the crucifixion (37:30). Initially, the swirling voices of a wordless choir suggest human and spiritual mourning. In a disturbing layered effect, the sound of laughter and banter from the Roman soldiers can be heard, and the coexistence of the two opposing emotions continues until the storm builds. With the addition of the storm sounds, the music rises to an emotional climax with brass chords, as Marcellus is touched by the blood of Christ and is forgiven in Christ's last words.

The Ten Commandments

Cecil B. DeMille's remake of *The Ten Commandments* (1956) marks a fitting and spectacular end to his directorial career, which spanned five decades. Grossing over forty million dollars, the most since *Gone With the Wind*, this film helped usher in the blockbuster era. Victor Young was the intended composer, but he had taken ill and recommended Elmer Bernstein to take his place. At this point, Bernstein's only major film credit was the jazz-influenced score for *The Man with the Golden Arm* (1955), not the experience necessary for one of the longest scores in film history. After viewing Bernstein's earlier film, DeMille said simply: "I thought you did a very nice job . . . But don't do anything like that in *The Ten Commandments*." The career of one of Hollywood's greatest composers was launched.

Figure 19.1 Moses parts the Red Sea in *The Ten Commandments*

Because of the length of production, Bernstein worked on the music for nearly a year. During that time, he crafted an exciting and unified score that played a major role in the film's success. Bernstein's music is most effective for the grand scenes appearing in the last hour of the film. The exodus begins with the sound of shofars, the rams' horns used in Jewish services (2:59:40/CD2 43:37), and continues with an exuberant march. The scene and music climax with the stunning parting of the Red Sea (3:21:00/CD2 1:05:15).

Ben Hur: The Narrative

The greatest of the religious epics is William Wyler's *Ben-Hur* (1959). The winner of eleven Academy Awards, including Best Picture and Best Scoring of a Dramatic Picture, *Ben-Hur* surpassed the record of ten Oscars garnered by *Gone With the Wind* (1939).

General Lew Wallace, a fascinating historic figure from the Civil War, created the original story in a popular novel published in 1880. A number of theatrical renditions of this story have been created, including a stage version with live horses pulling chariots on a treadmill and a spectacular silent film version directed by Fred Niblo (1925).

The film presents the lives of two men—Jesus Christ and Judah Ben-Hur. In addition to the interweaving of these two stories, the plot is fascinating for a number of parallels and reversals. In many ways, the second half is a mirror image of the first, with many of the roles reversed (Table 19.2).

Table 19.2

Plot reversals in *Ben-Hur*

EVENTS IN FIRST HALF	PARALLELS AND REVERSALS IN SECOND HALF
Birth of Christ, seen by Balthasar	Death of Christ, seen by Balthasar
Roman March for Messala	Roman March for Ben-Hur
The love of Judah and Esther begins to grow in the upstairs chamber	The love of Judah and Esther begins to diminish in the upstairs chamber
Judah's friendship turns to hatred	Judah's hatred returns to friendship
Messala triumphant, Ben-Hur sent to die	Ben-Hur triumphant, Messala dies
Death march of Ben-Hur, aided by water from Christ	Death march of Christ, aided by water from Ben-Hur
Ben-Hur in chains; Arrius is master	Arrius in chains; Ben-Hur is master

The Music

In dealing with the plot's diverse events, Rózsa maintains an overall stylistic unity by employing musical ideas that can be associated with Roman, Hebrew, and early Christian music. Many of the melodies are modal, meaning that they are based on old scale patterns that were abandoned in the seventeenth century. The most distinctive feature of modal scales is the lack of a leading tone, an essential element that creates tension and defines key areas in modern-era music. Rózsa also employs parallel harmonies, which retain the same pitch relationships from chord to chord and lack any sense of harmonic progression (see Example 19.1). Although historically connected to music from the Christian Church beginning nearly ten centuries after this story unfolds, the sound is an effective compromise between authenticity and the needs of a modern audience.

Example 19.1. Opening chords to *Ben-Hur*

The first three chords of the score establish this unique sound. Lacking the defining third of Western triads, these chords move in parallel motion, with each pitch moving down a whole step and then returning to the original pitch. Played by a strong brass section, the sound is both antique and awe-inspiring. The overture continues with a melody (the Redemption theme) that suggests the Phrygian mode, which sounds strange to modern ears. When Western triadic chords are employed, they too move in parallel fashion. A similar treatment of triads can be heard in the Christ theme and in several of the Roman marches. Also suggestive of Jewish and antique melodies are the numerous themes with strong pick-ups, accents on the second beats of a measure, dotted rhythms, and quick ornamental melodic turns.

Leitmotifs

In addition to the general stylistic uniformity, the score exhibits a complex and thorough system of leitmotifs. The story of Christ features two principal melodic ideas—the Christ and Redemption themes. The Christ theme (Example 19.3) is typically heard on an organ with a wavering sound. High strings with harmonics are frequently added, creating a halo effect around the melody. Also noteworthy is the pervasiveness of the number three in this theme. The number three is an important symbol for Christianity because of the Trinity; this theme has three-note chords, a melody using three pitches, and a meter with three beats in a measure, the only major theme in the film in triple meter.

Since there is no clear visual connection for the Redemption theme until the Sermon on the Mount, its exact meaning is initially unclear. Yet it shares a number of motives in common with the Christ theme and is easily associated with Christ. As shown in the Featured Film Guide, the opening phrases of the Christ and Redemption themes end with the same three notes. Moreover, the first three pitches of the Redemption theme are identical to the third measure of the Christ theme. This fall and return of a whole step is heard at the beginning of many of the major musical moments of the film, such as the overture, the prologue, the opening credits, and the entr'acte. The same gesture is also embedded in the themes for both Balthasar and Esther, and our ears will detect a Christian quality about their melodies and their characters.

If the interval of a major second is heard as a divine interval, then the open fifth, usually ascending, should be considered the human interval. It can be heard at the beginning of the Judea theme, the Esther theme, the Hate theme, and the Rowing theme. Miriam's theme rises and falls a fifth in its outline, Balthasar's theme descends a fifth twice, and Ben-Hur's theme also contains a rising fifth at its beginning.

The interval of a diminished fifth or tritone seems to represent man's fall from grace. The diminished fifth is the most disturbing interval in Western scales, and was once known as the devil's interval. In the film it is found primarily in music relating to Messala. The theme representing the friendship between Judah Ben-Hur and Messala has some warmth, especially in its early settings. But it also has some disturbing elements, such as the rigid dotted rhythm and the fall of a diminished fifth in its third measure. To be sure, this interval resolves to a perfect fifth in the next measure, but its presence foreshadows the Hate theme, which forcibly reiterates the tritone interval in a low, dark register. At Ben-Hur's lowest moment, when he is a slave in a Roman galley, Rózsa reduces the human motives to their essence. In an ostinato pattern, created by repeating the Rowing theme, we hear a rising fifth answered by a descent that creates two diminished fifths: A–D♯ and E–B♭.

Prologue and Exposition

The music for the overture and the opening credits helps to establish the overall mood of the film. For both sections, Rózsa provides a substantial orchestral medley featuring many of his principal themes. Most impressive is the powerful brass sound heard during the credits. Initially, this timbre is associated with the Roman Empire, but we soon discover that it also represents the heavenly kingdom, which has some well-known trumpet players of its own. This section climaxes with the Ben-Hur theme accompanied by ringing bells, a sound that is associated with the miracle at the conclusion of the film.

The prologue focuses on the world of Christ, with its vision of Joseph and Mary, the guiding light of the star of Bethlehem, and the adoration of the Child by the three wise men. This portion is dominated by Christian themes, including an extended presentation of Balthasar's theme with a wordless, heavenly choir, and a simple, childlike melody that underscores the Nativity tableau.

The mood of the prologue is abruptly shattered. After a shepherd sounds the Hebrew shofar, a mighty blast of trumpets responds with a Roman fanfare that accompanies the opening title. The conflict between Christ and Rome is further suggested during the exposition, when we hear the juxtaposition of a forceful Roman march and the gentle Christ theme. The exposition concludes with the reunion of Messala and his childhood friend Judah Ben-Hur. The Friendship theme here underscores both the warmth of their memories and the seeds of the personal conflict that will soon make them enemies.

The Fall of the House of Hur

The first series of complications juxtaposes love and hate. Love is kindled and burns quickly when Ben-Hur meets Esther. Rózsa composed an extended romantic cue based on the Esther theme for their encounter in an

Figure 19.2 A shepherd sounds a shofar, announcing the birth of Christ

upstairs room. There is also love and warmth in Messala's friendship theme when he first arrives at the House of Hur. In an ironic twist, the warm setting of this theme returns after Messala has coldly had the family arrested. It continues as Messala stands on the roof where he and Ben-Hur had, as children, thrown pebbles at people in the street. He discovers that the attack on the governor was indeed an accident, but still condemns the family in order to further his own ambitions.

The Hate theme first appears when Ben-Hur states that he will have to oppose Messala, rather than betray his Jewish friends. Foreshadowing the imminent turn of fate, a motive from the Hate theme heard in its second and third measures is embedded in the Roman march for Gratus, and it is reiterated repeatedly. After the accident, the Hate theme becomes more prominent.

During Ben-Hur's desert march, we hear a tortuous, chromatic melody with strong connections to the Hate theme. Ben-Hur's theme sounds desperate when he is refused water. At this moment, Christ intervenes and offers Ben-Hur water. This is one of two divine interventions during Ben-Hur's slavery that will lead to his turnaround. Both are accompanied by Christ's theme. As Ben-Hur is invigorated and intrigued by this kindness, his theme emerges fresh and energetic, and the scene closes with the Christ theme in a full orchestration.

The Galley Slave and Freedom

Once again, the sound of Christ is abruptly interrupted by the intrusion of Rome. The next scene opens with a view of Roman warships. Rózsa underscores this moment with a forceful fragment of the Rowing theme and an accompaniment that is clearly suggestive of "Mars" from *The Planets*, a set of symphonic poems by Gustav Holst. The connection to this concert work depicting the Roman god of war is certainly appropriate; John Williams, in his score to *Star Wars* (1977), uses the same piece for a similar effect.

In the galley, Rózsa builds incredible tension with the Rowing motive that is synchronized with the physical movement of the galley slaves. The ostinato (a repeating musical idea) changes speed as Arrius tests the skills of the slaves and of Ben-Hur in particular. Tension is built through repetition, the rising pitch, the crescendo, the accelerating tempo, and the growing dissonance above the ostinato. These sounds are later incorporated into the battle scene, the major turning point of the film. Having been unchained by orders of Arrius—the Christ motive suggests divine inspiration—Ben-Hur is able to escape and free other slaves.

A reversal occurs when Ben-Hur leaves the rowing bench and goes on deck. Amidst intense battle music, he saves the life of Arrius by diving into the water and dragging Arrius's body onto a makeshift raft. Believing that he is a failure, Arrius wants to commit suicide, but Ben-Hur is now the master and chains Arrius for his own protection. Completing the reversal, Judah even quotes a saying that the Romans used with slaves. Once the two are rescued, Arrius discovers that he won the battle, he is given a hero's welcome, and Ben-Hur is freed, eventually becoming Arrius's adopted son. Beginning the second half of the plot, Ben-Hur is now seen in a procession accompanied by a Roman march. Within this Roman section are two musical dances by Rózsa, an African fertility dance with African drums and a Roman dance with the orchestra imitating antique Roman instruments.

Returning Home and Revenge

Continuing with the plot reversals, Ben-Hur returns to Judea and is soon seen drinking water in the desert. His theme is heard in a setting similar to the moment just after Christ had given him water. His return to Judea also brings about the reprise of a number of earlier themes, including Judea, Balthasar, Esther, and Christ. Once Judah enters his house, the striking absence of music, even after he sees Esther, reflects the barren state of his home. In the upstairs chamber, where Ben-Hur and Esther first discovered their love, they talk again. The Esther theme appears in the same setting as in their first conversation, but it eventually gives way to the Hate theme, which dominates the next scenes.

Two new themes make their initial appearance in the subsequent scenes, both belonging to Miriam. When she and Tirzah are discovered to have leprosy, a dramatic, quickly descending motive appears that will follow them to the Valley of the Lepers. Later, as she makes Esther promise to keep her fate a secret from Ben-Hur, a dark, passionate theme appears that suggests a mother's love and sacrifice (see Example 19.9). The scene closes with an intense statement of the Hate theme.

After the entr'acte music, the dramatic chariot race becomes the focus of the story. Perhaps showing that hatred has driven out all other emotions, there is no non-diegetic music until the race is over and Judah sees the dying Messala. The scene does feature two Roman marches: the Circus March and the Parade of the Charioteers, which contains both the Hate and Ben-Hur motives. Once the race begins, only sound effects are heard, enhancing the realism of the remarkable stunt work. After Ben-Hur's triumph, the Circus March sounds briefly, and a phrase of the Parade of the Charioteers (the Ben-Hur phrase) sounds when Judah is given his laurels.

Finding Miriam and Tirzah

After his revenge on Messala, Ben-Hur's feelings are unresolved. Proving that he is a believer in neither stoicism nor existentialism, Ben-Hur feels that Messala is not at fault. Rather it was the Romans who had transformed his best friend into a hateful foe. Accordingly, Rózsa brings back the Friendship theme for the final scene between the two former friends, and the Hate theme is transferred to Judah's attitude towards Rome, especially after he learns that Miriam and Tirzah are lepers.

Figure 19.3 The climactic chariot race uses no underscoring

Ben-Hur's story has reached a desperate dead end. He has accomplished his goal of revenge, but discovers that this has only increased his bitterness. His mother and sister have leprosy, and his hatred for the Romans is destroying his love relationship with Esther. It is at this low point that the story of Christ reenters, and Christian themes become more prominent. Ben-Hur, filled with hate, passes by Christ's Sermon on the Mount, and the Christ and Redemption musical themes have their fullest expression here, foreshadowing the conclusion.

Climax and Resolution

The climax and resolution sections allow Rózsa to compose two musical climaxes, one for Christ and one for Ben-Hur. The former section begins with Christ's walk to Calvary carrying his cross, accompanied by a tortuous death march. As in Ben-Hur's desert march, chromaticism and dissonance underscore the bitterness of the moment. The Christ theme is heard when Ben-Hur offers Christ a cup of water, reversing their earlier roles, but it is rudely broken off as a guard kicks the water from their hands.

After the storm has raged at the death of Christ, Miriam and Tirzah are miraculously cured. The Christ theme enters, now in full orchestration accompanied by the sound of the rain, one of many water images in the film. As we see the water mix with the blood of Christ, carrying it throughout the land, imitation based on the Christ secondary motive builds to a grand, full brass statement of Christ's theme.

In the resolution, Ben-Hur has understood Christ's message, he has returned to Esther with a peaceful spirit, and he discovers that Christ has cured Miriam and Tirzah. In order to build an even bigger musical finish, Rózsa brings back the wordless chorus, suggesting a heavenly choir, and they present a rejuvenated Ben-Hur theme. The Christ theme reappears as the chorus sings "Alleluia," a word that not only comments on the preceding miracle, but also suggests the coming Resurrection.

Figure 19.4 Ben-Hur reverses his role with Christ, as we hear the Christ theme

Ben-Hur (1959)

Directed by William Wyler
Music by Miklós Rózsa

Principal Characters

Judah Ben-Hur, a Jewish Prince (Charlton Heston)
Messala, Ben-Hur's childhood friend (Stephen Boyd)
Esther, Ben-Hur's love interest (Haya Harareet)
Miriam, Ben-Hur's mother (Martha Scott)
Tirzah, Ben-Hur's sister (Cathy O'Donnell)

Religious Themes

Example 19.2 Redemption

Example 19.3 Christ

Example 19.4 Christ secondary motive

Example 19.5 Balthasar

Ben-Hur Themes

Example 19.6 Judah Ben-Hur

Example 19.7 Judea

Example 19.8 Esther/Love

Example 19.9 Miriam

Example 19.10 Messala/Friendship

Example 19.11 Hate

Example 19.12 Rowing

Prologue and Exposition

0:00–28:45; DVD Chapters 1–8

SCENE DESCRIPTION	MUSIC
Overture	Themes: Redemption, Judea (00:20), Esther (1:45), Miriam (3:20), Friendship (4:20), Redemption (5:50)
MGM logo	Redemption theme
Beginning in the year of Christ's birth, Balthasar tells of Rome's domination of Judea and of Jewish hopes for the promised savior. Joseph and Mary enter Jerusalem and leave for Bethlehem.	The Judea theme dominates, with brief Roman music for the fortress and a sacred vocal sound for the Temple. The Christ theme sounds briefly at the mention of the Redeemer.
The star shines on Bethlehem, as the Wise Men watch.	The orchestra and a wordless choir present Balthasar's theme.
The three Wise Men visit the nativity scene and present gifts.	The Adoration theme concludes with Balthasar's theme.
A shepherd signals with his shofar.	Source music: two notes sound.

The credits appear over the image of the Creation from Michelangelo's painting on the ceiling the Sistine Chapel.	A brass fanfare leads to the Redemption theme. Themes: Ben-Hur (12:20), Esther (13:05), and Ben-Hur.
In the year 26, a Roman legion led by Messala marches towards Jerusalem, passing through Nazareth.	The Redemption chords sound with the date. A march begins based on the Judea theme, but soon a Roman march appears. Judea returns at the end.
A friend asks Joseph the whereabouts of his son, and Joseph says that he is about his Father's business.	No music initially. With the glimpse of Jesus, the Christ theme is played with the organ.
The Roman legion arrives in Jerusalem, and is greeted by Sextus.	The March returns. Source music: Roman fanfare.
Messala, who grew up in Jerusalem, is replacing Sextus as tribune. Messala expresses his intent to bring order to the Jews by force. He is notified that Judah Ben-Hur has come to see him.	No music
The two childhood friends exchange greetings, talk about their youth, and throw spears at a crossbeam.	The Friendship theme is treated freely. The tone darkens as the discussion turns to Rome and Jerusalem.
The two friends argue, but at the end, they drink a toast.	No music until the Friendship theme underscores the toast.

Complications: The Fall of the House of Hur

28:45–1:05:30; DVD Chapters 9–18

SCENE DESCRIPTION	MUSIC
At the house of Hur, Messala, Judah, Miriam, and Tirzah reminisce. Messala gives Tirzah a ring and talks about his military triumphs.	The House of Hur theme is joined by the Friendship theme. The cue fades as Messala talks about conquering barbarians.
Ben-Hur and Messala talk privately. Messala wants his friend to betray Jewish dissidents, but Judah refuses.	Music is withheld until Ben-Hur declares that he is against Messala, when the Hate theme is heard.
Messala leaves, and Ben-Hur explains to his family what has happened.	The Hate and Friendship themes are interwoven.

Ben-Hur talks with his house steward Simonides, whose daughter Esther asks permission to marry.	The financial discussion has no music. The Love theme commences when Esther descends the stairs.
In an upstairs chamber, Esther and Judah talk about their childhood, recognize their love, and kiss.	The Love theme is sustained throughout the scene.
The new Roman governor Gratus enters Jerusalem. Messala greets him, and they parade through the streets. Judah and Tirzah watch from the rooftop.	Source music: a Roman march containing a motive from the Hate theme. The march begins with the entrance of Gratus and continues as they parade.
Tirzah accidentally knocks some tiles loose, causing Gratus to be hurt. Roman soldiers arrest Ben-Hur, Miriam, and Tirzah with Messala's consent. He goes to the roof and sees that it was an accident.	Music stops with the accident. After the arrest, music reenters warmly with the Friendship theme, suggesting that Messala is reminiscing about his childhood in this house.
Imprisoned, Ben-Hur wants to know the fate of his family. He escapes and confronts Messala, who confesses that he wants to use the incident to gain control of the people.	No music until soldiers retake Ben-Hur. The Hate theme enters, and turns to the Friendship motive as Ben-Hur is led under the crossbeam where they had thrown spears earlier.
Simonides and Esther ask Messala to release the Hur family, but he refuses and holds Simonides for questioning.	No music until the Hatred theme enters when Messala orders Simonides to be held.
Judah Ben-Hur and other prisoners are led on a tortuous desert journey to the sea. They pause in Nazareth for water. The soldiers and horses receive water first.	The ponderous, chromatic desert march incorporates intervals from the Hate theme. The music builds tension as the prisoners wait for water.
A guard refuses to let Ben-Hur have water. Collapsing, he asks God for help. Christ gives him water. The guard moves to strike Christ but cannot do so. The prisoners begin to march, and an invigorated Ben-Hur looks at Christ.	Ben-Hur's theme sounds weakly. Soon, Christ's theme appears in an extended statement. Ben-Hur's theme returns strongly at the end as he walks and stares at the figure of Christ. The Christ theme closes the scene.

Complications: The Galley Slave and Freedom

1:05:30–1:41:10; DVD Chapters 19–28

SCENE DESCRIPTION	MUSIC
The Roman fleet is at sea. Ben-Hur is a galley slave in one of the boats.	The Warship theme is followed by the Rowing theme.

The new commanding officer, Quintus Arrius, boards the ship and inspects the galley. Striking Ben-Hur, he praises his anger. The slaves begin to row. On deck, Arrius tells of their search for a Macedonian fleet.	Source music: a fanfare sounds for the arrival of Arrius. Silence follows until the men begin to row, accompanied by the Rowing theme. Ominous music underscores Arrius's revelation.
Arrius oversees a demonstration by the galley slaves, going through battle, attack, and ramming speeds. Ben-Hur remains strong and defiant throughout.	The Rowing theme is synchronized with the physical movement and accelerates, crescendos, and gets higher with the changes of speed.
Judah is sent to Arrius's cabin. Arrius learns of his background, his stubborn faith, and his desire for freedom.	The Warship theme is followed by quiet music until Arrius is startled awake, reinforced by a modest stinger.
The Macedonian fleet appears. Preparations are made for war, including chaining the slaves to their rowing positions. Arrius asks that Ben-Hur not be chained; Ben-Hur then recalls a similar unexpected kindness from Christ.	Intense war-like music predominates. The Rowing theme and variations on the motive are heard in the Galley. When Ben-Hur is unchained, we hear his theme and then the Christ theme, suggesting divine guidance.
The battle commences with initial successes for Arrius. A Macedonian boat rams that of Arrius. Ben-Hur releases some of his fellow slaves.	War music is sustained with some references to the Rowing theme. As Ben-Hur unlocks chains, we hear his theme.
Ben-Hur climbs on deck amidst fighting. Arrius falls overboard, and Judah dives after him, pulling him onto a raft. They watch the ship sink; Ben-Hur prevents Arrius from committing suicide.	Fighting music continues with a brief reference to Ben-Hur's theme when he dives into the sea. The Warship and Rowing themes are heard as the ship sinks.
A Roman ship rescues Arrius and Ben-Hur.	No music until they see the ship, when we hear the Rowing motive.
On board, Arrius learns that he was victorious and realizes that Ben-Hur has saved his life.	No music until the Rowing motive returns at the sight of the galley slaves.
In Rome, a procession leads to the Emperor, who praises Arrius and later pardons Ben-Hur.	Source music: Roman march music. No music for the dialogue.
At a lavish party, Arrius announces that he has adopted Ben-Hur as his son.	Source music: African and Roman dance music. No music for the announcement.
Ben-Hur tells Arrius of his desire to go home.	Esther's theme is followed by a lyric version of the Ben-Hur theme, ending with the Redemption chords.

Complications: Returning Home and Revenge

1:41:10–2:54:40; DVD Chapters 29–49

SCENE DESCRIPTION	MUSIC
Ben-Hur arrives in Judea.	The Judea theme is played.
Balthasar observes Ben-Hur, who gets water and lies down, enjoying his memories. Balthasar approaches, wondering if Judah is the Messiah.	The themes for Balthasar, Ben-Hur, and Esther appear in succession. As Balthasar speaks, we hear his theme followed by the Christ theme.
Balthasar introduces Ben-Hur to Sheik Ilderim, who asks Judah to race his horses against Messala in the Circus.	No music
Balthasar asks Judah not to seek hatred and talks again of the Messiah.	The themes for Balthasar and Christ underscore his talk.
Ben-Hur leaves and goes to Jerusalem, where he comes to his house.	The Judea and House of Hur themes are heard.
Inside, Judah reunites with Esther and Simonides.	The lack of music in this scene reflects the barrenness of the house.
Ben-Hur and Esther recall their last meeting and rekindle their love. Esther pleads with him not to give in to hatred, and tells of the teachings of Christ.	Esther's theme dominates until the mood darkens with the mention of Messala. The Hate theme and a brief phrase of Christ's theme are heard.
Ben-Hur confronts Messala, demanding to know the whereabouts of his mother and sister. In the prison, Miriam and Tirzah are found to have leprosy.	Music is withheld until the guard is startled to discover the lepers, whereupon we hear the Leper theme.
Released from prison, Miriam and Tirzah go to the house of Hur and speak with Esther. She promises not to tell Judah of their fate.	The Leper theme appears. Miriam's theme then dominates. Ben-Hur's theme lingers after he walks by, and Esther's theme is heard as mention is made of her love for Judah.
Esther tells Judah that Miriam and Tirzah are dead and pleads with him to forget Messala. Judah leaves.	No music until Ben-Hur leaves the house. The Ben-Hur and Hate themes are played.
Intermission	Hate theme

Entr'acte	Themes: Redemption, Judea, Esther, and Redemption. Much is the same as in the overture, except the entr'acte is shorter and the Redemption material is expanded.
In a Roman bath, Sheik Ilderim makes a wager with Messala.	No music
A montage shows the preparations on the day of the race.	Source music: the Circus March and fanfares announce that the race is about to begin.
The chariots parade around the racetrack.	Source music: Parade of the charioteers.
The horses are readied to begin. Pontius Pilate introduces the contestants.	No music other than a brief fanfare from the charioteer parade.
The race extends for nine laps around the track. At the climactic moment, Messala is spilled and trampled.	No music
Ben-Hur wins the race and is honored by Pontius Pilate.	Source music: the Circus March sounds with his triumph, and a phrase of the Parade of Charioteers (the Ben-Hur phrase) precedes the awarding of the laurels.

Complications: Finding Miriam and Tirzah

2:54:40–3:24:20; DVD Chapters 50–56

SCENE DESCRIPTION	MUSIC
Bloodied, Messala waits for Ben-Hur. Still hateful, before dying he tells Judah that Miriam and Tirzah are at the Valley of the Lepers.	The Friendship theme plays when Judah enters and more extensively after Messala dies. A trumpet plays a fragment of the Charioteer melody, mocking his false victory.
Judah goes to the Valley of Lepers seeking his mother and sister. He encounters Esther bringing food.	Dark, dissonant music, including the Leper motive, underscores his arrival.
Judah confronts Esther, who begs him not to show himself. He hides and observes Miriam and Tirzah.	Music halts for the conversation, but returns as Judah runs to see. The Leper theme leads to Miriam's theme.

Ben-Hur is prevented from seeing his mother and sister and leaves angry.	No music for the argument; an angry motive sounds at the end.
As they leave the valley, they see Christ preparing to give his Sermon on the Mount. Balthasar appears, saying that Christ is the Son of God.	With the vision of Christ in the distance, we hear his theme. Balthasar's theme accompanies his appearance.
Ben-Hur expresses his anger. He recalls an encounter with this man in the desert, but insists on going to Rome and leaves.	The music sours with the negative comments. The Christ theme returns with Judah's recollection, and Ben-Hur's theme is played as he goes.
People, including Esther, gather around Christ. Ben-Hur leaves in the distance.	Redemption music
In Jerusalem, Pontius Pilate warns Ben-Hur that he should leave Judea.	No music
Esther tells Judah of the hopeful message from Christ, and Judah talks of his desire for revenge. Esther says that she has lost him.	No music until Esther observes that hatred has turned Judah into Messala. The Hate theme appears, followed by Esther's theme.
At the Valley of the Lepers, Esther tells Miriam about Christ. Judah appears.	The Leper theme opens the scene and then fades. No other music.
Judah is told that Tirzah is dying. Esther wants to take them to Christ. Judah comforts Miriam and looks for Tirzah. He carries her out of the cave.	Music reenters, and the Christ theme is heard. Miriam's theme is played gently, and Ben-Hur's motive accompanies his search for Tirzah.

Climax and Resolution

3:24:20–3:42:25; DVD Chapters 56–61

SCENE DESCRIPTION	MUSIC
They enter Jerusalem, where the streets are deserted because of Christ's trial.	The music fades quickly.
Christ begins the long walk to his Crucifixion, carrying his cross. Ben-Hur arrives with Esther, Miriam, and Tirzah.	A somber funeral march is sustained.
As Christ passes, Ben-Hur recognizes him from the desert. Christ falls and is whipped by the soldiers.	The intense march continues through Christ's procession. Harsh music underscores his whipping.

Christ falls again, and Judah gives him water. The cup is kicked from Judah's hands, and he is pushed aside.	Christ's theme sounds during this parallel moment. An orchestra accent accompanies the Roman intrusion.
Christ is nailed to the cross.	No music
The cross is raised and the crowd watches sadly.	Motives from the Hate theme
Ben-Hur approaches and speaks to Balthasar, who suggests that this is just a beginning.	The Messala and Hate themes are combined. The Christ theme sounds briefly two times.
A storm rages at the death of Christ.	No music
Miriam and Tirzah discover that they have been miraculously cured. The blood of Christ flows out to the world.	The Christ and Redemption themes are combined in a joyous setting with ringing bells. The Christ secondary theme is treated in imitation.
Ben-Hur returns home. He tells Esther of Christ's comforting last words. He goes up the stairs and sees that Miriam and Tirzah are healthy.	Ben-Hur's theme opens the final scene, which also includes the Christ, Messala, Esther, and Miriam themes. A wordless choir leads to a climactic moment with a wordless chorus singing Ben-Hur's theme. The Christ/Redemption music is then sung with the word "Alleluia."

Trailer

Ben-Hur was a spectacular success, in which music played a large role. The early 1960s would see the production of additional religious epics, generally with traditional symphonic scores. But the quality and popularity of these films and of the classic musical score in general dwindled quickly, as a new era in American film was beginning to take shape.

Important Names and Terms

Cecil B. DeMille
Victor Young
modal harmony

Part 5

A New
American
Cinema,
1960–1976

20

Psycho

American society underwent a significant transformation during the 1960s. This tumultuous decade saw the peak of the Cold War and the threat of total nuclear annihilation, confrontations over civil rights and sexual liberation, assassinations, a moon landing, and the Vietnam War. Television cameras recorded many of these events, bringing horrifying visions into our living rooms. Rather than bonding us together, television illuminated the issues that separated us. Divisions based on race, sex, and age led to open and often violent confrontations. Traditions and authority were questioned in every aspect of American life.

In this environment of frustration and alienation, artists clung to the aesthetic voiced by Ezra Pound: "Make it new." Challenges to traditions in the art world had already escalated in the 1950s. Action painting, the Theater of the Absurd, and chance music had redefined the boundaries of their disciplines. Originality became the foremost element of an individual work of art, and the process of making art became as important as the product itself. With the continued growth of the university as patron supporting the professor/artist, the gulf between the so-called serious arts and the popular arts widened even further. The split is particularly apparent in music; "New Music" concerts attracted handfuls, while rock concerts were witnessed by thousands.

SIGNIFICANT FILMS

1959	*The 400 Blows*
	Hiroshima mon amour
1960	*L'Avventura*
	Breathless
	Psycho
1961	*Last Year at Marienbad*

Commercially oriented Hollywood films clearly lie in the realm of the popular arts. Yet filmmakers were not immune from revolutions in the arts. Moreover, they did not need to rebel against traditions—traditions were crumbling all around them. Hollywood studios were being taken over by large corporations, who were selling the movie lots to television. Increasingly, major studios financed and distributed pictures that were made abroad, especially in Great Britain. Studios no longer had exclusive contracts with actors or directors, and even the Hays Code was abandoned. Bare breasts were shown on the screen once again, beginning with *The Pawnbroker* (1964). Forced to be independent, filmmakers also became more original.

Figure 20.1 An action painting by Jackson Pollock

Another factor emerged that had an impact; film was developing a canon of classics. In the 1930s and 1940s, movies were made for immediate distribution, with little thought of creating classics. But once movies were shown on television, films such as *King Kong*, *Gunga Din*, *The Maltese Falcon*, and *The Wizard of Oz* were regarded as classics. Filmmakers now had films to study and be inspired by, but also films to compete with. Moreover, they had to deal with the issue that their films might be available for future generations to scrutinize. Composers of the early nineteenth century faced a similar crisis with the birth of so-called classical music, and they responded by turning to newer, more innovative compositional styles. Filmmakers reacted in a similar manner, and the films of the 1960s pulled away from the standard genres established in the Golden Age. Many films either redefined their genre or defied standard generic classification.

New Wave Cinema

Europeans led the way into the new era. In 1959, a new generation of filmmakers burst upon the scene in France, including François Truffaut, Jean-Luc Godard, and Alain Resnais. Known as New Wave Cinema, French films had an enormous impact on filmmaking around the world. At the heart of the movement is the concept of the auteur—the director/artist. Just as an author controls all aspects of a book, the auteur manipulates every detail of a film, including the script, cinematography, and music. For this new generation of auteurs, the traditional narrative techniques established in the 1930s were no longer viewed as adequate. Innovative plots with unclear beginnings and endings, ambiguous moral implications, and unconventional plot lines became vehicles in which to explore new visual effects, including slow motion, jump cutting, and freeze frames. As in the worlds of painting, music, theater, and dance, creativity sparkled.

New Wave directors showed great concern for the psychological importance of the mise-en-scène and music. For the most part, music was used to help establish an overall mood. Absent are the Hollywood clichés, such as mirroring the action, underscoring individual emotions, and loud endings. Applied sparingly, music—often diegetic—created atmospheric moods that remained detached from the details of an unfolding story. In light of this more limited role, directors rejected the musical traditions of the postromantics and embraced modern and popular styles.

Three of the most celebrated New Wave films contain distinctive modern musical scores. The music for Alain Resnais's *Hiroshima mon amour* (1959), composed by Georges Delerue, includes some popular musical cues as well as some suggestions of Japanese music. For the most part it maintains a serious, modern character, as befitting an intense drama set in the aftermath of the nuclear holocaust. Antonioni's *L'Avventura* (1960), with a moody score by Giovanni Fusco, relies heavily on the sound of a solo clarinet. The modern style captures the essence of the sensitive, psychological tale. Even more atmospheric is the predominant organ sound in *Last Year at Marienbad* (1961), also directed by Resnais. The music, like the interior and exterior images of the baroque hotel, plays a large role in creating the surrealistic aura of this film.

French filmmakers also embraced the sounds of American popular music, as can be heard in two landmark films: Truffaut's *The 400 Blows* (1959) and Godard's *Breathless* (1960). *The 400 Blows* (the title is part of a French colloquial expression freely translated as "to raise hell") follows the life of a troubled youth. The music, predominantly popular in nature, establishes a light-hearted, breezy mood throughout. When the film ends abruptly with a freeze frame, Truffaut forgoes the standard Hollywood big finish, as the last statement of the principal theme is performed by a single violin played pizzicato.

Figure 20.2 *The 400 Blows* ends abruptly with a freeze frame and the sound of a pizzicato violin

In *Breathless* the dominance of American-sounding jazz contributes to the setting of a Paris enamored with American pop culture. Ironically, Patricia, an American in Paris, is constantly attracted to European music, such as the Mozart Clarinet Concerto, and to European art. Music also helps accentuate the most startling technical device of the film—the jump cuts—since the abruptness of these cuts is set against smooth, continuous music.

A New American Era

The new era in European filmmaking began decisively in 1959. There is no such clear date for the emergence of a new American era. Arguments have been made for 1962, 1964, 1965, and 1967, but for all practical purposes we can say only that by 1967, Hollywood had absorbed the New Wave, and a new, invigorated production of films had begun. Between 1959 and 1967, the decline of Hollywood traditions and the emergence of a new style are intertwined, as will be discussed in Chapters 21 and 22. From the point of view of film music, the year 1960 makes a good dividing point. In 1959, Hollywood produced one of the last monumental film scores in the classic tradition (*Ben-Hur*) prior to the revival of the style in 1977 with *Star Wars*. In 1960, the first outstanding film score reflecting the newer conception appeared—*Psycho*.

Psycho

Matching the innovative spirit of his French and Italian counterparts, Alfred Hitchcock broke with many of the current Hollywood trends in making *Psycho*. He chose to shoot in black and white in order to highlight the starkness of the story and to lower production costs. Because of this, the visual images of *Psycho* can be linked with the European imports that were already having an impact in the country. Over the next few years, a significant number of America's finest films continued to use black-and-white film. The awarding of an Oscar for black-and-white cinematography continued until 1967.

 Psycho contains numerous other creative shots, including the opening city view that settles into a voyeuristic peep into a hotel window, fascinating mirror images, an overhead angle for the murder of Arbogast, and the superimposition of the face of death on a smiling Norman in the final scene. But the single most stunning effect is the shower montage, which rivals Eisenstein's Odessa steps montage in *Battleship Potemkin* (1925) for brilliance. In a sequence lasting forty-five seconds, Hitchcock rapidly moves between eighty-seven shots with a cutting technique that seems as violent as the scene itself. By the end, the audience imagines that it has seen nudity and a knife stabbing a body, but both are implied, not shown.

The Narrative

The visual shock of the shower scene is more than matched by Hitchcock's treatment of the narrative. The film stands as a classic model of the exploitation of sex and violence. The sexual tension of the opening segment of the film, showing an unmarried couple in a hotel room, is unprecedented since the Hays code. The scene even includes a never-shown-before backside of a bra; at the time, men were not supposed to know how such a contraption worked. Our protagonist is a woman who not only is having an affair, but who steals forty thousand dollars as well. When she is killed, our new protagonist seems to be a young man who, at best, is covering up a murder or, at worst, is a serial killer. The moral ambiguity in this film stands in stark contrast to the values expressed in *Ben-Hur*.

 In setting up the shower scene, Hitchcock lets us follow a standard narrative in which we align ourselves with Marion, despite her moral flaws. After several close calls, we expect her to succeed in either reaching Sam or returning safely to Phoenix with the money. Her murder forty-five minutes into the film is stunning. The story is no longer about Marion, Sam, and stolen money; it is now about Norman, a psychotic killer. In the process, Hitchcock redefines the horror genre. Instead of terror created by a monster, *Psycho* is the horrifying story of the boy next door. Hitchcock spends a substantial amount of time at the end of the film showing how such a horror could happen to anyone, and for a while, people all over the country stopped taking showers.

The Music

Supporting Hitchcock's visual and narrative effects is an innovative score by Bernard Herrmann. Reflecting the stark black-and-white cinematography, the music is written for a string orchestra, forgoing the variety of colors provided by wind and percussion instruments. Moreover, the treatment of the strings, reminiscent of Stravinsky's *Rite of Spring*, is often harsh and percussive, with frequent hard accents and pizzicato effects. Rarely are the strings allowed to play in the lyrical fashion normally associated with these instruments.

With these limited orchestral colors, Herrmann created a unified score that is consistently dissonant. There are certainly contrasts in mood, ranging from the tender, loving sound of the hotel room (4:35 and 6:00) to the terror of the shower (47:15). But all the cues project a common disturbed quality through the frequent use, both harmonically and melodically, of minor seconds and major sevenths. These related intervals are the most dissonant in traditional Western harmony. The harsh opening chords are built on the interval of a major seventh, and the following frantic eighth notes obsessively emphasize the half-step or minor second. The Stolen Money and Mother themes also center on these same intervals. The most striking use of this clash is the famous Murder theme. Herrmann creates a unique sound using the percussive-sounding strings, with a microphone close to the instrument to make the sound more strident, swooping to pitches that build a cluster of minor seconds and major sevenths (see Example 20.6).

Also essential to the understanding of this new approach in film scoring is the lack of contrast in a given cue. Once a cue begins, it is repetitive and does not change moods. Herrmann occasionally juxtaposes cues with different qualities, such as Lila's surprise in the cellar, but there are no gradual shifts within a cue. When Marion is trying to purchase a car (17:50), streams of chords similar to the opening of the story are heard. One might expect a rise in tension in the music when the highway patrolman stops to watch her, or at least some musical reaction when Marion first notices the officer. But the music remains aloof throughout and continues changing chords in a detached and neutral manner. Like the music of the New Wave films, the score for *Psycho* serves the primary function of creating a mood, while avoiding the standard Hollywood underscoring heard in films such as *Ben-Hur*.

Marion's Story

Hitchcock's division of the plot into two parts is reflected in the musical score. Each story has its own themes, and there are few overlapping cues. During Norman's story, reprises of the Flight and Transition themes provide momentary reminiscences of Marion themes, when first Arbogast (1:10:00) and then Sam (1:18:15) search for Marion.

The appearance of the Mother theme when Norman talks of a madhouse in the Marion story (40:35) serves as a foreshadowing of future events and marks the beginning of a musical transition to Norman's material. Other than these overlappings, there are no recurring ideas that pervade the entire film. The two parts of the story meet at the shower montage, when Herrmann introduces the terrifying murder theme that ends Marion's story and plunges us headlong into Norman's world.

The music for Marion is limited primarily to four musical ideas, one of which—the lover's theme—makes only two brief appearances early in the story. The most perplexing cue is the Transition theme (Eample 20.4). During the course of the film, it can be heard six times:

The opening view of Phoenix
The car lot (17:50)
Norman comes down from his house after arguing with Mother (32:50)
Norman balks at going into Marion's hotel room (33:55)
Marion calculates how much money she has spent (45:35)
Sam searches for Marion (1:18:15)

Because of the lack of a clear association within the story, the descending and ascending chords of the Transition theme have a reserved, stoic character. The unchanging character of the cue and its aimlessness contribute to the overall disquieting mood of the story.

The remaining two ideas in Marion's story are related. The Stolen Money theme is first heard at Marion's home, where the camera pans between the stolen money, a packed suitcase, and Marion, symbolically dressed in black underwear (10:45). The slow methodical movement of the strings against the slow descent and ascent of a minor second creates a strong feeling of foreboding. This musical idea returns when Marion takes money for the car (21:05) and when she hides the money in the newspaper (30:35). Once she is killed, this theme does not return, even though Hitchcock's moralizing camera focuses on the money in the newspaper just after the murder.

The Flight motive borrows the steady motion of the Stolen Money theme. One can almost hear it as the Stolen Money theme played at a frantic tempo. Added to this quick and steady pulse are some violent, syncopated chords, a brief and eerie melodic idea, and a low-pitched cadence. This theme kicks into action when Marion panics after being seen by her boss (13:00) and accompanies her as she drives to Los Angeles. The mood never changes, even when she imagines humorously what some of the reactions will be on Monday. Again, the music reflects her overall mood, not her moment-by-moment emotions. Contributing to the over-

all plot deception, Herrmann uses this theme, a theme associated with Marion, for the opening credits, thereby planting the idea in the viewer's mind that the film is about Marion. A less deceptive and less satisfactory introduction might have been composed using some of Norman's musical materials.

Norman's Story

The music for Norman has several distinct qualities. The dissonance level is more intense during this part of the film, and the extreme upper register of the violins is used extensively, both suggesting Norman's dementia. Norman's story also has more extended cues with few thematic references. Most striking is the music that appears in the overlapping of the two stories, just after Norman recognizes that Marion has used a fictitious name in signing in at the hotel—a moment that seems to trigger his lust (43:10). The music for this scene contains an unnerving rhythmic ostinato that combines with a variety of other ideas. When Norman watches Marion undressing with an unblinking eye, an eerie high pitch enters, suggesting his psychological state. As the cue continues, we can hear the Transition chords as Marion calculates her expenses, and it concludes only when Marion flushes the notes down the toilet, in a gesture that foreshadows what is about to happen to her life.

The two principal themes associated with Norman are the Mother theme and the Murder theme. The Mother theme consists of only three notes, and many manipulations of this motive can be heard, including statements of the theme backwards ("retrograde") and upside down ("inversion"). The motive is first heard in the low strings when Norman talks about the madhouse (40:35). A similar setting recurs at the end of the film, when Norman is waiting to be sent to a madhouse. In this setting, the music is quite ominous, especially as the last low pitch provides an inconclusive end to the film. Other prominent uses of the Mother theme accompany Arbogast, who sees Mother's shadow (1:10:00) and goes to find her in the house (1:13:40).

The Murder theme will always be associated with the shower montage. Initially, Hitchcock wanted no music for this scene, but after listening to what Herrmann wrote, he thankfully changed his mind. The passage has become one of the most recognizable in all film music. The strident swooping sounds have been linked with the sounds of birds, an obvious image in Norman's world; note also that Marion's last name is Crane, a type of bird. Herrmann, however, denied this connection, and perhaps it is better to think of the sound as the slashing of a knife. In addition to the shower montage, the theme appears three other times: during the murder of Arbogast (1:16:55), during the attempted murder of Lila (1:40:50), and, in varied form, when Norman is seen running from the house after Marion's murder (49:35).

Figure 20.5 Norman/Mother smiles at the end of the resolution

Psycho (1960)

Directed by Alfred Hitchcock
Music by Bernard Herrmann

Principal Characters

Marion Crane, a secretary tempted by money (Janet Leigh)
Sam Loomis, Marion's boyfriend (John Gavin)
Lila Crane, Marion's sister (Vera Miles)
Milton Arbogast, a detective (Martin Balsam)
Norman Bates, psychotic son of Mother (Anthony Perkins)

Marion's Themes

Example 20.1 Opening chords

Example 20.2 Flight

Example 20.3 Stolen Money

Example 20.4 Transition

Norman's Themes

Example 20.5 Mother

Example 20.6 Murder

Marion's Story

0:00–49:05; DVD Chapters 1–10
[Timing begin at the studio logo]

SCENE DESCRIPTION	MUSIC
Opening credits	Flight music
In Phoenix, we peer into a hotel window, where Marion and Sam have had a lunchtime liaison.	The Transition theme accompanies our view of the city and fades as we enter the hotel room.
Marion and Sam discuss their troubled relationship.	Two tender statements of a Love theme make their only appearance in the film.

Marion returns to work and is given forty thousand dollars to deposit.	No music
Marion is seen changing clothes and packing a suitcase with the money.	Stolen Money theme
Marion takes the money and begins to drive to Los Angeles. She sees her boss and becomes anxious.	No music until Marion is startled, which initiates the Flight theme.
Driving into the night, Marion pulls the car to the side of the road for rest. After a policeman talks to her, she continues her flight.	The music fades with the morning light, and there is no underscoring until the police car begins to follow her, as the Flight theme returns.
In Bakersfield, Marion hastily buys a new car with cash. As she drives away, she imagines a variety of conversations concerning her actions.	The Transition theme is played as she looks around. The Stolen Money theme is heard when she takes money. The Flight theme returns as she leaves.
In the rain, Marion stops at the Bates Motel. She sees Mother in a window and honks her horn. Norman runs out.	No music
Norman assigns her a cabin and helps her into her room. He invites her to have dinner with him in the house.	No music
Marion hides her money.	Stolen Money theme
Marion overhears Mother arguing with Norman. He brings sandwiches to the motel; she eats while they talk.	The Transition theme is played when Norman walks towards the motel, and it resumes when he hesitates about entering Marion's motel room.
The conversation turns sour when Norman thinks that Marion has suggested that her mother should be in a madhouse.	Most of the scene has no music. At the mention of the madhouse, Mother's theme makes its initial appearance.
Having decided to return the money, Marion goes into her room. Norman observes her undressing through a peephole, and he returns to his house.	As Norman watches, a disturbing high-pitched theme is played.
After making financial notes and then flushing them down the toilet, Marion takes a shower. She is suddenly attacked and killed by Mother.	The Transition theme is heard. Silence follows until we see Mother, which brings out the piercing Murder theme.

Norman's Story

49:05–1:48:00; DVD Chapters 11–26

SCENE DESCRIPTION	MUSIC
Norman discovers the body, cleans up the cabin, puts Marion and her belongings (including the money) into her car, and drives the car into a nearby lake.	A variation of the Murder theme is heard as Norman runs to the motel. New scurrying sounds accompany his cleanup. A stronger rhythmic idea is heard when he puts the body in the car. After a brief silence, Mother's theme appears in the low register.
Sam is writing a letter to Marion. Marion's sister Lila enters, followed by a private detective named Arbogast, who questions them about Marion.	No music
In a montage, Arbogast's investigation ends at the Bates Motel. He questions Norman and becomes suspicious. Seeing Mother, Arbogast wants to speak to her.	The Flight theme accompanies the montage, ending with cadences from the Transition theme. When Arbogast sees Mother, the Mother theme is played in the low strings. Ominous music follows.
Arbogast calls Lila, telling her where he is, and then goes to the house.	No music
Arbogast enters and goes up the stairs. Mother jumps at him with a knife and kills him.	Variations of Mother's theme are played. The Murder theme reappears briefly with the attack.
Sam goes to the Bates Motel, while Norman disposes of the body.	Transition theme
Sam and Lila talk to the skeptical deputy sheriff, who says that Mother has been dead for ten years.	No music
Norman moves Mother to the cellar.	Ominous chords
Sam and Lila go to the motel, meet Norman, and find evidence of Marion's presence.	Chords underscore their travel to Bates and return as they begin to investigate.
While Sam talks to Norman, Lila explores inside the house.	Tentative music is played as Lila goes to the house. The music stops when Lila enters, and resumes when she begins to explore Mother's room and then Norman's room.

Norman knocks out Sam and races to the house. Seeking refuge in the fruit cellar, Lila discovers that Mother is a preserved corpse. Norman enters dressed as Mother with a knife, but he is subdued by Sam.

The music plays loudly with the impact, and then scurrying sounds suggest Norman's frantic search for Lila. The music calms briefly when Lila first sees Mother, but the Murder theme returns as Norman attacks and is combined with the scurrying motive.

A psychiatrist explains what has happened to Norman. Norman is seen in a padded cell, and we hear Mother's final, ominous words.

Music, predominantly the Mother theme, appears only at the end, when Mother begins to speak.

Trailer

The juxtaposition of the scores of *Ben-Hur* and *Psycho* makes a startling contrast. The seeds for this seemingly abrupt change in musical style had been observed in a number of key films created before 1960, and the classical traditions certainly lingered beyond 1959. But clearly a new era was at hand, and, as seen with European films, the new American cinema would explore both modern and popular musical styles extensively.

Important Names and Terms

New Wave Cinema
Alain Resnais
Georges Delerue
Michelangelo Antonioni
François Truffaut
Jean-Luc Godard
Giovanni Fusco

21

Declining Traditions, 1960–1967

Traditional filmmaking in Hollywood did not disappear in the early 1960s as suddenly as Marion does in *Psycho*, but clearly the end was at hand. Although many films continued to exhibit features of the classic film score, most incorporated some of the newer trends. We can observe the fading traditions in the declining epics, in the turn towards popular music, and in the last glory years of the Hollywood musical.

Epic Films

With the enormous popularity and success of *Ben-Hur* (1959), Hollywood continued to produce epic stories set in antiquity, most of them Biblical stories. Foremost among these are *Spartacus* (1960), *King of Kings* (1961), *Cleopatra* (1963), *Sodom and Gomorrah* (1962), and *The Greatest Story Ever Told* (1965). Retaining the qualities of the 1950s, these films were lavish, featured a multitude of major stars, used wide-screen color cinematography, and were supported by musical scores by some of Hollywood's finest

SIGNIFICANT FILMS

1960	*Exodus* ♫ ✉
	Spartacus ✉
	The Magnificent Seven ✉
1961	*West Side Story* ★
	Breakfast at Tiffany's ♫♫
	El Cid ✉ ✉
	Days of Wine and Roses ♫
	Dr. No
1962	*Lawrence of Arabia* ★ ♫
1965	*Doctor Zhivago* ♫
1967	*Wait Until Dark*
1969	*Butch Cassidy and the Sundance Kid* ♫♫

composers. But the magic was gone, and these films tend to be weaker both artistically and in popular appeal than those of the previous decade.

Spartacus

The major exception to these generalizations is *Spartacus*, a powerful story about a slave rebellion against Rome. Part of the success of this film is its mood, which runs counter to the uplifting optimism of the other epics. The plot appears to be a mixture of the late 1950s epic with the pessimism of the 1960s. Instead of the hoped-for triumph of freedom-seeking slaves, we see their rebellious spirit crushed by the power of Rome. While the 1950s epics seem to symbolize freedom's victory over communism, *Spartacus* seems to have more ominous implications about contemporary American society.

This darker message is reflected in the musical score composed by Alex North. One of the most successful composers of the decade—he received five Oscar nominations in the 1960s—North creates a sound that is distinct from the epic film scores of Rózsa. Brass fanfares still dominate, but North includes prominent low brass instruments in addition to trumpets, a thicker texture, syncopated rhythms, and dissonances. Although this sound has often been equated with the decadence of Rome, it seems rather to suggest its brutality and cruel power. Historically, Rome was about to enter its most dominant era. The music leaves us with the feeling that while Rome, perhaps standing for America, is building its mighty Empire, it is also planting the seeds of its decay.

Other Epics

In general, the successful epics of the 1960s turned to subjects other than the Bible and Rome, including medieval history (*El Cid*, 1961), westerns (*How the West Was Won*, 1962), comedy (*It's a Mad Mad Mad Mad World*, 1963), and modern history (*Exodus*, 1960; *Lawrence of Arabia*, 1962; *55 Days at Peking*, 1963; *Zulu*, 1964; and *Doctor Zhivago*, 1965). The music for *Exodus* sets the standard for the new epic film score. Created by Ernest Gold, the Oscar-winning score centers on one prominent theme that became a popular hit. Featuring a solo piano in a concerto-like setting, the theme captures the spirit of Jews seeking a new homeland in Palestine. Unfortunately, the movie, with its apparent justification of Jewish terrorism, runs counter to modern sensibilities and has not retained its initial appeal.

Miklós Rózsa's score for *El Cid* is one of the finest epic scores of the post *Ben-Hur* era, and it is arguably one of the composer's best, though less celebrated, creations. As he had done with his earlier epics, Rózsa studied the music of medieval Spain and derived a number of melodies from historical materials, including a beautiful love theme that was nominated for Best Song. The film features a number of brilliant fanfares that recall the sounds of *Ben-Hur*. The most notable of these leads to a jousting match (46:00). In the moment just before the combat begins, fanfares are played in two different keys, representing the two sides that are in conflict.

Figure 21.1 Arabian landscapes are accompanied by Jarre's lush theme

Lawrence of Arabia

In several of the new epics, an exotic locale such as China, Africa, and Russia plays a major part in the story. Director David Lean was particularly adept at incorporating beautiful landscapes into his films and making them part of the story. For *Lawrence of Arabia* (1962), Lean filmed on location in the Arabian desert. Faced with enormous obstacles, foremost of which was the oppressive heat, he fashioned some of the most memorable visions in all of film history. Essential to the power of these landscapes is a lush score created by French composer Maurice Jarre featuring a beautiful and popular principal theme.

Lawrence of Arabia, considered to be one of America's finest films (rated No. 5 by the AFI), is a sweeping story that follows the odyssey of T. E. Lawrence during World War I, as described in his autobiography, *Seven Pillars of Wisdom*. Reflecting a trend towards realism, the film does not present the standard glorification of a British hero. Rather, the portrayal of this pivotal figure in the Middle East retains numerous contradictions. Was he a hero or a charlatan? Was he a voice for civilization or for barbarism? Was he a homosexual? All of these questions are left unanswered. At the heart of the film is a portrayal of two men, Lawrence from civilized England and Sherif Ali ibn el Kharish, who makes his initial appearance in the brutish act of killing Lawrence's guide (28:30). By the end of the film, we see both characters transformed, as Ali becomes a civilized politician, and Lawrence is committing barbaric acts.

Maurice Jarre was not Lean's first, second, or even third choice to compose the music. The impressive list of figures who for one reason or another declined to work on this film includes the English composers Malcolm Arnold, who had scored Lean's *The Bridge on the River Kwai* in 1957, William Walton, and Benjamin Britten; the American master of musicals, Richard Rodgers; and one of the Soviet Union's leading composers, Aram Khatchaturian.

In the tradition of the classic film score, Jarre employs a full symphony orchestra in this score. But unlike the fully scored epics of the 1950s, the music for *Lawrence of Arabia* is used with restraint. In addition, Jarre introduces unusual sounds by including an electronic instrument (ondes martenot), a plucked string instrument from the zither family (cithare), and, calling upon his own percussion background, an Arabian hand drum (darbuka). With these musical forces, Jarre creates two distinct types of melodies: English tunes representing the British side of Lawrence, and Arabian tunes representing both the land and Lawrence in Arabia. Both styles can be heard in the overture, played against a dark screen, and during the opening credits.

Once the story begins, music is withheld until Lawrence begins his initial trek through Arabia (17:50), where the eerie sounds of the ondes martenot and the cithare

Maurice Jarre (1924–2009)

Trained at the Paris Conservatory, Jarre began composing for French films in the 1950s. He was catapulted into international recognition with his scores for two grand epics in the 1960s, *Lawrence of Arabia* and *Doctor Zhivago*, and he later divided his time between composing in Europe and in Hollywood. In a number of films, such as *Witness*, he used a synthesizer effectively. He has received nine Academy nominations and three Oscars.

Important Film Scores

Lawrence of Arabia 1962 ★ ♫
Dr. Zhivago 1965 ♫
The Tin Drum 1979
The Year of Living Dangerously 1982
A Passage to India 1984 ♫
Witness 1985 ✉
Mad Max Beyond Thunderdome 1985
Fatal Attraction 1987
Dead Poets Society 1989
Ghost 1990 ✉

★ = Best Picture Oscar   ♫ = Best Music Oscar   ✉ = Music Oscar Nomination

lead to a lush statement of the Lawrence of Arabia theme (Example 21.1). As with all the Arabian themes in this film, this melody presents a mixture of Middle Eastern qualities (pitched drums, the melodic interval of an augmented second, and modal harmonies) with Western orchestration and harmonies. The augmented second interval between B-flat and C-sharp in the second measure is emphasized by an extended triplet rhythm. The versatility of this theme allows Jarre to imitate the sound of Middle Eastern music, such as when Lawrence talks to Tafas at night (21:15), and to use a sweeping gesture in the violins for the grandiose visions of the Arabian desert.

Much of the story in this film is told through striking images. During the scene in which Lawrence rescues Gasim (see Viewer Guide), Lean lets the camera and music sustain the drama. The visions of Gasim walking into the rising sun, discarding his belongings, and eventually collapsing are crosscut with segments showing Lawrence riding in his direction, Daud (Lawrence's servant) waiting in the heat, and the ever-brightening sun. Jarre's music unifies these images by sustaining certain recurring sounds, including the prominent sound of percussion. At the same time, Jarre is able to project the growing intensity of the heat. With each cut to the burning sun, the music produces a strong accent that gets louder throughout the scene, matching the sun's brightness. As Gasim becomes more desperate, the music begins to accelerate to a frantic pace.

The climax of the scene is set up by both cinematography and music. Just as the music and visions of Gasim reach their most dramatic moments, Lean cuts to the waterhole, where Ferraj, Ali, and the other Arabs are waiting. The sudden lack of music adds further tension. Cutting back to Daud, Jarre brings in a faint drumbeat, our first signal that Lawrence has been successful. Although we cannot see Lawrence in the distance, Daud reacts, suggesting that his Arabian eyes are sharper than ours. The music grows in excitement, and the full orchestra enters with the principal theme, underscoring the triumph of this defining moment for Lawrence. In the eyes of the Arabs, he has just become Lawrence of Arabia. Also note in this excerpt the brief appearance of the English theme and the use of other Arabian material, including the sound of the cithare.

Viewer Guide

Lawrence of Arabia: Rescue of Gasim

Timing

Excerpt: 1:13:00–1:22:40 (0:00 at overture); DVD Chapters 20–22

Key Points

- Musical depiction of arid desert
- Emotional reaction to rescue, based on Arabian theme
- Use of ondes martenot and cithare

Setting

Lawrence (Peter O'Toole) has designed a daring plan to take the city of Aqaba from the Turks by crossing the Nefud Desert and attacking by land. Although Sherif Ali ibn el Kharish (Omar Sharif) believes that the crossing is impossible, he joins Lawrence in the attempt. Lawrence takes two servants, Daud and Ferraj. They successfully cross the desert, but one man, Gasim, has fallen and has been left in the desert. Against all odds, Lawrence reenters the desert to rescue Gasim.

Principal Leitmotifs

Example 21.1 Lawrence of Arabia

Example 21.2 Lawrence of England

PLOT	MUSIC
Crosscutting shows Gasim walking into the rising sun, Lawrence riding into the desert, Daud waiting at the desert edge, and the searing sun.	The music depicts the desert with the sounds of percussion, the high register of violins, and the low register of a piano. With each vision of the sun, the music becomes louder and faster.
The other tribesmen and Ferraj are shown waiting at a waterhole.	No music
Daud sees the figures and gallops towards them on his camel.	A distant drum signals the successful rescue, joined by strings and the cithare playing motives from the Arabian theme. A crescendo and an accelerando lead into a full statement of the theme, accentuating the triumph.
At camp, Ferraj waits, and Ali is frustrated.	No music
Ferraj sees the riders and alerts the camp. They all rise to see Lawrence.	The Arabian theme is suggested along with other Arabian material.
Ferraj and Doud greet each other, and the focus returns to Lawrence.	Lawrence's English and Arabian themes are played by the orchestra.
Ali greets Lawrence with water, showing his acceptance of the Englishman as a fellow Arab.	The Lawrence of Arabia theme is played fully by the strings.
Lawrence declares: "Nothing is written."	The cithare briefly plays the melody, and the orchestra joins in.
Several Arabs offer their beds to Lawrence, and he accepts that of Ali. Symbolically, he tries to take off his English clothes, but he is too tired and collapses onto the bed.	Arabian music is heard, including motives of the Lawrence of Arabia theme.

Lean and Jarre also worked together on the epic *Doctor Zhivago* (1965), based on the Nobel Prize–winning novel by Boris Pasternak. Like the score for *Lawrence of Arabia*, the score for *Doctor Zhivago* includes a relatively sparse use of musical cues, the incorporation of a folk instrument (the balalaika), and the dominance of a single melody, Lara's theme. While the landscape is not quite as spectacular as Arabia, the combination of a romantic story with beautiful cinematography and music proved to be a popular success once again, and Jarre won his second Oscar.

Movie Themes: Instrumental

During the 1950s, Hollywood had discovered the financial rewards of having popular musical themes in film scores, especially if they appealed to the younger generation. Inspired also by the success of themes for television shows, many filmmakers began to consider a hit musical theme an essential element of a successful movie. The finest of these would not only appeal to the audience, but also capture the essence of the film, as in *Lawrence of Arabia* and *Doctor Zhivago*.

The best instrumental theme of the early 1960s is Elmer Bernstein's energetic theme for *The Magnificent Seven* (1960), Hollywood's adaptation of Kurosawa's *Seven*

Close-Up: Drive-In Theaters

Built for Families and Teens

A new facet of the movie experience of the 1950s and 60s was the drive-in theater. The first such theater was created in New Jersey in 1933, but it was after World War II that the idea proliferated throughout the country. For the parents of baby boomers, the drive-in was a convenient and inexpensive way to take kids to the movies. Playgrounds were built to encourage families to come early, and concession stands provided drinks, hot dogs, pizza, and lots of treats. By 1958, nearly five thousand drive-ins were active in the US. Many were huge and featured other entertainments, such as pony rides and miniature golf. The Troy Theater in Michigan was built for three thousand cars. One of the more curious theaters opened in 1948—Ed Brown's Drive-In and Fly-in, capable of holding five-hundred cars and twenty-five airplanes.

As baby boomers grew up, they discovered the intimacy of watching movies from the privacy of their cars. Many films catered to the young audience with scenes of teenage sexual encounters and frightening moments that would make a couple cling together. The popularity of drive-ins continued through the 1960s, but after the Vietnam War and the subsequent phenomenon of *Star Wars*, for which the stereo sound of an indoor theater is essential, drive-ins rapidly began to close.

Figure 21.2 The first drive-in theater

Samurai (1954). Kurosawa's film is a brilliant study of society in the midst of change, a topic well suited to America in 1960. *The Magnificent Seven* retains this theme, as seven men in various stages of their lives have difficulties adjusting to the changing world. Coming together, they defend a Mexican village of farmers, whose lives are the epitome of order. The final message—"The farmers are the winners, we are the losers"—is less forceful than in Kurosawa's film, but still meaningful in the context of

Figure 21.3 The theme for *The Magnificent Seven* is primarily associated with Chris

the film. For many, however, the message would be obscured by Hollywood's star power, the exciting action sequences, and the rousing musical score.

Seven Samurai had included indigenous Japanese music, and Bernstein similarly created Mexican folk sounds supported by a prominent role for guitars and other instruments associated with Mexican music. At one point, a village celebration is accompanied by an odd tune with a distinctly Asian character (48:45). This is perhaps a tribute to the final farmer's dance in *Seven Samurai*, as both have similar instrumentation. Overall, the score is dominated by Bernstein's energetic main theme. Heard in numerous transformations and primarily associated with Chris (Yul Brynner), the theme has become the signature sound of the western spirit. Clearly indebted to the American nationalism of Copland and to Moross's score for *The Big Country*, Bernstein's music established a western sound that was distinct from the ballads of Tiomkin, heard in *High Noon* (1954) and *The Alamo* (1960).

Figure 21.4 The Pink Panther is accompanied by Mancini's sassy saxophone theme

A number of other instrumental themes achieved prominence in the early 1960s. Bernstein created a different mood for *The Great Escape* (1963), in which the idea of humor in the face of adversity is depicted by a cocky march. On the lighter side, Henry Mancini's jazz theme for *The Pink Panther* (1963) remains one of the most humorous and memorable of all movie themes. Another entertaining theme by Mancini, unfortunately a bit of a mismatch for its story, is "Baby Elephant Walk" from *Hatari!* (1962).

Movie Themes: Songs

Although the orchestral themes mentioned above were successful, moviemakers soon recognized that songs are more popular with the general public than instrumental tunes. Moreover, the inclusion of a song makes a film eligible for one additional Academy nomination—Best Song. Since the number of Oscar nominations given to a film is a major marketing advantage, theme songs far outnumber instrumental themes.

Theme songs also can create dramatic liabilities. In evaluating the quality and suitability of a song for a film, a number of issues should be considered:

- Does the mood of the song represent the overall mood of the film?
- Do the words of the song reflect some aspect of the story?
- Does the song blend into the musical style of the film score as a whole?
- Does the placement of the song detract from the dramatic flow?
- Who sings the song—a character in the drama or an unseen voice?

Figure 21.5 Audrey Hepburn sings "Moon River"

Some films created workable solutions to these issues, but there were also many songs that were not appropriate for their films.

Breakfast at Tiffany's

At the beginning of the decade, Henry Mancini was the top songwriter in the film industry, winning Oscars for "Moon River" from *Breakfast at Tiffany's* (1961) and "The Days of Wine and Roses" from *The Days of Wine and Roses* (1962). The first of these meets every criterion for an outstanding theme song. The melody and lyrics of "Moon River" successfully capture the spirit of two drifters who meet and fall in love. The tune is presented without words during the opening credits. It is first heard played by a solo harmonica, a subtle suggestion that Holly (Audrey Hepburn) is not a sophisticated city woman but comes from the country. Presentations by the strings and a wordless choir follow.

The words of the song are first heard when Audrey Hepburn sings the tune while accompanying herself on a guitar (42:00). The untrained quality of her voice adds to the sincerity and impact of the melody. The tune, representing growing love, is then used in the underscoring, blending well with the overall popular style of the score. The only weakness of the tune from a commercial perspective is its title. Everyone knows the tune as "Moon River," but many would not be able to name the movie associated with it. Ideally, for maximum publicity a song should share the same name as the movie.

Other Mancini Scores

Two other Mancini themes match their movie titles but raise some dramatic difficulties. "The Days of Wine and Roses," another classic love song, perfectly represents the early love relationship of the film's protagonists, Joe and Kirsten. But since the film is about the destructiveness of alcoholism, the tune is an odd theme song for the movie as a whole. In the closing scene, when Joe talks to his daughter Debbie about her mother, Mancini places the tune in a child's instrument, a glockenspiel. The effect is potent, but the meaning is ambiguous. Anyone drawn to the film because of the song would have been surprised by the film's content.

Completely out of sync with its film is Mancini's "Wait Until Dark" from the 1967 thriller *Wait Until Dark*. A change of pace for both Henry Mancini and Audrey Hepburn, this film features a surprisingly modern score that includes two pianos tuned a quarter-step apart; the strong out-of-tune quality suggests the disturbed character of a psychotic killer. It also links musically to an out-of-tune doll, which is sought after by the film's antagonist. The moment that startled a nation, when the killer leaps at Susy (1:46:00), is accompanied by a sweeping glissando played on the strings inside the piano. The return to traditional harmonies at the end suggests that the danger has been resolved, but the appearance of a cheerful song during the closing credits is totally incongruous with the film as a whole.

Other Song Composers

Among the other successful composers of theme songs in the decade are Dimitri Tiomkin, John Barry, Miklós Rózsa, and Burt Bacharach. Tiomkin, who had begun the theme song fad with his ballad for *High Noon* (1952), continued to create outstanding tunes with the Oscar-nominated songs "The Green Leaves of Summer" from *The Alamo* (1960) and the teen-oriented "Town Without Pity" from *Town Without Pity* (1961). The latter is a complete mismatch with the dramatic story of rape committed by American soldiers in Germany. Other popular songs that more successfully capture the spirit of their namesake films are John Barry's "Born Free" (1966) and Rózsa's patriotic "The Green Berets" (1968).

By the end of the decade, Henry Mancini's reputation as Hollywood's finest songwriter would be seriously challenged by Burt Bacharach, who composed a string of successful songs, including "What's New, Pussycat?" (1965) and "Alfie" (1966), from movies with the same titles. He closed the decade with two Academy Awards for the score to *Butch Cassidy and the Sundance Kid* (1969) and the song "Raindrops Keep Fallin' on My Head" from the same film. While the tune is appealing, the Oscar for scoring reflects the state of film music in the new era. There are only a few musical cues in the film, and the popular nature of those passages do not allow for development. Even the appearance of the winning song disrupts the dramatic flow (26:50). The tune accompanies an extended scene, more like a music video, that has no function in the plot; the mood and words of the song are unrelated to the film, and its intrusive quality is emphasized by the fact that the melody does not appear in the rest of the film. The difference between this score and the score for *Ben-Hur*, which won an Academy Award one decade earlier, is staggering.

Bringing Up Baby Boomers

Another major factor in the declining traditions in Hollywood filmmaking was the changing audience. By the early 1960s, the babies born in the baby boom of the late 1940s were teenagers. The ever-rising middle class had produced an unprecedented number of young people with leisure time, money, and entertainment needs. Eager to capitalize on this phenomenon, Hollywood began to appeal directly to the younger market. While audiences in the early 1950s were largely middle-aged, theaters and drive-ins were now filled with teenagers.

Rock Music

Rock music had a strong impact on films during the 1960s. Elvis Presley, who began his movie career in 1956, starred in an average of three films a year from 1960 to 1968. The Beatles also got into the act with three memorable films: *A Hard Day's Night* (1964), *Help!* (1965), and *Yellow Submarine* (1968). The zany antics of Paul, George, Ringo, and John during the musical performances served as a model for later MTV music videos. Numerous other rock singers and groups were featured in films. Among the most popular rock films were a series of films beginning with *Beach Party* (1963) featuring Frankie Avalon and Annette Funicello.

James Bond

During the decade, rock music in movies extended beyond the limited role of serving as a performance vehicle for a prominent singer or group. In *Dr. No* (1962), the first Bond film, the James Bond theme created a great sensation, and it remains one of the most widely recognized movie themes today. The theme is first presented during the opening credits. During the film itself, a conventional orchestra underscores the drama, but the Bond theme returns on electric guitar with Sean Connery's first line in his signature role—"Bond, James Bond" (8:00)—and subsequently during action and lusty moments. Later James Bond movies expanded the role of rock music, primarily through the scoring of a young English rock musician, John Barry. His theme from *Goldfinger* (1964) achieved a particularly high level of popularity.

Musicals: *West Side Story*

As with most film genres, musicals were on the decline during the 1960s. But while their numbers cannot match those of earlier decades, the quality is still excellent. Prior to the 1960s, only three musicals had won the Oscar for Best Picture: *The*

Broadway Melody (1929), *An American in Paris* (1951), and *Gigi* (1958). During the 1960s, four Best Picture Awards went to musicals: *West Side Story* (1961), *My Fair Lady* (1964), *The Sound of Music* (1965), and *Oliver!* (1968). The first three of this group are also ranked among the AFI Top 100 American Films. Unlike the earlier musicals that won the Best Picture award, these four are not original works, but adaptations of Broadway shows. Original film musicals were rare during the decade.

Figure 21.6 The balcony scene from *West Side Story*

Pointing the way to the new film version of a Broadway musical is *West Side Story*. Winning ten Oscars, it broke away from the tradition of Rodgers and Hammerstein with athletic dancing, intense jazz, and a potent story of racial violence. Set in New York, the story is essentially an adaptation of Shakespeare's *Romeo and Juliet*. Director Robert Wise, choreographer Jerome Robbins, and composer Leonard Bernstein are the principal artistic talents behind the film. Stephen Sondheim wrote the lyrics; he later became the foremost American composer of musical theater, and he won an Oscar for his song "Sooner or Later" from *Dick Tracy* (1990).

Bernstein incorporates into his score both American and Latin American popular music, helping to delineate the racial conflict between the American and Puerto Rican gangs. The harsh accents of American bebop accompany the fighting scenes and the Jets' rendition of "Cool," while a Latin American mambo is heard in the gym (36:15), "Maria" is introduced as a cha-cha-cha (39:30), and "Tonight" is set to a beguine rhythm (58:20). Intermixed with these popular sounds is a modernistic harmonic treatment, highlighted by the "Cool" fugue, whose principal subject uses eleven of the possible twelve tones of the chromatic scale (1:57:10). All of this material is superbly held together by brilliant thematic transformation. The whistles heard at the outset of the film is the germ motive for much of the musical material that follows.

Trailer

The Hollywood epic and musical were just two of the numerous genres that faded rapidly in the 1960s. Changes in American film, some of which were suggested in the late 1940s, were now accelerated. In the years that followed, traditional scoring would virtually disappear, as Hollywood entered a new era.

Important Names and Terms

Ernest Gold

Maurice Jarre

ondes martenot

Burt Bacharach

John Barry

The Beatles

Stephen Sondheim

Suggested Viewing

Action: *The Alamo* (1960) ✉ ✉, *The Guns of Navarone* (1961) ✉, *The Great Escape* (1963), *55 Days at Peking* (1963) ✉ ✉, *Zulu* (1964), and *The Sand Pebbles* (1966) ✉

Thriller: *Cape Fear* (1962) and *Charade* (1963) ✉

Drama: *Elmer Gantry* (1960) ✉, *Lilies of the Field* (1963), and *The Agony and the Ecstasy* (1965) ✉

Romance: *Splendor in the Grass* (1961) and *Summer and Smoke* (1961) ✉

Comedy: *The Apartment* ★ (1960) and *It's a Mad Mad Mad Mad World* (1963) ✉ ✉

Epic: *King of Kings* (1961) ✉

22

The Emerging New Era, 1960–1967

While the traditions of the Golden Age were fading in the early 1960s, influences from the New Wave were increasingly felt on American films. Among the characteristics of the emerging new era are a mixture of serious and light-hearted moments, frank treatment of sexuality, and creative narratives and images. With these elements, American filmmakers forged a new film era that would become firmly established by 1967.

Among the best of the early manifestations of the new era are *Psycho* (1960), *The Hustler* (1961), *Lonely Are the Brave* (1962), *The Manchurian Candidate* (1962), *Hud* (1963), *Dr. Strangelove* (1964), *The Pawnbroker* (1965), and *Who's Afraid of Virginia Woolf?* (1966). All of these films are in black and white, and all use music sparingly. For the most part, music is limited to the following moments:

- opening and closing credits
- source music
- transitions
- montages
- landscape panoramas
- scenes of movement or action

SIGNIFICANT FILMS

1961	*The Hustler*
1962	*To Kill a Mockingbird* ✉
	The Manchurian Candidate
1963	*Tom Jones* ★ ♫
1964	*The Pawnbroker*
	The Umbrellas of Cherbourg ✉ ✉
1967	*Bonnie and Clyde*
	The Graduate

Music in the New Era

As we saw in *Psycho* (Chapter 20), the music in these films tends to create general moods rather than to depict individual or changing emotions. Both popular and modern musical styles are well suited to this end. While the general public may see these styles as opposite poles in entertainment, their function in film is often similar. Also common to both is a reliance on a performance ensemble smaller than the standard orchestra, providing financial savings in these economical years.

Three Early Films

These musical qualities can be seen in three films from the first half of the decade—*The Hustler*, *The Pawnbroker*, and *The Manchurian Candidate*.

Figure 22.1 Fast Eddie shoots pool with jazz underscoring in *The Hustler*

Typical of the new sound is the music for *The Hustler* created by the big band arranger Kenyon Hopkins. The sporadic cues are composed for small groups of instruments found in a swing band. Music is heard during transitions and beneath some dialogue, but it is most effective for montages showing extended pool games (20:30). Throughout, the mood of the music remains aloof and cool, as if in an alcoholic haze, and does not reflect the tension of the games or the tragic event that sets up the film's climax.

The prominence of jazz in films at this time provided the opportunity for a number of composers in the jazz world to create film scores. Jazz great Duke Ellington, who had already scored the music for *Anatomy of a Murder* (1959—see Chapter 18), received an Academy nomination for the score to *Paris Blues* (1961), which features a performance by Louis Armstrong. During the 1960s, filmmakers recruited another African-American jazz musician who would have a major impact on both film and television—Quincy Jones.

Jones composed his first score for one of the finest films of the decade, *The Pawnbroker* (1964). As in *The Hustler*, the musical cues are often scored for jazz ensembles, but Jones slips into a modern style as needed in this powerful drama. The plot centers on Sol Nazerman (Rod Steiger), a Holocaust survivor, and his struggle to deal with his lack of emotion and his work as a pawnbroker in Harlem. The jazz idiom runs counter to Sol's character and reinforces our perception of his inability to deal with the changing world. In one of the most effective moments in the film, a single cello plays an extended solo as Sol is unable to reach out to a female companion (1:25:30). The lack of accompaniment in this passage represents Sol's complete isolation from others.

One of the unique sounds in *The Pawnbroker* is that of a harpsichord. An obsolete eighteenth-century keyboard instrument, the harpsichord had a resurgence of popularity in the 1950s and 1960s. For the most part, the instrument was used to recreate music from the past for a more authentic sound, but some concert composers also incorporated the distinctive timbre into their works, a trend that is also reflected in a number of films from the 1960s, including *The Manchurian Candidate* (1962).

David Amram, who composed only a handful of film scores, created an intriguing score for *The Manchurian Candidate*, a remake of which appeared in 2004. The music employs various modern styles. An American nationalist style is used for scenes of the soldiers return-

Figure 22.2 A harpsichord accompanies the nightmare dream sequences in *The Manchurian Candidate*

ing to the US, and avant-garde styles accompany the disoriented nightmares experienced by some of the soldiers. In these scenes, Amram makes effective use of the harpsichord. The timbre of the instrument suggests the intellectual atmosphere of the tea party, while the discordant harmonies project the underlying mood of the recurring nightmares (11:30).

Composer Profile

Quincy Jones (b. 1933)

Born in Chicago, Quincy Jones attended the Berklee School of Music and the Schillinger School of Music (both in Boston). At the age of seventeen, he became a trumpeter and arranger for Dizzy Gillespie and later played with Lionel Hampton before organizing his own band. In addition to his film music, he composed for television, including *I Spy* and *Ironside*, and won an Emmy for his work on the miniseries *Roots*. He also produced Michael Jackson's video "Thriller" and the all-star benefit video *We Are the World*. He has received six Oscar nominations and was honored with the Jean Hersholt Humanitarian Award in 1995.

Film Scores

The Pawnbroker 1964
In the Heat of the Night 1967 ★
In Cold Blood 1967 ✉
The Wiz 1978 ✉
The Color Purple 1985 ✉ ✉

★ = Best Picture Oscar   ♫ = Best Music Oscar   ✉ = Music Oscar Nomination

To Kill a Mockingbird

To Kill a Mockingbird (1962) is one of the finest Hollywood adaptations of a novel. Originally appearing in 1960 and awarded a Pulitzer Prize in 1961, *To Kill a Mockingbird* is Harper Lee's only published book. Based on her experiences growing up in a small Alabama town, it captures the spirit of America in the 1930s. One of the characters, young Dill, is based on Lee's neighbor and fellow writer, Truman Capote. Although the story deals with issues of racism, the portrayal of youthful innocence and wisdom gives the novel an overall optimistic mood.

American nostalgia, family strength, and childish innocence are underlying themes that run throughout the film, themes that are supported by the black-and-white photography and the musical score. Gregory Peck plays one of the strongest roles in film—Atticus Finch, a small town lawyer and single parent of two young children. In 2003, the American Film Institute voted his character the greatest hero in American film history, just ahead of Indiana Jones, James Bond, Rick (*Casablanca*), and Will Kane (*High Noon*).

Composer Profile

Elmer Bernstein (1922–2004)

Elmer Bernstein was born in New York and only gradually showed interest in music. After studying with Roger Sessions, he began making musical arrangements for the Army Air Corps. His first film score was composed in 1951, and he quickly established his compositional diversity with such contrasting styles as the jazz score for *The Man With the Golden Arm* and the epic music for *The Ten Commandments*. During a career that spans over half a century, he has sustained a prolific output of high-quality scores that reflect a wide variety of musical styles. He has received fourteen Oscar nominations, but won the award only once, for the musical *Thoroughly Modern Millie*.

Important Film Scores

The Man with the Golden Arm 1955 ✉		*True Grit* 1969 ✉	
The Ten Commandments 1956		*Animal House* 1978	
The Magnificent Seven 1960 ✉		*Airplane!* 1980	
To Kill a Mockingbird 1962 ✉		*Trading Places* 1983 ✉	
The Great Escape 1963		*Ghostbusters* 1984	
Hawaii 1966 ✉		*Wild Wild West* 1999	
Thoroughly Modern Millie 1967 ♫		*Far from Heaven* 2002 ✉	

★ = Best Picture Oscar   ♫ = Best Music Oscar   ✉ = Music Oscar Nomination

The score by Elmer Bernstein, his personal favorite, plays a major role in creating the overall atmosphere of the film. Bernstein generates a variety of moods within the story. When young Scout asks her older brother Jem about their deceased mother (15:15), Bernstein gently underscores the poignancy of the loss for both the children and Atticus. Minutes later, an exuberant American nationalist sound with clear ties to Copland is heard accompanying the children's play that will result in Scout, rolling inside a tire, landing abruptly at the porch of feared Boo Radley (18:05).

Figure 22.3 African-Americans stand in salute to Atticus Finch

Two principal stories unfold in the film, both dealing with prejudice. Atticus has been asked to defend a black man wrongly accused of rape. In keeping with the tradition of courtroom dramas, there is no music for the trial scenes. When the verdict of guilty is read, Bernstein composes a gentle hymn, which resounds with dignity as the African-Americans in the gallery stand to honor Atticus's effort, emphasized when the minister admonishes Scout to stand because her "father's passing" (1:41:55).

Although the trial leads to a tragic conclusion, the other story ends with optimism. In his own way, the Finches' neighbor Boo Radley is subject to similar prejudices. As people with special needs were often treated in the 1930s, he was virtually locked up in his house with no outside contact. Without knowing what Boo looks like, the children and neighbors imagine him to be the dangerous town bogeyman. Bernstein depicts Boo Radley with a variety of motives, some of which suggest the mystery and potential danger of this unknown neighbor, and some of which—notably his waltz-like theme—suggest his innocence. At the end of the climactic scene (see Viewer Guide), we see Boo for the first time (Robert Duvall, in his screen debut) and learn of his gentle and protective spirit towards the children, as reflected in the waltz theme.

Despite the great variety of emotions and events in this film, Bernstein retains an overall mood of childlike simplicity and innocence. Both dramas are seen through the eyes of Scout, and the music reflects her point of view. The opening theme (labeled Innocence in the Guide) is first heard as a response to Scout's humming. It is set in 6/8 meter, as are many children's tunes, and the unusual melodic movement suggests a child singing randomly. In its initial presentation, a single sustained pitch can be heard in the accompaniment. For the most part, this theme and Boo Radley's waltz are given simple settings, often evoking the sound of a music box. Throughout, Bernstein writes for a small number of instruments, including a harmonica, in keeping with the Southern locale. The score stands as a model of how much can be achieved with minimal musical forces.

To Kill a Mockingbird: Climax

Timing

Excerpt: 1:51:05–2:01:25 (0:00 at logo);
DVD Chapters 33–36

Key Points

- General modern style
- A small group of instruments
- Mood of gentle innocence

Setting

The two principal stories of the film converge in this climactic scene. In a small southern town, lawyer Atticus Finch (Gregory Peck) is a single father of two children, Scout and Jem. In the adult world, Atticus has defended a black man for a crime he did not commit. Even though he lost the trial, Atticus has humiliated Bob Ewell, who lied in court. In the children's world, mysterious Boo Radley serves as the neighborhood bogeyman, and they have been increasingly daring in approaching his house.

Principal Leitmotifs

Example 22.1 Innocence

Example 22.2 Boo Radley

PLOT	MUSIC
The narrator, Scout as an adult, tells us that it is October and that Scout, shown staring over a fence at Boo's house, looks for Boo every chance that she gets.	Gentle music sounds on the piano and in the woodwinds. The tune and the repetitive two-note accompaniment have been associated with Boo during the film.
It is Halloween night, and Jem is accompanying Scout, dressed as a ham, to a pageant.	Source music: the pageant band is playing.
After the pageant, Scout cannot find her dress, so Jem walks her home through the park while she still wears her ham costume.	The Innocence theme is stated simply by a flute and then the full orchestra, similar to the presentation heard at the beginning of the film.
Jem hushes Scout as he thinks that he has heard a noise, but they resume their journey home.	The music softens, and motives (a rising and falling scale and the two-note alternation) associated with danger and Boo are heard. The Innocence theme resumes in the piano with the accompaniment of Boo's two-note theme on the harmonica.
Jem stops for a second time. Scout also hears the sound, but thinks that it is Cecil Jacobs.	No music
There is no response to Scout's shouting, so they continue walking.	The two danger motives are heard again, along with some tension-building motives.
Suddenly a man wearing dark clothes knocks Scout down and attacks Jem. Scout is unable to get out of her ham outfit. Jem tries to help her get up, but is grabbed again and knocked unconscious.	The music gets louder with a high-pitched trill and the addition of trombones. Syncopated rhythms are heard as Jem comes to Scout's aid, but the trill returns along with the timpani as Jem is grabbed again. Violent chords suggest his beating.
The attacker grabs Scout, still in the ham costume, but another adult wearing lighter clothes reaches out to protect her. The two adults struggle. The attacker again grabs for Scout, but is pulled away. Finally, the other adult triumphs.	Fighting music is built on a repeating pulse and syncopated accents. The trill returns as the attacker grabs for Scout a second time. Fighting music continues in the trombones, leading to a sustained chord that gets louder and ends with an accent, suggesting the falling of a body.
We see the legs of the protector. He picks up Jem and walks away. Scout gets out of her costume, sees the man taking Jem to her house, races home to the arms of Atticus.	A march pulse, which begins with the man walking, alternates with an eerie clarinet motive. The pulse quickens as Scout runs, and the music begins to fade when Scout embraces her father.

The doctor is called; Jem will be all right. Sheriff Tate arrives and identifies the attacker as Bob Ewell, who was stabbed and killed. He questions Scout as to the identity of the defender.	No music
Scout sees him hiding in the room behind the door. She recognizes that he must be Boo Radley, and she takes his hand.	Boo's two-note motive leads to his waltz theme gently played by the orchestra.

Landmarks of the New Era

By 1967, American filmmaking had entered a new age. Many histories point to *Bonnie and Clyde* (1967) as the watershed film of the era. Using explicit sexuality and graphic violence, the film tells of two young Depression-era adults who turn to crime, in part as a reaction to an oppressive society. In the end they are obliterated in a flurry of gunfire, as governmental forces once again triumph over rebellious individuals. Needless to say, the film found a responsive audience in young moviegoers, and the movie set the tone of American films for several years to come.

Close-Up: Producers and Directors

Great Names of the 1950s and 1960s

During the 1950s, the great directors of the Golden Age were creating their last works. A new generation of producers and directors emerged who would have a major impact in Hollywood, including the following:

Otto Preminger (1906–1986) was born in Vienna and came to the United States in 1935 to direct a play on Broadway. He soon began working in Hollywood for Twentieth Century Fox as a producer and director. His two major films for the studio, *Laura* (1944) and *Forever Amber* (1947), were both scored by David Raksin. Gaining independence from the studios in the 1950s, Preminger forged a number of powerful films that pushed the Hays Code to its limit. *The Man with the Golden Arm* (1955) deals with drug addiction, and *Anatomy of a Murder* (1959) contains frank discussions of sex and rape. Both, like *Laura*, are important films for their use of jazz in film scores.

Elia Kazan (1909–2003) is one of the most controversial figures in Hollywood. Born in Turkey to Greek parents, he came to the United States when he was four. He began acting on stage and soon established himself as one of Broadway's top directors. He directed his first feature film, *A Tree Grows in Brooklyn*, in 1945 and won an Oscar for his portrayal of anti-Semitism in America, *Gentleman's Agreement* (1947). In the 1950s, he directed his finest films, including *A Streetcar Named Desire* (1951), *On the Waterfront* (1954), and *East of Eden* (1955). These films used progressive musical styles and helped create a new Hollywood sound. In the 50s, he also admitted his Communist background and named other Hollywood figures (see Close-Up on page 212).

David Lean (1908–1991) worked his way up in the English film industry from tea boy to director. After a series of outstanding films in the 40s, he created a sensation with the epic film *The Bridge on the River Kwai* (1957). He solid-

The music for *Bonnie and Clyde* is by Charles Strouse, who is best known for composing musicals such as *Bye Bye Birdie* and *Annie*. As in many movies that were to follow, music is sparse. The only non-diegetic music cues are short passages that function as energetic transitions. Most feature instruments associated with country music, such as the banjo and fiddle. Typical is the first cue, which appears after Clyde robs a store and the two introduce themselves to each other and then flee in a stolen car (8:20). The music is used only as dabs of color, but it still helps set the location and contributes to the overall mood for the film.

Music plays a more substantial role in another landmark work of the era, *The Graduate* (1967). The folk-rock duo of Paul Simon and Art Garfunkel composed and performed the principal music for the film. The other music, prepared by Dave Grusin, is entirely diegetic, including the music emanating from Mrs. Robinson's stereo and various musical sources at the Taft Hotel. The Simon and Garfunkel songs successfully capture the spirit of the aimless, disillusioned youth of the 60s and are essential to the popularity of the film. The soundtrack album from this film became a top seller.

ified his reputation as the great director of epics with *Lawrence of Arabia* (1962) and *Doctor Zhivago* (1965). His last major triumph was *A Passage to India* (1984). Lean often employed lush film scores dominated by a single melody. The music for all four of these films won Oscars.

Mike Nichols (b. 1931), born in Berlin, came to America with his parents to avoid the Nazis. He eventually established himself in improvisational theater and turned to directing Broadway plays. His first three films created a great sensation: *Who's Afraid of Virginia Woolf?* (1966), *The Graduate* (1967), and *Catch-22* (1970). Each featured a different musical approach. *Who's Afraid of Virginia Woolf?* has a sparse, modern score, *The Graduate* features the songs of Simon and Garfunkel, and *Catch-22* has virtually no music at all. An extended break in his film career ended with *Silkwood* (1983), and he has remained an active director since that point.

Stanley Kubrick (1928–1999) was born in the Bronx. Entering film through his interests in photography, he began directing films in the 50s. Winning an Oscar for *Spartacus* (1960), Kubrick was launched into the forefront of American directors, justifiably earning a reputation for his unique creations. After his controversial *Lolita* (1962) and his comic masterwork *Dr. Strangelove* (1964), Kubrick produced his greatest work, *2001: A Space Odyssey* (1969). The use of adapted music in *2001* continued in his startling *A Clockwork Orange* (1971) and *Barry Lyndon* (1975). These films were followed by Jack Nicholson's darkest role in *The Shining* (1980), the powerful Vietnam War film *Full Metal Jacket* (1987), and his last film, the erotic *Eyes Wide Shut* (1999). His projected film *Artificial Intelligence: A.I.* was brought to fruition in 2001 by Steven Spielberg.

As shown in Table 22.1, the appearances of the tunes are primarily limited to accompanying credits and montages showing the passing of time and travel. The songs do not change moods or react to the story, but are used to set an overall mood, as the film is often adjusted to the music. Near the end, however, the guitar humorously suggests the idling of a car and subsequently Ben running out of gas (1:38:45), and it plays appropriate discords when Ben cannot get into the church.

Figure 22.4 The guitar indicates that Ben has run out of gas

Table 22.1

Simon and Garfunkel songs in *The Graduate*

SONG	PLACEMENT IN FILM
"The Sound of Silence"	Opening credits Summer montage (37:50) Closing credits
"April Come She Will"	Summer montage (40:50)
"The Big Bright Green Pleasure Machine"	Source music on radio (1:02:20)
"Scarborough Fair/Canticle"	Montage of Elaine leaving (1:10:10) Ben travels to Berkeley (1:13:10) Ben watches Elaine (1:17:00 and 1:20:15)
"Mrs. Robinson"	Whistled (1:30:00) Travel montage (1:33:45) Travel montage (1:36:10) Travel montage (1:38:00)

International Films

While American filmmakers were absorbing influences from abroad, international film centers were particularly receptive to American popular musical styles. The reverse was also true—popular movie themes from foreign films were often more successful in this country than the films themselves. Greece, a relatively small center for film, produced two movie themes that enjoyed widespread popularity in America: "Never on Sunday" from *Never on Sunday* (1960) by Manos Hadjidakis and the dance from *Zorba the Greek* (1964) by Mikis Theodorakis. Another popular success in this country was Nino Rota's theme for Franco Zeffirelli's *Romeo and Juliet* (1968). The intrusion of popular music into film was felt even in Japan, as Masaru Sato's eclectic score for Kurosawa's *Yojimbo* (1961) incorporates elements of American popular music.

France

French film music in the 1960s tends to utilize either a popular or modern musical style. The leading composer of the early years of the New Wave was Georges Delerue. He was one of a number of French film composers who would become active both in France and the United States, including Maurice Jarre, Michel Legrand, and Francis Lai.

Delerue created film scores for two of François Truffaut's most celebrated films: *Shoot the Piano Player* (1960) and *Jules and Jim* (1962). Both contain atmospheric scores that set general moods. In *Shoot the Piano Player*, a few simple leitmotifs unify the score. The principal character, played by singer/songwriter/actor Charles Aznavour, is depicted by a popular piano tune representing the superficial, detached world in which he begins and ends the film.

Michel Legrand created a great sensation with his music for *The Umbrellas of Cherbourg* (1964). With no spoken dialogue, this film is essentially an opera written for film. The music incorporates a variety of jazz styles. During the opening scene at a garage, for example, the dialogue is sung to the accompaniment of a jazz ensemble ostensibly coming from the radio. Humorously, one mechanic intones that he does not like opera because it has "too much singing." Throughout the film, the variety of musical styles matches the Matisse-like colors of the film, and, like the use of color, the music often has little to do with the dramatic situation. The musical highlight is Legrand's "I Will Wait For You," which makes a strong emotional impact in the underscoring at the end when the two lovers meet, each knowing that they did not wait.

Italy

Several Italian filmmakers turned towards the more commercial side of the industry by making inexpensive but profitable movies. The most successful of these works are Sergio Leone's "spaghetti westerns" starring Clint Eastwood. Freely using dubbing, works such as *A Fistful of Dollars* (1964), *For a Few Dollars More* (1965), and *The Good, the Bad, and the Ugly* (1966) scored major financial triumphs in both Europe and America.

These films helped launch the career of the Italian film composer Ennio Morricone (b. 1928). In these westerns, Morricone created a distinctive style that mixes a variety of musical styles, including popular and avant-garde. His scores often feature unusual solo instruments (Jew's harp, whistle, harmonica), and natural sounds, such

Figure 22.5 Morricone's music helps to create a monumental heroic character in *The Good, the Bad, and the Ugly*

as a howling coyote or a pistol shot. The best of these scores is for Leone's masterpiece *Once Upon a Time in the West* (1969), which includes a distinctive dissonant harmonica theme for the character Harmonica (Charles Bronson) and a beautiful, operatic theme set with strings and soprano voice for the bride/widow Jill (Claudia Cardinale).

The British Invasion

In the 1960s, Great Britain exerted a strong influence on American films. Half of the Academy Award winners for Best Picture in the decade have ties to England, either in story or production: *Lawrence of Arabia* (1962), *Tom Jones* (1963), *My Fair Lady* (1964), *A Man for All Seasons* (1966), and *Oliver!* (1968). The decade also witnessed the "British Invasion" in rock music. Headed by the Beatles and the Rolling Stones, English rock music created a frenzy for English pop culture. In this climate, the English secret agent James Bond captivated America.

A number of popular British films were also successful in this country, particularly *Tom Jones*. Its selection as Best Picture in 1963 may not have sparked the controversy that *Hamlet* had created in 1948, but it was a surprise, mostly because of its content, not its country of origin. The Oscar-winning musical score by John Addison that accompanies this sexual romp captures the lusty mood of the eighteenth-century novel, which fit the mood of the "swinging 60s." Addison's score features colorful combinations of instruments, and he matches the energy on the screen with lively melodic materials. Most humorous is his use of a harpsichord, an instrument prominent in the time period of *Tom Jones*, to punctuate the dialogue as if it were recitative in an opera.

Joining the impressive list of international composers who would have a significant impact on Hollywood is England's John Barry. A former rock musician, Barry established a reputation with the rock-oriented scores for James Bond films. The versatility of his compositional talents became apparent with his double Oscars for song and score for *Born Free* (1966) and his Oscar for Best Original Score for the epic *Lion in Winter* (1968). The music for the latter film, a story based on the lives of Henry II and Eleanor of Aquitaine, is strongly indebted to Carl Orff's setting of medieval texts entitled *Carmina Burana*. Orff's music has become a twentieth-century equivalent of medieval music, and Barry captures that sound in a haunting score complete with chorus and Latin texts.

Trailer

The new era of American film continued to reflect musical treatments similar to those in European centers. Music would be applied sparingly, symphonic scores with leitmotifs would be rare, and popular and modern musical styles would predominate. In general, there was a more serious tone to this new cinema, a tone that was necessary for expressing the serious issues facing this nation during the Vietnam War years.

Important Names and Terms

Kenyon Hopkins Simon and Garfunkel Francis Lai
Quincy Jones Dave Grusin Ennio Morricone
harpsichord Manos Hadjidakis John Addison
David Amram Mikis Theodorakis
Charles Strouse Michel Legrand

Suggested Viewing

Drama: *Judgment at Nuremberg* (1961), *A Raisin in the Sun* (1961), *Lonely Are the Brave* (1962), *The Miracle Worker* (1962), *The Man Who Shot Liberty Valance* (1962), *Zorba the Greek* (1964) ✉, *Who's Afraid of Virginia Woolf?* (1966) ✉, *Cool Hand Luke* (1967) ✉, *In the Heat of the Night* (1967) ★, and *Guess Who's Coming to Dinner* (1967) ✉

Biopic: *Becket* (1964) and *A Man for All Seasons* (1966) ★

Thriller: *What Ever Happened to Baby Jane?* (1962) and *Seconds* (1966)

Comedy: *Dr. Strangelove* (1964)

23

Crisis Years, 1968–1972

The five-year span from 1968 to 1972 was one of the most turbulent periods in American history. The year 1968 alone witnessed numerous shocking events. On April 4, Martin Luther King was assassinated, sparking nationwide riots. Two months later, Robert Kennedy, after winning the California presidential primary, was shot and killed. Public opinion about the Vietnam War changed dramatically after the story of the My Lai massacre was made public. President Lyndon Johnson, citing lack of support, decided not to run for another term, and war protests frequently became violent—for example, at the Democratic convention in Chicago. The United States was not the only center of unrest in 1968; France was hit by both student riots and a strike of over ten million workers, and Prague was invaded by the Soviet Union. The latter event added more fuel to the Cold War, bringing the world closer to nuclear holocaust.

SIGNIFICANT FILMS

1968	*Planet of the Apes* ✉
	2001: A Space Odyssey
1969	*Midnight Cowboy* ★
	Easy Rider
1970	*Patton* ★ ✉
1971	*The French Connection* ★
	Shaft ✉ ♫
	A Clockwork Orange
	Dirty Harry
1972	*The Godfather* ★
1974	*The Godfather: Part II* ★ ♫

Films from the Late 1960s

The new American cinema was well suited to express the frustrations and concerns of American society at this time. In maintaining a strong sense of realism, filmmakers continued to use traditional musical scoring sparingly, and the musical style remained predominantly either modern, as in *Planet of the Apes* (1968), or popular, as in *Midnight Cowboy* (1969) and *Easy Rider* (1969). In addition, Stanley Kubrick explored a new approach to music in his *2001: A Space Odyssey* (1968).

Figure 23.1 The upside-down world in *Planet of the Apes* is reflected in Goldsmith's score

Planet of the Apes

For contemporary audiences, *Planet of the Apes* was far more than just a clever science fiction story. The underlying symbolism of the plot, in which a white human is trapped in a world dominated by black apes, was clear; the struggles of Charlton Heston against prejudice and an oppressive government was an inversion of the current political situation for African-Americans. Moreover, the stunning twist at the end of the film delivered a strong message about our potential future in the nuclear age.

Jerry Goldsmith's music for *Planet of the Apes* reflects the nightmare-like experiences of the hero in an upside-down world. Set in avant-garde style, it stands as one of the most modernistic scores created for a popular Hollywood film. The numerous unusual musical sounds employed by Goldsmith include tuned aluminum mixing bowls, a ram's horn, and brass instruments blown with inverted mouthpieces. With these elements Goldsmith supports the drama while maintaining a consistent distorted mood. One of the most striking scenes shows the temporary escape of the hero (54:30). The music follows his actions, including pizzicato timbres to suggest his efforts to hide from view. Ultimately he is recaptured, and the music stops just before he stuns the apes by speaking.

Figure 23.2 "Everybody's Talkin'" hovers hauntingly over the streets of New York City in *Midnight Cowboy*

Midnight Cowboy and Easy Rider

Popular musical styles dominate the next two features. *Midnight Cowboy* (1969), the only X-rated film to win a Best Picture Oscar, takes a harsh look at the decadence of American life, both in a small town and in New York City. John Barry, who oversaw the music for this film, mixed a variety of popular styles, usually heard as source music, with a few passages of modern electronic music. The dominant musical idea is the song "Everybody's Talkin'" by Fred Neil. The tune is first heard during the opening travel montage, and reprises of the song and an instrumental rendition linger hauntingly in scenes of New York and the final trip to Florida.

Instead of a single hit song, *Easy Rider* contains an album's worth of songs by a variety of rock artists, including Steppenwolf and the Byrds. The drug-oriented rock style coincides with the prominence of drugs in the plot, and the songs generally accompany montages showing travel and the passing of time, as the two society dropouts ride their Harley-Davidson choppers through the countryside. One promotion described the story as: "A man went looking for America and couldn't find it anywhere." Unfortunately, at the tragic ending they may have found the true America of the 1960s. The music captures the spirit of rebellious youth in 1969, a year that also brought the music festival at Woodstock.

Figure 23.3 A travel montage to the music of the Byrds in *Easy Rider*

Close-Up: A New Rating System

Censorship vs. Self-Regulation

The Hays Code, which had helped shape films for over two decades, was officially abandoned in 1966. Clearly, the standards that it had created had been discarded years earlier, as scenes of sex and violence grew more graphic. In order to avoid government regulation, the Motion Picture Association of America created a new rating system on November 1, 1968. The four initial ratings were:

G for General audiences
M for Mature audiences
R for Restricted audiences (no one under seventeen without an adult)
X for films that could not admit anyone under seventeen

These ratings underwent a number of changes. The designation M became GP and eventually PG-13 in 1984 for parental guidance, and NC-17 replaced the X rating in 1990. Individual films also have been reevaluated. *Midnight Cowboy* (1969), with its explicit scenes of homosexuality, is the only X-rated film to receive an Oscar for Best Picture, but in subsequent years, as attitudes toward morality on film changed, the rating was changed to an R.

Controversy still surrounds this system. Since teenagers make up a substantial portion of the viewing audience, a restricted rating can have a major impact on the financial success of a film. Many films have modified their content in order to be open to the younger market. Recently, critic Roger Ebert and MPAA president Jack Valenti engaged in a public debate over Kubrick's *Eyes Wide Shut* (1999), in which an orgy scene was digitally altered by the studio in order to avoid an NC–17 rating. Ebert and others argue that the current system allows for censorship.

2001: A Space Odyssey

One of the most original films of the era is Stanley Kubrick's epic science fiction film, *2001: A Space Odyssey* (1968). Although the social criticisms are not as direct as in *Planet of the Apes*, *Midnight Cowboy*, or *Easy Rider*, the film still reflects the youthful spirit of the time, most strikingly in the hallucinatory visions of the last portion of the film. Starting from Arthur C. Clarke's short story "The Sentinel," Clarke and Kubrick expanded the idea into a grand science fiction tale of the evolution of ape into man, and man into a higher form. In essence, it is a science fiction version of Christian theology, which suggests that man will evolve into a higher form sometime after the turn of the second millennium (2001).

In addition to its remarkable visual effects, this film is also notable for its use of previously composed music, as it reestablishes the tradition of the adapted score. Kubrick, who had worked with Alex North on the epic film *Spartacus*, had asked the composer to create a score for *2001*. After a significant portion was composed, Kubrick decided to discard North's music and instead used music borrowed from the following sources:

Richard Strauss: opening to *Also Sprach Zarathustra* (1896)
Johann Strauss, Jr.: *Blue Danube Waltz* (1867)
Aram Khatchaturian: *Gayane* Ballet Suite (1942)
György Ligeti: *Atmospheres* (1961) [orchestra, no voices]
György Ligeti: *Lux Aeterna* (1966) [voices, no orchestra]
György Ligeti: *Requiem* (1965) [voices and orchestra]

In the process, Kubrick made the ultimate statement about music in the new age: Music no longer needed to be tailored to fit the film. By using previously composed works and leaving them intact, Kubrick allows the music merely to coexist with the visual elements. Music still retains its mood-setting function, but it remains detached from the drama (see Table 23.1). Also noteworthy is the use of source

Table 23.1

Music in *2001: A Space Odyssey*

SECTION OF FILM	MUSIC
Opening	Overture—*Atmospheres* (0:00) Title—*Also Sprach Zarathustra* (3:05)
Dawn of Man	Discovery of Monolith—*Requiem* (11:45) Ape becomes man, envisions a tool—*Also Sprach Zarathustra* (15:20)
A Trip to the Moon	Space Travel—*Blue Danube Waltz* (19:45 and 33:45) Travel to Excavation Site—*Lux Aeterna* (45:30 and 49:00) The Monolith—*Requiem* (50:45)
Jupiter Mission—Eighteen Months Later (The Odyssey)	Flight—*Gayane* Ballet Suite (54:35 and 1:03:20) Intermission—*Atmospheres* (1:27:40)
Jupiter and Beyond the Infinite	Following the Monolith—*Requiem* and *Atmospheres* (1:56:45) David's Rebirth—*Also Sprach Zarathustra* (2:18:45)
Closing Credits	*Blue Danube Waltz* (2:20:10)

music when HAL the computer is disconnected. HAL's rendition of "Daisy" is both humorous and poignant, as we watch one of film's great villains revert to infancy.

Since North's score has survived and been recorded,* it is intriguing to compare his music with Kubrick's choices. Most would agree that Kubrick's decision to open with *Also Sprach Zarathustra* is sensational, and it has become one of film music's most memorable musical moments. The Ligeti passages are also effective, but the montages

Figure 23.4 HAL's watchful eye in *2001: A Space Odyssey*

accompanied by the *Blue Danube Waltz* seem lengthy, and a number of scenes that could have been underscored seem dry without music. Listen to North's music while watching the Dawn of Man montage. Does it enhance the scene or detract from it?

Films of the Early 1970s

As tensions continued to rise in this country, films frequently turned to modern musical styles to underscore the nightmarelike world of the early 1970s. Even action films incorporated the style, suggesting the frustration of America over rampant crime and corrupt and inept government officials. Concurrently, the sounds of rock music were continuously becoming more acceptable as underscoring for a variety of film genres. Film music at this time also witnessed a few new trends as well, including the expanded use of adapted scores, the appearance of synthesizers in scoring, and the growing tendency towards hybrid film scores, referred to as eclectic scores in this text.

A Clockwork Orange

Stanley Kubrick returned to black comedy with *A Clockwork Orange* (1971). In 1964, Kubrick had created the classic satire *Dr. Strangelove*. As in the earlier film, *A Clockwork Orange* treats extreme violence and moral ambiguity in a shocking yet darkly humorous manner. In contrast to *Dr. Strangelove*, the later film is futuristic, is shot in color, and uses music to enhance the emotional impact. Kubrick employs an adapted score, but, unlike *2001*, the excerpts run counter to the mood on the screen. Classical favorites, such as Beethoven's Symphony No. 9 and Rossini's Overture to *La gazza ladra,* and a vocal rendition of "Singin' in the Rain" are chilling when used as background to scenes of rape and other violence. This film score is also significant for its inclusion of original music created with a synthesizer, an early exploration of a sound that will become an important part of film scoring within a decade. The composer of the original music is Walter (Wendy) Carlos, who had earlier recorded the album *Switched-On Bach* (1968) using a Moog Synthesizer.

---

* North's score is available on Varese Records B0000014T6.

Patton

In the heart of the Vietnam War, 1970, three war films were released: *Patton*, *Catch-22*, and *M*A*S*H*. None of them dealt with Vietnam directly, but the parallels between their stories and current events could not be missed. *Patton* deals with one of the most controversial American generals in World War II. Some have described the film as being anti-war in spirit, but the film seems to walk a thin line between honoring and criticizing the general, as a commercial film should in a controversial time. Many could see Patton's hard, direct thinking as a glorification of the ideal military man, hindered, like the US military in Vietnam, by his superiors.

Jerry Goldsmith's economical but effective score is a major element in sustaining this nearly three-hour drama. Goldsmith contrasts two principal kinds of music: a quiet, hymn-like melody, and a trumpet fanfare and military sound. In a way, these divergent qualities reflect one of the major contradictions of General Patton, who was a deeply religious person but lived to kill for his country. Because of the sparseness of the score, each entrance of music has a heightened impact. True to the spirit of the times, George C. Scott, who played Patton, refused to accept the Oscar awarded for one of the most memorable portrayals in American film, saying that the ceremony was a "meat market."

New Action Heroes

In 1971, three new action heroes appeared, each supported by distinctive musical sounds. Best Picture winner *The French Connection* presents a violent, racist, and mean-spirited narcotics officer—Popeye Doyle (Gene Hackman). His relentless pursuit of a major drug dealer and his ultimate failure reflect the frustrations of the time. Music is used sparingly in the film, but the few cues by Don Ellis move freely from dissonant, unsettling passages to the sounds of rock music. Both suggest the dark world Popeye Doyle has to deal with.

San Francisco detective Harry Callahan (Clint Eastwood) in *Dirty Harry* is similar to Popeye Doyle. He is unscrupulous when fighting with criminals and with the system for which he works. The film portrays hippies and peaceniks as a source of many of society's ills, a theme that was substantially toned down in the sequels. Lalo Schifrin, who created the music for *Dirty Harry*, excels at action pictures. His diverse talents and experience allow him to mix musical styles, creating what can be termed an eclectic score. Rather than maintaining a single musical style, he freely uses whatever style seems appropriate.

In *Dirty Harry*, popular music tends to be heard in the action scenes or as source music, while dissonant passages represent the distorted mind of the antagonist Scorpio. But even the most avant-garde sounds often develop a popular character with the addition of a drum set (1:09:00). A few years later, Schifrin composed another excellent eclectic score for Bruce Lee's last and greatest film, *Enter the Dragon* (1973). Mixing elements of Chinese music, including traditional instruments, with Western sounds, Schifrin created a fresh score that freely moves from modern to popular styles.

Also making an impact in 1971 was *Shaft*, featuring an African-American detective (Richard Roundtree) who is proud, angry, unafraid of white society, and sexually aggressive. *Shaft* became a model for a cinematic movement called "blaxploitation," in which stereotypes of ghetto images were exploited for Hollywood's gain in action stories, westerns, science fiction, and even horror films. Also exerting great influence was the music for *Shaft* by soul singer and keyboard player Isaac Hayes, one of the dominant African-American performers of the early 1970s. Hayes not only composed an Academy Award-winning song, but also created a landmark Oscar-nominated score. In keeping with the hero, advertised as "hotter than Bond and cooler than Bullitt," a rock ensemble plays all the underscoring, and the influence of this approach can be heard up to the present time.

Composer Profile

Lalo Schifrin (b. 1932)

Born in Argentina, Schifrin was a sensational jazz pianist and worked with artists such as Xavier Cugat and Dizzy Gillespie. He is perhaps best remembered for his energetic theme for the television series (and later movie) *Mission: Impossible*. His ability to work with modern, traditional, and popular music is apparent in his numerous scores for action films.

Major Film Scores

The Cincinnati Kid 1965
Cool Hand Luke 1967 ✉
Bullitt 1968
Dirty Harry 1971
THX 1138 1971
Enter the Dragon 1973
The Amityville Horror 1979 ✉
The Competition 1980 ✉
Mission: Impossible 1996
Rush Hour 1998

★ = Best Picture Oscar   ♫ = Best Music Oscar   ✉ = Music Oscar Nomination

The Godfather

The trilogy of films based on Mario Puzo's novel *The Godfather* stands as one of the greatest achievements of American filmmaking. This saga of organized crime in America, which begins in the first year of the twentieth century (1901), encompasses nearly one hundred years. The compelling story, superb acting, and beautiful visual effects helped catapult director Francis Ford Coppola into the forefront of contemporary filmmaking. *The Godfather* is considered to be America's third greatest film by the AFI. *The Godfather: Part II* is the only sequel to make the AFI Top 100 List (number 32), and it was the first sequel ever to win an Oscar for Best Picture, an honor that has been matched only by *The Lord of the Rings: The Return of the King* (2003). *The Godfather: Part III* (1990) won fewer accolades, but it too is a strong film.

In a time when conspiracy theories ran rampant, when the public felt helpless against the power of the rich, and when many turned to illegal activities to defy the establishment, *The Godfather* (1972) found an avid audience. The central figure of the first two films is not Don Vito Corleone (Marlon Brando), the current Godfather, but his son and successor Michael (Al Pacino). Michael is young, looks like a college boy, has just returned from World War II as a war hero, and wants no part of the family business. We are drawn to him, and, as he is pulled into the family business, we remain loyal to his character even as he brutally murders his enemies and lies to his wife. Michael stands as a classic antihero, someone we know is wrong but admire nonetheless.

The Music

The Italian composers Nino Rota and Carmine Coppola, the father of the director, created the music for the trilogy. Rota composed the score for *The Godfather*, the two co-authored *The Godfather: Part II*, and Coppola completed the music for *The Godfather: Part III* after Rota died in 1979. Rota's versatile musical style, evident in the earlier films he scored for Fellini, is well suited to the needs of *The Godfather*. Essential to the story are two related and chilling themes: Killing is a business, not personal, and it is a family business.

Figure 23.5 Crosscuts show Michael becoming a godfather in church and in the streets, accompanied by a church organ

In keeping with the second theme, family gatherings are often juxtaposed with business activities in the film. The film opens at a wedding celebration for Vito's daughter, against which we see a number of business transactions. Both Italian and American popular music is heard in the background. The first attempt on the Don's life happens at Christmastime while carols are in the air (39:45). The aftermath of Michael's first murders is shown through a montage accompanied by an out-of-tune piano playing "Pennies from Heaven" at a family gathering (1:29:25). In the film's most gripping moment, we see the systematic assassination of

Michael's foes, accompanied by Bach organ music (2:36:15). While Michael is becoming godfather to a baby child, he is also becoming the Godfather to organized crime.

There are three principal musical themes in *The Godfather* (see Viewer Guide). The Godfather theme has the character of an Italian folk melody. At the beginning of the film, it is played without accompaniment by a solo trumpet, a common instrument in Italian villages. The folk derivation of the tune is confirmed in *The Godfather: Part II*. After the young Vito begins his rise by killing Don Fanucci, he sits on his steps with his family—another juxtaposition of business and family—while an older Italian sings the tune while playing a guitar (2:05:15 of *The Godfather: Part II*).

The tune is versatile. In the first film, its triple meter allows it to be used as an elegant waltz (25:55), and, in a horrific moment, it is heard as a distorted carousel tune as we watch a Hollywood producer wake up to find the severed head of a horse in his bed (32:45). The melody represents the Godfather position, and does not belong just to Vito. The theme will be passed on to Michael, and, in *The Godfather: Part III*, to Vincent.

The other two themes also appear in all three films. Michael's theme is first heard when he goes to his family's compound after his father has been shot (52:25). It grows in intensity as Michael becomes more involved in the family business, building to a climax with his shooting of Sollozzo and Captain McCluskey (1:29:05). The theme also appears in scenes of revenge and death, such as the execution of the once-loyal Sal Tessio to avenge his betrayal (2:43:40). The third recurring theme is associated with Sicily (1:36:35). It is heard frequently during Michael's stay in the region and during his courtship of Apollonia. The same theme returns with scenes of Sicily in both sequels.

Composer Profile

Nino Rota (1911–1979)

A child prodigy, Rota established an international reputation as a contemporary composer of chamber music, concertos, and operas before he began composing for films. His studies in America introduced him to the popular world of Gershwin, and his music easily flows between European and American and classical and popular styles. He scored over one hundred fifty films, including sixteen for Fellini.

Major Film Scores

La Strada 1954	*Romeo and Juliet* 1968
Nights of Cabiria 1957	*The Godfather* 1972 ★
La Dolce vita 1960	*The Godfather: Part II* 1972 ★ ♫
8½ 1963	

★ = Best Picture Oscar   ♫ = Best Music Oscar   ✉ = Music Oscar Nomination

The Hospital

Michael's journey to the position of Godfather begins in the hospital (see Viewer Guide). His father, recovering from gunshot wounds, has been left unattended. Sensing another attempt on his father's life, Michael acts quickly and coolly, showing his aptitude for the family business. There are three musical ideas in the underscoring, each of which occurs twice: tension music, Michael's theme, and the Godfather theme. The tension music is heard when Michael first arrives at the hospital and later when he is waiting outside with the baker. Rota creates a mood of foreboding with long sustained pitches, against which chords in the piano and orchestra change slowly, often creating dissonances.

Michael's theme is presented as an Italian funeral procession. Against a slow, repetitive drumbeat, the brass instruments solemnly intone the tune as it might be heard in a small Sicilian village. After the tune has finished, the drumbeat continues in an ostinato pattern, as Michael takes charge of the situation. The rhythms are grouped into four-measure units, punctuated by an English horn motive every fourth measure. Michael's theme reappears after he has successfully foiled the assassination attempt.

The Godfather theme is presented as Michael reassures his father that he is with him, and again as Michael is symbolically taken into the Godfather's compound. In both instances, the accompaniment suggests a folk character, but the harmonies are dissonant, reflecting the seriousness of the situation.

Viewer Guide

The Godfather: The Hospital

Timing

Excerpt: 1:01:05–1:10:20 (0:00 at logo);
DVD Chapters 8–9

Key Points

- Leitmotifs for Michael and the Godfather
- Transformation of Michael's theme into a funeral procession
- Tension built through musical underscoring

Setting

Michael (Al Pacino), son of the Godfather Don Vito Corleone (Marlon Brando), is a hero just back from the war. He has vowed not to take part in criminal activities, but he will gradually be drawn into his family's business. His first step begins after his father is shot. Vito, barely alive, has been taken to a hospital. Unarmed and inexperienced in family matters, Michael comes to the hospital to find that his father has no protection, and another assassination attempt appears imminent.

Principal Leitmotifs

Example 23.1 Godfather

Example 23.2 Michael

Example 23.3 Sicily

PLOT	MUSIC
Michael arrives at the hospital, which is decorated with Christmas lights. When he enters, he sees that everyone has left hastily.	The orchestra and piano play tension-building music. The lowest pitch is sustained without change.
Michael races upstairs and finds no guards. He sees his father lying in a hospital room.	Michael's theme is played as a funeral dirge accompanied by a slow pulse.
After entering the room, Michael is joined by a nurse who informs him that everyone was ordered to leave. Michael calls his brother Sonny, and gets the nurse to help move Vito.	The funeral pulse continues in a four-measure ostinato, punctuated by an English horn phrase every fourth measure.
Michael and the nurse move Vito to another area just as footsteps are heard and a mysterious figure appears. It is the baker, who offers his services.	No music
Michael tells his father that he is with him. Vito smiles faintly, and Michael kisses his hand.	The Godfather theme is heard with a folk-like accompaniment and distorted harmonies.

Michael joins the baker outside, and they pose as guards with weapons. A vehicle drives up, the driver sees them, and leaves.	The tension music with orchestra and piano returns.
As the car drives off, Michael helps the baker with a cigarette.	An oboe plays Michael's theme.
Police arrive, and an angry Captain McCluskey hits Michael. Tom Hagan, the family lawyer, arrives with private guards and takes Michael home.	No music, until the orchestra punctuates McCluskey's frustration at the end.
Michael is driven into the Corleone compound.	A trumpet plays the Godfather theme with folk accompaniment and distorted harmony.

Trailer

During these crisis years, modern and popular musical styles dominated American film music; both would continue to exert a strong influence through the 1970s. In some instances, these two styles, formerly thought to be diametrically opposed, were juxtaposed in the same film, creating an eclectic score. *The Godfather*, for example, moves freely from Italian and American popular music to modern dissonances and quotations of Bach. There were numerous predecessors of eclectic scores, such as the mixture of modern music and jazz in *On the Waterfront* (1954) and *Rebel Without a Cause* (1955), but the 1970s produced a large number of film scores featuring mixtures of more diverse musical styles, generally involving rock music. Also indicative of future trends in film scoring were two developments observed in the works of Stanley Kubrick: the use of adapted music and of the synthesizer.

Important Names and Terms

Stanley Kubrick

Walter/Wendy Carlos

Don Ellis

Lalo Schifrin

eclectic score

blaxploitation

Isaac Hayes

Francis Ford Coppola

Carmine Coppola

Suggested Viewing

Drama: *Airport* (1970) ✉ and *Five Easy Pieces* (1970)

Thriller: *Rosemary's Baby* (1968) and *Deliverance* (1972)

Action: *The Thomas Crown Affair* (1968) ✉ ♫

Romance: *Romeo and Juliet* (1968) ✉, *Love Story* (1970) ♫, and *Summer of '42* (1971) ♫

24

The Postwar Years, 1973-1976

Several crises in American society came to a head in the early 1970s. In a series of cathartic events, the nation resolved many of the issues that had divided it during the 60s. The United States withdrew from Vietnam in 1973. Vice President Spiro Agnew resigned in 1973, and President Richard M. Nixon, under the weight of the Watergate scandal, resigned in 1974. The Civil Rights movement, which had made great strides with the Civil Rights Acts of 1964 and 1968, continued to make progress during the 70s. The healing of racial wounds was symbolized by the success of the television mini-series *Roots* (1977), showing the proud heritage of African-Americans. Women also saw progress in their quest for equal rights, headed by the controversial *Roe vs. Wade* Supreme Court ruling in 1973. Activism turned its attention towards the environment, as the nation celebrated its first Earth Day in 1970. Even world tensions were somewhat alleviated by Nixon's historic visit to China in 1972. Put to one of its greatest tests, America had survived the 1960s and early 1970s.

In these postwar years, the tone of American movies is mixed. Cynicism is prominent; stories of conspiracies and struggles against authority are frequent. An increasing trend towards escapism also developed, which can be seen in films dealing with nostalgia, horror, sports, and

SIGNIFICANT FILMS

1973	*The Sting* ★ ♫
	American Graffiti
	Mean Streets
	The Exorcist
1974	*Chinatown* ✉
1975	*One Flew Over the Cuckoo's Nest* ★ ✉
	Jaws ♫
1976	*Rocky* ★ ✉
	Taxi Driver ✉

disasters. Regardless of the subject, film scores are for the most part sparse and predominantly modern or popular in style.

Eclectic Scores

There are three important trends in film music from the postwar years—the innovative use of eclectic scores, the expanded role of adapted scores, and the sporadic but growing number of symphonic scores. Among the most highly regarded films featuring eclectic scores at this time are *One Flew Over the Cuckoo's Nest*, *Taxi Driver*, and *Chinatown*. The music for all three films moves freely from popular to modern musical styles.

One Flew Over the Cuckoo's Nest

One Flew Over the Cuckoo's Nest (1975), a winner of five Academy Awards, uses both popular and avant-garde musical styles. Contrasting popular styles support the basic conflict in an insane asylum between the controlled environment of Nurse Ratched and the free spirit of McMurphy (Jack Nicholson). During recreation time, Ratched plays records of soothing symphonic popular music that aurally sedates the inmates (3:20), but when McMurphy leads a group on an escape to the outside (54:00), energized popular music underscores the adventure.

Jack Nitzsche earned an Academy nomination for *Cuckoo's Nest*, primarily for one unique musical idea that appears at the beginning and end of the film. For the main credits, Nitzsche combines avant-garde colors, including a musical saw, a country and western melody with guitar, and an accompaniment that suggests traditional Native American dance music. At the end of the film, this music returns when Chief, a huge Native American, mercifully kills McMurphy (2:07:45) and escapes into the wilderness. The full orchestra joins in his melody as Chief gains freedom, but once he is in the distance, the timbre returns to that of the beginning. At this point, the meaning of both the opening image and the Native American musical qualities becomes clear.

Taxi Driver

Martin Scorsese turned to the city of New York for a story of urban decadence as seen through the eyes of a taxi driver (Robert De Niro). For this film, Scorsese employs a number of film noir characteristics, including frequent night scenes, wet streets, a sexually active woman (Jodi Foster portrays a twelve-year-old prostitute), and interior monologues. Fittingly, Scorsese called upon the services of a composer who had helped to create the film noir musical style, Bernard Herrmann. This would be Herrmann's last score. One day after finishing work on this film, on Christmas Eve, 1975, he passed away.

In the score, Herrmann incorporates a number of film noir qualities, including predominantly low ranges, dark but colorful combinations of instruments, and frequent dissonances. Indeed, there are a significant number of similarities to *Citizen Kane*, but with the distinctive addition of a jazz idiom. For the most part, the older musical elements fit well with the sound of current American films. The music primarily sets a dark mood, and the repetitiveness of the cues and the lack of contrasting materials underscore the monotonous world of the insomniac Travis, the ex-Marine taxi driver.

Figure 24.1 The orchestra responds to the bloody climax of *Taxi Driver* with a strong lament

The music for the opening credits establishes the two principal ideas of the score. At the onset, the music centers on two low, dissonant chords featuring a descent of a major second. Subsequently, a saxophone enters with a sultry blues solo. While this melody provides a strong contrast to the dark chords of the opening, the two ideas are related, both melodically and harmonically. Note that the saxophone melody begins with the descent of a major second heard in the first chordal idea.

The two principal themes recur frequently during the course of the film. The first idea is heard primarily at night with scenes of decadence. The saxophone solo pervades the entire film. It is heard during night montages, and it accompanies the two women that Travis meets, a woman of the night and a woman of the day. The latter is first described as an angel, and a harp solo appropriately introduces the saxophone solo (10:20). The most significant transformation occurs after the climactic bloodbath, when the tune is loudly played by French horns, reminiscent of Prokofiev's climax in the ballet *Romeo and Juliet*, expressing the frustrations of our protagonist and of the post-Vietnam era (1:44:00).

Common to all of the musical material is the use of instruments associated with jazz, including a prominent snare drum part. While the drum is a natural sound for popular music and there is a street musician on screen playing snares, it also serves as a subtle reminder of Travis's military background, like the jacket that he wears.

Chinatown

At the forefront of the revival of film noir is *Chinatown* (1974), Roman Polanski's first Hollywood film after the brutal murder of his wife Sharon Tate. The dark, cynical, and bleak tone of the film is typical of the conspiracy movies from this time. Set in Los Angeles in 1937, the story is loosely based on real events. One of the key figures, Hollis Mulwray, is modeled after the Los Angeles water engineer William Mulholland, the man who brought water to the San Fernando Valley. In capturing the mood of the 1930s, Polanski resurrects a number of film noir characteristics, and even casts John Huston, a former director of film noir, as the villainous Noah Cross. Typical for the genre, the story of *Chinatown* is convoluted and features a hard-boiled private

Jerry Goldsmith (1929–2004)

Jerry Goldsmith, one of film's most prominent composers, emerged during the 1960s. His career rivals that of Elmer Bernstein for longevity, versatility, and quality. During the 1960s, he created a number of scores using various modern musical styles, including a modified American nationalist sound for *Lonely Are the Brave* (1962), an all-percussion score for *Seven Days in May* (1964), and an avant-garde style for *Seconds* (1966). He also was comfortable with popular styles, and he became one of the first composers to return to full symphonic composition in the 1970s. Typical of his generation, the Los Angeles-born composer also worked for television, for which he scored *The Man from U.N.C.L.E.* and *The Waltons*.

Important Film Scores

Lonely Are the Brave 1962	*Alien* 1979
Freud 1962 ✉	*Poltergeist* 1982 ✉
Lilies of the Field 1963	*First Blood* 1982
Seven Days in May 1964	*Hoosiers* 1986 ✉
The Sand Pebbles 1966 ✉	*Basic Instinct* 1992 ✉
Planet of the Apes 1968 ✉	*Air Force One* 1997 ✉
Patton 1970 ★ ✉	*L.A. Confidential* 1997
Chinatown 1974 ✉	*Mulan* 1998 ✉
The Wind and the Lion 1975 ✉	*The Mummy* 1999
Omen 1976 ♫	*Star Trek: Nemesis* 2002

★ = Best Picture Oscar   ♫ = Best Music Oscar   ✉ = Music Oscar Nomination

---

detective and a beautiful, seductive woman. Unlike the earlier films, *Chinatown* is in color and can be seen as an example of neo-film noir.

In keeping with film noir traditions, Jerry Goldsmith's score features dissonant harmonies and unusual colors. The main theme, a sultry trumpet solo heard during the opening credits, suggests the blues style of popular music from the late 1930s. But Goldsmith avoids using only musical clichés of that era. Believing that the story was timeless, Goldsmith created a predominantly modern musical style, brilliantly mixing jazz and the avant-garde.

The score calls for an unusual combination of instruments—strings, four pianos, four harps, trumpet, and percussion—and unusual performance techniques. Some of the pianos are "prepared," so that their timbre is altered, and at times the pianist is asked to reach inside the piano and strum the strings. These instrumental colors soon begin to develop associations with aspects of the story: the high register of the strings, often with harmonics, and the wooden percussion instruments suggest the arid climate of the Valley; the piano, often with quick flourishes, represents water; and the harp is associated with Evelyn. Cues featuring an avant-garde style appear when Jake observes Hollis talking to a young boy (8:20), when Jake enters an orange grove (1:09:00), and when Jake spies on Evelyn and Katherine (1:29:40).

The musical highlight of the film is the beautiful principal theme (see Viewer Guide). While its basic nature is grounded in the music of the 1930s, which would seem incongruent with avant-garde music, the two divergent styles are combined effectively. The initial statement of the theme during the opening credits presents a subtle shift from avant-garde color to jazz harmonies just as the trumpet enters. Because the dissonant avant-garde harmonies are built from intervals of the melody, the switch from modern to traditional jazz is seamless. In a way, the dissonances in the score represent the distorted world that is controlled by the wealthy. In Jake's life, love does exist, but it cannot break out of the confining environment. The disturbed nature of the music clearly foreshadows the tragic conclusion, one of the darkest in all of film.

Viewer Guide

Chinatown: The Revelation

Timing

Excerpt: 1:45:45–1:54:40 (0:00 at logo);
DVD Chapters 12–14

Key Points

- Avant-garde musical style
- Prominence of Love theme
- Lack of underscoring during dramatic confrontation

Setting

Private detective Jake Gittes (Jack Nicholson) is trying to solve the murder of Hollis Mulwray, the chief engineer of the Los Angeles Water and Power Company. In the process, he has engaged in a love affair with the widow, Evelyn Mulwray (Faye Dunaway), even though she is a suspect. Thrown into the mix is a mysterious girl named Katherine, whom Evelyn protects. Jake is just about to solve a curious mystery surrounding Hollis's death: He was found drowned in a freshwater reservoir, but salt water was found in his lungs.

Principal Theme

Example 24.1 Love

PLOT	MUSIC
At the Mulwray home, Jake makes fun of the gardener's accent, until he realizes that he is complaining about the salt water in the backyard pond.	No music until Jake realizes the implications. Dissonant, colorful chords sound that have been associated with water throughout the film.
Jake sees a pair of glasses in the pond, which is retrieved by the gardener.	High string pitches, a piano chord, and percussion precede fragments of the Love theme in the low strings.
Believing that Evelyn is the murderer, Jake quickly drives to the house where she is staying in order to have her arrested.	The tempo quickens, and the orchestra expands to include bells, other percussion, and strings. The trumpet plays phrases of the Love theme. A harp glissando closes the cue.
Jake phones Lt. Escobar and tells him where they are. He asks Evelyn to confirm that the glasses were her husband's, and then asks her about the mysterious girl. Dramatically, Evelyn tells Jake that Katherine is both her sister and her daughter.	No music
Evelyn notes that the glasses are bifocals and could not belong to Hollis.	Against a sustained dissonant chord, the harp plays the Love theme.
Katherine descends the stairs.	A distant-sounding piano plays a lovely version of the principal theme.
Evelyn tells Jake the address where she is going and drives off.	The music crescendos with mention of the address, signifying that it is important. The Love theme returns in the trumpet.
Jake calls his associate Walsh. When Jake tells him the address, Walsh responds: "Jesus, that's Chinatown."	No music

Adapted Scores

Following the lead of Kubrick's *2001: A Space Odyssey* and *A Clockwork Orange*, a number of films with adapted scores appeared during the 1970s. Music for these films was borrowed from a wide range of sources. In addition to taking from the nineteenth-century classics, filmmakers explored music from the recent past, including avant-garde compositions and classic rock.

The Sting

With the decline of the traditional musical, the Academy Award category for scoring of a musical was expanded in 1971 to include any score that adapted previously composed music. *The Sting* (1973), with music created by Marvin Hamlisch, is the first non-musical to win this Academy Award; it also received an Oscar for Best Picture. The music for the film is drawn from Scott Joplin's piano rags. Joplin, an African-American barroom pianist who rose to prominence in the 1890s, composed dances in a style called ragtime. The energetic syncopated rhythms of these rags gave American popular music its defining characteristic.

Figure 24.2 Scott Joplin

Since the plot of the film begins in September 1936, music dating from 1890 is historically out of place. But the energy and spirit of the tunes fit well with the story, and the film brought attention to this outstanding and neglected American composer. The music is played both by a solo piano, as it was originally written, and in orchestrations for small ensembles. Hamlisch occasionally alters the tempo and style in order for the music to accompany scenes of romance, flight, and tragedy—for example, the death of Luther (23:15).

In 1973, Marvin Hamlisch won a record three musical Oscars. In addition to *The Sting*, he won awards for Best Song and Best Score for *The Way We Were*. As he was thrust into the spotlight, his engaging personality turned him into a national celebrity. Hamlisch was in high demand as a film composer and remains active professionally.

Classic Rock

Also appearing in 1973 are two films with adapted classic rock music: *American Graffiti* and *Mean Streets*. *American Graffiti* has an almost continuous soundtrack of rock songs dating from 1954 to 1962, including "The Great Pretender," "Get a Job," and "Barbara Anne." The movie opens with "Rock Around the Clock," the same tune that appeared in *Blackboard Jungle* (1955). The difference in America's attitude toward rock music, as represented in these two films, is striking. In 1955 the tune represented the dark side of juvenile delinquency; in 1973 it recalls the innocent age of the Kennedy era. Hearkening back to happy days, the songs reflect the nostalgia suggested by the advertising motto: "Where were you in '62?"

Martin Scorsese's breakthrough film *Mean Streets* is also packed with rock 'n' roll hits, often heard as source music coming from jukeboxes and radios. Unlike the music for *American Graffiti*, however, the moods of the rock songs often run counter to the tough scenes of city life. The playing of "Please Mr. Postman" by the Marvelettes during a poolroom brawl (31:30), for example, creates a contradiction of moods and a strong sense of detachment. Scorsese, who chose his favorite songs from his childhood collection of rock, also mixed in Italian popular songs, opera, and patriotic music. With views of seedy New York streets, realistic portrayals, and ambivalent moral issues, Scorsese established himself as a major auteur of the new generation.

The Exorcist

An adapted score is used for an entirely different effect in *The Exorcist* (1973). For this intense film about a young girl (Linda Blair) who is possessed by the devil, music was borrowed from some of the most radical works of the avant-garde movement, most notably from the celebrated Polish composer Krzysztof Penderecki. Among the borrowed works are the following:

George Crumb: *Black Angels* (1970)
Hans Werner Henze: *Fantasia for Strings* (1966)
Krzysztof Penderecki: String Quartet No. 1 (1960)
    Polymorphia (1961)
    Kanon for Orchestra and Tape (1962)
    Cello Concerto 1966–72
    Devils of Loudun (1968)
Mike Oldfield: *Tubular Bells* (1973)
Anton Webern: Five Pieces for Orchestra, Opus 10 (1911–13)

The pieces are not quoted in their entirety; rather, brief patches are borrowed to accompany movement and underlie dialogue. The resultant disturbing mood matches the shocking visions on the screen. A typical use of music occurs during the opening, when we hear three fleeting sounds: music by Penderecki, as we see Regan MacNeil's house in Georgetown and a statue of the Virgin Mary, representing Father Karras; Crumb for the credits; and indigenous music from Iraq as we prepare for the shift of location of the first scene. Shortly thereafter, a patch of sound from Penderecki is combined with the sounds of fighting dogs as we see Father Merrin squaring off with the statue of the demon Pazuzu (10:00), foreshadowing the climax of the film.

Toward the Classical Revival

In 1971 Hollywood hit an all-time economic low, and the traditional symphonic score seemed both too expensive and too old-fashioned for American cinema. Famed director William Wyler was quoted in 1972: "If a director allows a violin on today's soundtrack, he is considered something of a senile relic." But as the nation turned away from postwar realism, traditional symphonic underscoring began to reassert itself.

Rocky

One of the surprise successes of the mid-1970s was Best Picture winner *Rocky* (1976). Starring newcomer Sylvester Stallone, *Rocky* became the first great sports film since *The Hustler* (1962). Establishing a trend for sports films, a rock beat is heard during montages showing training sessions and competitions. As is typical of this time, music in the film is sparse, but the symphonic score created by Bill Conti, energized by rock influences, was a significant reminder of music's ability to elicit strong emotional reactions.

Composer Profile

Bill Conti (b. 1943)

Conti trained at Juilliard and was a bandleader by the age of fifteen. His background in both jazz and classical music led to a diverse scoring style. He is best known for his enduring energetic theme for *Rocky* and for his Oscar-winning score for *The Right Stuff*. He has also garnered three Emmy Awards, and he is highly regarded as a conductor. He has frequently served as Music Director for the televised Academy Award Ceremonies.

Important Film Scores

Rocky 1976 ★ ✉
Private Benjamin 1980
For Your Eyes Only 1981 ✉
The Right Stuff 1983 ♫
The Karate Kid 1984
Broadcast News 1987
The Thomas Crown Affair 1999

★ = Best Picture Oscar   ♫ = Best Music Oscar   ✉ = Music Oscar Nomination

Conti mixes a brass fanfare, the principal love song, and rock music to create the most memorable cue of the film, a passage that captures the rawness of boxing and of the film's principal character. During the early portions of the film, the Rocky theme is heard only in fragments. But as the Italian Stallion gains strength and confidence, the theme begins to take its full form. Compare the two training sequences that end at the Philadelphia Museum of Art. In the first (1:13:00), the piano and orchestra play in a moderate tempo and with subdued dynamics as Rocky struggles up the stairs. In the second (1:30:30), the orchestra, brass, and rock instruments create one of Hollywood's most energetic musical moments, a passage that is still used to inspire athletes.

Figure 24.3 Conti's energetic music accompanies a training montage in *Rocky*

The increased role of music can be detected in a number of other films from mid-decade. *The Godfather: Part II* (1974) is more fully scored than *The Godfather* (1972). *The Exorcist* (1973), as we noted, uses a pastiche score comprised of a variety of avant-garde works, while Goldsmith's Oscar-winning score for *The Omen* (1976) exploits the full power of orchestral music in horror films. Goldsmith continued to expand the role of music in his exceptional score for *The Wind and the Lion* (1975) and the music for the *Planet of the Apes* sequels. Goldsmith is a significant figure in the reemergence of the symphonic score, but his role is often overlooked because of the sensational popularity of John Williams.

John Williams

John Williams established himself as Hollywood's premiere composer for disaster films, beginning with *The Poseidon Adventure* (1972). Although this film contains only a limited number of musical cues, the escapist story, supported by symphonic music, appealed to the public and led to a series of films based on similar plots. John Williams also scored *The Towering Inferno* (1974), in which the role of music is substantially expanded. Underscoring the romance, humor, and terror shown on the screen, Williams began to resurrect the traditions of the classical film score in a series of films that also marked the return of the blockbuster film.

Jaws

Williams's most celebrated score prior to 1977 is for Steven Spielberg's *Jaws* (1975). In comparison to *Star Wars*, *Jaws* contains less music, but the audience's emotional response to the orchestral cues was a major factor in the blockbuster's success. At the heart of the score is a repeated two-note leitmotif for the shark. As with most of the music surrounding the predator, the theme is pitched in the orchestra's lowest register, suggesting both danger and the creature's home in the depths of the ocean.

A New Force in Hollywood

The film school at the University of Southern California became the meeting place for a number of figures who were to reshape Hollywood film. The first love of George Lucas (b. 1944) was auto racing, which may have had an effect on a number of his later films. Forced to abandon the sport after an accident, he came to USC, and with the financial help of Francis Coppola, made his first film, the critically acclaimed *THX 1138* (1971), with music by Lalo Schifrin. On the basis of his success, Universal Pictures asked him to direct *American Graffiti* (1973), which created an enormous sensation. This film also helped launch the acting career of Harrison Ford. Ford later paid homage to his friend in Coppola's *Apocalypse Now* (1979) by assuming the character name Colonel G. Lucas.

Lucas created his greatest sensation with *Star Wars* (1977). The spectacular special effects, use of sound, and brilliant musical score by John Williams changed the direction of Hollywood filmmaking. Lucas stayed on as producer for the *Star Wars* sequels, but did not direct. He also collaborated with Spielberg and Williams on the Indiana Jones trilogy, starring Harrison Ford. Lucas created the special effects team called Industrial Light and Magic and became the first to explore the use of computer graphics in film. He was also instrumental in advancements in sound technology, and his Skywalker Sound Company pioneered the sophisticated THX sound system.

Steven Spielberg (b. 1947) studied film at California State University, Long Beach, graduating in 2001. His student years were interrupted when he became the youngest director ever to sign a full-time contract with a major Hollywood studio. Later, Spielberg went back to school, completed his coursework, and submitted *Schindler's List* as a senior project. He passed.

Spielberg first worked in television, creating episodes for *Night Gallery*, *Columbo*, and *Marcus Welby, M.D.* He established a reputation with his made-for-TV film *Duel* (1971) with Dennis Weaver. But it was the spectacular success of *Jaws* (1975) that catapulted Spielberg into stardom. Spielberg, who had first teamed with John Williams for *The Sugarland Express* (1974), again hired the composer to create the sensational score for *Jaws*. Soon the two collaborated on another major financial and critical success, *Close Encounters of the Third Kind* (1977).

In the early 1980s, Spielberg and Williams redefined the action picture with the Lucas productions of the Indiana Jones movies, and they created one of the great masterworks of recent films, *E.T. the Extra-Terrestrial* (1982). Spielberg continued to create major films, producing *Poltergeist* (1982), *Back to the Future* (1985), and *Who Framed Roger Rabbit* (1988) and directing *The Color Purple* (1985), *Schindler's List* (1993), and *Jurassic Park* (1993). John Williams provided the scores for the last two, and the two have continued to work together up to the present. Spielberg founded the production company Dreamworks, which has had a major impact on films since the late 1990s.

At the onset of the film, two essential elements are established. During the initial credits, the Shark leitmotif is heard along with underwater sounds; the audience immediately associates the music with the shark. The music continues through the first image, an underwater view that we assume because of the music is from the perspective of the shark. These two elements—the music and images from the shark's perspective—are then combined in the sensational opening sequence, which exploits sex and violence.

A young woman goes skinny-dipping in the ocean, while a potential rescuer falls in a drunken stupor on the beach. Without seeing the shark, we know of his presence because of the underwater camera and the musical motive. As we observe the woman being devoured with horrifying helplessness, the music does not get frenzied. Strong musical accents and her screams are sufficient to carry the scene, as Spielberg and Williams give us only a sample of what is to come. Also effective in this scene are moments when the music is absent, such as when Chrissie begins to swim, when we cut to the comatose boy on the beach, and when she is pulled underwater for the last time. As terrifying as it feels when the motive appears, it is even harder on the nerves when we hear nothing and do not know what to expect.

Figure 24.4 The shark suddenly appears without musical warning in *Jaws*

Throughout the film, these elements are used to build tension. Underwater views of dangling legs suggest danger and for two thirds of the film, music warns us that the shark is present. Because of this association, the audience clings to the small comfort that music always precedes an attack. Breaking this comfort zone, the shark suddenly appears without musical warning as Chief Brody is throwing chum in the water (1:21:05). Stunned, Brody can only say: "You're going to need a bigger boat." Thereafter, music no longer prepares us for attacks. In particular, a sudden appearance of the shark out of nowhere prior to the climactic battle (1:37:50) is one of the most startling moments of the film.

During this last portion of the film, the shark combats three men: Chief Brody (Roy Scheider), ichthyologist Matt Hooper (Richard Dreyfuss), and Quint (Robert Shaw), a figure reminiscent of Captain Ahab from *Moby-Dick*. Williams assigns the men several musical ideas. Most notable is the British sea song "Spanish Ladies," first heard when the boat leaves the harbor (1:12:20) and later sung by Quint (1:33:15). As the men pursue the shark, exhilarating music is heard. For the final chase (1:39:00), an extended theme is presented in fugal texture. But as the tables are reversed, and the hunters become the hunted, the score reverts to the Shark theme (1:45:35).

International Films: *Das neue Kino*

The early 1970s saw the reemergence of Germany as a major center of filmmaking. Essentially dormant in the field since 1932, West Germany entered into a productive phase termed *Das neue Kino* (the New Cinema). Led by three young directors—Werner Herzog, Rainer Werner Fassbinder, and Wim Wenders—West Germany produced an impressive number of high-quality films during the 1970s. The musical scores for these works tend to follow the stylistic trends seen in American films: the score for Herzog's *Aguirre: The Wrath of God* (1972) contains a variety of musical sounds, including several passages on an ethnic instrument; Wenders's *Kings of the Road* (1976), modeled after *Easy Rider*, is accompanied by American rock music; and the score for Fassbinder's *The Marriage of Maria Braun* (1979) is predominantly in a modern style. One of the most popular German films from the 1970s is *The Tin Drum* (1979) by influential director Volker Schlöndorff. The musical score by Maurice Jarre features jarring contrasts of musical elements that match the charming child's fantasy set against grim visions of the Nazi occupation of Poland.

Trailer

Scores based on modern and popular musical styles could be heard in films from both Germany and Hollywood during the mid-1970s. In the following years, the creative use of popular music would continue to be a major thrust of film music in both countries. Although modern music would also still exert a forceful influence on American films, the height of modernism had been achieved during the volatile years surrounding the Vietnam War. No succeeding time period would create as many major films with extended modern scores, as the era of avant-garde music would soon give way to postmodernism.

Important Names and Terms

Jack Nitzsche

Martin Scorsese

neo-film noir

Scott Joplin

Marvin Hamlisch

Krzysztof Penderecki

Bill Conti

George Lucas

Steven Spielberg

John Williams

Das neue Kino

Suggested Viewing

Drama: *The Conversation* (1974), *The Wind and the Lion* (1975) ✉, *Dog Day Afternoon* (1975), *Three Days of the Condor* (1975), and *Network* (1976)

Romance: *The Way We Were* (1973) ♫ ♪

Mystery: *Murder on the Orient Express* (1974) ✉

Horror: *Omen* (1976) ♫

Musical: *Jesus Christ Superstar* (1973) ✉, *Tommy* (1975) ✉, and *The Rocky Horror Picture Show* (1975)

Part 6

The Classic Revival, 1977–1988

25

Star Wars and Postmodernism, 1977–1984

Postmodernism is a recent movement in art and literature that rejects a number of the aesthetic principles that governed the modern arts for most of the twentieth century. Traits of postmodernism can be traced back to the 1950s and the movement came into prominence in the late 1970s. The term, whose meaning largely depends on the varied definitions of modernism, is imprecise and vague. In general, postmodernism can be seen in three related principles. First, the movement dismisses the modernistic need for continual change and originality. Second, it embraces the entire spectrum of artistic styles, including the popular arts, which had been shunned by modernists. Third, postmodernism recognizes the importance of emotional appeal and has been linked with neoromanticism. A common characteristic, whether in literature, music, painting, or architecture, is playful humor.

Since film—at least Hollywood film—is already a popular artform, postmodernist tendencies are not as obvious as they are in the arts that were more open to modernism. Still, one may well argue that film shared a number of characteristics with the other postmodern arts, and perhaps even provided some influence on the movement as a whole; the period roughly coincides with the *Star Wars* phenomenon. In the 1980s, filmmakers embraced the traditions of earlier films, giving new life

SIGNIFICANT FILMS

1977	*Star Wars* ♫
	Close Encounters of the Third Kind ✉
1978	*Superman: The Movie* ✉
1979	*Star Trek: The Motion Picture* ✉
1980	*The Empire Strikes Back* ✉
1981	*Raiders of the Lost Ark* ✉
1982	*Star Trek: The Wrath of Khan*
1983	*Return of the Jedi* ✉

to old clichés. Heroes, superheroes, and wisecracking detectives, resurrected from the past, once again triumphed over bad guys.

Another tradition in filmmaking that had a major impact in the 1980s is the sequel. In the 1930s and 40s, sequels were common; sequels were created for such diverse films as *Frankenstein* and *The Thin Man*. With the general emphasis on uniqueness in the 1950s and 60s, the making of sequels declined. The *James Bond* series, beginning in 1962, marked a return to the idea, and *The Godfather: Part II* proved that a sequel does not have to have an original title and, more importantly, that it can equal the quality of the original.

The 1980s saw a flood of sequels. Among the successful films of the 1970s that became series in the 80s are *Star Wars*, *Superman*, *Rocky*, *Mad Max*, *Star Trek*, and *Halloween*. The last two films each had four sequels produced in the 80s. Films from the 1980s that spawned sequels during the decade include *Raiders of the Lost Ark* (1981), *First Blood* (1982), *The Karate Kid* (1984), *Ghostbusters* (1984), and *Back to the Future* (1985). The most prolific series of the decade are *A Nightmare on Elm Street* (1984) with four sequels, *Police Academy* (1984) with five sequels, and *Friday the 13th* (1980), which had seven sequels in the 1980s, ending with *Friday the 13th Part VIII: Jason Takes Manhattan* (1989).

The *Star Wars* Trilogy

The phenomenon of *Star Wars* is significant in the history of both film and the arts in general. In film, it marks the beginning of a neoclassic phase. Neoclassicism, denoting a return to and reinterpretation of the traditions of an earlier classical period, is common to all art forms. When *Star Wars* appeared, sound film was exactly fifty years old. Within this relatively short time span, film developed a golden age, rejected those traditions, and returned to them. Such is the accelerated pace of twentieth-century life and twentieth-century popular entertainment. *Star Wars* embraces the traditions of the past and unabashedly adopts clichés from westerns, medieval action/romances, martial arts films, and romantic comedies. These borrowings do not diminish the work, as the strands are woven into a brilliant new tapestry.

Star Wars also stands at the onset of a general trend in the arts to return to the emotional qualities of romanticism. The arts of the 1950s through the 1970s generally were dominated by intellectual structures; emotions were mistrusted. Beginning in the late 1970s, a significant number of composers, artists, and writers sought to endow their works with greater emotional content. The link to traditional romanticism in *Star Wars* is apparent in the first line: "A long time ago in a galaxy far, far away." The fascination with our mysterious past is one of the standard themes of romanticism. Thereafter, the audience is inundated with sights and sounds—both music and sound effects—created to stimulate an emotional response. The sensational financial success of this film opened the door for other filmmakers and artists to follow suit.

The music of *Star Wars* returns to the some of the basic features of the classical film score: use of a symphony orchestra, a postromantic musical style, wall-to-wall scoring, support for the drama, and unity through leitmotifs and thematic transformation. John Williams avoids employing a theme song or any reference to popular music, other than the saloon music on Tatooine (44:50). He writes for the traditional symphony orchestra in a standard yet colorful manner; the strings are used for their lyric qualities, the brass for their power, and the woodwinds for their individual colors.

Figure 25.1 Musicians on Tatooine playing popular music

John Williams is grounded in the traditions of Max Steiner and Erich Korngold, but he has also assimilated some of the qualities of twentieth-century concert music, particularly the American nationalist style of Aaron Copland. Within his general musical style, Williams is able to quote and imitate works by other twentieth-century composers. In *Star Wars*, the dramatic final chords from Gustav Holst's symphonic poem "Mars" from *The Planets* is the obvious model for the music accompanying the destruction of the Death Star (1:56:50), and a passage derived from Stravinsky's *Rite of Spring* appears just after the droids split up on Tatooine (10:25).

As in scores from the classic age, music underlies and supports much of the drama. Physical gestures are often mirrored, source music accompanies the saloon scene, and the many varied emotional states—love, concern, and triumph—are projected in the underscoring. In the dramatic fighting scenes, characteristics of Korngold's great adventure scores can be heard, including hard accents, syncopation, loud dynamics, and occasional thematic references. In these sequences, music often coordinates with sound effects. Sometimes, the sounds are so compelling—for example, the pulsating light sabers—that music is not necessary. In the climactic attack on the Death Star, music accompanies the early stages of the battle. Eventually, the music subsides, leaving just sound effects. This absence of music allows Williams to pinpoint the imminence of the climactic moment by having the music reenter with a horn call just before the last, desperate run at the Death Star (1:53:20).

Traditional film scores often feature one dominant leitmotif, like the Shark theme in *Jaws*. But for *Star Wars*, the first of a trilogy of films, Williams increased the number of themes and reused many of them in the subsequent films, just as Richard Wagner had done in his monumental *Der Ring des Nibelungen*. Of the three principal themes from *Star Wars* shown in the Viewer Guide, two will appear again in *The Empire Strikes Back* and *Return of the Jedi*. The theme that is dropped belongs to Princess Leia. The gentle, feminine quality of Leia's theme provides an effective contrast to the other themes and is certainly appropriate when Luke is first attracted to her. But the theme loses some of its

Figure 25.2 Princess Leia is accompanied by a gentle Princess theme effectiveness when she is blasting away at storm troopers. In *The Empire Strikes Back*, Leia loses her solo theme but gains a joint theme that she shares with Han Solo.

Luke Skywalker's theme is the best-known melody of the film and is often referred to as the Star Wars theme. It is heroically sounded at the beginning of all of the *Star Wars* movies, including the recent prequels. Luke's theme goes through many transformations, depending upon what is happening to his character. After his uncle tells him that he needs to stay at home for another year, woodwinds play his theme, suggesting his sad and isolated state (25:15). In the climactic attack on the Death Star, his theme can be heard sadly, pensively, and triumphantly.

Figure 25.3 The motive for the Force plays as Luke looks at the two suns

The other major theme belongs to Obi-Wan Kenobi. This theme is first heard when Leia sends a message to Obi-Wan through R2-D2 (4:50). The theme is clearly identified with Obi-Wan when he rescues Luke (30:15). Because of its unique minor mode, it creates an effective contrast in sound. When Luke looks up at the Tatooine sky with two suns, Obi-Wan's theme appears in a brief but lush setting (25:15). The meaning is unclear, but the emotional impact is effective. After Obi-Wan's death, the theme will signify either his spirit or Luke's use of the Force. Appropriately, Obi-Wan's theme is transformed into the closing triumphant march (1:58:20). As is made clear in *The Phantom Menace* (1999), Obi-Wan is the principal hero of *Star Wars*; Luke's most important heroics are yet to come.

The Empire Strikes Back

As happens with a significant number of sequels, *The Empire Strikes Back* is a stronger film than the original. In addition to the improvements in special effects, the story has better dialogue, stronger characters, and a more developed plot. Rather than following a single plotline from beginning to end, as in *Star Wars*, *The Empire Strikes Back* crosscuts between three plotlines: Luke seeks Yoda, a master Jedi teacher; Han and Leia flee from the Imperial forces; and Darth Vader plots against the heroes. The three strands of the story eventually reunite and propel the film to a dramatic climax.

The music for *The Empire Strikes Back* was one of the most anticipated scores in film history, and it did not disappoint. In addition to the reappearance of most of the principal themes of *Star Wars*, three new leitmotifs appear. Foremost among these is the sinister Darth Vader theme. In *Star Wars*, Vader lacks a distinctive theme; dark chords and a stuttering rhythm provide a generally unobtrusive background for this strong character. In the sequel, he becomes an even more dominant figure in the story, as suggested by the title, and hence needs a stronger musical presence. Keeping the stuttering rhythms from *Star Wars* as an accompaniment, Williams adds a powerful new tune, often intoned in the low brass.

Two other major developments in the film are also reflected in the music. Princess Leia and Han Solo fall in love, and they are given an appropriate Love theme. In addition, we are introduced to Yoda, another key figure in the *Star Wars* saga. His lyric theme suggests his wisdom and gentle strength. Each of the new themes represents one of the three strands of development in the plot, and each will recur in *Return of the Jedi*. The themes for Vader and Yoda will also be heard in the prequels.

The excerpt outlined in the Viewer Guide is taken from the crosscutting middle portion of the film. Four segments are included: Han and Leia, Vader and the Emperor,

Close-Up: Dolby Sound

Listening to Movies

Once the technology for sound was established in the late 1930s, there were relatively few new developments in this aspect of filmmaking. Movie theaters were reluctant to change their systems again, and World War II turned the nation's focus away from entertainment issues. But with the crisis of Hollywood in the 1950s, new technology was seen as a way to enhance the theater experience and distinguish it from television. Over the next decades, substantial improvements in the sound of film took place. There are three principal developments in sound enhancement.

The first step was a move towards stereo during the 1950s. Sound engineers began recording with five to six microphones and then played the sound back in the theaters through seven speakers—five were placed behind the screen and two were placed on the sides for a surround sound effect. In order to enhance the sound further, superior magnetic tapes were sometimes used. These effects proved most beneficial in large theaters, where the enhanced sound played a major factor in films such as *Ben-Hur* (1959), *Spartacus* (1960), *West Side Story* (1961), *Lawrence of Arabia* (1962), *The Sound of Music* (1965), and *2001: A Space Odyssey* (1968).

But the innovations of magnetic tape and stereo were not universally adopted, since smaller theaters refused to invest in the new technology. As the sound of home entertainment improved with FM radio and stereo by the early 1970s, many movie theaters lagged behind the quality of sound that could be achieved in the home.

The second major step was the development by the Dolby labs of a noise-reduction system for tape recording and reproduction. The system was first used by the film industry in the recording of Kubrick's *A Clockwork Orange* (1971), and later for the complete sound recording of *The Quiet Revolution* (1974). But the breakthrough film was *Star Wars* (1977), which made Dolby Sound a household name. The impact was tremendous. In 1977, there were one hundred theaters in the United States with Dolby Sound, one year later there were four hundred fifty, and by 1981, over two thousand theaters were equipped with Dolby Sound.

The third major development is computer-aided digital sound. Digital recording eliminates the extraneous noises that normally result from multiple recordings of sound necessary in creating a film; hence, the final sound has the clarity of the original recording. Among the pioneer films with digital sound are *Edward Scissorhands* and *Dick Tracy*, both from 1990. Dolby quickly adapted to the new technology and developed an optional playback system that could be used on most major systems, whether or not they were equipped for digital sound. The first film using Dolby Stereo with digital sound was *Batman Returns* (1992), and shortly afterwards the system was successfully used for *Aladdin* (1992) and *Jurassic Park* (1993).

Luke and Yoda, and back to Han and Leia. Each segment features a different musical approach. The first two center on single themes. For the initial scene of Han and Leia, Williams supplies a love theme that extends into a full ABA form. Following a crescendo when they kiss, the mood abruptly changes as C-3PO interrupts—a moment that strikes a common chord with parents of young children. A strong musical contrast coincides with the cut to Darth Vader. His theme is played twice, the second time more strongly. During Vader's conversation with the Emperor, Williams abandons any reference to leitmotifs and creates an ominous, mysterious mood largely through a colorful orchestration that underscores the darkness of the characters and the eeriness of a conversation with a hologram figure.

As we cut to the planet Dagobah, music disappears, allowing us to focus on the quiet sound of rainfall. After seeing poor R2-D2 pinging in the rain, we enter Yoda's humble hut. Unlike the other segments, here we are presented with multiple themes. As the discussion shifts between Yoda, Obi-Wan, and Luke, the themes for each character underscore their role in the conversation. The whole is unified by a quiet, subdued mood that is broken only when Yoda advises Luke that he will become afraid.

The last segment begins with musical silence. Having been kissed, Leia is by herself pondering the situation and listening to the distant explosions created by the Imperial forces. Once music enters, it supports two moods. At first, a mysterious and ominous atmosphere is created as she and Han begin to notice that the cave does not feel right. Once Han realizes that it is not a cave but a large worm-like creature, the music abruptly swings into action with a fast pulse, hard syncopated accents, and a prominent brass section. The exhilarating music creates tension as the Millennium Falcon barely squeezes out between the closing teeth of the creature. While attention may be drawn to Williams's use of themes in discussions of his music, these action sequences and other mood cues are also essential to the success of his scores for *Star Wars* and other fantasy/adventure films.

Viewer Guide

The Empire Strikes Back: "This is no cave"

Timing

Excerpt: 50:45–1:00:55 (0:00 at studio logo)
DVD Chapters 24–27

Key Points

- Three strands of plot are interwoven
- Leitmotifs for most of the principal characters

- Underscoring for a variety of emotions
- Wall-to-wall music

Setting

In one plotline, Han Solo and Princess Leia are trying to escape Imperial ships by taking refuge in a cave located on a large meteor in an asteroid field. This lull allows them to repair the ship and heat up their relationship. Overseeing the pursuit of both Han and Luke is Darth Vader, who is with the main Imperial fleet. Meanwhile, Luke has crash-landed on the planet Dagobah looking for the Jedi instructor Yoda. Unknown to Luke, the small irritating creature he encounters, with a voice like *Sesame Street*'s Grover, is the famed master.

Star Wars Leitmotifs

Example 25.1. Luke Skywalker

Example 25.2. Obi-Wan Kenobi/The Force

Example 25.3. Princess Leia

New Leitmotifs for *The Empire Strikes Back*

Example 25.4. Darth Vader

Example 25.5. Han Solo and Princess Leia

Example 25.6. Yoda

PLOT	MUSIC
Princess Leia is struggling with some equipment on the ship. Han makes romantic advances, and she weakly resists. They kiss.	After a brief lyric introduction, the love theme enters in the French horn. The theme is presented in a full ABA form, ending with a crescendo as they kiss.
C-3PO interrupts the romantic moment, and Leia slips away.	The mood changes. The low string pizzicato adds a bit of humor.
Darth Vader, insisting that Han and Leia are still alive, orders the search to continue. He leaves the asteroid field to communicate with the Emperor.	Darth Vader's theme is heard twice with its distinctive stuttering accompaniment, once under the dialogue and then more forcibly as the ship moves out of the asteroid field.
The Emperor expresses concern about Luke Skywalker. Vader promises that Luke will either turn to the Dark Side as an ally or die.	Dissonant chords and avant-garde timbres set an ominous mood for our encounter with the powerful Emperor.
On Dagobah, Yoda prepares food for an impatient Luke.	No music

Yoda expresses his reluctance about taking Luke as a student, and the voice of Obi-Wan responds.	Obi-Wan Kenobi's theme is heard in the woodwinds.
Luke recognizes that the diminutive creature is Yoda, and pleads to be taught.	Luke Skywalker's theme and quiet chords are played. As Yoda walks, a rhythmic pulse is heard.
Yoda says that he has been watching Luke and that he is not ready.	Yoda's theme is played in a low register.
Obi-Wan argues on Luke's behalf.	Obi-Wan's theme reappears.
Luke promises not to fail.	Luke's theme is played quietly.
Luke says that he will not be afraid, but Yoda disagrees.	Ominous music that will recur during a later training exercise is played.
Imperial ships continue to look for Han and Leia, while shooting meteors.	Action music can be heard underneath the sound effects. (The DVD has taken out the music.)
A creature outside the ship startles Leia; Han goes out to protect the ship.	No music
Exploring outside, they encounter and shoot a couple of Mynocks (flying creatures).	Mysterious and ominous music is sustained. With each appearance of a Mynock, the music provides a loud jolt.
Han shoots at the cave, and when it reacts, he realizes that it is really a large worm-like animal.	A fast rhythmic pulse begins in the low strings.
While everything is shaking, Han hurries them inside and starts the ship.	Hard syncopated chords, a dominant brass section, and a fast pulse project a sense of danger.
The ship races out, escaping safely just before the teeth close.	A dark brass tune is heard while they speed down the throat. The music climaxes as they reach safety.

Return of the Jedi

Return of the Jedi presents no new major themes. As in *The Empire Strikes Back*, a number of subsidiary themes are created, but the music centers on the principal themes from the earlier films. Still, this score contains some of the finest orchestration in the trilogy, such as heard in the music for the Ewoks. One of the musical highlights occurs at the death of Darth Vader (1:59:40). His weakened state is reflected in the music, as his once powerful theme is played quietly and slowly by solo woodwinds, string harmonics, and the harp, the instrument of angels, still an effective cliché for death.

Figure 25.4 The death of Darth Vader is accompanied by a transformation of his musical theme

Other Fantasy/Adventure Film Scores by John Williams

Often overlooked because of the *Star Wars* sensation is another outstanding musical score by John Williams from 1977, *Close Encounters of the Third Kind*. A cross between a conspiracy film and a fantasy, this classic science fiction film features a five-note musical theme that plays a critical role in communicating with the extraterrestrials. The theme appears in the chanting of the natives (37:20), in the child's instrument (48:30), and ultimately in an improvised duet between man and visitor (1:58:30). Along with the score to *Star Wars*, the more extensive use of music for *Close Encounters* marks a clear departure from recent trends in film music.

In the following year, Williams created another popular sensation with the score for a film about a comic book hero, *Superman*. As in *Star Wars*, Williams composed a stirring heroic theme for the principal character, presented at the beginning of the film and during action sequences. Williams also composed a beautiful love theme, which gained popularity as "Can You Read My Mind?" The latter is heard most strikingly when Superman takes Lois on an evening fly-around (1:32:00).

In the wake of John Williams's exhilarating scores to *Jaws*, *Star Wars*, *Close Encounters of the Third Kind*, and *Superman*, the virtuoso studio orchestra sound returned to Hollywood, and fantasy/adventures became Hollywood's biggest money-makers. Of the top ten box office winners in the 1980s, seven were fantasy/adventure films supported by full symphonic scores. As can be

Table 25.1

Major fantasy/adventure films, 1977–1989

YEAR	FANTASY/ADVENTURE	COMPOSER	OSCAR
1977	*Star Wars*	John Williams	♫
1977	*Close Encounters of the Third Kind*	John Williams	✉
1978	*Superman*	John Williams	✉
1979	*Star Trek: The Motion Picture*	Jerry Goldsmith	✉
1980	*The Empire Strikes Back*	John Williams	✉
1980	*Superman II*	Ken Thorne and John Williams	
1981	*Raiders of the Lost Ark*	John Williams	✉
1982	*E.T. the Extra-Terrestrial*	John Williams	♫
1982	*Star Trek: The Wrath of Khan*	James Horner	
1983	*Return of the Jedi*	John Williams	✉
1983	*Superman III*	Giorgio Moroder, Ken Thorne, and John Williams	
1984	*Indiana Jones and the Temple of Doom*	John Williams	✉
1984	*Star Trek III: The Search for Spock*	James Horner	
1986	*Star Trek IV: The Voyage Home*	Leonard Rosenman	✉
1987	*Superman IV: The Quest for Peace*	Alexander Courage and John Williams	
1989	*Indiana Jones and the Last Crusade*	John Williams	✉
1989	*Star Trek V: The Final Frontier*	Jerry Goldsmith	
1989	*Batman*	Danny Elfman	

seen in Table 25.1, the trend remained strongest until 1984, after which the quality and popularity of these types of films diminished.

Also evident from this list is the dominance of John Williams. During the 1980s, Williams solidified his position as Hollywood's premier composer. In that time, he received eleven Academy nominations, and he scored a remarkable six of the decade's top ten box office winners: the top three—*E.T. the Extra-Terrestrial* (1982), *Return of the Jedi* (1982), and *The Empire Strikes Back* (1980)—and the trilogy of Indiana Jones films—*Raiders of the Lost Ark* (1981), *Indiana Jones and the Temple of Doom* (1984), and *Indiana Jones and the Last Crusade* (1989).

Figure 25.5 Superman and Lois fly at night to the song "Can You Read My Mind?"

For the latter trilogy of films, Williams again combined a strong heroic theme, a beautiful love theme, and an abundance of action music. The "Raiders March" has become one of the most popular musical excerpts from the 1980s, and it is frequently performed in today's concert halls. The March is first heard in *Raiders of the Lost Ark* (1981), but not at the beginning. Rather than appearing full-blown at the opening, as in *Star Wars* and *Superman*, the Indiana Jones theme picks up momentum only gradually, coming to its fullest statement as the "Raiders March" during the end credits. With the expansion of the closing credits to include just about anyone associated with the film, composers now have an opportunity to create extended musical numbers unfettered by dramatic demands. Williams makes the most of these opportunities. For the middle section of the "Raiders March," Williams uses the Love theme associated with Marion, first heard when her name is mentioned at 21:30.

The *Star Trek* Enterprise

The other major fantasy/adventure series that began in the late 1970s is *Star Trek*, based on an immensely popular television series from the 60s. The two principal composers who worked on the initial films of the series are veteran Jerry Goldsmith and newcomer James Horner. While each composer has an individual approach and style, the principal musical theme of the television series, created by Alexander Courage, is incorporated into their scores.

Jerry Goldsmith has become the composer most closely associated with *Star Trek*. He composed music for the inaugural film and for four additional films extending from *Star Trek V: The Final Frontier* (1989) to *Star Trek: Nemesis* (2002). The score for *Star Trek: The Motion Picture* (1979) established some new thematic ideas that would become part of the *Star Trek* tradition. The theme for the opening credits was later adapted as the main theme for the television series *Star Trek: The Next Generation*, and the music for the initial battle with the Klingons (4:55), complete with electronic sounds, has been recycled in later films and television episodes. As a whole, the film

John Williams (b. 1932)

Born in New York, John Williams moved to California as a teenager. After serving in the Air Force, he studied at Juilliard and then returned to the West Coast. He worked as a pianist in both film and television studios. In the 1950s he began scoring for the television series *Kraft Theatre*. His early film scores were largely for comedies, such as *Gidget Goes to Rome* (1963), *A Guide for the Married Man* (1967), and *The Paper Chase* (1973). He won his first Oscar for adapting and orchestrating, for film, the Harnick and Bock score from the Broadway musical *Fiddler on the Roof* (1971). Following his work on *The Poseidon Adventure* (1972), he earned a reputation as a specialist in disaster films. This led to his scores for *The Towering Inferno* (1974) and *Jaws* (1975). Steven Spielberg recommended Williams to George Lucas for *Star Wars* (1977), and the association of these three creative artists produced some of the major films in recent decades. Throughout his career, Williams has employed a wide variety of musical styles ranging from the avant-garde (*Images*) to jazz (*Catch Me If You Can*). Williams has also served as the principal conductor of the Boston Pops for a number of years and is still active as both a composer and conductor. In all, Williams has received nearly forty Academy Award nominations, and he has won five Oscars.

Important Film Scores

Valley of the Dolls 1967 ✉
Fiddler on the Roof 1971 ♫
The Poseidon Adventure 1972 ✉
Images 1972 ✉
The Towering Inferno 1974 ✉
Jaws 1975 ♫
Close Encounters of the Third Kind 1977 ✉
Star Wars 1977 ♫
Superman: The Movie 1978 ✉
The Empire Strikes Back 1980 ✉
Raiders of the Lost Ark 1981 ✉
E.T.: the Extra-Terrestrial 1982 ♫
Return of the Jedi 1983 ✉
Empire of the Sun 1987 ✉
Home Alone 1990 ✉
JFK 1991 ✉
Hook 1991 ✉

Schindler's List 1993 ★ ♫
Jurassic Park 1993
Saving Private Ryan 1998 ✉
Star Wars: Episode I—The Phantom Menace 1999
Harry Potter and the Sorcerer's Stone 2001 ✉
Artificial Intelligence: A.I. 2001 ✉
Star Wars: Episode II—Attack of the Clones 2002
Catch Me If You Can 2002 ✉
Harry Potter and the Prisoner of Azkaban 2004 ✉
Memoirs of a Geisha 2005 ✉
Munich 2005 ✉
War of the Worlds 2005
The Adventures of Tintin (2011)
War Horse (2011)

★ = Best Picture Oscar   ♫ = Best Music Oscar   ✉ = Music Oscar Nomination

is notoriously slow-moving, but the music is memorable. The futuristic story allows Goldsmith to employ a variety of adventurous colors, the extended montages give him time to create substantial musical units, the brief action sequences contain strong action music, and the beautiful Lt. Ilia prompts Goldsmith to create one of his most lyrical love themes.

James Horner scored the next two films of the series: *Star Trek: The Wrath of Khan* (1982) and *Star Trek III: The Search for Spock* (1984). The opening of *The Wrath of Khan* directly quotes the theme from the television show, thereby gaining immediate approval from the multitude of devoted Trekkies. The television theme recurs in several stirring moments, the most dramatic of which is the death of Spock (1:39:00). The music for the opening credits contains three additional themes that are loosely associated with the starship Enterprise. Containing more underscoring and more melodic material, Horner's score is closer to the spirit of John Williams than to that of Jerry Goldsmith. Particularly effective is the music for the battle in the nebula (1:22:00), which contrasts action music with sustained orchestral colors that match the striking visual images. As in the *Star Wars* trilogy, a number of the musical themes from this film will reappear in *The Search for Spock*.

Trailer

With these two films, James Horner established himself as a major Hollywood composer. His breakthrough coincided with the return of the classical symphony score, and he would continue to excel with such scores into the twenty-first century. In the succeeding decades, new musical sounds and approaches would emerge in Hollywood, but the traditional symhonic score would remain as a viable choice for filmmakers to the present time.

Important Names and Terms

postmodernism
sequel
James Horner
Dolby Sound

Suggested Viewing

Adventure/Fantasy: *Mad Max* (1979), *Mad Max 2: The Road Warrior* (1981), *Dragonslayer* (1981), *Conan the Barbarian* (1982), *Starman* ✉ (1984), *Dune* (1984), and *Mad Max Beyond Thunderdome* (1985)

26

E.T. the Extra-Terrestrial

E.T. the Extra-Terrestrial marks the high point for the revival of the classic film score. Combining elements of the fantasy/adventure and children's genres, *E.T.* captured the nation's imagination and provided high-quality entertainment that appealed to the entire family. The film currently stands fourth on the list of all-time box-office successes. In 2002, twenty years after its first release, *E.T.* was rereleased with enhanced images and some added scenes. The timings of both versions are given in the Featured Film Guide.

The Narrative

The story presents a double plot. In the principal story, an extraterrestrial being, known as E.T., is inadvertently abandoned on Earth. The central conflict deals with his attempt to return home before government agents capture him and before his health deteriorates. The subsidiary plot involves Elliot, a young boy whose name begins with E and ends with T. Elliot develops a symbiotic relationship with his new friend, and his story can be seen as a human parallel to that of E.T. Like the extra-terrestrial visitor, Elliot is alone, abandoned by his father, and unable to relate to his family or connect with any adult. In the end, just as E.T. goes home, we see that Elliot too has come home, having bonded with his siblings and acquired a new father figure.

Despite the fantasy elements, *E.T.* deals with a genuine contemporary problem. Set in suburbia, the film focuses on a child growing up in a broken home. Other than the mother, no adult face is shown until Agent Keys—appropriately named, since he is identified by his jangling keys—reaches out to Elliot. Agent Keys undergoes one of the most significant changes in the film. At the onset, he is seen relentlessly pursuing E.T. By the end, he has put aside his official duties and observes E.T.'s departure without interference. One of the most important lines of the film comes from Keys: "He came to me too. I've been wishing for this since I was ten years old." In this film, we see an adult recalling his youthful dreams, and a child leading the way to understanding through the wisdom of innocence.

Critical to the effectiveness of *E.T.* is the underlying tone. Although the film touches upon a full range of emotions, a gentle, magical character dominates. Bathed in blue light, embraced by visual images of circles, soothed by John Williams's delicate orchestration, the audience is given psychological comfort throughout E.T.'s adventure on Earth. For this film, John Williams, who excels in music for both fantasy/adventure and children's films, provided one of his greatest scores.

The Music

The childlike mood of the music is largely accomplished through orchestration. The E.T. theme is heard predominantly in the piccolo, harp, and celesta, all of which produce delicate sounds. Throughout the film, the colorful yet gentle sounds of woodwinds play a leading role. The full force of the orchestra is reserved for moments of exhilaration and awe, and the menacing sounds that accompany the federal agents and even the death scene are scored relatively lightly.

In addition to the consistency of sound and mood, Williams unifies the score thematically. Rather than presenting several independent themes, as in *Star Wars*, Williams focuses primarily on a single theme that has a number of variations. The principal variations (see Feature Film Guide) are used interchangeably, depending on the desired effect. The opening statement of the theme appears in a mysterious, magical setting, while the second version is often heard in exhilarating passages. The third variation appears at times of contemplation or sadness. These generalizations are not completely consistent through the film, but the variations of the basic motive create a sense of both unity and variety.

In addition, the E.T. theme provides the basis for much of the other material in the film. Notice how each version of the E.T. motive begins with a leap upward followed by a descent of at least one note. The upward leap in each instance is the interval of a fifth, and this same interval can be found in each of the other themes shown in the Featured Film Guide. Indeed, the second Bicycle theme can be heard as an elaborate variation of the E.T. theme.

Much of the other musical material is similarly derived from the E.T. theme: The fanfares invert the E.T. intervals, the chase music is based on a transformation of the Bicycle theme, and even the closing timpani solo emphasizes the interval of a fifth. Of course, the audience is not expected to hear all of these relationships, even after multiple viewings. But the resultant continuity of material creates a smooth flow of ideas that is comforting to the ear and contributes greatly to the magical effect of the film as a whole.

Exposition

The mood of the film is established at the outset. For audiences expecting to hear the heroic sounds of *Star Wars* and *Superman*, the opening music for *E.T. the Extra-Terrestrial* was a surprising change. Instead of a powerful opening theme, we hear mysterious, colorful sounds. The musical style evokes the avant-garde styles of the post-World War II generation with its unique colors, dissonances, and sliding pitches. Two goals are accomplished: The unexpected mood stimulates the audience's imagination, and the nontraditional timbres suggest the presence of extraterrestrials.

In the exposition, Williams provides themes for both the protagonist and antagonist. The E.T. theme appears first in the piccolo. The high register contributes to the magical, mysterious quality of this visitor from far away, and the initial monophonic texture suggests the simplicity of E.T.'s character. The theme for Keys is presented in a low register, which contributes to its menacing character. But Keys's theme is not overpowering in the sense of the Darth Vader theme from *The Empire Strikes Back*. First presented in the bassoons, the theme becomes loud and raucous only when E.T. is frightened and runs. The forceful presentation at that point is more a reflection of E.T.'s state of mind than a portrayal of Keys's character. After the ship has left, Williams presents the themes for the protagonist and antagonist one more time, as we view the suburb where the story will unfold.

First Encounters and Bonding

The initial complications are intertwined with Elliot's own exposition. As the story begins to unfold, we learn valuable background information about Elliot's parallel story. We are constantly reminded of Elliot's isolation; he is unable to play with the older boys, he has trouble relating to his family, and his father has left. There is no underscoring for these family moments, as there is no magic in Elliot's life. Ultimately, we see him looking out the kitchen window in need of a friend, and we hear the E.T. theme for the first time since the exposition.

Figure 26.1 The search for E.T. is represented by Keys's theme

E.T. and Elliot begin to show signs of their symbiotic relationship: Both scream when they first meet, E.T. mimics Elliot's hand gestures, E.T. is tired and they both fall asleep, and in the morning Elliot feels startled downstairs when E.T. opens an umbrella upstairs. In their first encounters, the music underscores the uncertainty of meeting an alien. But once they have communicated through candy diplomacy, E.T.'s gentle, magical theme becomes more pronounced, leading to a full orchestral statement when E.T. levitates fruit in front of the three children. Periodically we are reminded of the ongoing search for E.T. by the sight of Keys, accompanied by his ominous theme. Also introduced for the first time are the Bicycle themes, heard when Elliot rides to the forest.

Figure 26.2 Elliot begins to bond with his siblings after meeting E.T.

Developing a Plan

This section presents an amusing crosscutting scene showing Elliot at school and E.T. at the house. Initially, the scenes of Elliot have no music, while humorous music accompanies the scenes of E.T. But as E.T.'s explorations begin to affect Elliot, music begins to play over the cuts. Williams adds slurred trombone effects to suggest the inebriation of both E.T. and Elliot. At school, Elliot begins to see the frog as a little E.T., and E.T.'s theme is given to the frog. At the end of the scene, Elliot frees all the frogs, while E.T. watches a romantic scene from *The Quiet Man*. Williams borrows a portion of Victor Young's score for this 1952 classic, but concludes the quotation with the cadence of the E.T. theme.

In addition to the humor, this section provides important plot developments. E.T. envisions a plan for calling home, and he learns to speak. Meanwhile, Keys is closing in on E.T.'s location, accompanied by his ever-present theme, and we learn that E.T.

Figure 26.3 E.T. discovers beer

is growing weaker. Particularly touching is the scene of E.T. listening to Peter Pan, a story about lost boys and returning home. During the reading and the healing of Elliot's finger, a harp gently plays E.T.'s theme.

Implementing the Plan, Capture, and Death

The mood in these scenes shifts from humor and optimism to sadness and tragedy. The early portions continue the light-hearted mood established earlier. On Halloween, E.T. leaves the house in order to phone home. On the way he sees a youngster dressed in a Yoda costume and begins repeating "home, home, home." Williams underscores this humor by quoting Yoda's theme, first heard in *The Empire Strikes Back* (1980). This brief tribute to the George Lucas film is reciprocated in *The Phantom Menace* (1999), in which we can see E.T. figures sitting in the Imperial Senate.

An early emotional climax occurs with the thrilling bicycle ride. As they ride through the forest, we hear music suggesting the E.T. theme, but when the bicycle begins to go out of control, the music turns tense. Suddenly, Elliot and E.T. soar into the air, where we see them as silhouettes against the moon. For this exhilarating moment, Williams presents the first full-length, full-orchestra statement of the E.T. theme in A-B-A

Figure 26.4 E.T. goes out on Halloween

form. The E.T. motive is initially heard three times as they fly. The orchestra then plays contrasting material that is thematically derived from the E.T. theme. Dramatically, the E.T. theme returns with three more statements of the motive just before they land.

The abrupt changes of mood that follow are reinforced by the music. Slower, more melancholy statements of the E.T. theme underscore the sadness of an impending farewell, the lack of response to his call, and E.T.'s failing health. The invasion of the house and ultimate capture of E.T. is scored with forceful music, centering on Keys's theme, featuring a pounding timpani. A prevailing sense of tragedy accompanies the apparent death of E.T.

Climax and Resolution

The final section of the film contains one of the finest examples of Hollywood film scoring. In an extended cue that lasts nearly twenty minutes, Williams takes us from Elliot's tragic sense of loss to jubilation at E.T.'s resurrection; humor and action as they escape; exhilaration when they fly; and sadness, joy, and awe at E.T.'s departure. Much of this music has been adapted by John Williams into a concert piece entitled "Adventures on Earth." Once again, the symphonic ABA version of the E.T. theme is heard while the boys are flying, and the final build-up of repeating variations of the E.T. theme leads to a powerful climax at the end of the film. Throughout the final passage, listen to the strong emotional painting of the music, the colorful orchestration, and the appearances of our now familiar musical themes.

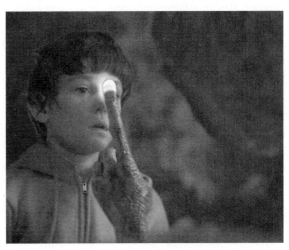

Figure 26.5 E.T. and Elliot say farewell

E.T. the Extra-Terrestrial (1982)

Directed by Steven Spielberg
Music by John Williams

Principal Characters

E.T., an extraterrestrial visitor
Elliot, a ten-year-old boy (Henry Thomas)
Mary, Elliot's mother (Dee Wallace)
Gertie, Elliot's younger sister (Drew Barrymore)
Michael, Elliot's older brother (Robert MacNaughton)
Keys, a government agent (Peter Coyote)

Principal Leitmotifs

Example 26.1. E.T. theme

Example 26.2. E.T. theme

Example 26.3. E.T. theme

Example 26.4. Keys theme

Subsidiary Themes

Example 26.5. Alien theme

Example 26.6. Bicycle theme

Example 26.7. Lyrical Bicycle theme

Exposition

0:00–8:00 (1982)/0:00–8:15 (2002); DVD Chapters 1 and 2
[timings begin at the Universal logo]

SCENE DESCRIPTION	MUSIC
Opening credits	The avant-garde style creates an unworldly character.
View of the starry sky	E.T.'s theme is heard in the piccolo.
View of a spaceship on Earth	The Alien theme is intoned.
Extraterrestrial beings are collecting samples of plant life. E.T. is shown.	The woodwinds create a magical quality.

The peaceful scene is interrupted by the arrival of vehicles with Keys and others. E.T. is startled and runs toward the ship.	The music becomes ominous, and Keys's theme is heard in the low woodwinds. The chase music features the Keys theme.
The spaceship takes off, leaving E.T. alone. The agents begin to look for him.	The Alien theme is presented in the brass. The piccolo and horn play the E.T. theme. Keys's theme is heard in the low woodwinds as the agents look toward E.T.

Complications: First Encounters

8:00–19:20 (1982)/8:15–19:35 (2002); DVD Chapters 3–5

SCENE DESCRIPTION	MUSIC
Elliot is excluded from a game of "Dungeons and Dragons." He is sent outside to meet the pizza delivery man. As he returns to the house he hears a sound. Elliot tosses a ball into the shed, and it is thrown back. Startled, he runs into the house. The boys and Elliot's mom investigate, but they find only mysterious footprints.	No underscoring initially. There are two brief moments of source music: music from the radio, and the boys singing the theme from the T.V. show "The Twilight Zone."
Later in the night, Elliot goes to the backyard. He encounters E.T., terrifying both equally.	Mysterious, unworldly music is heard at the outset; there is no music for the encounter.
The next morning, Elliot rides his bicycle to the woods and leaves candy. Seeing Keys, Elliot rapidly returns home, as E.T. watches from behind a tree.	The Bicycle themes appear as Elliot goes to the woods. Keys's theme is heard when Elliot sees him searching.
At the dinner table, no one believes Elliot's story. His isolation is even more pronounced, as we learn that his father has recently run off with another woman to Mexico. Mary, still hurting from the breakup of her marriage, is upset by the news. In need of a friend, Elliot stares out the kitchen window.	No music in this scene until Elliot looks out the window, when we hear the E.T. theme, played once again by the piccolo.

Complications: Bonding

19:20–41:10 (1982)/19:35–44:00 (2002); DVD Chapters 6–8

SCENE DESCRIPTION	MUSIC
That night Elliot sleeps on the porch, and E.T. comes to him, returning the candy. Elliot leaves a trail of candy, enticing E.T. to his room. E.T. mimics Elliot. Both are fatigued and fall asleep. Meanwhile, agents look in the woods; Keys discovers some candy.	The music is ominous but turns more magical as E.T. reveals the candy. E.T.'s theme is heard delicately when he enters the house. After some sleepy music, Keys's theme returns.
In the morning, Elliot feigns illness and stays home from school. Elliot shows E.T. some of his possessions. Elliot begins to make food for both of them, but drops the food downstairs when E.T. is startled upstairs.	No music until E.T. appears, accompanied by his theme. There is no music in the food episode.
Added Scene in 2002: Elliot talks back to his mother on the phone and E.T. submerges in the bath.	The E.T. theme appears briefly in the piccolo.
Elliot shows E.T to Michael. Gertie intrudes and is startled. Everyone screams just as Mary comes into the house. Elliot distracts his mom and then joins the others in the closet. As Keys continues to look for E.T., the children gather in Elliot's room. Elliot shows a picture of Earth, saying, "Home, home, home." E.T. levitates food, creating a model solar system, while Keys and agents pass the house. A bit later, E.T., still the botanist, heals a dying geranium plant.	No music in this scene until we hear the E.T. theme when they are in the closet. This theme also reappears when E.T. levitates the fruit and cures the geranium. Keys's theme is heard both times that we see his image.

Complications: Developing a Plan

41:10–1:00:25 (1982)/44:00–1:03:15 (2002); DVD Chapters 8–11

SCENE DESCRIPTION	MUSIC
In the morning, the children go to school, leaving E.T. alone. In a crosscutting scene, Elliot experiences every sensation that E.T. encounters. In a science class, Elliot is preparing to dissect a frog, but becomes drunk when E.T. drinks a few beers. Elliot speaks to his frog as he spoke to E.T. Watching television, E.T. learns about beaming up and telephones. He also sees a Buck Rogers comic strip with a panel showing an antenna sending radio signals.	A little suspense music as Mary looks in the closet. The music turns playful when E.T. begins to explore, and swooping pitches suggest drunkenness. Source music is heard from the television. E.T.'s theme appears when Elliot talks to the frog and when E.T. thinks of calling home.
In class, Elliot lets his frog escape and begins to free all the frogs. Paralleling a scene that E.T. is observing on television, Elliot romantically kisses a girl in class as the frogs escape.	E.T.'s theme and playful music. Music quoted from *The Quiet Man* accompanies the kissing, but has an E.T. cadence.
Mom and Gertie return home. While imitating Gertie, who is watching *Sesame Street*, E.T. says his first two words: the letter "B" and "good." By the time Elliot comes home, E.T. has his expanded vocabulary: "E.T. phone home."	No music other than source music from the television until E.T. phones home, accompanied by the E.T. and Alien themes.
Agents, still searching, eavesdrop on the boys as they look for items to make a transmitter. E.T. overhears Mary reading a Peter Pan story to Gertie, and when Elliot hurts his finger ("Ouch"), E.T. heals the wound. E.T. builds the transmitter, but his health begins to deteriorate.	Keys's theme accompanies the various views of the agents. The harp plays the E.T. theme during the reading of Peter Pan and the healing of Elliot's finger. It recurs while E.T. builds the transmitter.

Complications: Implementing the Plan

1:00:25–1:11:25 (1982)/1:03:15–1:15:04 (2002); DVD Chapters 12 and 13

SCENE DESCRIPTION	MUSIC
It is Halloween. In a trick-or-treating scene, a bewildered E.T. sees a familiar sight, a costumed Yoda, and begins repeating the word "home."	Playful music is heard when they go outside. Yoda's theme from *The Empire Strikes Back* is quoted and then developed.
Elliot takes E.T. to the woods on his bicycle, and soon E.T. has them flying, silhouetted against the moon. After landing in the woods, E.T. builds a transmitter. Elliot's mom is upset that Elliot has not returned. When she leaves to contact authorities, Keys and other agents enter the house.	Music accompanies the bicycle riding and builds to a full statement of the E.T. theme in ABA form when they fly. Keys's theme plays as agents enter the house.
Added Scene in 2002: Wild Halloween revelries are humorously contrasted with the calm demeanor of Mary as she finds Michael and Gertie in the midst of chaos.	Playful music
E.T.'s transmission is successful, but as agents are inspecting the house, no one responds to the message. Both E.T. and Elliot are sad.	E.T.'s theme gives way to dissonance to accompany the agents. E.T.'s theme is presented more sadly as they wait.

Complications: Capture and Death

1:11:25–1:30:20 (1982)/1:15:04–1:34:00 (2002); DVD Chapters 14–16

SCENE DESCRIPTION	MUSIC
When Elliot wakes up in the woods the next morning, E.T. is gone. As a policeman interviews his mother, Elliot returns home and tells Michael to find him.	No music
Michael rides his bicycle, eluding an agent's car. He discovers E.T.'s dying body in a riverbed, and takes it home. Concerned, Michael shows the deteriorating body to Mary. As she takes the kids out of the house, they run into agents in space suits invading the home.	Bicycle riding themes accompany Michael. E.T.'s theme is heard anxiously when he finds the body. The Alien theme and a sad E.T. theme are heard when Mary sees him. Keys's theme continues to be interspersed.

Agents set up a perimeter and prepare to isolate the house with a protective plastic covering. Keys enters and befriends Elliot—the first adult face shown in the film other than Mary's. Elliot's health is also deteriorating, but he improves as E.T. turns worse. Michael observes the geranium plants wilt. Despite the doctor's efforts, E.T. seemingly dies.

Dissonant music is played during the invasion of the house. The Keys and Alien themes can be heard. E.T.'s theme appears as he says farewell. The music droops with the flowers, and sad music accompanies the death scene.

Climax

1:30:20–1:43:20 (1982)/1:34:00–1:47:00 (2002); DVD Chapters 17 and 18

SCENE DESCRIPTION	MUSIC
Elliot is allowed to spend a few moments alone with E.T.'s body. Elliot says his farewell, but as he leaves he sees the geraniums return to life, indicating that E.T. is alive.	Quiet, somber music accompanies this tearful scene. E.T.'s theme is played by the celesta and then by a solo clarinet. Music turns joyful when Elliot notices the flowers.
ET begins to jabber, and Elliot tries to cover him. Elliot tells Michael.	Humorous, playful music, then more joyful statements of the E.T. theme.
Gertrude delivers a note to Mary, as Elliot enters the back of the van with E.T. Michael takes the wheel, and they drive off, pulling some agents with them. Gertie tells Keys that they are going to the space ship. Elliot manages to get rid of the agents clinging to the van.	Tentative music for Gertie with a crescendo at the end. The two Bicycle themes accompany the escape. Several stingers sound as Elliot pulls the plugs on the agents.
Michael's friends meet E.T. at the park and promise to help. Agents arrive and approach the truck.	A piccolo and then the orchestra play the E.T. theme. Humorous music follows. Tension increases with the arrival of the agents.
The boys begin to ride bicycles with E.T. The police are in hot pursuit. Just as they are about to be caught, E.T. makes all four bicycles fly, creating silhouettes against the setting sun.	The orchestra creates the sound of bicycle riding. Action/chase music includes the Bicycle theme, some of Keys's theme, and E.T.'s theme. As the boys fly, we return to the full A-B-A statement of the E.T. theme.

Resolution

1:43:20–1:50:20 (1982)/1:47:00–1:54:00 (2002); DVD Chapter 19

SCENE DESCRIPTION	MUSIC
They arrive in the forest, and the spaceship lands.	A bassoon plays the E.T. theme. The music is a mixture of joy and sadness. The E.T. theme is heard repeatedly.
Keys arrives with Mary and Gertie. Gertie ("Be good") and Michael ("Thank you") say goodbye.	A brief statement of the Keys theme is followed by sad music, largely based on the E.T. theme.
Elliot and E.T. sadly express their feelings ("Ouch"). After a final hug, E.T. says: "I'll be right here."	Music begins to swell, building in waves to the E.T. theme played by the French horn. The brass build to another climax.
ET boards the spaceship. The door closes, and the ship leaves.	E.T.'s theme is played by the full orchestra, then by the piccolo and French horn. The full orchestra accompanies the ship's departure.

Trailer

John Williams's music for *E.T. the Extra-Terrestrial* is not as monumental as his action-packed underscoring for the *Star Wars* trilogy, but the score's gentle nature, brilliant color combinations, and strong emotional content make this one of his finest and most popular efforts. Williams maintained a remarkable output of scores into the twenty-first century, and he is still seen as Hollywood's premier composer. Consistent in his scores from these years are a wide variety of musical styles and the evident mastery of his craft.

27

In the Shadow of *Star Wars,* 1977–1984

The *Star Wars* phenomenon exerted an enormous influence on Hollywood filmmaking. While the impact of this film is still being felt today, the frenzy for fantasy/adventure films began to wane in 1984. One of the outgrowths of the genre's immense appeal in 1977–84 was a widening schism between critical and public tastes. The films that critics applauded were no longer the same films that the public preferred. Prior to the 1970s, the public and the critics were generally in agreement. As late as 1972 and 1973, the winners of the Best Picture award, *The Godfather* and *The Sting*, were also among the top ten box-office successes of the decade. But for the remainder of the 1970s, all of the 1980s, and most of the 1990s, no winner of the Best Picture award finished in the top ten financial successes of their respective decade. The only exceptions in the 1990s are *Forrest Gump* (1994) and *Titanic* (1997). The disparity is largely due to the dependence of blockbuster films upon repeated viewing by young teens, whose tastes generally run counter to those of adult critics.

Many filmmakers hence did not feel the need to use symphonic underscoring in order to create a first-quality film. Indeed, between the Oscars given to John Williams for *Star Wars* (1977) and *E.T.* (1982), all four winners of the award for music are pointedly non-symphonic: *Midnight*

SIGNIFICANT FILMS

1977	*Saturday Night Fever*
1978	*Midnight Express* ♫
	Halloween
1979	*Apocalypse Now*
	A Little Romance ♫
1980	*The Shining*
1981	*Chariots of Fire* ★ ♫
	Excalibur
1982	*Blade Runner*
1984	*Amadeus* ★

Express (1978), *A Little Romance* (1979), *Fame* (1980), and *Chariots of Fire* (1981). In general, four non-symphonic kinds of musical scores can be observed during this time:

- synthesized scores
- popular music scores
- eclectic scores
- adapted scores

Synthesized Scores

The synthesizer has had a major impact on film music. In addition to its usefulness in the creative process and in the practical production of scores and parts, the synthesizer offers film composers a wider variety of musical colors than a symphony orchestra. There are three principal styles of synthesizer music heard in film music.

- Modern: In keeping with its original association with electronic music, the synthesizer can be used to create an electronic score with new colors.
- Traditional: Using its ability to imitate acoustic instruments, the synthesizer can replace the sound of an orchestra, create the sounds of individual instruments within an orchestra (piano, harp, drums, etc.), or augment the sounds of an instrument family in a recording, such as the violins. In these roles, the musical style imitates the traditional sounds of postromanticism.
- Popular: Largely through its association with rock musicians, the synthesizer has become an important element of the popular music film score.

Midnight Express and *Halloween*

In 1978, two completely synthesized scores demonstrated the versatility of the instrument—*Midnight Express* and *Halloween*. Italian-born Giorgio Moroder, one of the principal figures in the creation of disco, showcased a variety of synthesizer sounds and styles in the nightmarish film *Midnight Express*. Based on a true story, this film shows the grim experiences of an American youth imprisoned in Turkey. In the score, Moroder incorporates both modernistic dissonances, for tension and the expression of anguish, and popular melodic material. In the process, he mimics the sound of musical instruments, such as the piano, violin, and electric guitar, and he explores new timbres.

Is It Real, or Is It Synthesized?

The synthesizer is an electronic instrument typically incorporating a keyboard. It is capable of imitating the sound of traditional acoustic musical instruments and of creating new sounds. Robert Moog developed a synthesizer in 1964 that was intended for the composition of electronic music and took the place of a large electronic studio. In 1970, Moog developed a portable model, and rock musicians soon began using the instrument in live performances.

A number of significant developments have expanded the instrument's capabilities. In 1971, a digital synthesis appeared that allowed performers to program their own colors (called "voices" or "patches") into the machine. Through the 1980s, companies created software with additional colors or programming capabilities. In 1983, the Yamaha DX 7 introduced MIDI (Musical Instrument Digital Interface), which allows the synthesizer to be connected to other synthesizers, drum machines, and computers. The early 1980s also saw the development of synthesizers that not only had synthesized sounds, but were also capable of recording external sounds (called "samples") and recreating them through a digital process. In this way, one can record a musical instrument, such as a viola, or an external sound, such as a barking dog, and replay the timbre through the synthesizer. The net result of these developments was a tremendous expansion of the variety and quality of sounds.

The synthesizer has had a huge impact on film composition. On the practical level, it allows the composer to explore a variety of orchestrations with relative ease and to create orchestral parts with the aid of a computer. Film directors discovered that they could hear the basic qualities of the score without hiring an orchestra, and directors who had a background in music could create their own music, as John Carpenter did for the film *Halloween* (1978).

The sounds of the synthesizer were first heard in film scores in the 1970s. Stanley Kubrick employed a synthesizer in *A Clockwork Orange* (1970). In 1978, Giorgio Moroder became the first composer to win an Oscar for a synthesized score. In addition to the well-known film scores of Vangelis, important synthesizer scores of the 80s include Tangerine Dream's *Thief* (1981), Howard Shore's *Scanners* (1981), Thomas Newman's *Reckless* (1984), and Maurice Jarre's *Witness* (1985). Since rock musicians tended to be knowledgeable about synthesizers, a significant number of film composers from the late 80s and 90s have been drawn from the world of popular music. The synthesizer still plays a major role in the creation and sound of film scores, but the newness of the sound has been diluted by its overuse in television.

Figure 27.1 Composer/conductor Gershon Kingsley demonstrates the new Moog Synthesizer in 1969

Figure 27.2 A later model Moog synthesizer

The final cue is one of the most intriguing. As Brad makes his final break from a Turkish prison (1:55:15), a ballad is played quietly. When he opens the prison door, the tune picks up a Turkish character, reflecting the world outside the prison, but soon a Western popular style returns in a full synthesized orchestration as he joyfully makes his escape. For this effort, Moroder became one of the few composers to receive an Oscar for his first score.

While *Midnight Express* won critical praise, *Halloween* (1978) became a popular sensation, particularly with teenage audiences. Made on a limited budget, the film eventually grossed over $18 million, a record at that time for an independent film. Director John Carpenter, who came from a strong musical background, composed a number of synthesized cues. The opening theme, associated with the psychotic murderer Michael, contains a repetitive ten-beat pattern (1-2-3, 1-2-3, 1-2, 1-2) that unnervingly suggests Michael's presence and his cold, unrelenting, murderous nature. The piano timbre heard in the main theme is sometimes combined with original sounds,

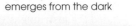

Figure 27.3 Michael slowly emerges from the dark

often in the low register, in order to create a suspenseful character.

The climactic sequence (1:21:00), beginning with an ominous alternation of two notes, introduces a variety of effects, including moments of terrifying silence, that lead to the multiple climaxes. At the end, when Michael's body mysteriously disappears after being stabbed three times, shot six times, and falling off a balcony, we are left with only his haunting ten-beat theme. This melody reappears in all the sequels.

Vangelis

The Greek composer Vangelis achieved both critical and popular success with his synthesized scores to *Chariots of Fire* (1981) and *Blade Runner* (1982). *Chariots of Fire*, winner of the award for Best Picture for 1981, also earned Vangelis an Oscar, largely on the strength of its main theme. Heard during the opening credits while we view Olympic athletes running on a beach, the theme features pulsating rhythms and a simple anthem, suggesting the joy of amateur athletics. For most of the film, the synthesizer recreates the sounds of acoustic instruments, such as the piano, violin, horn, and wind chimes, but the sound lacks the vibrancy and inherent emotional energy of acoustic instruments. The contrast in timbre between the synthesized cues and the source music further exposes the novelty of the synthesized sound.

Vangelis's most successful score is for *Blade Runner*. Since the film is set in the future (2019), the synthesizer is essential to the vision of a mechanized, futuristic world. Compared to the earlier Vangelis films, *Blade Runner* has a more sophisticated and varied score, including modern, symphonic, popular, and ethnic (Japanese) vocal and instrumental sounds. Although many remain critical of all synthesized soundtracks, the score to *Blade Runner*, "composed, arranged, performed, and produced" by Vangelis, stands as a virtuoso achievement in film scoring.

Popular Music: *Saturday Night Fever*

In the wake of *Star Wars*, popular music did not disappear from film. Rather, musical tastes turned towards rock's own version of escapism—disco. *Saturday Night Fever* created a great sensation with its disco dancing by John Travolta and songs by the Bee Gees, including the hit "Staying Alive." In a way, *Saturday Night Fever* is a throwback to the old Fred Astaire movies. The principal character is a dancer, and the plot is designed to provide multiple opportunities for dancing and the playing of popular music.

Disco had just begun to make an impact on the rock scene in 1975, and this film brought the style into the mainstream. The soundtrack by the Bee Gees sold over thirty million albums, demolishing all sales records for film music. Among the best films influenced by *Saturday Night Fever* are the popular musical *Grease* (1978); *Fame* (1980), which won Oscars for Best Score and Best Song; and *Flashdance* (1983), winner of an Oscar for Best Song.

Eclectic Scores: *Apocalypse Now*

The diversity of the eclectic score is readily apparent in Francis Coppola's *Apocalypse Now* (1979). Based on a novel by Joseph Conrad set on the Congo River (*Heart of Darkness*, 1902), Coppola's film deals directly with the question of why America lost the Vietnam War, and music helps to deliver this message. The underscoring, created by both Carmine and Francis Coppola, is largely synthesized and often dissonant, establishing a disturbed mood that runs throughout the film. In contrast, we hear Jim Morrison's voice during the prologue singing "The End" from the 1967 album *The Doors*. The song not only sets up the apocalyptic vision of Vietnam, but also poignantly serves as a reminder of Morrison's own tragic death in 1971.

Figure 27.4 Wagner's music accompanies the helicopter attack in *Apocalypse Now*

A river voyage is at the center of this episodic plot. Early in the trip, Americans rudely blare the Rolling Stones' 1965 hit "Satisfaction" (23:00) from their radio, providing a cultural jolt to the peaceful Vietnamese on the riverside. American popular music is also heard when girls from Playboy entertain the troops (1:03:00). As the scene turns ugly, dissonant underscoring gradually overwhelms the popular source music.

The most memorable music of the film is neither popular nor modern, but Wagner's "Ride of the Valkyrie." In the opera *Die Walküre*, this theme accompanies women warriors riding flying horses in search of heroes to bring

to Valhalla. In *Apocalypse Now*, the theme is played over loudspeakers as American helicopters fly into combat (38:15). In a stunning moment, Coppola stops the music in mid-phrase and cuts to the quiet, innocent Vietnamese village that will shortly be destroyed. In each of these uses of source music, Coppola reinforces the vision of the arrogant intrusion of Western society into a gentle Asian culture.

Adapted Scores

In the late 1970s and early 1980s, music from the Baroque era achieved a level of popularity. Numerous excerpts from works created during the eighteenth century were adapted into films, as the style of the Baroque era served as a distinctively fresh sound in a medium that had been dominated by romantic, modern, and popular styles.

Among the many films that feature Baroque music are the 1979 Best Picture winner *Kramer vs. Kramer*, which uses Vivaldi and Purcell, the 1980 Best Picture winner *Ordinary People*, which contributed to the immense popularity of Pachelbel's Canon; and a gripping Australian film from 1981, *Gallipoli* which uses Albinoni's Adagio.

The most successful adaptation of Baroque music can be heard in *A Little Romance* (1979). Vivaldi's Guitar Concerto serves as a leitmotif for the young lovers, and excerpts

Composer Profile

Georges Delerue (1925–1992)

A student of the famed French composer Darius Milhaud, Delerue was one of the leading composers for New Wave films. He achieved recognition in America for the scores for two Best Picture winners, and he received five Academy nominations, winning for the enchanting *A Little Romance*.

Important Film Scores

Hiroshima mon amour 1959
Shoot the Piano Player 1960
Jules and Jim 1962
A Man for All Seasons 1966 ★
Julia 1977 ✉
A Little Romance 1979 ♫
Agnes of God 1985 ✉
Platoon 1986 ★
Steel Magnolias 1989

★ = Best Picture Oscar   ♫ = Best Music Oscar   ✉ = Music Oscar Nomination

from Vivaldi's Mandolin Concerto and one of his violin concertos make sense when we discover that the children's destination is Venice, the home of Vivaldi. Additional music is supplied by veteran French film composer Georges Delerue, who creates a light-hearted score with a mixture of Baroque and popular styles. Although there is a significant amount of adapted music, Delerue won the Oscar for Best Original Score.

The Shining

Kubrick's *The Shining* (1980) is a horror film featuring one of Jack Nicholson's most memorable roles. As in *A Clockwork Orange*, the score mixes borrowed excerpts with original synthesized music created by Wendy Carlos. All of the borrowed compositions are from the twentieth century: Bartók's *Music for Strings, Percussion, and Celesta* (1936), Ligeti's *Lontano* (1967), and six works by the Polish avant-garde composer Penderecki. The musical styles of Ligeti and Penderecki are similar; both employ swooping gestures and sliding pitches. The excerpt from Bartók is one of his most colorful movements; all of the works blend well together stylistically in the film.

Figure 27.5 Adapted music plays a prominent role in Kubrick's *The Shining*

Unlike the borrowed material in *2001: A Space Odyssey*, these works are consistently altered by cuts, deletions, and extensions. Kubrick also edited the film to match certain passages in the music. As a result, the music not only establishes a horrific atmosphere but also punctuates dialogue, reflects physical movement, and reveals emotional reactions. For example, when Danny, the psychic son of the writer (Jack Nicholson), rides his bigwheel, encounters the twins, and envisions their mutilated bodies (41:05), the entire scene is tailored to work within the structure of Penderecki's *De Natura Sonoris No. 1*.

The synthesizer also plays a significant role, especially in the early portions of the film. Ominous cues, similar to the simple ideas heard in *Halloween*, tell us of Danny's special abilities and warn us about the dangers lurking in the Overlook Hotel. Especially effective is the music for the opening credits, which presents a synthesized setting of "Dies irae" ("Day of Wrath"), the Gregorian chant from the Requiem Mass.

Excalibur

John Boorman's *Excalibur*, based on Thomas Malory's *Le Morte Darthur*, is a visually stunning interpretation of the Arthurian legend. With the aid of South African composer Trevor Jones, Boorman put together a brooding score that is based largely on borrowed music. Emerging as the most recognizable music from the film is "O Fortuna" from Carl Orff's *Carmina Burana*. The original work is a piece for chorus and orchestra based on medieval texts written in Latin and Old German. Although filled with twentieth-century harmonies and colors, the music contains a number of medieval qualities, and the energetic chanting retains a strong suggestion of western Europe's mysterious past, often with malevolent connotations. In the film, this music is heard three times, all of which accompany Arthur and his men as they ride to battle.

The other excerpts are taken from three Wagner operas—*Parsifal*, *Tristan und Isolde*, and *Die Götterdämmerung*. The choice of these operas is made not only for their appropriate musical moods, but also because of the similarities between their plots and that of *Excalibur*. Parsifal is the Germanic name for Perceval,

Figure 27.6 Music of Wagner appears with the sword in *Excalibur*

one of the principal characters in *Excalibur*. His quest for the Holy Grail is treated in both dramas, and the music from Wagner's *Parsifal* underscores Perceval's ultimate success (1:52:05). The prelude to *Tristan und Isolde* is used as a leitmotif for the illicit love between Queen Guinevere and Sir Lancelot. It is initially heard the first time they meet (57:55). In Wagner's opera, Isolde is married to King Mark but falls in love with his most trusted warrior, Tristan, creating an obvious parallel to the film. From Act III of *Die Götterdämmerung*, "Siegfried's Funeral" is the first and most frequently used music in the film. Wagner's drama deals with a great hero, a powerful sword, and death, subjects that are developed in *Excalibur* as well.

Amadeus

One of the most highly regarded films of the decade is the 1984 Best Picture winner, *Amadeus*. Based on a play of the same name by Peter Shaffer, the film depicts aspects of the life of Mozart as seen through the eyes of a jealous contemporary, Antonio Salieri. Filmed in Prague by Czech director Milos Forman, the lavish production gives great attention to authenticity in clothes, sets, decorations, food, and music. From the candle-lit theater to the narrow winding streets, the atmosphere of the late eighteenth century is realistically captured. There is also a great deal of authenticity in detailing Mozart's life: he was a brilliant child prodigy; he was able to memorize music at first hearing; and he did compose drafts of great masterpieces with few corrections or alterations. Even some of the dialogue, such as Joseph's famous "Too many notes," is taken from contemporary anecdotal accounts. But there are also a few licenses taken. The vision of a conductor waving his arms, for example, makes good theater, but is inaccurate for the time.

Figure 27.7 18th-Century Painting of Wolfgang Amadeus Mozart

The film explores two aspects of Mozart's life that are oddities. One is his lack of support in Vienna. Although he was recognized as Europe's greatest musical genius, he did not have the financial backing of a strong patron. The film suggests that this may be due to his erratic character. While his use of foul language can be documented, the ill-mannered behavior and hyena laugh we see in the film are strictly a dramatic interpretation.

More troubling are issues surrounding Mozart's death at the age of thirty-five. The presence of a mysterious stranger commissioning a Requiem Mass is part of

Mozart's legend, although the figure has since been identified as the Count Walsegg-Stupach, not Salieri. Mozart's death is attributed to rheumatic-inflammatory fever, but arguments that his symptoms are also consistent with poisoning have been persistent. Although there is no credible evidence that Mozart was murdered, and certainly none to link his death to Salieri, the burial of Europe's greatest composer in an unmarked pauper's grave still raises questions.

The plot is revealed in a series of flashbacks. Former court composer Antonio Salieri, who attempts suicide in the opening scene, now resides in an insane asylum, left with just the memories of his fame. An ineffectual priest trying to bring him comfort serves as the catalyst for his recollections. The story begins to unfold as Salieri becomes increasingly aware of his mediocrity in comparison to Mozart. Angry with God for giving him the ability to recognize genius, Salieri decides to seek his revenge by attacking God's chosen one—Mozart. The title *Amadeus*, taken from one of Mozart's middle names, suggests this central theme. Literally meaning "God's love," *Amadeus* presents a war between Salieri and God, with Mozart as the battleground. The film serves as a powerful allegory of the struggle between genius and mediocrity, both in society as a whole and within us as individuals. In the end, Salieri, the patron saint of mediocrity, absolves all those around him, including the priest, the inmates, and us.

Figure 27.8 Portrait of the Italian Composer Antonio Salieri

The film contains no newly composed music; essentially all the music in the film is by Mozart. Mozart's music is interwoven with the plot in a brilliant manner. At times, such as the opening section when we hear the Symphony in G Minor and the burial scene with the Requiem Mass (2:28:50), extended passages of his music are used as underscoring, requiring the film to be cut to match the flow of the music. In other moments, only brief excerpts are quoted. The film begins with the dark opening chords of *Don Giovanni*, and these four chords become the leitmotif for Mozart's father, Leopold.

Mozart's music is also heard frequently as source music. The most intriguing use occurs when music represents the thoughts of either Salieri or Mozart. When Salieri first reads a Mozart score (22:25), the music is diegetic—we are hearing what Salieri is reading. The music stops abruptly when Mozart snatches the score from Salieri's hands. At the turning point of the plot (54:40), Salieri decides to take his revenge on Mozart by seducing his wife, who seems receptive to the idea. But his attitude changes after he begins to read Mozart's music. Desperately looking at page after page of sublime music, Salieri hears each piece in his mind, and we, in turn, hear every change of composition. Confronted with first versions of absolute masterpieces without corrections, Salieri is stunned. He leaves the room and, in a powerful moment, burns his cross, vowing to hurt God by destroying Mozart.

In the dictation scene (see Viewer Gude), Mozart is too weak to write the music and relates his ideas to Salieri, who copies them down. Line by line, we hear the "Confutatis" from the Requiem Mass constructed, sometimes as Mozart reads the music off the page and sometimes as he dictates the parts. Once the "Confutatis" and "Voca me" sections are completed, he asks to hear the music from the beginning. At that point, the complete version is heard for the first time. The music here serves a double purpose; it reveals the finished work as heard in Mozart's mind, and it underscores Constanza's urgent race home. At this point, the film is edited to coincide with the music. Note how the cuts often occur with changes of mood in the music. At the end, the "Confutatis" section moves to its quiet conclusion, suggesting Mozart's exhausted state.

The opening and closing of this scene contain two powerful moments, both highlighted by the absence of music. In the first, Salieri admits to believing in eternal damnation, a fate, as we have seen, that has already taken its toll while he is alive. In the final moment, Mozart apologizes to Salieri for being unkind. The moment is stunning for both Salieri and us. Mozart's last words before dying were to ask for forgiveness from the man who has murdered him.

Viewer Guide

Amadeus: Dictation

Timing

2:16:35–2:24:35 (0:00 at studio logo);
DVD/side 2 33:35–41:35, Chapters 10–11

Key Points

- Music is taken from Mozart's Requiem Mass
- The dictation allows us to hear the music created line by line
- The Requiem serves as source music and suggests emotional qualities
- The film is edited to match the music

Setting

Antonio Salieri (F. Murray Abraham) has plotted to take the life of Mozart (Tom Hulce), steal his final composition (the Requiem Mass), and present it as his own memorial tribute for the funeral. In a weakened condition, Mozart dictates the Mass to Salieri, which means that the Mass will appear from Salieri's hands. Meanwhile, Constanza, who had temporarily left her husband, is racing back to rejoin him.

PLOT	MUSIC
A weary Mozart is struggling to focus. He asks Salieri if he believes in eternal damnation, and then dictates.	No music
Mozart sings the bass line and then asks to see the music.	As Mozart looks at the music, we hear the bass line sung by a chorus.
Mozart dictates the tenor line.	The tenor line is heard as he dictates.
When Mozart describes the instrumental parts, Salieri has difficulties.	The trombone and bassoon parts are heard.
Salieri does not understand, so Mozart sings the harmony.	The trumpet and timpani chords are played as Mozart gestures with his hand.
Mozart dictates the fiery string part.	The unison strings play an energetic line.
Mozart dictates the contrasting "Voca me" section.	The soprano and alto lines are heard, followed by the orchestral accompaniment.
Mozart wants to see the music from the beginning. Crosscutting shows Constanza coming home in a carriage and Mozart reading the music.	The opening of the "Confutatis" begins with the cut to Constanza, suggesting her urgency. After we return to Mozart, the gentler "Voca me" section enters.
We cut back to the carriage, and then to Constanza holding their child.	The urgent "Confutatis" returns with the cut, and the image of Constanza and child coincides with the gentle "Voca me" reprise.
Exhausted, Mozart continues to read the remainder of the movement and then wants to take a break.	The closing portion of the movement is performed. As it grows softer, the music suggests Mozart's physical condition.
Mozart asks Salieri to remain with him while he rests, and Salieri agrees. Mozart asks for Salieri's forgiveness.	No music

Trailer

Amadeus takes us back to a distant time and place. In this film, Mozart's music helps to establish a sense of reality for our vision of eighteenth-century Vienna. No other musical style—postromantic, modern, popular—could have succeeded quite so well. Other epic films created around this time took us to distant lands and ages, and the music in these films would fill a similar role, as will be seen in chapter 28.

Important Names and Terms

synthesizer
Giorgio Moroder
John Carpenter
Vangelis
disco
Trevor Jones

Suggested Viewing

Drama: *The Deer Hunter* (1978) ★, *Norma Rae* (1979) ♫, *Raging Bull* (1980), *The Elephant Man* (1980) ✉, *On Golden Pond* (1981) ✉, *Ragtime* (1981) ✉, and *Sophie's Choice* (1982) ✉

Comedy/Drama: *Annie Hall* (1977) ★, *Manhattan* (1979), *Breaking Away* (1979) ✉, *The Competition* (1980) ✉ ✉, and *Terms of Endearment* (1983) ★ ✉

Romance: *Somewhere in Time* (1980)

Horror/Science Fiction: *Alien* (1979), *Altered States* (1980) ✉, *Scanners* (1981), and *Poltergeist* (1982) ✉

Action: *Escape from New York* (1981) and *Thief* (1981)

Musical: *Grease* (1978) ✉, *Fame* (1980) ♫ ♫, *Victor/Victoria* (1982) ♫, and *Flashdance* (1983) ♫

28

Settings Far and Near, 1982–1988

As interest in escapist fantasies waned in the mid-1980s, filmmakers turned toward more down-to-earth stories. Films about real people and recent history became increasingly popular. The settings of these films, generally in faraway, exotic lands or in America's recent past, still provided some element of escapism, but the focus was on realistic portrayals of actual events. For the most part, these films featured full symphonic scores that sometimes incorporated elements of either ethnic or popular musical styles.

Exotic Epics

Central to the exotic settings are beautiful landscape panoramas accompanied by lush orchestral underscoring. The extent to which ethnic music is reflected in these scores varies greatly. The following are among the options facing the composer and director:

- Ignore the indigenous culture and use a Western style only, whether postromantic, modern, or popular

SIGNIFICANT FILMS

1982	*Gandhi* ★ ✉
	The Year of Living Dangerously
1983	*The Right Stuff* ♫
1984	*A Passage to India* ♫
	Once Upon a Time in America
	The Natural ✉
1985	*Out of Africa* ★ ♫
1986	*The Mission*
1987	*The Last Emperor* ★ ♫
	Empire of the Sun ✉
	The Untouchables ✉

- Include diegetic music reflecting the music of the non-Western culture
- Add ethnic instruments to the studio orchestra
- Incorporate stylistic characteristics of the other culture in the underscoring
- Create a score using the musical style of the region exclusively

Composers from earlier decades had already explored this range of solutions. Maurice Jarre, using a Western symphony orchestra, managed to create a distinctive Arabian sound for *Lawrence of Arabia* (1963) and incorporated a balalaika in *Doctor Zhivago* (1965). The score for *The Third Man* (1949) is played entirely by a zither, and *The Naked Prey* (1966) uses only African music. More typical is Victor Young's *Around the World in 80 Days* (1956), which relies on Western musical clichés to suggest the various locales.

By the 1980s, much more was known about world music, and respect for other cultures was growing. Moreover, composers discovered that the unique timbres of music from other regions could add freshness to a musical score. Although the degree of use of non-Western elements is inconsistent, a trend was established that would continue to the present time.

India

In the early 1980s, India was the setting for two acclaimed films, *Gandhi* (1982) and *A Passage to India* (1984). The latter film, with music by Maurice Jarre, won an Oscar for its sparse musical score. Following his 1960s formula, Jarre created one central melody— a popular tune associated with erotic visions. There is little to suggest the India of 1924 in the score, and, overall, the music is not as impressive as Jarre's other Oscar winners.

Gandhi (1982), which won the Oscar for Best Picture and is one of film's finest biopics, deals with the life of the great political and spiritual leader of twentieth-century India. The landmark score includes a substantial amount of Indian music, largely created by Ravi Shankar. Shankar, who became famous in the West during the 1960s and 70s as the teacher of Beatles guitarist George Harrison and for his collaborations with other Western artists, supplies a number of passages for sitar and Indian drums. Indian

Figure 28.1 Ravi Shankar playing a sitar

music is often heard during montages, such as Gandhi's journey on a train (48:30). Functioning much like the songs in *Easy Rider* (1969), the music creates an Indian ambiance as we watch the passing countryside.

George Fenton contributed Western music cues to the film; they generally underscore dramatic moments. The two styles are sometimes combined. In the opening scene, Indian music initiates the underscoring. Soon, Western strings enter unobtrusively, playing dissonant material that foreshadows the assassination of Gandhi. When the opening scene concludes, mournful Indian music accompanies Gandhi's funeral procession. In a similar

Figure 28.2 The funeral procession following the assassination of Gandhi

but more extended passage, the music for the march to the Indian Ocean begins quietly as a song (2:09:00). Then Indian instruments enter, and the music climaxes with the addition of Western orchestral instruments.

China

Two excellent films set in China appeared in 1987—*Empire of the Sun* and *The Last Emperor*. The eighth collaboration of Steven Spielberg and John Williams, *Empire of the Sun* combines plot elements of *E.T.* (1982) and *Schindler's List* (1993). Set in Shanghai during World War II, the film portrays a Japanese internment camp for British prisoners as seen through the eyes of a young boy. Like *Gandhi*, the story deals with British culture in a non-Western region, but this time from the perspective of the British. The music reflects this point of view. At the outset, we hear an English boys' choir singing the Welsh lullaby "Suo Gan," followed by the sounds of Jim's mother playing Chopin on the piano; the music is as much a part of Western culture as the English manor where they live and the Western architecture in the banking district of Shanghai.

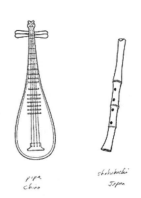

Figure 28.3 A pipa from China and a shakuhachi from Japan

The diverse musical styles are soon combined. In Jim's journey to the masquerade party (10:10), Williams mixes the Chopin with a newly composed melody. For their surreal visions of the city, Williams adds dissonant harmonies, a wordless boys' choir, and a children's tune in a fascinating musical collage. Such musical diversity is also reflected in the contrast between the next two cues. As Jim plays in a downed airplane, beautiful ethereal music is heard (15:30). In contrast, when Jim sees Japanese soldiers, avant-garde Western music features the timpani, additional Western percussion, and a shakuhachi, Japanese flute (17:55). Throughout the film, Williams paints a vivid musical portrayal of the mixture of the three distinct cultures: Chinese, Japanese, and Western.

The Last Emperor was nominated for nine Oscars and won all nine, including Best Picture and Best Original Score. Extending from 1908 to 1967, the film tells the story of Pu Yi, the last Chinese emperor, whose power was usurped by the revolution. Filled with fascinating visions of Chinese culture, this was the first Western film allowed to shoot in the Forbidden City.

Figure 28.4 An erhu, a two-stringed Chinese instrument

Befitting such a story and setting, the music, created by the combined efforts of David Byrne, Ryuichi Sakamoto, and Cong Su, thoroughly incorporates the ethnic sounds of Chinese music. For the opening credits, a haunting melody is played on an erhu, a Chinese string instrument similar in sound to a violin, but with only two strings. The melody, accompanied by Chinese percussion and a xylophone, is later played by a pipa, a Chinese plucked string instrument. Within the Forbidden City, traditional Chinese music is heard almost exclusively. Outside those walls, Western music, often popular in nature, has a more prominent role.

Figure 28.5 The young Emperor looks out at the Forbidden City

Other Regions

Among the other non-Western settings for major films in the 1980s are *The Year of Living Dangerously* (1982) and *Out of Africa* (1985). In the former, a young Mel Gibson plays a reporter in Indonesia during the 1965 coup against President Sukarno. A gamelan orchestra is heard during the opening credits and plays periodically throughout the drama. Matching these colors, Maurice Jarre created a synthesizer score that sometimes imitates and plays with the gamelan sound.

Figure 28.6 A gamelan player

Out of Africa features John Barry's Oscar-winning score. Drawn from the life and writings of Danish author Isak Dinesen, this beautiful epic was nominated for eleven Academy Awards and received seven. The music is used primarily for establishing moods during the numerous beautiful visions of Africa. The two most memorable musical moments are the playing of Barry's lush principal theme during a montage of Africa as viewed from Hatton's airplane (1:53:00) and the haunting sound of Mozart's Clarinet Concerto in the African wilderness as the film opens.

The Mission

One of the most forceful epics of the decade is *The Mission* (1986), the winner of the Palme d'Or at the Cannes Film Festival. The film is based on actual events surrounding the 1750 Treaty of Madrid, which gave part of the Spanish territory in South America to Portugal, making the newly baptized natives subject to slavery. Although the Church officially approved of this turn of events, a number of Jesuit priests decided to remain at the mission and protect the natives. Framed by a scene showing Bishop Altamirano dictating a letter, this tragic story embraces both a personal drama and an historical struggle. This controversial film is a masterful artwork, combining brilliant cinematography, a powerful story, and an outstanding film score.

Composer Ennio Morricone freely mixes historical, ethnic, avant-garde, and traditional Western symphonic and choral styles in a masterful eclectic score. This combination is an essential element of the powerful climactic scene (see Viewer Guide). Filled with contradictions, the climax shows priests defending the natives with weapons and prayer. Both fail, as the mercenary slave traders massacre natives and priests. In the underscoring, Morricone employs two peaceful ideas that run counter to the violence. A Catholic motet (*Ave Maria*) is heard *a capella*—that is voices without instruments, a common sound in the Renaissance. In the final moments, the Gabriel theme is played joyfully as the missionary meets his death with serene resignation. Surrounding this material is a distorted avant-garde sound that includes drums and an ethnic instrument, the Andean flute.

Ennio Morricone (b. 1928)

The Italian composer Ennio Morricone studied music in Rome and began his career scoring Italian films. His work for the famed director Sergio Leone, including the spaghetti western classic *A Fistful of Dollars*, brought him international attention. Active in Europe and Hollywood, Morricone is one of the most prolific of all film composers; he has worked on over four hundred movies. His ability to write in diverse musical idioms has made it difficult to ascribe a distinctive style to him. Despite creating a large number of outstanding film scores, he has received only five Academy nominations and no Oscars.

Important Film Scores

A Fistful of Dollars 1964	*The Untouchables* 1987 ✉
The Good, the Bad, and the Ugly 1966	*Cinema Paradiso* 1989
Once Upon a Time in the West 1968	*Bugsy* 1991 ✉
Days of Heaven 1978 ✉	*In the Line of Fire* 1993
Once Upon a Time in America 1984	*The Legend of 1900* (1998)
The Mission 1986 ✉	*Malèna* 2000 ✉

★ = Best Picture Oscar   ♪ = Best Music Oscar   ✉ = Music Oscar Nomination

The diverse musical styles are held together by a handful of musical themes (see Viewer Guide). The motives for the priests and for the natives are similar, as both are set within the limited range of a fourth. The Priests theme, heard during the opening credits, has a sense of warmth and dignity that we associate with the Jesuits. In contrast, the Native theme is sprightly and suggests the basic joyful nature of these people. The popular oboe theme of Gabriel, first heard when he attempts to convert the natives (11:00), provides a fresh contrast to the other material.

Perhaps the most intriguing aspect of the score is the layered effect that Morricone creates when he combines several themes. In these passages, the musical strands do not blend together as in a contrapuntal work but instead retain their own distinctive sound, so that we hear them as independent units played simultaneously. One such moment occurs when Mendoza, a slave trader, in the midst of a village festival, learns that his lover is having an affair with his brother. At first, we hear the diegetic festival music (22:40). Later, we see the festive celebrations, but hear only the underscoring depicting Mendoza's

Figure 28.7 Gabriel befriends the natives with his oboe

inner rage (24:20). Shortly thereafter, the two combine, creating an ominous effect that foreshadows Mendoza's murder of his brother.

Gabriel's theme is combined with the native motive, usually accompanied by drums, on several occasions, reflecting the unity of Gabriel and the natives. In addition, the climactic scene features layered effects combining the *Ave Maria* and dissonant underscoring. The most impressive layered effect is saved for last, during the closing credits. Here Morricone presents three layers—the traditional motet chorus *Ave Maria*, Gabriel's oboe theme, and the native melody with drums.

Viewer Guide

The Mission: Climax

Timing

1:47:50–1:57:30 (0:00 at studio logo); DVD Chapters 30–32

Key Points

- Use of folk instruments
- Avant-garde sytle
- Layered music
- Music runs counter to the mood

Setting

Defying Church orders, several priests remain with the Indians at the mission. Gabriel (Jeremy Irons) leads a group in peaceful prayer, while Mendoza (Robert De Niro) and Fielding (Liam Neeson) help others to defend the area. A mercenary army has successfully scaled the cliffs and is attacking on land and on the river that leads to the magnificent falls. At this point, the battle has turned against the natives.

Principal Leitmotifs

Example 28.1. Gabriel's theme

Example 28.2. Priests theme

Example 28.3. Native theme

PLOT	MUSIC
A group of mercenaries arrive at the mission. They launch fire arrows, and the church begins to burn.	The native choir sings *Ave Maria*, a motet on a Catholic Latin text. Several drumbeats suggest the ominous situation.
At the river, mercenaries pursue Fielding's boat. Fielding is shot and killed. The natives continue to paddle, and they and the mercenaries plunge over the falls.	No music
Another round of fire arrows strikes the church. The natives leave and are shot upon.	An Andean flute plays a syncopated idea. The drumbeats sound again, and a dissonant high pitch is added.
While one group of natives attacks the mercenaries, Gabriel peacefully leads others as he holds a monstrance. In the battle, the native attack is repulsed.	A steady drumbeat suggests the military, and high-pitched dissonances continue to create a nightmare mood. Low-pitched sounds accompany visions of the dead.
Mendoza kills four mercenary snipers.	Voices begin that lead to *Ave Maria*.
Mendoza runs to the next line of defense, an explosive device under a bridge, which he prepares to detonate.	The *Ave Maria* and avant-garde timbres are combined. A strong rhythmic pulse builds tension.
Mendoza sees a wounded child and runs to save him. He is wounded, and his line to the explosives is cut. Mendoza is shot repeatedly.	A variety of avant-garde sounds are played, including a high pitch that adds intensity when Mendoza understands that all is lost.
The dying Mendoza watches Gabriel lead the peaceful natives in a procession.	In a layered effect, the *Ave Maria* returns as source music, while a dissonant mixture of sounds is in the background.

The natives are systematically shot and killed, and so is Gabriel.	Gabriel's theme, suggesting his serene nature, is joyfully played, accompanied by a low, steady drumbeat.
A native picks up Gabriel's monstrance and walks to certain death. The camera shows the village as it burns down.	Gabriel's theme comes to a religious cadence. After the music fades, silence is broken only by the slow pulse of the drum.

Stories of America

During the 1980s, filmmakers also created numerous films based on American subjects. Vivid stories of baseball, twentieth-century wars, and our exploration of space were shown to audiences eager to see realistic portrayals of the recent past. Also successful at the box office at this time were films showing the violence of the Prohibition era.

Gangster Movies

Two notable films set in the Prohibition era feature symphonic scores by Ennio Morricone: *Once Upon a Time in America* (1984) and *The Untouchables* (1987). The music for Sergio Leone's *Once Upon a Time in America* is more tuneful than that of *The Untouchables* or the *Godfather* scores. Morricone musically links this film to Leone's earlier epic *Once Upon a Time in the West* (1968) by using a similar texture—a single instrument playing a plaintive melody with accompaniment—and by the use of a wordless soprano accompanied by strings to represent the love interest. Contrasting musical styles are provided by the jazz from nightclubs, ethnic Chinese music in the opium den, several renditions of the Beatles' "Yesterday," and a quotation of Rossini's light-hearted overture to *La gazza ladra*.

The Untouchables is based on a popular television series. While director Brian De Palma carefully recreates the ambiance of the 1930s, Morricone's Oscar-nominated score makes no reference to the time period other than a few extended solos for saxophone. The music during the opening credits clearly establishes a contemporary style, as Morricone combines the Al Capone theme, faintly reminiscent of the *Godfather* theme, with aggressive sounds supported by a rock drumbeat. Throughout the film, the drums underscore violence. For contrast, Morricone supplies some beautiful scoring, especially for the scenes of Eliot Ness with his family.

Other American Subjects

In a different vein, the American epic *The Right Stuff* (1983) features an extensive Oscar-winning score by versatile Bill Conti. *The Right Stuff* contains both popular and

Great Names of the 1970s and 1980s

Francis Ford Copolla (b. 1939), the son of an Italian-American composer, was born in Detroit and raised in New York. He earned a master's degree from the UCLA film school and wrote a number of screenplays, winning an Oscar for his contributions to *Patton*. His first major break was Paramount's offer to direct *The Godfather*. He made the most of the opportunity, and the film stands as one of the finest works by an American director. He followed that success with perhaps the greatest sequel ever, *The Godfather: Part II*, and the critically acclaimed *The Conversation*. *Apocalypse Now* proved to be a turning point in his career. Although this film is generally seen as a masterpiece, the difficulties in production and the spiraling budget hurt Copolla's reputation. Since that time, he has produced several successful films, but also a number of box-office failures.

Martin Scorsese (b. 1942) was born in New York and attended the film school at NYU. After teaching at his alma mater for a short period, he moved to Hollywood. His first masterpiece is *Mean Streets* (1973), a tough vision of life on the streets based partly on his own experiences. The same gritty visions propelled *Taxi Driver* (1976) to international acclaim, as it won the Palme d'Or at the Cannes Film Festival. In 1980 he created a film that, according to the AFI Top 100 rankings, is the greatest film of that decade, *Raging Bull*, a biography of the boxer Jake LaMotta. Since then he has created such diverse films as *The Color of Money* (1986), *GoodFellas* (1990), *The Last Temptation of Christ* (1988), *The Age of Innocence* (1993), *Kundun* (1997), *Gangs of New York* (2002), and *The Aviator* (2004).

Woody Allen (b. 1935) was born in Brooklyn with the name Allen Stewart Konigsberg. Like Scorsese, he attended the film school at NYU, but failed a course entitled Motion Picture Production. He quit school and began working as a writer for comedians and for several television series, including the classic *Your Show of Shows*. Despite receiving an Emmy nomination, he moved on to stand-up comedy and eventually films, in which he acted, wrote the screenplays, and directed. He performed all three roles in his first major success, *Take the Money and Run* (1969). His rising reputation climaxed with the bittersweet comedy *Annie Hall* (1977), which eclipsed *Star Wars* and won the Best Picture Oscar. Another masterpiece, *Manhattan* (1979), followed, and Allen began to diversify his subjects. Among his other highly rated features are *A Midsummer Night's Sex Comedy* (1982), *Hannah and Her Sisters* (1986), and *Crimes and Misdemeanors* (1989). The 1990s were a difficult decade for Allen. His films have had mixed reviews, and his personal life has been marked by scandal. After he married the adopted daughter of his former girlfriend, actress Mia Farrow, it was alleged that Allen had also molested another daughter.

Oliver Stone (b. 1946) is yet another New York product. After a year at Yale, he dropped out and went to Vietnam, where he taught English. In 1967, he returned to Vietnam as a soldier and received a Bronze Star and Purple Heart. Back in the United States, he attended NYU and studied filmmaking under Martin Scorsese. He won his first Oscar for the screenplay for *Midnight Express* (1978). He continued writing for a variety of films, including *Conan the Barbarian* (1982), prior to his directorial debut with *Platoon* (1986). This film was a spectacular success, winning Oscars for Best Film and Best Director. He later completed the trilogy of films about Vietnam with the Oscar-winning *Born on the Fourth of July* (1989) and *Heaven & Earth* (1993). His other films, which are characterized by masterful technique and frequent controversy, include *The Doors* (1991), *JFK* (1991), *Natural Born Killers* (1994), and *Nixon* (1995).

symphonic material. Popular songs, heard throughout the film, help date the plot-line, which extends from the 1940s through the 1960s. The symphonic music, which has a wide range of emotional effects, is successful in creating an overall patriotic mood for the film. The score also contains several adaptations of classical music, including a quote from "The Russian Sailor's Dance" by Glière after the Russians successfully launch a rocket.

While not as patriotic as *The Right Stuff*, *The Natural* (1984) is one of the finest examples of Americana in the decade. Set in 1939, the film follows the baseball season of Roy Hobbs (Robert Redford), a thirtyfive-year old rookie. Although he has enormous talent, his career was derailed before it got started, and he has one last chance to play major-league ball. Mixed into this mythological baseball yarn are two women who fulfill the archetypal roles of females in male-oriented films, the seductress (Kim Basinger) and the redeemer (Glenn Close).

The music for *The Natural* was created by a composer from a familiar family—Randy Newman, the nephew of the famed film composer Alfred Newman. For montages showing games, a standard place for rock music in most contemporary sports films, Newman chose a jazz idiom reflecting the era. There are montages for two

Composer Profile

Randy Newman (b. 1943)

The nephew of Alfred Newman, Randy began his career as a songwriter and was recently given a lifetime achievement award by the American Society of Composers, Authors, and Publishers. He received Academy nominations for both song and score for his second film, *Ragtime* (1981), primarily on the strength of a waltz. Since then, he has composed a number of Oscar-nominated scores, most notably for animated features. He won an Oscar for the song "If I Didn't Have You" from *Monsters, Inc.*

Important Film Scores

Ragtime 1981 ✉ ✉
The Natural 1984 ✉
Parenthood 1989 ✉
Toy Story 1995 ✉ ✉
A Bug's Life 1998 ✉
Meet the Parents 2000 ✉
Monsters, Inc. 2001 ✉ ♫
Cars 2006 ✉
The Princess and the Frog (2009) ✉ ✉
Toy Story 3 (2010) ♫
★ = Best Picture Oscar   ♫ = Best Music Oscar   ✉ = Music Oscar Nomination

losing streaks; in the first, we hear a humorous steady-moving bass line (called a walking bass), reflecting the ineptitude of the team (31:05); in the second, a swanky romantic tune suggests that romance is distracting Roy (1:09:20). More energetic and upbeat music accompanies the visions of winning streaks.

For the rest of the score, Newman turned primarily to the style of Aaron Copland, whose musical style suggests values that are fundamental to Americana. Newman's melodic gifts are apparent in the flashbacks at the beginning of the film, and much of this material achieves prominence later, when Roy returns to his roots. In his musical choices, Newman avoided many of the clichés of sports films and helped to project a story that is about America's recent past.

Figure 28.8 Hobbs hits an electrifying home run in *The Natural*

International Films

Because of the growing internationalism of Hollywood films and the rise of multiple production centers for films, it has become more difficult to define national schools of filmmaking. Already considered in this chapter are several films from two or more regions, including *Gandhi* (England and India) and *The Last Emperor* (China, Italy, England, and Hong Kong). In general, the finest European films from this time tend to focus on stories about the immediate past, just like contemporary American films. Unlike the American films, however, music often plays a minimal role.

Among the prominent European films with sparse musical scores are Truffaut's acclaimed *The Last Metro* (1980), which deals with France during the Nazi occupation, and the celebrated German film *Das Boot* (1981). The most joyful musical moment in the latter is the singing of "It's a Long Way From Tipperary" by the crew of the German U-boat. Ingmar Bergman's last film, *Fanny and Alexander* (1982), depends primarily on source music, as did Bergman's earlier *Autumn Sonata* (1978). The moving simplicity of the Danish/French film *Babette's Feast* (1987), about a nineteenth-century political refugee, also emphasizes source music, primarily singing. Composer Per Norgaard provides a few additional musical cues for small chamber groups that function as a touch of spice for this sumptuous film feast.

One of the most highly acclaimed international film scores from this time is for the French/Italian film *Cinema Paradiso* (1989). Created by Ennio Morricone and including a love theme composed by his son Andrea Morricone, the score is light-hearted and melodic. Morricone's score successfully captures the humor, nostalgia, and romance in this tale of a movie theater in a small Italian community.

Trailer

The trend of creating films set in exotic locations and in America's recent past continued through the 1990s and into the twenty-first century. For film composers, the epic nature of these visions allowed them to compose more substantial scores with wider musical resources. The settings in other locales in particular encouraged the incorporation of ethnic musical styles and instruments. As we will observe in the next unit, indigenous national styles would become an important tool in creating fresh sounds in the ever-changing world of film music.

Important Names and Terms

Ravi Shankar
George Fenton
sitar
shakuhachi
erhu
pipa
gamelan
Andean flute
layered music
Randy Newman
Per Norgaard

Suggested Viewing

Drama: *Agnes of God* (1985) ✉ and *Dangerous Liaisons* (1988) ✉
Romance: *A Room With a View* (1985)
Thriller: *Fatal Attraction* (1987)
Western: *Silverado* (1985) ✉
War: *Platoon* (1986) ★

29

New Box-Office Kings, 1984–1988

In 1984, *Beverly Hills Cop* and *Ghostbusters* were bigger hits than *Indiana Jones and the Temple of Doom* and *Star Trek III: The Search for Spock*, thereby signaling the end of the reign of fantasy/adventure films. In the following year, *Back to the Future* was another box-office sensation, and these three films, along with their sequels, brought a new spirit to Hollywood films.

Comedy/Adventure Films

Common to *Beverly Hills Cop*, *Ghostbusters*, and *Back to the Future* is the casting of comedians from television as heroes of action and adventure films. In these new box-office successes, there is more emphasis on comedy, the characters are realistic and easy to relate to, the films are relatively short, and the scores feature popular music, either exclusively or in combination with orchestral music.

SIGNIFICANT FILMS

1984	*Ghostbusters* ✉
	Beverly Hills Cop
1985	*Back to the Future*
	Witness
1986	*'Round Midnight* ♫
	Top Gun ♫
	Hoosiers ✉
1987	*Lethal Weapon*
1988	*Rain Man* ★ ✉
	Die Hard
	The Milagro Beanfield War ♫
	Who Framed Roger Rabbit

Beverly Hills Cop

Eddie Murphy brought the ad-libbed humor, colorful language, and rock sound of *Saturday Night Live* to the detective genre in *Beverly Hills Cop*. The soundtrack, created by Harold Faltermeyer, contains only rock music, which reinforces the image of a ghetto-tough Detroit cop bringing his street smarts and his hip music to laid-back Beverly Hills. Throughout the film, music has four roles: to accompany the credits; to underscore movement, such as action or travel; to underscore the hero's character; and to serve as source music.

The first four cues of the film, while Axel, the Eddie Murphy character, is still in Detroit, illustrate these roles. The first cue is the song "The Heat Is On," which appears during the opening credits. Sung by Detroit native Glenn Frey, the words and the images of Detroit establish the urban background that is essential to define our protagonist. Action begins within minutes (4:45), and the long, destructive truck chase allows time for a second song to be performed in its entirety. The third cue (10:55) is a four-measure ostinato that becomes Axel's theme. Its funky character, amusing variations, and looping quality—it always leads back to the beginning—provide excellent support for Axel's character. For the final cue (13:15), diegetic rock music is heard in the poolroom as Axel and Zach become reacquainted. Although limited in its roles, the music sustains high energy, contains an immediate appeal to younger audiences—those who see films multiple times—and contributes to both the setting and characterization in the drama. Of course, the music made money as a popular album as well.

Ghostbusters

Elmer Bernstein, a versatile musician who had created outstanding scores for science fiction, adventure, and comedy films, combined the sounds of all three in the music for *Ghostbusters*. Mixed in with his traditional symphonic style are a number of high-energy popular tunes. The free movement from one style to the other can be seen as a typical postmodernist trait. Another characteristic of postmodernism can be seen within the film itself—the prominent use of an advertising icon, the Stay-Puft Marshmallow Man.

The opening brings these diverse musical elements together. Combining the timbres of an orchestra and a synthesizer, dissonant alien sounds suggest the supernatural while we observe a librarian at work. The full orchestra takes over as cards begin to fly from the catalogue—a librarian's nightmare—and action music accompanies her subsequent flight. Just at the dramatic moment when she screams, a drum roll ushers in a rendition of Ray Parker Jr.'s Oscar-nominated song "Ghostbusters."

Figure 29.1 The popular theme song bursts out at the title credits

This mixture of musical styles, which becomes commonplace during the decade, is evident throughout the film. A romantic melody played by a solo cello accompanies

Building on the Foundation of Rock

In the 1960s, the age of rock and roll passed, and a new rock era emerged. Just as jazz developed a number of distinct styles in the late 1940s, rock music quickly splintered into a myriad of different types, some defined by a single performer or group. Among the most prominent rock styles of the 60s are the following:

hard rock (Rolling Stones): a hard beat with a strong message about sex and drugs

soft rock (Pat Boone): easy listening for background music

soul music (Ray Charles): an extension of the traditions of blues singing

Motown (Diana Ross): from Detroit, fused gospel, rock, and blues

folk rock (Bob Dylan): a fusion of rock and folk with a message of rebellion

Each succeeding decade brought more innovative rock styles, and Hollywood absorbed them and sometimes provided springboards to success. *Saturday Night Fever*, for example, gave an enormous boost to disco.

Because of the increasing splintering of rock into distinct styles, filmmakers began to expand the role of the popular sounds beyond appealing to young audiences. The choice of a rock number could create a specific atmosphere. The plots of both *The Graduate* and *Easy Rider* deal with disillusioned individuals, but the divergent moods of their stories are established by their style of rock music. Since rock music is now a half-century old, the choice of a particular tune can help set the time of a story. *Forrest Gump* (1994), for example, is a virtual history of rock, as the story opens with a vision of Elvis and progresses beyond the Vietnam War. The music consistently dates the events in Forrest's life. An individual's character can also be defined by the style of music that he listens to. In *Boyz n the Hood* (1991), the no-nonsense father (Laurence Fishburne) listens to jazz; the less intellectual neighbor Mrs. Baker listens to the music of her youth, Motown; and the younger generation listens to rap.

Recent years have brought some fascinating fusions of rock with other styles, including those of contemporary art music. The easy transitions between heavy metal and minimalism in *The Matrix* (1999), and the now familiar sound of a drum set during intense passages of dissonance point to an exciting new age of eclectic film music, in which rock music will maintain a strong presence.

the cellist Dana (17:00), dark brass chords suggest the powerful dark world of Gozer, the ancient Sumerian deity (48:45), and energetic music rocks New York as it looks to be saved by the Ghostbusters (1:18:55).

Back to the Future

Back to the Future (1985) launched the film career of Michael J. Fox, who was already an established television star for his role in *Family Ties*. Because of his youthful looks, the twenty-four year old Fox successfully plays a seventeen-year-old who travels back in time and meets his parents as teenagers. The film mixes considerable fun and humor with serious action and life-threatening situations. Supporting these divergent moods is a score that combines rock and symphonic music.

In addition to filling the roles described above, rock music serves an additional purpose in this film. The film can be divided into three time periods: 1985, 1955, and back to 1985. In each, rock music helps to establish the time period, along with the clothes, the cars, and the furniture. Near the opening of the film, the contemporary song "The Power of Love" underscores a travel montage as Marty (Michael J. Fox) skates to school (5:50) and later when he returns. Other 80s rock sounds can be heard at Marty's band audition (8:15) and from his clock radio (17:30).

When Marty walks downtown in the past, he hears two hits from 1955, "Mr. Sandman" (35:15) and "The Ballad of Davy Crockett" (37:20). Later, he joins Marvin Berry's band and performs another hit from 1955, "Earth Angel" (1:24:30). In a playful musical gag, Marty then leads the band in a rendition of "Johnny B. Goode" (1:27:15), which prompts Marvin to call his cousin Chuck to have him listen to this new sound. Chuck Berry would record this hit song in 1958. A final bit of musical humor occurs when Marty returns to 1985. As he wakes, his clock radio features the contemporary rock sound of a song entitled "Back in Time" (1:46:35).

Also critical to the success of this film is a strong symphonic score by Alan Silvestri. Standard orchestral clichés underscore the seriousness of the action scenes and lend credence to the bond between Marty and Doc, the eccentric scientist. Silvestri also creates a theme reminiscent of *Superman* that is heard in triumphant moments, such as the antagonist Biff's encounter with manure (1:06:45). The theme, which is subject to a variety of transformations, is heard in a romantic setting when Marty's parents kiss for the first time (1:23:30).

Who Framed Roger Rabbit

Among Alan Silvestri's film credits is the score for a comedy/action/animation film, *Who Framed Roger Rabbit* (1988). Perhaps the ultimate in postmodernism, this film combines animation and live action to an unprecedented degree. Moreover, the cartoon characters come from various competing studios. Just the presence of Mickey Mouse and Bugs Bunny on the screen at the same time was outrageous.

The film combines characteristics of two opposing film styles, animation and film noir. From the traditions of the latter, we have a setting in the 1940s, a burned-out private detective, an alluring and suspicious dame, and a convoluted plot with a surprising twist at the end. Indeed, the film has several intended parallels to *Chinatown*: a conspiracy story set in Los Angeles, dirty pictures propelling the plot, and a previous incident in Toontown (Chinatown) that leads the detective to avoid the area. To reinforce this connection, the detective Eddie is given a jazz trumpet solo as his theme, like Jake in *Chinatown*. Among the other principal themes are a sleazy saxophone theme for Jessica, and a standard bad-guy theme for Judge Doom.

Figure 29.2 The music of Franz Liszt will never be the same after the Duck duet

Silvestri's score combines three principal styles: cartoon, jazz, and traditional. Cartoon music differs from other film music in that it is continuous and usually underlines each physical gesture without much subtlety. Other than the opening cartoon within a cartoon, starring Roger Rabbit and Baby Herman, Silvestri wisely employs this style sparingly, primarily for brief antics by Roger. Much of the score is dominated by a jazz sound created by a quartet of musicians, which primarily accompanies scenes featuring Eddie the detective. Traditional underscoring appears during action scenes and romantic moments. One further postmodern factor in this mix is the quotation of two nineteenth-century classics. Early in the film, the brooms from *Fantasia*'s "Sorcerer's Apprentice" clean the studio to the sound of their famous theme by Dukas played on a saxophone (9:00). In one of the humorous highlights of the film, the duo of Donald and Daffy Duck dazzles in a performance of the *Hungarian Rhapsody* No. 2 by Franz Liszt (15:00).

New Action Heroes

The above action and adventure films featured unconventional heroes in humorous stories, accompanied by popular music that appealed to a young, hip generation. Some of the other new action heroes at this time were more conventional, at least in physical appearance, and they are generally given symphonic support. One of the finest composers of such scores is Michael Kamen, who provided the music for two new action films and their sequels—*Lethal Weapon* (1987) and *Die Hard* (1988).

Composer Profile

Michael Kamen (1948–2003)

Michael Kamen had a background in classical music—he studied the oboe at Juilliard—and rock music—he was the music director for David Bowie. Kamen excelled at creating action scores. During the 1980s, he composed more than twenty-five film scores, including *Lethal Weapon* and *Die Hard*. He is perhaps best known for the music to *Mr. Holland's Opus*. He received two Oscar nominations for Best Song.

Important Film Scores

Lethal Weapon 1987	*Don Juan DeMarco* 1995 ✉
Die Hard 1988	*Mr. Holland's Opus* 1995
Robin Hood: Prince of Thieves 1991 ✉	*X-Men* 2000
Last Action Hero 1993	

★ = Best Picture Oscar   ♫ = Best Music Oscar   ✉ = Music Oscar Nomination

A number of similarities link these films together. Both feature an action hero who is undergoing personal problems. In *Lethal Weapon*, Riggs (Mel Gibson) is struggling to deal with his wife's death; in *Die Hard*, John (Bruce Willis) is estranged from his wife. For both, the Christmas season and all of its trappings exacerbate their emotional states. At the conclusion of the films, both characters resolve their personal problems by surviving an excessively violent struggle against well-organized and well-trained criminals—so much for needing an analyst.

The scores for each film also contain a number of similarities. Christmas songs are heard at the beginning and end of each in order to reinforce the pervading Christmas spirit that surrounds our heroes. Kamen also supplies suspense and action cues with appropriate orchestral noise, generally dominated by the brass section. But an important contrast in the two plots allows Kamen to supply more variety of musical sounds in *Lethal Weapon*.

In this film, a second character serves as a heroic counterpart to Riggs—Roger Murtaugh (Danny Glover). When we are first introduced to them, they are both unclothed: Roger is in a bath surrounded by his loving family, and Riggs is in his trailer with his dog. Roger eats bacon for breakfast, and Riggs drinks beer. Reinforcing such contrasts, Kamen provides each character with a unique musical timbre. A saxophone solo performed by David Sanborn represents Roger, and a guitar solo played by Eric Clapton accompanies Riggs. The two timbres, linked by their common improvisational jazz character, are heard throughout the film, providing a strong contrast to the action music. Since the two figures are often on the screen at the same time, the two soloists provide some improvised duos. Solo orchestral instruments are sometimes added as well, allowing Kamen to slip effortlessly into orchestral underscoring as needed.

Die Hard has more bullets and explosions than *Lethal Weapon*, and the action is more unrelenting. Some contrast is provided by source music, which shifts from Bach to rap, but, on the whole, the score is dominated by suspense and action cues. The musical highlight is the use of Beethoven's Symphony No. 9 as a leitmotif for the German terrorists/thieves. Beethoven was of course a German composer. Hints of the theme, its first four notes, are heard in the early portions of the film as the terrorists make their preparations (18:00). When the terrorists enter the elegant Christmas party, a string quartet is conveniently playing an arrangement of their theme as source music (22:50). When the vault is finally opened, a full orchestral rendition of the Beethoven classic signifies the momentary triumph of the terrorists (1:43:25). The music returns once again, with voices, during the closing credits. In *Die Hard 2* (1990), *Finlandia* by Sibelius serves a similar function and ties in with the freezing winter weather.

Figure 29.3 Beethoven's Symphony No. 9 suggests victory for the German thieves in *Die Hard*

Witness

The musical treatment in the preceding films is standard for the action films of the period; Maurice Jarre, however, proved that other approaches could also be effective. In *Witness* (1985), an Amish boy witnesses a murder in Philadelphia, and detective John Book (Harrison Ford) takes him and his mother back to the Amish countryside for safety, where the final confrontation takes place. Deciding not to use an orchestral score, Jarre created the music for an ensemble of synthesizers.

Figure 29.4 Building a barn in *Witness* to the music of Maurice Jarre

Jarre also avoids the standard Hollywood musical support for violence and tension. Instead, the music appears as patches of sound setting a single mood. Low pitches suggest danger, and higher pitches accompany visions of Amish life. An Amish theme is heard four times in the film. It is presented in the opening in a hymn-like setting as we watch the simple life of the Amish. Later, in one of the most beautiful cues in any film of the decade, Jarre gives this tune a strong Baroque character as the Amish, with Book's help, build a barn (1:10:30). A repetitive bass line makes the passage sound like a passacaglia, a Baroque form built on a repeating bass line, and the thick contrapuntal texture and hymn-like theme evoke the strength of religious conviction in the Baroque era. For this passage, the synthesizers recreate the timbres of orchestral instruments. The theme appears twice more near the end, beginning when the Amish men appear at the climactic moment. The music, like the film itself, treats the Amish life with great respect.

The Widening Scope of Popular Music

By the mid-1980s, film composers had at their disposal more variety of styles and combinations of styles than ever before. Much of this variety is due to the continuous appearance of new popular styles and to the expanding presence of popular music in film. Rock music continued to generate hits both at the box office and in record sales. Rock instrumentals and popular songs performed by unseen singers appeared increasingly within the body of a film, both as source music and as underscoring. While in general the use of diegetic rock music is similar to that of earlier decades, now there seems to be less consideration for the relationship of the music to the drama. Many of the tunes are chosen for their ability to sell soundtracks rather than for the appropriateness of their lyrics or style for the drama.

Action and Sports Films

Two important influences from television can be seen. In the summer of 1981, MTV began broadcasting on cable television. Rock videos, such as Michael Jackson's "Thriller" (1982), created an enormous sensation. Films, which already had MTV moments ("Raindrops Keep Fallin' on My Head" from *Butch Cassidy and the Sundance Kid*, 1969), now embraced the concept of cutting montage scenes to match the length of a rock tune. A second major influence from television was Jan Hammer's rock-oriented music for *Miami Vice*. As a result, popular music in movies can be heard accompanying divergent montage scenes showing travel, the passing of time, fighting, and lovemaking.

The most successful film using the MTV approach is *Top Gun* (1985), with music created by Giorgio Moroder and Harold Faltermeyer. Rock music accompanies dizzying flying sequences that, along with Tom Cruise, made a great impression on young audiences. Moroder, who had received an Academy Award for his innovative synthesizer score for *Midnight Express* (1978), won his second Oscar for Best Song with "Take My Breath Away," written for *Top Gun*. Faltermeyer also created several of the musical numbers, including the "Top Gun Anthem," which serves as an effective theme song played on electric guitar. In the climactic scene, an energized rock beat accompanies all the action after Maverick (Tom Cruise) takes off (1:31:45) until the music erupts into the "Top Gun Anthem" eight minutes later, following the victory.

A surprise box-office hit from 1986 was the uplifting sports drama *Hoosiers*, with an Oscar-nominated score by Jerry Goldsmith. As in *Top Gun*, rock music generates high energy in action montages—in this case, scenes of basketball practices and games, the last of which is augmented with the sounds and energy of cheering crowds. Unlike *Top Gun*, this eclectic score also contains some beautiful cues created by a synthesizer to accompany scenic Indiana landscapes. This is the story of an American sport in its heartland. Appropriately, Goldsmith mixes a variety of American sounds, from Coplandesque nationalism to rock. In the music's most dramatic moment, just after the team wins the state championship, Goldsmith turns off the rock music and then the celebration noise, leaving only the orchestra, as the victory theme is sounded first in the French horns and then in the strings (1:48:05). The victory means much more than just a game.

Dramatic Films

Increasingly, popular music began to be used in dramatic films. The scores that won Oscars in 1986 and 1987 are both based on a popular music idiom, both deal with serious issues, and neither uses rock music. *'Round Midnight* is one of the finest films to come out of the 1980s. Inspired by the lives of a number of jazz musicians, the film depicts a burned-out jazz musician in Paris and his friendship with an adoring fan. The realism of the views of two great cities—Paris and New York (Martin Scorsese has a

Dave Grusin (b. 1934)

Dave Grusin is active in both film and television. The former jazz pianist and accompanist to Andy Williams created scores for a number of the most endearing films of the 1980s. He received six Oscar nominations, winning his only award in 1988.

Important Film Scores

The Graduate 1967
Three Days of the Condor 1975
Heaven Can Wait 1978 ✉
On Golden Pond 1981 ✉
Tootsie 1982 ✉
The Milagro Beanfield War 1988 ♫
The Firm 1993 ✉

★ = Best Picture Oscar   ♫ = Best Music Oscar   ✉ = Music Oscar Nomination

---

cameo, in which he extols the virtues of his beloved city)—extends to the principal actor Dexter Gordon. Gordon is a jazz musician with no acting experience, yet his realistic portrayal earned him an Oscar nomination. There is little underscoring in the film, but there are abundant jazz performances, projecting moods of both warmth and sadness. Herbie Hancock, one of the leading figures in recent jazz history, prepared the music and also played the role of the pianist Eddie.

Dave Grusin won an Oscar for his enjoyable score for *The Milagro Beanfield War*. Grusin's experience as a jazz musician and a composer of popular music in films since the 1960s are brought together in this unpretentious film. Mixing American and Mexican popular and folk sounds, Grusin created a warm atmosphere that pervades this basically serious look at Hispanic life in New Mexico. The film is an example of magic realism, a literary movement primarily from Mexico, in which fantasy and realism are mixed, creating a sense of instant mythology. The music sustains a magical quality throughout. The film avoids announcing a stern moral which makes it vastly different from the populist films in the 1940s and the liberal themes of the 1970s.

Rain Man

Box-office success, critical recognition, a serious theme, and rock music came together in the 1988 Best Picture winner, *Rain Man*. A tale of two brothers, the film follows the transformation of Charlie Babbitt (Tom Cruise) after meeting his brother Raymond (Dustin Hoffman), who has a condition currently known as savant syndrome. At the beginning of the film, Charlie is a slick talking, self-serving, emotionally detached businessman. After his father dies, he learns that the three-million-dollar inheritance has been left in a trust to his brother, who he did not know existed. Charlie kidnaps Raymond and begins a journey from Cincinnati to California. In the process, Charlie learns much about his brother, savant syndrome, and his past. Dustin Hoffman won an Oscar for his brilliant portrayal of this real-life figure.

The music for this film, by newcomer Hans Zimmer, created a great sensation for its understated use of rock music idioms. The score features a number of vocal soloists in a wide variety of popular styles, raging from calypso to Gershwin. Extended instrumentals created by the synthesizer are also employed. As observed in other popular music scores, the cues establish single moods, whether joyful, sad, or nostalgic. There are no contrasts within a given cue. A simple, gentle theme featuring a flute serves as the principal theme, which recurs periodically during the journey and

Composer Profile

Hans Zimmer (b. 1957)

Born in Germany, Hans Zimmer moved to London and worked as a rock musician. His natural talent for the synthesizer led him to film composition, and his Oscar-nominated score for *Rain Man* made him one of Hollywood's top young composers. The light popular quality of his score helped establish a film sound that has been widely imitated. In the following year, he provided the music for another Best Picture winner, *Driving Miss Daisy*. During the 1990s, Zimmer would become one of Hollywood's most successful film composers, winning an Oscar for his score for *The Lion King* (1995).

Important Film Scores

Rain Man 1988 ★ ✉
Driving Miss Daisy 1989 ★
Thelma and Louise 1991
A League of Their Own 1992
The Lion King 1994 ♫
As Good as It Gets 1997 ✉
The Thin Red Line 1998 ✉
The Prince of Egypt 1998 ✉
Gladiator 2000 ✉
Black Hawk Down 2001
Pearl Harbor 2001
The Last Samurai 2003

Madagascar 2005
The Da Vinci Code 2006
Pirates of the Caribbean: Dead Man's Chest 2006
The Dark Night (2008)
Sherlock Holmes (2009) ✉
Inception (2010) ✉

★ = Best Picture Oscar   ♫ = Best Music Oscar   ✉ = Music Oscar Nomination

at the end of the film. Predominantly, music is heard during travel montages, but it also underscores serious moments in the dialogue. In most of these cues, the music is subdued in mood, tempo, and volume.

At the opening of the card-counting episode (see Viewer Guide), a country and western song is heard in the background as source music. Charlie at his most desperate moment is initially irritated with Raymond's behavior, but his mood quickly brightens when he realizes that Raymond's ability to memorize would serve him well in Las Vegas. During the montage of the trip to Vegas, the instrumental underscoring, created by a synthesizer, projects renewed energy, reflecting both Charlie's spirits and their intended destination. Once they arrive, voices are added, and the energy remains high throughout the card game. Without changing the mood, Zimmer allows room for dialogue and humor by bringing the vocals and melody in and out of the texture.

Viewer Guide

Rain Man: Counting Cards

Timing

1:23:10–1:32:20 (0:00 at studio logo); DVD Chapters 24–26

Key Points

- Use of source music
- Rhythmic pulse for driving montage
- Added vocals for Las Vegas
- Lack of contrast in the mood

Setting

Charlie (Tom Cruise) needs money to save his business. Desperate, he kidnaps his savant brother Raymond (Dustin Hoffman), who has inherited three million dollars from their father. While traveling, Charlie has learned many of Raymond's idiosyncrasies and suddenly realizes that his amazing ability to memorize can earn money at the blackjack tables in Las Vegas.

PLOT	MUSIC
In a restaurant, Raymond irritates Charlie until he realizes that Raymond has memorized the jukebox selections.	Source music: a country and western song comes from the jukebox.

At their car, Charlie tests Raymond's memory with cards.	No music
While driving to Las Vegas, Charlie explains the rules for the game and their betting signals.	A strong rhythmic pulse begins and underscores the dialogue.
They arrive in Las Vegas, Charlie pawns his watch for cash, and they enter the hotel.	Vocals enter, both a soloist and an ensemble. With the image of the archangel Gabriel with a trumpet, the singer mimics a siren.
They enter the hotel. Charlie gets new clothes and a haircut.	The music gets quieter, but the vocals reenter as the two dapper men descend the escalator.
Entering the casino, they are bombarded by the sights and sounds of gambling. They approach the card table, ready to begin.	The music again gets quieter, allowing the sound effects from the casino to be more prominent. Vocals announce their arrival at the card table.
Early on, Raymond makes a mistake, but he helps Charlie win a double down.	The music is reduced to the rhythm section, but crescendos with the victory.
A montage shows them winning over $80,000 as casino officials try to figure out how they are cheating. Finally, a gambling wheel distracts Raymond.	The music continues without pause, but it fades in and out to allow for dialogue.

Trailer

By the end of the 1980s, film music had expanded its palette to include traditional symphonic scores, numerous types of popular music, both disturbing and accessible modern sounds, and a range of ethnic musical styles. Musical diversity continued to expand through the next decade, as filmmakers and film composers built on the accomplishments of the past and created distinct, innovative scores that would carry us into the twenty-first century.

Important Names and Terms

Harold Faltermeyer   MTV
Alan Silvestri   Herbie Hancock
Michael Kamen   Hans Zimmer

Suggested Viewing

Drama: *The Color Purple* (1985) ✉ ✉
Comedy/Drama: *Tootsie* (1982) ✉, *The Breakfast Club* (1985), *The Accidental Tourist*
    (1988) ✉, and *Big* (1988)
Children/Drama: *The Karate Kid* (1984) and *The Princess Bride* (1987)
Musical: *Purple Rain* (1984) ♫ ✉ and *Dirty Dancing* (1987)
Action/Adventure: *Romancing the Stone* (1984)
Horror/Science Fiction: *Gremlins* (1984) and *Aliens* (1986) ✉

Part 7

Fin de Siècle and the New Millennium, 1989-2004

30

Symphonic Scores, 1989–1996

The decade of the 1990s was one of the most remarkable periods in American history. The Cold War that had dominated international politics since the 1950s came to an abrupt end with the fall of the Berlin Wall in 1989, the unification of the two Germanys in 1990, and the collapse of the Soviet Union in 1991. The "Evil Empire," as President Ronald Reagan called it, had simply vanished, and the ever-present threat of nuclear holocaust subsided greatly. Because of these developments, the United States assumed political, economic, and even cultural leadership in the world. The country finally entered an era that President John Kennedy had once envisioned— "Pax Americana." The era would last a dozen years.

The 1990s saw tremendous developments in technology and science. It is estimated that there were one hundred million computers in use in 1990. By mid-decade, that number had doubled. New concepts such as "surfing the net," e-mail, and Amazon.com quickly became a central part of American life and critical to America's preeminent international position. The information highway now leads to every part of the globe, and the full implication of the Internet is just beginning to be realized. But perhaps even more stunning are the medical discoveries of recent years, insuring that life in 2015 will be very different from life today.

SIGNIFICANT FILMS

1989	*Batman*
	Glory
1990	*Dances with Wolves* ★ ♫
	Home Alone ✉ ✉
1991	*Hook* ✉
1992	*The Last of the Mohicans*
1993	*Schindler's List* ★ ♫
	Jurassic Park
	Blue
1995	*Braveheart* ★ ✉

Close-Up: Technology and Home Entertainment

VCR, HBO, and DVD

Since the 1970s, technology has revolutionized our movie-watching habits. Prior to that time, movies could be viewed in one of two ways—either by going to the theater to see a new release or by waiting for a television network to broadcast an older movie. Other options became available in the mid-1970s when the VCR went on sale. In 1975, a Betamax VCR with a recording capability of one hour cost $2,295. Competition from the VHS model drove prices down and recording times up. Within a decade, the VHS format dominated the market, and the VCR was a standard companion to the television in American homes. The impact on movie watching was twofold. You could now record movies shown on television, view them at your own convenience, and keep the tape as part of your permanent collection. One could also go to a video store and rent relatively new films, bypassing the television networks completely.

Also bringing greater access to recent movies were the cable movie channels. The cable television phenomenon began in 1972 with the initial broadcasts of the "Home Box Office" (HBO) channel. After HBO began to distribute its programming with the aid of a satellite in 1975, it became a dominant force in cable television. Soon other movie channels appeared on cable, including Showtime (1978), The Movie Channel (1979), Cinemax (1980), and The Disney Channel (1983).

The 1980s and 90s brought about more changes. In 1988, CDs outsold LPs for the first time. The disc format was then applied to films, and in 1997, DVDs became available for public sale in the United States. The clarity and convenience of the DVD has enabled us to study, appreciate, and understand the art of filmmaking in a way that was never possible before. Yet, even as new innovations continue to improve our home entertainment centers, movie theaters continue to thrive. Technology, it appears, will never replace the public theater experience.

As with the change in filmmaking from the 1950s to the 1960s, it is difficult to specify a single year as a demarcation point marking a new film age. For our purposes, we have chosen 1989, a year that coincides with the fall of the Berlin Wall. In that year a number of key films appeared that point to important trends of the 1990s, most notably the tendencies towards dark moods, historical realism, and graphic violence. Through the early years of the 1990s, symphonic scores remained a dominant force; their ability to underscore both dark and light stories can be heard in divergent films, including fantasies, historical dramas, and comedies.

Fantasies

Fantasy films had lost their mass appeal by the middle of the 1980s. Fantasies continued to appear occasionally into the 1990s, paving the way for the eventual return of the fantasy blockbuster—films such as the *Star Wars* prequels, the *Harry Potter* series, and the *Lord of the Rings* trilogy. Among the most successful of these earlier fantasies are *Batman* (1989) and *Jurassic Park* (1993).

Batman

One of the key films of 1989 is Tim Burton's *Batman*, which appeared only two years after the last *Superman* sequel (*Superman IV: The Quest for Peace*, 1987). Both *Superman* and *Batman* are based on superheroes from D.C. Comics. The differences between these movies, however, point to the changing mood of Hollywood films. Superman lives in the thriving city of Metropolis, has a bright secret Fortress of Solitude, goes on a formal and gentlemanly first date with Lois, and saves lives. Batman lives in the dark and decaying world of Gotham City, has a dark secret Bat Cave, sleeps with Vickie on their first date, and vengefully kills people. While the fantasy/action subject links *Batman* to the traditions of the 1980s, the film's darkness points to the prevailing mood of the 1990s.

Essential to the brooding character of *Batman* is the musical score by Danny Elfman, one of several bright young composers to emerge in the 1980s. Elfman's friendship with director Tim Burton led to his initial opportunities to score major films, as the two collaborated on *Pee-wee's Big Adventure* (1985) and *Beetlejuice* (1988). The score to *Batman* marked a significant step in Elfman's growth as a film composer.

Composer Profile

Danny Elfman (b. 1953)

Danny Elfman is one of a number of new film composers who did not receive formal training in music. His career began because Tim Burton was a fan of his rock group Oingo Boingo, and the two have established an extended collaboration. For *The Nightmare Before Christmas*, Elfman not only composed the music, but sang the role of Jack as well. A gifted melody writer, Elfman has scored a significant number of popular films, including *Spider-Man* and Best Picture winner *Chicago*. He has received three Oscar nominations. Among his television credits is the theme for the cartoon series *The Simpsons*.

Important Film Scores

Pee-wee's Big Adventure 1985	*Men in Black* 1997 ✉
Beetlejuice 1988	*Planet of the Apes* 2001
Batman 1989	*Spider-Man* 2002
Edward Scissorhands 1990	*Chicago* 2002 ★
The Nightmare Before Christmas 1993	*Big Fish* 2003 ✉
Mission: Impossible 1996	*Spider-Man 2* 2004
Good Will Hunting 1997 ✉	*Charlie and the Chocolate Factory* 2005
	Milk (2008) ✉

★ = Best Picture Oscar   ♫ = Best Music Oscar   ✉ = Music Oscar Nomination

Orchestration plays an essential role in the creation of a dark score. Like the composers for film noir, Elfman generally features low-pitched instruments, and, when higher-pitched instruments are employed, they are heard in their lower registers. Unlike film noir composers, Elfman also uses the full power of the orchestra, with dominating parts given to the brass and percussion. At the opening, the bassoon, the lowest-pitched member of the woodwinds, sets an ominous mood with the Batman motive (Example 30.1). As the title appears, the full orchestra quickly turns to a dark minor chord, supported by an organ sound. The latter not only adds a gothic effect, but also foreshadows the location of the climax—a dark cathedral. The prevailing minor keys and the recurring motive contribute to the overall mood. Even at the end of the film, when Batman's triumphant music is sounding, an abrupt turn to minor closes the film in a shroud of chilling darkness.

Figure 30.1 The music covers the ending of *Batman* with a chilling shroud of darkness

The Batman motive begins with four rising pitches; the first three rise by step, and the last is a leap. As with motivic themes heard in earlier films, this theme is subject to numerous variations. At times, only the first four notes are played. The motive can be heard in counterpoint, at the beginnings of new melodies, and transformed into a variety of moods. Within a two-minute time span (37:55), the motive introduces a waltz for the killing of Grissom, becomes a romantic piano melody as lovers linger in bed, and appears played by a music box for the Joker's triumph. Further manipulations of the motive can be heard in the drive to the Bat Cave (1:12:20), where the motive is played quickly, as an accompaniment, and slowly, as the melody. During the closing credits, the motive can also be heard as a constant accompaniment to the theme song "Scandalous," sung by Prince.

Example 30.1 Batman motive

Jurassic Park

Escapist action films continued to enjoy great box-office appeal in the 1990s. Four of the decade's top ten films mix elements of action and disaster: *Jurassic Park* (1993), *Independence Day* (1996), *Twister* (1996), and *The Lost World: Jurassic Park* (1997). All these films have substantial symphonic scores, fully exploiting the remarkable virtuosity of the contemporary studio orchestra. While some of the musical effects may be lost in the sheer length of the wall-to-wall music, many of the excerpts are exhilarating and play a large role in the success of the special-effect action sequences.

The most memorable score among these films was written for *Jurassic Park* by John Williams. This Spielberg film has a number of parallels to *King Kong* (1933), including a setting on an exotic island, visions of a variety of dinosaurs, a gate separating the beasts from the humans—one of the characters in *Jurassic Park* even points out the similarity of the gate—the initial introduction to the beast through the sound of his footsteps, and the patient but intense build-up to the action, which, once started, becomes unrelenting. There is one difference—viewers have to wait for the sequel (*The Lost World: Jurassic Park*) to see the beast transplanted to the United States.

Figure 30.2 Action and music combine for a box-office smash in *Jurassic Park*

Like Max Steiner's music for the earlier classic, Williams's action music contributes to the horrific effects through loud dynamics dominated by brass and percussion, harsh syncopated accents, and strong dissonances. The major difference between the two scores is the inclusion of more contrast in *Jurassic Park*. Both films use minimal music in the openings, but Williams also withholds music for the initial views of the tyrannosaurus rex. In this way, the music lends a greater sense of realism to the first attacks, and the early silence allows Spielberg and Williams to turn up the intensity by adding music to the later sequences.

Williams also includes two themes that provide contrast to the action music. When the helicopter arrives at Jurassic Park, the awe-inspiring view of the island is supported by an exhilarating trumpet theme (16:35). This theme returns later in the film when the t-rex ironically saves the lives of the remaining survivors (1:57:00). The other contrasting theme is the warm melody associated with the brontosaurus (20:15). Appearing in the scenes with the gentler dinosaurs, this beautiful cue also underscores our relief when they escape.

Historical Dramas

The trend towards realism has led to numerous films with historical settings. Stories have focused on historic events—*Apollo 13, Titanic, Pearl Harbor*; historic figures—*Nixon, Malcolm X, A Beautiful Mind*; and historical backgrounds—*Dances with Wolves, Braveheart*, and *Gladiator*. In the quest for a greater sense of reality, scenes of graphic violence are frequent. Clint Eastwood's *Unforgiven*, a dark portrayal of the old west, exposes the myth of the western hero; *Saving Private Ryan* creates a realistic sense of the terror of D-Day; and *Dances with Wolves* shows us with horrifying accuracy how makeshift hospitals functioned at battles in the Civil War.

Glory

Within a short time span, three excellent films appeared that focused on historical events in America: *Glory* (1989), *Dances with Wolves* (1990), and *The Last of the Mohicans* (1992). Based on the true story of the first all-black regiment to fight in the Civil War, *Glory* paints a grim picture of this horrendous conflict. Images of rigidly formalized warfare, bloodshed, and makeshift hospitals show us the past with vivid realism. Readings from actual letters written by Col. Robert Gould Shaw (Matthew Broderick), the white commander of the regiment, add to the sense of realism. The efforts to recreate scenes with authenticity even extend to the source music cues, which are played on instruments from the Civil War era.

James Horner composed a gripping score for the film. As in many of his works, Horner employs distinct musical sounds that represent some aspect of the story. At the onset, we hear a solo trumpet and snare drums, standard sounds for military stories. These are immediately followed by the ethereal sounds of the Harlem Boys' Choir, and it is this timbre that hauntingly lingers over the entire film. The vocal timbre suggests innocence and, in this film, serves as a constant reminder of how modern society is built on the sacrifices of others.

The most powerful musical moments appear at the end of the film. As the regiment parades by the white Union soldiers, a former adversary yells "Give 'em hell, 54" leading to a stirring presentation of the principal theme (1:37:50). During the battle, music is withheld until Shaw, the white commander, is killed (1:49:35). At this point, the music, which too closely resembles the opening of Orff's *Carmina Burana*, creates an intriguing mood. Rather than reflecting the tragedy of the ensuing slaughter, it suggests the triumph of the African-Americans, who have finally earned the right to fight and die for their country. In the closing moments, we see Shaw thrown into a mass grave with his company (1:54:00). Next to him is thrown the most rebellious of the black soldiers, played by Denzel Washington. As the Boys' Choir sings the *Glory* hymn, we are reminded of the equality of death for blacks and whites, officers and soldiers.

Dances with Wolves

Dances with Wolves (1990), directed by Kevin Costner, won seven Academy Awards, including Best Picture and Best Original Score. After a grimly realistic opening scene set in the Civil War, the film follows John Dunbar (Kevin Costner) going west. Reversing the traditional roles of westerns, Dunbar finds the Indians civilized and the whites savage. In creating this epic, Costner painstakingly researched and recreated Native American rituals; he even used Lakota dialogue with subtitles, lending a strong air of authenticity to the story. In the process, Costner replaced the usual historical inaccuracies with new, politically correct inaccuracies. Still, the treatment is both fascinating and respectful.

John Barry (1933–2011)

English composer John Barry began his musical career in a military band and later formed a rock band. After arranging music for *Dr. No*, he scored a number of other Bond films. His versatility became apparent with *Born Free*, a winner of Academy Awards for both song and score. In all, he has received five Oscars, and he has worked on four films that won the Best Picture award.

Important Film Scores

Dr. No 1962
Zulu 1964
Goldfinger 1964
Born Free 1966 ♬ ♬
The Lion in Winter 1968 ★ ♬
Midnight Cowboy 1969 ★
Out of Africa 1985 ★ ♬
Dances with Wolves 1990 ★ ♬
Chaplin 1992 ✉

★ = Best Picture Oscar   ♬ = Best Music Oscar   ✉ = Music Oscar Nomination

A large part of the success of the film is due to the music by John Barry, arguably his finest score. Calling upon his gifts for lyricism and orchestration, Barry brings the lush, serene sound of *Out of Africa* to the beauty of the west and to the dignity of Native Americans. The film's numerous visions of landscapes, settlers, and Indians allowed Barry the freedom to write extended melodic cues with warm orchestrations. Particularly striking are the Wolf theme, a slow waltz first heard at 35:10, the vision of the Native American encampment (51:45), and the discovery and subsequent hunt of buffalo (1:22:15).

The Last of the Mohicans

Set during the French and Indian War, *The Last of the Mohicans* (1992) is based on James Fenimore Cooper's classic novel, which centers on a real incident—the massacre of more than two hundred people after they had surrendered to the French. Trevor Jones composed much of the score, and there are some additional cues provided by Randy Edelman.

The darkly beautiful title theme pervades the film. It has no single association, as it underscores a variety of moments. Most effective is the combination of the theme with beautiful panoramas showing America's natural beauty. The short-long rhythm heard in the third measure of the theme and in the subsequent measures is often referred to as a "Scottish snap," which serves as a subtle connection to the Munro family, which comes from Scotland. A prominent dance tune also signifies the presence of European immigrants. First heard as source music (56:05), the dance tune is soon combined with a variation of the title theme played on a solo violin, as we watch Hawkeye (Daniel Day-Lewis) and Cora (Madeleine Stowe) in a moment of passion.

Both melodies return in the climactic scene of the film when Hawkeye and his Mohican family pursue a band of Hurons, who have taken Cora's sister (see Viewer Guide). Supporting this breathtaking chase sequence is the dance tune placed over an eight-measure basso ostinato in a manner that strongly suggests the Baroque era. Adding to the suggestion of that period is the sound of a harpsichord reproduced by a synthesizer. The repetitive nature of this cue creates a sense of inevitability, and the music remains detached from the stunning dramatic developments.

The unrelenting motion of the dance tune is broken twice. Early in the chase, the title theme momentarily overwhelms the chase music, as we are shown another view of America's natural beauty. In that moment we are reminded of the absolute beauty of nature, while watching the brutality of man. Later, the dance is suspended to reflect two tragic moments. Magua slays Uncas, leaving his father to be the "last of the Mohicans," and Alice quietly moves to the edge of the cliff and walks off as her sister watches from a distance. The dance resumes as Chingachgook takes his revenge by killing Magua.

Viewer Guide

The Last of the Mohicans: Climax

Timing

1:38:05–1:48:05 (0:00 at studio logo);
DVD Chapters 28–30

Key Points

- Repeating bass line
- Mixture of Baroque, Scottish, and Native American elements
- Contrast of nature's beauty to man's cruelty
- Mood of music runs counter to the action

Setting

European-born Hawkeye (Daniel Day-Lewis) was raised as the son of Chingachgook and the brother of Uncas, who are the last of the proud tribe of Mohicans. The three hunters have witnessed the massacre of the remnants of a British brigade, including the commander, Col. Edmund Munro, by a Huron war party. The Huron leader Magua, who planned the ambush, has captured Munro's two daughters, Cora (Madeleine Stowe) and Alice (Jodhi May), as well as a British officer, Major Duncan Heyward. Just prior to the climactic scene, Magua has presented the prisoners to the tribal chief, expecting that the three would be burned. Hawkeye daringly enters the encampment and argues for their lives.

Principal Themes

Example 30.2 Repeating bass

Example 30.3 Fiddle tune

Example 30.4 Title theme

PLOT	MUSIC
The Huron chief disagrees with Magua's violent ways. He compromises by giving Alice to him as a prize, deciding to burn only Cora.	No music

Hawkeye and Heyward, both in love with Cora, offer to take her place at the stake. Magua leaves angrily. Hawkeye is surprised when the chief accepts the British officer as a substitute.	A steady drum pulse begins.
Hawkeye hurries Cora away from the camp and joins Chingachgook and Uncas. Taking his rifle, he shoots Heyward, who is already burning at the stake.	The repeating bass line begins with the dance tune melody.
Hawkeye, Chingachgook, Uncas, and Cora race up the mountain in order to catch up with Magua's party and Alice.	The music continues to repeat with added orchestral instruments.
A panoramic vision of the American mountains and a waterfall intrudes upon the chase scene.	The lush title theme overwhelms the chase music.
The chase continues. Uncas is the first to engage the war party, but is killed by Magua and thrown off the cliff, to the anguish of his father.	The chase music reemerges. At the end of the fight, the dance tune disappears.
Alice walks to the edge of the cliff and leaps to her death. Cora sees this tragic moment.	The chase music is suspended while Alice lingers at the edge of the cliff.
The pursuit continues, and Chingachgook engages Magua in a fight and kills the Huron. He now stands as the last of the Mohicans.	The chase music resumes and comes to a final cadence with the death of Magua.

Schindler's List

Graphically realistic recreation of past events reaches an artistic peak in Steven Spielberg's *Schindler's List* (1993), generally acknowledged to be the finest film of the 1990s. Based on a true story from World War II Poland, the dramatic transformation of the German businessman Oskar Schindler (Liam Neeson) is seen against a backdrop of the various stages of the Holocaust. In a daring move, Spielberg shot the film primarily in black and white, lending a greater sense of authenticity. To maintain a strong sense of realism, horrific scenes are shown with great attention to detail and accuracy.

For this powerful story of the Holocaust, John Williams created a score unlike anything else he has composed. For his efforts, he won his only Academy Award of the 1990s. Absent are his usual trademarks—fanfares, lush melodies, and intricate interweaving of leitmotifs. Instead, Williams constructed a hauntingly beautiful and introspective score. If there had been any doubts that Williams could create effective concert hall music, they were certainly laid to rest with the score for *Schindler's List*, which has become a staple in the repertoire of a new generation of violinists.

Williams employs elements of klezmer, the traditional sound of Jewish popular music. Klezmer ensembles generally feature a solo violin or clarinet, both of which are found in the score. Giora Feidman, clarinetist for the Israel Philharmonic and a recognized master of klezmer music, was brought to Hollywood to record the clarinet solos. But the dominant instrument of the score is the solo violin. Even the source music, from the opening sounds of the radio to the accompaniment of the singer at Schindler's birthday celebration, consistently brings in the sound of a solo violin. The interplay of the solo violin, played by Itzhak Perlman, and the orchestra in the background music suggests the relationship between a cantor and his congregation. The choice of a violin as the solo instrument links the sound to the proud tradition of Jewish violinists, including names such as Heifetz and Perlman.

The supporting orchestration, featuring strings, harp, and selected winds such as the clarinet and English horn, retains a dark, somber coloring. The orchestral violins and even the soloist remain in the lower register, the darkest and richest. The rhythmic, harmonic, and melodic elements also reflect Jewish traditions. The prevailing minor mode, the occasional augmented-second intervals, and the expressive use of the minor second all suggest the klezmer traditions.

Another unusual element of the score is its static quality. In each of the extended cues, Williams establishes an overall mood, but the music does not directly interact with the drama. In one of the early scenes, we see both the gathering of Jews into the ghetto and the rising fortunes of Schindler (19:10). The entire segment is accompanied by dance rhythms and a klezmer tune. The satirical character of the music matches some of the humorous touches in the scene, but the mood of the music never changes, in spite of the seriousness of some of the other moments. In effect, the musical sound remains aloof from the dramatic action and creates an overall atmosphere. The story is a flashback; there will be no surprises, no rescues, and no happy endings. The pervading sense of sadness in the music matches the starkness of the black-and-white photography and brilliantly captures the essence of the film.

Braveheart

Braveheart is based on the life of the Scottish hero William Wallace. It is difficult to separate fact from fiction in the tales of this legendary figure. It is known that Wallace was a strong leader in the Scottish rebellion that led to its independence, and that he was captured and cruelly executed by the English. While the film does little to settle the historical questions, it does depict the strong sense of freedom expressed by the Scots of the time, and it creates a passionate story of heroism, betrayal, and triumph.

During the opening scenes of Scottish mountains, James Horner uses the sound of a bagpipe to help establish the setting of Scotland and the sense of freedom associated with the instrument outlawed by the English. Indigenous sounds of Scotland are further exploited with the use of a harp (both as accompaniment and as a solo instrument at Murron's burial; 54:15), as well as the kena (a wooden flute) and the whistle (a high-pitched flute). The melodic material also suggests folk music with frequent Scottish snaps, quick turns, and ornaments. Also striking is the music as the Scottish army prepares for battle (1:23:15). The combination of sustained modern dissonance with the traditional bagpipes, field drums, and blaring brass instruments creates a tremendous build-up to the action.

Principal Themes

Example 30.5 Outlaw theme

Example 30.6 Love theme

Example 30.7 Braveheart theme

Throughout the film, Horner skillfully supports the action and mood with his orchestration and musical materials. At the beginning, a wordless choir suggests the importance of the story, dark brass chords foreshadow the betrayal that awaits William Wallace, and the poignant dissonances of the string passages establish the somber mood of both Scotland and Wallace's fate. Elsewhere, action music, such as the sustained dissonances combined with the bagpipe and sharp attacks of the kena during Wallace's revenge scene (46:00) does not fall into clichés. For the bigger battle scenes, Horner omits music, allowing the rhythmic pulse of the sound effects to dominate.

Unity is created through the use of leitmotifs. There are three principal themes. The Outlaw theme, so named by William's uncle, is played by bagpipes at the opening of the film and is clearly associated with Wallace and his army. The love theme is first heard when Murron gives William a flower when they are children (12:00). The theme dominates the early section of the story after they meet as adults. It later recurs when William speaks to Isabelle about Murron (1:50:00), and the theme is given to Isabelle as their relationship becomes intimate (2:22:20).

The Braveheart theme does not make an appearance until Wallace's "Sons of Scotland" speech (1:16:55). At this point, the theme sounds fresh and dramatic, and it will become the principal melody for the remainder of the film. After his first victory, a solo horn, traditionally associated with heroes, intones the noble Braveheart theme (1:31:50). At the end,

Figure 30.3 Wallace's "Sons of Scotland" speech

the theme is associated with Robert the Bruce, who will take up Braveheart's mantle and win freedom for Scotland. Horner's compositional skills shine in his contrapuntal passages. He combines the Irishman Stephen's sprightly jig with the Outlaw theme (1:14:45), later plays two versions of the Outlaw theme simultaneously, and finally presents both the Outlaw and the Braveheart themes together in a grand climax (2:49:15).

Comedies

Serving as a counterbalance to the dark themes of the era are a number of successful comedies. For the most part, comedies tend to employ popular music. But a number of excellent symphonic scores can be heard in comedies as well, particularly in films that contain an underlying message.

Home Alone

Rather than just settling for a humorous farce as the kid outsmarts the bad guys, *Home Alone* treats serious issues of family relationships and the spirit of Christmas. John Williams's score lends an amusing yet sophisticated aura to the story. The music begins with a quotation from the television Christmas classic *How the Grinch Stole*

Figure 30.4 John Williams displays a lighter side with his score for *Home Alone*

Christmas, and then moves into a darkly jolly theme with a magical orchestration featuring sleigh bells and a celesta, a sound that Williams will use later in the Harry Potter films.

Throughout the film, Williams deftly crafts musical materials out of traditional Christmas tunes. In one extended cue (1:13:00), Kevin races home from the church where the choir has been rehearsing the "Carol of the Bells." Williams plays with motives from the tune as Kevin declares, "This is my house!" and begins to create defenses. At one point, Williams even introduces a brief fugue to suggest the scurrying activity.

Hook

More fully developed is the tuneful score for *Hook*. An adult fantasy, *Hook* is the story of Peter Pan, who has grown up to be a lawyer. The magical tale of the rediscovery of the innocence and joy of youth is energized by the combined talents of three box-office giants—Robin Williams, Dustin Hoffman, and Julia Roberts. The score contains four principal themes. Two are associated with Peter. A gentle theme, beginning with a falling minor third, the interval we use to sing "Yoo-hoo," is associated with memories of Peter's boyhood. It is first heard when we see Grandma Wendy (10:30), and later as Peter flies to Neverland (35:00). His second theme is the exuberant adventure melody, heard most frequently after Peter regains his confidence, flies, and fights pirates (1:40:15).

The remaining principal themes are associated with the other two stars in the film. Captain James Hook has a delightfully sinister theme in the low register. The tune provides a comic counterpoint to Peter's arrival on Hook's ship (37:45), and it accompanies Hook's appearances right up to his demise from the falling crocodile (2:04:00). The other major theme in the film is the whimsical melody associated with Tinkerbell, which is played on a piano at the beginning of the film at the children's play. When she makes her first appearance, John Williams engages in a bit of musical fun by adapting a passage from Stravinsky's *Firebird* ballet, since Peter initially thinks that she is a firefly (31:00).

International Films

During the 1990s, international centers produced a number of significant film scores, many of which were set for symphony orchestras. Particularly noteworthy are the products of two traditional centers, France and Italy, and a young but strong school of filmmaking in Australia.

France

France continued to produce a significant number of high-quality films in the 1990s. Among the most celebrated works is the trilogy of films created by director Krzysztof Kieslowski entitled *Three Colors: Blue* (1993), *White* (1993), and *Red* (1994). The colors, which visually dominate each of the respective films, are the colors of the French flag, symbolizing liberty (blue), equality (white), and fraternity (red). These themes are the central focus of each film. The Polish composer Zbigniew Preisner, who created the music for the trilogy and another internationally successful film, *The Double Life of Veronique* (1991), has become one of the most popular European film composers today.

Music plays a particularly important role in *Blue*, in which the death of a famous composer allows his wife to come into her own. Haunted by the music of her husband's incomplete work that was to have been performed simultaneously by twelve different orchestras in twelve different European cities, she finally decides to complete the project, revealing that she was the true creative force behind his fame.

Italy

Two Italian films have received Academy Awards for Best Musical Score in the 1990s, *Il Postino* (1994) and *Life Is Beautiful* (1998). Luis Bacalov, a Spanish film composer, created the music for *Il Postino*. Bacalov's score features the sound of a bandoneon, a type of accordion common in South America, which is often heard in duets with other instruments such as a clarinet, mandolin, violin, or piano in this tale of friendship between a postman and the Nobel Prize winning poet from Chile, Pablo Neruda. For *Life Is Beautiful*, Nicola Piovani composed a light-hearted comic score that provides a fitting sound for the bittersweet story.

Down Under

Two exceptional films from Down Under have featured a piano—*The Piano* (1993) from New Zealand and *Shine* (1996) from Australia. The former is an intense, erotic story set in New Zealand during the Victorian age. Michael Nyman successfully created romantic piano pieces that could actually be played by the talented actress Holly Hunter. *Shine* is a biography of David Helfgott, a remarkable solo pianist who has mental problems resembling Tourette's syndrome. Numerous works from the classical repertoire, ranging from Vivaldi through the Romantics, are heard throughout the film, and Rachmaninov's Piano Concerto No. 3 plays a central role in the story. Australian composer David Hirschfelder provided the original music.

Trailer

Entering the 1990s, a number of excellent symphonic scores appeared, most of which maintained the traditions of the classic film score. In particular, stories of historical realism embraced the style, and this trend would soon culminate in the sensational success of *Titanic* (1997). As will be observed in Chapter 31, popular music also continued to play a significant role in film music during this time.

Important Names and Terms

Danny Elfman

Randy Edelman

klezmer

Zbigniew Preisner

Luis Bacalov

Nicola Piovani

Michael Nyman

David Hirschfelder

Suggested Viewing

Biopics: *My Left Foot* (1989), *Born on the Fourth of July* (1989) ✉, *JFK* (1991) ✉, *Chaplin* (1992) ✉, *Ed Wood* (1994), *Apollo 13* (1995) ✉, and *Michael Collins* (1996)

Historical: *The English Patient* (1996) ★ ♫

Western: *Unforgiven* (1992) and *Tombstone* (1993)

Drama: *Howard's End* (1992) ✉, *A River Runs Through It* (1992) ✉, *Philadelphia* (1993) ✉, and *Mr. Holland's Opus* (1995)

Romance: *Ghost* (1990) ✉, *The Remains of the Day* (1993) ✉, *The Age of Innocence* (1993) ✉, and *Notebook* (1994)

Sports: *Field of Dreams* (1989) ✉ and *Rudy* (1994)

Science Fiction/Action: *The Abyss* (1989), *The Hunt for Red October* (1990), *Basic Instinct* (1992) ✉, *The Fugitive* (1993) ✉, and *Independence Day* (1996)

Fantasy: *Edward Scissorhands* (1990) and *The Nightmare Before Christmas* (1993)

31

Popular Music, Animation, and Realism, 1989–1996

Alternatives to the traditional symphonic score continued to be explored in Hollywood films throughout the 1990s. In the early years of the decade, the creative use of popular music provided a fresh sound, both in the resurgence of animated features and in realistic dramas. In addition, the changing sounds of contemporary concert music gave the film composer new styles to assimilate.

Animated Films

In the 1980s, animated movies were infrequent, musicals were out of fashion, and high-quality children's films were limited primarily to the Muppets. All of these trends ended abruptly in 1989 with the sensational success of *The Little Mermaid*. Apparently, while adults felt too sophisticated to watch a musical by themselves, they would quietly enjoy one with their children. The resurgence of the animated musical is the single most important musical development in the early 1990s, and it has proven to be both a financial and artistic success.

SIGNIFICANT FILMS

1989	*The Little Mermaid* ♫♫ ✉
	Do the Right Thing
1990	*GoodFellas*
1991	*The Silence of the Lambs* ★
	Beauty and the Beast ♫♫ ✉ ✉
	Boyz n the Hood
1994	*Forrest Gump* ★
	The Lion King ♫♫ ✉ ✉
	The Shawshank Redemption ✉
	Pulp Fiction

Alan Menken (b. 1949)

Born in New York, Menken has won a remarkable number of Oscars in a very short period of time. Having studied both piano and violin, Menken became interested in musical theater and was first known as a songwriter. He wrote the music for a successful Broadway musical, *Little Shop of Horrors*, and when that was made into a movie (1986), he began to score films. He has a close association with the Disney studios, and his music for animation films would garner him eight Oscars, second only to Alfred Newman in music and third on the all-time list for any category.

Important Film Scores

Little Shop of Horrors 1986 ✉
The Little Mermaid 1989 ♪♪ ✉
Beauty and the Beast 1991 ♪♪ ✉ ✉
Aladdin 1992 ♪♪ ✉
Pocahontas 1995 ♪♪
The Hunchback of Notre Dame 1996
Hercules 1997 ✉
Enchanted (2007) ✉ ✉ ✉
Tangled (2010) ✉

★ = Best Picture Oscar   ♪ = Best Music Oscar   ✉ = Music Oscar Nomination

---

The principal force in the revival of animation features is the Disney Studio. Since 1989, Disney has produced at least one animation film in every year but 1993. With *The Little Mermaid* (1989), Disney returned to several characteristics of past classics: the recreation of a fairy story with a strong female role, comic sidekicks for both the antagonist and protagonist, the casting of well-known entertainment figures as voices, and the incorporation of a number of engaging songs. The principal composer behind Disney's second renaissance is Alan Menken, who has become one of the most honored figures in the Academy's history.

The Little Mermaid

The Little Mermaid retells a Hans Christian Andersen story, but with an added happy ending. Like many of the most successful animated films of this time, the setting is exotic, allowing Menken to incorporate a distinct non-Western sound. Exploiting the underwater locale, Menken mixes a number of popular Caribbean musical elements with other traditional styles. In the opening concert created by the crabby conductor Sebastian, Menken mimics the sound of a Gilbert and Sullivan operetta. Later,

Sebastian cuts loose in two calypso numbers, both of which were nominated for best song: "Under the Sea" and "Kiss the Girl." In addition to the effective songs, Menken supplies strong underscoring that ignores many of the clichés associated with cartoons, such as non-stop music and mirroring physical movement.

Beauty and the Beast

Many of these same elements are apparent in *Beauty and the Beast* (1991). Based on a French fairy tale, the film mixes serious adult themes with standard features of Disney animation, making this one of the studio's high points. It received six Oscar nominations, including the first Best Picture nomination for an animated feature and four music nominations for Alan Menken.

Menken won the only two Oscars awarded to the film, for Best Original Score and Best Song. In the latter category, "Beauty and the Beast" was selected over the other two nominees from the same film, "Belle" and "Be Our Guest." In several of the musical numbers, Menken, as in *The Little Mermaid*, incorporates musical characteristics reflecting the locale—France. In addition to French folk instruments, one of the principal singers, Lumiere, mimics the voice of Maurice Chevalier. With that distinctive gravelly vocal quality, Lumiere leads the kitchen objects in a rousing rendition of "Be Our Guest," set to a dazzling waltz tempo (38:15). The extravagant entertainment is an enjoyable spoof of the spectacular dance sequences created by Busby Berkeley in the 1930s. In this, and all of the musical numbers, the story is effectively enhanced, either by developing the characters or advancing the plot.

Menken provides effective underscoring throughout the film. Appropriate moods are established for sequences of humor, action, and romance. In one action sequence, an invasion by the people of the village is repulsed to an energetic instrumental ver-

Figure 31.1 Lumiere leads the dishes in a Busby Berkeley spoof in *Beauty and the Beast*

sion of "Be Our Guest" (1:14:30). Quotations of songs in the underscoring provide a sense of familiarity to the ear, such as the use of "Beauty and the Beast" as a leitmotif for the rose. Menken also crafts new themes for leitmotifs. The most important of these is the theme for the enchanted spell, which is heard at the beginning of the film, played by a music box. At the climax of the story, this motive is transformed into a thrilling brass fanfare and joyful acclamation, as the Beast transforms into an overly handsome prince (1:21:15).

Other Menken Scores

In the next several years, Disney continued to span the world for stories. Menken lent his golden touch to two films, *Aladdin* (1992) and *Pocahontas* (1994). *Aladdin*, from the *Arabian Nights*, provides excellent entertainment, led by the sidesplitting voice of Robin Williams as the genie. Menken mixes Arabian sounds with other popular musical styles in an Oscar-winning score, and two of his songs were also nominated, with the award going to "A Whole New World." Similarly, Menken received Oscars for his score for *Pocahontas* and its principal song, "Colors of the Wind." Loosely based on the epic poem "Song of Hiawatha" by Henry Wadsworth Longfellow, the story allowed Menken to intermix musical sounds of England and of Native Americans. In a musical highlight, the song "Mine, Mine, Mine" begins as a simple minuet, an aristocratic English dance, and builds to Governor Ratcliffe's intense song of greed, mirrored by John Smith's song of discovery (25:50).

Table 31.1

Major Disney animation features, 1989–2003

YEAR	ANIMATED FEATURE	COMPOSER	SCORE	SONG
1989	The Little Mermaid	Alan Menken	♪	♪✉
1990	The Rescuers Down Under	Bruce Broughton		
1991	Beauty and the Beast	Alan Menken	♪	♪✉✉
1992	Aladdin	Alan Menken	♪	♪✉
1994	The Lion King	Hans Zimmer/Elton John	♪	♪✉✉
1995	Pocahontas	Alan Menken	♪	♪
1995	Toy Story	Randy Newman	✉	✉
1996	The Hunchback of Notre Dame	Alan Menken		
1997	Hercules	Alan Menken		✉
1998	Mulan	Goldsmith/Wilder/Zippel	✉	
1998	A Bug's Life	Randy Newman	✉	
1999	Tarzan	Mark Mancina/Phil Collins		♪
1999	Toy Story 2	Randy Newman	✉	
2000	The Emperor's New Groove	Debney/Hartley/Sting		✉
2001	Atlantis: The Lost Empire	James Newton Howard		
2001	Monsters, Inc.	Randy Newman	✉	♪
2002	Lilo & Stitch	Alan Silvestri		
2003	Finding Nemo	Thomas Newman	✉	

Disney's next two productions, *The Hunchback of Notre Dame* (1996) and *Hercules* (1997), were less popular than their predecessors. Despite the sophisticated and moving score, *The Hunchback of Notre Dame* created some controversy over its dark adult themes. Still, the music, at times operatic in nature, is considered by many to be the finest and most sophisticated that Menken ever wrote for Disney. Particularly striking are the numbers that combine soloists and chorus. In the Notre Dame cathedral, Esmerelda sings an impassioned "God Help the Outcasts," while church members pray for wealth and glory (35:40). An even more striking contrast occurs when Judge Frollo sings "Beata Maria," a traditional Catholic Latin text, with a priestly chorus; the music soon turns into the lustful "Hellfire," with images of Esmerelda dancing in the flames (47:50). The dark spirit of the 1990s had now touched even Disney animations. In a rebuff, the film received no Academy nominations. The reception for *Hercules* was also modest, although Menken was nominated for his song "Go the Distance." After this film, Alan Menken took a seven-year hiatus from film scoring, but returned with Disney's traditional animated production of *Home on the Range* (2004).

The Lion King

Two major Disney animated features appeared in mid-decade without music by Menken. Both exhibited traits that look to future developments. Turning to an African legend, *The Lion King* (1994) provided Disney with another critical and popular hit. A new approach was taken to the music of the film. Rather than contracting a single composer, the studio hired a scorer, Hans Zimmer, and a songwriter, Elton John. The move paid great dividends, as Zimmer won an Academy Award for the score, and Elton John received three nominations for his songs: "Circle of Life," "Hatuna Matata," and the Oscar winner "Can You Feel the Love Tonight?"

In another innovation for this recent series of Disney films, several musical numbers are sung by unseen voices, not by characters. Typically, the film opens with a choral number, but the music for "The Circle of Life" is presented as underscoring for the birth of Simba and is not sung by any of the characters. In this scene, African choral singing combines with a Western popular music style. Elsewhere, the African choral sound gives a fresh quality to this outstanding musical score.

Realism

Contemporary audiences, raised on cable television and videos, had become too sophisticated for standard film clichés. As a result, filmmakers created works with stronger emotional impact, real contemporary stories, and scenes of graphic violence. The need for realism even led the creators of *Fargo* (1996) to make a false claim that their drama was based on actual events, and the sense of reality accounts for the phenomenal popularity of *The Blair Witch Project* (1999) and the success of the television series *Survivor* and other reality shows. In many realistic dramas, popular music heightens the sense of realism, as it provides us with the sounds that many people hear in daily life.

Forrest Gump

Forrest Gump is the engaging story of a mentally retarded man (Tom Hanks) and of America during its most turbulent time. The contrast between the two subjects is fascinating, as Forrest maintains his childlike wisdom, while the nation undergoes major upheavals. Through Forrest's eyes we see the innocent early years of Elvis Presley, the struggle for integration, the tragedy of the Vietnam War, and the ultimate maturation of the baby boomers. In addition, his relationship with his girfriend Jenny and his war buddy Lt. Taylor allows the film to touch upon serious personal issues, such as child abuse, disabilities, and death.

Music plays several critical roles in this drama. As the film moves freely through a variety of flashbacks, popular music helps to provide smooth transitions and establish the various time periods. In the process we hear a miniature history of rock, beginning with Elvis Presley's Gump-inspired rendition of "Hound Dog" (11:40). Popular music also provides an energetic background for several montages, such as Gump's early experiences in Vietnam (40:35).

The composer, Alan Silvestri, reserves his orchestral underscoring for the quieter and more joyful moments of the film. The film is framed by a floating feather, first gathered by Forrest at a municipal bus stop and placed into his *Curious George* book, and ultimately released from the book, now in the hands of Forrest Jr., at a school bus stop. Silvestri's Feather theme, the most memorable original tune of the film, makes its only two appearances at these points. The gentle character of the melody, played in the upper register of the piano with delicate syncopations, suggests the simplicity and innocence of Forrest.

A light quality is sustained throughout the underscoring. The timbre of the piano's upper register frequently accompanies Forrest, especially in scenes with his mother. Several other themes also recur. When Forrest first sees Jenny (13:45), the strings play a lyrical melody that will follow her through her many changes. Forrest also has a running theme, first heard when he breaks his braces (16:45) and later when he runs for the Alabama football team, in Vietnam, and across the country. In a way, the gentle underscoring reflects Forrest's consistent view of the world, while the popular music reflects the changing nation.

Spike Lee

In 1989, another seminal film appeared, director Spike Lee's critically acclaimed *Do the Right Thing*. Within a few years, Spike Lee completed a series of outstanding films, including *Mo' Better Blues* (1990), *Jungle Fever* (1991), and *Clockers* (1995). All of

Alan Silvestri (b. 1950)

A drummer and guitar player, Silvestri studied at the Berklee School of Music in Boston and began his scoring career in television. His first major film, *Romancing the Stone* (1984), contains a mixture of traditional music, dissonances, rock, and Latin American popular sounds, largely created using a synthesizer. Silvestri is equally adept at scoring for acoustic instruments and synthesizer; his versatility can be heard in the wide range of musical styles he commands.

Important Film Scores

Romancing the Stone 1984
Back to the Future 1985
Who Framed Roger Rabbit 1988
The Abyss 1989
Forrest Gump 1994★ ✉
Cast Away 2000
The Polar Express 2004
Night at the Museum (2006)
The Avengers (2012)

★ = Best Picture Oscar   ♫ = Best Music Oscar   ✉ = Music Oscar Nomination

these films deal realistically with grim aspects of urban life, including prejudice and drugs. While the primary focus is on African-Americans, Lee's visions also encompass Italians and other New York ethnic groups, and his stories generally deal with problems faced by all of society. *Jungle Fever*, for example, is a compelling story of an interracial affair outside of marriage. While the race issue ultimately dooms the relationship, the story embraces topics of love and marriage that touch the lives of a wide spectrum of America.

Music by African-American jazz and rock performers, such as Spike's father Bill Lee and Stevie Wonder, form a significant portion of the soundtracks for these films. Yet Spike Lee also allows for a number of traditional symphonic cues that effectively touch the full range of emotions from humor to tragedy. Among the musical highlights in these films are the extended jazz sequences composed by Bill Lee for *Mo' Better Blues*, and the performances of Terence Blanchard (trumpet) and Branford Marsalis (saxophone).

Figure 31.2 Denzel Washington and Wesley Snipes play jazz musicians in Spike Lee's *Mo' Better Blues*

Close-Up: African-Americans and Film

The Black Experience

Throughout the history of American film, the industry has been torn between the racist attitudes of whites and the potential significant audience of blacks. This conflict was evident even to distributors and exhibitors of the earliest films. In many theaters, especially in the South, the answer was segregation. Whites sat on the main level and blacks in the balcony. Another solution, called "the midnight ramble," had showings for white audiences during the day and evening, and for black audiences late at night. Segregation appeased white audiences, but there still remained the problem of enticing black audiences to the theater. Standard movie fare rarely featured African-Americans, and when a black character was included in a story, he was most likely a stereotype and sometimes even played by a white actor in blackface.

One of the remarkable artistic achievements in American film is the work of African-American director Oscar Micheaux. Inspired and supported by the Harlem Renaissance movement in New York, Micheaux became one of the most prolific filmmakers in America during the 1920s and 30s. Using black actors, he dealt with serious subjects, such as interracial marriage, racism, and alcoholism. It is likely that jazz musicians accompanied the showing of many of these films.

Gradually, racial stereotyping lessened in Hollywood films. By the late 1940s, racism was one of the many social issues that were brought to the screen. Sidney Poitier, a talented African-American actor, became a major Hollywood star during the 1950s. He appeared in a number of important films dealing with the black experience in America, including *The Defiant Ones* (1958), a story about the flight of two convicts, one white and one black, who are chained together; *A Raisin in the Sun* (1961), an adaptation of a Broadway play with an all-black cast about an African-American family moving to an all-white suburb; and Best Picture winner *In the Heat of the Night* (1967), a drama about a black

Philadelphia police detective and a white Mississippi sheriff solving a murder case.

In succeeding decades, two trends can be observed. African-American actors, such as Louis Gossett Jr., were increasingly cast in roles that could have been filled by white actors. A second trend, beginning in the 1970s, dubbed "blaxploitation," targeted black audiences by featuring black heroes who triumph over the white establishment. The most successful of these was *Shaft* (1971). In addition, black issues continued to be addressed through the 80s in films such as *Ragtime* (1981), *The Cotton Club* (1984), *A Soldier's Story* (1984), and *The Color Purple* (1985).

The late 80s and the 90s have seen the emergence of a distinctive new style of black filmmaking. John Singleton's *Boyz n the Hood* (1991) focuses on life in South Central Los Angeles. Steve James created a sensational documentary in *Hoop Dreams* (1994), and Spike Lee rose to major director status with *Do the Right Thing* (1989). Lee, the son of the prominent jazz musician Bill Lee, was raised in Brooklyn. The most important black director since Micheaux, he was the first to create commercially successful films based on African-American stories, as well as stories dealing with life in New York in general. Among his best-known films are *Mo' Better Blues* (1990), *Jungle Fever* (1991), the epic *Malcolm X* (1992), *Clockers* (1995), *Summer of Sam* (1999), and *25th Hour* (2002). During this era, a new generation of African-American actors has emerged. In 2002, the Oscars for best actor and actress were awarded to Denzel Washington and Halle Berry, the first time two African-Americans were honored jointly.

When black composers were asked to create a film score, it was generally because of their background in jazz or rock. Among the most prominent film scores created by African-Americans are Duke Ellington's *Anatomy of a Murder* (1959), Miles Davis's *Elevator to the Gallows* (1958), Isaac Hayes's *Shaft* (1971), and Terence Blanchard's *Malcolm X* (1972). The film scores of Quincy Jones are discussed in Chapter 22.

Boyz n the Hood

In *Boyz n the Hood* (1991), John Singleton's riveting drama of life in South Central Los Angeles, source music also plays a significant role. Ranging from jazz to Motown to rap, the music defines the barriers between generations and between neighbors. When popular music is used as background, the choice of styles is often dictated by who is on the screen or what activity is being undertaken. Considering that Ice Cube plays one of the central figures and that the movie is named after one of his rap albums, there is a surprising balance of musical styles that include some sparse but effective symphonic music by Stanley Clarke. The most extended passage of rap appears in the closing credits.

Crime Films

In the 1990s, realism extended to stories about crime, in which cities and prisons were depicted with graphic visions of violence. Gruesome scenes, as shown in Best Picture winner *The Silence of the Lambs* (1991), thrilled audiences. Mob crime continued to hold its fascination for the American movie going public as well, as evidenced by films such as *GoodFellas* (1990), *The Godfather: Part III* (1990), and *Bugsy* (1991).

GoodFellas

Of the last three films, Martin Scorsese's *GoodFellas* provided the freshest look and sound for this traditional genre. Rejecting symphonic underscoring, Scorsese used only adapted popular music on the soundtrack, following the successful pattern of *Mean Streets* (1973). Matching the innovative camera techniques, the music blurs scene changes and obscures the distinction between source music and underscoring. Scorsese primarily chose songs, such as the opening Tony Bennett 1953 hit "Rags to Riches," that suggest an adult, middle-class taste—what one might hear in a Las Vegas lounge. The moods of the songs run counter to the scenes of extreme violence, reinforcing Scorsese's not-too-subtle message about the superficial manner in which violence is treated in modern society. The only intense popular music occurs after Henry begins dealing with drugs. In a somewhat humorous jolt, the closing credits begin with "My Way," a signature song for Frank Sinatra, but instead of the rendition by the famed Italian crooner that would match the mood established throughout the film, we hear a raspy performance by Sid Vicious of the Sex Pistols.

Pulp Fiction

Quentin Tarantino's *Pulp Fiction* (1994) is considered to be one of the most influential films of the 1990s. Unlike *GoodFellas*, *Pulp Fiction* is not based on an actual event, and the film constantly juxtaposes images and sounds of popular culture with vivid scenes of violence. Three separate plot lines are intertwined and linked by two hit men, played by Samuel L. Jackson and John Travolta. Abrupt jumps in time create a jigsaw plot, in which the viewer can finally fit the various pieces into a proper chronological order only near the end of the film.

As in *GoodFellas*, the soundtrack is limited to classic rock, but two aspects of the music are distinctive. Rather than selecting the relaxed mood of lounge music, Tarantino chose the upbeat sound of surf music. Moreover, all of the music in this film can clearly be heard as source music. Tarantino establishes this effect with the title credits, which open with "Misirlou" performed on electric guitar by Dick Dale. The tune ends abruptly with the sound of a car radio changing channels to "Jungle Boogie" performed by Kool & the Gang. The divergent nature of the two songs reflects the musical tastes of the two hit men we see in a car in the opening scene; "Jungle Boogie" quickly and quietly fades under their loquacious chatter. Music is not as omnipresent as it is in *GoodFellas*, but the linking of pop music with violence supports a similar theme about the superficiality of violence in American culture.

Figure 31.3 John Travolta's comeback in *Pulp Fiction* includes a twist competition, a reference to his most famous role in *Saturday Night Fever*

The Silence of the Lambs

A dark thriller, *The Silence of the Lambs* tells of the pursuit of a serial killer who skins his women victims. Desperate to catch him, the FBI solicits the help of another serial killer, Dr. Hannibal Lecter, nicknamed "Hannibal the Cannibal." This character, played brilliantly by Anthony Hopkins, was recently voted No. 1 on the American Film Institute's list of Hollywood's all-time greatest villains. The chemistry between Lecter and Clarice (Jodie Foster) makes this film one of the best of the decade.

Supporting the often-grisly images is an effective musical score by Howard Shore. As in *Batman*, the music for *The Silence of the Lambs* is predominantly in a low register, but it has a more subdued character. Shore avoids extended melodies and unifies the score through the repetitive use of motives. In the opening scene, the principal theme is heard ascending and descending. Soon it appears as an ostinato pattern, over which ominous chords shift. The theme reappears when Clarice sees pictures of

Figure 31.4 Hannibal Lecter quietly conducts Bach after brutally murdering two guards

mutilated bodies, the victims of the serial killer, "Buffalo Bill" (5:05). Throughout the score, numerous variations are derived from this brief idea, sometimes heard in counterpoint. At the end, Shore continues to play with these motivic elements, as Hannibal is about to "have a friend for dinner."

Source music is used effectively throughout the film. Buffalo Bill prefers a more contemporary rock style than the killers in *GoodFellas* and *Pulp Fiction*. Hannibal Lecter

David (b. 1954) and Thomas (b. 1955) Newman

David and Thomas Newman, the sons of Alfred Newman, were raised in Los Angeles and attended the School of Music at USC. Both emerged as successful film composers in the mid-1980s, working largely on comedies. In the 1990s, they have become among the most prolific composers in Hollywood, and have worked on many popular films in recent years.

Important Film Scores

David Newman	Thomas Newman
Critters 1986	*Revenge of the Nerds* 1984
Throw Momma from the Train 1987	*Fried Green Tomatoes* 1991
The War of the Roses 1989	*The Shawshank Redemption* 1994 ✉
Bill & Ted's Excellent Adventure 1989	*Red Corner* 1997
The Mighty Ducks 1992	*The Green Mile* 1999
Anastasia 1997 ✉	*American Beauty* 1999 ★ ✉
Galaxy Quest 1999	*Erin Brockovich* 2000
Bowfinger 1999	*Road to Perdition* 2002 ✉
Dr. Dolittle 2 2001	*Finding Nemo* 2003 ✉
Ice Age 2002	*Lemony Snicket's A Series of Unfortunate*
Dr. Seuss' The Cat in the Hat (2003)	*Events* 2004 ✉
Alvin and the Chipmunks:	*The Good German* (2006) ✉
The Squeakquel (2009)	*WALL/E* (2008) ✉

★ = Best Picture Oscar   ♪ = Best Music Oscar   ✉ = Music Oscar Nomination

---

likes Bach. In the most stunning portion of the film, Hannibal is listening to Bach's *Goldberg Variations* just prior to his escape (1:14:05). The choice of music is not arbitrary. Bach is considered one of the most brilliant of all composers, and the *Goldberg Variations*, one of his most complex works, is suitable listening for a psychopathic genius. Once Hannibal takes action, the underscoring overwhelms the source music and reflects the horror of the scene and the terror of the guards. As the underscoring subsides, the sounds of Bach reemerge, suggesting that Hannibal has been cold and calculating throughout.

Moments later, when the dead guard is discovered, the low brass darkly intone the descending version of the theme (1:19:50). Not done with this horrific scene, the police—and the audience—think that Hannibal has been killed, but a sudden cut takes us to the ambulance (1:24:25). Since the music crescendos over the cut, we sense that something is wrong. Building in intensity with pounding timpani strokes, the music ultimately lets us imagine what happens without actually having to witness it.

The Shawshank Redemption

Adapted from a Stephen King novella, *The Shawshank Redemption* (1994) reflects a number of the characteristics of the 1990s, including dark tones, realism in its depiction of prison life, and a twisting plotline. The musical score by Thomas Newman has been described as understated because of its subdued and repetitive qualities. The music rarely reflects details of the drama, but rather establishes background moods with melodic fragments and sustained pitches. Contrasting musical styles are heard, including the divergent sounds of Hank Williams and a duet from Mozart's *Marriage of Figaro*. The playing of the latter (1:07:30) provides a sublime moment in the film that sparks a debate about the value of art and hope. But for the most part, Newman maintains a cold and distant mood. At various times, this tone represents Andy's numbness, which the judge describes as "icy and remorseless," the hopelessness of prison life, and Andy's calculating plan of escape.

The detached mood is established in the opening scene. At first, we hear the 1939 hit "If I Didn't Care," sung by the Inkspots, which we learn is emanating from Andy's car radio. The film soon begins to crosscut in time between the night that the wife of Andy Dufresne (Tim Robbins) was murdered and his trial for that crime. At times we are watching Andy in his car, while listening to the trial. When we first begin to hear the voices of the trial, underscoring emerges and quickly replaces the song. The nondiegetic music primarily consists of a single pitch, called a pedal, and a repetitive and somewhat dissonant piano part. By sustaining these elements across the time cuts, Newman helps to connect the two events and lends a sense of unity to the opening.

Throughout the film, the combination of a pedal and melodic fragments played on a piano creates a somber mood. In one of the most moving scenes of the film, an elderly inmate named Brooks is released (1:00:35). He tries to cope with the fast-paced modern world but eventually gives up and hangs himself. During the entire scene, melodic fragments are heard in a setting similar to the opening. Later, when long-time inmate Red is released and tries to deal with life outside of prison, the same material returns (2:08:30). Other than this, the connection of melodic ideas to specific characters or aspects of the drama tends to be vague.

In the scene showing Andy's escape (see Viewer Guide), the music continues to create general moods rather than reflect specific actions. When the flashback first shows Andy digging a hole, the music from the opening scene returns; the cue lacks any change of mood that might have been suggested by his discovery of the soft plaster and his formation of a plan. Similarly, the music does not indulge in dramatic chords as he makes his escape. Rather, the music simply gets louder and, because of the reserved quality of the music up to this point, the climactic moment of freedom has a powerful impact. For the remainder of the escape scene, music remains unobtrusive.

In the final moments of the film, as Red joins Andy by the Pacific Ocean, a full melodic theme emerges that reflects the joy of their reunion. By Hollywood standards, the sound is still understated, but within the context of this film, the cue is quite effective. Although

The Shawshank Redemption: Escape

Timing

1:52:00–2:02:15 (0:00 at studio logo);
DVD Chapters 31–33

Key Points

- Repetitious musical cues sustain moods
- The music climaxes with Andy's escape

Setting

Andy Dufresne (Tim Robbins), falsely imprisoned for the murder of his wife, is serving two life sentences in Shawshank prison. He has befriended Red (Morgan Freeman), but he also is abused by both inmates and officials. Most recently, a man who could have proven his innocence was killed by order of the warden. Andy has quietly made plans to escape. Using a small rock pick, he has over the years dug a hole in his cell behind large posters. He has also used his knowledge of banking to gain access to and control of the warden's illegal financial dealings. In the process, he has established a fictitious identity on the outside. One stormy night, he makes his escape. In the morning the guards find that his cell is empty; he has seemingly disappeared.

PLOT	MUSIC
Stunned by Andy's disappearance, the warden yells at the guards and questions Red. In frustration he throws one of Andy's rocks. The rock penetrates the poster, revealing the escape hole.	Music is withheld until everyone stares at the hole in the poster. Sustained pitches enter, suggesting their surprise.
Police arrive, and Red narrates their fruitless search for Andy.	The strings play a dance-like passage in a lower register.
Red continues to narrate, as flashbacks show Andy conceiving of his plan to dig a hole and his actions on the night of his escape.	Sustained pitches suggest Andy's thinking of a plan. The piano enters with the material from the beginning of the film as he implements the plan. The music pauses briefly as Andy switches the financial records in the warden's office.
Andy crawls through the hole into the sewer passageway. With a rock, he breaks the sewage pipe.	The low strings slowly reiterate fragments of a melody.

Andy enters the pipe and crawls five hundred yards to a stream outside the prison.	A dissonance signifies that the pipe is broken. The above material returns and crescendos as he emerges.
Andy runs through the stream, takes off his prison shirt, and holds up his arms exuberantly.	The earlier music is now played strongly by the full orchestra, climaxing in a triumphant sound as he raises his arms.
Andy enters a bank, withdraws money, and asks that a package containing evidence of the warden's fradulent activities be mailed.	Quiet, gentle music underscores Andy's activities.
The package arrives at a newspaper, and the story is published.	No music
The warden looks at a sign on his wall saying "His Judgement Cometh and that Right Soon," as police cars approach the prison. Looking at Andy's Bible, the warden sees a note to him and a hole where the pick was hidden in the book of Exodus.	A low-pitch rhythmic pulse suggests the inevitable outcome of this turn of events.

the melody sounds fresh and new, it was originally suggested in a scene when the prisoners sat on a rooftop, drank beer, and momentarily felt normal (56:00).

Trailer

The musical scores for films described in Chapters 30 and 31, extending from 1989 to 1996, are characterized by diverse styles and creative approaches. Masterful symphonic scores by veterans such as John Williams and James Horner and newcomer Danny Elfman underscore both historical dramas and fantasies. Popular music, both classic rock and original music, appeared in films ranging from animated features to violent crime stories. In 1997, the score to *Titanic* made an enormous sensation, and the symphonic score continues to exert a strong influence on Hollywood filmmaking. In a striking backlash to this success, however, alternate musical sounds would be explored in many of the films leading up to the new millennium.

Important Names and Terms

Alan Menken

Elton John

Phil Collins

Spike Lee

Bill Lee

Terence Blanchard

rap music

Stanley Clark

Howard Shore

Thomas Newman

David Newman

Suggested Viewing

Crime/Action: *La Femme Nikita* (1990), *Bugsy* (1991) ✉, *Speed* (1994), and *Fargo* (1996)

Drama: *Driving Miss Daisy* (1989) ★, *Dead Poets Society* (1989), and *Leaving Las Vegas* (1995)

Romantic comedy: *Pretty Woman* (1990), *Sleepless in Seattle* (1993) ✉, and *Groundhog Day* (1993)

32

The Sinking *Titanic*, 1997–2000

Living up to its name, *Titanic* (1997) was a colossal phenomenon. No film has matched its box-office success, both in this country and around the world. This sensational achievement invites comparisons to Hollywood's two earlier great epics, *Gone With the Wind* (1939) and *Ben-Hur* (1959). These three films, along with *The Lord of the Rings: The Return of the King* (2003), are the all-time top Oscar winners. *Titanic* and *Ben-Hur* each won eleven awards, and *Gone With the Wind* received ten. These three films are extravagant historical epics that reflect their era: *Gone With the Wind* is a Golden Age production with messages for pre-World War II America; the story of *Ben-Hur* provided inspiration for Cold War audiences; and *Titanic* typifies the 1990s trend of portraying, in graphic detail, tragic events in the recent past.

SIGNIFICANT FILMS

1997	*Titanic* ★ ♫♫
1998	*Shakespeare in Love* ★ ♫
	Run Lola Run
1999	*American Beauty* ★ ✉
	Star Wars: Episode I—The Phantom Menace
	The Matrix
2000	*Gladiator* ★ ✉
	Chocolat ✉
2002	*Star Wars: Episode II—Attack of the Clones*

Titanic

Great expense was taken in bringing the story of the Titanic to the screen. Indeed, the production of the film cost more than the original ship. Elaborate details were recreated from the interior of the luxury liner, actual people—the captain, the musicians, and passengers—

were portrayed, and the collision, sinking, and horrifying deaths were recreated with grim accuracy. As with *Gone With the Wind* and *Ben-Hur*, *Titanic* also seems to signal the end of a line. Unlike *Star Wars*, which sparked a revolution in filmmaking, there were no major color epics following *Gone With the Wind*, *Ben-Hur* imitators were few and generally weak, and *Titanic* caused a negative reaction, as the film's reputation sank nearly as fast as the ship itself.

The scores for these three films also share a number of characteristics, including a largely symphonic setting and a reliance on leitmotifs. Max Steiner's *Gone With the Wind* is the definitive classic film score, with a beautiful main melody and a multitude of other significant themes. Miklós Rózsa's *Ben-Hur* also employs numerous themes, but he subjects them to more vigorous manipulation and incorporates aspects of twentieth-century compositional techniques. James Horner's *Titanic* retains a close relationship to current popular music trends. The synthesizer is used frequently, and the principal melodies are loosely applied in the drama and generally remain intact. Their strength is in their beauty, not in their potential thematic manipulations.

The four principal themes of *Titanic* can be heard in pairs. The Titanic and Southampton themes belong to the ship in all her glory. Initially, the soaring Titanic melody appears by itself played by a French horn behind scenes of the salvage boat (8:40 and 13:05). With the first flashback to Southampton, the English port from which the Titanic departed, the Titanic and Southampton themes are both energetically presented (21:10).

Principal Themes

Example 32.1 Titanic

Example 32.2 Southampton

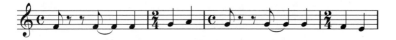

Example 32.3 Rose

Example 32.4 Love (Verse)

Example 32.5 Love (Chorus)

The most extended statement of the Southampton theme occurs as the ship begins the trip in earnest and picks up speed (31:15). Horner successfully captures the excitement of the event, as man's "largest moving object" races with dolphins, who manage to swim in tempo. When Jack excitedly calls out, the *Titanic* theme soars forth once again. The magnificence of this scene, along with the stunning view of the ship, is given musical support by the full symphony, wordless vocals, and bells. Except for a brief reference to the Titanic theme at the end of the film, neither melody is heard again, as the ship has just enjoyed its finest moment.

The Rose and Love themes are also frequently paired together. The Rose theme is performed hauntingly and wordlessly at the beginning of the film by a solo soprano voice. The tune is given a strong Irish folk quality, although Rose is neither Irish nor a member of the folk class. The association of this theme with the character is vague. Perhaps it is better to think of it as representing Rose's story. Nonetheless, the theme is hauntingly beautiful and serves as a needed contrast to the other material.

The Love theme has its initial full presentation in one of the most romantic scenes in all of film. In the Titanic's last sunset, the two lovers stand at the bow of the boat and kiss for the first time (1:20:20). In keeping with its relationship to the folk-like Rose theme, the melody is initially presented on a pennywhistle. The full orchestra eventually enters, but fades as the solo voice finishes the tune. As the image of the sunken ship replaces the flashback, the voice and the pennywhistle take on a ghostly character. The Love theme returns in a piano rendition when Jack sketches Rose in the nude (1:26:50), and an oboe plays it delicately when they make love in the back seat of a car (1:33:35).

Later, the two themes appear together in some of the most potent scenes of the film. When Rose is being lowered in a lifeboat (2:17:55), we hear her theme. Suddenly, she leaps back onto the *Titanic*, and the Rose and Love themes are combined contrapuntally. For the climactic moment when Rose realizes that Jack is dead and releases her hand from his frozen grip (2:55:35), the Rose theme adds a strong emotional element. As she whistles for help, we can also hear a fragment of the Love theme. The two themes are

Figure 32.1 Rose and Jack fall in love on the *Titanic*

again heard in counterpoint more joyfully at the end of the film, when Rose apparently joins Jack on the *Titanic*. Also note the reference to the Rose theme during the closing credits, as the Love theme is transformed into "My Heart Will Go On," one of the most popular melodies of the 1990s and certainly one of the most effective of all movie themes.

In addition to these melodies, the score for *Titanic* contains good underscoring for action sequences, mood-evoking colors, and effective source music. Most notable are the haunting sounds of the opening segment showing the sunken ship, the vocals suggesting ghostly spirits, the trombone choir depicting the cold of the iceberg, the water, and the dead, and the intense dissonance mixed with distorted references to the Love theme as the *Titanic* breaks and sinks.

Source music helps to define the class system on board. When we see the upper decks, we often hear elegant chamber music; for the lower regions of the ship, Irish dance music is played (1:05:40). In another emotional moment, the string quartet decides to keep playing despite their impending deaths (2:30:30). While the ensemble plays the hymn "Nearer My God to Thee," we see a montage of people calmly preparing to die, including the crew, an elderly couple holding each other in bed, and a mother telling her children a story.

Composer Profile

James Horner (b. 1953)

James Horner was born in Los Angeles. His parents took him to London, where he eventually attended the Royal Conservatory of Music. Returning to California, he studied music as an undergraduate at USC and received a Ph.D. in composition and theory at UCLA. He began scoring small-budget films in the late 1970s, and in 1982 he had a major breakthrough with the score to *Star Trek: The Wrath of Khan* (1982). Since then, he has become one of Hollywood's most respected and successful composers of symphonic scores.

Important Film Scores

Star Trek: The Wrath of Khan 1982	*Apollo 13* 1995 ✉
48 Hrs. 1982	*Braveheart* 1995 ✉
Aliens 1986 ✉	*Titanic* 1997 ★ ♫ ♫
The Name of the Rose 1986	*A Beautiful Mind* 2001 ★ ✉
Glory 1989	*House of Sand and Fog* 2003 ✉
Field of Dreams 1989 ✉	*Troy* 2004
Honey, I Shrunk the Kids 1989	*Apocalypto* 2006
	Avatar (2009) ✉

★ = Best Picture Oscar   ♫ = Best Music Oscar   ✉ = Music Oscar Nomination

A Rose by Any Other Name

Shakespeare in Love

Despite the enormous success of *Titanic*, the next few years in Hollywood were marked by a reactionary trend towards simplicity. The shift in mood can be seen in the winners of the Best Picture award for the two years immediately following *Titanic*, both of which have "rose" themes: *Shakespeare in Love* (1998) and *American Beauty* (1999). Like Titanic, *Shakespeare in Love* involves real-life people, has action set against a historical background (Shakespeare's Rose Theater), presents a love story that ends unhappily, and has an Oscar-winning musical score. But the mood is entirely different. *Shakespeare in Love* is a warm and humorous tale that draws strength from the simplicity of its story and setting. Much of this tone is the result of Stephen Warbeck's score, which is consistently light and warm. The incorporation of Renaissance instruments such as the recorder contributes to the fresh sound of this period film.

Figure 32.2 Love blooms in the Rose Theater

American Beauty

In a different tone, *American Beauty* takes a dark comedic look at life in suburbia. Through the lives of three members of a dysfunctional family, a cynical view of the superficial values and insecurities of fin de siècle America is presented. A wide variety of diegetic popular music reflects the divergent tastes of the family members and further suggests the superficial facades that surround each of their lives. The Oscar-nominated score by Thomas Newman also contributes to the stagnant quality of the film, in which people are trapped by their self-images.

In *The Shawshank Redemption*, we observed how Newman employed repetitive musical elements in order to sustain moods. This quality is even more evident in *American Beauty*, as Newman more fully embraces a contemporary musical style called minimalism. Emerging as a major movement in concert music in the mid-1980s, minimalism is characterized by the constant repetition of small motivic units, often with a link to popular music through syncopation. At the beginning of *American Beauty*, for example, a lively two-measure motive is repeated for over three minutes, suggesting the repetitive nature of Lester's life. At times, the mesmerizing sound of a Javanese gamelan orchestra is employed; this sound is particularly effective as underscoring to Lester's rose fantasies (19:00). The resultant sound is creative and fresh, matching the spirit of the film itself.

Figure 32.3 Lester enjoys an erotic rose fantasy

Fresh Musical Sounds

In the final years of the twentieth century, film music continued to create unique colors and styles, often dictated by the source music. The following films reflect some of the variety of musical colors in recent years:

- *Elizabeth* (1998): Renaissance music
- *The Legend of 1900* (1998): Piano music, including extended jazz cues
- *He Got Game* (1998): Adapted score with music by Aaron Copland
- *Eyes Wide Shut* (1999): Adapted score with evocative piano music by Franz Liszt
- *Almost Famous* (2000): Contemporary rock music
- *O Brother, Where Art Thou?* (2000): American folk music

Some of the diversity of musical sounds employed in scores at the end of the century can also be heard in three popular films: *Chocolat* (2000), *The Matrix* (1999), and *Run Lola Run* (1998).

Close-Up: Independent Films

American Independents

The term "independent film" is vague, but it basically refers to a film that is made outside of the film establishment. In the early history of American film, the establishment was Thomas Edison's Motion Picture Patents Company, and many of the independent filmmakers not affiliated with Edison moved to California and founded the Hollywood studio system. Within twenty years, the "independent" California filmmakers had become the establishment and actively discouraged new independents. The decline of studio power in the 1950s forced Hollywood to incorporate the work of independents, and independent filmmaking has steadily gained prominence up to the present time.

There are three principal types of independent films: documentaries, avant-garde films, and narratives. Documentaries, non-fiction films, can be made on a wide variety of subjects, from simple weddings and celebrations to elaborate events like a political gathering or the making of a movie. One of the best known of all independent films is *Woodstock* (1970), a documentary of the historic rock concert. A recent documentary by filmmaker Michael Moore, *Fahrenheit 9/11* (2004), created a storm of controversy over its negative portrayal of the Bush administration's handling of the 9/11 crisis. The film won the Palme d'Or from the Cannes Film Festival and has set box-office records for a documentary.

Avant-garde films are closely allied to art movements, and tend to be experimental and innovative.

Chocolat

Like *American Beauty*, *Chocolat* exposes the facades and pretentiousness of a community, but the setting is a French village in 1959, and the overall mood is warm and uplifting. The Oscar-nominated score by Rachel Portman effectively sets the tone for this magical tale. With elegant simplicity, Portman employs a number of light melodic ideas that create evocative moods. Many of the tunes have folk features, such as dance-like accompaniments. The folk qualities link up both to the river people and to the South American origin of the chocolate recipe. Some folk instruments are used, but for the most part, solo woodwinds play the melodies, notably the flute, clarinet, and English horn. A number of the recurring melodies are associated with aspects of the story, such as the wind, magic, and the village mayor.

The Matrix

One of the most intriguing scores in recent years accompanies *The Matrix* (1999). Blending science fiction and martial arts, the film is a slick, highly polished view of the future. Ironically, while we observe a disturbing scenario about machines taking over the world, we also marvel at the incredible technology that went into the making of the film. The music by Don Davis matches the vision of a machine world with mechanical-sounding music. Mixing the modern concert hall sounds of minimalism with the popular sounds of techno and heavy metal, Davis creates an effective score that supports the dramatic action and sets an overall mood.

France is the principal center for such works, but there has been a small but strong avant-garde film movement in the United States since the late 1940s.

The independent narrative often incorporates non-Hollywood elements into the story. Perhaps the most significant independent element is the focus on ethnic subjects. Black filmmakers, dating back to the silent film era (see Close-Up on page 420), have recorded the experience of being African-American. Similarly, there are numerous excellent films developed from the perspective of Asian American, Native American, and Chicano filmmakers.

Many independent filmmakers produce films hoping to attract the financial backing of a Hollywood studio. Independent film festivals, such as the Sundance Festival, are held yearly and are attended by Hollywood scouts.

Among the independent films that achieved significant financial success are *Easy Rider* (1969), *Hoop Dreams* (1994), and *The Blair Witch Project* (1999).

Modern technology has proven to be an incredible boost to independent filmmaking. Today many home computers contain film-editing programs, and camera equipment is becoming less expensive. As a result, there has been a flood of independent films in recent years, often available over the Internet. Obviously the quality is not consistent, and film schools cannot keep up with the interest shown by young, eager students. Funding stands as the biggest problem facing the independent filmmaker. Among the most common solutions are government and private grants, university funding, and borrowing from family members.

Rachel Portman (b. 1960)

Rachel Portman was born in England and studied music at Oxford University. She began scoring films while she was still a student, and later worked for the BBC. She became the first woman to win an Academy Award for music with her score to *Emma* (1996) and has received two other nominations.

Important Film Scores

The Joy Luck Club 1993
Emma 1996 ♫
The Cider House Rules 1999 ✉
Chocolat 2000 ✉
Nicholas Nickleby 2002
The Manchurian Candidate 2004

★ = Best Picture Oscar   ♫ = Best Music Oscar   ✉ = Music Oscar Nomination

---

Among the number of recurring musical ideas are fast, repetitive scales that accompany the rapidly moving numbers of the matrix, and ominous dark and unrelated chords that accompany Agents, the humanized forms of the machines. In the training combat between master Morpheus and apprentice Neo (49:00), the music begins with Taiko drums and a gong, a clear reference to the Asian origin of kung fu. As the battle commences, techno music by the group Lunatic Calm is introduced. By the end, minimalist sounds from the orchestra have taken over. The transitions between these distinct musical styles are nearly seamless, as Davis merges the popular and concert styles.

Figure 32.4 Neo and Morpheus battle in a training exercise, accompanied by a variety of musical styles

Run Lola Run

Techno sounds also play a large role in the popular German film *Run Lola Run* (*Lola Rennt*). The story deals with fundamental philosophical questions about meaning and randomness in life. Lola must get 100,000 deutsche marks to her boyfriend Manni in twenty minutes or he will face serious consequences. Through the sheer willful force of the young Lola, we see her race to the rescue three separate times. Each time there are slight variations of coincidences that have enormous consequences on the lives of the people that Lola encounters and on the final outcome.

Director Tom Tykwer created his own techno-propelled score primarily with the aid of the synthesizer. The upbeat pulse provides a perfect background for the energized running scenes and the youthful appeal of the movie. Unlike the classical Hollywood score, Tykwer's music does not change for nuances of the story. In the excerpt described in the Viewer Guide, a window is almost broken, a gun fires accidentally, the police surround Lola and Manni, and yet the mood of the music is unaltered during all those moments. Within these minimal parameters, Tykwer makes slight modifications to the sound that emphasize significant moments, such as the addition of a high pitch when Manni is about to go into the supermarket, the entrance of a violin sound when Lola arrives too late, and the sound of a drum when Lola is forced into action.

Matching the film's postmodern images that mix black and white, color, and animation, the music incorporates diverse musical styles in a few selected moments. As Lola and Manni make their escape from the supermarket, we hear Dinah Washington sing the 1959 classic "What a Difference a Day Makes." Not only does the mood of this song run counter to the visual images; the words are also quite humorous in light of the movie as a whole. After Lola has been shot, we hear a passage from Charles Ives's *The Unanswered Question*, a work that deals with the meaning of life. Once again, the borrowed music has implications for the essential theme of the movie. This excerpt is repeated at the end of Lola's second run, when an ambulance hits Manni. Fortunately, circumstances change just enough for a happy ending after Lola's third run.

Viewer Guide

Run Lola Run: Robbing a Store

Timing

Excerpt: 25:10–32:00 (0:00 at studio logo);
CD Chapters 10–13

Key Points

- Scoring primarily for a synthesizer
- Techno music
- Music does not reflect specific actions or emotions
- Adaptations of two borrowed works

Setting

Manni (Moritz Bleibtreu) has lost 100,000 deutsche marks that belong to a local criminal. He has twenty minutes to replace the money or he faces a reprisal. He calls his girlfriend Lola (Franka Potente), who immediately runs to her father's bank to obtain some money. She is unsuccessful, and runs to meet Manni.

PLOT	MUSIC
Lola runs alongside an ambulance, and both avoid hitting a windowpane. In a crosscut, we see Manni waiting and Lola running.	A techno beat is heard throughout.
Manni surveys a supermarket. A split screen shows Manni, Lola, and the clock.	Vocals and a high pitch string sound are added.
When time runs out, Manni enters the store and pulls out his gun.	The music crescendos.
Just as Lola arrives, the guard pulls a gun.	A string sound is added to the timbre.
Lola hits the guard, takes his gun, and accidentally shoots it.	A drum sound is added.
Lola and Manni escape as police arrive.	Dinah Washington sings "What a Difference a Day Makes."
Lola is accidentally shot.	Stunned silence
Lola falls.	The strings play *The Unanswered Question* by Charles Ives.

Symphonic Scores

The first half of the 1990s saw a large number of orchestral scores created for films, culminating in epics such as *Braveheart* (1996) and *Titanic* (1997). After *Titanic*, the number of orchestral scores declined, as other musical styles and colors were explored in a search for fresh sounds. The most notable composers of traditional symphonic scores in the years immediately following *Titanic* are Hans Zimmer and John Williams.

Gladiator

Hans Zimmer created a strong symphonic score for *Gladiator* (2000), an epic that bears a number of similarities to *Braveheart*. Like *Braveheart*, *Gladiator* won the award for Best Picture, is set in the distant past, has extended battle scenes with graphic violence, and tells of a man who is killed at the end, seeking revenge against a powerful enemy for the death of his wife. One of the principal differences between the two films is the overall tone. While *Braveheart* is set against the beauty of Scotland, *Gladiator* projects the dark, brutal reality of the Roman era.

In keeping with this tone, Zimmer's abundant melodic ideas are predominantly in lower registers and frequently in minor keys. The opening of the film establishes a distinctive musical timbre. The initial sound of a plucked instrument symbolizes the telling of a story, the dissonances suggest that it is a painful story, and the beautiful wordless solo voice establishes a mournful tone. The principal theme for Maximus, the hero, is soon heard (2:40). Set in D minor, it has a strong character and represents his heroic role in the film. The score contains a great variety of colors and thematic ideas, many of which are related. In particular, note the transformation of the Maximus theme into a gentle warm melody as he thinks of his family (30:45).

The *Star Wars* Prequels

At the turn of the century, the long-awaited prequels to the *Star Wars* trilogy finally appeared: *The Phantom Menace* (1999), *Attack of the Clones* (2002), and *Revenge of the Sith* (2005). John Williams, who may be the most prolific composer for orchestra in all of music history, created the scores for all three films. Perhaps because of the unrelenting nature of the wall-to-wall music, neither the score from *The Phantom Menace* nor *Attack of the Clones* was nominated for an Oscar. Yet the experience of this master craftsman is abundantly evident in his handling of thematic material and orchestration. To be sure, many passages resort to clichés, as would be expected in maintaining the traditions of *Star Wars*, but there are also many unique colors and combinations of sounds that challenge the limits of the virtuoso Hollywood orchestra.

In writing these scores, Williams faced a major problem—creating a new sound while maintaining ties to the original trilogy. Tradition is followed at the beginning and end of each film, as Williams quotes the original music for the opening credits and the initial section of the closing credits. A number of familiar themes also appear, most notably the Force theme and, less frequently, Yoda's theme. Near the end of *The Phantom Menace*, we hear Darth Vader's theme as Yoda worries about Anakin's future (2:06:40). This theme becomes more pronounced in *Attack of the Clones*, as Anakin heads towards the Dark Side. Also in the latter film, the image of young Boba Fett (50:45) brings out his brief motive from *The Empire Strikes Back*. Periodically, Williams quotes Luke Skywalker's theme during a battle scene, with no reference to his character.

For the most part, however, Williams creates a distinctively new sound in these films. Much of this newness stems from his use of voices, which have a minimal role in the original trilogy. Most striking is the dark Orff-like Duel of the Fates theme that underscores the battle with the Sith in *The Phantom Menace* (1:50:20) and makes a brief reappearance in *Attack of the Clones* (1:14:40). Numerous new leitmotifs for people and places also appear. The evil characters are given low-pitched themes, the same general range used for Darth Vader's theme in *The Empire Strikes Back*. Curiously, the theme for Senator Palpatine is similar in shape to that of Lord Sidious (almost like the Sidious theme in disguise), adding further fuel to the speculation that these two men are the same.

Figure 32.5 The Duel of the Fates theme accompanies an action sequence in *The Phantom Menace*

For each of the first two prequels, Williams composed a new lyrical melody. In *The Phantom Menace*, Anakin is accompanied by a gentle tune appropriate for the innocence of a young child (32:55). The final cadence of the theme, however, comes very close to becoming Darth Vader's theme, hinting at what we know lies in the future for Anakin. This connection is withheld until the end of the closing credits, for those who stay to the last moment. Here, the cadence of Anakin's theme is quietly transformed so that it resembles Darth Vader's theme. In case the point was missed, the motive is repeated several times as the music fades, and the sound of Darth Vader breathing is added in the background.

Examples 32.6–32.9. Anakin's theme becomes Darth Vader's theme in *The Phantom Menace*

Example 32.6 Anakin

Example 32.7 Altered cadence

Example 32.8 Ending form

Example 32.9 Darth Vader's theme

Anakin's theme makes only a brief appearance in *Attack of the Clones*. Instead, Anakin now has a beautiful love theme that he shares with Padme. Perhaps the most beautiful melody in all the *Star Wars* movies, this theme is first heard when Anakin and Padme begin to speak on a more personal level (29:20), and it grows in intensity as their relationship develops. The triplet rhythm in the second and third measures is sometimes isolated and used in action sequences involving the two lovers. One might also note that the same descending triplet is one of the distinctive characteristics of the theme for Luke Skywalker, who will be a product of their love and marriage.

Example 32.10 Anakin and Padme from *The Attack of the Clones*

Trailer

The twentieth century closed with numerous musical highlights. The symphonic score still demonstrated enough flexibility to underscore a wide variety of films. The mastery of John Williams continued to be on display for many of those, but other composers, including Hans Zimmer, made significant contributions to the repertory. Particularly invigorating were the numerous new musical sounds coming from innovative sources. The search for new musical sounds would continue to characterize film music of the twenty-first century.

Important Names and Terms

Stephen Warbeck

minimalism

Rachael Portman

Don Davis

techno

Tom Tykwer

Suggested Viewing

Comedy: *As Good as It Gets* (1997) ✉, *Men in Black* (1997) ✉, *Being John Malkovich* (1999), and *O Brother, Where Art Thou?* (2000)

Action/Thrillers: *L.A. Confidential* (1997) ✉, *The Mask of Zorro* (1998), *The Sixth Sense* (1999), and *Memento* (2000)

Fantasy: *X-Men* (2000)

Animated: *Princess Mononoke* (1997), *Mulan* (1998) ✉, *A Bug's Life* (1998) ✉, and *The Prince of Egypt* (1998) ✉

Drama: *Good Will Hunting* (1997) ✉, *The Truman Show* (1998), *Magnolia* (1999) ✉, *The Cider House Rules* (1999) ✉, and *Erin Brockovich* (2000)

History/Biopic: *Amistad* (1997) ✉ and *Elizabeth* (1998) ✉

War: *The Thin Red Line* (1998) ✉ and *Saving Private Ryan* (1998) ✉

33

The Red Violin

The postmodern era rejected the modernist notion that the popular arts have only transient value. By the end of the twentieth century, most universities offered courses in popular music and film, and many had even established film departments—developments that would have been unthinkable in earlier decades. As the artistic value of film music was recognized, the traditional stigma of composing for film diminished.

American Concert Composers

Over the last two decades, it has become more common for American concert composers to write film scores. Among those who have achieved recognition for both concert music and film music in recent years are Philip Glass, Tan Dun, Elliot Goldenthal, and John Corigliano.

Philip Glass

Philip Glass (b. 1937) is one of the key figures in the early years of minimalism. Beginning in the 1960s and rising to importance in the 1980s, minimalism features music with a deliberately simplified melodic, harmonic, and rhythmic

SIGNIFICANT FILMS

1997	*Kundun* ✉
1998	*The Red Violin* ♫
2000	*Crouching Tiger, Hidden Dragon* ♫✉
2002	*Frida* ♫✉
	The Hours ✉

character. Its repetitive nature creates a hypnotic sound reminiscent of a machine or computer. In adopting this new style, Glass was influenced by the music of Ravi Shankar, the renowned sitar player from India. By the mid-1970s Glass had created a significant repertoire of works, including the landmark

Figure 33.1 Minimalism and Tibetan music mix in Philip Glass's score to *Kundun*

opera *Einstein on the Beach* (1976). Assimilating some aspects of popular music, minimalism reflects the postmodern trend towards making art music accessible to the general public. The movement has had an impact on a number of film scores, as has already been noted in the discussions of *American Beauty* and *The Matrix*.

Glass created a sensation with the music for two fascinating documentaries: *Koyaanisqatsi* (1983), which addresses ecological issues; and *Powaqqatsi* (1988), which deals with third world problems. He later became involved with commercially oriented films, such as the horror slasher *Candyman* (1992) and the media satire *The Truman Show* (1998), and he achieved critical recognition with the Oscar-nominated scores to *Kundun* (1997) and *The Hours* (2002).

Martin Scorsese's *Kundun* is a biopic about the Dalai Lama, beginning with the discovery of his identity in a remote Tibetan village at the age of two and extending to his escape from Tibet after China had overrun his country. Glass incorporates the sounds of several Tibetan instruments, and his own repetitive minimalist style suggests the meditative nature of Buddhist contemplation. Most effective are the numerous scenes of rituals and ceremonies.

In *The Hours*, Glass links together the related stories of three women with similar musical cues that often extend over the abrupt cuts of time. As each woman faces the issue of suicide, Glass builds tension through accelerating tempos and increasing dynamics. Glass creates some of his most unabashedly emotional music for this well-acted psychological drama.

Tan Dun

Chinese-born Tan Dun (b. 1957) was raised during the Cultural Revolution and, as a composer, began to explore Western musical styles when restrictions were loosened. Still, the Chinese government banned public performances of Tan Dun's works in 1983, and he came to the United States shortly thereafter in order to study music at Columbia University. Among his best-known works are the opera *Marco Polo* (1995), which mixes Western avant-garde sounds with those of Beijing Opera; the *Symphony 1997: Heaven*

Earth Mankind, composed for the ceremony marking the return of Hong Kong to China; and *2000 Today: A World Symphony for the Millennium*, a work commissioned by the BBC, PBS Television, and Sony Classical, that was broadcast to the world on January 1, 2000, on more than fifty-five international television networks.

Figure 33.2 Jen leaps to her death to the mournful sound of an erhu

Using a mixture of Western and Chinese musical styles, Tan Dun created the sensational Oscar-winning score for *Crouching Tiger, Hidden Dragon* (2000). Tan Dun combines traditional Chinese instruments, such as the two-stringed erhu, and the flute-like bawu and dize, with Western instruments, most notably a solo cello played by the Chinese-American musician Yo-Yo Ma. The melodic material for the cello, featuring slides and quick ornaments, reflects some of the vocal traditions of Beijing Opera. Throughout the film, Tan Dun freely mixes traditional Western harmony, Western popular music rhythms, avant-garde timbres, and ethnic Chinese sounds.

An excellent martial arts fantasy with stunning visual effects, the story tells of two sets of doomed lovers. The mixture of action, romance, and tragedy allows Tan Dun to incorporate a variety of musical effects. Chinese drumming propels scenes of combat (16:00), and lyric duets between an erhu and cello accompany both sets of lovers (1:09:45). The timbre of these duets recalls a similar sound in the celebrated Chinese musical work *The Butterfly Concerto*. The music achieves a timeless beauty during the final Liebestod scene (1:52:15). During the ensuing closing credits, the love theme, originally heard as a traditional Chinese melody, is transformed into a Western popular song, "A Love Before Time," which received a nomination for Best Song.

Elliot Goldenthal

Born in Brooklyn in 1954, Elliot Goldenthal studied composition with John Corigliano at the Manhattan School of Music and had informal lessons with Aaron Copland as well. His best-known concert work is the *Vietnam Oratorio*, commissioned and performed by the Pacific Symphony in 1995 to commemorate the twentieth anniversary of the end of the Vietnam War. In addition, Goldenthal has composed for the theater and for film. Among his film credits are *Pet Sematary* (1989), *Interview with the Vampire: The Vampire Chronicles* (1994), *Batman Forever* (1995), *Heat* (1995), *Michael Collins* (1996), and *Frida* (2002).

In these films, Goldenthal mixes a variety of musical styles, including postromantic, avant-garde, minimalist, and ethnic. It is primarily because of the last that Goldenthal received an Oscar for his score to *Frida*. This film is a biopic about Frida Kahlo (1907–1954), a creative artist who gained international stature despite being a woman and coming from a third-world country—Mexico. Her turbulent marriage to the famed Mexican muralist Diego Rivera, her strong communist sympathies, and her ties to her culture allow for glimpses into this fascinating country and era.

Goldenthal's score, like Kahlo's artwork, is grounded in Mexican folk traditions. In both diegetic and non-diegetic passages, traditional Mexican dances and melodic styles energize the film. As needed, Goldenthal also incorporates dissonant underscoring for dramatic situations. The Oscar-nominated duet "Burn It Blue," heard during the closing credits, is one of the musical highlights.

Figure 33.3 *Broken Column* by Kahlo

John Corigliano

John Corigliano (b. 1938) is among the leading musical figures in America today. A composer of symphonies, chamber music, and the highly regarded opera *Ghosts of Versailles* (1987), he recently received a Pulitzer Prize for his Symphony No. 2 (2001). He is also recognized as an excellent teacher, and has been associated with the Manhattan School of Music and Juilliard. Corigliano has composed three film scores: *Altered States* (1980), *Revolution* (1985), and *The Red Violin* (1999). The first of these created a sensation, as his modernistic musical style created a fitting support to this out-of-body story. The film received an Oscar nomination for Best Dramatic Score.

The Red Violin: The Narrative

Directed by François Girard, *The Red Violin* (1998) has an episodic plot that follows the journey of a violin from its creation in seventeenth-century Cremona to its sale at an auction in twentieth-century Montreal. Between these two framing events are three principal episodes:

- Delivered to a monastery, the violin is played by generations of orphan boys. Eventually Kaspar Weiss, a young violin prodigy, is given the violin, and Georges Poussin, a violin teacher, takes him to Vienna.
- Stolen by gypsies, the violin eventually is brought to England in the late nineteenth century. Frederick Pope, a famed violinist, obtains the instrument and performs virtuoso compositions with it.
- The violin is taken to China, where it remains through the early years of the twentieth century. During the Cultural Revolution, it is secretly given to an old man who collects musical instruments.

At first glance, the film would appear to have a loose structure. The time period spans over three hundred years, and the location encompasses five countries, necessitating the use of five different languages. As with many recent films, *The Red Violin* contains numerous jumps of time and location. Intermixed with the three principal episodes are recurring scenes of the violin's origin and its twentieth-century fate.

Yet there are a number of elements that unify these various events. Each of the episodes has an association with the color red. The orphan monastery and the music that is made there can easily be associated with the Italian Baroque composer Antonio Vivaldi, whose nickname was "The Red Priest." Frederick Pope of the second episode is clearly modeled after the nineteenth-century virtuoso Niccolò Paganini, who was seen by some as a red devil. In the third episode, the violin finds a home in Red China. We can also observe a clear progression in the owners of the violin. It is originally intended for a baby, and then it passes to a boy, a man, and finally an old man. In the end, it will return to a child as the cycle is completed. In addition, all the stories deal with the mortality of man, while the violin survives. One can see a basic theme dealing with the transience of human life and the enduring power of man's artistic creations.

The Music

John Corigliano's remarkable Oscar-winning score also supports the overall structure of the film. Indeed, because of delays in production, much of the music was created prior to the filming. As a result, the score is one of the most unified in all of film.

The Principal Theme

For this story about a violin, Corigliano limits the orchestra to a solo violin, played by Joshua Bell, and a string orchestra. The principal theme (Example 33.1) belongs to both Anna Bussotti and the Red Violin. Anna sings the haunting tune several times, but it is heard primarily on the violin during the episodes. The melody is modal, lacking a leading tone, and hence can easily be heard as a Renaissance tune or as a modern melody. The theme begins on D, and, in subsequent phrases, cadences on G, A, and E. These four principal pitch points are also the four open strings of a violin.

Anna's melody appears over a recurring bass line in an old form called a Chaconne (Example 33.2). The exact rhythm of the chaconne varies, but the rising seven-note pattern is maintained throughout the film. A chaconne is a variation structure dating from before 1800, in which a pattern of harmonies is constantly repeated. At times, chaconnes also featured a repeated bass in an ostinato pattern. In *The Red Violin*, the chaconne melody can be heard by itself and underlying the first two phrases of Anna's theme (4:45). A third recurring idea, the lament, derives its descending motion from the second measure of Anna's theme and is also set above the chaconne bass (15:45).

Figure 33.4 Anna sings the Red Violin theme

Exposition: Cremona and Montreal

Most of the musical material for this film is related to Anna's theme. In a way, one can view the entire score as a theme and variation structure. All of the principal ideas are presented during the opening sections of the film, in which we shift from seventeenth-century Cremona to twentieth-century Montreal, and then back to Cremona. At the onset, only the chaconne and fragments of Anna's theme are presented. Most strikingly, the opening pitches of her theme, played freely and quickly by the string orchestra, are heard as we enter Bussotti's workshop, suggesting that these fragments are the voices of the violins hanging in the shop.

Anna's theme is presented fully with the accompaniment of the chaconne line when the film moves to Montreal. More significant, however, is the vocal version of the theme sung by the pregnant Anna. It is at this moment that we understand that the principal theme belongs to both Anna and the Red Violin. With the sudden and tragic death of Anna, the Lament theme appears for the first time. This theme always appears at the end of the subsequent episodes, essentially functioning as a closing theme for each story.

Episode: Vienna

In the first episode, we hear some of the most creative variations of Anna's theme. The setting for this episode is split between an isolated monastery and the city of Vienna. When we first see the monastery (21:45), we hear a Baroque concerto played by young boys. The solo part, which is always played by an orphan on the Red Violin, is an embellished version of Anna's theme. The violin finally ends up in the hands of the child prodigy Kaspar. When Kaspar auditions for master violin teacher Poussin, he plays a

Figure 33.5 The Red Violin theme is played in Baroque style

wonderful adaptation of Anna's theme that resembles the opening prelude of Bach's Sonata No. 1 for unaccompanied violin (25:40).

In Vienna, we hear two other distinct variations of the theme. As we arrive at the city, the theme is played in the underscoring in an elegant classical Viennese style (28:30). Later, once Kaspar has settled into Poussin's house, the boy begins to practice a difficult exercise known as an étude. Aided by a mechanical device, a prototype of the metronome, Kaspar gradually builds up speed until he reaches a breathtaking tempo (38:30). The melody of this exercise piece is also derived from Anna's theme.

Episodes: Oxford and Shanghai

Figure 33.6 The Red Violin is played by Frederick Pope while Joshua Bell, in a cameo, listens in the orchestra on the left

The musical style continues to change, matching the time period of the succeeding episodes. The second episode presents the theme in two distinct yet related styles. Initially, after gypsies have stolen the Red Violin, the theme is heard embedded within the improvised dance music played by the gypsies (49:10). The theme is particularly noticeable when the violin is playing in its lowest register. Later, the theme becomes part of the fantasies played by violin virtuoso Frederick Pope (56:35), both when he is in concert and when he is being inspired. During the concert scenes, note the young-looking violinist playing in the front row of the orchestra; this is a cameo appearance by the real soloist, Joshua Bell.

With the third episode, we enter the twentieth century, and Anna's theme is immediately presented with more dissonant, twentieth-century accompaniments (1:12:00). In China, we hear children sing during the Cultural Revolution (1:14:50). The tune, which is also heard in *The Last Emperor*, is well chosen. Upon close examination, we can hear that it vaguely follows the melodic contour of Anna's theme. This episode provides a fascinating glimpse into the turmoil that was created during that time.

Climax and Resolution: Montreal

The final portion of the film generally places Anna's theme in avant-garde settings. Harsh dissonances reflect not only the contemporary time period, but also the moral dilemma facing violin appraiser Morritz and the anguish shown in the flashback to Montreal, revealing the secret behind the Red Violin. After the intense sounds of the climax, the theme returns to a simple statement, performed on the violin and with a singing voice. The story has completed its cycle, as the Red Violin is once again in the hands of a child.

The Red Violin (1998)

Directed by François Girard
Music by John Corigliano

Principal Characters

Charles Morritz, violin expert (Samuel L. Jackson)
Nicolo Bussotti, famous violinmaker (Carlo Cecchi)
Anna Bussotti, young wife of Nicolo (Irene Grazioli)
Cesca, fortune reader (Anita Laurenzi)
Kaspar Weiss, violin prodigy (Christoph Koncz)
Georges Poussin, violin teacher (Jean-Luc Bideau)
Frederick Pope, English violin virtuoso (Jason Flemyng)
Victoria Byrd, novelist and Pope's lover (Greta Scacchi)
Xiang Pei, leader in Cultural Revolution (Sylvia Chang)
Chou Yuan, old music teacher (Liu Zi Feng)

Principal Themes

Example 33.1 Anna Bussotti/Red Violin

Example 33.2 Chaconne

Example 33.3 Lament

Exposition: Cremona and Montreal

0:00–20:40; DVD Chapters 1–3
[Timing begins at the studio logo]

SCENE DESCRIPTION	MUSIC
During the opening credits, we see a seventeenth-century violin shop in Cremona. Nicolo Bussotti is inspecting the work of his apprentices.	The first five notes of Anna's theme are played in the upper register. Numerous statements of the beginning of her theme are heard, representing the voices of all of the violins in the shop. The Chaconne theme is then played four times in various rhythms, and the section closes with the opening five notes in a lower register.
Unhappy with the work of a student, Bussotti smashes a violin.	No music
Following the title, we jump to twentieth-century Montreal and observe Charles Morritz.	Anna's theme is played, accompanied by the Chaconne.
Morritz enters an auction, where the Red Violin goes on sale.	No music
Back in Cremona, a pregnant Anna Bussotti sings.	Source music: Anna's theme
Anna asks Cesca to read her future. Anna picks five tarot cards.	No music
Reading the first card, Cesca tells Anna that she will live a long, full life and have a long journey.	The first five notes of Anna's theme are played quietly in the upper register.
Anna visits her husband in the shop, and he shows her his latest violin, his greatest masterpiece.	No music
Nicolo says that he will give the violin to their child. Later that night they look at the moon.	Fragments of Anna's theme lead to a full statement by the lower strings.
As Nicolo is finishing work on the violin, Anna sings.	Source music: Anna's theme
Anna goes into labor. A boy runs to tell Nicolo, who rushes home.	Dissonances and the Chaconne are heard during the running scenes.
Nicolo discovers that both his wife and child have died.	The Lament theme is accompanied by the Chaconne.

Later that night, Nicolo completes the violin by applying a distinctive red varnish.	No music until he applies the varnish, when we hear Anna's theme with the Chaconne.
We return to Montreal and observe Morritz entering the room again. Bidding begins on the Red Violin.	The music concludes and fades away. No music for the remainder of the scene.

Episode: Vienna

20:40–48:00; DVD Chapters 4–7

SCENE DESCRIPTION	MUSIC
At a late eighteenth-century monastery, young orphan boys are trained to play the violin.	Source music: a Baroque concerto derived from Anna's theme.
The Red Violin is donated to the monastery and passed from child to child until it reaches the hands of Kaspar Weiss.	Source music: the concerto begins with a variation of Anna's theme as the solo line. No music for the arrival of the violin
The story cuts back to Cremona, and Cesca reads the second tarot card, seeing a curse, danger, and illness.	No music
The eminent violin teacher Georges Poussin arrives at the monastery.	No music
Kaspar plays for Poussin, who agrees to take him to Vienna as a student.	Source music: a Baroque unaccompanied prelude based on Anna's theme
Poussin and Kaspar travel to Vienna.	Anna's theme is heard in an elegant Viennese style.
Kaspar is brought to Poussin's house, where he will live and study. Poussin obtains an audition for him.	No music
Kaspar begins a rigorous training routine with a metronome.	Source music: an étude derived from Anna's theme
Poussin learns that Kaspar sleeps with his violin.	Source music: Kaspar is practicing the étude.
Kaspar is told that he cannot sleep with the violin. At night he has heart problems, and his violin is returned.	A drumbeat (his heart) and sustained pitches accompany the doctor's visit. There is no other music in the scene.
Kaspar continues practicing with intensity.	Source music: the étude

Kaspar sleeps with his treasured violin the night before the audition.	A fragment of Anna's theme enters as he sleeps.
On the way to the audition, Kaspar and Poussin sing.	Source music: ear training music with timpani
At the audition, Kaspar is invited to perform. As he is about to play, he collapses and dies.	Source music: various notes from a cello and recorder. As Kaspar is about to play, the drumbeat (his heart) returns.
Kaspar is buried at the monastery.	The Lament theme returns.
Poussin learns that the Red Violin is buried with the body.	The Lament enters again after Poussin learns what has happened to the violin.
Cesca continues reading and sees lust and energy.	The Lament concludes.

Episode: Oxford

48:00–1:10:40; DVD Chapters 7–9

SCENE DESCRIPTION	MUSIC
Gypsies rob Kaspar's grave. The Red Violin is passed through several generations, and eventually crosses the channel to England.	Source music: the gypsies play improvisatory music and then a dance. Embedded in the dance in the low register is Anna's theme.
At the Montreal auction, modern-day priests from the monastery are bidding for the Red Violin.	No music
Back in Cremona, Cesca reads the third tarot card and sees a man that she describes as the devil.	Source music: the gypsy violin is heard briefly.
In nineteenth-century England, violin virtuoso Frederick Pope obtains the Red Violin from the gypsies.	Source music: a gypsy plays a variation of Anna's theme.
The gypsies enter a concert hall.	Source music: an orchestra is tuning.
Veronica enters backstage and talks with Pope.	No music
The orchestra and audience wait while Pope is being "inspired."	Source music: Pope plays improvisatory music with fragments of Anna's theme.
Pope performs the virtuoso fruits of his inspiration.	Source music: Pope plays a virtuosic fantasy based on Anna's theme.

Pope interrupts Victoria's work, seeking more inspiration.	Source music: Pope plays a slower variation of the theme.
Victoria tells Pope that she must travel to Russia.	Anna's theme is heard in a lush, late romantic setting.
Victoria and Pope exchange letters; he becomes depressed.	The Anna and Chaconne themes mix together, maintaining the postromantic style.
Popes cancels a concert performance.	No music
Victoria returns and finds Pope being "inspired" by another woman. She gets a gun.	Source music: further improvisations on Anna's theme
Confronting the lovers, Victoria shoots the Red Violin.	Dissonant music builds tension.
In a final letter, Pope writes that he will commit suicide and is giving away some of his possessions to pay off debts.	A variation of the Lament theme returns.
A representative of the Frederick Pope Foundation arrives at the Montreal auction and bids.	The strings enter in a modern style as the film segues into the next section.

Episode: Shanghai

1:10:40–1:33:10; DVD Chapters 9–12

SCENE DESCRIPTION	MUSIC
Pope's Chinese servant sails to Shanghai and sells the violin to a pawnshop, where it remains until a Chinese woman buys it for her daughter.	Anna's theme is played in a modern, dissonant setting. The Chaconne is also prominent.
Reading the fourth tarot card, Cesca sees justice, a trial, guilt, and fire.	At the end, we can hear the beginning of the Chinese music.
In China, young children pay homage to the Cultural Revolution.	Source music: the children sing accompanied by three accordions.
Chou Yuan is reprimanded for clinging to Western music. Xiang Pei speaks on his behalf and proposes that he concentrate on traditional Chinese instruments. All agree, and Yuan throws his violin into a fire.	No music

Xiang Pei goes to her apartment.	Source music: parade music with Chinese instruments
Xiang Pei destroys her Western musical possessions. She takes the Red Violin out of hiding. Ming enters.	No music
Xiang Pei shows Ming the violin.	Source music: Pei plays Anna's theme.
Ming tells his father about the violin, and he brings members of the Red Guard to Pei's apartment.	Source music: a recording of Anna's theme is playing.
Xiang Pei takes the Red Violin to Chou Yuan.	Source music: a variety of Chinese music can be heard in the streets.
Yuan accepts the instrument.	Strings play the Revolutionary song.
At the Montreal auction, we see an older Ming and a companion bid on the violin.	No music

Climax and Resolution: Montreal

1:33:10–2:11:00; DVD Chapters 12–18

SCENE DESCRIPTION	MUSIC
Cesca reads the fifth card and sees an end of the journey and a rebirth.	No music
The Red Violin is found in Chou Yuan's attic along with other musical instruments, following his death.	The Chaconne theme is played repeatedly. The Lament is also heard briefly.
In Montreal, Morritz arrives to appraise the collection of violins from China prior to the auction.	No music
He is drawn to the Red Violin and immediately suspects its origin.	Harsh dissonances and Anna's theme create a somber mood.
Morritz, with the help of Evan, studies the instrument, but does not tell anyone of his suspicion.	No music
Morritz continues to study the violin intently and asks that a copy of the Red Violin in England be purchased.	Avant-garde music with hints of Anna's theme accompanies his research. His dealings with other people have no music.
Virtuoso violinist Ruselsky inspects the violin collection. He plays the Red Violin, but Morritz convinces him that it is not right for him.	Source music: random arpeggios and Anna's theme with accompaniment when he tries the Red Violin.

Scientific tests show that the Red Violin is remarkable. Morritz talks about finding something that he has long been seeking. More tests.	No music for the tests. Another variation of Anna's theme is played while Morritz philosophizes.
Returning to his hotel, Morritz receives the results of tests on the varnish and discovers the source of the red color.	A portion of the Chaconne theme is heard in a high register along with scurrying figures, similar to the film's opening.
A flashback to Cremona shows Nicola carrying Anna's dead body into his shop. He cuts her hair and makes a brush. He slashes her wrists and drains blood. Mixing it into the varnish, he applies it to the violin.	The Chaconne is repeated numerous times. The Lament theme can also be heard. New material leads to a statement of Anna's theme.
Back in Montreal, Morritz confesses to the auctioneer that the instrument is the famous Red Violin.	No music
Ruselsky reads the news and is angry with Morritz for the deception.	A variation of the Chaconne theme is heard.
While the auction begins, Morritz thinks about the violin and Anna.	A new melody emerges in the lower register as a cello is about to be auctioned. Music stops for the auction, but Anna's theme returns as Morritz looks at her portrait.
Changing his mind, Morritz comes to the auction with the copy of the Red Violin under his arm. He switches the two instruments.	Low pitches are sustained and gradually get louder and pick up a faster tempo.
While bidding begins, security is called because the Red Violin is missing its auction tag. The tag is found and Ruselsky buys the fake violin for $2,400,000.	Tension continues to rise, climaxing when Morritz is given his coat and the missing tag is found.
Morritz leaves in a cab, calls home, and says he has a new instrument for his own little girl.	Anna's theme is played by the solo violin. As Morritz talks to his daughter, the orchestra enters.
In Cremona, Anna leaves Cesca, who places the tarot cards back into a stack. The closing credits follow.	Anna's theme continues, ending with her singing voice.

Trailer

The Oscars for Best Score awarded to *The Red Violin* (1999), *Crouching Tiger, Hidden Dragon* (2000), and *Frida* (2002) are partially a reflection of the fine craftsmanship brought to film music by these three concert composers. Characteristic of each of these scores is a distinctive new sound that provides a fresh alternative to standard orchestral or popular music scores. Scores by American concert composers represent one of the many positive trends in today's film music.

Important Names

Philip Glass
Tan Dun
Elliot Goldenthal
John Corigliano

34

The New Millennium, 2001–2004

America entered the twenty-first century as the dominant political, economic, and cultural force in the world. The first two of these areas are a natural outgrowth of winning the Cold War and the country's leadership in technology. Cultural dominance, however, is a surprise. In seeking a cultural identity, America has traditionally turned to Europe. American composers and artists studied in Europe, and Europeans were brought to our country as teachers and creators. When the film industry needed composers in the 1930s, it immediately sought out foreign-born musicians such as Korngold, Steiner, Rósza, and Tiomkin. As American artists began to assert themselves, they excelled at the more revolutionary styles of traditional European art forms; abstract expressionism and American avant-garde music gained international recognition.

But while we were preoccupied with emulating European art, the world was embracing our popular culture. McDonald's, Hollywood movies, and American pop music carried the American image abroad more effectively than all the politicians, diplomats, and military leaders together. Ironically, in some regions that

SIGNIFICANT FILMS

2001	*The Lord of the Rings: The Fellowship of the Ring* ♫ ✉
	Harry Potter and the Sorcerer's Stone ✉
	Black Hawk Down
	Pearl Harbor ✉
	Monsters, Inc. ✉ ♫
	Shrek
	Moulin Rouge
2002	*Chicago* ★ ✉
	Spider-Man
	The Lord of the Rings: The Two Towers
2003	*The Lord of the Rings: The Return of the King* ★ ♫ ♫
	Finding Nemo ✉
	The Triplets of Belleville ✉
	Kill Bill: Vol. 1
2004	*Spider-Man 2*
	Kill Bill: Vol. 2
	Harry Potter and the Prisoner of Azkaban ✉

consider America to be an enemy by day, Hollywood films attract large audiences at night. Europe also experienced a wave of Americanization, and, as a consequence, a European backlash against American culture has developed. This attitude is readily apparent in the French satirical animated feature *The Triplets of Belleville* (2003).

The assimilation of American popular music in non-Western regions has followed a consistent formula. The harmony, rhythm, and accompanying instruments are borrowed from American rock music. An ethnic melodic instrument may be added, and the voice, singing in the native language, reflects the tonal quality and performance style of the region, usually producing a more nasal sound than Western singing. The Mandarin version of "A Love Before Time" from *Crouching Tiger, Hidden Dragon* provides a good example of this hybrid style. Examples are abundant in films from India, in which characters are likely to break out in song at any moment. *Lagaan: Once Upon a Time in India,* (2001), in particular, is an entertaining and fresh fusion of musical cultures.

Despite the general popularity of American music abroad, America's role as an economic and political power has faced serious challenges. The events of September 11, 2001, the wars in Afghanistan and Iraq, and the constant threat of terrorism have had a major impact on daily life in the United States. Initially, Hollywood did not know how to respond (see Close-Up). But in the turbulent years of the early twenty-first century, the film industry turned to a number of the successful formulas of the 1990s, including realism, in the showing of both historical and violent events, and escapist entertainment, including musicals, animations, and fantasies.

Realism

Black Hawk Down

One of a handful of war movies to appear after the tragic events of 9/11, *Black Hawk Down* provides a realistic look at a battle between the technologically equipped Americans and the forces of a third-world country. Recapturing a moment in recent American history, the film depicts a skirmish in Somalia in 1993. Supporting this clash between two diverse societies is a score that contains musical elements of both cultures. Traditional Muslim music is heard at prayer time, and American popular music blares from radios at the US base. The most intriguing sounds, however, are a mixture of the two. Just as the city streets show both non-Western and Western features—architecture, clothes, a car—the music frequently combines elements of Middle Eastern and American popular music, as we hear during the preparations for battle (37:35).

Close-Up: 9/11 and Hollywood

America Goes to War

The tragic events of September 11, 2001, brought the Pax Americana to a devastating end. Within a few years, the United States was engaged in active combat in both Afghanistan and Iraq. Life in the US has been altered dramatically; the impact of the War on Terrorism on individual rights has been pronounced, and divisive debates continue.

During the two World Wars and the Korean War, Hollywood rallied to glorify America's cause. Americans were shown as heroes, and enemies were depicted as savage beasts—villains capable of cold-blooded murder, treachery, and rape. During the Vietnam War, such stories lost their appeal in view of the scenes shown daily on television. Today, it is difficult for Hollywood to make films about current events. The destruction of the World Trade Center has not been the subject of a theatrical release, and filmmakers have avoided contributing to the serious problem of prejudice against Arabs in the US.

Rather than giving Hollywood new subject matter for films, these events have been inhibiting. Immediately after 9/11, production was delayed on a number of movies. Among the films that were affected were *Sidewalks of New York*, a romantic comedy set in New York City; *Big Trouble*, a story about an atomic bomb on a plane; *Windtalkers*, a World War II action picture; and *Collateral Damage*, in which Arnold Schwarzenegger fights terrorists. Spike Lee, whose many films pay homage to New York, effectively uses 9/11 as a backdrop to the provocative drama *25th Hour*.

In this careful climate, fantasy/adventure stories were a safe choice. Here, our heroes can kill hundreds of clones, droids, or orcs without offending any ethnic group. But even in the adventures of our comic-book heroes, references to current struggles are not completely avoided. At Spider-Man's most desperate moment, the citizens of New York rally to his aid and one of them exclaims, "You mess with one of us, you mess with all of us." While the heroic stories of how New York coped with this crisis have not been tapped by Hollywood, judging by history, it will not be long before some thoughtful and powerful dramas about 9/11 are brought to the big screen.

Pearl Harbor

Hans Zimmer, who contributed to the music of *Black Hawk Down*, was the principal musical figure in another war film from 2001, *Pearl Harbor*. This film follows a formula similar to that of *Titanic*—a love story set against a horrific event from our recent past. Even more money was spent on this lavish epic, but, despite the stunning special effects, it could not repeat the magic of the earlier film. Musically, *Pearl Harbor* also has a number of similarities to *Titanic*, most notably the inclusion of a beautiful love song, "There You'll Be," in the closing credits. To create this song, the filmmakers turned to one of Hollywood's top songwriters, Diane Warren, who earned her fifth Academy nomination for her effort. Unlike the theme from *Titanic*, her melody is not integrated into Zimmer's musical score, and the song causes both a thematic and stylistic jolt, as its contemporary style is half a century removed from the time period of the story.

In the narrative portion of the film, Zimmer provides two compelling love themes. The first initially accompanies the boyhood friendship of Rafe and Danny. As a love triangle develops, Rafe and Evelyn are given a new lyrical love theme, while Danny and Evelyn borrow the theme representing the two best friends. Judging just from the themes, one can easily speculate which love will last to the end of the film. In the scenes dealing with the war, Zimmer does an excellent job of mixing symphonic, choral, and ethnic sounds. The sensitive portrayal of the Japanese leaders as thoughtful and not simply evil is projected through Zimmer's music. The most powerful moment of the film, all love stories aside, is the montage of the destruction of Pearl Harbor. Functioning like the chorus in a Greek tragedy, a sublime chorale laments the suffering and loss of life (2:02:00).

Kill Bill

Realistic portrayals of violence continued to characterize films of the early twenty-first century. *Gangs of New York* (2002) shows the brutal reality of life in nineteenth-century New York, *The Pianist* (2002) recreates with horrific detail visions of the Warsaw ghetto of World War II, and *The Passion of the Christ* (2004) dwells on the torturous last hours of Jesus Christ, including his crucifixion. Of the nonhistorical films, the most sensational visions of violence appear in Quentin Tarantino's two-part martial arts fantasy, *Kill Bill: Vol. 1* (2003) and *Kill Bill: Vol. 2* (2004).

For these films, Tarantino creates a clearly delineated episodic plot, in which each segment of the story is denoted as a chapter and given a subtitle. Maintaining the successful formula that he used in earlier films such as *Reservoir Dogs* (1992) and *Pulp Fiction* (1994), these chapters do not follow a strict chronological sequence. Reinforcing the segmented nature of the plot, some chapters are set apart from the others through the use of animation and black-and-white cinematography. In addition to creating visual variety, these contrasting techniques help tone down the extreme violence shown in their segments.

The music in these films is predominantly borrowed and represents a wide range of styles. Some of the musical ideas recur in the story, such as a passage composed by Quincy Jones for the television show *Ironside* (1967–75), a series about a detective who, like the Bride in *Kill Bill*, survives a crippling assassination attempt. Featuring loud, swooping sounds, this brief quotation serves as an effective revenge motive. For the most part, however, music is used to create patches of color for individual chapters, and there is little musical connection between the two films.

For the bloody tale of revenge shown in animation during "Chapter 3: The Origin of O-Ren" (*Vol. 1*, 35:55), Tarantino adds music by Luis Bacalov from the spaghetti western *The Grand Duel* (1972). With this borrowing, Tarantino links the traditions of martial arts films to that of westerns. Reinforcing this relationship, Tarantino brings in music composed by Morricone for *Death Rides a Horse* (1968) just prior to the showdown at the House of Blue Leaves (1:13:30). This quotation is especially meaningful, since the plot for *Death Rides a Horse* was the direct model for the plot of this chapter.

Several other musical moments are striking. Underscoring the wickedly beautiful assassin Elle Driver, the whistled theme from Bernard Herrmann's music for *Twisted Nerve* (1968) creates an unnerving effect. Still, the most memorable music appears at the beginning of *Vol. 1*. Just after we see Bill shoot the Bride, Nancy Sinatra sings the haunting tune "Bang Bang (My Baby Shot Me Down)," and the captivating story of survival and revenge commences.

Musical Reprise

Seventy-four years after the first film musical *The Jazz Singer* (1927) changed film history, *Moulin Rouge* (2001) seemingly revitalized the genre. One year later, *Chicago* (2002) became the first musical to win a Best Picture Oscar in thirty-four years. As is typical with the genre, both films involve performers whose acts are part of the story. Beyond this, these two films treat the traditional genre in creatively different ways.

Moulin Rouge

Moulin Rouge is a fascinating postmodern film. The title is the name of a famous cabaret in Paris, known for its dazzling and extravagant shows. The characters are drawn from a variety of sources. Christian and his colleagues parallel the male figures in a popular nineteenth-century story best known in its operatic version, Puccini's

Figure 34.1 The love duet from *Moulin Rouge*

La Bohème (1896). In both stories the lead male is a writer, and, in a distinct postmodern twist, we see Christian writing the story as it unfolds. His closest friends, as in *La Bohème*, are artists of various types. In the film, the painter is Toulouse-Lautrec, who is an actual postimpressionist painter famous for his posters created for the Moulin Rouge, which can be seen in the background. Satine, the heroine, is a courtesan, a high-class female companion, and her role is similar to that of Violetta in another operatic classic, Verdi's *La Traviata* (1852). In keeping with the plots of both operas, Satine is ill and dies at the end. In nineteenth-century literature, women who had sexual relationships outside of marriage invariably suffered that fate.

Postmodernism can also be seen in the kaleidoscope of stunning visual effects, which effortlessly jump through time and space, and in the pastiche of music, most of which is borrowed from other sources. As in the traditional musical, songs are used either as part of an entertainment act or as a natural means of expression. Early in the film (14:30), at the Moulin Rouge, Satine performs "Diamonds Are a Girl's Best Friend" from *Gentlemen Prefer Blondes* (1953), a signature song for Carol Channing, but she inserts a passage from Madonna's hit, "Material Girl," from 1985. Later, Satine and Christian sing an intimate love duet (49:10) that includes Lennon and McCartney's "All You Need Is Love," Phil Collins's "One More Night," U2's "Pride (In the Name of

Love)," Jack Nitzsche's "Up Where We Belong," David Bowie's "Heroes," Dolly Parton's "I Will Always Love You," and the only original song in the film, David Baerwald's "Come What May."

Chicago

Unlike *Moulin Rouge*, *Chicago* is a film adaptation of a Broadway show. Its underlying theme seems to be an elaboration of a line from another musical by composer John Kander: "Life is a cabaret." Two women murderers use embellished versions of their sordid life stories to build successful entertainment careers. In the process, we learn that show business encompasses the media, the law, and indeed all of life. The film's most celebrated scene drives this message home, as lawyer Billy Flynn (Richard Gere) argues in the courtroom while dazzling us with tap dancing (1:30:25).

Figure 34.2 Courtroom razzle-dazzle in *Chicago*

Animation

Animated movies continue to be among the most successful and creative films in the new millennium. During the early 2000s, Disney produced a number of entertaining features, including two outstanding films, *Monsters, Inc.* (2001) and *Finding Nemo* (2003). Both were box-office successes, and both won Academy Awards for Best Animated Feature. Following the lead of *Toy Story*, neither film incorporates songs in the manner of a musical. Randy Newman created the score for *Monsters, Inc.*, for which he was nominated for Best Score and won the Best Song Oscar. The popular "If I Didn't Have You" does not appear in the narrative, but is sung during the closing credits. Elsewhere, Newman employs a variety of musical styles to support this fantasy. Especially noteworthy are the jazz-inspired cues. The amusing trombone and saxophone duet during the opening credits can be heard as representing the two characters in the story.

Finding Nemo

Finding Nemo (2003) became the top-grossing box-office winner in Disney's history. For this undersea story that begins near the Great Barrier Reef and ends near Sydney, Australia, Disney employed a musical sound that is strikingly different from its other animated films. Forgoing the typical melody-dominated score and even the standard theme song, composer Thomas Newman mixed a number of relatively subdued styles, ranging from somber passages that recall his score to *The Shawshank Redemption* to subtle sounds of rock. Much of the thematic material is repetitious, but Newman maintains variety through the changing timbres, as he utilizes a full range of instrumental colors. He also indulges in a number of musical jokes, the most striking of which is the use of the *Psycho* shower theme as the leitmotif for the terrifying little girl Darla (1:15:40). Like cousin Randy, Thomas received an Oscar nomination for Best Score.

Shrek and *Triplets*

Competing with the above Disney films for Best Animation awards were two creative features, *Shrek* (2001) and *The Triplets of Belleville* (2003). In *Shrek*, the wall-to-wall music of traditional animation is avoided, as the fantasy adventure is treated in a more dramatic fashion. Although limited, the underscoring still plays an important role in projecting the serious nature of the adventure. *Shrek*, aimed at older children and adults, also incorporates a number of rock and roll hits, highlighted by the final rendition of "I'm a Believer," performed by many unbelievable characters from fairy tales. While the film lost to *Monsters, Inc.* in the Academy Awards, it won a large following. The sequel *Shrek 2* (2004) is currently third on the all-time US Box-office list and another sequel is projected to appear in 2006.

Figure 34.3 Shrek's sidekick Donkey sings "I'm a Believer"

Disagreeing with the Academy, both the New York Film Critics Circle and the Los Angeles Film Critics Association gave awards to *The Triplets of Belleville* over *Finding Nemo* as the Best Animated Feature in 2003. This offbeat French film, which sparkles with quirky and irreverent humor, satirizes the influence of American culture on postwar France. The most visible manifestation of this pointed humor is the image of an obese Statue of Liberty with a hamburger held in her lower hand (34:15). The animation technique is also anti-Hollywood in style, and the muted principal characters are reminiscent of comic characters in the French films by Jacques Tati (see Chapter 17).

A variety of musical styles are employed in this film, either as underscoring or as source music. The Kyrie from Mozart's Mass in C Minor, K. 437, for example, accompanies Grandma Souza's stormy ocean trip on a paddleboat (32:30). This musical quotation is foreshadowed during several earlier cues, beginning with the ominous music accompanying the image of passing time (8:00). Elsewhere, divergent musical styles, including folk, Baroque, and modern, can be heard.

Ultimately, the jazz-inspired passages are the most distinctive of the score. The title of the film refers to three elderly sisters who are former vaudeville singers and who still perform at a local nightclub. Their opening toe-tapping rendition of "Belleville Rendez-Vous," aided by caricatures of Josephine Baker and Fred Astaire, establishes the energy and the bizarrerie of the film. Later, Souza joins the ladies in a jazz quartet performance that features a newspaper, refrigerator, vacuum cleaner, and the spokes of a bicycle wheel (55:40). Jazz is also used as underscoring, most notably in the thematic material representing the gangster bad guys. Canadian-French composer Benôit Charest created the score, which has become a great sensation in France, Canada, and the United States. In addition to composing the music, Charest is credited with playing the guitar, drums, piano, and vacuum cleaner.

Escapist Films

As many box-office analysts predicted, escapist films have fared well in the post-9/11 era. In seeking new heroes, Hollywood has turned to comics and to children's novels. These films have enjoyed considerable success.

Spider-Man

Created by Marvel Comics in August 1962, Spider-Man was an ideal hero for the 1960s—young, bright, creative, and misunderstood by adults. The timelessness of this teenage vision of the world is evidenced by the great box-office appeal of the web-slinger forty years later in both *Spider-Man* (2002) and *Spider-Man 2* (2004).

Principal themes

Example 34.1 Spider-Man

Example 34.2 Responsibility

Spider-Man is filled with action, humor, and romance. Danny Elfman's score supports each mood well, as he freely moves from the dark sounds of brass and wordless vocals to energized action music. The score is unified by several thematic ideas (Examples 34.1–2). The principal theme, representing Spider-Man, is a four-note motive played by the upper strings during the opening logo. A fuller theme, with a warm descending motion at the end, represents Peter's responsibility in possessing great power. It also suggests his relationship with his uncle and aunt.

Figure 34.4 Spider-Man and Mary Jane kiss

In addition, a subdued Love theme, which can be heard when Mary Jane kisses an upside-down Spider-Man (1:20:40), suggests Peter's love for her. At the end of the film, romance is put on hold, as Peter shoulders the responsibilities of his unique gifts. At this point, the Love theme gives way to the Responsibility theme played by a solo French horn; this instrument traditionally denotes heroes, and the solo suggests that he has chosen a lonely path.

The music for *Spider-Man 2* (2004) retains these principal themes and adds a more forceful antagonist theme (41:50). Doctor Octopus and his eight arms are represented by a dynamic dark melody that often mimics his powerful movement with strong musical accents. The Love theme is also scored more fully in the sequel, as the relationship between Peter and M. J. heats up. But at the end, the Spider-Man theme still dominates, as we, like M. J., are left watching the superhero chase yet another siren.

Harry Potter

Fantasy/adventure films have retained their general popularity in the twenty-first century. In addition to the success of the *Star Wars* prequels (Chapter 32), two new popular series of films have appeared, each based on a series of novels: *Harry Potter* and *The Lord of the Rings*. The *Harry Potter* phenomenon is recent. The author, J. K. Rowling, was a struggling English writer until her first novel, initially entitled *Harry Potter and the Philosopher's Stone*, was published in 1997. Within three years, Rowling earned over $400 million, and sales of her initial book and the first two sequels exceeded thirty million copies. By contrast, J. R. R. Tolkien has enchanted readers for over a half a century. An English professor specializing in Old and Middle English, Tolkien published *The Hobbit* in 1937 and the trilogy of novels *The Lord of the Rings* in 1954–55. While both series are read by young and old, *Harry Potter* is considered to be children's literature, and *The Lord of the Rings* is aimed at young adults. The difference in intent is reflected in both the movies and in the film music.

As of this writing, three Harry Potter films have appeared: *Harry Potter and the Sorcerer's Stone* (2001), *Harry Potter and the Chamber of Secrets* (2002), and *Harry Potter and the Prisoner of Azkaban* (2004). More are in the planning stages. The films have justifiably enjoyed great box-office success. They are well acted, have dazzling special effects, and have been faithful to the intent of the popular novels.

In creating the three Oscar nominated scores, John Williams might have modeled the music after *Star Wars*—after all, the stories do have some similarities. Both focus on the struggle between evil forces and an orphan boy who is destined for greatness. Thankfully, Williams chose to preserve the atmosphere of children's literature by evoking the musical style heard in films such as *Home Alone* and *Hook*. Distinctive to this character is the music box sound created by the celesta or by a synthesizer and the memorable and somewhat quirky melodic material.

Some of Williams's melodies are used as leitmotifs, while others are applied more loosely in the drama. The principal theme, which is heard during various magical scenes, has been given the title Hedwig, the name of Harry's white owl. While Hedwig has not played an active role in the films, evidence, including musical hints, suggests that the owl's watchful eye may become more prominent before the series is complete. Hedwig's extended song-like theme is in E minor and has numerous twists in its melodic contour. In its fullest form, it has two parts. The second, marked Hedwig B, can also be heard independently. Both are subject to variations of orchestration and rhythm.

Principal themes

Example 34.3 Hedwig

Example 34.4 Hedwig B

Example 34.5 Harry

Example 34.6 Parents

Example 34.7 Sorcerer's Stone (Tom Riddle)

A number of other prominent themes are shown here. The Harry theme is usually heard in moments of joy and triumph, while the Parents theme is clearly associated with Harry's mother and father. The darker themes include a three-note motive that symbolizes the sorcerer's stone in the first film and Tom Riddle in the second. While the music for the first two films share much of the same thematic material, the score for *The Prisoner of Azkaban* explores new timbres and styles, including several Renaissance-inspired cues and a frolicking jazz sound for the ride on the Knight bus (9:45).

Figure 34.5 Harry Potter with Hedwig

The *Lord of the Rings* Trilogy

Tolkien's *The Lord of the Rings* is an epic story that extends through three novels. Filmmaker Peter Jackson skillfully crafted a film based on each book:

The Lord of the Rings: The Fellowship of the Ring (2001)
The Lord of the Rings: The Two Towers (2002)
The Lord of the Rings: The Return of the King (2003)

The story is set in Middle-earth, a world invented by Tolkien, populated by hobbits, elves, dwarves, trolls, orcs (an enhanced species of goblin), men, and sorcerers. Much of the fascination of the story is its incorporation of details from medieval times, which gives the tale a mythical quality. Middle-earth, for example, is the actual Middle English term for the world, as they knew it. The books thus reflect one of the traditional themes of romanticism—returning to the mysterious, magical world of the Middle Ages. These stories contain a number of striking parallels to one of the greatest products of nineteenth-century romanticism, Wagner's *Der Ring des Nibelungen*.

As in Wagner's operatic cycle, *The Lord of the Rings* centers on a cursed ring. In the Tolkien tale, the evil Sauron forged an all-powerful ring in an earlier age. Both the ring, which has fallen into hobbit hands, and Sauron are once again regaining power, and they threaten to take over Middle-earth. The only way to defeat these evil forces is to destroy the ring where it was made, at Mount Doom in Mordor. This task falls to a young hobbit named Frodo, who is joined by a fellowship of eight others. At times, the episodic plotline resembles an extended video game, complete with leaps to safety and multiple levels of combat. Needless to say, sales of video games have created another lucrative resource for filmmakers.

Howard Shore's music for the three films invites comparisons to John Williams's scores for the *Star Wars* trilogy. The music for both of these mythical fantasies is monumental in scope and features wall-to-wall scoring, full symphonic coloring and numerous recurring themes. Yet, Shore has created a distinctive sound, which can partially be attributed to his extended use of voices, including both solo and choral forces.

The Fellowship of the Ring opens with the singing of Gregorian chant, a musical repertory that dates back to the earliest years of the Christian church. With this sound, Shore establishes the sense of mystery and magic of Tolkien's conception and provides an immediate aural link to the Middle Ages, just as the clothes and weapons of the humans and the gothic architecture later provide visual links. Also invoking the sound of the Middle Ages are the numerous chanting choral cues in the style of Orff's *Carmina Burana*, which are typically assigned to visions of the evil forces of Sauron. Among the other distinctive uses of voices are the moving laments at the apparent death of Gandalf (2:09:05, extended II/41:55) and the death of Boromir (2:38:55, extended II/1:23:05), the serene chanting accompanying our visions of Rivendell (1:16:05, extended I/1:26:35) and Lothlórien (2:13:10, extended II/47:45), and the hauntingly beautiful solo sung by Enya during the love scene of Aragorn and Arwen (1:24:55, extended I/1:35:55).

Shore's use of thematic material also differs from that of John Williams in *Star Wars*. In the latter, most of the principal characters have clearly defined themes. One can often tell who is on the screen by merely hearing the music. In *The Lord of the Rings*, Shore applies his themes more generally. The principal characters, including Frodo, Gandalf, and Aragorn, do not have individual themes. Frodo shares a Hobbit theme with his uncle Bilbo, his companions, and the Shire. Gandalf, along with the others who accompany Frodo, are represented by the single Fellowship theme. The King of Gondor theme will eventually be given to Aragorn, but the broader implications of the theme are that it belongs to the world of men in general.

In a way, the music reflects one of the remarkable aspects of this trilogy—the strength of its ensemble acting in which no single actor dominates. For all of the accolades that these three films received, there was only one Oscar nomination for acting: Ian McKellen, in the role of Gandalf, was nominated for Best Supporting Actor for his work in the first film of the trilogy. In the stunning eleven-Oscar sweep for *The Return of the King*, there were no nominations for acting.

The story of *The Lord of the Rings* centers on the struggle between good and evil. The forces of evil have a number of musical ideas, which tend to be short, repetitive,

Howard Shore (b. 1946)

Howard Shore was the music director for *Saturday Night Live* in the late 1970s. In the 1980s, he created a sensational synthesizer score for *Scanners* (1981) and provided music for a number of popular films in the decade. The piano jazz improvisation on "Heart and Soul" during the closing credits of *Big* is one of the most entertaining musical moments of the decade. Shore sustained a steady output of scores in the 1990s and won an Oscar the first time he was nominated, for *The Lord of the Rings: The Fellowship of the Ring*. He later won two Oscars for *The Lord of the Rings: The Return of the King*.

Important Film Scores

Scanners 1981
Big 1988
The Silence of the Lambs 1991 ★
Mrs. Doubtfire 1993
Philadelphia 1993
Ed Wood 1994
The Lord of the Rings: The Fellowship of the Ring 2001 ★ ♫
The Lord of the Rings: The Two Towers 2002
Gangs of New York 2002 ✉
The Lord of the Rings: The Return of the King 2003 ★ ♫ ♫
The Aviator 2004
The Twilight Saga: Eclipse (2010)
Hugo (2011) ✉
★ = Best Picture Oscar   ♫ = Best Music Oscar   ✉ = Music Oscar Nomination

and played by the low brass. The most powerful of these themes is the leitmotif given to the orcs (first heard at 1:04:50, extended I/1:15:10). This theme is set against a menacing rhythmic accompaniment that has a disturbing pattern of five beats in a measure. Played with clanging metal sounds that recall the anvils from underground Nibelheim in Wagner's *Ring* cycle, the pattern alternates three beats and two beats: 1 2 3 1 2. With the heavy accent on the first beat of each group, an awkward lopsided effect is created that suggests lumbering orcs. Against this intense rhythmic background, the low brass instruments play short melodic ideas. As shown in the Viewer Guide, the theme contains a long note that crescendos. This gesture, in which a lengthy note or chord gets louder, is heard throughout *The Fellowship of the Ring* and is used to represent a variety of moods, including danger and solemnity.

Sauron, the Lord of the Rings, is often represented by a harsh four-note theme, although this motive is applied to the land of Mordor as well. In one of Shore's most striking moments, this dark motive is transformed into a triumphant chorale when

Sauron and Mordor are destroyed in *The Lord of the Rings: The Return of the King* (2:46:30, extended II/1:27:25). By far the most beautiful of the themes representing evil is the Ring theme, a sinuous nine-note melody that seductively weaves in an out of the score. This theme is clearly related to the Sauron theme; the initial three notes of both themes are identical, and each concludes with a downward leap. The Black Riders who search for the ring on behalf of Sauron are given several themes, one of which resembles the *Dies irae*.

The three principal themes representing good, the Fellowship, the King of Gondor, and the Hobbit are also related in sound. The Fellowship and King of Gondor themes have the same modal character with a lowered leading tone. This quality, characteristic of music before 1600, once again links the musical sound of this film to the Middle Ages. Indeed the Fellowship theme begins and ends with a shift down to the lowered leading tone and back to the home pitch. You may recall a similar gesture at the beginning of *Ben-Hur*, where it also suggested the sound of an ancient time period. By contrast the Hobbit theme is in a modern key (D major), but it is related thematically to the Fellowship theme. In the latter, note the three-note motive beginning at the end of the second measure that establishes a rhythmic pattern: short–short–long. The pattern is heard three times in succession in this theme.

The Hobbit theme begins with the same three-note rhythmic idea, although it is slower. Part of the effect of this tune, especially when it is heard following the Fellowship theme, results from the raised third note, making the tune clearly in a major key, and the continued rise in the melodic contour. The resultant melody is warm, tender, and hymn-like. The Hobbit theme is subject to numerous variations, such as the sprightly solo violin version heard in the Shire (8:50, extended I/9:25).

Many of the above themes are heard in the Council of Elrond scene (see Viewer Guide). The sounds of evil dominate the beginning; dark chords, voices, a Black Rider theme, and the Sauron theme set an ominous mood for the council. In the extended DVD edition of the film, the Ring theme also makes an appearance. After Frodo volunteers to be the ring-bearer, the Fellowship theme swells forth, and the mood changes to optimism. Near the end of the scene, the Hobbit theme enters and provides its usual comic relief, as do the little characters themselves. The fellowship has now grown to nine, matching the number of Black Riders.

When Boromir addresses the council, a solo French horn, the instrument of heroes, intones the solemn King of Gondor theme. In contrast to the Fellowship theme, the King of Gondor theme is heard only briefly in the first two films of the trilogy. The melody finally achieves prominence in the last film, *The Return of the King* (2003). At the moment of Aragorn's crowning (2:53:45, extended II/1:35:35), a solo French horn once again plays the theme, recalling its initial appearance in the Elrond scene. Considering the length of the three wall-to-wall epic scores, it is remarkable that Shore has kept the music fresh through subtle thematic variations and avoiding the overuse of any single theme. When the King of Gondor theme soars in the last film, it sounds new, yet its seeds were carefully planted in the earlier films.

The Lord of the Rings: The Fellowship of the Ring: **The Council of Elrond**

Timing

1:26:30–1:33:25 (0:00 at studio logo); DVD Chapter 23
1:37:25–1:45:30 (Extended Edition); DVD Chapter I/27

Key Points

- Dark orchestration with use of brass instruments
- Appearance of numerous leitmotifs

Setting

The young hobbit Frodo (Elijah Wood) has completed his mission of delivering the powerful ring created by the evil Mordor to the land of the elves. Here, leaders representing various species, including man, debate what to do. The evil within the ring begins to work immediately on those who have gathered, and they begin to bicker. Seemingly, only the hobbit, in his simplicity and purity, can withstand the ring's seductive power.

Principal Leitmotifs

Example 34.8 Fellowship

Example 34.9 King of Gondor

Example 34.10 Hobbit

Example 34.11 Sauron

Example 34.12 Ring

Example 34.13 Orcs

PLOT	MUSIC
Elrond describes the seriousness of the situation.	Ominous low chords appear in the midst of his speech.
Frodo sets the ring on the central table.	Solemn chords are played with crescendos.
The group is taken aback by the appearance of the ring.	Voices and other mysterious sounds are added to the chords.
Boromir approaches to take the ring. As he reaches out, Gandalf speaks angrily in the evil language of Mordor. Gandalf defends his use of the words (this section is in the extended edition only).	The Ring theme sounds as Boromir talks of the ring. The music crescendos into the speaking voices.
Boromir argues that the ring can be useful in fighting Sauron.	A solo horn plays the King of Gondor theme.
Aragorn, the heir to the human throne, argues against Boromir. Boromir refuses to acknowledge Aragorn as king.	The King of Gondor theme continues. Dark chords return.
Elrond concludes that destroying the ring is the only choice. The dwarf Gimli tries to smash it with his ax, but fails.	The King of Gondor theme is played in the low strings.

Elrond tells the group that the ring, made in Mount Doom, must be destroyed there.	The Black Riders theme is joined by voices, suggesting the creation of the ring at Mount Doom.
Boromir talks of the impossibility of going to Mordor, and soon the group begins to argue violently.	Dark chords continue and get louder. As the argument begins, a quick pulse is established.
Frodo stares at the ring and hears voices. He decides to take it to Mordor.	Mixed with the dissonant background, Sauron's theme is stated twice. The orchestra crescendos as Frodo stands.
All become quiet when Frodo volunteers.	Solemn chords underscore the moment.
First Gandalf and then four others volunteer to accompany him.	The Fellowship theme appears. Voices sing the solemn chords as Boromir joins.
The other hobbits—Sam, Merry, and Pippen—volunteer as well, making nine for the fellowship of the Ring.	The Hobbit theme is played with the entrance of the three. The scene concludes with the Fellowship theme.

Trailer

It is fitting that our survey ends with a trilogy of films about a ring that recalls the great *Ring* cycle of Wagner. In a way, we have completed our own cycle. Over 130 years after the completion of the operatic masterpiece, Wagner's voice remains vibrant and strong, surviving fads, trends, and national crises. To be sure, the classic symphonic score has been just one of many musical voices in the one hundred and ten years of film history. The ever-changing styles of modern, popular, historical, and ethnic music have provided us with rich and varied sounds for our movies, as evident in the scores to recent films such as *Black Hawk Down*, *Kill Bill*, *Moulin Rouge*, and *The Triplets of Belleville*. Yet regardless of the style or length of the score, music remains an integral part of the filmmaking process—a process that still reflects Wagner's grand vision of the total artwork.

Important Names

Diane Warren   J. K. Rowling
Benôit Charest   J. R. R. Tolkien

Suggested Viewing

Science Fiction/Fantasy: *Artificial Intelligence: A.I.* (2001) ✉, *Donnie Darko* (2001), *Minority Report* (2002), *Signs* (2002), *Big Fish* (2003) ✉, *Batman Begins* (2005), *The Chronicles of Narnia: The Lion, the Witch, and the Wardrobe* (2005), and *Star Wars: Episode III—Revenge of the Sith* (2005)

Drama: *Far from Heaven* (2002) ✉, *The Hours* (2002) ✉, *Road to Perdition* (2002) ✉, *Million Dollar Baby* (2004) ★, *Sideways* (2004), *Brokeback Mountain* (2005) ♪, *Crash* (2005) ★, *Memoirs of a Geisha* (2005) ✉, and *Pride and Prejudice* (2005) ✉

Biopic: *Catch Me If You Can* (2002) ✉, *Seabiscuit* (2003), *The Aviator* (2004), *Finding Neverland* (2004) ♪, *Ray* (2004), *Capote* (2005), *Cinderella Man* (2005), and *Walk the Line* (2005)

Action/Thriller: *Insomnia* (2002), *The Last Samurai* (2003), *Munich* (2005) ✉, and *Sin City* (2005)

Comedy: *Amélie* (2001) and *Love Actually* (2003)

Animated: *Spirited Away* (2001), *The Incredibles* (2004), *Madagascar* (2005), and *Cars* (2006)

Selected Bibliography

Elements of Drama, Film, and Music

Barsam, Richard. *Looking at Movies*. New York: W. W. Norton & Company, 2004.

Boggs, Joseph M. *The Art of Watching Films*, 5th ed. New York: McGraw-Hill, 1999.

Cameron, Kenneth M., and Patti P. Gillespie. *The Enjoyment of Theater*, 5th ed. Boston: Allyn and Bacon, 2000.

Giannetti, Louis. *Understanding Movies*, 9th ed. Upper Saddle River, NJ: Prentice Hall, 2001.

Machlis, Joseph, and Kristine Forney. *The Enjoyment of Music*, 9th ed. New York: W. W. Norton & Company, 2003.

Film History

Cook, David A. *A History of Narrative Film*, 4th ed. New York: W. W. Norton & Company, 2004.

Harpole, Charles, ed. *History of American Cinema*, 10 vols. New York: Scribner's, 1990–2003.

Mast, Gerald, and Bruce F. Kawin. *A Short History of the Movies*, 7th ed. Boston: Allyn and Bacon, 2000.

Nowell-Smith, Geoffrey, ed. *The Oxford History of World Cinema*. New York: Oxford University Press, 1996.

Thompson, Kristin, and David Bordwell. *Film History: An Introduction*, 2nd ed. Boston: McGraw-Hill, 2003.

General Studies of Film Music

Brown, Royal S. *Overtones and Undertones: Reading Film Music*. Berkeley: University of California Press, 1994.

Burt, George. *The Art of Film Music*. Boston: Northeastern University Press, 1994.

Darby, William, and Jack Du Bois. *American Film Music: Major Composers, Techniques, Trends, 1915–90*. Jefferson, NC: McFarland & Company, 1990.

Gorbman, Claudia. *Unheard Melodies: Narrative Film Music*. Bloomington, IN: Indiana University Press, 1987.

Kalinak, Kathryn. *Settling the Score: Music and the Classical Hollywood Film*. Madison, WI: University of Wisconsin Press, 1992.

Karlin, Fred. *Listening to Movies: The Film Lover's Guide to Film Music*. New York: Schirmer Books, 1994.

MacDonald, Laurence E. *The Invisible Art of Film Music: A Comprehensive History*. New York: Ardsley House, 1998.

Marmorstein, Gary. *Hollywood Rhapsody: Movie Music and Its Makers, 1900 to 1975*. New York: Schirmer Books, 1997.

Palmer, Christopher. *The Composer in Hollywood*. New York: Marion Boyars, 1990.

Prendergast, Roy. *Film Music: A Neglected Art*, 2nd ed. New York: W. W. Norton & Company, 1992.

Thomas, Tony. *Music for the Movies*, 2nd ed. Los Angeles: Silman-James Press, 1997.

Timm, Larry M. *The Soul of Cinema*. Englewood Cliffs, NJ: Prentice Hall, 2003.

Reference Sources on Film Music

Bloom, Ken. *Hollywood Song: The Complete Film and Musical Companion*. New York: Facts on File, Inc., 1995.

Cooke, Mervyn. "Film Music," in *The New Grove Dictionary of Music and Musicians*, 2nd ed. London: Macmillan Publishing, 2001.

Craggs, Stewart R. *Soundtracks: An International Dictionary of Composers for Film*. Ashgate, England: Ashgate Publishing, 1998.

McCarty, Clifford. *Film Composers in America: A Filmography, 1911–1970*, 2nd ed. Oxford: Oxford University Press, 2000.

Stilwell, Robynn J. "Music in Films: A Critical Review of Literature, 1980–1996." *The Journal of Film Music*, I/1 (Summer 2002), 19–61.

Wagner and Film

Brockett, Oscar G., and Robert R. Findlay. *A History of European and American Theater and Drama since 1870*. Englewood Cliffs, NJ: Prentice Hall, 1973.

Collier, Jo Leslie. *From Wagner to Murnau: The Transposition of Romanticism from Stage to Screen*. Ann Arbor, MI: UMI Research Press, 1988.

Huckvale, David. "The Composing Machine: Wagner and Popular Culture," in *A Night at the Opera*, ed. Jeremy Tambling. London: John Libbey & Company, 1994, 113–143.

Paulin, Scott D. "Richard Wagner and the Fantasy of Cinematic Unity: The Idea of the *Gesamtkunstwerk* in the History and Theory of Film Music," in *Music and Cinema*, ed. James Buhler, Caryl Flinn, and David Neumeyer. Hanover, NH: Wesleyan University Press, 2000, 58–84.

Music for Silent Film

Altman, Rick. "The Living Nickelodeon," in *The Sounds of Early Cinema*, ed. Richard Abel and Rick Altman. Bloomington, IN: Indiana University Press, 2001, 232–240.
Marks, Martin Miller. *Music and the Silent Film; Contexts and Case Studies, 1895–1924*. New York: Oxford University Press, 1997.

Internet Sources

All Movie Guide. www.allmovie.com
Film Music on the Web. www.musicweb.uk.net/film/
The Internet Movie Database. www.imdb.com
Music and Moving Pictures. www.mailbase.ac.uk/lists/music-and-moving-pictures/

Glossary

a cappella: In choral music, without the accompaniment of instruments. The sound of an a cappella choir is associated primarily with music from the Renaissance.

adaptation: The borrowing of a substantial portion of an existing composition for use in a film score. The music should remain largely intact and recognizable, although it can be altered or adapted to suit the needs of the film. *Amadeus* has an adapted score based on music by Mozart.

American nationalism: A modern musical style associated with the concert works and film scores of Aaron Copland.

antagonist: The adversary in a drama who is in a conflict with the protagonist. Darth Vader is the antagonist in *Star Wars*.

arrangement: A new setting of a previously composed melody. Unlike an adaptation, in an arrangement the film composer borrows only the melody and creates a new accompaniment.

auteur: A director who molds all aspects of filmmaking into a unified and distinctive artistic style.

avant-garde: A term associated with experimental artistic styles, such as electronic music. The 1950s and 1960s saw the peak of avant-garde arts.

biopic: A film that presents a biography; a common film genre.

blockbuster: A film that costs an extraordinary amount of money to make with the hope of producing a major box-office success. *Titanic* (1997) is the most successful blockbuster hit, while *Cleopatra* (1963) is a blockbuster that failed.

cadence: A resting moment in music. The various types of cadences are analogous to punctuation marks in prose.

causal plot: A story in which each incident leads logically to the next with a clear cause-and-effect relationship. Most stories are told in this fashion.

chord: The simultaneous sounding of three or more pitches.

chorus: In performance, the term refers to a group of singers. In a solo song, the term designates the memorable portion of the tune that follows the verse.

chromatic: Using notes not found in the diatonic scales of the Western musical system. Chromatic melodies and harmonies can sound unstable, experimental, or exotic.

cinematography: The art of photography with moving pictures.

compilation score: A type of musical score, common in the silent film era, in which most of the music is borrowed from other sources.

concert composer: A term applied to composers who create music such as symphonies, string quartets, and cantatas, for performances in concert and opera houses.

conjunct: Moving primarily by small intervals, without large leaps, creating a smooth quality.

contrapuntal: The adjective form of the noun "counterpoint."

counterpoint: The art of combining two or more equal melodies together.

crosscut: See *cut*.

cut: The connection between two shots. There are three principal types of cuts. One is the narrative cut, in which our vision is focused on different objects or people in a continuous scene. A second type of cut joins different times (flashback or forward) or places. The third type is the crosscut, which moves quickly back and forth between two or more related events.

diegetic music: See *source music*.

dies irae: A well-known medieval chant from the Requiem Mass. It is frequently quoted in films to suggest death.

disjunct: Moving by wide intervals, often creating a disjointed character.

dissonance: The harmonic clash between pitches that creates tension. Sounds of unrest, e.g. intervals of seconds and sevenths; the opposite of consonance. In traditional music, dissonances resolve into consonances, creating a sense of closure. Expressionism is a musical style that remains dissonant throughout.

dubbing: The recording and synchronization of dialogue, singing, and sound effects during postproduction.

eclectic score: A musical score that contains a wide range of musical styles, typically rock music and one of the radical modern styles, such as avant-garde.

electronic music: Music created with the aid of electronic instruments that either manipulate existing sounds or generate new musical sounds through electronic means.

epic: A lengthy story that treats the achievements of an individual, region, or time period. In film, the term also suggests a lavish production featuring several well-known stars.

episodic plot: A story in which many of the incidents are loosely connected and are not the result of cause and effect. Such a plot often centers on a journey.

ethnic music: Music from non-Western regions, such as Asia, Africa, or the Middle East. In film music, a geographic area is often suggested by the use of instruments indigenous to the region.

expressionism: A movement in painting, literature, theater, music, and film that explores the dark regions of the subconscious mind. Common themes are nightmares, perversions, and insanity. *The Cabinet of Dr. Caligari* (1919) is the foremost example of the movement in film. In music, the term is most closely associated with Arnold Schoenberg, who created a style that is consistently dissonant.

feature film: In our context, any film over four reels in length. In modern filmmaking, a feature film can extend from ninety minutes to over three hours.

flashback: A cut backwards in time in a narrative film, often revealing something about the present. The inserted vision may be momentary, as if a character has a fleeting memory, or substantial in length—for example, the Paris montage in *Casablanca* (1942) and much of the story of *Titanic* (1997).

film noir: A term coined by French critics to denote a dark trend in American filmmaking beginning in the 1940s. Common features include strong dark shadows, nighttime urban settings, and dark, twisted plots. The term can be applied to a detective genre from this time as well.

flutter-tonguing: A performance technique in which the tongue is moved rapidly while air is blowing into the instrument. With brass instruments, the technique can create an agitated, horrific effect.

fugue and **fugal**: A fugue is a formal process from the Baroque era that develops one or more themes in imitative counterpoint. Full-length fugues are rare in film; passages that use this procedure are called fugal.

gamelan: An instrumental ensemble from Java or Bali consisting of a variety of percussion instruments, flutes, stringed instruments, and occasionally singers. The non-Western pitches and the repetitive performance style create a hypnotic character, often suggestive of Eastern philosophies.

genre: A general term denoting the category of film based on its plot, form, or content. Some standard genres are westerns, romances, and action/adventure films.

Gesamtkunstwerk: A German term coined by Richard Wagner meaning the "Total Artwork," the synthesis of all the arts in one theatrical conception. For Wagner, this idea was inherent in his music dramas. Today, we can see the principles in film.

glissando: A musical sound created by playing a series of adjacent notes together in a single quick gesture. Common on harps, pianos, and strings, this technique often creates a swooping effect.

Gregorian chant: Unaccompanied, monophonic liturgical chants, largely from the medieval era, created for use in the religious services of the Catholic Church. Chant is traditionally sung by males.

harmonics: A performance technique for string players, in which the basic sound is altered by lightly touching the string at certain designated spots. The resulting sound has a soft, ringing quality.

harmony: The element of music dealing with the sound of two or more simultaneous pitches.

homophonic: A term for musical texture dominated by a single melody with accompaniment. The texture is common in Western music in general, and especially in film music.

imitation: A type of contrapuntal texture in which two or more melodies are heard that are similar to each other. It is the basis of the fugue.

interval: The distance between two pitches. For additional information, see chapter 3.

jazz: The term, which has developed many implications since the 1920s, is largely associated with African-American musicians. Originally, it designated a performance style in which a given melody is subject to numerous improvisations. In the 1930s, sophisticated jazz bands, called big bands or swing bands, were created featuring saxophones, trumpets, trombones, and a rhythm section (piano, bass, and drums). In this style,

improvisation was more limited, and formal compositional techniques, such as orchestration, were more important.

key: In traditional Western harmony, the central or home pitch that governs the melodic and harmonic movement. If, for example, the home pitch is C, the music is considered to be in the key of C major or minor.

leading tone: In traditional Western harmony, the leading tone is the seventh and last note of the major and minor scales. Under normal circumstances, it possesses a harmonic tension that leads strongly to the home pitch of the scale.

leitmotif: A German term associated with Richard Wagner that designates a recurring theme linked with some aspect of a drama. The technique can be found in numerous film scores. Some of the most famous leitmotifs in film are the themes for Darth Vader (*The Empire Strikes Back*, 1980), the shark (*Jaws*, 1975), and Tara (*Gone With the Wind*, 1939).

linear plot: A story that is told in strict chronological sequence.

major and **minor**: The primary scales of traditional Western music. Each consists of seven pitches derived from a specific pattern of whole and half steps. Minor scales and harmonies are often used to create dark moods or reflect sad situations.

melody: The element of music that deals with the horizontal connection of pitches. Any group of notes that can be perceived as a unit is considered to be a melody.

meter: Recurring patterns of strong and weak pulses in music. Traditional Western music is generally organized into duple (two- or four-beat groupings) or triple (three-beat groupings) meters.

Mickey Mousing: A derogatory term for the mimicking of physical action in film music to such an extent as to suggest cartoon music—for example, creating musical accents for footsteps.

minimalism: A musical movement that achieved prominence in the 1970s, in which short melodic, harmonic, or rhythmic ideas are repeated with little variation. The style can be heard in such diverse films as *Halloween* (1978), *Kundun* (1997), and *American Beauty* (1999).

mise-en-scène: A theatrical term that refers to the visual elements of film. It encompasses aspects such as lighting, costumes, and décor, the relationship of these elements to each other, and how they are photographed.

modal: A term for a melody or a harmonic system that suggests music created before 1600 or music from other cultures. A distinctive element of a modal sound is the lowered leading tone.

monophonic: Characterized by a musical texture featuring a single melodic line with no accompaniment. It is commonly found in music from the medieval era and music of non-Western cultures.

montage: Originally a French term meaning editing, it now generally designates the relatively quick cutting of images that are related in some manner. It is effective in showing the passing of time or the frantic character of large action scenes.

motive: In music, a motive is a small melodic unit that is treated as a theme or used to build a larger melodic idea. The first movement of Beethoven's Symphony No. 5 is largely based on the famous four-note motive.

narrative film: A film that relates some type of story.

neoclassic: In all arts, the term designates a return to the principles of an earlier classical age.

neorealism: A movement in Italian filmmaking immediately following World War II that primarily used outdoor settings and non-actors.

Das neue Kino: The resurgence of film in West Germany beginning in the late 1960s.

New Wave cinema: An influential new approach to filmmaking in France beginning in 1959 that explored innovative plots and visual effects.

nickelodeon: In the early film era, a shop that was converted into a movie theater. The usual admission price was a nickel.

non-diegetic music: See *underscoring*.

nonlinear plot: A story that is told out of chronological order—for example, with flashbacks.

ondes martenot: An electronic instrument played with the aid of a keyboard. It can play only one pitch at a time, and has a variety of colors. It has been used in numerous film scores, most notably in Jarre's *Lawrence of Arabia* (1962).

orchestration: The act of assigning instruments or voices to the various musical ideas that have been created. A specialist in this task is called an orchestrator.

ostinato: A melodic, rhythmic, or harmonic idea that is repeated throughout a portion of a musical composition.

pan: Horizontal movement of the camera.

pedal: A long sustained pitch, generally in the lowest register.

phrase: A melodic unit.

pizzicato: A sound created by string instruments when the pitches are plucked with the fingers rather that played with a bow. The resultant sound is similar to that of a guitar.

plot: The order and structure of a story.

postmodernism: A movement in the arts that can be seen as a reaction against the modernistic values held during much of the twentieth century.

postproduction: The phase of filmmaking that occurs after the film has been shot.

protagonist: The principal character of a drama, around whom the plot and theme unfolds.

rhythm: The musical element that deals with the dimension of time. The term can refer to the relative length of notes, and it also encompasses the concept of meter.

running counter to the action: In film, the term describes the effect when the mood of the music contradicts the mood of the projected images or the plot.

serialism: In its most common use, the term is associated with a system developed by Arnold Schoenberg that ordered the twelve pitches of the Western musical system into a series that can be manipulated in a variety of ways. The sound of such music, like expressionistic music, tends to be totally dissonant.

soundtrack: Strictly speaking, this term designates all of the sound in a film, including dialogue, sound effects, and music. In its more general usage, it refers only to the musical portion of the sound, and sometimes just the popular songs in a given movie.

source music: Music that has a logical source within the narrative of the film, such as a radio, dance band, or jukebox. Also known as diegetic music, it can be thought of as a type of sound effect.

syncopation: Placing musical accents on weak beats or between beats of an established meter.

synthesizer: An electronic instrument capable of generating and reproducing sounds. Controlled by a keyboard, it is capable of imitating the sounds of acoustic instruments, replacing an entire orchestra, or creating unique new sounds. Vangelis won an Oscar for his synthesized score to *Chariots of Fire* (1981).

tempo: The speed of beats in a musical composition.

texture: The element of music dealing with the melodic lines and the combination of melodic lines in a composition. A single melody by itself is considered a monophonic texture, a dominant melody with accompaniment is called a homophonic texture, and a passage with two or more equal melodies is contra puntal.

theme: A recognizable melodic idea that recurs, thereby lending shape to a musical composition.

theremin: An electronic instrument that changes pitches as the player moves his hand closer or further from a central antenna. The instrument can be heard in Rózsa's scores to *The Lost Weekend* (1945) and *Spellbound* (1945) and Herrmann's *The Day the Earth Stood Still* (1951).

timbre: The element of music dealing with the colors or tone qualities produced by voices, instruments, and the various combinations of voices and instruments.

tritone: Also known as a diminished fifth or augmented fourth, this interval is considered to be the most unstable interval in traditional Western harmony.

underscoring: Music in film that does not emanate from a source seen (or implied) on the screen. It is also known as non-diegetic music.

Credits

(Film grabs are identified by: *Film title* (year), director, studio)

Figure 1.1: Archivo Iconografico, S. A./Corbis

Fig. 1.2: Jerry Cooke/Corbis

Fig. 1.3: Courtesy of the author

Fig. 1.4: *Pirates of the Caribbean: The Curse of the Black Pearl* (2003), Gore Verbinski, Disney Studios

Fig. 2.1: *Indiana Jones and the Temple of Doom* (1984), Steven Spielberg, Paramount Pictures

Fig. 2.2: *Annie Hall* (1977), Woody Allen, MGM/UA

Fig. 2.3: *Laura* (1944), Otto Preminger, Twentieth Century Fox

Fig. 2.4: *Lady in the Lake* (1947), Robert Montgomery, MGM/UA

Fig. 3.1: Hulton-Deutsch Collection/Corbis

Fig. 3.2: Bettmann/Corbis

Fig. 3.3: Michael Boys/Corbis

Fig. 4.1: *Steamboat Willie* (1928), Walt Disney and Ub Iwerks, Disney Studios

Viewer Guide Ch. 4 (p.45): *Gone With The Wind* (1939), Victor Fleming, MGM/UA

Fig. 5.1: Corbis

Fig. 5.2: Museum of Modern Art, Film Stills Archive

Fig. 5.3: *The Kiss* (1896), d. W. K. L. Dickson, The Edison Manufacturing Company

Fig. 5.4: Museum of Modern Art, Film Stills Archive

Fig. 5.5: Untitled experimental film (1894/1895), W. K. L. Dickson, The Edison Manufacturing Company

Fig. 5.6: *Departure from the Lumière Factory* (1894), Louis and Auguste Lumière

Fig. 5.7: Corbis

Fig. 5.8: *A Trip to the Moon* (1902), Georges Méliès

Fig. 5.9: *The Great Train Robbery* (1903), Edwin Porter, The Edison Manufacturing Company

Fig. 5.12: Museum of Modern Art, Film Stills Archive

Fig. 6.1: Hulton-Deutsch Collection/Corbis

Fig. 6.2: Theatre Historical Society of America, Elmhurst, IL. Ben Hall Collection

Fig. 6.3: courtesy of the author

Fig. 6.4: Corbis

Fig. 6.5: *L'Assassinat du Duc de Guise* (1908), André Calmettes and Charles Le Bargy, Film D'Art

Fig. 6.6: Les *Amours de la reine Élisabeth* (1912), Henri Desfontaines and Louis Mercanton, Film D'Art; released in the U. S. as Queen Elizabeth by Adolph Zukor.

Figs. 7.1, 7.2, 7.4, and Featured Film Ch. 7 (p.80): *The Birth of a Nation* (1915), D. W. Griffith

Fig. 7.3: courtesy of the author

Fig. 8.1: Theatre Historical Society of America, Elmhurst, IL. Ben Hall Collection

Fig. 8.2: Theatre Historical Society of America, Elmhurst, IL. Ben Hall Collection

Fig. 8.3: National Gallery, Oslo, Norway. (c) 2004 The Munch Museum/The Munch-Ellingsen Group/ Artists Rights Society (ARS), NY—Photo: Erich Lessing/Art Resource,

Fig. 8.4: *The Cabinet of Dr. Caligari* (1920), Robert Wiene, Decla-Bioskop (merged with UFA in 1921)

Fig. 8.5: *Battleship Potemkin* (1925), Sergei Eisenstein and Grigori Aleksnadrov

Fig. 8.6: *Napoléan* (1927), Abel Gance, Société Génerale des Films

Viewer Guide Ch. 9 (p.99): *Don Juan* (1926), Alan Crosland, MGM/UA

Fig. 9.1: Edison National Historic Site, National Park Service

Fig. 9.2: Museum of Modern Art, Film Stills Archive

Fig. 9.3: Bettmann/Corbis

Viewer Guide Ch. 9 (p.103): *The Jazz Singer* (1927), Alan Crosland, Warner Bros. Studio

Fig. 9.4: *Sunrise: A Song of Two Humans* (1927), F. W. Murnau, Twentieth Century Fox

Fig. 9.5: *City Lights* (1931), Charles Chaplin, Twentieth Century Fox

Fig. 10.1: *Blackmail* (1929), Alfred Hitchcock, British International Pictures

Fig. 10.2: *Hallelujah* (1929), King Vidor, Warner Bros. Studio

Fig. 10.3: *Blue Angel* (1930), Joseph von Sternberg, UFA

Fig. 10.4: *The Hollywood Review of 1929* (1929), Charles Reisner, MGM/UA

Fig. 10.5: 42nd Street (1933), Busby Berkeley, Warner Bros. Studio

Fig. 10.6: *Steamboat Willie* (1928), Walt Disney and Ub Iwerks, Disney Studios

Fig. 11.1: *Mutiny on the Bounty* (1935), Frank Llyod, Warner Bros. Studio

Fig. 11.2: *The Informer* (1935), John Ford, RKO Pictures

Viewer Guide Ch. 11 (p. 130): *The Bride of Frankenstein* (1935), James Whale, Universal Studios

Viewer Guide Ch. 11 (p. 135): *The Adventures of Robin Hood* (1938), Michael Curtiz and William Keighley, Warner Bros. Studio

Fig. 11.3: *Snow White and the Seven Dwarfs* (1939), Walt Disney, Disney Studios

Fig. 12.1: *Mr. Smith Goes to Washington* (1939), Frank Capra, Columbia Pictures

Fig. 12.2: *Stagecoach* (1939), John Ford, Warner Bros. Studio

Viewer Guide Ch. 12 (p.145): *Wuthering Heights* (1939), William Wyler, MGM/UA

Fig. 12.3: *The Wizard of OZ* (1939), Victor Fleming, MGM/UA

Fig. 12.4: *Gone With The Wind* (1939), Victor Fleming, MGM/UA

Fig. 13.1: *Alexander Nevsky* (1938), Sergei Eisenstein and Dmitri Vasilyev

Figs. 13.2, 13.3, 13.4, 13.5, and Viewer Guide Ch.13 (p.163): *Citizen Kane* (1940), Orson Welles, RKO Pictures

Figs. 14.1–14.4, and Featured Film Ch.14 (p.172): *Casablanca* (1940), Michael Curtiz, Warner Bros. Studio

Fig. 15.1: *Laura* (1944), Otto Preminger, Twentieth Century Fox

Fig. 15.2: *The Lost Weekend* (1945), Billy Wilder, Universal Studios

Fig. 15.3: *Spellbound* (1945), Alfred Hitchcock, Selznick International Pictures

Fig. 15.4 and Viewer Guide Ch.15 (p.189): *The Best Years of Our Lives* (1946), William Wyler, MGM/UA

Fig. 15.5: *The Red Shoes* (1948), Michael Powell and Emeric Pressburger, Paramount Pictures

Fig. 16.1: Courtesy of www.tvhistory.tv

Fig. 16.2: Schenectady Museum; Hall of Electrical History Foundation/Corbis

Fig. 16.3: Bettmann/Corbis

Fig. 16.4: *A Streetcar Named Desire* (1951), Elia Kazan, Warner Bros. Studio

Fig. 16.5 and Viewer Guide Ch.16 (p.204): *High Noon* (1952), Fred Zinnemann, Republic Studios

Fig. 16.6: *Singin' in the Rain* (1952), Stanley Donen and Gene Kelly, MGM/UA

Fig. 17.1: *Sunset Boulevard* (1950), Billy Wilder, Paramount Pictures

Fig. 17.2: *A Place in the Sun* (1951), George Stevens, Paramount Pictures

Viewer Guide Ch.17 (p.216): *On the Waterfront* (1954), Elia Kazan, Columbia Pictures

Fig. 17.3: *Rebel Without a Cause* (1955), Nicholas Ray, Warner Bros. Studio

Fig. 17.4: *Forbidden Planet* (1956), Fred M. Wilcox, Warner Bros. Studio

Fig. 18.1: *Around the World in 80 Days* (1956), Michael Anderson, Warner Bros. Studio

Fig. 18.2: *Some Like it Hot* (1959), Billy Wilder, MGM/UA

Fig. 18.3 and Viewer Guide Ch.18 (p.230): *Touch of Evil* (1958), Orson Welles, Universal Studios

Fig. 18.4: *Vertigo* (1958), Alfred Hitchcock, Universal Studios

Fig. 18.5: *North by Northwest* (1959), Alfred Hitchcock, Warner Bros. Studio

Fig. 18.6: *The Seventh Seal* (1957), Ingmar Bergman

Fig. 19.1: *The Ten Commandments* (1956), Cecil B. DeMille, Paramount Pictures

Figs. 19.2, 19.3, 19.4, and Featured Film Ch.19 (p.246): *Ben Hur* (1959), William Wyler, Warner Bros. Studio

Fig. 20.1: Musee National d'Art Moderne, Centre Georges Pompidou. (c) 2004 The Pollock-Krasner Foundation/Artists Rights Society (ARS), NY. Photo: (c) CNAC MNAM/ Dist. Réunion des Musées Nationaux/Art Resource, NY

Fig. 20.2: *The 400 Blows* (1959), François Truffaut

Figs. 20.3, 20.4, 20.5, and Featured Film Ch.20 (p.266): *Psycho* (1960), Alfred Hitchcock, Universal Studios

Fig. 21.1 and Viewer Guide Ch.21 (p.275): *Lawrence of Arabia* (1962), David Lean, Columbia Pictures

Fig. 21.2: Bettmann/Corbis

Fig. 21.3: *The Magnificent Seven* (1960), John Sturges, MGM/UA

Fig. 21.4: *The Pink Panther* (1963), Blake Edwards, MGM/UA

Fig. 21.5: Photofest

Fig. 21.6: *West Side Story* (1961), Robert Wise and Jerome Robbins, MGM/UA

Fig. 22.1: *The Hustler* (1961), Robert Rossen, Twentieth Century Fox

Fig. 22.2: *The Manchurian Candidate* (1962), John Frankenheimer, MGM/UA

Fig. 22.3 and Viewer Guide Ch.22 (p.290): *To Kill a Mockingbird* (1962), d. Robert Mulligan, Universal Studios

Fig. 22.4: *The Graduate* (1967), Mike Nichols, MGM/UA

Fig. 22.5: *The Good, the Bad, and the Ugly,* (1966-67), Sergio Leone, MGM/UA

Fig. 23.1: *The Planet of the Apes* (1968), Franklin J. Schaffner, Twentieth Century Fox

Fig. 23.2: *Midnight Cowboy* (1969), John Schlesinger, MGM/UA

Fig. 23.3: *Easy Rider* (1969), Dennis Hopper, Columbia Pictures

Fig. 23.4: *2001: A Space Odyssey* (1968), Stanley Kubrick, MGM/UA

Fig. 23.5 and Viewer Guide Ch.23 (p.308): *The Godfather* (1972), Francis Ford Coppola, Paramount Pictures

Fig. 24.1: *Taxi Driver* (1976), Martin Scorsese, Columbia Pictures

Viewer Guide Ch.24 (p.317): *Chinatown* (1974), Roman Polanski, Paramount Pictures

Fig. 24.2: Courtesy John Edward Hasse

Fig. 24.3: *Rocky* (1976), John G. Avildsen, MGM/UA

Fig. 24.4: *Jaws* (1975), Steven Spielberg, Universal Studios

Figs. 25.1, 25.2, and 25.3: *Star Wars* (1977), George Lucas, Twentieth Century Fox

Viewer Guide Ch.25 (p.334): *The Empire Strikes Back* (1980), Irvin Kershner, Twentieth Century Fox

Fig. 25.4: *Return of the Jedi* (1983), Richard Marquand, Twentieth Century Fox

Fig. 25.5: *Superman: The Movie* (1978), Richard Donner, Warner Bros. Studio

Figs. 26.1, 26.2, 26.3, 26.4, 26.5, and Featured Film Ch.26 (p.348): *E. T. the Extra-Terrestrial* (1982), Steven Spielberg, Universal Studios

Fig. 27.1: Bettmann/Corbis

Fig. 27.2: Courtesy the author

Fig. 27.3: *Halloween* (1978), John Carpenter, Compass International

Fig. 27.4: *Apocalypse Now* (1979), Francis Ford Coppola, Paramount Pictures

Fig. 27.5: *The Shining* (1980), Stanley Kubrick, Warner Bros. Studio

Fig. 27.6: *Excalibur* (1981), John Boorman, Warner Bros. Studio

Fig. 27.7: Bettmann/Corbis

Fig. 27.8: Archivo Iconografico, S.A./Corbis

Viewer Guide Ch.27 (p.366): *Amadeus* (1984), Milos Forman, Warner Bros. Studio

Fig. 28.1: AFP/Getty Images

Fig. 28.2: *Gandhi* (1982), Richard Attenborough, Columbia Pictures

Fig. 28.3: Stapleton Collection/Corbis

Fig. 28.4: Stapleton Collection/Corbis

Fig. 28.5: *The Last Emperor* (1987), Bernardo Bertulucci, Columbia Pictures

Fig. 28.6: Michael Freeman/Corbis

Fig. 28.7 and Viewer Guide Ch.28 (p.374): *The Mission* (1986), Roland Joffé, Warner Bros. Studio

Fig. 28.8: *The Natural* (1984), Barry Levinson, Columbia Pictures

Fig. 29.1: *Ghostbuster* (1984), Ivan Reitman, Columbia Pictures

Fig. 29.2: *Who Framed Roger Rabbit* (1988), Robert Zemeckis, Disney Studios

Fig. 29.3: *Die Hard* (1988), John McTiernan, Twentieth Century Fox

Fig. 29.4: *Witness* (1985), Peter Weir, Paramount Pictures

Viewer Guide Ch.29 (p.391): *Rain Man* (1988), Barry Levinson, MGM/UA

Fig. 30.1: *Batman* (1989), Tim Burton, Warner Bros. Studio

Fig. 30.2: *Jurassic Park* (1993), Steven Spielberg, Universal Studios

Viewer Guide Ch.30 (p.404): *The Last of the Mohicans* (1992), Michael Mann, Twentieth Century Fox·

Fig. 30.3: *Braveheart* (1995), Mel Gibson, Paramount Pictures

Fig. 30.4: *Home Alone* (1990), Chris Columbus, Twentieth Century Fox

Fig. 31.1: *Beauty and the Beast* (1991), Gary Trousdale and Kirk Wise, Disney Studios

Fig. 31.2: *Mo' Better Blues* (1990), Spike Lee, Universal Studios

Fig. 31.3: *Pulp Fiction* (1994), Quentin Tarantino, Miramax

Fig. 31.4: *Silence of the Lambs* (1991), Jonathan Demme, MGM/UA

Viewer Guide Ch. 31 (p.425): *The Shawshank Redemption* (1994), Frank Darabont, Castle Rock Entertainment

Fig. 32.1: *Titanic* (1997), James Cameron, Paramount Pictures

Fig. 32.2: *Shakespeare in Love* (1998), John Madden, Miramax

Fig. 32.3: *American Beauty* (1999), Sam Mendes, Dreamworks SKG

Fig. 32.4: *The Matrix* (1999), Andy and Larry Wachowski, Warner Bros. Studio

Viewer Guide Ch.32 (p.437): *Run, Lola, Run* (2001), Tom Tykwer, Columbia/Tristar

Fig. 32.5: *Star Wars Episode I: The Phantom Menace* (1999), George Lucas, Twentieth Century Fox

Fig. 33.1: *Kundun* (1997), Martin Scorsese, Touchstone Pictures

Fig. 33.2: *Crouching Tiger, Hidden Dragon* (2000), Ang Lee, Columbia/Tristar

Fig. 33.3: Fundacion Dolores Olmedo, Mexico City, D.F. (c) Banco de Mexico Trust. Photo: Schalkwijk/Art Resource, NY

Figs. 33.4, 33.5, 33.6, and Featured Film Ch.33 (p.450): *The Red Violin* (2001), François Girard, Universal Studios

Fig. 34.1: *Moulin Rouge* (2001), Baz Luhrmann, Twentieth Century Fox

Fig. 34.2: *Chicago* (2002), Rob Marshall, Miramax

Fig. 34.3: *Shrek* (2001), d. Andrew Adamson and Vicky Jenson, Dreamworks SKG

Fig. 34.4: *Spider-man* (2002), Sam Raimi, Columbia/Tristar

Fig. 34.5: *Harry Potter and the Sorcerer's Stone* (2001), Chris Columbus, Warner Bros. Studio

Viewer Guide Ch.34 (p.473): *The Lord of the Rings: The Fellowship of the Ring* (2000), Peter Jackson, New Line Cinema

Index

on Atticus Finch character, 288
on *Godfather*, 306
on Hopkins as villain, 422
on *Lawrence of Arabia*, 273
and 1939 films, 141
and 1960s musicals, 282
on *Raging Bull*, 377
on *Some Like It Hot*, 227
American films, ascent of, 64
American Graffiti, 313, 319, 323
American nationalism, 157–58, 186–92, 209, 213–15, 232
and *Magnificent Seven*, 278
and Williams, 331
American in Paris, An, 195, 197, 207, 282
American in Paris, An (Gershwin symphonic poem), 207
American Psycho, 399
Amfitheatrof, Daniele, 211
Amistad, 441
Amityville Horror, The, 305
"Among My Souvenirs," 187
Amram, David, 287
Anastasia, 423
Anatomy of a Murder, 223, 226–27, 228, 286, 292, 420
ancient Greece, music of (*Quo Vadis*), 238
Andersen, Hans Christian, 414
Andrews, Dana, 189
Andrews Sisters, 206
Andromaque (Racine), 70
Animal House, 288
Animals in Motion (Muybridge), 52
animated films, 137–39, 413–17, 464–466
see also at Disney
Annie, 293
Annie Get Your Gun, 227
Annie Hall, 368, 377
antagonist, 13
anthologies, 68–69
Anthony Adverse, 132, 133, 139
antihero, Michael Corleone as, 306
Antonioni, Michelangelo, 261
Apartment, The, 227, 283
Apocalypse Now, 7, 15, 323, 357, 361–62, 377
Apollo 13, 401, 412, 432
Appalachian Spring (Copland), 4, 5, 157
"April Come She Will," 294

Aristotle, 4, 11
Arlen, Harold, 146, 148
Armstrong, Louis, 286
Armstrong, Robert, 119
Arnold, Malcolm, 225, 273
Around the World in 80 Days, 223, 224–25
music and locale in, 42, 370
theme song in, 201, 224, 226
and Young, 225
"Around the World in 80 Days" (tune), 224
arrangements, 38
in *Birth of a Nation*, 77–78
Arrival of a Train at La Ciotat Station, The, 56
Artificial Intelligence: A.I., 293, 340, 475
artwork, total, 4, 105
see also Wagner, Richard
As Good as It Gets, 390, 441
Asphalt Jungle, 185, 213, 222
Assassinat du Duc de Guise, L', 63, 70, 73
Astaire, Fred, 137, 361
caricature of in *Triplets of Belleville*, 465
Astaire-Rogers musicals, 122
"As Time Goes By," 38, 169, 170, 171, 172, 175, 176, 177
Atlantis: The Lost Empire, 416
Atmospheres (Ligeti), 302
Attack of the Clones (Star Wars: Episode II), 340, 429, 439, 440–41
aulos, 238
"Auprès de ma blond," 224
Auric, Georges, 193, 221
Australia, films from, 411
auteur, 6, 260
Griffith as, 64
Autry, Gene, 137
Autumn Sonata, 379
"Avalon," 173, 175
Avalon, Frankie, 281
avant-garde films, 434–35
avant-garde music, 209, 220–21, 325
in *Chinatown*, 316, 317
and *E.T.*, 345, 349
in *The Mission*, 372
in *One Flew Over the Cuckoo's Nest*, 314
Ave Maria (motet), 372, 374, 375
"Ave Maria" (Schubert), 129
Aviator, The, 377

Khatchaturian, Aram, 273, 302

Kieslowski, Krzysztof, 410

Kill Bill, 462–63, 475

Kill Bill: Vol. 1, 459

Kill Bill: Vol. 2, 459, 462

Killers, The, 184, 185, 195

Kinetophone, 51, 55, 61

Kinetoscope, 51, 53, 54–55

King, Martin Luther Jr., assassination of, 299

Kingdom of the Fairies, 57

King of Kings, The, 92, 106, 192, 271, 283

King Kong, 3, 111, 112, 117–21, 123, 150

    as classic, 260

    and *Jurassic Park*, 401

    as RKO production, 122

Kingsley, Gershon, 359

Kings of the Road, 325

Kings Row, 133, 165

Kinobibliothek (*Kinothek*), 69

Kiss, The, 54

"Kiss the Girl," 415

Kiss Me Deadly, 222

klezmer, 407

"Knock on Wood," 169, 170, 173, 174

Koncz, Christoph, 450

Kool & the Gang, 422

Korda, Alexander, 185

Korngold, Erich, 125, 132, 133

    and *Adventures of Robin Hood*, 132, 134

    and classical film score, 141

    as foreign-born, 459

    and Friedhofer, 188

    and Wagner, 3, 133

    and Warner Bros., 122

    and Williams, 331

Korngold, Julius, 133

Kosma, Joseph, 154

Koyaanisqatsi, 444

Kraft Theatre television series, 340

Kramer vs. Kramer, 362

Kubrick, Stanley, 293

    A Clockwork Orange, 31, 303

    Dr. Strangelove, 293, 303

    Eyes Wide Shut, 301

    and future trends, 310

    The Shining, 363

    and synthesizer (*Clockwork Orange*), 359

    2001, a Space Odyssey, 200, 300, 302

Kundun, 377, 443, 444

Kurosawa, Akira, 14, 197, 221, 277, 278, 295

Lanchbery, John, 79

L.A. Confidential, 316, 441

La dolce vita, 234, 307

Lady in the Lake, 17, 18

Lady from Shanghai, 195

Lady and the Tramp, 138, 208

Lagaan: Once Upon a Time in India, 460

Lai, Francis, 295

Lanchester, Elsa, 130

Landmarks of Early Films, 62

Lang, Fritz, 91, 92

Lantz, Walter, 116

Lasky, Jesse, 66, 92, 192

Last Action Hero, 385

Last Emperor, The, 369, 371, 379

    and *The Red Violin*, 449

Last Laugh, The, 69, 92

Last Metro, The, 379

Last of the Mohicans, The, 14, 397, 402, 403–6

Last Samurai, The, 390

Last Temptation of Christ, The, 377

Last Year at Marienbad, 259

Laugh-O-Grams, 138

Laughton, Charles, 126

Laura, 17, 43, 181, 183–84, 199, 292

    as film noir, 182

Laurenzi, Anita, 450

Lawrence, T. E., 273

Lawrence of Arabia, 31, 271, 272, 273–77, 277, 293, 296, 333, 370

layered effect, 107

League of Their Own, A, 390

Lean, David, 225, 273, 277, 292–93

Leaving Las Vegas, 427

Lee, Bill, 419, 420

Lee, Harper, 288

Lee, Spike, 418–19, 420, 461

Legend of 1900, The, 373, 434

Legends of the Fall, 32

mood, 15, 41

Moog, Robert, 359

Moog Synthesizer, 303, 359

    see also synthesizer

"Moon River," 279

Moorehead, Agnes, 163

More Treasures from American Film Archives, 1894–1931, 62, 73

Morocco, 123

Moroder, Giorgio, 338, 358, 359, 388

Moross, Jerome, 232, 278

Morricone, Andrea, 379, 462

Morricone, Ennio, 28, 295–96, 372, 373, 376, 379

Morrison, Jim, 361

Morte Darthur, Le (Malory), 363

Mother Courage and Her Children (Brecht play), 212

Mother India (Bharati Mata), 235

"Mother of Mine," 102

Motion Picture Association of America, 301

Motion Picture Moods for Pianists and Organists, 69, 90

Motion Picture Patents Company, 53, 434

Motion Picture Piano Music: Descriptive Music to Fit the Action, Character, or Scene of Moving Pictures, 68–69

Motion Picture Producers and Distributors of America, Inc., 149

motive, 24, 71

    in *American Beauty*, 433

    in *Batman*, 400

    in *Ben-Hur*, 241–42, 244, 245, 246–47, 251, 255

    in *Best Years of Our Lives*, 188, 190

    in *Bride of Frankenstein*, 128, 129, 131, 132

    in *Citizen Kane*, 161, 162, 164

    in *E.T.*, 347

    in *Hamlet*, 194

    in Harry Potter films, 469

    in *High Noon*, 203, 205

    in *Psycho*, 264, 265

    in *Silence of the Lambs*, 422

    in *To Kill a Mockingbird*, 289, 291

    in *Touch of Evil*, 230

Motown, 383

Moulin Rouge, 459, 463–64, 475

"movie palaces," 88

Movietone sound system, 104, 122

Moving Picture World (publication), 60

Mozart, Wolfgang Amadeus, 68, 77

    Marriage of Figaro, 424

Mass in C Minor, 465

Mass In G (Gloria), 81, 86

    in *Out of Africa*, 372

    in *Rules of the Game*, 154

Mr. Deeds Goes to Town, 193

Mr. Holland's Opus, 385, 412

Mr. Hulot's Holiday, 221

Mr. Lucky television series, 231

"Mr. Sandman," 384

Mrs. Doubtfire, 471

Mrs. Miniver, 147, 165, 193

Mr. Smith Goes to Washington, 141, 142, 143, 148, 193, 202

"Mrs. Robinson," 294

MTV, 388

Mulan, 316, 416, 441

Mulholland, William, 315

Mummy, The, 316

Munch, Edvard, 93

Muppets, 413

Murder, My Sweet, 182, 195

Murder on the Orient Express, 325

Murnau, F. W., 91, 92, 104, 106, 212

Murphy, Eddie, 382

music, elements of, 21

    harmony, 25–27

    melody, 23–25

    notation, 22–23

    texture, 25

music, types of for silent films, 61

musical accompaniment, 59, 65, 67

    in 1920s, 87–89

musical comedy (musicals), 114–15, 134, 137, 139, 206–7, 281–82

musical unity, 43–44

music anthologies, 65

Music in Film: National Public Radio Milestones of the Millenium (1 CD), xiii

music for films, *see* film music

"Music Popularity Chart," 206

Music for Strings, Percussion, and Celesta, (Bartok), 363

music videos, 281

Mussolini, Benito, 71–72

Mussorgsky, Modest, 148

mute, 30

Mutiny on the Bounty (1935), 125, 126–27, 147

Muybridge, Eadweard, 51, 52–54

"My Darling Clementine," 142
My Fair Lady, 282, 296
"My Gal Sal," 102
"My Heart Will Go On," 432
My Left Foot, 412
"My Mammy," 102, 103, 104
My Uncle, 221
"My Way," 421

Naked Prey, The, 32, 320
Name of the Rose, The, 40, 432
Napoléon, 87, 88, 95–96
narrative film, 11, 57–60
    live music with, 61
National Film Preservation Foundation, 62
nationalism, American, 157–58, 186–92, 232
    and *Magnificent Seven*, 278
    and Williams, 331
national schools, 156
National Velvet, 147
Native American stereotype, 143
Natural, The, 369, 378
Natural Born Killers, 377
NBC, 198
"Nearer My God to Thee," 432
Neeson, Liam, 374, 406
Neil, Fred, 300
neoclassicism, 330
neo-film noir, 316
neorealism, 194
Network, 325
neue Kino, Das, 324–25
Never on Sunday, 295
"Never on Sunday," 294
New Babylon, The, 87, 95
Newman, Alfred, 122, 125, 143, 144
    and *David and Bathsheba*, 238
    and Friedhofer, 188
    and *Grapes of Wrath*, 182
    and *How the West Was Won*, 223
    and Oscars, 144, 414
    and *The Robe*, 237–38, 238, 239
    and *Wuthering Heights*, 143–44, 145
Newman, David, 144, 423

Newman, Emil, 144
Newman, Lionel, 122, 144
Newman, Randy, 144, 378–79, 416, 464
Newman, Thomas, 144, 359, 416, 423, 424, 433, 464–65
"New Music" concerts, 259
New Wave cinema, 260–61, 285
    and Delerue, 295, 362
    and *Psycho*, 262, 263
Niblo, Fred, 240
Nicholas Nickleby, 436
Nichols, Mike, 18, 293
Nicholson, Jack, 293, 314, 317, 363
nickelodeons, 51, 59, 61
Night on Bald Mountain (Mussorgsky), 148
Night Gallery (television series), 323
Night of the Hunter, 222
Nightmare Before Christmas, The, 399, 412
Nightmare on Elm Street, A, 330
Night at the Opera, A, 139, 147
Nights of Cabiria, 234, 307
9/11 events, 461
1960s, 259, 299
    and *Spider-Man*, 466
Ninotchka, 152
Nitzsche, Jack, 314, 464
Nixon, 377, 401
Nixon, Richard M., 313
Noble, Ray, 173
Noche de los mayas, La, 153, 156
Nogaard, Per, 379
Noguchi, Isamu, 4
Nolan, Christopher, 18
non-diegetic music, 37
    see also underscoring
nonfiction films, 16
nonlinear plot, 13, 18
Nordgren, Erik, 235
Nordhoff, Charles, 126
Norma (Bellini), 77
Norma Rae, 368
North, Alex, xiv, 199, 200, 213, 272, 302
North by Northwest, 158, 193, 223, 232, 233–34
Northwest Mounted Police, 225
Northwest Passage, 92, 147
Nosferatu, 7, 88, 91, 92, 96, 106

Porter, Cole, 137, 173

Portman, Rachel, 435, 436

Poseidon Adventure, The, 108, 322, 340

Postino, Il, 411

postmodern critics, x

postmodernism, 325, 329

    in *Ghostbusters*, 382

    of *Moulin Rouge*, 463

    and popular arts, 443

    in *Run Lola Run*, 437

    Who Framed Roger Rabbit as, 384, 385

postproduction, 18

postromantic music style, 39, 39–40, 44, 153

    in *Star Wars*, 331

    and Wagner, 8

Potente, Franka, 437

Pound, Ezra, 259

Powaqqatsi, 444

"Power of Love," 384

Preisner, Zbigniew, 410

Prelude to the Afternoon of a Faun (Debussy), 93

Preludes, Les (Liszt), 106

Preminger, Otto, 183, 228, 292

Prendergast, Roy, x, xi

Presley, Elvis, 192, 206, 281, 418

Pretty Woman, 427

Previn, Charles, 122

Pride and Prejudice, 165

Pride of the Yankees, The, 165, 192

"Pride (In the Name of Love)," 463–64

Prince of Egypt, The, 390, 441

Princess Bride, The, 393

Prisoner of Zenda, The, 71, 144

Private Benjamin, 321

Private Life of Henry VIII, 123

Prokofiev, Sergei, 28, 33, 155, 155–56, 315

protagonist, 13

Psycho, 259, 262–70, 285

    dissonance in, 26, 263

    and *Finding Nemo*, 464

    and Herrmann, 158

    and Hitchcock, 193

    homophonic texture in, 25

    and mood, 15, 41, 263, 286

    string instruments in, 28, 43, 263

Public Enemy, The, 113, 123

Puccini, Giacomo, 133, 463

Pulp Fiction, 43, 413, 421–22, 462

Purcell, Henry, 362

Purple Rain, 393

Puzo, Mario, 306

Queen Elizabeth, 63, 66, 70–71, 71

"Que Será, Será," 201

Quiet Man, The, 193, 208, 225

    in *E.T.*, 346, 352

Quiet Revolution, The, 333

Quo Vadis, 185, 237, 238

Rachmaninov, Sergei, 40

    Piano Concerto No. 3, 411

Racine, Jean, 70

racism, 76, 420

radio, 111

Radio City Music Hall, 88

Raging Bull, 368, 377

"Rags to Riches," 421

Ragtime, 368, 378, 420

Raiders of the Lost Ark, 329, 330, 338, 339, 340

"Raiders March," 339

"Raindrops Keep Fallin' on My Head," 280, 388

Rain Man, 381, 389–92

Rains, Claude, 135, 172

Raisin in the Sun, A, 297, 420

Raksin, David, 108, 122, 183, 292

range, 23

Rap, 386

    in *Boys n the Hood*, 383, 421

Rapée, Erno, 69, 90, 93, 106

Rashômon, 209, 221–22

Rathbone, Basil, 135

rating system, 149, 301

Rauschenberg, Robert, 5

Ray, Nicholas, 219

Ray, Satyajit, 235

RCA, 198

Reagan, Ronald, 212, 397

realism, 417–19, 420, 460–63